The Aims of Argument

A RHETORIC AND READER

Third Edition

Timothy W. Crusius / Carolyn E. Channell

Southern Methodist University

Mayfield Publ

Mountain

London

LIBRARY OF CONGRESS CATALOGING-IN-PUBLICATION DATA
Crusius, Timothy W.
The aims of argument : a rhetoric and reader / Timothy W. Crusius, Carolyn E. Channell.—3rd ed.
p. cm.
Includes index.
ISBN 0-7674-1131-5
1. English language—Rhetoric. 2. Persuasion (Rhetoric). 3. College readers. 4. Report writing. I. Channell, Carolyn E. II. Title.
PE1431.C78 1999
808'.0427—dc21 99-27621
CIP

Manufactured in the United States of America
10 9 8 7 6 5 4 3 2

Mayfield Publishing Company
1280 Villa Street
Mountain View, CA 94041

Sponsoring editor, Renée Deljon; production, Strawberry Fields Publishing; manuscript editor, Tom Briggs; design manager, Glenda King; photo researcher, Rennie Evans; cover designer, Linda Robertson; manufacturing manager, Randy Hurst. The text was set in 10.5/12 Bembo by Thompson Type and printed on 45# Custom LG by The Banta Book Group.

Cover image: Jasper Johns, *Target with Four Faces.* 1955. Assemblage: encaustic on newspaper and collage on canvas with objects, 26 × 26" (66 × 66 cm) surmounted by four tinted plaster faces in wood box with hinged front. Box, closed, 3¾ × 26 × 3½" (9.5 × 66 × 8.9 cm). Overall dimensions with box open, 33⅝ × 26 × 3" (85.3 × 66 × 7.6 cm). The Museum of Modern Art, New York. Gift of Mr. and Mrs. Robert C. Scull. Photograph © 1999 The Museum of Modern Art, New York. © Jasper Johns/Licensed by VAGA, New York, NY.

Text and illustration credits continue at the back of the book on pages 773–776, which constitute an extension of the copyright page.

For W. Ross Winterowd

PREFACE

In 1980 an author could justify a new argumentation textbook for first-year college students simply by saying that it filled a void; now prospective authors must ask themselves, Does the profession really need yet another book on argumentation? Moreover, they had better have a good answer to a question that experienced instructors of argument will surely ask: How, specifically, is your text different from—and better than—the one I am using?

People write textbooks for many reasons, but probably the most important reason—the one that keeps authors going long after the initial enthusiasm (and advances) are spent—is the chance of satisfying a need. With over thirty years of teaching experience between us, we have tried most of the argumentation texts currently available. Some of them are quite good, and we have learned from them. However, we found ourselves adopting a text not so much out of genuine enthusiasm but rather because it had fewer liabilities than any of the others under consideration. True, all textbook selection involves comparisons of the "lesser evil" sort. But we wondered why we were so lukewarm about even the best argumentation textbooks. What was it exactly that put us off?

We found many problems, both major and minor. But our dissatisfaction boiled down to a few major criticisms:

Most treatments were too formalistic and prescriptive.
Most failed to integrate class discussion and individual inquiry with written argumentation.
Apart from moving from simple concepts and assignments to more complicated ones, no book offered a learning sequence.
Despite the fact that argument, like narrative, is clearly a mode or means of development, not an end in itself, no book offered a well-developed view of the aims or purposes of argument.

We thought that these shortcomings had many undesirable results in the classroom, including the following:

The overemphasis on form confused students with too much terminology, made them doubt their best instincts, and drained away energy and interest from the process of inventing and discovering good arguments. Informal argumentation is not cut-and-dried but open-ended and creative.

The separation of class discussion from the process of composition created a hiatus (rather than a useful distinction) between oral and written argument so that students had difficulty seeing the relation between the two and using the insights learned from each to improve the other.

The lack of a learning sequence—of assignments that begin by refining and extending what students can do without help and that then build on these capacities with each subsequent assignment—meant that courses in argumentation were less coherent and less meaningful than they could be. Students did not understand why they were doing what they were doing and could not envision what might reasonably come next.

Finally, inattention to what people actually use argument to accomplish resulted in too narrow a view of the functions of argument and thus in unclear purposes for writing. Because instruction was mainly limited to what we call arguing to convince, too often students saw argument only as a monologue of advocacy. Even when their viewpoint was flexible, too often they assumed a pose of dogmatism and ignored any true spirit of inquiry.

We set out consciously to solve these problems—or at least to render them less problematical—when we wrote the first edition of this book. The result was a book different in notable respects from any other argument text available. In Chapter 1 we define and explain four aims of argument:

Arguing to inquire, the process of questioning opinions
Arguing to convince, the process of making cases
Arguing to persuade, the process of appealing to the whole person
Arguing to negotiate, the process of mediating between or among conflicting positions

The book's increasing popularity through its first and second editions tells us that we have satisfied a need. We're gratified that our approach has proven useful.

We have found that instructors have certain questions about these aims, especially in terms of how they relate to one another. No doubt we have yet to hear all the questions that will be asked, but we hope that by answering the ones we have heard, we can clarify some of the implications of our approach.

1. *What is the relative value of the four aims? Since negotiation comes last, is it the best or most valued?* Our answer is that no aim is "better" than any other aim. Given certain needs or demands for writing and certain audiences, one aim can be more appropriate than another for the task at hand. We treat negotiation last because it involves inquiry, convincing, and persuading and thus comes last in the learning sequence.

2. *Must inquiry be taught as a separate aim?* Not at all. We have designed the text so that it may be taught as a separate aim (the use of argument Plato and Aristotle called *dialectic*), but we certainly do not intend this "may" to be interpreted as a "must." We do think that teaching inquiry as a distinct aim has certain advantages. Students need to learn how to engage in constructive dialogue, which is more disciplined and more focused than class discussion usually is. Once they see how it is done, students seem to enjoy dialogue with one another and with texts. Dialogue helps students think through their arguments and imagine reader reaction to what they say, both of which are crucial to convincing and persuading. Finally, as with the option of teaching negotiation, teaching inquiry offers instructors another avenue for assignments other than the standard argumentative essay.
3. *Should inquiry come first?* For a number of reasons, inquiry has a certain priority over the other aims. Most teachers are likely to approach inquiry as a prewriting task, preparatory to convincing or persuading. And very commonly, we return to inquiry when we find something wrong with a case we are trying to construct, so the relation between inquiry and the other aims is as much recursive as it is a matter of before and after.

   However, we think inquiry also has psychological, moral, and practical claims to priority. When we are unfamiliar with an issue, inquiry comes first psychologically, often as a felt need to explore existing opinion. Regardless of what happens in the "real world," convincing or persuading without an open, honest, and earnest search for the truth is, in our view, immoral. Finally, inquiry goes hand-in-hand with research, which, of course, normally precedes writing in the other aims of argument.

   In sum, we would not defend Plato's concept of the truth. Truth is not simply "out there" in some wordless realm waiting to be discovered; rather, our opinion is what we discover or uncover as we grapple with a controversial issue and results largely from how we interpret ourselves and our world. We agree, therefore, with Wayne Booth that truth claims ought to be provisional and subject to revision, held for good reasons until better ones change our minds. Moreover, we agree with Plato that rhetoric divorced from inquiry is dangerous and morally suspect. The truth (if always provisional—some person's, some group's, or some culture's version of the truth) must count for more than sheer technical skill in argumentation.
4. *Isn't the difference between convincing and persuading more a matter of degree than of kind?* Fairly sharp distinctions can be drawn between inquiry and negotiation and between either of these two aims and the monologues of advocacy: convincing and persuading. But convincing and persuading do shade into one another, so that the difference is only clear at the extremes, with carefully chosen examples. Furthermore, the "purest" appeal to reason—a legal brief, a philosophical or scientific argument—appeals in ways beyond the sheer cogency of the case being made. Persuasive techniques are typically submerged but not absent in arguing to convince.

   Our motivation for separating convincing from persuading is not so much theoretical as pedagogical. Students usually have so much difficulty with case-making that individual attention to the logical appeal by itself is justified. Making students focally conscious of the appeals of character, emotion, and style while they are struggling to cope with case-making is too much to ask and can overburden them to the point of paralysis.

Regardless, then, of how sound the traditional distinction between convincing and persuading may be, we think it best to take up convincing first and then persuasion, especially since what students learn in the former can be carried over more or less intact into the latter. And, of course, it is not only case-making that carries over from convincing into persuading. Since one cannot make a case without unconscious appeal to character, emotional commitments (such as values), and style, teaching persuasion is really a matter of exposing and developing what is already there in arguing to convince.

The central tenets of an approach based on aims of argument may be summarized as follows:

Argumentation is a mode or means of discourse, not an aim or purpose of discourse; consequently, our task is to teach the aims of argument.

The aims of argument are linked in a learning sequence, so that convincing builds on inquiry, persuasion on convincing, and all three contribute to negotiating; consequently, we offer this learning sequence as an aid to conceiving a course or courses in argumentation.

We believe in the learning sequence as much as we do in the aims of argument. We think that anyone giving it an honest chance will come to prefer this way of teaching argument over any other ordering currently available.

At the same time, we recognize that textbooks are used selectively, as teachers and programs need them for help in achieving their own goals. As with any other text, this one can be used selectively, ignoring some parts, playing up others, designing other sequences, and so on. If you want to work with our learning sequence, it is there for creative adaptation. If not, the text certainly does not have to be taught as a whole and in sequence to be useful and effective.

We conclude with some notes on the readings. You will discover that many of the issues around which these essays are organized unavoidably involve students in issues of race, class, and gender difference. This slant is not intended to be political, nor does it reflect a hidden agenda on our part. Rather, we think students can come to feel more deeply about issues of this sort than they do about others we have tried. Class debates are livelier, maybe because such issues hit closer to home—the home and community they came from, the campus they live on now. Whatever the case, we have found that the issues work, both for students and for us.

They work, we think, because such issues help expose something obvious and basic about argumentation: People differ because they are different, and not just on the basis of race, class, and gender. Without some confrontation with difference, students may miss the deep social and cultural roots of argument and fail to understand why people think in such varied ways about immigration, education, welfare, abortion, and other issues that turn on difference, as well as issues such as the environment, which may seem at first to have nothing to do with difference.

We have consciously avoided the "great authors, classic essays" approach. We have tried instead to find bright, contemporary people arguing well from diverse viewpoints—articles and chapters similar to those that can be found in our better journals and trade books, the sort of publications students will read most in doing research on the issues. We have also tried to bring students into the argument as it currently stands, recognizing that the terms of the debate are necessarily always changing. Finally, we have not presented any issue in a simple pro-and-con fashion, as if there were only two sides to a question. We want the readings to provide models for writing not too far removed from what students can reasonably aspire to, as well as stimulation toward thinking through and rethinking positions on the issues in question.

Included in this range of approaches are arguments made not only with words but with images. We therefore include some examples of editorial cartoons, advertisements, and photographs; students may want to experiment with making their own nonverbal arguments.

Some reviewers and users have called our approach innovative. But is it better? Will students learn more? Will instructors find the book more satisfying and more helpful than what they currently use? Our experience—both in using the book ourselves and in listening to the responses of those who have read it or tested it in the classroom for us—is that they will. Students complain less about having to read this book than about having to read others used in our program. They do seem to learn more. Teachers claim to enjoy the text and find it stimulating, something to work with rather than around. We hope your experience is as positive as ours has been. We invite your comments and will use them in the process of perpetual revision that constitutes the life of a text and of our lives as writing teachers.

NEW TO THE THIRD EDITION

The major changes from the second edition are the following:

Previously, in Part 1, we devoted a few pages to images that make arguments and persuade in other ways—together with, of course, photographs and cartoons dispersed throughout Part 2, the readings chapters. We have retained the latter—indeed, added some—while expanding the few pages into a new chapter, "Image and Argument: Visual Rhetoric," complete with examples of visual rhetoric in "living color." This new Chapter 8 moves students from understanding visual persuasion in general to writing critiques of ads, political cartoons, and public monuments. It also includes material on graphics and an article that uses them effectively, coupled with writing assignments that encourage students both to create "free-standing" visual rhetoric and to integrate graphics with texts. The result is a chapter unique in textbooks of this kind, one long overdue given the significance of visual rhetoric in our culture and the sensitivity of contemporary students to it. Students know that in our society the image counts as much as the word; consequently, they want to understand visual rhetoric and use it effectively. We think you will enjoy teaching this chapter as much as we have.

We changed Part 1 in other notable ways, too. We expanded and moved what had been Appendix A, "Researching Arguments," into the main text, making it Chapter 9, the last in Part 1 and an effective transition to Part 2's readings. The former Appendix B is now Appendix A, "Editing and Proofreading," and we have a new Appendix B, "Keeping a Writer's Notebook" (formerly a very brief Chapter 2). Chapter 9's research coverage reflects the most current MLA and APA guidelines.

In Part 2 we provide new readings chapters. Because things change, and what was fresh becomes subtly and not-so-subtly stale, especially for teachers who use the book semester after semester, it was time for some new chapters and for some new readings to replace some of the old ones. Chapters on the family, the news media, higher education, and the future are new, while other chapters, most notably those on feminism and on race and class, have been brought up to date with new readings. We know that some of you will miss individual selections and chapters dropped to make room for the new material; we hope you will find the overall gain worth the sacrifice.

We have learned a great deal from the comments of both teachers and students who have used this book, so please continue to share your thoughts with us.

We wish to acknowledge the work of the following reviewers: L. Bensel-Meyers, University of Tennessee at Knoxville; Mary F. Chen-Johnson, Tacoma Community College; Matilda Cox, University of Maryland at College Park; Charles Watterson Davis, Kansas State University; Peggy B. Jolly, University of Alabama at Birmingham; and Anne Williams, Indiana University-Purdue University Indianapolis.

The work of Melanie Field, our production editor, and Tom Briggs, our copyeditor, went far beyond the call of duty in helping us to refine and develop the revised manuscript. At Mayfield, Marty Granahan's work with permissions and Rennie Evans's photo research also deserve special recognition and our deepest gratitude. Rick Roehrick's assistance with Chapter 9 was invaluable. Finally, Renée Deljon, our editor, showed her usual brilliance and lent her unflagging energy throughout a long and sometimes trying process that led to this new edition of *Aims*.

NOTE TO STUDENTS

Our goal in this book is not just to show you how to construct an argument but to make you more aware of why people argue and what purposes that argument serves in our society. Consequently, Part 1 of this book introduces four specific aims that people may have in mind when they make arguments: to inquire, to convince, to persuade, and to negotiate. Preceding the chapters on each specific aim of argument are three relatively short chapters that offer an overview of the four aims and prepare you for working with assignments in the aims.

Chapter 1 explains the aims and how they fit into the larger concept of *rhetoric,* the persuasive use of language.

Chapter 2 offers an approach to reading any argument.

Chapter 3 shows you, step by step, how to analyze the logic of any argument.

Because critical reading and analysis prepare you for the first aim, arguing to inquire, Chapters 2 and 3 lead directly into Chapter 4, and each subsequent chapter on the aims assumes and builds on the previous one. Chapter 8 covers not an aim but a kind of argument that can contribute to achieving any of the aims of argument: visual rhetoric. Part 1 concludes with Chapter 9, "Researching Arguments," a guide to both conducting research and writing researched arguments.

Part 2 of this book consists of readings, most by professional writers. As examples of the aims of argument, the selections offer something for you to emulate. All writers learn from studying the strategies of other writers. The object is not so much to imitate what a more experienced writer does as it is to understand the range of approaches and tactics you might use in your own way and for your own purposes.

Included in this range of approaches are arguments made not only with words but also with images. Part 2 therefore includes some examples of editorial cartoons, advertisements, and photographs.

The readings serve another function as well. To learn about argument, we have to argue; to argue, we must have something to argue about. So we have grouped essays around some central issues of current public discussion.

We selected these particular issues rather than other widely debated ones for two main reasons. One is that they have worked well in our own classes, better than others we tried and rejected. The other reason is that most of these issues deal centrally with society and more or less require us to think about difference, about what leads people to disagree with one another in the first place.

Basically, people argue with one another because they do not see the world the same way, and they do not see the world the same way because of their different backgrounds. Therefore, in dealing with how people differ, a book about argument must deal with what makes people different, with the sources of disagreement itself—including gender, race, ethnicity, class, and religion. Rather than ignoring or glossing over difference, we hope the readings in Part 2 will help you better understand difference—as well as provide interesting and significant subjects to argue about.

This book concludes with two appendixes, each a reference that you will want to consult repeatedly as you work through the assignments in the main parts of the text. Appendix A focuses on editing, the art of polishing and refining prose, and on proofreading for some common errors. Appendix B offers advice about how to keep a writer's notebook.

Arguing well is difficult for anyone. For many college students it is especially challenging because they have had little experience writing arguments. We have tried to write a text that is no more complicated than it has to be, and we welcome your comments so that we may improve future editions. Please write us at the following address:

The Rhetoric Program
Dallas Hall
Southern Methodist University
Dallas, Texas 75275

You may also e-mail your comments to the following address:

cchannel@post.cis.smu.edu

CONTENTS

Part One

THE AIMS OF ARGUMENT

CHAPTER ONE

An Overview of Key Terms

Commonly, the word *argument* refers to a verbal conflict, a dispute involving two or more people. In this book we will use the word in a sense closer to that of the Latin verb from which it derives: *arguere,* "to make clear."

WHAT IS ARGUMENT?

Argument is the process of making what we think clear to ourselves and to others. It takes us from a vague, private viewpoint to a clearly stated position that we can defend publicly in speech or writing. Like any journey, the process provides us with discoveries and new knowledge. If we undertake this process in a spirit of honesty and openness, we can compare it to a search for truth.

Argument in this sense of seeking clarity has a two-part form or structure: (1) the statement of an opinion and (2) the statement of one or more reasons for holding that opinion. If you say, for example, "Student loans for college ought to be more widely available," you have stated an opinion. In doing so, you have made one thing clear—namely, your position on the issue of student loans. But as yet, you have not made an argument in our particular sense of the word. Not until you add to your opinion a reason for holding it—for example, "because rising costs are preventing too many capable but impoverished students from attending"—do you construct an argument. By adding your reason, you have made something else clear—namely, *why* you take the position you do.

As we will see in detail in later chapters, arguments require more than simply an opinion coupled with a reason. But this basic form is fundamental to accomplishing any of the aims of argument.

HOW SHOULD WE APPROACH ARGUMENT?

Argument is . . . in principle the renunciation of violence.

—JAMES CROSSWHITE, *The Rhetoric of Reason*

Obviously, no argument can begin until someone asserts something—or "ventures an opinion," as we say. But merely asserting by itself is not enough. Some other person has to respond, challenging the assertion by asking for a reason or by making a counter-assertion. Otherwise, nothing happens.

Sometimes when we challenge a claim, the person who offered it says defensively, "Well, that's *my* opinion," as if we didn't know that already, or "That's *just* my opinion," which implies, of course, that we should let it slide. Either response stops argument dead in its tracks—as does a hostile challenge along the lines of "What sort of stupid idea is that?" or a sneering "Oh, yeah, sure."

So arguments can fail right at the beginning, before they have a chance to go anywhere. When this happens, everybody loses. The person who retreats from a thoughtful challenge loses the chance to rethink an opinion that may need rethinking; the person who meets the opinions of other people with hostility or indifference loses the chance to understand and learn from other points of view. Ultimately, society loses if arguments fail too often, for the quality of a society depends on the quality of its conversations. People who can't resolve differences through argumentation resort to threats and force. When arguments fail, violence increases.

How, then, should we approach argument? What attitudes can help an argument at least get off the ground and maybe even soar? We must care enough about our opinions to want them heard—this is part of self-respect. We must also try not to get our feelings hurt or become defensive when our opinions are questioned; other people can respect us, like us, even love us and still reasonably disagree with something we've said. Often their disagreement is the key to our own outlook maturing. Finally, if we want our own views to be heard and responded to thoughtfully, we must listen to others and offer responses intended to help rather than hurt. Approached this way, argument can be something we look forward to rather than something we dread or avoid. Approached this way, everyone wins.

WHAT ARE THE AIMS OF ARGUMENT?

Argument is not in itself an end or a purpose of communication. It is rather a *means* of discourse, a way to develop what we have to say. In this book we use the term *aim* to refer to the various purposes that argument helps us accomplish.

We all know people who seem to argue just for the sake of argument; they would "argue with a post," we say. But even these people have an aim beyond argument itself. It may be to vent hostility or resentment or outrage. Or it may be to show off, to display what they know, or to dominate (or enliven) a discussion. We may feel that such contentious people are arguing inappropriately, but they are clearly not arguing simply to argue. They are arguing to express themselves.

An argument may be almost entirely self-expression. Some speakers and writers are satisfied just to have their say; they don't care about influencing other people. Consider the letters to the editor in your local paper. A few attempt to influence the viewpoints of others, but most only state an opinion, with perhaps minimal justification. Newspaper editors appropriately give these sections titles such as "Sounding Off."

All arguments are expressive to some degree. Nothing tells us more about people than the opinions they hold and their reasons for holding them. Our opinions play a large role in making us what we are: conservative, liberal, or middle-of-the-road in politics; a believer, an atheist, or an agnostic in religion; and so on. Because what we think is so much what we are, we typically hold our opinions with deep conviction and genuine passion—so much so that we often fail to question our own opinions or to listen to the arguments of other people who disagree with us.

In societies that value freedom of speech, argument as self-expression is common. It is also quite spontaneous: we learn it much as we learned our first language, simply by attempting it, with little thought about the form of the argument or the process that brought us to our position. For this reason we have not singled out argument as expression for special concern in this book.

We assume most of your arguments will be expressive, or at least will begin as self-expression. But when you examine your own opinions or the opinions of someone who disagrees with you, when you try to get others to change their positions, and when you explore avenues of compromise between competing positions, you are moving beyond self-expression to one of the following four aims of argument: to inquire, to convince, to persuade, or to negotiate.

Arguing to Inquire

The ancient Greeks called argument as inquiry *dialectic;* today we might think of it as *dialogue,* or serious conversation. Arguing to inquire can also be done in writing and may even work best when we can scrutinize our thoughts "out there" on the page.

Arguing to inquire helps us to form opinions, to question opinions we already have, and to reason our way through conflicts or contradictions. It enables us to decide what we will accept as the truth about a given issue. It requires an attitude of patient questioning under nonthreatening circumstances and is therefore something we most often do alone or among trusted friends and associates.

In everyday life we most commonly argue to inquire when we face a complicated decision, such as buying the right car or deciding which major to take in college. We want to make an intelligent decision, one that seems reasonable to us and to others whose opinions we respect. What do we do? We argue with ourselves; we try out arguments on our friends; we offer a tentative opinion to someone we respect, whose insight we'd like to have.

We also use argument as inquiry when we think through dilemmas, whether personal or public—when one voice inside says one thing and another says something that conflicts with the first. For example, we have been taught to be tolerant of others, to respect the opinions of people who disagree with us. But when we encounter opinions that are themselves intolerant, that are racist or sexist in an aggressive and even potentially violent way, we are confronted with a dilemma: How much tolerance is too much tolerance? Where do we draw the line between differences that must be respected, and even encouraged, and opinions that are dangerous and should be actively opposed, and even suppressed? Should we protest a Nazi group's demonstration on Main Street? Should we challenge a campus group that destroys every copy of a school-supported newspaper it finds offensive?

Sometimes college courses ask us to confront such basic philosophical dilemmas as the limits of tolerance. More commonly, though, the purpose of inquiry in college is to help us form opinions about issues requiring some kind of research. We become acquainted with an issue through lectures and assigned reading; then, to assess what we have heard and read, we must seek out additional information and opinions. Argument as inquiry helps us read and listen more critically so that we can arrive at our own position with confidence. Because inquiry engages us in dialogues with others and with ourselves, its success depends on the art of asking questions, the principal concern of Chapter 4.

Finally, argument as inquiry plays a role in our professional lives. A research scientist may devote years, even a lifetime, to formulating, testing, and reformulating hypotheses that explore a single set of phenomena—black holes, for example. Businesspeople must find solutions to practical problems (How can we increase sales in our southern region?), resolve dilemmas based on changing societal and political attitudes (How can we achieve our goals for affirmative action and still hire the best people?), and meet new and often unanticipated challenges that have a direct impact on success or failure (How should we respond to the evolving economic and political conditions in Eastern Europe?). Basic to such research and decision-making is arguing to inquire.

Arguing to Convince

Some inquiry never stops, remaining permanently open-ended; the goal of most inquiry, however, is to reach some kind of conclusion. This conclusion can go by many names, but we'll call it a *conviction* and define it as "an earned opinion, achieved through careful thought, research, and discussion." Once we arrive at a conviction, we ordinarily want others to share it—that is, the aim of further argument is to secure the assent of people who do not share our conviction (or who do not share it fully). Such assent is an agreement of minds secured by reason rather than by force.

Arguing to inquire centers on asking questions; we use argument as inquiry to expose and examine what we think. Arguing to convince centers on making a case, which, as we shall see in Chapter 5, involves an elaboration of the basic structure "*x* because *y*"; we use argument as convincing in an effort to get others to agree with what we think. Inquiry is the search for what is true; convincing is the attempt to get others to accept the truths we claim to have reached.

Examples of arguing to convince are all around us. The purest may be found in scholarly and professional writing (for example, when a historian interprets the causes of an event in the past and makes a case for his or her interpretation or when a judge writes up a justification for a particular ruling). But we see examples in everyday life as well: on editorial pages, where writers make a case for their position on local issues or candidates for office, and at school, when a student appeals a grade.

Whenever we encounter a stance supported by reasons that asks for our assent to the position being argued, we are dealing with argument as convincing. Whenever our intent as writers is primarily to gain the intellectual assent of our reader (when we want a reader to respond with "I agree" or "You're right"), we are arguing to convince.

Arguing to Persuade

More than to earn the assent of readers, persuasion tries to influence their behavior as well, to move them to act upon the conviction to which they have assented. An advertisement for Mercedes-Benz aims to convince us not only that the company makes a high-quality car but also that we should go out and buy one. A Sunday sermon asks for more than agreement with some interpretation of a biblical passage; the minister wants the congregation to apply the message to their lives. Persuasion asks us to *do* something—spend money, live a certain way, cast a vote, join a movement. Because we don't always act on our convictions, persuasion cannot rely on reasons alone; it must appeal in broader and deeper ways.

Persuasion appeals to readers' emotions. We may be convinced by an argument that starving children deserve our help, but actually getting us to send money may require a photograph of a child with skeletal limbs and a hunger-bloated stomach. The intent of such tactics is clear: to reinforce reasons with pity, the better to move us to action.

To a greater extent than convincing, persuasion also relies on the personal appeal of the writer. To convince, a writer must earn the reader's respect and trust; to persuade, a writer must get the reader to identify his or her own interests with those of the writer. A writer's personal charm may help, but such identification requires much more than the reader liking the writer. Any good feeling must be joined to something "higher" or "larger" than the writer, to something that the writer represents and that the reader would like to be associated with. A majority of Americans identified with Ronald Reagan, for example; his appeal combined personal likableness with a larger anti-government sentiment, deeply rooted in American history. Of course, few of

COMPARING THE AIMS: A SUMMARY

The aims of argument have much in common. For example, besides sharing argument, they all tend to draw on sources of knowledge (research) and deal with controversial issues. But the aims also differ from one another, mainly in terms of purpose, audience, situation, and method, as summarized here and on the inside front cover.

	Purpose	*Audience*	*Situation*	*Method*
Inquiry	Seeks truth	Oneself, friends, and colleagues	Informal; a dialogue	Questions
Convincing	Seeks assent to a thesis	Less intimate; wants careful reasoning	More formal; a monologue	Case-making
Persuading	Seeks action	More broadly public, less academic	Pressing need for a decision	Appeals to reason and emotions
Negotiating	Seeks consensus	Polarized by differences	Need to cooperate, preserve relations	"Give and take"

We offer this chart as a general guide to the aims of argument. Think of it as the "big picture" you can always return to as you work your way through Part 1, which deals with each of the aims in detail.

We hope you will explore on your own how the aims converge and diverge and how they overlap and interact in specific cases.

us have the persuasive advantage of being a public figure. Nevertheless, we can ally ourselves with causes and values that our readers find sympathetic. Chapter 6 investigates the resources of identification in more detail.

Finally, in addition to relying on emotional and personal appeals, persuasion exploits the resources of language more fully than convincing does. To convince, our language must be clear and cogent so that readers can follow our case; to persuade, we need language that readers will remember and that will appeal by its sound and by the images it creates. In Chapter 6 we will also explore the persuasive resources of language, traditionally called *style.*

Arguing to Negotiate

By the time we find ourselves in a situation where our aim is to negotiate, we will have already attempted to convince an opponent of our case and to persuade that opponent to settle a conflict or dispute to our satisfaction. Our opponent will no doubt also have used convincing and persuading in an attempt to move us similarly. Yet neither side will have been able to secure the assent of the other, and "agreeing to disagree" is not a practical solution because the participants must come to some agreement in order to pursue a necessary course of action.

In most instances of negotiation, the parties involved try to work out the conflict themselves because they have some relationship they wish to preserve—as employer and employee, business partners, family members, neighbors, even coauthors of an argument textbook. Common differences requiring negotiation include the amount of a raise or the terms of a contract, the wording of a bill in a congressional committee, and trade agreements among nations. In private life, negotiation helps roommates to live together and families to decide on everything from budgets to vacation destinations.

Just like other aims of argument, arguing to negotiate requires sound logic and the clear presentation of positions and reasons. However, negotiation challenges our interpersonal skills more than do the other aims. Each side must listen closely to understand not just the other side's case but also the other side's emotional commitments and underlying values. Initiating such a conversation and keeping it going can sometimes be so difficult that an outside party, a mediator, must assist in the process. With or without a mediator, when negotiation works, the opposing sides begin to converge. Exchanging viewpoints and information and building empathy enable all parties to make concessions, to loosen their hold on their original positions, and finally to reach consensus—or at least a resolution that all participants find satisfactory.

As Chapter 7 makes clear, this final aim of argument brings us full circle, back to *dialogue,* to the processes involved in arguing to inquire. The major difference is that in negotiation we are less concerned with our own claims to truth than we are with overcoming conflict, with finding some common ground that will allow us to live and work together.

WHAT IS RHETORIC?

Argument is a rhetorical art. *Rhetoric* originally meant "the art of persuasive *speaking,*" but the term has come to include written discourse as well. Whether oral or written, rhetoric always aims to influence an audience. By *art* we mean not "fine art" (painting, sculpture, music, and so on) but the principles underlying some activity that requires education, experience, and judgment—the art of medicine, for example. Like medicine, rhetoric is a practical art: the art of speaking or writing well.

Studying rhetoric involves learning and applying a body of knowledge that originated in ancient Greece and has existed for about 2,400 years. Like all academic and professional fields, this body of knowledge has changed over time. However, in his analysis of persuasion, the ancient Greek philosopher Aristotle identified three basic types of appeals that have remained useful to the study of rhetoric through the centuries: (1) *logos,* the use of logic, which appeals to the audience's reason and intellect; (2) *ethos,* the speaker's attempts to project his or her own character as wise, ethical, and practical; and (3) *pathos,* the appeal to the emotions or sympathies of the audience.

In addition to these basic concepts, other principles appeared as rhetoric responded to developments in psychology, literature, and philosophy: principles for inventing and organizing arguments, for anticipating the needs of audiences, for building logical cases, and for polishing style and language. Rhetoric has also been influenced by historical developments, such as the spread of democracy and the rise of electronic media. This book combines current principles with classical tradition to present a contemporary rhetoric for argument.

To a degree, you have been practicing the art of rhetoric all your life. For example, even as a small child you figured out how to convince your parents that you should be able to stay up an hour later or that you "deserved" a certain new toy. Formal rhetoric builds on your aptitudes and experiences, allowing you to develop a more conscious and therefore more discriminating awareness of what you can achieve with argument.

Some people who speak or write well claim to have taught themselves. But most of us need more than our natural ability and experience, and even the talented few can improve by joining natural talents with conscious knowledge and informed feedback from others. Learning rhetoric means consciously applying knowledge about arguments and the aims of argument to what you already understand from experience. You will become more critical of what you do when you argue. You will also become a more critical listener to and reader of the arguments of others.

We want to stress that arguing well is an ethical act, for the authentic art of rhetoric is highly ethical. The principles of rhetoric oblige a speaker or writer to make the best possible case and to respect the audience, rather than pander to or manipulate it. As we will show, all of the aims of argument require sensitivity to questions of right and wrong.

Each of the major aims of argument has its own rhetoric—its own focus, principles, and methods—and in Chapters 4 through 7 we will take them up one by one, as though they were separate from one another. But we will also explore how they connect with each other and how they often work together in practice. Moreover, we will see how convincing builds on inquiry, how persuasion builds on convincing, and how negotiation integrates inquiry, convincing, and persuading.

Following Through

Recall a recent argument you made, either spoken or written. What was your point? Who was your audience? What was your main aim in arguing? merely to express your opinion? to convince your audience to assent to your view on the issue? to get your audience to take some action? to negotiate a compromise? Can you think of another recent argument in which your aim was different?

CHAPTER TWO

Reading an Argument

Throughout this book you will be reading both professional and student-written arguments that exemplify ways to argue. Many also offer multiple viewpoints on contemporary issues—conversations you will join when you write arguments of your own. You should read these arguments *critically,* taking on the role of a critic by *analyzing* (to see how the argument is put together) and by *evaluating* (to decide how well the argument achieves its aim and whether it advances a position that merits respect). Critical reading is not casual, and you should not undertake it when you are tired or distracted. Critical reading skills are essential to understanding the aims and methods of argument; in this chapter we focus on some specific methods for you to practice.

BEFORE YOU READ

Experts have found that readers who have the greatest success comprehending the ideas in any text meet two criteria: (1) they have some *prior knowledge* of the subject matter, and (2) they are able to see a piece of writing in its *rhetorical context.* Such readers use context to determine the meaning of unfamiliar words, and they "read between the lines," recognizing ideas and assumptions that are only implied. Let's look at these two practices with an eye toward argument.

Recalling Prior Knowledge

Every piece of writing is part of an ongoing conversation involving a number of participants who represent a range of opinions and who have each contributed a variety of ideas, facts, and authoritative citations to the debate. The greater a reader's familiarity with this background, the easier it is for him or her to approach a new argument from a critical perspective, filling in any gaps in the information and recognizing a writer's assumptions and biases.

Therefore, it makes sense to take some time before you start reading to recall what you already know about the topic: the basic issues involved and the perspectives you have read or heard expressed. Use your writer's notebook (see Appendix B) to record what you remember. And don't neglect to consider your own opinions about the issue. If you are conscious of the attitudes and ideas you bring to your reading, you can better see an argument in its own light.

Following Through

You are about to read an argument entitled "Making the Mosaic." What does the title tell you? A *mosaic*—a design composed of many small pieces of stone or tile—is often used as a metaphor for American society, emphasizing that we are a people with many distinct ethnic backgrounds. But many people question whether the mosaic metaphor is appropriate. An earlier metaphor, comparing America to a melting pot, suggests a different picture, a society in which ethnic differences disappear and immigrants assimilate to the single identity of "American." There is also debate about whether a common identity is possible or desirable.

In your writer's notebook jot down some arguments you have heard about issues relating to legal immigration. Have you heard arguments for or against putting higher limits on legal immigration? What sort of limits do some people argue for? What reasons are offered? If you have heard arguments in favor of immigrants either maintaining or losing their ethnic identity, can you recall some of the reasons on either side? How might one's background or personal experience affect one's perspective on these questions? Which metaphor—melting pot or mosaic—fits your own view of America? How might your background affect your view?

Considering the Rhetorical Context

Critical readers breathe life into a written argument by seeing it as part of a dynamic activity. They view the author as a human being with hopes, fears, biases, ambitions, and—most importantly—a purpose that his or her words on the page are intended to accomplish. The argument becomes an action, aimed at affecting a particular audience in a particular place and time.

Publishers' notes and editorial headnotes often include information and clues that can help you answer the following questions about rhetorical context:

When was this argument written? (If not recently, how might it be helpful to know something about the time it first appeared?)
Why was it written? What prompted its creation?
Who is the author, and what are his or her occupation, personal background, and political leanings?

Where does the article appear? If it is reprinted, where did it appear originally?
For whom do you think the author is writing?
What purpose does the author have in writing? What does he or she hope to accomplish through argument?

Following Through

Read the following editorial headnote for the argument "Making the Mosaic":

> Anna Quindlen, a novelist and syndicated columnist who won a Pulitzer Prize in 1992, comments on contemporary issues from the perspective of a liberal, a feminist, and a mother. The following column appeared in the *New York Times* in November 1991.

In your writer's notebook make some notes about what this headnote tells you about the argument's rhetorical context. Do you think that immigration issues were much the same in 1991 as they are today? What do you know about the *New York Times* and its readership? What does it mean to have a liberal perspective in general? What viewpoints would you anticipate finding in the writing of someone with a liberal perspective on immigration?

As you read the essay, you will fill in your understanding of its rhetorical context and revise some of the expectations you had about it based on prior knowledge and the headnote. All reading involves the revision of preconceptions, but it is better to define some initially rather than to begin with none or with only vague ones.

AS YOU READ

Critical reading involves reading a text at least three times. Here we will suggest goals for each reading, but you are likely to have your own way of noting ideas and making connections. Be ready to record whatever thoughts come to mind.

The First Reading

The first reading of any text explores new territory. You might prefer to start at the beginning and simply read the selection straight through. But it's a good idea to look first at the opening and closing paragraphs, where you will often find explicit statements of the author's thesis and additional clues to help you construct the rhetorical context. You might also scan the text, looking at major headings (if any) and the first sentences of paragraphs. Then read through the essay at a moderate pace.

During this first reading, except for circling words to look up, don't feel compelled to make marks in the text. But don't hesitate to make marginal notes if thoughts or questions occur to you.

Following Through

Before you read "Making the Mosaic," look at the first and last paragraphs and at the first sentence of each body paragraph. Try to determine Quindlen's main point and purpose, as well as her intended audience—those whom she is trying to persuade. Then, after you have read through the essay once, use your writer's notebook to record your responses to the six questions on rhetorical context listed on pages 12–13.

ANNA QUINDLEN

Making the Mosaic

THERE IS some disagreement over which wordsmith first substituted 1
"mosaic" for "melting pot" as a way of describing America, but it is undoubtedly a more apt description. And it undoubtedly applies in Ms. Miller's third-grade class and elsewhere in the Lower East Side's Public School 20.

The neighborhood where the school is located is to the immigrant experience what Broadway is to actors. Past Blevitzky Bros. Monuments ("at this place since 1914"), past Katz's Delicatessen with its fan mail hung in the window, past the tenement buildings where fire escapes climb graceful as cat burglars, P.S. 20 holds the corner of Essex and Houston.

Its current student body comes from the Dominican Republic, Cambodia, Bangladesh, Puerto Rico, Colombia, mainland China, Vietnam and El Salvador. In Ms. Miller's third-grade class these various faces somehow look the same, upturned and open, as though they were cups waiting for the water to be poured.

There's a spirit in the nation now that's in opposition to these children. It is not interested in your tired, your poor, your huddled masses. In recent days it has been best personified by a candidate for governor and the suggestion in his campaign that there is a kind of authentic American. That authentic American is white and Christian (but not Catholic), ethnic origins lost in the mists of an amorphous past, not visible in accent, appearance or allegiance.

This is not a new idea, this resilient form of xenophobia. "It is but too 5
common a remark of late, that the American character has within a short time been sadly degraded by numerous instances of riot and lawless violence," Samuel F. B. Morse wrote in an 1835 treatise called "Imminent Dangers to the

Free Institutions of the United States through Foreign Immigration," decrying such riffraff as Jesuits.

Times are bad, and we blame the newcomers, whether it's 1835 or 1991. Had Morse had his way, half of me would still be in Italy; if some conservatives had their way today, most of the children at P.S. 20 would be, in that ugly phrase, back where they came from. So much for lifting a lamp beside the golden door.

They don't want to learn the language, we complain, as though the old neighborhoods were not full of Poles and Italians who kept to their mother tongue. They don't want to become American, we say, as though there are not plenty of us who believe we lost something when we renounced ethnicity. "Dagos," my mother said the American kids called them, American being those not Italian. "Wops." How quickly we forget as we use pejoratives for the newest newcomers.

Our greatest monument to immigration, the restored Ellis Island, seems to suggest by its display cases that coming to America is a thing nostalgic, something grandparents did. On the Lower East Side it has never been past tense, struggling with English and poverty, sharing apartments with the bathroom in the hall and the bathtub in the kitchen.

They send their children to school with hopes for a miracle, or a job, which is almost the same thing. This past week the School Volunteer Program, which fields almost 6,000 volunteer tutors, sponsored the first citywide Read Aloud: 400 grown-ups reading to thousands of kids in 90 schools. In P.S. 20, as so many have done before, the kids clutched their books like visas.

10 It is foolish to forget where you come from, which, in the case of the United States, is almost always somewhere else. The true authentic American is a pilgrim with a small "p," armed with little more than the phrase "I wish. . . ." New ones are being minted in Ms. Miller's class, bits of a mosaic far from complete.

The Second Reading

The goals for your second reading are to recognize the structure of the argument and to wrestle with any difficult passages.

Analyzing Structure

By *structure* we mean the writer's plan or arrangement. Arguments seldom divide into anything like the formulaic "five-paragraph essay" with thesis and reasons in predetermined places. Arrangements for arguments are practically infinite, and good writers make their own decisions about what should go where in any given situation. But in a well-written argument, it should be clear that different parts have different jobs to do. These may include:

Providing background
Offering and developing a reason
Giving an opposing view
Rebutting an opposing view

If the writer's case has been tightly crafted, breaking the essay into its parts can be like breaking a Hershey's bar into its already well-defined segments. However, other arguments are more loosely structured, with their divisions less readily discernible. But even with these, close analysis will generally reveal some fault lines that indicate specific divisions, and it will be possible to see the roles played by the various chunks. As you read a second time, draw lines between the paragraphs where you detect dividing points. (Some chunks may be single paragraphs, and others may be groups of as many as five or more paragraphs.) Then, drawing on your understanding of the author's purpose and audience, try to describe the function of each part.

This brief essay by Quindlen seems informal and loosely structured, but a careful look reveals that it is a well-crafted argument with a structure of four main parts, each with its own role to play. Paragraphs 1–3 form the introduction. They work together to open with a positive and sympathetic look at an ethnically diverse immigrant community, but they do not present Quindlen's main point. Paragraph 4 introduces an opposing view that current trends in immigration may bring too much poverty and too much ethnic diversity. Paragraphs 5–9 offer reasons and evidence for rejecting this opposing view, and paragraph 10 concludes with Quindlen's main point, that America ought to be a country where people with nothing can have an opportunity to fulfill their dreams.

Quindlen's audience most likely consists of educated professionals who read the *New York Times.* They would know there is debate about how an influx of poor and ethnically diverse immigrants will affect American society. Quindlen recognizes that her readers don't want to be lectured to, so she makes her case in an indirect and even entertaining way. Looking in more detail at the four subdivisions of her essay, we can appreciate her strategy in appealing to this audience.

1. Paragraphs 1–3 introduce the argument by giving a colorful description of an immigrant neighborhood. Quindlen wants to emphasize the continuity of the immigrant experience, so she reminds readers that the Lower East Side of New York has historically been the home of poor immigrants (nothing new or threatening here). And the immigrants she portrays are a class of hopeful third-graders.
2. Paragraph 4 introduces an opposing view, that the United States should not continue to admit large numbers of poor and ethnically diverse people. Quindlen's presentation of this view shows that she wants to discredit it. To emphasize how unfair it is, she has placed it in sharp juxtaposition to her description of the children's "upturned and open" faces. Notably, she doesn't name the politician who personifies this viewpoint because that would aim the argument too directly at a single individual.
3. Paragraphs 5–9 are the heart of the argument, as they offer reasons and evidence for rejecting what Quindlen calls the "conservative" opposing view. Notice that she presents the reasons indirectly. She does not say, "This

fear of difference is unfair and irrational because first, second, and third." Instead of spelling them out, she presents the reasons *through* the details. A careful reader extracts the reasons—a skill known commonly as reading between the lines. We have paraphrased the reasons in italics here. You can decide what the essay would have gained—or lost—if Quindlen had been more explicit about spelling them out.

In paragraphs 5 and 6 Quindlen offers one reason: *Similar arguments against ethnic groups in the past now appear as examples of obvious bigotry and paranoia.* As evidence she offers Samuel Morse's quotation from 1835 and cites examples of the Jesuits and her own Italian grandparents.

Quindlen gives a second reason in paragraph 7: *The belief that there is only one true kind of American makes immigrants give up their cultural heritage.* This idea makes three appearances in the essay, here and in paragraphs 5 and 10, but it goes largely without concrete support. Perhaps she believes that her readers, if they are Americans with an "amorphous past," will regret that they have lost touch with some part of their heritage, too.

Finally, in paragraphs 8 and 9, Quindlen offers a final reason: *Today's immigrants have the same determination to achieve the American dream that all earlier waves of immigrants had.* As evidence she cites some of the hardships of daily life for poor immigrant families and shows their children's eagerness to learn how to read.

4. Paragraph 10 sums up what Quindlen is really arguing for: It shouldn't matter where immigrants come from; wanting to make something of oneself through hard work is the only requirement for being a true American.

Working through Difficult Passages

In every text or piece of writing, a reader will find some passages that are less accessible than others. As you read another person's writing, you may feel a little shaky about what the author means. You may encounter new words to look up. Other factors outlined in the following sections also contribute to comprehension difficulty. In many cases *paraphrasing*—putting the passage into your own words—can increase reading comprehension and confidence. (Paraphrasing is a useful skill for any writer working with other written texts; in Chapter 9, "Researching Arguments," we offer more detailed advice on how to paraphrase.)

Metaphors One obstacle to reading comprehension may result from a writer's use of metaphors. A *metaphor* is a way of seeing one thing in terms of something else. For example, we commonly describe the act of beginning to love someone in terms of "falling in love." The meanings we associate with literal falling—loss of control, being a victim of circumstance—are carried over into the new context of describing an emotional state. We tend not to notice such common metaphors (and similes, which employ the words *like* or *as* to make the comparison more plainly), but a new metaphor in an unfamiliar context will make a reader stop and think.

We have already pointed out that Quindlen uses the metaphors "melting pot" and "mosaic," which are common enough in our culture to pose no barrier to most readers' understanding. The term *dead metaphor* is sometimes used to describe metaphorical expressions that are so common we do not even think of them as metaphors. But we *should* think about them because, in a very concise but powerful way, all metaphors are arguments. That is, they argue for a particular perspective on something, just as the "falling" metaphor argues that we should view love as a condition beyond our control. Dead metaphors are particularly dangerous because we do not even think about how they shape our attitudes.

Consider how the common metaphors "America is a melting pot" and "America is a mosaic" make different arguments about how immigrants should act and how they should be treated. Appreciating the full impact of these metaphors will help your critical reading of Quindlen's essay.

In the last sentence of paragraph 4, Quindlen uses metaphors that are fresh and unusual. Some Americans' ethnic origins, she says, are "lost in the mists of an amorphous past." "Mists" is a metaphor for the vague sense some people have of their ancestors; they cannot see their pasts clearly. To speak of the past as amorphous, or shapeless, is also metaphorical: Can the past, an abstract concept, ever have a shape? She is saying that a shapeless past has nothing to distinguish it from everyone else's. In both metaphors she uses concrete terms as a way of expressing something abstract. Something is lost by putting the idea into nonmetaphorical words of our own, but it helps us appreciate the persuasive effects of Quindlen's phrasing.

Remember that metaphors are everywhere, not just in poetry and fiction. You may find a passage of argumentative writing difficult if you read too literally.

Unusual Syntax *Syntax* simply means the order of words in a sentence. In English, readers expect something close to a subject-verb-object sequence, with some modifiers here or there. But writers vary syntax to avoid monotony or to achieve a certain effect. They use sentence fragments. They create long sentences with many modifiers. They invert the expected word order. And they leave out words they think the reader can fill in: To err is human, to forgive divine. Sometimes a sentence is complicated because the idea expressed is complicated. In all these cases, paraphrasing can help. Casting an idea into plainer syntax will make it clearer to you; in particular, it is a good idea to break a long sentence into several shorter ones of your own. Let's look again at the last sentence of Quindlen's fourth paragraph:

> That authentic American is white and Christian (but not Catholic), ethnic origins lost in the mists of an amorphous past, not visible in accent, appearance or allegiance.

This sentence starts out simply enough, but after the comma, Quindlen makes an unusual grammatical choice—an absolute phrase. That's a phrase containing a noun and modifiers, but the phrase does not modify anything itself. Here is a clearer but less dramatic way of expressing this same idea:

> Authentic Americans are white Protestants whose looks and speech show no trace of their ethnic origins and who have no feelings of loyalty toward any ethnic group.

Multiple Voices Most texts include quotations, either direct or indirect, from other speakers or written texts. With direct quotations, if the speaker is clearly named, readers will not be confused; however, indirect quotations can be tricky. For example, in paragraph 5, Quindlen quotes Samuel Morse both directly and indirectly. When she describes the Jesuits as "riffraff," this is clearly not her own opinion but Morse's. On your second reading of any argument, you might notice passages in which you are uncertain whose point of view is being presented. These problems clear up on repeated readings and through discussions with other readers.

Allusions Many arguments contain brief references to people, events, songs, art—anything in the culture that the author assumes he or she shares with the readers. Such *allusions* are one way for the author to form a bond with the readers—provided the readers' and the author's opinions are the same about what is being alluded to. For example, most Americans are proud of the Statue of Liberty and familiar with the words that appear on its base, the closing lines of Emma Lazarus's 1883 poem "The New Colossus":

> Give me your tired, your poor,
> Your huddled masses yearning to breathe free.
> The wretched refuse of your teeming shore.
> Send these, the homeless, tempest-tost to me,
> I lift my lamp beside the golden door.

Notice how Quindlen borrows freely from this poem in paragraphs 4 and 6, clearly assuming her readers' familiarity with it. You might consider how directly mentioning Lazarus or the Statue of Liberty would have changed the effect.

Following Through

Paragraph 5 is a difficult passage, partly because of vocabulary but also because of the archaic nineteenth-century phrasing in the quotation from Morse. Paraphrase this entire paragraph, quoting Morse indirectly and using your own diction and syntax as much as possible. Make it clear that Morse is connecting lawlessness with immigration.

READING ARGUMENTS CRITICALLY

1. Note the *main claim,* or *thesis,* of the argument, if it appears explicitly. If it does not, paraphrase it in the margin.
2. Pick out and mark the *main reasons* in support of the thesis. (Don't expect to find many major reasons; in a good argument, much space and effort may go toward developing and supporting only one reason.)
3. Consider the *evidence* offered, and write marginal comments about the reasons themselves and how well they are supported. Question evidence in terms of both quantity and quality.
4. Note *key terms* and how the writer defines (or fails to define) them. Would most readers agree with the definitions? How would you define or illustrate key terms that need clarification?
5. If the writer presents any *analogies,* ask whether the things being compared are truly similar. Note any problems.
6. Look for any *contradictions.* Does any evidence cited in the text contradict other evidence in the text or from other sources?
7. Identify the *assumptions* on which the thesis and reasons are based. Does the argument, or any of its reasons, rest on an assumption that all readers may not share?
8. Ask whether any *opposing views* are represented. Are they depicted fairly?
9. Think about your *personal response.* What do you agree with? What do you disagree with? Why?

The Third Reading

In Chapter 4 we explore how a reader can enter into a dialogue with the writer of an argument by posing questions to the writer and using the text itself as a basis for imagining the writer's responses. Such an extended dialogue is the best inquiry into a written argument, but a faster alternative is to raise questions and note the anticipated objections of those with opposing views directly in the margins of the printed text. In your third reading you should raise such questions even if you agree with the writer's argument. It may be easier (and more fun) to challenge arguments you disagree with, but if you are studying arguments as claims to truth, it is even more important to challenge the views you find most sympathetic.

Even if you oppose a writer's position, be open in your third reading to recognizing valid points and good reasoning. This kind of critical reading will enlarge your understanding of an issue and open your mind to new perspectives. In fact, it may cause you to change your mind. The box "Reading

Arguments Critically" lists some things to look for when annotating an argument.

We have annotated the first four paragraphs of Quindlen's essay as an example.

ANNA QUINDLEN

Making the Mosaic

THERE IS some disagreement over which wordsmith first substituted "mosaic" for "melting pot" as a way of describing America, but it is undoubtedly a more apt description. And it undoubtedly applies in Ms. Miller's third-grade class and elsewhere in the Lower East Side's Public School 20.

So she favors preserving difference.

The neighborhood where the school is located is to the immigrant experience what Broadway is to actors. Past Blevitzky Bros. Monuments ("at this place since 1914"), past Katz's Delicatessen with its fan mail hung in the window, past the tenement buildings where fire escapes climb graceful as cat burglars, P.S. 20 holds the corner of Essex and Houston.

Analogy suggests all pass through on their way to success.

Its current student body comes from the Dominican Republic, Cambodia, Bangladesh, Puerto Rico, Colombia, mainland China, Vietnam and El Salvador. In Ms. Miller's third-grade class these various faces somehow look the same, upturned and open, as though they were cups waiting for the water to be poured.

I think this would pose a language problem.

Metaphor suggests optimism.

There's a spirit in the nation now that's in opposition to these children. It is not interested in your tired, your poor, your huddled masses. In recent days it has been best personified by a candidate for governor and the suggestion in his campaign that there is a kind of authentic American. That authentic American is white and Christian (but not Catholic), ethnic origins lost in the mists of an amorphous past, not visible in accent, appearance or allegiance.

But is it fair to say that her opponents are against the children?

Like my own.

shapeless

Following Through

Read "Making the Mosaic" a third time, writing marginal annotations as you go. Refer to the sample marginal annotations and use the suggestions listed in the box "Reading Arguments Critically." In addition, make a special effort to consider the following: We have offered paraphrases of the main point and the reasons. How would you put them into your own words? Would you add anything to Quindlen's definition of "authentic American"? How thoroughly and fairly has Quindlen presented the opposing view? What is she assuming about the chances for success for this new wave of immigrants? Has she given enough evidence to suggest that the public schools can handle the variety of ethnic groups she describes? Does she need more evidence to show that earlier waves of immigrants also learned English only reluctantly?

AFTER YOU READ

A person who invests time and effort in critical reading usually becomes engaged enough in the text and the issue it deals with to be curious about others' reactions to the same argument. As a student in a college course, you will be able to compare your responses to arguments with the responses of other students and your instructor. Thus, critical reading is a way for you to enter the ongoing conversation that serves to create knowledge itself. For professionals in all fields, conversations about one another's arguments take place all the time—orally, in meetings and at conferences, and in writing, through both informal critiques and articles in popular and professional journals. Ultimately, such conversations establish and refine the bodies of knowledge that constitute the various disciplines and professions.

Finally, any reading should point you in the direction of further reading. For example, you might find references to other books or articles on the topic; many scholarly arguments conclude with a bibliography showing works the author consulted. Or you can use the research methods described in Chapter 9 to find other articles and arguments.

Following Through

In your writer's notebook respond to Quindlen's argument. Do you accept her position? Do you find the argument convincing? If you do, why? If not, why not? Much of the debate today about legal immigration centers on a change in immigration policy that occurred in 1965 and its effects since then. What more would you need to know before you could take a more informed position on U.S. immigration policy?

CHAPTER THREE

Analyzing an Argument: A Simplified Toulmin Method

In Chapter 2 we discussed the importance of reading arguments critically: breaking them down into their parts to see how they are put together, noting in the margins key terms that are not defined, and raising questions about the writer's claims or evidence. Although these general techniques are sufficient for analyzing many arguments, sometimes—especially with intricate arguments and with arguments we sense are faulty but whose weaknesses we are unable to specify—we need a more systematic technique.

In this chapter we explain and illustrate such a technique based on the work of Stephen Toulmin, a contemporary philosopher who has contributed a great deal to our understanding of argumentation. This method will allow you to analyze the logic of any argument, whether written or spoken; you will also find it useful in examining the logic of your own arguments as you draft and revise them. Keep in mind, however, that because it is limited to the analysis of logic, the Toulmin method is not sufficient by itself. It is also important to question an argument through dialogue (see Chapter 4) and to look at the appeals of character, emotion, and style (see Chapter 6).

A PRELIMINARY CRITICAL READING

Before we consider Toulmin, let's first explore the following argument carefully, using the general process for critical reading we described in Chapter 2.

WILLIAM F. MAY

Rising to the Occasion of Our Death

William F. May (b. 1927) is a distinguished professor of ethics at Southern Methodist University. The following essay appeared originally in The Christian Century *(1990).*

1 FOR MANY parents, a Volkswagen van is associated with putting children to sleep on a camping trip. Jack Kevorkian, a Detroit pathologist, has now linked the van with the veterinarian's meaning of "putting to sleep." Kevorkian conducted a dinner interview with Janet Elaine Adkins, a 54-year-old Alzheimer's patient, and her husband and then agreed to help her commit suicide in his VW van. Kevorkian pressed beyond the more generally accepted practice of passive euthanasia (allowing a patient to die by withholding or withdrawing treatment) to active euthanasia (killing for mercy).

Kevorkian, moreover, did not comply with the strict regulations that govern active euthanasia in, for example, the Netherlands. Holland requires that death be imminent (Adkins had beaten her son in tennis just a few days earlier); it demands a more professional review of the medical evidence and the patient's resolution than a dinner interview with a physician (who is a stranger and who does not treat patients) permits; and it calls for the final, endorsing signatures of two doctors.

So Kevorkian-bashing is easy. But the question remains: Should we develop a judicious, regulated social policy permitting voluntary euthanasia for the terminally ill? Some moralists argue that the distinction between allowing to die and killing for mercy is petty quibbling over technique. Since the patient in any event dies—whether by acts of omission or commission—the route to death doesn't really matter. The way modern procedures have made dying at the hands of the experts and their machines such a prolonged and painful business has further fueled the euthanasia movement, which asserts not simply the right to die but the right to be killed.

But other moralists believe that there is an important moral distinction between allowing to die and mercy killing. The euthanasia movement, these critics contend, wants to engineer death rather than face dying. Euthanasia would bypass dying to make one dead as quickly as possible. It aims to relieve suffering by knocking out the interval between life and death. It solves the problem of suffering by eliminating the sufferer.

5 The impulse behind the euthanasia movement is understandable in an age when dying has become such an inhumanly endless business. But the movement may fail to appreciate our human capacity to rise to the occasion of our death. The best death is not always the sudden death. Those forewarned of death and given time to prepare for it have time to engage in acts of

reconciliation. Also, advanced grieving by those about to be bereaved may ease some of their pain. Psychiatrists have observed that those who lose a loved one accidentally have a more difficult time recovering from the loss than those who have suffered through an extended period of illness before the death. Those who have lost a close relative by accident are more likely to experience what Geoffrey Gorer has called limitless grief. The community, moreover, may need its aged and dependent, its sick and its dying, and the virtues which they sometimes evince—the virtues of humility, courage, and patience—just as much as the community needs the virtues of justice and love manifest in the agents of care.

On the whole, our social policy should allow terminal patients to die but it should not regularize killing for mercy. Such a policy would recognize and respect that moment in illness when it no longer makes sense to bend every effort to cure or to prolong life and when one must allow patients to do their own dying. This policy seems most consonant with the obligations of the community to care and of the patient to finish his or her course.

Advocates of active euthanasia appeal to the principle of patient autonomy—as the use of the phrase "voluntary euthanasia" indicates. But emphasis on the patient's right to determine his or her destiny often harbors an extremely naïve view of the uncoerced nature of the decision. Patients who plead to be put to death hardly make unforced decisions if the terms and conditions under which they receive care already nudge them in the direction of the exit. If the elderly have stumbled around in their apartments, alone and frightened for years, or if they have spent years warehoused in geriatrics barracks, then the decision to be killed for mercy hardly reflects an uncoerced decision. The alternative may be so wretched as to push patients toward this escape. It is a huge irony and, in some cases, hypocrisy to talk suddenly about a compassionate killing when the aging and dying may have been starved for compassion for many years. To put it bluntly, a country has not earned the moral right to kill for mercy unless it has already sustained and supported life mercifully. Otherwise we kill for compassion only to reduce the demands on our compassion. This statement does not charge a given doctor or family member with impure motives. I am concerned here not with the individual case but with the cumulative impact of a social policy.

I can, to be sure, imagine rare circumstances in which I hope I would have the courage to kill for mercy—when the patient is utterly beyond human care, terminal, and in excruciating pain. A neurosurgeon once showed a group of physicians and an ethicist the picture of a Vietnam casualty who had lost all four limbs in a landmine explosion. The catastrophe had reduced the soldier to a trunk with his face transfixed in horror. On the battlefield I would hope that I would have the courage to kill the sufferer with mercy.

But hard cases do not always make good laws or wise social policies. Regularized mercy killings would too quickly relieve the community of its obligation to provide good care. Further, we should not always expect the law to provide us with full protection and coverage for what, in rare circumstances, we may morally need to do. Sometimes the moral life calls us out into a no-man's-land where we cannot expect total security and protection under the law. But no one said that the moral life is easy.

A STEP-BY-STEP DEMONSTRATION OF THE TOULMIN METHOD

The Toulmin method requires an analysis of the claim, the reasons offered to support the claim, and the evidence offered to support the reasons, along with an analysis of any refutations offered.

Analyzing the Claim

Logical analysis begins with identifying the *claim,* the thesis or central contention, along with any specific qualifications or exceptions.

Identify the Claim

First ask yourself, *What statement is the author defending?* In "Rising to the Occasion of Our Death," for example, William May spells out his claim in paragraph 6:

> Our social policy should allow terminal patients to die but it should not regularize killing for mercy.

In his claim May supports passive euthanasia (letting someone die by withholding or discontinuing treatment) but opposes "regularizing" (making legal or customary) active euthanasia (administering, say, an overdose of morphine to cause a patient's death).

Much popular argumentation is sometimes careless about what exactly is being claimed: untrained arguers too often content themselves with merely taking sides ("Euthanasia is wrong"). Note that May, a student of ethics trained in philosophical argumentation, makes a claim that is both specific and detailed. Whenever an argument does not include an explicit statement of its claim, you should begin your analysis by stating the writer's claim yourself. Try to state all claims fully and carefully in sentence form, as May's claim is stated.

Look for Qualifiers

Next ask, *How is the claim qualified?* Is it absolute, or does it include words or phrases to indicate that it may not hold true in every situation or set of circumstances?

May qualifies his claim in paragraph 6 with the phrase "on the whole," indicating that he recognizes possible exceptions to the application of his claim. Other possible qualifiers include "typically," "usually," and "most of the time." Careful arguers are generally wary of making absolute claims. Although unqualified claims are not necessarily faulty, they do insist that there are no cases or circumstances in which the claim might legitimately be contradicted.

Qualifying words or phrases are often used to restrict a claim and improve its defensibility.

Find the Exceptions

Finally ask, *In what cases or circumstances would the writer not press his or her claim?* Look for any explicit exceptions the writer offers to qualify the claim.

May, for example, is quite clear in paragraph 8 about when he would not press his claim:

> I hope I would have the courage to kill for mercy—when the patient is utterly beyond human care, terminal, and in excruciating pain.

Once he has specified these conditions in abstract terms, he goes further and offers a chilling example of a case in which he believes mercy-killing would be appropriate. Nevertheless, he insists that such exceptions are rare and thus do not justify making active euthanasia legal or allowing it to become common policy.

Critical readers respond to unqualified claims skeptically—by hunting for exceptions. With qualified claims they look to see what specific exceptions the writer will admit and what considerations make restrictions necessary or desirable.

Summarize the Claim

At this point it is a good idea to write out the claim, its qualifiers, and its exceptions in your writer's notebook so that you can see all of them clearly. For May they look like this:

(qualifier)	"On the whole"
(claim)	"our social policy should allow terminal patients to die but it should not regularize killing for mercy"
(exception)	"when the patient is utterly beyond human care, terminal, and in excruciating pain"

Record the claim and its qualifiers and exceptions in whatever way helps you see them best, but do not skip this step. Not only will it help you remember the results of your initial claim analysis, but you will also be building on this summary when you analyze the argument in more detail.

Analyzing the Reasons

Once you have analyzed the claim, you should next identify and evaluate the reasons offered for the claim.

List the Reasons

Begin by asking yourself, *Why is the writer advancing this claim?* Look for any statement or statements that are used to justify the thesis. May groups all of his reasons in paragraph 5:

The dying should have time to prepare for death and to reconcile with relatives and friends.

Those close to the dying should have time to come to terms with the impending loss of a loved one.

The community needs examples of dependent but patient and courageous people who sometimes do die with dignity.

The community needs the virtues ("justice and love") of those who care for the sick and dying.

When you list reasons, you need not preserve the exact words of the arguer; often doing so is impossible, because reasons are not always explicit but may have to be inferred. Be very careful, however, to adhere as closely as possible to the writer's language. Otherwise, your analysis can easily go astray, imposing a reason of your own that the writer did not have in mind.

Note that reasons, like claims, can be qualified. May does not say, for instance, that "the aged and dependent" *always* show "the virtues of humility, courage, and patience." He implicitly admits that they can be ornery and cowardly as well. But for May's purposes it is enough that they sometimes manifest the virtues he admires.

Use your writer's notebook to list the reasons following your summary of the claim, qualifiers, and exceptions. One possibility is to list them beneath the summary of the claim in the form of a tree diagram (see the diagram on page 29).

Examine the Reasons

There are two questions to ask as you examine the reasons. First ask, *Are they really good reasons?* A reason is only as good as the values it invokes or implies. A value is something we think is good—that is, worth pursuing for its own sake or because it leads to attaining other goods. For each reason you should specify the values involved and then determine whether you accept those values as generally binding.

Second ask, *Is the reason relevant to the thesis?* In other words, does the relationship between the claim and the reason hold up to examination? For example, the claim "You should buy a new car from Fred Freed" cannot be supported by the reason "Fred is a family man with three cute kids" unless you accept a relationship between an auto dealer's having cute children and his or her reliability in dealing with customers.

Be careful and deliberate as you examine whether reasons are good and whether they are relevant. No other step is as important in assessing the logic of an argument, and no other can be quite as tricky.

To illustrate, consider May's first reason: Those who know they are about to die should have time to prepare for death and to seek reconciliation with people from whom they have become estranged. Is this a good reason? Most of us would probably think so, valuing the chance to prepare for death and to reconcile ourselves with estranged friends or family members. Not to do so would seem immature, irresponsible, unforgiving.

A Toulmin Model for Analyzing Arguments

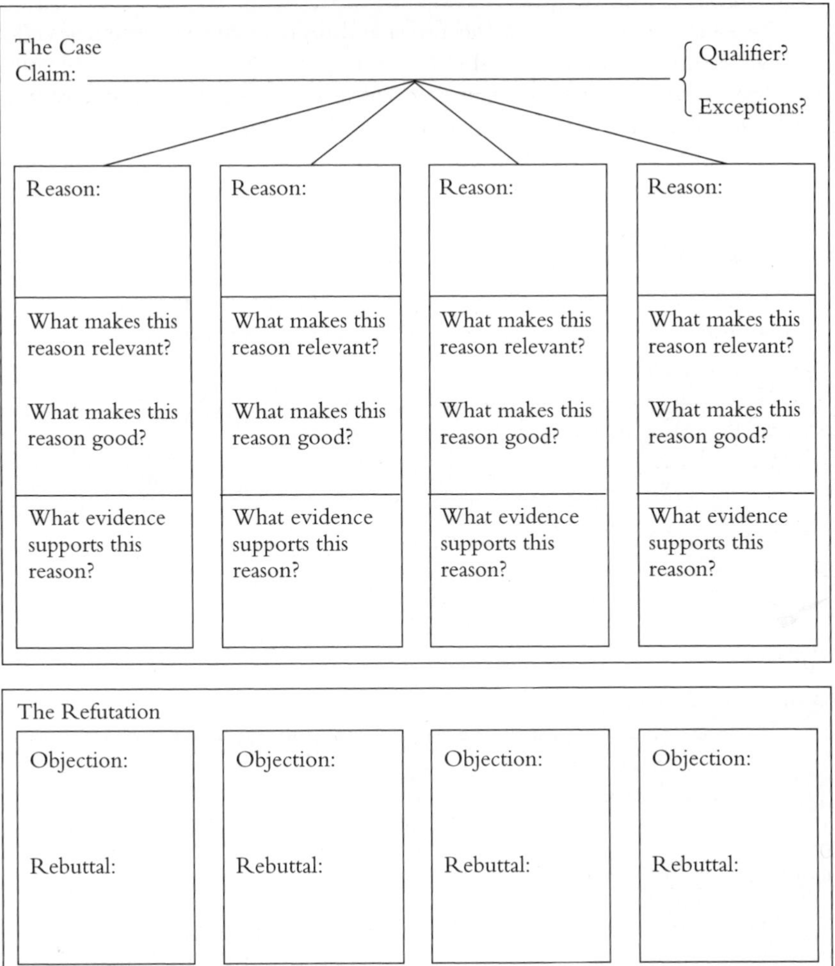

But is the reason relevant? May seems to rule out the possibility that a dying person seeking active euthanasia would be able to prepare for death and reconcile with others. But this is obviously not the case. Terminally ill people who decide to arrange for their own deaths may make any number of preparations beforehand, so the connection between this reason and May's claim is really quite weak. To accept a connection, we would have to assume that active euthanasia necessarily amounts to a sudden death without adequate preparation. Because we cannot do so, we are entitled to question the relevance of the reason, no matter how good it might be in itself.

Following Through

Now examine May's second, third, and fourth reasons on your own, as we have just examined the first one. Make notes about each reason, evaluating how good each is in itself and how relevant it is to the thesis. In your writing notebook create your own diagram based on the model on page 29.

Analyzing the Evidence

Once you have finished your analysis of the reasons, the next step is to consider the evidence offered to support any of those reasons.

List the Evidence

Ask, *What kinds of evidence (data, anecdotes, case studies, citations from authority, and so forth) are offered as support for each reason?* Some arguments advance little in the way of evidence. May's argument is a good example of a moral argument from and about principles; such an argument does not require much evidence to be effective. Lack of evidence, then, is not always a fault. For one of his reasons, however, May does offer some evidence: after stating his second reason in paragraph 5—the chance to grieve before a loved one dies can be helpful for those who must go on living after the patient's death—he invokes authorities who agree with him about the value of advanced grieving.

Examine the Evidence

Two questions apply. First ask, *Is the evidence good?* That is, is it sufficient, accurate, and credible? Second ask, *Is it relevant to the reason it supports?* Clearly, the evidence May offers in paragraph 5 is sufficient; any more would probably be too much. We assume his citations are accurate and credible as well. We would generally also accept them as relevant, because apart from our own experience with grieving, we have to rely on expert opinion. (See Chapter 5 for a fuller discussion of estimating the adequacy and relevance of evidence.)

Noting Refutations

A final—and optional—step is to assess an arguer's refutations. In a refutation a writer anticipates potential objections to his or her position and tries to show why they do not undermine the basic argument. Refutations do not relate directly to claims, reasons, and evidence. A skilled arguer typically uses them not as part of the main logic of an argument but as a separate step to deal with any obvious objections a reader is likely to have.

First ask, *What refutations does the writer offer?* Summarize all refutations and list them on your tree diagram of claims, reasons, and evidence. Then ask, *How does the writer approach each objection?* May's refutation occupies paragraph 7. He recognizes that the value of free choice lends weight to the pro-euthanasia position, and so he relates this value to the question of "voluntary euthanasia."

Because in our culture individual freedom is so strong a value, May doesn't question the value itself; rather, he leads us to question whether voluntary euthanasia is actually a matter of free choice. He suggests that unwanted people may be subtly coerced into "choosing" death or may be so isolated and neglected that death becomes preferable to life. Thus, he responds to the objection that dying people should have freedom of choice where death is concerned.

Summarizing Your Analysis

Once you have completed your analysis, it is a good idea to summarize the results in a paragraph or two. Be sure to set aside your own position on the issue, confining your summary to the argument the writer makes. In other words, whether you agree with the author, attempt to assess his or her logic fairly.

Although May's logic is strong, it doesn't seem fully compelling. He qualifies his argument and uses exceptions effectively, and his single use of refutation is skillful. However, he fails to acknowledge that active euthanasia need not be a sudden decision leading to sudden death. Consequently, his reasons for supporting passive euthanasia can be used to support at least some cases of active euthanasia as well. It is here—in the linkage between reasons and claim—that May's argument falls short. Furthermore, we may question whether the circumstances under which May would permit active euthanasia are in fact as rare as he suggests. Experience tells us that many people are beyond human care, terminal, and in pain, and many others suffer acute anguish for which they might legitimately seek the relief of death.

Following Through

Following is a student-written argument on capital punishment. Read it through once, and then use the Toulmin method as described in this chapter to analyze its logic systematically.

Student Sample: An Argument for Analysis

AMBER YOUNG

Capital Punishment: Society's Self-Defense

JUST AFTER 1:00 A.M. on a warm night in early June, Georgeann, a pretty college student, left through the back door of a fraternity house to walk the ninety feet down a well-lighted alley to the back door of her sorority house. Lively and vivacious, Georgeann had been an honor student, a 1 cheerleader, and Daffodil Princess in high school, and now she was in the middle of finals week, trying to maintain her straight A record in college. That evening several people saw Georgeann walk to within about forty feet of the door of her sorority house. However, she never arrived. Somewhere in that last forty feet, she met a tall, handsome young man on crutches, his leg in a cast, struggling with a brief case. The young man asked Georgeann if she could help him get to his car which was parked nearby. Georgeann consented. Meanwhile, a housemother sleeping by an open window in a nearby fraternity house was awakened by a high-pitched, terrified scream that suddenly stopped. That was the last anyone ever heard or saw of Georgeann Hawkins. Her bashed skull and broken body were dumped on a hillside many miles away, along with the bodies of several other young female victims who had also been lured to their deaths by the good looking, clean-cut, courteous, intelligent, and charming Ted Bundy.

By the time Ted Bundy was caught in Utah with his bashing bar and other homemade tools of torture, he had bludgeoned and strangled to death at least thirty-two young women, raping and savaging many of them in the process. His "hunting" trips had extended into at least five Western states, including Washington, Oregon, Idaho, Utah, and Colorado, where he randomly selected and killed his unsuspecting victims.

Bundy was ultimately convicted of the attempted kidnapping of Carol DeRonche and imprisoned. For this charge he probably would have been paroled within eighteen months. However, before parole could be approved, Bundy was transferred to a jail in Colorado to stand trial for the murder of Caryn Campbell. With Bundy in jail, no one died at his hands or at the end of his savagely swung club. Young women could go about their lives normally, "safe" and separated from Ted Bundy by prison walls. Yet any number of things could have occurred to set Bundy free—an acquittal, some sympathetic judge or parole board, a psychiatrist pronouncing him rehabilitated and safe, a state legislature passing shorter sentencing or earlier parole laws, inadequate prison space, a federal court ruling abolishing life in prison without any possibility for parole, or an escape.

In Bundy's case, it was escape—twice—from Colorado jails. The first time he was immediately caught and brought back. The second time Bundy made it to Florida, where fifteen days after his escape he bludgeoned and strangled Margaret Bowman, Lisa Levy, Karen Chandler, and Kathy Kleiner in their Tallahassee sorority house, tearing chunks out of Lisa Levy's breast and buttock with his teeth. Ann Rule, a noted crime writer who became Bundy's confidant while writing her book *The Stranger Beside Me,* described Bundy's attack on Lisa Levy as like that of a rabid animal. On the same night at a different location, Bundy sneaked through an open window and so savagely attacked Cheryl Thomas in her bed that a woman in the apartment next door described the clubbing as seeming to reverberate through the whole house for about ten seconds. Then, three weeks later, less than forty days after his escape from the Colorado jail, Bundy went hunting again. He missed his chance at one quarry, junior high school student Leslie Ann Parmenter, when her brother showed up and thwarted her abduction. But Bundy succeeded the next day in Lake City, where he abducted and killed twelve-year-old Kimberly Diane Leach and dumped her strangled, broken body in an abandoned pig barn.

The criminal justice system and jails in Utah and Colorado did not 5
keep Margaret Bowman, Lisa Levy, Karen Chandler, Kathy Kleiner, Cheryl Thomas, Leslie Ann Parmenter, or little Kimberly Leach safe from Ted Bundy. The state of Florida, however, with its death penalty, has made every other young woman safe from Ted Bundy forever. Capital punishment is society's means of self-defense. Just as a person is justified in using deadly force in defending herself or himself against a would-be killer, so society also has a right to use deadly force to defend itself and its citizens from those who exhibit a strong propensity to kill whenever the opportunity and the urge arise.

However, while everyone wants a safe society, some people would say that capital punishment is too strong a means of ensuring it. Contemporary social critic Hendrick Hertzberg often attacks the death penalty, using arguments that are familiar, but not compelling, to those who do not share his absolute value-of-life position. For example, in one article he tries to paint a graphic picture of how horrible and painful even the most modern execution methods, such as lethal injection, are to the prisoner ("Premeditated"). Elsewhere he dismisses the deterrence argument as "specious," since "[n]o one has ever been able to show that capital punishment lowers the murder rate" ("Burning" 4). But the Florida death penalty has, in fact, made certain that Ted Bundy will never again go on one of his hunting trips to look for another young woman's skull to bash or body to ravage. A needle prick in the arm hardly conjures up images of excruciating pain so great as to be cruel and unusual. Thousands of good people with cancer and other diseases or injuries endure much greater pain every day until death. Therefore, waiting for death, even in pain, is more a part of a common life experience than a cruel or unusual punishment.

Of course, the possibility of mistakenly executing an innocent person is a serious concern. However, our entire criminal justice system is tilted heavily toward the accused, who is protected from the start to the end of the criminal justice procedure by strong individual-rights guarantees in the Fourth, Fifth, Sixth, and Seventh Amendments of the U.S. Constitution. The burden of proof in a criminal case is on the government, and guilt must be proved beyond a reasonable doubt. The chances of a guilty person going free in our system are many times greater than those of an innocent person being convicted. Those opposed may ask, "How do we know that the number of innocent people found guilty is really that low?" The number must be low because when the scandal of an innocent person being convicted comes to light, the media covers it from all angles. The movie *The Thin Blue Line* is an example of such media attention. In addition, the story of *The Thin Blue Line* is illustrative in that the U.S. Supreme Court caught the error and remanded the case, and Randall Adams is no longer subject to the death penalty.

If, however, such a mistake should occur in spite of all the protections guaranteed to the accused, such an innocent death would certainly be tragic, just as each of the nearly 50,000 deaths of innocent people each year on our highways are tragic. As much as we value human life, we inevitably weigh and balance that value against social costs and benefits, whether we like to admit it or not. If the rare, almost nonexistent, chance that an innocent person might be executed is such a terrible evil as to require abolition of capital punishment, then why don't we also demand the abolition of automobiles as well? Because we balance the value of those lives lost in traffic accidents against the importance of automobiles in society. In doing so, we choose to accept the thousands of automobile deaths per year in order to keep our cars. It is interesting to note that even opponents of capital punishment, like Hertzberg, do not demand abolition of the automobile, which leads to the observation that even they may not be at the extreme, absolute end of the life-value scale, where preservation of life takes precedence over *all* other social concerns.

Just as we, as a society, have decided that the need for automobiles outweighs their threat to innocent life, we can decide that capital punishment is necessary for the safety and well-being of the general populace. The most legitimate and strongest reason for capital punishment is not punishment, retribution, or deterrence, but simply society's right to self-defense. Society has a right to expect and demand that its government remove forever those persons who have shown they cannot be trusted to circulate in society, even on a limited basis, without committing mayhem. First degree murderers, like Bundy, who hunt and kill their victims with premeditation and malice aforethought must be removed from society permanently as a matter of self-defense.

10 Having made that decision, there are only two alternatives available—life in prison or death. We base our approval or disapproval of capital punishment as an option on fundamental values and ideals relating to life itself, rather than on statistics or factual evidence. Most of us are a long way from the extreme that considers life to have no value; instead, we crowd more closely to the other side, where life is viewed as inviolable. However, few in our society go so far as to believe that life is sacrosanct, that its preservation is required above all else. Our founding fathers wrote in the Declaration of Independence that all men are endowed by their Creator with unalienable rights, including "life, liberty, and the pursuit of happiness." However, there is no indication that life was more sacred to them than liberty. In fact, Patrick Henry, who would later be instrumental in the adoption of the Bill of Rights to the U.S. Constitution, is most famous for his defiant American Revolutionary declaration "I know not what course others may take, but as for me, give me liberty or give me death!"

The sentiment that some things are worse than death remains pervasive in this country where millions of soldiers and others have put themselves in harm's way and even sacrificed their lives to preserve and defend freedom for themselves or for the people they leave behind. Many people will readily or reluctantly admit to their willingness to use deadly force to protect themselves or their families from a murderer. The preservation of life, any life, regardless of everything else, is not an absolute value that most people in this country hold.

In fact, many prisoners would prefer to die than to languish in prison. While some might still want to read and expand their minds even while their bodies are confined, for those who are not intellectually or spiritually oriented, life in prison would be a fate worse than death. Bundy himself, in his letters from prison to Ann Rule, declared, "My world is a cage," as he tried to describe "the cruel metamorphosis that occurs in captivity" (qtd. in Rule 148). After his sentencing in Utah, Bundy described his attempts to prepare mentally for the "living hell of prison" (qtd. in Rule 191). Thus, some condemned prisoners, including Gary Gilmore, the first person to be executed after the U.S. Supreme Court found that Utah's death penalty law met Constitutional requirements, refused to participate in the appeals attempting to convert his death sentence to life in prison because he preferred death over such a life. In our society, which was literally founded and sustained on the principle that liberty is more important than life, the argument that it is somehow less cruel and more civilized to deprive someone of liberty for the rest of his or her life than just to end the life sounds hollow. The Fifth Amendment of the U.S. Constitution prohibits the taking of either life or liberty without due process of law, but it does not place one at a higher value than the other.

The overriding concerns of the Constitution, however, are safety and self-defense. The chance of a future court ruling, a release on parole, a pardon, a commutation of sentence, or an escape—any of which could turn the murderer loose to prey again on society—creates a risk that society should not have to bear. Lisa Levy, Margaret Bowman, Karen Chandler, Kathy Kleiner, Cheryl Thomas, and Kimberly Leach were not protected from Bundy by the courts and jails in Utah and Colorado, but other young women who were potential victims are now absolutely protected from Bundy by the Florida death penalty.

The resolutions of most great controversies are, in fact, balancing acts, and capital punishment is no exception. There is no perfect solution; rather, the best answer lies on the side with the greatest advantages. It comes down to choosing, and choosing has a price. Capital punishment carries with it the slight risk that an innocent person will be executed; however, it is more important to protect innocent, would-be victims of already convicted murderers. On balance, society was not demeaned by the execution of Bundy in Florida, as claimed by Hertzberg ("Burning" 49). On the contrary, society is, in fact, better off with Ted Bundy and others like him gone.

WORKS CITED

Hertzberg, Hendrick. "Burning Question." *The New Republic* 20 Feb. 1989: 4+.

———. "Premeditated Execution." *Time* 18 May 1992: 49.

Rule, Ann. *The Stranger Beside Me.* New York: Penguin, 1989.

The Thin Blue Line. Dir. Errol Morris. HBO Video, 1988.

FROM ANALYSIS TO INQUIRY

No method for analyzing arguments is perfect, and no method can guarantee that everyone using it will assess an argument the same way. Uniform results are not especially desirable anyway. What would be left to talk about? The point of argumentative analysis is to step back and examine an argument carefully, to detect how it is structured, to assess the cogency and power of its logic. The Toulmin method helps us move beyond a hit-or-miss approach to logical analysis, but it cannot yield a conclusion as compelling as mathematical proof.

Convincing and persuading always involve more than logic, and, therefore, logical analysis alone is never enough to assess the strength of an argument. For example, William May's argument attempts to discredit those like Dr. Jack Kevorkian who assist patients wishing to take their own lives. May depicts Kevorkian as offering assistance without sufficient consultation with the patient. Is his depiction accurate? Clearly, we can answer this question only by finding out more about how Kevorkian and others like him work. Because such questions are not a part of logical analysis, they have not been of concern to us in this chapter. But any adequate and thorough analysis of an argument must also address questions of fact and the interpretation of data.

Logical analysis as we have been discussing it here is a prelude to arguing to inquire, the focus of the next chapter. Analysis helps us find some of the questions we need to ask about the arguments we read and write. Such "stepping back" is good discipline, but we think you will agree that "joining in," contributing to dialogue about arguments, is both more fun and more rewarding. So, not forgetting what we have learned in this chapter, let's move on to the more interesting and more human art of *dialogue*.

CHAPTER FOUR

Preparing to Write: Arguing to Inquire

In Chapter 1 we distinguished four aims or uses of argument: inquiring, convincing, persuading, and negotiating. Argument as inquiry, the focus of this chapter, has the following characteristics.

Its end or purpose is truth. Truth is a claim about what we believe or ought to believe—what we take to be right or correct. When we argue to inquire, we are not attempting to support a belief or position we hold already; rather, we are seeking to define our position on an issue or examining a tentatively held position to discover if it is really the one we should take. Inquiry is a means of finding the position on some issue that both satisfies us personally and holds up under the scrutiny of others.

Its audience is primarily the inquirer along with fellow inquirers concerned with the same controversial issue. In inquiry we argue with ourselves or with other people whose minds are open and who share our interest in some question. Such people might include friends, classmates, counselors, parents, and teachers—anyone who will cooperate with us in a patient questioning of opinion.

Its medium is dialogue. Inquiry requires participating in a conversation, instead of simply doing research, because no claim to truth about a topic exists outside of human conversation, free of opinions and values. Even a factual news report of an event—for example, an assisted suicide—comes to our attention in a way that challenges a set of values, complete with quoted opinions from involved parties and interested authorities. Our opinions result partly from our responses to these other opinions. When we go on to do library research, we extend the conversation as we question and interpret information and arguments in the print media. Inquiry is interactive, a question-and-answer process that can take a variety of forms. The most common forms are one-on-one dialogues and small-group discussions, but inquiry can also take the form of imaginary dialogues that you carry on with yourself. Further, when you base your inquiry on a written text, you should also engage in "conversation"—listening to what the text says and trying to detect its strengths and weaknesses.

Its art consists of discovering the right questions and the best answers. Inquiry is the process through which we form and test our opinions and earn our claims to truth, our convictions. Therefore, the "right" questions are those that improve our understanding and that reveal weak or misleading parts of an argument. The best answers in inquiry are those that are direct and honest, not evasive, convoluted, defensive, or dogmatic. Inquiry is friendly interrogation: its aim is *not* to prove that we are right and someone else is wrong, but rather to examine opinions in a search for truth.

In sum, then, argument as inquiry is a dialogue with oneself, another person, or a text—a way of examining competing claims of truth through a process of questioning and answering.

THE IMPORTANCE OF INQUIRY

We begin with argument as inquiry for several reasons. First, inquiry is often where we must start a writing project, especially when we know relatively little about the topic at hand. Even when we know enough to have formed an opinion about the topic, we still need to examine what we claim to know and what stance we want to take.

More importantly, we start with inquiry because, alone among the aims of argument, it has truth as its single goal. Before trying to move an audience toward a position we advocate, we have a moral responsibility to first examine that position and the reasons we hold it. Convincing and persuading become immoral when people have no regard for the truth—when they set out to gain advantage by glossing over or distorting what they know to be true or when they make no effort to distinguish truth from error in the first place. Of course, there is nothing wrong with the desire to influence other people. But we need only look around us to see a world full of irresponsible advocacy. Advertising agencies promote products without questioning their effectiveness or even their safety. Politicians appeal to voters' prejudices and willingly change their positions with the shifting winds of public opinion. Television preachers take advantage of gullible and uneducated viewers, persuading them to send money in return for prayers and miracles. Special interest groups thwart the public interest by coercing votes from policymakers fearful of their influence and dependent on their campaign contributions.

Less obviously, perhaps, as individuals we shirk our moral responsibility when we accept uncritically as truth the beliefs of others—whether parents, teachers, or so-called experts. Questioning received truths takes effort and may make us uncomfortable, but we must do it if we are to earn our convictions and responsibly exercise our right to free speech.

No amount of thoughtful inquiry can prevent us from being mistaken some of the time; what we take to be true will often turn out to be false or only partly true. But at least if we commit ourselves to serious inquiry, we can avoid unethical argumentation, the kind that has no regard for the truth.

Finally, inquiry is fundamental to the academic environment in which you now find yourself. No other contemporary institution is dedicated to inquiry to the extent that higher education is. Here people are valued not only for their knowledge but also, and more importantly, for the searching questions they ask. Research methods in the various fields of study differ greatly, but all claims to knowledge are arguments, and all arguments are subject to question, to inquiry. Consequently, what we are about to discuss—argument as inquiry—applies to anything you might study in college, as well as to the arguments you encounter elsewhere.

QUESTIONS FOR INQUIRY

How do we go about inquiring into our own or someone else's position on an issue? There is no single procedure to follow, because a conversation is a natural act and does not run according to a script or pattern. But while every conversation takes its own course, the quality of the dialogue will depend on the kinds of questions posed. The following list suggests what you should ask when you want to open an argument to scrutiny.

1. *Ask if you have understood the arguer's position on the issue.* The best way to do this is to restate, paraphrase, or summarize the thesis. (Face-to-face you might say, "I believe that you are saying . . . Am I understanding you?") Be sure to note how strongly the claim is made. Has the arguer qualified it by suggesting conditions or exceptions? If you are inquiring into your own argument, ask if you have stated your own position clearly. Do you need to qualify it in any way?
2. *Ask about the meaning of any words that seem central to the argument*. You can do this at any point in a conversation and as often as it seems necessary. When dealing with a written text, try to discern the meaning from the context. For instance, if an author's case depends on the fairness of a proposed solution, you'll need to ask what "fair" means, because the word has a range of possible applications. You might ask, "Fair to whom?"
3. *Ask what reasons support the thesis.* Paraphrasing reasons is a good way to open up a conversation to further questions about assumptions, values, and definitions.
4. *Ask about the assumptions on which the thesis and reasons are based.* Most arguments are based on one or more unstated assumptions. For example, if a college recruiter argues that the school he or she represents is superior to most others (thesis) because its ratio of students to teachers is low (reason), the unstated assumptions are (1) that students there will get more attention, and (2) that more attention results in a better education. As

you inquire into an argument, note the assumptions and ask if they are reasonable.

5. *Ask about the values expressed or implied by the argument.* For example, if you argue that closing a forest to logging operations is essential even at the cost of dozens of jobs, you are valuing environmental preservation over the livelihoods of the workers who must search for other jobs.
6. *Ask how well the reasons are supported.* Are they offered as opinions only, or are they supported with evidence? Is the evidence recent? sufficient? What kind of testimony is offered? Who are the authorities cited? What are their credentials and biases? Are there other facts or authoritative statements that might weaken the argument?
7. *Consider analogies and comparisons.* If the author makes an argument by analogy, does the comparison hold up? For example, advocates of animal rights draw an analogy with civil rights when they claim that just as we have come to recognize the immorality of exploiting human beings, so we should recognize the immorality of exploiting other species. But is this analogy sound?
8. *Ask about the arguer's biases and background.* What past experiences might have led the arguer to take this position? What does the holder of this position stand to gain? What might someone gain by challenging it?
9. *Ask about implications.* Where would the argument ultimately lead should we accept what the speaker advocates? For example, if someone contends that abortion is murder, asking about implications would lead to the question, Are you willing to put women who get abortions on trial for murder and, if they are convicted, to punish them as murderers are usually punished?
10. *Ask whether the argument takes opposing views into account.* If it does, are they presented fairly and clearly or with mockery and distortion? Does the author take them seriously or dismiss them? Are they effectively refuted?

Use the preceding questions as a checklist as you inquire into arguments; it is a good idea to memorize them or write them down in your writer's notebook for easy reference. Keep in mind, however, that effective inquiry requires much more than a list of questions. First, you must read or listen attentively, taking in what other arguers have to say without being too anxious to assert your own point of view. Of course, you will usually have some sort of gut reaction to any argument, but be careful to listen rather than rush to judgment, just as you would want others to hear you out. Inquiry is more than an exchange of opinion; it is an exploration of opinion. Clearly, no exploration can occur without first listening.

Second, you must ask thoughtful questions and be genuinely engaged in the argument at hand. Because each argument is unique, you cannot apply a checklist of questions mechanically, the same way in every case. To open up a particular argument, you must find the "right" questions to ask, those that reveal the argument's strengths and weaknesses. To reiterate, the art of inquiry, unlike a mechanical process, is a dialogue with oneself, another person, or a text.

INQUIRY AND WRITTEN ARGUMENTS: THE PROCESS OF DIALOGUE

We have said that it is possible to have a "conversation" with writers of written arguments. Doing so requires some imagination on the part of the inquirer, who must not only pose questions but also supply plausible answers from the writer's point of view. Such an imagined dialogue is a good way to evaluate arguments you encounter in your research and to decide which arguments you may want to adapt in support of your own position.

A Preliminary Critical Reading

Suppose you encounter the following argument by Michael Levin while researching the topic of international terrorism and the various antiterrorism policies adopted by nations around the world. First read Levin's argument critically, following the procedure discussed in Chapter 2. Start by skimming, reading the first and last paragraphs and the first sentence or two of each paragraph in between to get a quick overall idea of Levin's point. Then read the argument sequentially, at a moderate pace. Finally, after putting it aside for awhile, read the argument a second time, underlining whatever seems most important and writing down your responses in the margins and in your writer's notebook. If you have trouble following the argument's logic, use a Toulmin analysis as described in Chapter 3. Such an analysis will help prepare you for a dialogue with Levin's case.

MICHAEL LEVIN

The Case for Torture

Michael Levin is a philosophy professor at the City College of New York. This argument was written in 1982 and originally published in Newsweek *magazine.*

IT IS generally assumed that torture is impermissible, a throwback to a more brutal age. Enlightened societies reject it outright, and regimes suspected of using it risk the wrath of the United States. 1

I believe this attitude is unwise. There are situations in which torture is not merely permissible but morally mandatory. Moreover, these situations are moving from the realm of imagination to fact.

Death. Suppose a terrorist has hidden an atomic bomb on Manhattan Island which will detonate at noon on July 4 unless . . . (here follow the usual demands for money and release of his friends from jail). Suppose, further, that he is caught at 10 A.M. of the fateful day, but—preferring death to failure—won't disclose where the bomb is. What do we do? If we follow due process—wait for his lawyer, arraign him—millions of people will die. If the only way to save those lives is to subject the terrorist to the most excruciating possible pain, what grounds can there be for not doing so? I suggest there are none. In any case, I ask you to face the question with an open mind.

Torturing the terrorist is unconstitutional? Probably. But millions of lives surely outweigh constitutionality. Torture is barbaric? Mass murder is far more barbaric. Indeed, letting millions of innocents die in deference to one who flaunts his guilt is moral cowardice, an unwillingness to dirty one's hands. If *you* caught the terrorist, could you sleep nights knowing that millions died because you couldn't bring yourself to apply the electrodes?

Once you concede that torture is justified in extreme cases, you have 5
admitted that the decision to use torture is a matter of balancing innocent lives against the means needed to save them. You must now face more realistic cases involving more modest numbers. Someone plants a bomb on a jumbo jet. He alone can disarm it, and his demands cannot be met (or if they can, we refuse to set a precedent by yielding to his threats). Surely we can, we must, do anything to the extortionist to save the passengers. How can we tell 300, or 100, or 10 people who never asked to be put in danger, "I'm sorry, you'll have to die in agony, we just couldn't bring ourselves to . . ."

Here are the results of an informal poll about a third, hypothetical, case. Suppose a terrorist group kidnapped a newborn baby from a hospital. I asked four mothers if they would approve of torturing kidnappers if that were necessary to get their own newborns back. All said yes, the most "liberal" adding that she would like to administer it herself.

I am not advocating torture as punishment. Punishment is addressed to deeds irrevocably past. Rather, I am advocating torture as an acceptable measure for preventing future evils. So understood, it is far less objectionable than many extant punishments. Opponents of the death penalty, for example, are forever insisting that executing a murderer will not bring back his victim (as if the purpose of capital punishment were supposed to be resurrection, not deterrence or retribution). But torture, in the cases described, is intended not to bring anyone back but to keep innocents from being dispatched. The most powerful argument against using torture as a punishment or to secure confessions is that such practices disregard the rights of the individual. Well, if the individual is all that important—and he is—it is correspondingly important to protect the rights of individuals threatened by terrorists. If life is so valuable that it must never be taken, the lives of the innocents must be saved even at the price of hurting the one who endangers them.

Better precedents for torture are assassination and preemptive attack. No Allied leader would have flinched at assassinating Hitler, had that been possible.

(The Allies did assassinate Heydrich.[1]) Americans would be angered to learn that Roosevelt could have had Hitler killed in 1943—thereby shortening the war and saving millions of lives—but refused on moral grounds. Similarly, if nation A learns that nation B is about to launch an unprovoked attack, A has a right to save itself by destroying B's military capability first. In the same way, if the police can by torture save those who would otherwise die at the hands of kidnappers or terrorists, they must.

Idealism. There is an important difference between terrorists and their victims that should mute talk of the terrorists' "rights." The terrorist's victims are at risk unintentionally, not having asked to be endangered. But the terrorist knowingly initiated his actions. Unlike his victims, he volunteered for the risks of his deed. By threatening to kill for profit or idealism, he renounces civilized standards, and he can have no complaint if civilization tries to thwart him by whatever means necessary.

Just as torture is justified only to save lives (not extort confessions or 10
recantations), it is justifiably administered only to those *known* to hold innocent lives in their hands. Ah, but how can the authorities ever be sure they have the right malefactor? Isn't there a danger of error and abuse? Won't We turn into Them?

Questions like these are disingenuous in a world in which terrorists proclaim themselves and perform for television. The name of their game is public recognition. After all, you can't very well intimidate a government into releasing your freedom fighters unless you announce that it is your group that has seized its embassy. "Clear guilt" is difficult to define, but when 40 million people see a group of masked gunmen seize an airplane on the evening news, there is not much question about who the perpetrators are. There will be hard cases where the situation is murkier. Nonetheless, a line demarcating the legitimate use of torture can be drawn. Torture only the obviously guilty, and only for the sake of saving innocents, and the line between Us and Them will remain clear.

There is little danger that the Western democracies will lose their way if they choose to inflict pain as one way of preserving order. Paralysis in the face of evil is the greater danger. Some day soon a terrorist will threaten tens of thousands of lives, and torture will be the only way to save them. We had better start thinking about this.

A Sample Dialogue

Begin your dialogue with Michael Levin by questioning the gist of his position in "The Case for Torture." As with any written argument, you must

[1]Reinhard Heydrich, deputy chief of the Gestapo in Hitler's Germany, was known as "the Hangman of Europe." He was assassinated by Czech patriots.

take special care in doing so because the author is not present to correct you if you go wrong. The questioner should always begin with what the answerer has said, gaining the assent of the answerer at every step in the line of reasoning: "Did I understand you to say . . . ?" "Yes." "And did you also assert . . . ?" "I did." These preliminary questions are important because they set the stage for exploring the argument itself and help ensure the mutual understanding necessary for dialogue.

In "The Case for Torture" you don't have to search for a thesis; Levin states his central position explicitly in paragraph 2: "There are situations in which torture is not merely permissible but morally mandatory." You might begin the dialogue by paraphrasing that main idea:

Q: Professor Levin, the way I hear it, you believe that given certain conditions, the *only* right thing to do is to torture someone.

[At this point, you can feel confident that Levin would agree.]

A: Yes, it would be immoral not to.

[Now you are ready to ask another question to explore more fully the point to which Levin has just assented. Asking for definitions is often a good way to probe more deeply. Does anything in Levin's position statement need clarification?]

Q: I'd like to know what you mean by situations or conditions in which torture must occur.

[Here, again, Levin makes the question relatively easy to answer by stating these conditions explicitly in his essay. You can paraphrase them.]

A: Innocent people would be about to die at the hands of terrorists, and the captured terrorist would have to be obviously guilty and have information that would save their lives.

[You are now ready to ask Levin a question about his reasons.]

Q: Why is it morally mandatory to torture a terrorist under the circumstances you describe above?

[This reason is stated most explicitly in paragraph 5.]

A: The torture will save the lives of innocent people.

[Now that you have elicited Levin's reason, you might ask about the assumptions underlying his position. For example, what is he assuming about the information to be gained through torture?]

Q: Aren't you assuming that the person being tortured will tell the truth? If a person is willing to die for a cause, wouldn't he or she also lie—mislead the authorities until the bomb explodes?

[By challenging this assumption, have you deflated Levin's whole argument? Recall that in inquiry you are not seeking to destroy an argument but rather to examine it. This goal requires that you attempt to find the best response to any question. In this case you must make an honest effort to answer the question as Levin would.]

A: The torturer does assume that the terrorist will tell the truth in an effort to get the pain over with as soon as possible. Pain weakens a person's will to resist.

[You might press further on this point, particularly if you know something about how the victims of torture generally respond to their captors' demands for information. But you could just as well question at this point the values inherent in Levin's thesis.]

Q: I see that while you value civilized behavior over brutality, you value innocent lives most of all. Is that right?

[Again you should try honestly to respond as Levin would.]

A: Yes. I suggest that we substitute for our current principle "thou shalt never torture" a new principle: "The decision to use torture is a matter of balancing innocent lives against the means needed to save them" (paragraph 5). In other words, the moral principle underlying my argument is essentially "act always to protect the lives of innocent people."

[At this point, remembering that Levin has illustrated his principle with examples—innocent airline passengers and innocent citizens of Manhattan facing nuclear annihilation—you might be ready to say, "Yes, I see that you have a point." But inquiry obligates you to press further: Is it really *right* to accept this principle?]

Q: What about our constitutional right to due process?

A: Torture probably is unconstitutional, but the number of lives saved justifies the violation of constitutional rights.

Q: But in paragraph 6 you suggest that if kidnappers threatened to kill even one newborn baby, torture would be justified. Is the number of lives saved through torture a factor or not?

[Because an argument must be consistent, finding a satisfactory answer to this question is obviously crucial to defending Levin's position. Levin would probably deny that quantity was a factor.]

A: I believe that once you accept the principle that saving innocent lives justifies torture, it does not matter if it is one or one million that you save. I began with the extreme case to persuade you to agree with the principle.

[You might also ask a further question about constitutional rights.]

Q: The Constitution also prohibits cruel and unusual punishment. Obviously, torture is cruel. What specific means are you advocating? Only once do you offer any concrete example of what you have in mind, when you refer in paragraph 4 to applying electrodes. Let's be more concrete. Is any sort of torture allowable? In addition to electric shock, could we also, say, apply acid to the skin? or beat the captured terrorist with a rubber hose, perhaps concentrating on the genitalia? or sever a limb? Furthermore, if one form of torture fails to work, may we try another, more painful one? Exactly how far can we take it? And when do we give up trying to extract the information we want?

[You might assume that Levin would step back a bit from his position at this point and respond with some qualification.]

A: I am not advocating gruesome or disfiguring forms of torture. Electric shock was what I had in mind. And, clearly, we can only take it as far as unconsciousness. We stop when the possibility of saving innocent lives is past.

[But this is not, in fact, consistent with what Levin actually says in paragraph 9, where he suggests that we may use "whatever means necessary" to thwart terrorist activity. To represent Levin's position accurately, we must say something like the following.]

A: I set no limits. We should use any means at our disposal. However, I advocate torture not as a punishment but as a means of preventing the loss of innocent lives.

[Once it is clear that the brutality can be unlimited, your next question might center on the issue of determining guilt.]

Q: But what if we only *believe* the captured terrorist is guilty? Maybe he or she has been mistakenly identified.

[Levin seems to have anticipated this objection. In paragraphs 11 and 12 he maintains that we should torture only the "obviously guilty" and claims that terrorists' desire for publicity makes this error nearly impossible. Accepting Levin's qualification, you might still be troubled by the fact that others—legitimate soldiers in a war, for example—may cause the death of innocent people. How are terrorists more "guilty" than soldiers?]

Q: What are the reasons that terrorists blow up airplanes?

[You can paraphrase Levin's response in paragraph 9.]

A: Terrorists operate for profit or idealism, that is, out of political motives. Often terrorists are attempting to secure the release of "freedom fighters" or the safety of people fighting for their own political views or disputed land.

Q: Is it possible that terrorists see themselves as soldiers at war?

A: Yes, they might see themselves as guerrillas.

Q: If our country were at war and our military captured enemy soldiers who had information about a planned attack on some American city or base, would our military be able to torture these prisoners of war? Would they not be forbidden to do so under Geneva Convention rules?

A: Of course, we should treat our enemies in a declared war according to these principles, but terrorists are not ordinary soldiers; terrorists take the lives of innocent civilians, not other soldiers.

Q: Do not soldiers in declared wars sometimes take the lives of innocent civilians? Would you have advocated that the Japanese torture a captured American who could have given them information about the bombing of Hiroshima?

A: No, I would not advocate torture in a declared war.

Q: So you are saying that in some circumstances it is mandatory to protect the lives of innocents through torture but that in others it is immoral to protect the lives of innocents through torture?

A: Yes, that is what I am saying.

The dialogue with Michael Levin could go on indefinitely, exploring the definition of war and the rights of people who fight and kill for political reasons, assuming that both sides were interested in pursuing the truth about whether torture is indeed ever justified. In your dialogues with texts and other people, try to remember that the point is not to attack or defend but to probe—to uncover the uncomfortable spots that make both questioner and answerer think harder. Such dialogue tends to reveal the full complexity of a topic, which is exactly what is required to find the best position and make the most truthful argument.

Following Through

1. In your writer's notebook continue the dialogue with Levin. You might pursue one of the following areas of questioning or one of your own.

   Does Levin offer any evidence? What might you ask him about it? What might he have included that he did not?

   In paragraphs 7 and 8 Levin contrasts torture with capital punishment and also compares it with assassination and preemptive attacks. What similarities and differences might there be among these acts?

2. Select one of the two essays from the following list, and do a critical reading as described in Chapter 2 and an analysis as described in Chapter 3. Annotate the text, and make notes in your writer's notebook. With another student or in a small group, create a dialogue with the writer based on the questions outlined on pages 39–40. Then share your questions and answers with the rest of the class, comparing results and focusing on the variety of paths dialogues can take.

   "Rising to the Occasion of Our Death," William May, pages 57–58

   "Capital Punishment: Society's Self-Defense," Amber Young, pages 31–36

EVALUATING AN ARGUMENT: AN ANALYSIS BASED ON INQUIRY

A dialogue can take you in many directions and open up a great deal you may not have thought about carefully before. Writing an essay after a dialogue can help bring your best insights together and enable you to decide how much of an argument to accept. Sometimes an informal paragraph or two in your writer's notebook is enough. However, to assess an argument for other readers, you will need to write a more formal evaluation.

The audience for such an evaluation will be other people interested in the issue who, like you, are trying to decide what they think. You should assume that they have read the argument and are also trying to evaluate it. In other words, think of your audience and yourself as peers, as fellow truth-seekers. Your tone should be critical but impartial. Your goal is to evaluate, but you should also be interested in helping your readers understand the argument. There is no lockstep process for an essay evaluating an argument, but we can offer some suggestions.

Preparing to Write

First, of course, read the argument thoroughly and critically, until you feel confident about your own understanding of it. Review the definition of critical reading (page 11) and our other suggestions in Chapter 2.

As you read, you should mark up the text of the argument (make a photocopy for this purpose if necessary). Identify the claim, the reasons, and any evidence; mark the sections that the essay breaks down into; note whether (and how) terms are defined; and so on. See Chapter 3 for more advice about analyzing arguments.

If the argument is particularly difficult, summarize and paraphrase the parts you find troublesome (refer to the section in Chapter 9 entitled "Using Sources"). Raise questions about these passages in class or in conference with your instructor.

Next, in addition to discussing the essay with others, you should write out a dialogue with the writer as we have illustrated in this chapter, posing questions and providing careful responses that accurately reflect the writer's position. You will not reproduce the dialogue in your essay, but what you learn and conclude from it will certainly be useful.

From Dialogue to Draft

Analytical essays are not just summaries. Readers are looking for your insights into the argument and your assessment of the writer's claim. Your thesis, therefore, will be some statement evaluating the overall worth of the argument you are analyzing. To arrive at it, review your annotations and recall your dialogue with the text. What strengths and weaknesses did you uncover?

Support your thesis with comments (either negative or positive) that have resulted from your reading of the argument and your dialogue with it. You may focus your critical reading on key aspects of the argument that will form natural topics for paragraphs or groups of paragraphs in your written analysis. For example, you might build a part of your analysis around an evaluation of the argument's main reason, around an important analogy in the argument, or around an assumption of the writer's that you do not share. One way to discover points to include in your analysis is to recall your dialogue with the writer: What questions proved most fruitful? You will also need to support and develop your comments with specific references to passages in the argument, making use of brief summaries and paraphrases as well as direct quotations.

Remember that you may not be able to include every critical observation in your analysis. Attempting to work in everything can result in an analysis that is more like an inventory or a laundry list—not very readable. It is better to concentrate on related points so that your analysis has unity and focus. Above all, emphasize the main qualities that make the argument succeed or fail in your estimation.

A Sample Analysis

Because we have already illustrated dialogue by questioning Michael Levin's "The Case for Torture," we follow up with a sample analysis of it.

Michael Levin's "The Case for Torture": A Dangerous Oversimplification

TORTURE IS one topic about which the truth seems clear. Enlightened people the world over believe that torture is immoral and barbaric. However, Michael Levin in his essay "The Case for Torture" challenges Americans to rethink their position that nothing could ever justify torture. Levin's case is thought-provoking, but his position is not one that we should accept. 1

Levin's reason for justifying torture appears in paragraph 5: the end, saving innocent people's lives, justifies the means, denying terrorists their right not to be subjected to cruel and unusual punishment. This reason (and therefore his entire case) rests on two assumptions: that authorities will have terrorists in custody and that torturing them will yield information that could save innocent lives. But if we assent to torture based on these conditions, can we be sure that it will be put into practice only in situations that are equally clear-cut? How would we know, for example, that a "terrorist" was not insane or simply bluffing? What if the terrorist never did speak? And even if he or she did, how would we know that the information was the truth and not a desperate lie aimed at buying time or getting revenge for the torture? No actual situation is likely to be as neat as the one Levin poses, and assenting to torture could result in horrible abuses.

Even if we grant that torture would save lives in such a situation, can we accept Levin's argument? He attempts to win our assent through three hypothetical cases (paragraphs 2–6) in which he claims torture would be "morally mandatory." He first tries to get the reader to accept his argument based on millions of lives being at stake. Levin then extends the principle to a situation in which hundreds of lives are at stake and finally to one in which just one life, a newborn baby's, is at stake. By the time he gets to the baby in paragraph 6, he seems to have forgotten that he justified torture's barbarity earlier on the grounds that "millions of lives surely outweigh constitutionality" and that "mass murder" is more barbaric than torture (paragraph 4). Is Levin saying that quantity matters—or not? Because of this inconsistency, Levin's argument here relies more upon emotional appeal than good reasoning.

Another major section of Levin's argument turns on the distinction between torture and punishment. We may agree that torture, unlike the death penalty, might save the lives of potential victims (paragraph 7). However, when Levin says torture is like a preemptive military strike (paragraph 8), he exposes his argument to serious questions. If we can torture a terrorist to save innocent lives, why not torture a soldier to accomplish the same ends? Perhaps Levin would say the difference is one of guilt and innocence, that the soldier is also an innocent.

However, Levin's use of the terms *guilt* and *innocence* can also be ques- 5
tioned. He defines the innocent as those who have not asked to be put in danger, using newborn babies as one example. Certainly, a soldier, at least one who volunteers to fight, is not innocent according to this definition. Levin would probably argue that soldiers put themselves at risk for better reasons than terrorists do. But Levin admits that terrorists kill for "idealism" (paragraph 9) or for the release of their "freedom fighters" (paragraph 11). This is killing for political reasons, making a terrorist akin to a soldier. And if we try to make a distinction based on who gets killed, civilians or soldiers, we must acknowledge that American soldiers have killed civilians, even infants, in many of our wars, most notably in the bombing of Hiroshima and Nagasaki, but also in Vietnam and more recently in Iraq. Suddenly, Levin's goal of keeping the line clear between "Us and Them" (paragraph 11) becomes more complicated. Just who is eligible for torture?

Admitting that most terrorists are more like soldiers than they are like criminals does not justify terrorism, but it does help us see the problem of terrorism in its political complexity. It also leads us to examine some implications of the decision that torture can be right. Can we assent to using it in warfare? Is torture right depending on whose "civilization," "idealism," and "order" it preserves?

Ultimately, Levin's argument fails to convince. It raises some interesting issues, but even in the most clear-cut situation he presents, Levin is not able to establish the morality of torture. Torture is something we might wish to use given certain circumstances; but defending it as a moral choice, much less as "morally mandatory," does not work.

Following Through

Find an argument on a topic that you are currently researching. Read the argument critically, annotating the text, and write a dialogue with the author. Rather than merely pairing questions and answers, try to make chains of questions and answers that follow naturally from one another, as we did with the Levin argument. While you must find justification in the text for every response you have the writer make, you should also push beyond the surface of the text. The dialogue should dig more deeply into the argument, uncovering both what is implied and what is stated directly. If you get stuck, consult the list of questions on pages 39–40 to help you start a new chain of questioning.

Look over your dialogue and your annotations for points to make about what the argument actually is and how well it stands up to inquiry. Finally, draft an analytical essay based on your inquiry. Before you write, read student Cindy Tarver's analysis of an argument by William Murchison, both of which follow.

WILLIAM MURCHISON

City Shouldn't Ignore Morality

William Murchison is a syndicated columnist whose work appears often in the Dallas Morning News, *where this argument was originally published.*

AND SO another U.S. city bellies up to the gay rights issue. Dallas' City Council asks: Should we or shouldn't we hire gay cops? The answer up to now has been an automatic no. Police work is public in nature. Public law forbids the sexual practices that define homosexuality: in addition to which, police officers function as role models. 1

Advocates of homosexual rights are nonetheless voluble and persistent. They want action. Americans are having to think carefully about a moral issue long regarded as settled. How should they think? Here is one view.

The homosexual cop issue, it seems to me, is only superficially about civil rights and hiring policy. Deeper down, it is about the legitimation of homosexuality as just another modern "lifestyle."

It is all part of a great design: claim accredited victim status, repeal the anti-sodomy laws, depict practicing homosexuals as appropriate role models, intimidate doubters by smearing them as "homophobic," drop the very word "homosexual" in favor of the positive, upbeat-sounding "gay."

As heterosexuals acquiesce in this design, out of fear or the desire to 5
be politically correct, they move homosexuality further down the road to legitimation.

The campaign has succeeded in marked degree. Various cities prohibit various kinds of "discrimination" against homosexuals. The ordination of practicing (as distinguished from celibate) homosexuals is a hot issue among Methodists, Presbyterians, Episcopalians, and others. Traditional prohibitions, such as the military's ban on homosexual personnel, are under legal and political attack.

Non-homophobic foes of homosexual "rights" sometimes don't know what to do. They don't want to injure the feelings of homosexual friends, and they don't want to countenance a radical redrafting of the moral laws. And so they worry.

Why? Can't the moral law be changed by a good old democratic vote? To say so evidences a dramatic misreading of the moral law.

The moral law—peculiar to no religious tradition; rather, innate in the human species—is no set of icky-picky prescriptions made up by kill-joys.

The moral law is an owner's manual for the human body—and soul. 10
You follow it for the reason you change (or should change) your automobile's oil every 3,000 miles: because if you don't, things start to happen, things you may not like.

The human "owner's manual" says—always has, actually—that heterosexual monogamy works. It does not work perfectly by the standards of an imperfect world; yet, on the historical record, the alternatives work less satisfactorily and sometimes injuriously. This is as true of, for instance, heterosexual adultery as of other misadventures.

Ten years ago, a well-known homosexual activist paid a call on me to press the case for "gay rights." He grew livid during our visit, all but pounded on the table. Whose business was it, he demanded to know, what sexual preference he evinced? He would do as he wanted. I had never anticipated otherwise. A few years later, he was dead. Of AIDS.

That is not a smug, God-struck-him-dead kind of remark. It is a painful observation about the necessary sequence of cause and effect: If you do "A," expect "B." Or "C." Or "D." Or various permutations and combinations of same.

The great irony of AIDS, the vast majority whose incidences result from anal copulation, is that it occurs in the midst of the ongoing national celebration of the "gay lifestyle." It is like Poe's *Masque of the Red Death*. While inside the nobles whoop it up, the great destroyer enters, unnoticed.

What a waste! My caller of 10 years ago was a talented and probably, 15
when he wasn't yelling at me, genial man. The world was better off with than without him, as could be said of numberless AIDS victims.

Anyone who hates or physically torments practicing homosexuals is, in theological or secular terms, a swine. The moral law—remember it?—calls hatred wrong. Wrong likewise is the failure to draw meaningful distinctions among different species of conduct and conviction. American society is being offered that precise temptation today. We should resist to the uttermost.

Student Sample: An Analysis Based on Inquiry

CINDY TARVER

An Appeal to Prejudice

HOMOSEXUALITY EXISTED in biblical times and continues to be 1
viable today. Indeed, the open expression of homosexuality is now so prevalent that gay rights have become a major concern of the American public. Evidence of this concern can be seen specifically in the question recently posed by the Dallas City Council: Should we or shouldn't we drop the ban on gay police officers?

William Murchison, a columnist for the *Dallas Morning News,* states in his editorial "City Shouldn't Ignore Morality" that there is no reason homosexuals should be permitted to serve on the Dallas police force. Nevertheless, Murchison's is not a strong argument as it is based upon faulty reasoning, distorted evidence, and broad assumptions.

Murchison presents several reasons to justify his stance against homosexual cops. His first and most effective reason deals with the questionable legality of allowing gays to serve as officers of the law. Murchison cites the state sodomy law, which declares relations with someone of the same sex a misdemeanor. In doing so, he argues that gays, who must be considered repeat offenders under this law, do not qualify to serve as police.

Murchison's second reason deals with his perception of gay police as poor role models. However, Murchison does not clearly state why he feels homosexual police would be poor role models. One must assume it is because he sees homosexuality as wrong and fears that children would become too accepting of the gay lifestyle were they to embrace gay role models. Moreover, Murchison may fear that children would actually become gay in an effort to imitate their role models. If so, he is assuming that an officer's sexual orientation would be apparent during the performance of his or her professional duties. Furthermore, scientific evidence has begun to point toward a biological basis for homosexuality. If this is in fact the case, society need not worry about children choosing to become homosexual because they think it is "cool."

However, the most destructive flaw in Murchison's argument results from 5
the assumptions upon which he bases his main reason: that homosexuality violates "the moral law." First, Murchison assumes that "moral law" exists.

This is a major fault because the existence of moral law cannot be proven. It hinges upon individual beliefs about the human condition. Thus, people who believe that humans are innately good are likely to believe in moral law, while those who believe that humans are innately evil are unlikely to believe in moral law. Thus much of Murchison's argument is ineffective if the audience does not believe in moral law.

Murchison also assumes that all of mankind shares the same moral law. However, this is not necessarily the case. In fact, many would argue that morality is shaped by religion and can thus vary as greatly as do religious beliefs and practices. Another assumption which relates to this concept is the premise that homosexuality is against moral law. If all of humanity does not share the same moral law, then homosexuality may not be against everyone's moral law.

Murchison's final assumption is that homosexuality is a choice, and while that may be, there is mounting evidence that biological factors play a large role in determining sexual orientation. If this is in fact the case and sexual preference is actually determined before birth, then how can homosexuality be considered wrong? Wouldn't it have to become amoral, and of no more consequence than the color of one's eyes?

As evidence to support his point that homosexuality violates the moral law, Murchison argues that AIDS is a logical outcome of engaging in homosexual activities. Evidently, Murchison has forgotten about the tremendous number of people who have contracted AIDS through heterosexual sex, blood transfusions, and sharing needles, as well as the many practicing homosexuals who have not contracted AIDS. The belief that homosexuality and AIDS are intrinsically linked is a massive distortion of the truth.

Thus, what at first appears to be a thoughtful and well executed argument is actually full of weaknesses and contradictions. Murchison's reasoning is faulty, his evidence is distorted, and the assumptions upon which he bases his argument are not necessarily true. It is clear that Murchison designed his argument to appeal to those already entrenched in antihomosexual prejudice. Murchison's argument is nothing more than an emotional appeal, and thus he fails to convince the reader of the validity of his claim.

INQUIRING INTO A RANGE OF POSITIONS

When preparing to write an argument of your own, you should review a variety of published arguments and informative articles about your issue. As you read conflicting points of view, you will discover that the debate surrounding an issue seldom involves two distinct sides, for and against. Instead, you will find a range of positions, varying with the particular interests and insights of the participants in the debate. Writers who disagree on some points, for example, will agree on others. To determine your own best position, you will need to explore a full range of opinions. But sorting through the many positions can be a challenge. We suggest that as you inquire into the various positions on an issue, you use your writer's notebook or index cards to record your responses based on the following advice.

1. *Read the sources critically.* Be sure that they are addressing the same issue, not just the same topic. For example, one issue growing out of the topic of acquaintance rape is whether incidents of acquaintance rape on college campuses should be handled by college judicial boards or turned over to local police; a different issue on the same topic is whether acquaintance rape can be distinguished from other types of rape. Be able to write a clear statement of the issue being addressed.
2. *Identify the important facts involved in the debate.* Factual information can be verified: names, numbers, locations, dates, and so on. Note if any sources disagree about some of the facts. Which sources seem most reliable?
3. *Identify the positions.* If your sources are arguments, paraphrase each writer's main claim, or thesis. If you have a source that is an informative article, several positions may be given, including the names of people or groups who hold those positions. Paraphrase each of these positions as well. Extreme contrasts among positions will be readily apparent; but also try to note more subtle differences among positions that are similar.
4. *Note interactions among the different positions.* As you compare arguments on a common issue, you will find topics addressed by several if not all voices in the debate. Cutting across the arguments, look at how questions raised by one writer are also addressed by other writers. The idea is to note the threads of conversation that weave through the entire debate and see where the writers agree and where they disagree.

   As you move back and forth across the arguments, you may want to work with different-colored highlighters to code the major questions of the debate. Another practical method for making comparisons is to use index cards, recording on one card what writer A has to say on the question of X, on another card what writer B has to say about the same question, and so on.
5. *Conclude your exploration with a tentative position for your own argument.* Which sources have contributed to your thinking? What arguments have you accepted and why?

Following Through

Read two or three arguments on a single issue. Then write a dialogue in which you have the writers set forth and challenge each other's ideas. You might also include yourself in the conversation, posing questions and listening to the alternating voices as they agree and disagree (see the questions for inquiry on pages 39–40). You need not take a side, but you do want to be a critical inquirer.

The Exploratory Essay

As a step toward composing an argument of your own, you may be assigned to write an essay that explores the various positions you have encountered in your reading. Such an essay begins not with a thesis but with a description of the issue under debate and an overview of the conflicting positions. The purpose of the essay is to discover what you accept and reject among the arguments that make up public debate on the issue. Writing such an essay should help you find a position you can feel confident defending.

Whether your essay is an informal notebook entry or a piece revised for your classmates or instructor, it ought to take the following shape:

Introduction: defining and describing the issue. The paragraphs in this section should introduce the topic and the issue. Include relevant factual information upon which everyone seems to agree. Also paraphrase the positions of the leading voices in the debate.

Inquiry: comparing points of disagreement. The paragraphs in this section should compare the basic points of disagreement among the positions you have just described. Instead of devoting one or two paragraphs to each writer or position, try to organize your paragraphs around particular questions or points on which the writers differ: ("On the question of X, writer A and others who agree with her position argue . . . Writer B, on the other hand, thinks . . ."). Comment on the strengths and weaknesses of the contrasting views.

Conclusion: taking your own position. Your exploratory essay should end with a statement of your own tentative position on the issue and an explanation of why you think it the best. You may support one of the arguments you have analyzed, modify one of those arguments, or offer a different argument of your own. The important thing is not to leave your readers hanging or yourself sitting on the fence. Make it clear what you think and why.

Three Opposing Positions

Following are three arguments on the topic of euthanasia. They all address the same issue: Should assisted suicide, what some call "active euthanasia," be made legal in the United States? You may already have read the first argument, which appears in Chapter 3; the others offer additional viewpoints on the issue. A sample exploratory essay comparing the three immediately follows the third argument.

WILLIAM F. MAY

Rising to the Occasion of Our Death

FOR MANY parents, a Volkswagen van is associated with putting chil- 1
dren to sleep on a camping trip. Jack Kevorkian, a Detroit pathologist, has now linked the van with the veterinarian's meaning of "putting to sleep." Kevorkian conducted a dinner interview with Janet Elaine Adkins, a 54-year-old Alzheimer's patient, and her husband and then agreed to help her commit suicide in his VW van. Kevorkian pressed beyond the more generally accepted practice of passive euthanasia (allowing a patient to die by withholding or withdrawing treatment) to active euthanasia (killing for mercy).

Kevorkian, moreover, did not comply with the strict regulations that govern active euthanasia in, for example, the Netherlands. Holland requires that death be imminent (Adkins had beaten her son in tennis just a few days earlier); it demands a more professional review of the medical evidence and the patient's resolution than a dinner interview with a physician (who is a stranger and who does not treat patients) permits; and it calls for the final, endorsing signatures of two doctors.

So Kevorkian-bashing is easy. But the question remains: Should we develop a judicious, regulated social policy permitting voluntary euthanasia for the terminally ill? Some moralists argue that the distinction between allowing to die and killing for mercy is petty quibbling over technique. Since the patient in any event dies—whether by acts of omission or commission—the route to death doesn't really matter. The way modern procedures have made dying at the hands of the experts and their machines such a prolonged and painful business has further fueled the euthanasia movement, which asserts not simply the right to die but the right to be killed.

But other moralists believe that there is an important moral distinction between allowing to die and mercy killing. The euthanasia movement, these critics contend, wants to engineer death rather than face dying. Euthanasia would bypass dying to make one dead as quickly as possible. It aims to relieve suffering by knocking out the interval between life and death. It solves the problem of suffering by eliminating the sufferer.

The impulse behind the euthanasia movement is understandable in an 5
age when dying has become such an inhumanly endless business. But the movement may fail to appreciate our human capacity to rise to the occasion of our death. The best death is not always the sudden death. Those forewarned of death and given time to prepare for it have time to engage in acts of reconciliation. Also, advanced grieving by those about to be bereaved may ease some of their pain. Psychiatrists have observed that those who lose a loved one accidentally have a more difficult time recovering from the loss than those who have suffered through an extended period of illness before the death. Those who have lost a close relative by accident are more likely to experience what

Geoffrey Gorer has called limitless grief. The community, moreover, may need its aged and dependent, its sick and its dying, and the virtues which they sometimes evince—the virtues of humility, courage, and patience—just as much as the community needs the virtues of justice and love manifest in the agents of care.

On the whole, our social policy should allow terminal patients to die but it should not regularize killing for mercy. Such a policy would recognize and respect that moment in illness when it no longer makes sense to bend every effort to cure or to prolong life and when one must allow patients to do their own dying. This policy seems most consonant with the obligations of the community to care and of the patient to finish his or her course.

Advocates of active euthanasia appeal to the principle of patient autonomy—as the use of the phrase "voluntary euthanasia" indicates. But emphasis on the patient's right to determine his or her destiny often harbors an extremely naïve view of the uncoerced nature of the decision. Patients who plead to be put to death hardly make unforced decisions if the terms and conditions under which they receive care already nudge them in the direction of the exit. If the elderly have stumbled around in their apartments, alone and frightened for years, or if they have spent years warehoused in geriatrics barracks, then the decision to be killed for mercy hardly reflects an uncoerced decision. The alternative may be so wretched as to push patients toward this escape. It is a huge irony and, in some cases, hypocrisy to talk suddenly about a compassionate killing when the aging and dying may have been starved for compassion for many years. To put it bluntly, a country has not earned the moral right to kill for mercy unless it has already sustained and supported life mercifully. Otherwise we kill for compassion only to reduce the demands on our compassion. This statement does not charge a given doctor or family member with impure motives. I am concerned here not with the individual case but with the cumulative impact of a social policy.

I can, to be sure, imagine rare circumstances in which I hope I would have the courage to kill for mercy—when the patient is utterly beyond human care, terminal, and in excruciating pain. A neurosurgeon once showed a group of physicians and an ethicist the picture of a Vietnam casualty who had lost all four limbs in a landmine explosion. The catastrophe had reduced the soldier to a trunk with his face transfixed in horror. On the battlefield I would hope that I would have the courage to kill the sufferer with mercy.

But hard cases do not always make good laws or wise social policies. Regularized mercy killings would too quickly relieve the community of its obligation to provide good care. Further, we should not always expect the law to provide us with full protection and coverage for what, in rare circumstances, we may morally need to do. Sometimes the moral life calls us out into a no-man's-land where we cannot expect total security and protection under the law. But no one said that the moral life is easy.

SIDNEY HOOK

In Defense of Voluntary Euthanasia

Sidney Hook (1902–1989) was a philosophy professor at New York University. This essay was originally printed in the New York Times *in 1987.*

A FEW short years ago, I lay at the point of death. A congestive heart 1
failure was treated for diagnostic purposes by an angiogram that triggered a stroke. Violent and painful hiccups, uninterrupted for several days and nights, prevented the ingestion of food. My left side and one of my vocal cords became paralyzed. Some form of pleurisy set in, and I felt I was drowning in a sea of slime. At one point, my heart stopped beating; just as I lost consciousness, it was thumped back into action again. In one of my lucid intervals during those days of agony, I asked my physician to discontinue all life-supporting services or show me how to do it. He refused and predicted that someday I would appreciate the unwisdom of my request.

A month later, I was discharged from the hospital. In six months, I regained the use of my limbs, and although my voice still lacks its old resonance and carrying power I no longer croak like a frog. There remain some minor disabilities and I am restricted to a rigorous, low-sodium diet. I have resumed my writing and research.

My experience can be and has been cited as an argument against honoring requests of stricken patients to be gently eased out of their pain and life. I cannot agree. There are two main reasons. As an octogenarian, there is a reasonable likelihood that I may suffer another "cardiovascular accident" or worse. I may not even be in a position to ask for the surcease of pain. It seems to me that I have already paid my dues to death—indeed, although time has softened my memories they are vivid enough to justify my saying that I suffered enough to warrant dying several times over. Why run the risk of more?

Secondly, I dread imposing on my family and friends another grim round of misery similar to the one my first attack occasioned.

My wife and children endured enough for one lifetime. I know that for 5
them the long days and nights of waiting, the disruption of their professional duties and their own familial responsibilities counted for nothing in their anxiety for me. In their joy at my recovery they have been forgotten. Nonetheless, to visit another prolonged spell of helpless suffering on them as my life ebbs away, or even worse, if I linger on into a comatose senility, seems altogether gratuitous.

But what, it may be asked, of the joy and satisfaction of living, of basking in the sunshine, listening to music, watching one's grandchildren growing into adolescence, following the news about the fate of freedom in a troubled world, playing with ideas, writing one's testament of wisdom and folly for posterity? Is not all that one endured, together with the risk of its recurrence, an acceptable price for the multiple satisfactions that are still open even to a person of advanced years?

Apparently those who cling to life no matter what think so. I do not.

The zest and intensity of these experiences are no longer what they used to be. I am not vain enough to delude myself that I can in the few remaining years make an important discovery useful for mankind or can lead a social movement or do anything that will be historically eventful, no less event-making. My autobiography, which describes a record of intellectual and political experiences of some historical value, already much too long, could be posthumously published. I have had my fill of joys and sorrows and am not greedy for more life. I have always thought that a test of whether one had found happiness in one's life is whether one would be willing to relive it—whether, if it were possible, one would accept the opportunity to be born again.

Having lived a full and relatively happy life, I would cheerfully accept the chance to be reborn, but certainly not to be reborn again as an infirm octogenarian. To some extent, my views reflect what I have seen happen to the aged and stricken who have been so unfortunate as to survive crippling paralysis. They suffer, and impose suffering on others, unable even to make a request that their torment be ended.

10 I am mindful too of the burdens placed upon the community, with its rapidly diminishing resources, to provide the adequate and costly services necessary to sustain the lives of those whose days and nights are spent on mattress graves of pain. A better use could be made of these resources to increase the opportunities and qualities of life for the young. I am not denying the moral obligation the community has to look after its disabled and aged. There are times, however, when an individual may find it pointless to insist on the fulfillment of a legal and moral right.

What is required is no great revolution in morals but an enlargement of imagination and an intelligent evaluation of alternative uses of community resources.

Long ago, Seneca observed that "the wise man will live as long as he ought, not as long as he can."[1] One can envisage hypothetical circumstances in which one has a duty to prolong one's life despite its costs for the sake of others, but such circumstances are far removed from the ordinary prospects we are considering. If wisdom is rooted in knowledge of the alternatives of choice, it must be reliably informed of the state one is in and its likely outcome. Scientific medicine is not infallible, but it is the best we have. Should a rational person be willing to endure acute suffering merely on the chance that a miraculous cure might presently be at hand? Each one should be permitted to make his own choice—especially when no one else is harmed by it.

[1]Seneca (4 B.C.E.–65 C.E.) lived in Rome and taught a philosophy known as Stoicism, which advocated duty, self-discipline, and adherence to the natural order of things.

The responsibility for the decision, whether deemed wise or foolish, must be with the chooser.

MATTHEW E. CONOLLY

Euthanasia Is Not the Answer

Matthew E. Conolly, a professor of medicine at UCLA, delivered this speech before a 1985 conference sponsored by the Hemlock Society, an organization that advocates voluntary euthanasia.

1 FROM THE moment of our conception, each of us is engaged in a personal battle that we must fight alone, a battle whose final outcome is never in any doubt, for, naked, and all too often alone, sooner or later we *all* must die.

We do not all make life's pilgrimage on equal terms. For some the path is strewn with roses, and after a long and healthy life, death comes swiftly and easily; for others it is not so. The bed of roses is supplanted by a bed of nails, with poverty, rejection, deformity, and humiliation the only lasting companions they ever know.

I know that many people here today carry this problem of pain in a personal way, or else it has been the lot of someone close to you. Otherwise you would not be here. So let me say right at the outset, that those of us who have not had to carry such a burden dare not criticize those who have, if they should plead with us for an early end to their dismal sojourn in this world.

HARD CASES MAKE BAD LAWS

Society in general, and the medical profession in particular, cannot just turn away. We must do *something;* the question is—what?

5 The "what" we are being asked to consider today, of course, is voluntary euthanasia. So that there be no confusion, let me make it quite clear that to be opposed to the active taking of life, one does not have to be determined to keep the heart beating at all costs.

I believe I speak for all responsible physicians when I say that there clearly comes a time when death can no longer be held at bay, and when we must sue for peace on the enemy's terms. At such a time, attending to the patient's comfort in body, mind, and soul becomes paramount. There is no obligation, indeed no justification, for pressing on at such a time with so-called life-sustaining measures, be they respirators, intravenous fluids, CPR, or whatever. I believe that there is no obligation to continue a treatment once it has been started, if it becomes apparent that it is doing no good. Also, withholding useless treatment and letting nature take its course is *not* equivalent to active euthanasia. Some people have attempted to blur this distinction by creating the term "passive euthanasia." The least unkind thing that can be said about this term is that it is very confusing.

Today's discussion really boils down to the question—do hard and tragic cases warrant legalization of euthanasia? There can be no doubt that hard and tragic cases do occur. However, the very natural tendency to want to alleviate human tragedy by legislative change is fraught with hazard, and I firmly believe that every would-be lawmaker should have tattooed on his or her face, where it can be seen in the mirror each morning, the adage that HARD CASES MAKE BAD LAWS.

If we take the superficially humane step of tailoring the law to the supposed wishes of an Elizabeth Bouvia (who, incidentally, later changed her mind),[1] we will not only bring a hornet's nest of woes about our own ears, but, at a stroke, we will deny many relatives much good that we could have salvaged from a sad situation, while at the same time giving many *more* grief and guilt to contend with. Even worse, we will have denied our patients the best that could have been offered. Worst of all, that soaring of the human spirit to heights of inspiration and courage which only adversity makes possible will be denied, and we will all, from that, grow weaker, and less able to deal with the crisis of tomorrow.

Unleashing Euthanasia

Let's look at these problems one by one. The first problem is that once we unleash euthanasia, once we take to ourselves the right actively to terminate a human life, we will have no means of controlling it. Adolf Hitler showed with startling clarity that once the dam is breached, the principle somewhere compromised, death in the end comes to be administered equally to all—to the unwanted fetus, to the deformed, the mentally defective, the old and the unproductive, and thence to the politically inconvenient, and finally to the ethnically unacceptable. There is no logical place to stop.

10 The founders of Hemlock no doubt mean euthanasia only for those who feel they can take no more, but if it is available for one it must be available for all. Then what about those precious people who even to the end put others before themselves? They will now have laid upon them the new and horrible thought that perhaps they ought to do away with themselves to spare their relatives more trouble or expense. What will they feel as they see their 210 days of Medicare hospice payments run out, and still they are alive. Not long ago, Governor Lamm of Colorado suggested that the old and incurable have a *duty* to get out of the way of the next generation. And can you not see where these pressures will be the greatest? It will be amongst the poor

[1]Elizabeth Bouvia, chronically ill with cerebral palsy and crippling arthritis, was well known in the 1980s for her legal battles for the right to starve herself to death while she was hospitalized.

and dispossessed. Watts will have sunk in a sea of euthanasia long before the first ripple laps the shore of Brentwood. Is that what we mean to happen? Is that what we want? Is there nobility of purpose there?

It matters to me that my patients trust me. If they do so, it is because they believe that I will always act in their best interests. How could such trust survive if they could never be sure each time I approached the bed that I had not come to administer some coup de grace when they were not in a state to define their own wishes?

Those whose relatives have committed more conventional forms of suicide are often afterwards assailed by feelings of guilt and remorse. It would be unwise to think that euthanasia would bring any less in its wake.

A Better Way

Speaking as a physician, I assert that unrelieved suffering need never occur, and I want to turn to this important area. Proponents of euthanasia make much of the pain and anguish so often linked in people's minds with cancer. I would not dare to pretend that the care we offer is not sometimes abysmal, whether because of the inappropriate use of aggressive technological medicine, the niggardly use of analgesics, some irrational fear of addiction in a dying patient, or a lack of compassion.

However, for many, the process of dying is more a case of gradually loosing life's moorings and slipping away. Oftentimes the anguish of dying is felt not by the patient but by the relatives: just as real, just as much in need of compassionate support, but hardly a reason for killing the patient!

But let us consider the patients who do have severe pain, turmoil, and 15
distress, who find their helplessness or incontinence humiliating, for it is these who most engage our sympathies. It is wrong to assert that they must make a stark choice between suicide or suffering.

There is another way.

Experience with hospice care in England and the United States has shown repeatedly that in *every* case, pain and suffering can be overwhelmingly reduced. In many cases it can be abolished altogether. This care, which may (and for financial reasons perhaps must) include home care, is not easy. It demands infinite love and compassion. It must include the latest scientific knowledge of analgesic drugs, nerve blocks, antinausea medication, and so on. But it can be done, it can be done, it can be done!

Life Is Special

Time and again our patients have shown us that life, even a deformed, curtailed, and, to us, who are whole, an unimaginable life, can be made noble and worth living. Look at Joni Earickson—paraplegic from the age of seventeen—now a most positive, vibrant and inspirational person who has become world famous for her triumph over adversity. Time and time again, once symptoms are relieved, patients and relatives share quality time together, when forgiveness can be sought and given—for many a time of great healing.

Man, made in the image of his Creator, is *different* from all other animals. For this reason, his life is special and may not be taken at will.

We do not know why suffering is allowed, but Old and New Testament 20
alike are full of reassurances that we have not been, and will not ever be, abandoned by our God. "Yea, though I walk through the valley of the shadow of death, I will fear no evil *for thou art with me.*"

CALL TO CHANGE DIRECTION

Our modern tragedy is that man has turned his back on God, who alone can help, and has set himself up as the measure of all things. Gone then is the absolute importance of man, gone the sanctity of his life, and the meaning of it. Gone too the motivation for loving care which is our responsible duty to the sick and dying. Goodbye love. Hello indifference.

With our finite minds, we cannot know fully the meaning of life, but though at times the storms of doubt may rage, I stake my life on the belief that to God we are special, that with Him, murder is unacceptable, and suicide (whatever you call it) becomes unnecessary.

Abandon God, and yes, you can have euthanasia. But a *good* death it can never be, and no subterfuge of law like that before us today can ever make it so.

My plea to the Hemlock Society is: Give up your goal of self-destruction. Instead, lend your energy, your anger, your indignation, your influence and creativity to work with us in the building of such a system of hospice care that death, however it come, need no longer be feared. Is not this a nobler cause? Is not this a better way?

A Sample Exploratory Essay

Exploring the Issue of Voluntary Euthanasia

THE QUESTION I am exploring is whether active euthanasia—assisted 1
suicide—should be legalized as it is in some foreign countries, such as the Netherlands. Debate on this issue has been stirred by the activities of a Michigan pathologist, Jack Kevorkian, who is under criminal indictment for helping several terminally or chronically ill Americans to take their own lives. The arguments that I read are devoted exclusively to the kind of euthanasia in which the patient is conscious and rational enough to make a decision about terminating his or her life.

I encountered two basic positions on this issue. Sidney Hook, a philosopher, represents the view that assisted suicide should be a legal option for the patient. After recovering from a life-threatening illness, Hook decided that each patient must "be permitted to make his own choice" and to ask that his or her suffering be ended (60). The other two writers take the opposing view that legalizing active euthanasia is bad social policy. However, their positions differ slightly. Matthew Conolly, a professor of medicine, argues that even the most extreme and tragic cases do not justify legalizing assisted suicide. His view is that proper medical and hospice care totally eliminates suicide as the only alternative to suffering. William May qualifies his opposition to active euthanasia by adding that in extreme cases it would be moral to break the law and to help someone die.

One question all three writers address is whether a patient's suffering justifies giving him or her the right to choose death. Hook argues that suffering can be too horrible to bear, and he supports this reason convincingly with evidence from his own experience with heart failure and stroke. The other writers counter by trying to see some inherent value in suffering. Both argue that it brings out distinctively human virtues, such as courage and patience. I find Hook more convincing on this question; an intelligent man, he did not "soar to heights of inspiration" as Conolly puts it (62), but rather felt he was "drowning in a sea of slime" as pleurisy filled his lungs (59). I agree that humans do have great capacity to carry on in spite of adversity, but that does not mean we should demand that they bear it. Their genuine feelings, from my own observations of dying relatives, are more likely fear and impatience, even self-pity.

The writers on both sides agree that the effects on loved ones of a patient's suffering are terrible. Hook offers this as the second of his two reasons for active euthanasia, claiming that his family's life during his illness was "a grim round of misery" (59). Conolly agrees that the family may feel more anguish than the patient (63). However, when he says that this grief does not justify "killing the patient," he overlooks that the patient would be the one making the choice. And the life the patient is sacrificing for the sake of loved ones is not one he or she finds worth living.

5 All three writers also touch upon the relationship between the larger community and those within it who are sick and dying. Conolly and May see these people in terms of how they benefit the community, while Hook sees them in terms of what they cost. Conolly and May argue that a civilized society must accept its duty to care for the sick and dying. In this sense, having the sick and dying around gives society a chance to practice a virtue that is in too short supply as it is. Legalizing assisted suicide would make it all too easy for our society to further ignore its duty; as May says, we would "kill for compassion only to reduce the demands on our compassion" (58). He is right that Americans do not have a good record on compassion for the elderly. Typically, ailing grandparents are institutionalized rather than cared for in the homes of family. And as Conolly points out, the poor suffer the most from our society's indifference (62–63). But to argue as May does that a society needs to have sick and dying members in order to bring forth the virtues of caring and compassion asks too much of the sick and dying. It is like saying

that we need to have the poor around in order to give the rich an opportunity to be charitable.

Hook agrees that the community has a "moral obligation" to "look after its disabled and aged" (60). But he sees these people more as a burden on community resources; caring for them can become costly, reducing the quality of life for the rest, especially the young. I admire the selflessness of this man, but his argument makes me ask, Is it right to let individuals choose to sacrifice themselves for the sake of the rest?

The answer to this question turns upon one other question that all three writers take up: How freely could one make the choice to die? Hook seems to assume that the choice for everyone would be as unpressured as he feels it would be in his case. But he wrote his argument as an old man with a highly successful life behind him—a man who had enjoyed so much he was in a position to be generous with his life. I tend to agree with Conolly that in poor families, guilt may replace generosity as the motive when insurance or Medicare funds run out (62). And May argues that elderly people who have lived alone or in institutions for years may choose death out of sheer despair (58). It is as if the whole society has coerced them into dying.

Hook, Conolly, and May touch on other points in common, but the preceding strike me as the questions most central to the debate. I approached this topic with an inclination to take a position in favor of legalizing assisted suicide. These readings made me see that this policy may bring with it certain dangers.

I agree with Conolly that the medical profession could do more to reduce the suffering of the terminally ill, and I agree with May that society needs to become more compassionate and responsible for quality of life among the aged and terminally ill. However, I do not see either of these desirable goals as alternatives to the option of active euthanasia. Extreme cases of suffering will continue, and they are not as rare as Conolly implies.

However, Conolly and May helped me to see that the apparent individ- 10
ual freedom of choice involved in assisted suicide may be an illusion, so I would want to qualify my position to include a process whereby the courts would be involved to protect the interests of the dying patient. This step may prolong the process of obtaining relief, but I think it ensures justice. Assisted suicide should be a choice, but it must involve more than simply patient, family, and doctor.

USING INQUIRY BY PEERS IN WRITING AN ARGUMENT

After some research into a topic you are preparing to write about, you will find that inquiry by your peers can help you reach a position you can defend. We will illustrate how inquiry works in class discussion with an example of one student's presentation of her tentative position and her responses to the questions raised by her classmates.

Dana's topic was harassment codes, which many colleges and universities have recently enacted to restrict language or behavior that is offensive to minorities and other groups by making such behavior a punishable offense. For example, a code in effect at Southern Methodist University states that harassment "directed towards one or more individuals because of race, ethnicity, religion, sex, age, sexual orientation, or handicap is strictly prohibited. Harassment includes but is not limited to physical, psychological, oral, or written abuse." Although such codes have been ruled unconstitutional at some public schools, a number of private schools have been able to defend them successfully.

In preparation for writing an argument on this topic, students did some assigned reading and outside research. Following is a transcript of how Dana presented her initial position to the class in a brief statement.

Dana: I believe the antiharassment code is well-intentioned but dangerous because it threatens the atmosphere of free expression and inquiry that is vital to a great university. The code is vague about what is prohibited, and students will worry too much about expressing opinions that might be described as abusive.

[Next, to help Dana think through her argument, her classmates questioned her position, even if they agreed with it, and Dana tried to answer their objections.]

Q: Dana, I understand you to say that you are against the code, but you admit it is well intentioned. So you are saying that it would be a good thing to curb harassment? [question about thesis]

A: I'm saying it is bad to harass, but it is also bad to have these codes because it's hard to draw the line between what should be allowed and what should not. Some opinions may hurt, but people should be allowed to say them. For example, I found a case at one university where a gay student complained because another student in the class said homosexuality was a disease that was treatable. That's an opinion, and to prohibit its expression is a blow against academic freedom.

Q: Are you assuming that our code actually does prohibit students from expressing such opinions? [question about reasons and the assumptions behind them]

A: Our code says psychological abuse is harassment. If a gay person was offended by the opinion that homosexuality is an illness, he could claim to be psychologically abused.

Q: So when you said "the spirit of free expression and inquiry" is vital at a great university, you include the right to express offensive opinions? How far would you take that? Would you include the opinions of the Ku Klux Klan? Of Adolf Hitler? [question about definition and implications of the argument]

A: Yes, it has to include offensive opinions—even those of the Klan and Hitler.

Q: Wouldn't these make some people very uncomfortable and even fearful? [question about implications]

A: Yes, but the academic environment requires that there be no restrictions on thought and its expression.

Q: So you are saying that it is more important to have academic freedom at a university than to have a climate where people are not made to feel abused? [question about values]

A: Yes, but to say so makes me sound insensitive. I'm not defending harassment; I just think it is essential that a university guarantees students the right to express opinions.

Q: If the line between offensive opinions and harassment could be drawn more clearly, do you think you could support the code? [question about thesis]

A: I don't think so. Anyway, I don't think it could be done.

Q: Would you say calling someone a "fag" was an opinion that should be protected? Can calling people names possibly be a part of the spirit of academic inquiry? [question about definition]

A: I agree that name-calling and epithets don't belong in an academic environment, but I have to think more about whether that kind of expression should be restricted and how a code might be worded to eliminate that sort of thing, but not free expression. I plan to look at the wording of some codes from other schools.

This dialogue, like all dialogues, could go on indefinitely. But from this brief exchange, you can see that if Dana is to be confident that she has arrived at the best position on the issue, she has to think more about her definition of "free inquiry" and her priorities regarding free expression versus protection from harassment. She also will have to consider the meaning of "harassment"; if she can think of examples of expressions and behavior that would constitute clear harassment, she will have to admit that a different wording of the code might be more defensible.

Following Through

If your class has been exploring topics for argument, write a statement of fifty to one hundred words on the position you are planning to take. As Dana did in the preceding example, include in your statement your main claim, or thesis, and explain why you feel the way you do. Then present your statement to a classmate or small group and together construct a written "conversation" about your position. Or present your statement to the whole class for inquiry.

CHAPTER FIVE

Making Your Case: Arguing to Convince

The last chapter ended where inquiry ends—with the attempt to formulate a position, an opinion that we can assert with some confidence. Once our aim shifts from inquiry to convincing, everything changes.

The most significant change is in audience. In inquiry our audience consists of our fellow inquirers—generally, friends, classmates, and teachers we can talk with face-to-face. We seek assurance that our position is at least plausible and defensible, a claim to truth that can be respected whether the audience agrees with it or not. In convincing, our audience now consists of readers whose positions differ from our own or who have no positions at all on the issue. The audience shifts from a small, inside group that helps us develop our argument to a larger, public audience that will either accept or reject it.

As the audience changes, so does the situation or need for argument. Inquiry is a cooperative use of argument; it cannot take place unless people are willing to work together. Convincing, conversely, is competitive. We pit our case against the case(s) of others in an effort to win the assent of readers who will compare the various arguments and ask, Who makes the best case? With whom should I agree?

Because of the change in audience and situation, our thinking also changes, becoming more strategic and calculated to influence the readers. In inquiry we try to make a case we can believe in; in convincing we must make a case that readers can believe in. What we find compelling in inquiry will sometimes also convince our readers, but we will always have to adapt our reasoning to appeal to their beliefs, values, and self-interest. We will also likely offer reasons that did not occur to us at all in inquiry but that come as we attempt to imagine the people we hope to convince. This shift to convincing does not, however, mean abandoning the work of inquiry. Our version of the truth, our convictions, must first be earned through inquiry before we can seek to convince others in the public arena.

In this chapter we look first at the structure and strategy of complete essays that aim to convince. Then we provide a step-by-step analysis of the kind of thinking necessary to produce such an essay.

THE NATURE OF CONVINCING: STRUCTURE AND STRATEGY

In Chapter 1 we defined argument as an assertion supported by a reason. To convince an audience, writers need to expand on this structure. They usually have to offer more than one reason and support all reasons with evidence. In this chapter we use the term *case structure* to describe a flexible plan for making any argument to any audience that expects sound reasoning. We use the term *case strategy* to describe the moves writers make to shape a particular argument, including selecting reasons, ordering them, developing evidence, and linking the sections of the argument to have maximum impact on an audience.

Case Structure

All cases have at least three levels of assertion. The first level is the thesis, or central claim, which everything else in the case supports. The second level provides the reason or reasons the arguer advances for holding the thesis. The third level is the evidence offered to support each reason, typically drawn from some authoritative source.

In the abstract, then, cases look like this:

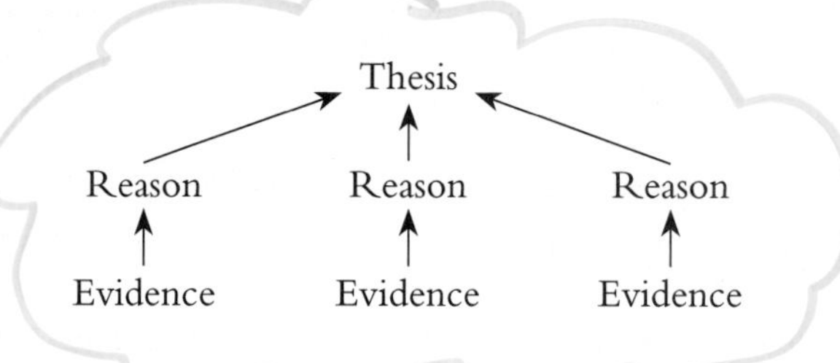

Our diagram shows three reasons, but because case structure is flexible, a good case could be built with only one reason or more than three.

Case Strategy

In Chapter 2 we explained that you can read an argument with greater comprehension if you begin with a sense of the rhetorical context in which the writer worked. Likewise, in preparing to write an argument, you should consider the following rhetorical issues:

Who is your intended audience? What preconceptions and biases might they hold about your topic?

What is your aim for writing?
What claim do you want your readers to accept? How strong a claim can you realistically expect them to accept?
What reasons are likely to appeal to this audience?
How should you arrange the reasons to make the greatest impression on your readers?
How should you lead into the argument? How should you conclude it?
What can you do to present yourself as a person the audience can trust and respect?

By working out answers to these questions in your writer's notebook, you will create a rhetorical prospectus that will help you envision a context within which to write and a tentative plan to follow.

To demonstrate case strategy, we will look at an argument by Anne Marie O'Keefe, a psychologist and lawyer, that deals with drug testing in the workplace. It was published originally in *Psychology Today* in 1987. As a lawyer O'Keefe clearly is concerned about employees' rights to privacy; as a psychologist she is sensitive to what drug testing does to human relationships. After careful inquiry, including library research, she reached the position that despite the dangers of drugs, the practice of testing people for drug use in the workplace should be prohibited.

Thinking about Audience

To make an effective case for her position, O'Keefe envisions an audience that may favor workplace drug screening, and her strategy is to use reasons and evidence to convince readers who initially disagree with her. Therefore, she had to consider their likely responses. To develop a strategy, she had to pose questions like these:

Who will my readers be?
How will they be predisposed to view drug testing?
What will they have on their minds as soon as they see that my argument is against testing?

Based on these questions, O'Keefe probably assumes something like the following about her intended audience:

> Most people feel that drugs are a serious problem in the United States; widespread sentiment exists that something must be done, and drug testing is specific action. But given American suspicion of authority and high regard for individual rights, support for drug testing cannot run very deep. People may feel that it is necessary under the circumstances but also regard it as an invasion of privacy.

Strategy, then, must begin with thoughts about the audience and its values and preconceptions. Next we will examine how O'Keefe shapes the elements of case structure—thesis, reasons, and evidence—to appeal to her readers.

Formulating the Thesis

Assuming that her audience shares her esteem for constitutional rights, O'Keefe refines her position to a more specific thesis. Although it may not appear word for word in the text of the argument, a thesis forecasts how a case will be made. Because you need a clear sense of what you are claiming to build the rest of your case, you should write out a thesis as the first level of your argument's structure. O'Keefe's thesis does not appear explicitly in the text of her argument, but it can be summarized easily: Drug testing unjustifiably intrudes upon the privacy of workers.

Choosing Reasons

O'Keefe's thesis must show that drug testing is an invasion of privacy and thus a policy that cannot be justified. She builds her case on three reasons, aimed strategically at appealing to her audience and undermining their support for drug testing.

Thesis: Drug testing unjustifiably intrudes upon the privacy of workers.

Reason 1: Drug abuse is actually declining, and the push for drug testing is motivated solely by politics and profit making. (Strategy: O'Keefe wants her readers to question the need for testing and the motives of those who advocate testing.)

Reason 2: Drug tests are highly unreliable. (Strategy: O'Keefe wants to undermine any confidence her readers may have in the technology of drug testing.)

Reason 3: Drug testing violates our constitutional right to privacy and destroys employee morale. (Strategy: O'Keefe wants to appeal to American values and the self-interest of employers.)

While O'Keefe does mention the high cost to employers of drug testing, she has not chosen this as a main reason, because she is not writing primarily for the business leaders she criticizes. Rather, she builds her case on other points.

As you read O'Keefe's argument, note how she has arranged her three reasons. We will have more to say later about her strategies for introducing each reason and supporting it with evidence.

ANNE MARIE O'KEEFE

The Case against Drug Testing

1 DURING 1986, the nation's concern over illegal drug use reached almost hysterical proportions. The U.S. House of Representatives passed legislation that, had the Senate agreed, would have suspended certain constitutional protections and required the death penalty for some drug offenses. The

President issued an executive order calling for the mass drug testing of federal employees in "sensitive" positions. Federal courts have deemed such testing to be illegal for some classes of federal workers; however, these decisions are still being appealed, and the administration is determined to forge ahead with its drug-testing program. And private employers have turned increasingly to chemical laboratories to determine who is fit for hiring, promotion, and continuing employment. Between 1982 and 1985, the estimated proportion of Fortune 500 companies conducting routine urinalysis rose from 3 to nearly 30 percent—a figure expected to reach 50 percent by this year or next year.

While there are issues of legitimate concern about drug use and public safety, the speed and enthusiasm with which many of our elected representatives and business leaders have embraced drug testing as a panacea has left many questions unanswered. Why did our national drug problem so rapidly become the focus of political and business decisions? Did this change reflect a sudden, serious worsening of the problem? Why did mass drug testing suddenly gain favor? Was it shown to be particularly effective in detecting and deterring illegal drug use? And finally, what are the costs of making employees and job applicants take urine tests?

Our country has a serious drug problem. The National Institute on Drug Abuse (NIDA) estimates that nearly two-thirds of those now entering the work force have used illegal drugs—44 percent within the past year. But ironically, the drug-testing craze has come just when most types of drug use are beginning to wane. NIDA reports that for all drugs except cocaine, current rates are below those of 1979, our peak year of drug use.

Why the furor now? The drug-testing fad might be viewed as the product of both election-year posturing and well-timed and well-financed marketing efforts by test manufacturers. During the 1970s, the relatively low-cost chemical assay (called EMIT) that promised to detect drugs in urine was first manufactured. In the beginning, these tests were used only by crime laboratories, drug-treatment programs and the military. By the early 1980s, a handful of private employers were also using them. But more recently, sales of drug tests have gotten a big boost from the attitudes and edicts of the Reagan administration. On March 3, 1986, the President's Commission on Organized Crime recommended that all employees of private companies contracting with the federal government be regularly subjected to urine testing for drugs as a condition of employment. Then came the President's executive order on September 15, requiring the head of each executive agency to "establish a program to test for the use of illegal drugs by employees in sensitive positions." It remains unclear how many millions of federal workers will be subject to such testing if the President gets his way.

Strangely, drug testing is becoming widespread despite general agree- 5
ment that the results of mass tests are often highly inaccurate. Error rates reflect both inherent deficiencies in the technology and mistakes in handling and interpreting test results. In a series of studies conducted by the federal Centers for Disease Control (CDC) and NIDA, urine samples spiked with drugs were

sent periodically to laboratories across the country serving methadone treatment centers. Tests on these samples, which the labs knew had come from CDC, revealed drug-detection error rates averaging below 10 percent. However, when identical samples subsequently were sent to the same laboratories, but not identified as coming from CDC, error rates increased to an average of 31 percent, with a high of 100 percent. These errors were "false negatives," cases in which "dirty" urine samples were identified as "clean."

Independent studies of laboratory accuracy have also confirmed high error rates. One group of researchers reported a 66.5 percent rate of "false positives" among 160 urine samples from participants in a methadone treatment center. False-positive mistakes, identifying a "clean" urine sample as containing an illegal drug, are far more serious in the context of worker screening than are false-negative mistakes. This is because false positives can result in innocent people losing their jobs. Ironically, since the error rates inherent in the drug tests are higher than the actual rate of illegal drug use in the general working population, as reported by NIDA, the tests are more likely to label innocent people as illegal drug users than to identify real users.

Many of the false-positive results stem from a phenomenon known as "cross-reactivity." This refers to the fact that both over-the-counter and prescription drugs, and even some foods, can produce false-positive results on the tests. For example, Contac, Sudafed, certain diet pills, decongestants, and heart and asthma medications can register as amphetamines on the tests. Cough syrups containing dextromethorphan can cross-react as opiates, and some antibiotics show up as cocaine. Anti-inflammatory drugs and common painkillers, including Datril, Advil, and Nuprin, mimic marijuana. Even poppy seeds, which actually contain traces of morphine, and some herbal teas containing traces of cocaine can cause positive test results for these drugs.

Commercial testing companies almost always claim very high accuracy and reliability. But because these laboratories are not uniformly regulated, employers who buy their services may find it hard to confirm these claims or even to conduct informed comparative shopping. Companies that mass-market field-testing kits such as EMITs (which cost an estimated $15 to $25 per test) usually recommend that positive test results be confirmed with other laboratory procedures, which can run from $100 to $200 per test. But relatively few employers seem to be using the expensive back-up procedures before firing employees who test positive. Even when employers do verify positive results, employees who turn out to be drug-free upon retesting will already be stigmatized.

The tests have other critical failings, particularly their limited sensitivity to certain drugs, a shortcoming the drug-test manufacturers readily admit. Consider cocaine, for example. Despite great concern in the 1980s over the use of cocaine, the only illicit drug whose use is on the rise, this is the drug to which the tests are least sensitive since its chemical traces dissipate in a few days. Alcohol, which is legal but potentially detrimental to job performance, is also hard to detect, since traces disappear from within 12 to 24 hours. By contrast, urine testing is, if anything, overly sensitive to marijuana; it can detect the drug's chemical byproducts (not its active ingredient) for weeks after its use and can even pick up the residue of passive inhalation. Drug testing does not indicate the recency of use, nor does it distinguish between chronic and one-time use. Most important, though urinalysis can reveal a lot about off-the-job activities, it tells nothing about job performance.

Mass drug testing is expensive, but its greatest costs are not financial and 10
cannot be neatly quantified. The greatest costs involve violations of workers' rights and the poor employee morale and fractured trust that result when workers must prove their innocence against the presumption of guilt.

The most important cost of drug testing, however, may be the invasion of workers' privacy. Urinalysis may be highly inaccurate in detecting the use of illegal drugs, but it can reveal who is pregnant, who has asthma, and who is being treated for heart disease, manic-depression, epilepsy, diabetes, and a host of other physical and mental conditions.

In colonial times, King George III justified having his soldiers break into homes and search many innocent people indiscriminately on the grounds that the procedure might reveal the few who were guilty of crimes against the Crown. But the founders of our nation chose to balance things quite differently. An important purpose and accomplishment of the Constitution is to protect us from government intrusion. The Fourth Amendment is clear that "the right of the people to be secure in their persons . . . against unreasonable searches and seizures, shall not be violated. . . ." Searches are permitted only "upon probable cause, supported by Oath or affirmation, and particularly describing the place to be searched, and the persons or things to be seized."

The U.S. Supreme Court has ruled that extracting bodily fluids constitutes a search within the meaning of this Amendment. Therefore, except under extraordinary circumstances, when the government seeks to test an employee's urine, it must comply with due process and must first provide plausible evidence of illegal activity. People accused of heinous crimes are assured of this minimum protection from government intrusion. Because employees in our government work force deserve no less, most courts reviewing proposals to conduct mass tests on such employees have found these programs to be illegal.

Unfortunately, workers in the private sector are not as well protected. The Constitution protects citizens only from intrusions by government (county, state, and federal); it does not restrict nongovernmental employers from invading workers' privacy, although employers in the private sector are subject to some limitations. The constitutions of nine states have provisions specifically protecting citizens' rights to privacy and prohibiting unreasonable searches and seizures. Several private lawsuits against employers are now testing the applicability of these shields. Local governments can, if they wish, pass legislation to protect private employees from unwarranted drug tests; in fact, San Francisco has done so. In addition, union contracts and grievance procedures may give some workers protection from mass drug testing, and civil-rights laws could block the disproportionate testing of minorities. Nonetheless, private employees have relatively little legal protection against mandatory drug testing and arbitrary dismissal.

Civil libertarians claim that as long as employees do their work well, 15
inquiries into their off-duty drug use are no more legitimate than inquiries into their sex lives. Then why has drug testing become so popular? Perhaps because it is simple and "objective"—a litmus test. It is not easily challenged because, like the use of lie detectors, it relies on technology that few understand. It is quicker and cheaper than serious and sustained efforts to reduce illegal drug use, such as the mass educational efforts that have successfully reduced cigarette smoking. And finally, while drug testing may do little to address the real problem of drug use in our society, it reinforces the employer's illusion of doing something.

Apparently some employers would rather test their employees for drugs than build a relationship with them based on confidence and loyalty. Fortunately, there are employers, such as the Drexelbrook Engineering Company in Pennsylvania, who have decided against drug testing because of its human costs. As Drexelbrook's vice president put it, a relationship "doesn't just come from a paycheck. When you say to an employee, 'you're doing a great job; just the same, I want you to pee in this jar and I'm sending someone to watch you,' you've undermined that trust."

Arranging Reasons

Throughout her argument O'Keefe deals with the likely preconceptions of her readers. After two introductory paragraphs, paragraphs 3 and 4 counter the justification for drug testing based on the belief that the problem of drug abuse is so great that extraordinary measures are required to cope with it. Yes, we have a substance-abuse problem, she admits, but illegal drug use is actually declining and has been declining without drug testing. Having weakened this underlying rationale, she goes on to expose what she sees as the genuine motives behind drug testing—hysteria, political advantage, and money. Her strategy here—to discredit the politicians and business leaders who advocate drug testing—plays to the prejudices of many Americans who view the Washington political establishment and big business as motivated by self-interest.

O'Keefe next seeks to destroy her readers' confidence in the technology of drug testing. She devotes much space (paragraphs 5–9) to this reason, probably because she assumes her readers share the common faith in the ability of technology to provide clean, efficient, and relatively simple solutions for complex social problems. To undermine this faith, O'Keefe calls attention to the "inherent deficiencies" in drug testing technology.

O'Keefe's third and final reason (paragraphs 10–16) achieves its full force based on Reasons 1 and 2. If (1) there is no compelling need for drug testing and the people pushing it are acting out of self-interest and (2) the technology is by nature faulty, then (3) we have to take more seriously the violation of constitutional rights and the undermining of trust between employee and employer that are inherent in drug testing.

Using Evidence

How well has O'Keefe used the third level of case structure, the supporting evidence for each reason? For her first reason she briefly cites NIDA reports that the rate of drug use in 1987 was lower than that in 1979, a "peak year." She acknowledges that cocaine is an exception, but the authority of the source and the overall statistical trends would sway most readers. She then alleges that businesses and politicians are benefitting from the testing fad; she supports this claim with a chronological presentation of facts about the advocacy of these tests by the Reagan administration up to 1986, an election year. The strategy here is simply to make the obvious political connection.

O'Keefe offers a wealth of evidence to support her second reason: that drug tests are unreliable (paragraphs 5–9). Her strategy in presenting this evidence is simple and effective. She divides her evidence into two parts and begins with the less serious charge: that drug tests can result in false negatives, or failures to detect the presence of illegal drugs. After calling our attention to the failure of drug testing in achieving its primary purpose—to identify users—she goes on to describe the more serious problem of false positives, which can cause innocent people to lose their jobs or be stigmatized. She further contrasts error rates in labs that know they are being monitored with error rates in labs that don't, encouraging readers to conclude that the labs are careless and therefore untrustworthy.

In paragraph 8 O'Keefe recognizes a contradictory piece of evidence that defenders of drug testing would likely point out: that relatively more reliable, but also more expensive, tests exist. In granting the existence of such tests, O'Keefe strengthens her own case by suggesting that rather than go to the expense of double-checking, most employers will choose simply to fire employees based on the less expensive, less reliable test.

In backing up her third reason, a more abstract point about the right to privacy, O'Keefe appeals strongly and concretely to her readers' fears and values. Urinalysis reveals "who is pregnant, who has asthma, and who is being treated for heart disease," and so on (paragraph 11), information that has nothing to do with illegal drugs and that most people feel is their own business. Finally, O'Keefe invokes the authority of history and the Fourth Amendment's protection from unwarranted government intrusion, a basic American value associated with the founders of our nation.

Introducing and Concluding the Argument

We have analyzed O'Keefe's strategic use of the three levels of case structure—thesis, reasons, evidence—to build an argument that will convince her audience not to support drug testing. Arguing to convince also requires that a writer think strategically of ways to open and close his or her presentation of the case.

The Introduction O'Keefe's opening strategy is to cast her argument in terms of reasoned reaction as opposed to emotional overreaction. Note the careful choice of words in her opening sentence: "During 1986, the nation's concern over illegal drug use reached almost hysterical proportions." She goes on in the rest of the paragraph to "prove" her point with sentences that amount to a list: The U.S. House of Representatives did this . . . the president did that . . . private employers have done this. In other words, each of her points after her opening assertion is designed to strengthen our acceptance of "almost hysterical" as an accurate and plausible description of the reaction during 1986 to illegal drug use.

In paragraph 2 O'Keefe poses questions having to do with her three areas of discussion that advocates of drug testing have not answered: Why are the tests being done? How well do they work? What effects do they have? This opening strategy accomplishes two purposes. First, it provokes the reader to think, to share in her skepticism. Second, it predicts the rest of her essay, which goes on to answer these questions.

The Conclusion O'Keefe's strategy in concluding her complex argument is fairly simple: she attempts to present a fair and rational evaluation of drug testing as a solution to the drug problem. First, in paragraph 15 she again questions why these tests have become so popular. This time her tone is less accusatory, and she seems to be trying to understand her well-intentioned but ill-informed opposition. In the final paragraph she effectively presents a flat alternative: Either we can test employees for drugs or we can build employer-employee relationships based on mutual respect. She then closes with an image that cannot fail to stick: the humiliation of urinating in a jar while someone watches to make sure the sample is not tampered with. The lack of trust and the cold impersonality of corporate drug testing comes through in a conclusion of real power, made all the more effective because she actually quotes a corporate executive critical of drug testing.

Following Through

A successful essay has smooth transitions between its opening and its first reason and between its last reason and its conclusion, as well as between each of the reasons in the body of the essay. In your writer's notebook describe how O'Keefe (1) announces that she is moving on from her introduction to her first reason, from her first reason to her second, and so on and (2) at the same time links each section with what has come before.

THE PROCESS OF CONVINCING

Few people draft an essay sequentially, beginning with the first sentence of the first paragraph and ending with the last sentence of the last paragraph.

But the final version of any essay must read as if it had been written sequentially, with the writer fully in control throughout the process.

A well-written essay is like a series of moves in a chess game, each made to achieve some end or ends, to gain a strategic advantage, as part of an overall plan to win. In the case of convincing, the overall plan is to win the agreement of the reader.

While readers may not be fully aware of the moves that make up a convincing argument, the writer probably created most of them more or less consciously. As we have seen in this chapter, we can learn much about how to convince by studying finished essays—polished arguments that convince. However, it is one thing to understand how something works and quite another to produce it ourselves. In part, the difficulty is that we cannot see from the final product everything that went into making it work so well. Just as the audience for a movie typically cannot imagine all the rehearsals, the many takes, and the editing that make a scene so powerful, so it is hard for us to imagine all the research and thinking, the many drafts, and the process of editing and proofreading that O'Keefe must have gone through to make "The Case against Drug Testing" worth printing. Yet it is precisely this process you must understand and immerse yourself in if you are to go beyond appreciating the structure and strategies of someone else's writing to actually produce convincing arguments of your own.

The following discussion of the composing process assumes that the work of inquiry (Chapter 4) and research (Chapter 9) has already been done. It also assumes that you have worked out a rhetorical prospectus to guide you in combining structure with strategy.

Preparing a Brief

Before you begin to draft, it is a good idea to prepare a brief. Recall that we defined case structure as the basic components of any case. In a brief you adapt case structure to make a particular argument. The brief shows the thesis and reasons that you plan to use and gives some indication of how you will support each reason with evidence. The brief ought to indicate a tentative plan for arranging the reasons, but that plan may change as you draft and revise. In this section we will take you through the process of creating a brief.

Working toward a Position

First, we need to distinguish a position from a thesis. A *position* (or a stance or opinion) amounts to an overall, summarizing attitude or judgment about some issue. "Universities often exploit student athletes" is an example of a position. A *thesis* is not only more specific and precise but also more strategic, designed to appeal to readers and to be consistent with available evidence. For example, "Student athletes in revenue-generating sports ought to be paid for their services" would be one thesis representing the preceding position, perhaps for an audience of college students. Because a case is nothing more than the reasons and evidence that support a thesis, we cannot construct a case without one. But without a position we do not know where we stand in general on an issue and so cannot experiment with various thesis formulations. Typically, a position precedes a thesis.

The goal of inquiry is to earn an opinion, to find a stance that holds up in dialogue with other inquirers. What often happens in inquiry, however, is that we begin with a strong opinion, usually unearned, find it failing under scrutiny, discover positions advanced by others that do not fully satisfy us, and so emerge from inquiry uncertain about what we do think. Another common path in inquiry is to start out with no opinion at all, find ourselves attracted to several conflicting positions, and so wind up in much the same condition as the person whose strong initial position collapses under scrutiny—unsure, confused, even vexed because we can't decide what we think.

In such situations resolve first to be patient with yourself. Certainty is often cheap and easy; the best, most mature positions typically come to us only after a struggle. Second, take out your writer's notebook and start making lists. Look over your research materials, especially the notecards on which you have recorded positions and evidence from your sources. Make lists in response to these questions:

> What positions have you encountered in research and class discussion?
>
> What seems strongest and weakest in each stance? What modifications might be made to eliminate or minimize the weak points? Are there other possible positions? What are their strong and weak points?
>
> What pieces of evidence impressed you? What does each of these imply or suggest? What connections can you draw among the pieces of evidence given in various sources? If there is conflict in the implications of the evidence, what is that conflict?

While all this list-making may seem at times to be only doodling, you can often begin to see convergences as your mind begins to sort things out.

Bear in mind that emotional commitment to ideas and values is important to a healthy life but is often an impediment to clear thought and effective convincing. Sometimes we find our stance by relinquishing a strongly held opinion that proves hard to make a case for—perhaps for lack of compelling reasons or evidence that can appeal to readers outside the group that already agrees with us. The more emotional the issue—abortion, pornography, affirmative action, among others—the more likely we are to cling to a position that is difficult to defend. When we sense deep conflict, when we want to argue a position even in the face of strong contradictory evidence and counterarguments we cannot respond to, it is time to reconsider our emotional commitments and perhaps even to change our minds.

Finally, if you find yourself holding out for the "perfect" position, the one that is all strength and no weakness, the best advice is to give up. Controversial issues are controversial precisely because no one stance convinces everyone, because there is always room for counterargument and for other positions that have their own power to convince.

Student Sample: Working toward a Position Justin Spidel's class began by reading many arguments about homosexuality and discussing issues related to gay rights. Justin decided to investigate whether same-sex marriage should be legal. His initial perspective on the issue was that same-sex marriage ought to be legal because he thought that gays and lesbians should be treated as equals and that no harm would result. As he did research, he learned that a majority of Americans strongly oppose same-sex marriage, mainly because they believe its legalization would change a long-standing definition of marriage and alter its sacred bond. Justin read articles opposing gay marriage by such well-known public figures as William Bennett, but he also read many in favor. He found especially convincing the arguments by gays and lesbians who were in long-standing, loving, monogamous relationships but who were barred from marrying their partners. Justin's initial round of research led him to the position "Gays and lesbians should be able to marry."

During the inquiry stage Justin discussed his position with his classmates and instructor. Knowing that gays and lesbians do sometimes get married in churches, Justin's classmates asked him to clarify the phrase "able to marry." Justin explained that he meant legal recognition of same-sex marriages by individual state governments and, therefore, all states, since marriage in any one state is usually recognized by the rest. When asked if other countries recognize same-sex marriage, Justin admitted that only Denmark does. He decided to argue for his position anyway on the grounds that the United States should take the lead in valuing equality and individual rights. He was asked about the implications of his position: Would granting legal status to same-sex marriage devalue the institution? Justin responded that the people who are fighting for legalization have the deepest respect for marriage and that marriage is about love and commitment rather than sexual orientation.

Following Through

Formulate a tentative position on a topic that you have researched and inquired into. Write it up with some brief explanation of why you support this stand. Be prepared to defend your position in class or with a peer in a one-on-one exchange of position statements.

Analyzing the Audience

Before you decide on a thesis, give some thought to the rhetorical context of your argument. Who needs to hear it? What are their values? What common ground might you share with them? How might you have to qualify your position to influence their opinions?

To provoke thought, people occasionally make cases for theses that they know have little chance of winning significant assent. One example is the argument for legalizing all drug use; although reasonably good cases have been made for this position, most Americans find it too radical to be convincing. If you want to convince rather than provoke, you must formulate a thesis that both represents your position and creates as little resistance in your readers as possible. Instead of arguing for legalizing drugs, for example, you might argue that much of the staggering amount of money spent on enforcement, prosecution, and imprisonment be diverted to rehabilitation and social problems connected with drug abuse. Because most positions allow for many possible theses, writers need to analyze their audience before settling on one.

Student Sample: Analyzing the Audience Justin knew that many people would view same-sex marriage as a very radical idea. Some possible audiences, such as conservative Christians, would never assent to it. So Justin targeted an audience he had some chance of convincing—people who opposed same-sex marriage but were not intolerant of homosexuals. Justin sketched the following audience profile.

> My audience would be heterosexual adults who accept that some people are homosexual or lesbian; they may know people who are. They would be among the nearly forty-seven percent of Americans who do not object to same-sex relationships between consenting adults. They may be fairly well educated and could be any age from college students to their grandparents. They are not likely to have strong religious objections, so my argument will not have to go deeply into the debate about whether homosexuality is a sin. However, these readers oppose legalizing marriage between gays and lesbians because they think it would threaten the traditional role of marriage as the basis of family life. They think that marriage has come into enough trouble lately through divorce, and they want to preserve its meaning as much as possible. Their practical position would be that if same-sex couples want to live together and act like they're married, there is nothing to stop them, so they are really not being hurt by leaving things as they are. They believe in the value of heterosexual marriage for the individual and society, so I can appeal to that. They also hold to basic American principles of equal rights and the right to the "pursuit of happiness." But mainly I want to show my readers that gays and lesbians are missing out on some basic civil rights and that letting them marry would have benefits for everyone.

Following Through

Write a profile of the audience you hope to reach through an argument you are currently planning. Try to be as specific as possible, including any information—age, gender, economic status, and so forth—that may contribute to your audience's outlook and attitudes. What interests, beliefs, and values may be influencing them? How might you have to alter your position or phrase your thesis to give your argument a chance of succeeding? What reasons might they be willing to consider? What would you have to rule out?

Developing a Thesis

A good thesis grows out of a combination of things: your position, your research, your exploration of reasons to support your position, and your understanding of the audience. Later on, during the process of drafting, you may refine the thesis by phrasing it more precisely, but for now you should concentrate only on stating a thesis that represents your position clearly and directly.

We would advise you against trying to make your thesis do more than simply present the claim. Naturally, your mind runs to reasons in support, but hold off on these. It makes more sense to save the reasons until you can present them thoroughly as the body of the paper unfolds.

Student Sample: Developing a Thesis Justin's original statement, "Gays and lesbians should be able to marry," expresses a position, but it could be more precise and more directed toward the readers Justin defined in his audience profile. He already had some reasons to support his argument, and he wanted the thesis to represent his current position accurately, without locking him into some rigid plan. He refined his position to the following:

> A couple's right to marry should not be restricted based on sexual preference.

This version emphasized that marriage is a right everyone should enjoy, but it did not go far enough in suggesting why the readers should care or recognize it as a right. Justin tried again:

> Every couple who wishes to commit to each other in marriage should have the right to do so, regardless of sexual preference.

Justin was fairly satisfied with this version because it appealed to a basic family value—commitment.

He then started thinking about how committed relationships benefit society in general, an argument that would appeal to his readers. He wondered if he could point the thesis not just in the direction of rights for homosexuals and lesbians but also in the direction of benefits for everyone, which would broaden his appeal. It would also allow him to develop his essay more by using some good arguments he had encountered in his reading. He tried one more time and settled on the following thesis:

> Everyone, gay and straight, will benefit from extending the basic human right of marriage to all couples, regardless of sexual preference.

Following Through

1. Write at least three versions of a tentative thesis for the essay you are currently working on. For each version, write an evaluation of its strengths and weaknesses. Why is the best version the best?
2. As we saw in analyzing William May's case against assisted suicide (Chapter 3), sometimes a thesis needs to be qualified and exceptions to the thesis need to be stated and clarified. Now is a good time to think about qualifications and exceptions.

   Basically, you can handle qualifications and exceptions in two ways. First, you can add a phrase to your thesis that puts some limitations on it, as William May did in his argument on assisted suicide: "*On the whole,* our social policy . . . should not regularize killing for mercy." May admits that a few extreme cases of suffering justify helping someone die. The other method would be to word the thesis in such a way that exceptions or qualifications are implied rather than spelled out. As an example consider the following thesis: "Life sentences with no parole are justifiable for all sane people found guilty of first-degree murder." Here, the exceptions would be "those who are found insane" and "those tried on lesser charges."

   Using your best thesis statement from the previous exercise, decide whether qualifications and exceptions are needed. If they are, determine how best to handle them.

Analyzing the Thesis

Once you have a thesis, your next task is to *unpack* it to determine what you must argue. To do this, put yourself in the place of your readers. In order to be won over to that position, what are they going to have to find in your argument? Answering that question requires looking very closely at both what the thesis actually says and what it implies. It also requires thinking about the position and attitudes of your readers, as you described them earlier in your audience profile.

As an example consider Anne Marie O'Keefe's thesis, "Drug testing in the workplace is an unjustifiable intrusion on individuals' privacy." Because there is no qualifier, the reader is going to expect an argument opposing *all* drug testing in the workplace. The argument will have to give good reasons that the intrusion on privacy is not justified. But O'Keefe realized that her readers might not believe that privacy is necessary in the workplace, so establishing workers' rights to privacy was another area of development required by this thesis.

Many thesis sentences appear simple, but analysis shows that they are quite complex. Let's consider a thesis on the issue of whether Mark Twain's *Huckleberry Finn* should be taught in the public schools. Some have argued that

Twain's classic novel should be removed from required reading lists because a number of readers, especially African Americans, find its subject matter and language offensive. In fact, in some schools the novel is not assigned at all, while in others it may be assigned but students have the option of choosing to study another novel of the same period instead. In our example thesis the writer supports the teaching of the novel: "Mark Twain's *Huckleberry Finn* should be required reading for all high school students in the United States."

Unpacking this thesis, we see that the writer must first argue for *Huckleberry Finn* as *required* reading—not merely as a good book but as one that is indispensable to an education in American literature. The writer must also argue that the book be required at the high school level, rather than middle school or college. Finally, knowing that some people find certain passages offensive, the author must defend the novel from charges of racism, even though the thesis does not explicitly state, "*Huckleberry Finn* is not a racist book." Otherwise, these charges stand by default; to ignore them is to ignore the context of the issue.

Student Sample: Analyzing the Thesis By analyzing his thesis—"Everyone, gay and straight, will benefit from extending the basic human right of marriage to all couples, regardless of sexual preference"—Justin realized that his main task was to explain specific benefits that would follow from allowing gays to marry. He knew that he would have to cite ways in which society will be better off, as well as those in same-sex relationships who want to marry. He knew that his readers would agree that marriage is a "basic human right" for heterosexual adults, but he could not assume that they would see it that way for homosexual couples. Therefore, he had to make them see that same-sex couples have the same needs as other couples. He also wanted to make certain that his readers understood that he was arguing only that the law of the land recognize such marriages, not that all churches and denominations sanctify them.

Following Through

Unpack a tentative thesis of your own or one that your instructor gives you to see what key words and phrases an argument based on that thesis must address. Also consider what an audience would expect you to argue, given a general knowledge about the topic and the current context of the dispute.

Finding Reasons

For the most part no special effort goes into finding reasons to support a thesis. They come to us as we attempt to justify our opinions, as we listen to the arguments of our classmates, as we encounter written arguments in research, and as we think about how to reach the readers we hope to convince. Given good writing preparation, we seldom formulate a thesis without already having some idea of the reasons we will use to defend it. Our problem, rather, is usually selection—picking out the best reasons and shaping and stating them in a way that appeals to our readers. When we do find ourselves searching for reasons, however, it helps to be aware of their common sources.

The Audience's Belief System Ask yourself, What notions of the real, the good, and the possible will my readers entertain? Readers will find any reason unconvincing if it is not consistent with their understanding of reality. For example, people will accept or reject arguments about how to treat illness based on their particular culture's notions about disease. Likewise, people have differing notions of what is good. Some people think it is good to exploit natural resources so that we can live with more conveniences; those who place less value on conveniences see more good in conserving the environment. Finally, people disagree about what is possible. Those who believe it is not possible to change human nature will not accept arguments that certain types of criminals can be rehabilitated.

Special Rules or Principles Good reasons can also be found in a community's accepted rules and principles. For example, in the United States citizens accept the principle that a person is innocent until proven guilty. The Fifth Amendment states that no one may be "deprived of life, liberty, or property, without due process of law." We apply this principle in all sorts of nonlegal situations whenever we argue that someone should be given the benefit of the doubt.

The law is only one source of special rules or principles. We also find them in politics ("one person, one vote"), in business (the principle of seniority, which gives preference to employees who have been on a job longest), and even in the home, where each family formulates its own house rules. In other words, all human settings and activities have their own norms, and we must ask ourselves in any search for reasons what norms may apply to our particular topic or thesis.

Expert Opinion and Hard Evidence Probably the next most common source of reasons is expert opinion, which we must rely on when we lack direct experience with a particular subject. Most readers respect the opinion of a trained professional with advanced degrees and prestige in his or her field. And when you can show that experts are in agreement, you have an even better reason.

Hard evidence can also provide good reasons. Readers generally respect the scientific method of gathering objective data upon which conclusions can be drawn. Research shows, for example, that wearing a bicycle helmet significantly reduces the incidence of head injuries from accidents. Therefore, we can support the thesis "Laws should require bicycle riders to wear helmets" with the reason "because statistics show that fewer serious head injuries occurred in bicycle accidents when the riders were wearing helmets than when no helmets were worn."

When you argue about any topic, you will be at a disadvantage if you don't have detailed, current information about it in the form of expert opinion and hard evidence.

Tradition We can sometimes strengthen a position by citing or alluding to well-known sources that are part of our audience's cultural tradition—for example, the Bible, the Constitution, and the sayings or writings of people our readers recognize and respect. Although reasons drawn from tradition may lose their force if many audience members identify with different cultures or are suspicious of tradition itself, they will almost always be effective when readers revere the source.

Comparison A reason based on similarity argues that what is true in one instance should be true in another. For example, we could make a case for legalizing marijuana by showing that it is similar in effect to alcohol, which is legal—and also a drug. The argument might look like this:

> *Thesis:* Marijuana use should be decriminalized.
>
> *Reason:* Marijuana is no more harmful than alcohol.

Many comparison arguments attempt to show that present situations are similar to past ones. For example, many who argue for the civil rights of gays and lesbians say that discrimination based on sexual preference should not be tolerated today just as discrimination based on race, common thirty years ago, is no longer tolerated.

A special kind of argument based on similarity is an *analogy,* which attempts to explain one thing, usually abstract, in terms of something else, usually more concrete. For example, in an argument opposing sharing the world's limited resources, philosopher Garrett Hardin reasons that requiring the wealthy nations of the world to feed the starving nations is analogous to requiring the occupants of a lifeboat filled to a safe capacity to take on board those still in the water, until the lifeboat sinks and everyone perishes.

Arguments of comparison can also point to difference, showing how two things are not the same, or not analogous. For example, many Americans supported participation in the 1992 Persian Gulf War by arguing that unlike the disastrous conflict in Vietnam, this war was winnable. The argument went as follows:

> *Thesis:* America can defeat Iraq's military.
>
> *Reason:* Warfare in the deserts of Kuwait and Iraq is very different from warfare in the jungles of Vietnam.

The Probable or Likely Of course, all reasoning about controversial issues relies on making a viewpoint seem probable or likely, but specific reasons drawn from the probable or likely may often come into play when we want to defend one account of events over another or when we want to attack or support a proposed policy. For example, defenders of Supreme Court nominee

Clarence Thomas attempted to discredit Anita Hill's accusations of sexual harassment in a number of ways, all related to probability: Is it likely, they asked, that she would remember so clearly and in such detail events that happened as long as ten years ago? Is it probable that a woman who had been harassed would follow Thomas from one job to another, as Hill did?

Because a proposed policy may have no specific precedent, particularly if it is designed to deal with a new situation, speculating about its probable success or failure is sometimes all a writer arguing for or against the new policy can do. For example, the collapse of communism in eastern Europe and the former Soviet Union has left the United States in the unusual position of having no serious military threat to its own or its allies' security. What, then, should we do—drastically reduce our armed forces, especially the nuclear arsenal? redirect part of what we once spent on defense into dealing with pressing domestic problems? Any proposal for confronting this new situation is defended and attacked based on what we are likely to face in the foreseeable future.

Cause and Effect People generally agree that most circumstances result from some cause or causes, and they also agree that most changes in circumstances will result in some new effects. This human tendency to believe in cause-and-effect relationships can provide reasons for certain arguments. For example, environmentalists have successfully argued for reductions in the world's output of hydrofluorocarbons by showing that the chemicals damage the earth's ozone layer.

Cause-and-effect arguments are difficult to prove; witness the fact that cigarette manufacturers have argued for years that the connection between smoking and lung disease cannot be demonstrated. Responsible arguments from cause and effect depend on credible and adequate hard evidence and expert opinion. And they must always acknowledge the possible existence of hidden factors; smoking and lung disease, for example, may be influenced by genetic predisposition.

Definition All arguments require definitions for clarification. However, a definition can often provide a reason in support of the thesis as well. If we define a term by placing it in a category, we are saying that whatever is true for the category is true for the term we are defining. For example, Elizabeth Cady Stanton's landmark 1892 argument for women's rights ("The Solitude of Self") was based on the definition "women are individuals":

> *Thesis:* Women must have suffrage, access to higher education, and sovereignty over their own minds and bodies.
>
> *Reason:* Women are individuals.

If Stanton's audience, American congressmen, accepted that all individuals are endowed with certain inalienable rights, Stanton's definition reminded them that women fit into the category of "individual" just as much as men do and so deserve the same rights.

Almost all good reasons come from one or some combination of these eight sources. However, simply knowing the sources will not automatically provide you with good reasons for your argument. Nothing can substitute for thoughtful research and determined inquiry. Approach each of these sources as an angle from which to think about your thesis statement and the results of your research and inquiry. They can help you generate reasons initially or find better reasons when the ones you have seem inadequate.

Finally, do not feel that quantity is crucial in finding good reasons. While it is good to brainstorm as many reasons as you can, you will want to focus on those that you think will appeal most to your audience and that you can develop thoroughly. A good argument is often based on just one or two good reasons.

Student Sample: Finding Reasons Justin used the eight sources listed in the preceding section to help find some of his reasons. He also considered his audience and the beliefs they would likely hold. Here are the possible reasons he found; note that each reason is stated as a complete sentence.

From the audience's belief system:

Marriage is primarily about love and commitment, not sex.
Marriage is a stabilizing influence in society.

From rules or principles the audience would likely subscribe to:

Everyone has an equal right to life, liberty, and the pursuit of happiness.

From expert opinion (in this case, a lawyer and some noted authors on gay rights):

Denying gays and lesbians the right to marry is an incredible act of discrimination.
Allowing gays and lesbians to marry will promote family values such as monogamy and the two-parent family.

From comparison or analogy:

Just as we once thought marriage between blacks and whites should be illegal, we now think same-sex marriage should be illegal.
Gay and lesbian couples can love each other just as devotedly as heterosexual couples.

From cause and effect:

Marriage is a way for people to take care of each other rather than being a burden on society should they become ill or unemployed.

Clearly, Justin now had far more ideas for his case than he needed. He now had to evaluate his list to check the fit between the reasons he thought were best and his thesis sentence.

Following Through

Here is one way of brainstorming for reasons. First, list the eight sources for finding reasons, discussed on pages 86–88, in your writer's notebook, perhaps on the inside front cover or on the first or last page—someplace where you can easily find them. Practice using these sources by writing your current thesis at the top of another page and then going through the list, writing down reasons as they occur to you.

Exchange notebooks with other class members. See if you can help each other generate additional reasons.

Selecting and Ordering Reasons

Selecting reasons from a number of possibilities depends primarily on two considerations: your thesis and your readers. Any thesis demands a certain line of reasoning. For example, the writer contending that *Huckleberry Finn* should be required reading in high school must offer a compelling reason for accepting no substitute—not even another novel by Mark Twain. Such a reason might be, "Because many critics and novelists see *Huckleberry Finn* as the inspiration for much subsequent American fiction, we cannot understand the American novel if we are not familiar with *Huckleberry Finn.*" A reason of this kind—one that focuses on the essential influence of the book—is likely to appeal to teachers or school administrators.

It is often difficult to see how to order reasons prior to drafting. Because we can easily reorder reasons as we write and rewrite, in developing our case we need only attempt to discover an order that seems right and satisfies us as an overall sequence. The writer advocating *Huckleberry Finn,* for example, should probably first defend the novel from the charge that it is racist. Readers unaware of the controversy will want to know why the book needs defending, and well-informed readers will expect an immediate response to the book's critics because it is their efforts to remove the book from classrooms that has created the controversy. Once the charge of racism has been disposed of, readers will be prepared to hear the reasons for keeping the book on required reading lists.

The readers' needs and expectations must take precedence in all decisions about sequencing reasons. We should also consider relationships among the reasons themselves, how one may lead to another. For instance, Anne Marie O'Keefe's case against drug testing first establishes the unreliability of the tests and then focuses on the damage such tests inflict on innocent employees and the violation of civil rights they represent. This sequence is effective because each reason prepares the reader for the next one. If drug tests are often inaccurate, then innocent people will be falsely accused; if innocent people are falsely accused, the unwarranted invasion of privacy seems much worse—indeed, indefensible.

Besides thinking about what your readers need and expect and how one reason may gain force by following another one, you should also keep in mind a simple fact about memory: We recall best what we read last and next best what we read first. A good rule of thumb, therefore, is to begin and end your defense of a thesis with your strongest reasons, the ones you want to emphasize. A strong beginning also helps keep the reader reading, while a strong conclusion avoids a sense of anticlimax.

Student Sample: Selecting and Ordering Reasons Justin generated eight possible reasons to support his position on gay and lesbian marriage. To help decide which ones to use, he looked again at his audience profile. What had he said about the concerns of people who oppose same-sex marriage? Which of his potential reasons would best address these concerns?

Because his audience did not believe that the ban on same-sex marriage was a great loss to gays and lesbians, Justin decided to use the lawyer's point about how the ban is discriminatory. The audience's other main concern was with the potential effect of gay marriage on the rest of society, particularly traditional marriage and family. Therefore, Justin decided to use the reasons about the benefits of same-sex marriage to society: how family values would be reinforced and how marriage keeps people from burdening society if they become unable to support themselves.

Justin noticed that some of his reasons overlapped one another. For example, the point about marriage being a stabilizing influence was merely a general statement that was better expressed in combination with his more specific reasons about economic benefits and family values. And his reason that mentioned discrimination overlapped his point that it is wrong to deny "life, liberty, and the pursuit of happiness." Overlapping is common, because there are many ways of saying the same idea.

What would be the best strategy for arranging these reasons? Initially, Justin wanted to begin with the point about discrimination, but then he decided to soften up his audience and appeal to their interests by listing the advantages first. Saving the argument about discrimination until the second half of his essay would let him end more strongly with an appeal to the readers' sympathy and sense of fairness.

Then Justin rechecked his thesis to confirm that the reasons really supported it. He decided that his readers might not buy that marriage is a "basic human right" for those of the same sex, so he decided to add one more reason in support of the similarities between heterosexuals and homosexuals.

Justin wrote up the following brief version of his argument:

Thesis: Everyone, gay and straight, will benefit from extending the basic human right of marriage to all couples, regardless of sexual preference.

> *Reason:* It would reinforce family values such as monogamy and the two-parent family.

Reason: It would provide a means of keeping people from burdening society.

Reason: Denying people the right to marry is discrimination.

Reason: The love homosexuals have for each other is no different from love between heterosexuals.

Following Through

We call the case structure a flexible plan because as long as you maintain the three-level structure of thesis, reasons, and evidence, you can change everything else at will: throwing out one thesis for another or altering its wording, adding or taking away reasons or evidence, or reordering both to achieve the desired impact. Therefore, when writing your brief, don't feel that the order in which you have found your reasons and evidence should determine their order in your essay. Rather, make your decisions based on the following questions:

What will my audience need or expect to read first?
Will one reason help set up another?
Which of my reasons are strongest? Can I begin and conclude my argument with the strongest reasons I have?

To a thesis you have already refined, now add the second level of your brief, the reason or reasons. Be ready to explain your decisions about selection and arrangement. Final decisions about ordering will often be made quite late in the drafting process—in a second or third writing. Spending a little time now, however, to think through possible orderings can save time later and make composing less difficult.

Using Evidence

The skillful use of evidence involves many complex judgments. Let's begin with some basic questions.

What Counts as Evidence? Because science and technology rely on the hard data of quantified evidence—especially statistics—some people assume that hard data is the only really good source of evidence. Such a view, however, is far too narrow for our purposes. Besides hard data, evidence includes the following:

Quotation from authorities: expert opinion, statements from people with special knowledge about an issue, and traditional or institutional authorities such as respected political leaders, philosophers, well-known authors, and people who hold positions of power and influence. Besides books and other printed sources, you can gather both data and quotations from interviews with experts or leaders on campus and in the local community.

Constitutions, statutes, court rulings, organizational bylaws, company policy statements, and the like.

Examples and case histories (that is, extended narratives about an individual's or an organization's experience).

The results of questionnaires that you devise and administer.

Personal experience.

In short, evidence includes anything that confirms a good reason or that might increase your readers' acceptance of a reason advanced to justify your thesis.

What Kind of Evidence Is Best? What evidence is best depends on what particular reasons call for. To argue for bicycle helmet legislation, we need to cite facts and figures—hard data—to back up our claim that wearing helmets will reduce the number of serious head injuries caused by bicycling accidents. To defend *Huckleberry Finn* by saying that it is an indictment of racism will require evidence of a different kind: quoted passages from the novel itself, statements from respected interpreters, and so forth.

When you have many pieces of evidence to choose from, what is best depends on the quality of the evidence itself and its likely impact on readers. In general—especially for hard data—the best evidence is the most recent. Also, the more trusted and prestigious the source, the more authority it will have for readers. Arguments about the AIDS epidemic in the United States, for example, often draw on data from the Centers for Disease Control in Atlanta, a respected research facility that specializes in the study of epidemics. And because the nature of the AIDS crisis changes relatively quickly, the most recent information would be the most authoritative.

Finally, always look for evidence that will give you an edge in winning reader assent. For example, given the charge that *Huckleberry Finn* is offensive to blacks, its vigorous defense by an African American literary scholar would ordinarily carry more weight than its defense by a white scholar.

How Much Evidence Is Needed? The amount of evidence required depends on two judgments: (1) the more crucial a reason is to your case and (2) the more resistant readers are likely to be to a reason. Most cases have at least one pivotal reason, one point upon which the whole case is built and upon which, therefore, the whole case stands or falls. Anne Marie O'Keefe's case against drug testing in the workplace turns on our accepting the inherent inaccuracy of the tests themselves. Such a pivotal reason needs to be supported at length, regardless of the degree of reader resistance to it; about one-third of O'Keefe's essay supports her contention that drug tests are unreliable. Compare this with the relatively small amount of space she devotes to showing that drug use is on the decline.

Of course, a pivotal reason may also be the reason to which readers will be most resistant. For instance, many arguments supporting women's right to abortion turn on the reason that a fetus cannot be considered a human being until it reaches a certain point in its development and, therefore, does not qualify for protection under the law. This reason is obviously both pivotal and likely to be contested by many readers, so devoting much space to evidence for the reason would be a justified strategy.

Student Sample: Using Evidence Justin took the brief showing his case so far and on a large table laid out all of his notecards and the material he had photocopied and marked up during his research. He needed to find the expert opinions, quotations, statistics, dates, and other hard evidence that would support the reasons he intended to use. Doing this before starting to draft is a good idea because it reveals where evidence is lacking or thin and what further research is necessary. If you have a lot of sources, it may help to use different-colored markers to indicate which passages will work with which of your reasons. Justin was now able to add the third level—evidence—to his case structure, including the sources from which he took it. When an article was longer than one page, he included page numbers to turn to as he drafted his paper.

Thesis: Everyone, gay and straight, will benefit from extending the basic human right of marriage to all couples, regardless of sexual preference.

- *Reason:* It would reinforce family values such as monogamy and the two-parent family.
  - *Evidence:* Marriage stabilizes relationships. (Sources: Rauch 23; Dean 114)
  - *Evidence:* Children of gays and lesbians should not be denied having two parents. (Sources: Dean 114; Sullivan; Salholz)
  - *Evidence:* If gays can have and adopt children, they should be able to marry. (Source: Salholz)
- *Reason:* It would provide a means of keeping people from burdening society.
  - *Evidence:* Spouses take care of each other. (Source: Rauch)
- *Reason:* Denying gays and lesbians the right to marry is discriminatory.
  - *Evidence:* Marriage includes rights to legal benefits. (Source: Dean 112)
  - *Evidence:* Domestic partnerships fail to provide these rights. (Sources: Dean 112; Salholz)
  - *Evidence:* Barring these marriages violates many democratic principles. (Sources: "Declaration"; Dean 113; Salholz)
- *Reason:* The love homosexuals have for each other is no different from love between heterosexuals.

Evidence: Many gays and lesbians are in monogamous relationships. (Source: Ayers 5)
Evidence: They have the same need to make a public, legal commitment. (Source: Sullivan)

Following Through

Prepare a complete brief for an argument. Include both reasons and some indication of the evidence you will use to support each one, along with a note about sources. Remember that a brief is a flexible plan, not an outline engraved in stone. The plan can change as you begin drafting.

From Brief to Draft

Turning a rough outline, or brief, of your argument into a piece of prose is never easy. Even if you know what points to bring up and in what order, you will have to (1) determine how much space to devote to each reason, (2) work in your evidence from sources, and (3) smoothly incorporate and correctly cite all quotations, summaries, and paraphrases. Furthermore, you will have to create parts of the essay that are not represented in the brief, such as an introduction that appeals to your audience and a conclusion that does not simply rehash all that you have said before. As you draft, you may also see a need for paragraphs that provide background on your topic, clarify or define an important term, or present and rebut an opposing argument. Following are some suggestions and examples that you may find helpful as you begin to draft.

The Introduction

Some writers must work through a draft from start to finish, beginning every piece of writing with the introductory paragraph. They ask, How can you possibly write the middle unless you know what the beginning is like? Other writers feel they can't write the introduction until they have written the body of the argument. They ask, How can you introduce something until you know what it is you are introducing? Either approach will eventually get the job done, as long as the writer takes the rhetorical context and strategy into account when drafting the introduction and goes back to revise it when the draft is completed.

Introductions are among the hardest things to write well. Remember that an introduction need not be one paragraph; it is often two or even three short ones. A good introduction (1) meets the needs of the audience by setting up the topic with just enough background information and (2) goes right to the heart of the issue as it relates to the audience's concerns.

Should the introduction end with the thesis statement? This strategy works well in offering the easiest transition from brief to draft in that it immediately sets the stage for the reasons. However, the thesis need not be the last sentence in the introduction, and it may not appear explicitly until much later in the draft—or even not at all, provided that readers can tell what it is from the title or from reading the essay.

Student Sample: The Introduction Our student writer Justin had to consider whether he needed to provide his readers with a detailed history of the institution of marriage and even whether people feel strongly about the value of marriage. Because they oppose same-sex marriage, he assumed that his readers were familiar with the traditions underpinning the institution. What would these readers need to be told in the introduction? Essentially that the gay and lesbian rights movement calls for extending to same-sex couples the legal right to marry and that Justin's argument supported its position.

For example, if Justin had opened with, "Americans' intolerant attitudes toward homosexuality are preventing a whole class of our citizens from exercising the right to marry," he would have been assuming that there are no valid reasons for denying same-sex marriage. Such a statement would offend his target audience members, who are not homophobic and might resent the implication that their arguments are based only in prejudice. Rather than confronting his readers, Justin's introduction attempts to establish some common ground with them:

> When two people fall deeply in love, they want to share every part of their lives with each other. For some, that could mean making a commitment, living together, and maybe having children together. But most people in love want more than that; they want to make their commitment public and legal through the ceremony of marriage, a tradition thousands of years old that has been part of almost every culture.
>
> But not everyone has the right to make that commitment. In this country, and in most others, gays and lesbians are denied the right to marry. According to many Americans, allowing them to marry would destroy the institution and threaten traditional family values. Nevertheless, "advances in gay and lesbian civil rights [are] bringing awareness and newfound determination to many," and hundreds of same-sex couples are celebrating their commitment to each other in religious ceremonies (Ayers 6). These couples would like to make their unions legal, and we should not prohibit them. Everyone, gay and straight, will benefit from extending the basic human right of marriage to all couples, regardless of sexual preference.

Justin's first paragraph builds common ground by offering an overview of marriage that his readers are likely to share. In the second paragraph he goes on to introduce the conflict, showing his own awareness of the main objections offered by thoughtful critics of same-sex marriage. Notice the even tone with which he presents these views; this sort of care is what we defined in Chapter 1 as paying attention to ethos—in other words, presenting your own character as fair and responsible. Finally, Justin builds common ground by showing the gay and lesbian community in a very positive light, as people who love and commit to each other just as heterosexuals do.

A good introduction attracts the reader's interest. To do this, writers use a number of techniques, some more dramatic than others. They may open with the story of a particular person whose experience illustrates some aspect of the topic. Or they may attempt to startle the reader with a surprising fact or opinion, as Jonathan Rauch, one of Justin's sources, did when he began his essay this way: "Whatever else marriage may or may not be, it is certainly falling apart." Generally, dictionary definitions are dull openers, but a *Newsweek* writer used one effectively to start her article on gay marriage: "Marry. 1 a) to join as husband and wife; unite in wedlock, b) to join (a man) to a woman as her husband, or (a woman) to a man as his wife." The technique works partly because the writer chose to use the definition not in an opening sentence but rather as an *epigraph*—words set off at the beginning of a piece of writing to introduce its theme. Pithy quotations work especially well as epigraphs. All of these are fairly dramatic techniques, but the best and most common bit of advice about openings is that specifics work better than generalizations at catching a reader's notice; this same *Newsweek* article had as its first sentence, "Say marriage and the mind turns to three-tiered cakes, bridal gowns, baby carriages."

How you choose to open will depend on your audience. Popular periodicals like *Newsweek* are a more appropriate setting for high drama than are academic journals and college term papers, but every reader appreciates a writer's efforts to spark his or her attention.

The Body: Presenting Reasons and Evidence

We now turn to drafting the body paragraphs of the argument. While it is possible in a short argument for one paragraph to fully develop one reason, avoid thinking in terms of writing only one paragraph per reason. Multiple paragraphs are generally required to develop and support a reason.

The key thing to remember about paragraphs is that each one is a unit that performs some function in presenting the case. You ought to be able to say what the function of a given paragraph is—and your readers ought to be able to sense it. Does it introduce a reason? Does it define a term? Does it support a reason by setting up an analogy? Does another paragraph support the same reason by offering examples or some hard data or an illustrative case?

Not all paragraphs need topic sentences to announce their main point. Worry instead about opening each paragraph with some hints that allow readers to recognize the function of the paragraph. For example, some transitional word or phrase could announce to readers that you are turning from one reason to a new one. When you introduce a new reason, be sure that readers can see how it relates to the thesis. Repeating a key word or offering a synonym for one of the words in the thesis is a good idea.

Student Sample: Presenting Reasons and Evidence As an example let's look at how Justin developed the first reason in his case. Recall that he decided to put the two reasons about benefits to society ahead of his reasons about discrimination. Of the two benefits he planned to cite, the one about strengthening family values seemed the stronger reason, so he decided to lead off with that one. Notice how Justin uses a transitional phrase to connect his first reason with the introductory material (printed earlier), which had mentioned opposing views. Also observe how Justin develops his reason over a number of paragraphs and by drawing upon multiple sources, using both paraphrase and direct quotation. (See Chapter 9 for guidelines on quoting and citing sources.)

> In contrast to many critics' arguments, allowing gays and lesbians to marry actually promotes family values because it encourages monogamy and gives children a two-parent home. As Jonathan Rauch, a gay writer, explains, marriage stabilizes relationships:
>
> > One of the main benefits of publicly recognized marriage is that it binds couples together not only in their own eyes but also in the eyes of society at large. Around the partners is woven a web of expectations that they will spend nights together, go to parties together, take out mortgages together, buy furniture at Ikea together, and so on—all of which helps tie them together and keep them off the streets and at home. (23)
>
> Some people would say that gays and lesbians can have these things without marriage simply by living together, but if you argue that marriage is not necessary for commitment, you are saying marriage is not necessary for heterosexuals either. Many people think it is immoral to live together and not have the legal bond of marriage. If gays and lesbians could marry, they would be "morally correct" according to this viewpoint. Craig Dean, a Washington, D.C. lawyer and activist for gay marriage, says that it is "paradoxical that mainstream America stereotypes Gays and Lesbians as unable to maintain long-term relationships, while at the same time denying them the very institutions to stabilize such relationships" (114).
>
> Furthermore, many homosexual couples have children from previous marriages or by adoption. According to a study by the American Bar Association, gay and lesbian families with children make up six percent of the population in the United States (Dean 114). A secure environment is very important for raising children, and allowing same-sex couples to marry would promote these children having two parents, not just one. It would also send these children the positive message that marriage is the foundation for family life. As Andrew Sullivan, a senior editor of *The New Republic* asks, why should gays be denied the very same family values that many politicians are arguing everyone else should have? Why should their children be denied these values? *Newsweek* writer Eloise Salholz describes a paradox: If "more and more homosexual pairs are becoming parents . . . but cannot marry, what kind of bastardized definition of family is society imposing on their offspring?"

At this point Justin is ready to take up his next reason: Marriage provides a system by which people take care of each other, lessening the burden on society. Justin's entire essay appears on pages 102–106. You may wish to look it over carefully before you begin to draft your own essay. Note which paragraphs bring in the remaining reasons and which paragraphs smoothly present and rebut some opposing views.

The Conclusion

Once you have presented your case, what else is there to say? You probably do not need to sum up your case; going over your reasons one more time is not generally a good strategy and will likely bore your readers. And yet you know that the conclusion is no place to introduce new issues.

Strategically, you want to end by saying, "Case made!" Here are some suggestions for doing so:

1. Look back at your introduction. Perhaps some idea that you used there to attract your readers' attention could come into play again to frame the argument—a question you posed has an answer, or a problem you raised has a solution.
2. Think about the larger context your argument fits into. For example, an argument about why *Huckleberry Finn* should be taught in public high schools, even if some students are offended by its language, could end by pointing out that education becomes diluted and artificial when teachers and administrators design a curriculum that avoids all controversy.
3. If you end with a well-worded quotation, try to follow it up with some words of your own, as you normally would whenever you quote.
4. Be aware that too many conclusions run on after their natural endings. If you are dissatisfied with your conclusion, try lopping off the last one, two, or three sentences. You may uncover the real ending.
5. Pay attention to style, especially in the last sentence. An awkwardly worded sentence will not have a sound of finality, but one with some rhythmic punch or consciously repeated sounds can wrap up an essay neatly.

Student Sample: The Conclusion Following is Justin's conclusion to his argument on same-sex marriage.

> It's only natural for people in love to want to commit to each other; this desire is the same for homosexuals and lesbians as it is for heterosexuals. One recent survey showed that "over half of all lesbians and almost 40% of gay men" live in committed relationships and share a house together (Ayers 5). As Sullivan, who is gay, explains, "At some point in our lives, some of us are lucky enough to meet the person we truly love. And we want to commit to that person in front of family and country for the rest of our lives. It's the most simple, the most natural, the most human instinct in the world. How could anyone seek to oppose that?" And what does anyone gain when that right is denied? That's a question that everyone needs to ask themselves.

Justin's conclusion is unusual because although reasons usually appear in the body paragraphs of a written argument, Justin offers his fourth reason in the last paragraph: Gay and lesbian couples can love each other with the same devotion and commitment as can heterosexual couples. This reason and its development as a paragraph make an effective conclusion because they enable Justin to place the topic of same-sex marriage into the larger context of what marriage means and why anyone wishes to enter into it. Also, Justin was able to find a particularly moving quotation to convince his audience that this meaning is the same for homosexuals. The quotation could have ended the essay, but Justin wanted to conclude with words of his own that would make the readers think about their own positions.

Following Through

Using your brief as a guide, write a draft version of your argument to convince. In addition to the advice in this chapter, refer to Chapter 9, which covers paraphrasing, summarizing, quoting, and incorporating and documenting source material.

Revising the Draft

Too often revising is confused with editing. Revising, however, implies making large changes in content and organization, not simply sentence-level corrections or even stylistic changes, which fall into the category of editing.

To get a sense of what is involved in revising, you should know that the brief of Justin Spidel's essay on pages 94–95 is actually a revised version. Justin had originally written a draft with his reasons presented in a different order and without three of the sources that now appear in his paper. When Justin exchanged drafts with another classmate who was writing on the same topic, he discovered that some of her sources would also help him develop his own case more solidly. The following paragraph was the original third paragraph of Justin's draft, immediately following the thesis. Read this draft version, and then note how in the revised essay, printed on pages 102–106, Justin improved this part of his argument by developing the point more thoroughly in two paragraphs and by placing them toward the end of the paper.

> Not to allow same-sex marriage is clearly discriminatory. The Human Rights Act of 1977 in the District of Columbia "prohibits discrimination based on sexual orientation. According to the Act, 'every individual shall have an equal opportunity to participate in the economic, cultural, and intellectual life of the District and have an *equal opportunity to participate in all aspects of life*'" (Dean 112). If politicians are going to make such laws, they need to recognize all their implications, and follow them. Not allowing homosexuals to marry is de-

nying the right to "participate" in an aspect of life that is important to every couple that has found love in each other. Also, the Constitution guarantees equality to every man and woman; that means non-discrimination, something that is not happening for gays and lesbians in the present.

Reading Your Own Writing Critically

As we explained in Chapter 2, being a critical reader of arguments means being an analytical reader. In that chapter we made suggestions for reading any argument; here we focus on what to look for in reading your own writing critically.

Read with an Eye toward Structure Remember, different parts of an argument perform different jobs. Read to see if you can divide your draft easily into its strategic parts, and be sure you can identify what role each group of paragraphs plays in the overall picture. The draft should reflect your brief, or you should be able to create a new brief from what you have written. If you have trouble identifying the working parts and the way they fit together, you need to see where points are overlapping, where you are repeating yourself, or what distant parts actually belong together. This may be the time for scissors and paste, or electronic cutting and pasting if you are working at a computer.

Read with an Eye toward Rhetorical Context You may need to revise to make the rhetorical context clearer: why are you writing, with what aim, and to whom? You establish this reader awareness in the introduction, and so you need to think about your readers' values and beliefs, as well as any obvious personal data that might help explain their position on the issue—age, gender, race, occupation, economic status, and so on. You may need to revise your introduction now, finding a way to interest your readers in what you have to say. The more specific you can make your opening, the more likely you are to succeed.

Inquire into Your Own Writing Have a dialogue with yourself about your own writing. Some of the questions that we listed on pages 39–40 will be useful here:

1. Ask what you mean by the words that are central to the argument. Have you provided definitions when they are needed?
2. Find the reasons, and note their relation to the thesis. Be able to state the connection, ideally, with the word "because": *thesis* because *reason*.
3. Be able to state what assumptions lie behind your thesis and any of your reasons. Ask yourself, What else would someone have to believe to accept this as valid? If your audience is unlikely to share the assumption, then you must add an argument for it—or change your thesis.
4. Look at your comparisons and analogies. Are they persuasive?
5. Look at your evidence. Have you offered facts, expert opinion, illustrations, and so on? Have you presented these in a way that would not raise doubts but eliminate them?

6. Consider your own bias. What do you stand to gain from advocating the position you take? Is your argument self-serving or truth-serving?

Getting Feedback from Other Readers

Because it is hard to be objective about your own work, getting a reading from a friend, classmate, teacher, or family member is a good way to see where revision would help. An unfocused reading, however, usually isn't critical enough; casual readers may applaud the draft too readily if they agree with the thesis and condemn it if they disagree. Therefore, have your readers use a revision checklist, such as the one outlined in the box "Reader's Checklist for Revision."

Following Through

1. After you have written a draft of your own argument, revise it using the preceding suggestions. Then exchange your revised draft with a classmate's and use the "Reader's Checklist for Revision" to guide you in making suggestions for each other's drafts.
2. Read the final version of Justin Spidel's argument on pages 102–106. Then apply the questions for inquiry listed on pages 39–40 to inquire into the case presented in his argument.
3. You may or may not agree with Justin Spidel's views on same-sex marriage; however, if you were assigned to give him suggestions on how to improve his written argument, what would you advise him to do? Reread his audience profile, and use the "Reader's Checklist for Revision" to help you decide how his presentation could be improved.

Editing and Proofreading

The final steps of writing any argument are editing and proofreading, which we take up in Appendix A.

Student Sample: An Essay to Convince

JUSTIN SPIDEL

Who Should Have the Right to Marry?

WHEN TWO people fall deeply in love, they want to share every part of their lives with each other. For some, that could mean making a commitment, living together, and maybe having children together. But most people in love want more than that; they want to make their commitment public and 1

READER'S CHECKLIST FOR REVISION

1. Be sure you understand the writer's intended audience, by either discussing this with the writer or reading any notes the writer has provided. Then read through the entire draft. It is helpful to number the paragraphs so you can later refer to them by number.
2. If you can find an explicit statement of the author's thesis, underline or highlight it. If you cannot find one, ask yourself whether it is necessary that the thesis be stated explicitly, or would any reader be able to infer it easily? If the thesis is easily inferred, put it in your own words at the top of the draft.
3. Think about how the thesis could be improved. Is it offensive, vague, or too general? Does it have a single focus? Is it clearly stated? Suggest more concrete diction, if possible.
4. Circle the key terms of the thesis—that is, the words most central to the point. Could there be disagreement about the meaning of any of these terms? If so, has the author clarified what he or she means by these terms?
5. Look for the structure and strategy of the argument. Underline or highlight the sentences that most clearly present the reasons, and write Reason 1, Reason 2, and so forth in the margin. If identifying the reasons is not easy, indicate this problem to the author. Also think about whether the author has arranged the reasons in the best order. Make suggestions for improvement.
6. Identify the author's best reason. Why would it appeal to the audience? Has the author strategically placed it in the best position for making his or her case?
7. Look for any weak parts in the argument. What reasons need more or better support? Next to any weakly supported reasons, write questions to let the author know what factual information seems lacking, what sources don't seem solid or credible, what statements sound too general, or what reasoning—such as analogies—seems shaky. Are there any reasons for which more research is in order?
8. Ask whether the author shows an awareness of opposing arguments. Where? If not, should this be added? Even if you agree with this argument, take the viewpoint of a member of the opposition: What are the best challenges you can make to anything the author has said?
9. Evaluate the introduction and conclusion.

legal through the ceremony of marriage, a tradition thousands of years old that has been part of almost every culture.

But not everyone has the right to make that commitment. In this country, and in most others, gays and lesbians are denied the right to marry. According to many citizens and politicians, allowing them the right to marry would destroy the institution and threaten traditional family values. Nevertheless, "advances in gay and lesbian civil rights [are] bringing awareness and newfound determination to many," and hundreds of same-sex couples are celebrating their commitment to each other in religious ceremonies (Ayers 6). These couples would like to make their unions legal, and we should not prohibit them. Everyone, gay and straight, will benefit from extending the basic human right of marriage to all couples, regardless of sexual preference.

In contrast to many critics' arguments, allowing gays and lesbians to marry actually promotes family values because it encourages monogamy and gives children a two-parent home. As Jonathan Rauch, a gay writer, explains, marriage stabilizes relationships:

> One of the main benefits of publicly recognized marriage is that it binds couples together not only in their own eyes but also in the eyes of society at large. Around the partners is woven a web of expectations that they will spend nights together, go to parties together, take out mortgages together, buy furniture at Ikea together, and so on—all of which helps tie them together and keep them off the streets and at home. (23)

Some people would say that gays and lesbians can have these things without marriage simply by living together, but if you argue that marriage is not necessary for commitment, you are saying marriage is not necessary for heterosexuals either. Many people think it is immoral to live together and not have the legal bond of marriage. If gays and lesbians could marry, they would be "morally correct" according to this viewpoint. Craig Dean, a Washington, D.C. lawyer and activist for gay marriage, says that it is "paradoxical that mainstream America stereotypes Gays and Lesbians as unable to maintain long-term relationships, while at the same time denying them the very institutions to stabilize such relationships" (114).

Furthermore, many homosexual couples have children from previous marriages or by adoption. According to a study by the American Bar Association, gay and lesbian families with children make up six percent of the population in the United States (Dean 114). A secure environment is very important for raising children, and allowing same-sex couples to marry would promote these children having two parents, not just one. It would also send these children the positive message that marriage is the foundation for family life. As Andrew Sullivan, a senior editor of *The New Republic,* asks, why should gays be denied the very same family values that many politicians are arguing everyone else should have? Why should their children be denied these values? *Newsweek* writer Eloise Salholz describes a paradox: If "more and more homosexual pairs are becoming parents . . . but cannot marry, what kind of bastardized definition of family is society imposing on their offspring?"

Also, binding people together in marriage benefits society because mar- 5
riage provides a system for people to take care of each other. Marriage means that individuals are not a complete burden on society when they become sick, injured, old, or unemployed. Jonathan Rauch argues, "If marriage has any meaning at all, it is that when you collapse from a stroke, there will be at least one other person whose 'job' it is to drop everything and come to your aid" (22). Rauch's point is that this benefit of marriage would result from gay marriages as well as straight, and in fact, may be even more important for homosexuals and lesbians because their relationships with parents and other relatives may be strained, and they are also less likely than heterosexuals to have children to take care of them in their old age. Same-sex couples already show such devotion to each other; it's just that the public recognition of legal marriage helps to keep all spouses together through hard times.

In spite of these benefits, many people say that same-sex marriage should not be allowed because it would upset our society's conventional definition of marriage as a bond between people of opposite sexes. As William Bennett has written, letting people of the same sex marry "would obscure marriage's enormously consequential function—procreation and childrearing." Procreation may be a consequence of marriage, but it is not the main reason anymore that people get married. Today "even for heterosexuals, marriage is becoming an emotional union and commitment rather than an arrangement to produce and protect children" ("Marriage" 770). And what about heterosexual couples who are sterile? No one would say that they should not be allowed to marry. If the right to marry is based on the possibility of having children, "then a post-menopausal woman who applies for a marriage license should be turned away at the courthouse door" (Rauch 22). No one would seriously expect every couple who gets married to prove that they are capable of having children and intend to do so. That would be a clear violation of their individual rights.

In the same way, to outlaw same-sex marriage is clearly discriminatory. According to Craig Dean, "Marriage is an important civil right because it gives societal recognition and legal protection to a relationship and confers numerous benefits to spouses" (112). Denying same-sex marriage means that gays and lesbians cannot enjoy material benefits such as health insurance through a spouse's employer, life insurance benefits, tax preferences, leaves for bereavement, and inheritance. In some states, laws about domestic partnership give same-sex couples some of these rights, but they are never guaranteed as they would be if the couple were legally next-of-kin. Thomas Stoddard, a lawyer, says that domestic partnership is the equivalent of "second-class citizenship" (qtd. in Salholz).

Aside from these concrete types of discrimination, denying same-sex marriage keeps gay and lesbian citizens from enjoying the basic human right to "life, liberty, and the pursuit of happiness." The Human Rights Act of 1977 in the District of Columbia makes one of the strongest stands against discrimination based on sexual orientation. According to the Act, "every individual shall have an equal opportunity to participate in the economic, cultural, and intellectual life of the District and have an equal opportunity to participate in all aspects of life" (qtd. in Dean 113). Not allowing homosexuals to marry does deny them the right to "participate" in an aspect of life that is important to most every couple that has found love in each other. The Hawaii Supreme Court ruled in 1993 that the ban on gay marriage is probably in violation of the Constitution (Salholz).

Of course, many churches will never agree to perform these marriages because they believe that homosexuality is a sin. It is possible to debate the interpretations of the Bible passages that these people cite as evidence, and many religious leaders do. The separation of church and state allows all churches to follow their own doctrines, and many things that are legal in this country are disapproved of by some churches. My point is that the government should not deny the *legal* right to marry in relationships where couples want to express their love towards each other.

It's only natural for people in love to want to commit to each other; this 10
desire is the same for homosexuals and lesbians as it is for heterosexuals. One recent survey showed that "over half of all lesbians and almost 40% of gay men" live in committed relationships and share a house together (Ayers 5). As Sullivan, who is gay, explains, "At some point in our lives, some of us are lucky enough to meet the person we truly love. And we want to commit to that person in front of family and country for the rest of our lives. It's the most simple, the most natural, the most human instinct in the world. How could anyone seek to oppose that?" And what does anyone gain when that right is denied? That's a question that everyone needs to ask themselves.

WORKS CITED

Ayers, Tess, and Paul Brown. *The Essential Guide to Lesbian and Gay Weddings*. San Francisco: Harper, 1994.

Bennett, William, "Leave Marriage Alone." *Newsweek* 3 June 1996: 27.

Dean, Craig R. "Gay Marriage: A Civil Right." *The Journal of Homosexuality* 27.3-4 (1994): 111–15.

"Marriage." *The Encyclopedia of Homosexuality*. Ed. Wayne R. Dynes. New York: Garland, 1990.

Rauch, Jonathan. "For Better or Worse?" *The New Republic* 6 May 1996: 18–23.

Salholz, Eloise. "For Better or For Worse." *Newsweek* 24 May 1993: 69.

Sullivan, Andrew. "Let Gays Marry." *Newsweek* 3 June 1996: 26.

CHAPTER SIX

Appealing to the Whole Person: Arguing to Persuade

In Chapter 1 we defined persuasion as "convincing *plus*" to suggest the three forms of appeal in addition to reason that are required for persuasion: the appeals (1) to the writer's character, (2) to the emotions of the audience, and (3) to style, the artful use of language itself. Building on what you learned about making cases in Chapter 5, this chapter's goal is to help you understand and control this wider range of appeals. But why? Shouldn't reason be enough?

Perhaps it would be if human beings were like *Star Trek*'s Mr. Spock, truly rational creatures. But human beings are only sometimes rational—and even then imperfectly. We often agree with an argument but lack the courage or motivation to translate our assent into action.

Persuasion, then, aims to close the gap between assent and action. Because persuasion seeks a deeper and stronger commitment from readers, it appeals to the whole person, to our full humanity, not just to the mind. It offers reasons, of course, because people respond to good reasons. But it also encourages the reader to identify with the writer, because people respond not only to the quality of an argument but also to the quality of the arguer. In addition, the persuader wants to stir the reader's emotions, because strong feelings reinforce the will to act; persuasion works on the heart as much as the mind. Finally, choices about style matter in persuasion, because human beings are language-using animals whose response to what is said depends on how well it is said.

A MATTER OF EMPHASIS: WHEN TO CONVINCE AND WHEN TO PERSUADE

When should you aim to persuade rather than to convince? Always notice what an academic assignment calls for, because the full range of persuasive appeal is not always appropriate for written arguments in college. In general, the more academic the audience or the more purely intellectual the issue, the less appropriate it is to appeal to the whole person. A philosophy or science paper often requires you to convince but rarely to persuade. In such cases you should confine yourself primarily to thesis, reasons, and evidence.

But when you are working with public issues, with matters of policy or questions of right and wrong, persuasion's fuller range of appeal is usually appropriate because such topics address a broader readership and involve a more inclusive community. Arguments in these areas affect not just how we think but how we act, and the heightened urgency of persuasion goes further in sparking action or fundamental change.

Convincing primarily requires that we control case-making. But persuasion asks us to make conscious decisions about three other appeals as well: (1) we must gain our readers' confidence and respect through the deliberate projection of our good character, (2) we must touch our readers' emotions, and (3) we must focus on language itself as a means of affecting people's thoughts and behavior. The writer who aims to persuade integrates these other forms of appeal with a well-made case, deliberately crafting the essay so that they all work together.

As with convincing, writing a persuasive argument begins with inquiry and research—a patient search for the truth as preparation for earning a claim to truth. However, before you can move from a general idea of your own position to a specific thesis, you must think about the audience you seek to persuade.

ANALYZING YOUR READERS

Persuasion begins with difference and, when it works, ends with identity. That is, we expect that before reading our argument, our readers will differ from us not only in beliefs but also in attitudes and desires. A successful persuasive argument brings readers and writer together; it creates a sense of connection between parties that were previously separate in viewpoint. But what means can we use to overcome difference and create a sense of identity? First, we need to focus on our readers and attempt to understand their frame of mind by asking certain key questions.

Who Is the Audience, and How Do They View the Topic?

The first step is to identify possible appeals to your readership. Keep in mind that good persuaders are able to empathize and sympathize with other people, building bridges of commonality and solidarity. To aid your audience analysis, ask these questions:

Who are my readers? How do I define them in terms of age, economic and social class, gender, education, and so forth?

What typical attitudes or stances toward my topic do they have?

What in their background or daily experiences helps explain their point of view?
What are they likely to know about my topic?
How might they be uninformed or misinformed about it?
How would they like to see the problem, question, or issue resolved, answered, or handled? Why? That is, what personal stake do they have in the topic?
In what larger framework—religious, ethical, political, economic—do they place my topic? That is, what general beliefs and values are involved?

What Are Our Differences?

Audience analysis is not complete until you can specify exactly what divides you from your readers. Sometimes specifying difference is difficult to do before formulating a detailed case; understanding exactly what divides you from your readers comes later, at the point of the first draft. But as soon as you can, you must clarify differences; knowing exactly what separates you from your readers tells you what to emphasize in making your case and in choosing other strategies of appeal. These questions can help:

Is the difference a matter of assumptions? If so, how can I shake my readers' confidence in their assumptions and offer another set of assumptions favorable to my position?
Is the difference a matter of principle, the application of general rules to specific cases? If so, should I dispute the principle itself and offer a competing one the audience will also value? Or should I show why the principle should not apply in some specific instance relevant to my case?
Is the difference a matter of a hierarchy of values—that is, do we value the same things but to different degrees? If so, how might I restructure my readers' values?
Is the difference a matter of ends or of means? If of ends, how can I show that my vision of what ought to be is better or that realizing my ends will also secure the ends my readers value? If a difference of means, how can I show that my methods are justified and effective, more likely to bear fruit than others?
Is the difference a matter of interpretation? If so, how can I shake my readers' confidence in the traditional or common interpretation of something and show them that my interpretation is better, that it accounts for the facts more adequately?
Is the difference a matter of implications or consequences? If so, how can I convince my readers that what they fear may happen will not happen, that it will not be as bad as they think, or that other implications or consequences outweigh any negatives?

What Do We Have in Common?

In seeking to define the common ground you and your readers share, the key point to remember is that no matter how sharp the disagreements that divide you from those you hope to persuade, resources for identification always exist. Ask these sorts of questions:

Do we have a shared local identity—as members of the same organization, for example, or students at the same university?

Do we share a more abstract, collective identity—as citizens of the same region or nation, as worshippers in the same religion, and so forth?

Do we share a common cause—such as promoting the good of the community, preventing child abuse, or overcoming racial prejudice?

Is there a shared experience or human activity—raising children, caring for aging parents, helping a friend in distress, struggling to make ends meet?

Can we connect through a well-known event or cultural happening—a popular movie, a best-selling book, something in the news that would interest both you and your readers?

Is there a historical event, person, or document that we both respect?

READING A PERSUASIVE ESSAY

To illustrate the importance of audience analysis, we will turn to a classic essay of the twentieth century, Martin Luther King's "Letter from Birmingham Jail," a brilliant example of the art of persuasion. As we will see, King masterfully analyzed his audience and used the full range of appeals to suit that particular readership.

Background

To appreciate King's persuasive powers, we must first understand the events that led up to the "Letter" and also the actions King wanted to move his readers to take. As president of the Southern Christian Leadership Conference, a civil rights organization dedicated to nonviolent social change, King had been organizing and participating in demonstrations in Birmingham, Alabama, in 1963. He was arrested, and while he was in jail, eight white Alabama clergymen of various denominations issued a public statement reacting to his activities. Published in a local newspaper, the statement deplored the illegal demonstrations of King and his organization as "unwise and untimely":

> We the undersigned clergymen are among those who, in January, issued "An Appeal for Law and Order and Common Sense," in dealing with racial problems in Alabama. We expressed understanding that honest convictions in racial matters could properly be pursued in the

courts, but urged that decisions of those courts should in the meantime be peacefully obeyed.

Since that time there had been some evidence of increased forbearance and a willingness to face facts. Responsible citizens have undertaken to work on various problems which cause racial friction and unrest. In Birmingham, recent public events have given indication that we all have opportunity for a new constructive and realistic approach to racial problems.

However, we are now confronted by a series of demonstrations by some of our Negro citizens, directed and led in part by outsiders. We recognize the natural impatience of people who feel that their hopes are slow in being realized. But we are convinced that these demonstrations are unwise and untimely.

We agree rather with certain local Negro leadership which has called for honest and open negotiation of racial issues in our area. And we believe this kind of facing of issues can best be accomplished by citizens of our own metropolitan area, white and Negro, meeting with their knowledge and experience of the local situation. All of us need to face that responsibility and find proper channels for its accomplishment.

Just as we formerly pointed out that "hatred and violence have no sanction in our religious and political traditions," we also point out that such actions as incite to hatred and violence, however technically peaceful those actions may be, have not contributed to the resolution of our local problems. We do not believe that these days of new hope are days when extreme measures are justified in Birmingham.

We commend the community as a whole, and the local news media and law enforcement officials in particular, on the calm manner in which these demonstrations have been handled. We urge the public to continue to show restraint should the demonstrations continue, and the law enforcement officials to remain calm and continue to protect our city from violence.

We further strongly urge our own Negro community to withdraw support from these demonstrations, and to unite locally in working peacefully for a better Birmingham. When rights are consistently denied, a cause should be pressed in the courts and in negotiations among local leaders, and not in the streets. We appeal to both our white and Negro citizenry to observe the principles of law and order and common sense.

Signed by:
C. C. J. Carpenter, D.D., LL.D., *Bishop of Alabama*
Joseph A. Durick, D.D., *Auxiliary Bishop, Diocese of Mobile, Birmingham*
Rabbi Milton L. Grafman, *Temple Emanu-El, Birmingham, Alabama*

Bishop Paul Hardin, *Bishop of the Alabama-West Florida Conference of the Methodist Church*
Bishop Nolan B. Harmon, *Bishop of the North Alabama Conference of the Methodist Church*
George M. Murray, D.D., LL.D., *Bishop Coadjutor, Episcopal Diocese of Alabama*
Edward V. Ramage, *Moderator, Synod of the Alabama Presbyterian Church in the United States*
Earl Stallings, *Pastor, First Baptist Church, Birmingham, Alabama*

In his cell King began his letter on the margins of that newspaper page, addressing it specifically to the eight clergymen in the hope that he could move them from disapproval to support, from inaction to a recognition of the necessity of the demonstrations. As a public figure King knew that his letter would reach a larger audience, including the demonstrators themselves, who were galvanized by its message when 50,000 copies were later distributed by his supporters. In the years since, King's letter has often been published, reaching a global audience with its argument for civil disobedience in the service of a higher, moral law.

The Basic Message

King's letter is long; he even apologizes to his readers for having written so much. Its length is not due to its basic message, however, but to its persuasive appeals—to the way the main points are made. Before turning to King's "Letter from Birmingham Jail," read the following summary, which differs as greatly from King's prose as a nursery song differs from a Beethoven symphony.

> Because I am the leader of an organization that fights injustice, it is most appropriate for me to be in Birmingham, where human rights are being violated. Our campaign of nonviolent civil disobedience was not rash and unpremeditated but the result of a history of failed negotiations and broken promises. We aim to increase tensions here until the city leaders realize that dialogue must occur. Our actions are not untimely but long overdue, given that blacks have been denied their civil rights in this country for over 340 years.
>
> While we advocate breaking some laws, we distinguish between moral laws and immoral laws that degrade the human personality. The former must be obeyed, the latter disobeyed openly and lovingly. We may be extremists, but people who accomplish great things are often so labeled, and our nonviolent protests are preferable to inaction.
>
> In failing to support us, white Southern religious leaders such as yourselves fail to meet the challenges of social injustice. You should not praise the police for their work at breaking up the demonstrations, but rather praise the demonstrators for standing up for their human dignity.

MARTIN LUTHER KING, JR.

Letter from Birmingham Jail

April 16, 1963

My Dear Fellow Clergymen:

WHILE CONFINED here in the Birmingham city jail, I came across 1
your recent statement calling my present activities "unwise and untimely." Seldom do I pause to answer criticism of my work and ideas. If I sought to answer all the criticisms that cross my desk, my secretaries would have little time for anything other than such correspondence in the course of the day, and I would have no time for constructive work. But since I feel that you are men of genuine good will and that your criticisms are sincerely set forth, I want to try to answer your statement in what I hope will be patient and reasonable terms.

I think I should indicate why I am here in Birmingham, since you have been influenced by the view which argues against "outsiders coming in." I have the honor of serving as president of the Southern Christian Leadership Conference, an organization operating in every southern state, with headquarters in Atlanta, Georgia. We have some eighty-five affiliated organizations across the South, and one of them is the Alabama Christian Movement for Human Rights. Frequently we share staff, educational, and financial resources with our affiliates. Several months ago the affiliate here in Birmingham asked us to be on call to engage in a nonviolent direct-action program if such were deemed necessary. We readily consented, and when the hour came we lived up to our promise. So I, along with several members of my staff, am here because I was invited here. I am here because I have organizational ties here.

But more basically, I am in Birmingham because injustice is here. Just as the prophets of the eighth century B.C. left their villages and carried their "thus saith the Lord" far beyond the boundaries of their home towns, and just as the Apostle Paul left his village of Tarsus and carried the gospel of Jesus Christ to the far corners of the Greco-Roman world, so am I compelled to carry the gospel of freedom beyond my own home town. Like Paul, I must constantly respond to the Macedonian call for aid.

Moreover, I am cognizant of the interrelatedness of all communities and states. I cannot sit idly by in Atlanta and not be concerned about what happens in Birmingham. Injustice anywhere is a threat to justice everywhere. We are caught in an inescapable network of mutuality, tied in a single garment of destiny. Whatever affects one directly, affects all indirectly. Never again can we afford to live with the narrow, provincial "outside agitator" idea. Anyone who lives inside the United States can never be considered an outsider anywhere within its bounds.

You deplore the demonstrations taking place in Birmingham. But your 5
statement, I am sorry to say, fails to express a similar concern for the conditions that brought about the demonstrations. I am sure that none of you would want to rest content with the superficial kind of social analysis that deals merely

with effects and does not grapple with underlying causes. It is unfortunate that demonstrations are taking place in Birmingham, but it is even more unfortunate that the city's white power structure left the Negro community with no alternative.

In any nonviolent campaign there are four basic steps: collection of the facts to determine whether injustices exist; negotiation; self-purification; and direct action. We have gone through all these steps in Birmingham. There can be no gainsaying the fact that racial injustice engulfs this community. Birmingham is probably the most thoroughly segregated city in the United States. Its ugly record of brutality is widely known. Negroes have experienced grossly unjust treatment in the courts. There have been more unsolved bombings of Negro homes and churches in Birmingham than in any other city in the nation. These are the hard, brutal facts of the case. On the basis of these conditions, Negro leaders sought to negotiate with the city fathers. But the latter consistently refused to engage in good-faith negotiation.

Then, last September, came the opportunity to talk with leaders of Birmingham's economic community. In the course of the negotiations, certain promises were made by the merchants—for example, to remove the stores' humiliating racial signs. On the basis of these promises, the Reverend Fred Shuttlesworth and the leaders of the Alabama Christian Movement for Human Rights agreed to a moratorium on all demonstrations. As the weeks and months went by, we realized that we were the victims of a broken promise. A few signs, briefly removed, returned; the others remained.

As in so many past experiences, our hopes had been blasted, and the shadow of deep disappointment settled upon us. We had no alternative except to prepare for direct action, whereby we would present our very bodies as a means of laying our case before the conscience of the local and the national community. Mindful of the difficulties involved, we decided to undertake a process of self-purification. We began a series of workshops on nonviolence, and we repeatedly asked ourselves: "Are you able to accept blows without retaliating?" "Are you able to endure the ordeal of jail?" We decided to schedule our direct-action program for the Easter season, realizing that except for Christmas, this is the main shopping period of the year. Knowing that a strong economic-withdrawal program would be the by-product of direct action, we felt that this would be the best time to bring pressure to bear on the merchants for the needed change.

Then it occurred to us that Birmingham's mayoral election was coming up in March, and we speedily decided to postpone action until after election day. When we discovered that the Commissioner of Public Safety, Eugene "Bull" Connor, had piled up enough votes to be in the run-off, we decided again to postpone action until the day after the run-off so that the demonstrations could not be used to cloud the issues. Like many others, we waited to see Mr. Connor defeated, and to this end we endured postponement after postponement. Having aided in this community need, we felt that our direct-action program could be delayed no longer.

You may well ask: "Why direct action? Why sit-ins, marches and so 10
forth? Isn't negotiation a better path?" You are quite right in calling for negotiation. Indeed, this is the very purpose of direct action. Nonviolent direct action seeks to create such a crisis and foster such a tension that a community which has constantly refused to negotiate is forced to confront the issue. It seeks so to dramatize the issue that it can no longer be ignored. My citing the creation of tension as part of the work of the nonviolent-resister may sound rather shocking. But I must confess that I am not afraid of the word "tension." I have earnestly opposed violent tension, but there is a type of constructive, nonviolent tension which is necessary for growth. Just as Socrates felt that it was necessary to create a tension in the mind so that individuals could rise from the bondage of myths and half-truths to the unfettered realm of creative analysis and objective appraisal, so must we see the need for nonviolent gadflies to create the kind of tension in society that will help men rise from the dark depths of prejudice and racism to the majestic heights of understanding and brotherhood.

The purpose of our direct-action program is to create a situation so crisis-packed that it will inevitably open the door to negotiation. I therefore concur with you in your call for negotiation. Too long has our beloved Southland been bogged down in a tragic effort to live in monologue rather than dialogue.

One of the basic points in your statement is that the action that I and my associates have taken in Birmingham is untimely. Some have asked: "Why didn't you give the new city administration time to act?" The only answer that I can give to this query is that the new Birmingham administration must be prodded about as much as the outgoing one, before it will act. We are sadly mistaken if we feel that the election of Albert Boutwell as mayor will bring the millennium to Birmingham. While Mr. Boutwell is a much more gentle person than Mr. Connor, they are both segregationists, dedicated to maintenance of the status quo. I have hope that Mr. Boutwell will be reasonable enough to see the futility of massive resistance to desegregation. But he will not see this without pressure from devotees of civil rights. My friends, I must say to you that we have not made a single gain in civil rights without determined legal and nonviolent pressure. Lamentably, it is an historical fact that privileged groups seldom give up their privileges voluntarily. Individuals may see the moral light and voluntarily give up their unjust posture; but, as Reinhold Niebuhr has reminded us, groups tend to be more immoral than individuals.

We know through painful experience that freedom is never voluntarily given by the oppressor; it must be demanded by the oppressed. Frankly, I have yet to engage in a direct-action campaign that was "well timed" in the view of those who have not suffered unduly from the disease of segregation. For years now I have heard the word "Wait!" It rings in the ear of every Negro with piercing familiarity. This "Wait" has almost always meant "Never." We must come to see, with one of our distinguished jurists, that "justice too long delayed is justice denied."

We have waited for more than 340 years for our constitutional God-given rights. The nations of Asia and Africa are moving with jetlike speed toward gaining political independence, but we still creep at horse-and-buggy pace toward gaining a cup of coffee at a lunch counter. Perhaps it is easy for those who have never felt the stinging darts of segregation to say, "Wait." But when you have seen vicious mobs lynch your mothers and fathers at will and drown your sisters and brothers at whim; when you have seen hate-filled policemen curse, kick, and even kill your black brothers and sisters; when you see the vast majority of your twenty million Negro brothers smothering in an airtight cage of poverty in the midst of an affluent society; when you suddenly find your tongue twisted and your speech stammering as you seek to explain to your six-year-old daughter why she can't go to the public amusement park that has just been advertised on television, and see tears welling up in her eyes when she is told that Funtown is closed to colored children, and see ominous clouds of inferiority beginning to form in her little mental sky, and see her beginning to distort her personality by developing an unconscious bitterness toward white people; when you have to concoct an answer for a five-year-old son who is asking: "Daddy, why do white people treat colored people so mean?"; when you take a cross-country drive and find it necessary to sleep night after night in the uncomfortable corners of your automobile because no motel will accept you; when you are humiliated day in and day out by nagging signs reading "white" and "colored"; when your first name becomes "nigger," your middle name becomes "boy" (however old you are), and your last name becomes "John," and your wife and mother are never given the respected title "Mrs."; when you are harried by day and haunted by night by the fact that you are a Negro, living constantly at tiptoe stance, never quite knowing what to expect next, and are plagued with inner fears and outer resentments; when you are forever fighting a degenerating sense of "nobodiness"—then you will understand why we find it difficult to wait. There comes a time when the cup of endurance runs over, and men are no longer willing to be plunged into the abyss of despair. I hope, sirs, you can understand our legitimate and unavoidable impatience.

You express a great deal of anxiety over our willingness to break laws. 15
This is certainly a legitimate concern. Since we so diligently urge people to obey the Supreme Court's decision of 1954 outlawing segregation in the public schools, at first glance it may seem rather paradoxical for us consciously to break laws. One may well ask: "How can you advocate breaking some laws and obeying others?" The answer lies in the fact that there are two types of laws: just and unjust. I would be the first to advocate obeying just laws. One has not only a legal but a moral responsibility to obey just laws. Conversely, one has a moral responsibility to disobey unjust laws. I would agree with St. Augustine that "an unjust law is no law at all."

Now, what is the difference between the two? How does one determine whether a law is just or unjust? A just law is a man-made code that squares with the moral law or the law of God. An unjust law is a code that is out of harmony with the moral law. To put it in the terms of St. Thomas Aquinas: An unjust law is a human law that is not rooted in eternal law and natural law. Any law that uplifts human personality is just. Any law that degrades human personality is unjust. All segregation statutes are unjust because segregation distorts the soul and damages the personality. It gives the segregator a false sense of superiority and the segregated a false sense of inferiority. Segregation, to use the terminology of the Jewish philosopher Martin Buber, substitutes an "I–it" relationship for an "I–thou" relationship and ends up relegating persons to the status of things. Hence, segregation is not only politically, economically, and sociologically unsound, it is morally wrong and sinful. Paul Tillich has said that sin is separation. Is not segregation an existential expression of man's tragic separation, his awful estrangement, his terrible sinfulness? Thus it is that I can urge men to obey the 1954 decision of the Supreme Court, for it is morally right; and I can urge them to disobey segregation ordinances, for they are morally wrong.

Let us consider a more concrete example of just and unjust laws. An unjust law is a code that a numerical or power majority group compels a minority group to obey but does not make binding on itself. This is *difference* made legal. By the same token, a just law is a code that a majority compels a minority to follow and that it is willing to follow itself. This is *sameness* made legal.

Let me give another explanation. A law is unjust if it is inflicted on a minority that, as a result of being denied the right to vote, had no part in enacting or devising the law. Who can say that the legislature of Alabama which set up that state's segregation laws was democratically elected? Throughout Alabama all sorts of devious methods are used to prevent Negroes from becoming registered voters, and there are some counties in which, even though Negroes constitute a majority of the population, not a single Negro is registered. Can any law enacted under such circumstances be considered democratically structured?

Sometimes a law is just on its face and unjust in its application. For instance, I have been arrested on a charge of parading without a permit. Now, there is nothing wrong in having an ordinance which requires a permit for a parade. But such an ordinance becomes unjust when it is used to maintain segregation and to deny citizens the First-Amendment privilege of peaceful assembly and protest.

20 I hope you are able to see the distinction I am trying to point out. In no sense do I advocate evading or defying the law, as would the rabid segregationist. That would lead to anarchy. One who breaks an unjust law must do so openly, lovingly, and with a willingness to accept the penalty. I submit that an individual who breaks a law that conscience tells him is unjust, and who willingly accepts the penalty of imprisonment in order to arouse the conscience of the community over its injustice, is in reality expressing the highest respect for law.

Of course, there is nothing new about this kind of civil disobedience. It was evidenced sublimely in the refusal of Shadrach, Meshach, and Abednego to obey the laws of Nebuchadnezzar, on the ground that a higher moral law was at stake. It was practiced superbly by the early Christians, who were willing to face hungry lions and the excruciating pain of chopping blocks rather than submit to certain unjust laws of the Roman Empire. To a degree, academic freedom is a reality today because Socrates practiced civil disobedience. In our own nation, the Boston Tea Party represented a massive act of civil disobedience.

We should never forget that everything Adolf Hitler did in Germany was "legal" and everything the Hungarian freedom fighters did in Hungary was "illegal." It was "illegal" to aid and comfort a Jew in Hitler's Germany. Even so, I am sure that, had I lived in Germany at the time, I would have aided and comforted my Jewish brothers. If today I lived in a Communist country where certain principles dear to the Christian faith are suppressed, I would openly advocate disobeying that country's antireligious laws.

I must make two honest confessions to you, my Christian and Jewish brothers. First, I must confess that over the past few years I have been gravely disappointed with the white moderate. I have almost reached the regrettable conclusion that the Negro's great stumbling block in his stride toward freedom is not the White Citizen's Counciler or the Ku Klux Klanner, but the white moderate, who is more devoted to "order" than to justice; who prefers a negative peace which is the presence of tension to a positive peace which is the presence of justice; who constantly says: "I agree with you in the goal you seek, but I cannot agree with your methods of direct action"; who paternalistically believes he can set the timetable for another man's freedom; who lives by a mythical concept of time and who constantly advises the Negro to wait for a "more convenient season." Shallow understanding from people of good will is more frustrating than absolute misunderstanding from people of ill will. Lukewarm acceptance is much more bewildering than outright rejection.

I had hoped that the white moderate would understand that law and order exist for the purpose of establishing justice and that when they fail in this purpose they become the dangerously structured dams that block the flow of social progress. I had hoped that the white moderate would understand that the present tension in the South is a necessary phase of the transition from an obnoxious negative peace, in which the Negro passively accepted his unjust plight, to a substantive and positive peace, in which all men will respect the dignity and worth of human personality. Actually, we who engage in nonviolent direct action are not the creators of tension. We merely bring to the surface the hidden tension that is already alive. We bring it out in the open, where it can be seen and dealt with. Like a boil that can never be cured so long as it is covered up but must be opened with all its ugliness to the natural medicines of air and light, injustice must be exposed, with all the tension its exposure creates, to the light of human conscience and the air of national opinion before it can be cured.

In your statement you assert that our actions, even though peaceful, must 25
be condemned because they precipitate violence. But is this a logical assertion? Isn't this like condemning a robbed man because his possession of money precipitated the evil act of robbery? Isn't this like condemning Socrates because his unswerving commitment to truth and his philosophical inquiries precipitated the act by the misguided populace in which they made him drink hemlock? Isn't this like condemning Jesus because his unique God-consciousness and never-ceasing devotion to God's will precipitated the evil act of crucifixion? We must come to see that, as the federal courts have consistently affirmed, it is wrong to urge an individual to cease his efforts to gain his basic constitutional rights because the quest may precipitate violence. Society must protect the robbed and punish the robber.

I had also hoped that the white moderate would reject the myth concerning time in relation to the struggle for freedom. I have just received a letter from a white brother in Texas. He writes: "All Christians know that the colored people will receive equal rights eventually, but it is possible that you are in too great a religious hurry. It has taken Christianity almost two thousand years to accomplish what it has. The teachings of Christ take time to come to earth." Such an attitude stems from a tragic misconception of time, from the strangely irrational notion that there is something in the very flow of time that will inevitably cure all ills. Actually, time itself is neutral; it can be used either destructively or constructively. More and more I feel that the people of ill will have used time much more effectively than have the people of good will. We will have to repent in this generation not merely for the hateful words and actions of the bad people but for the appalling silence of the good people. Human progress never rolls in on wheels of inevitability; it comes through the tireless efforts of men willing to be co-workers with God, and without this hard work, time itself becomes an ally of the forces of social stagnation. We must use time creatively, in the knowledge that the time is always ripe to do right. Now is the time to make real the promise of democracy and transform our pending national elegy into a creative psalm of brotherhood. Now is the time to lift our national policy from the quicksand of racial injustice to the solid rock of human dignity.

You speak of our activity in Birmingham as extreme. At first I was rather disappointed that fellow clergymen would see my nonviolent efforts as those of an extremist. I began thinking about the fact that I stand in the middle of two opposing forces in the Negro community. One is a force of complacency, made up in part of Negroes who, as a result of long years of oppression, are so drained of self-respect and a sense of "somebodiness" that they have adjusted to segregation; and in part of a few middle-class Negroes who, because of a degree of academic and economic security and because in some ways they profit by segregation, have become insensitive to the problems of the masses.

The other force is one of bitterness and hatred, and it comes perilously close to advocating violence. It is expressed in the various black nationalists groups that are springing up across the nation, the largest and best-known being Elijah Muhammad's Muslim movement. Nourished by the Negro's frustration over the continued existence of racial discrimination, this movement is made up of people who have lost faith in America, who have absolutely repudiated Christianity, and who have concluded that the white man is an incorrigible "devil."

I have tried to stand between these two forces, saying that we need emulate neither the "do-nothingism" of the complacent nor the hatred and despair of the black nationalist. For there is the more excellent way of love and nonviolent protest. I am grateful to God that, through the influence of the Negro church, the way of nonviolence became an integral part of our struggle.

If this philosophy had not emerged, by now many streets of the South would, I am convinced, be flowing with blood. And I am further convinced that if our white brothers dismiss as "rabble-rousers" and "outside agitators" those of us who employ nonviolent direct action, and if they refuse to support our nonviolent efforts, millions of the Negroes will, out of frustration and despair, seek solace and security in black-nationalist ideologies—a development that would inevitably lead to a frightening racial nightmare.

Oppressed people cannot remain oppressed forever. The yearning for 30
freedom eventually manifests itself, and that is what has happened to the American Negro. Something within has reminded him of his birthright of freedom, and something without has reminded him that it can be gained. Consciously or unconsciously, he has been caught up by the *Zeitgeist,* and with his black brothers of Africa and his brown and yellow brothers of Asia, South America, and the Caribbean, the United States Negro is moving with a sense of great urgency toward the promised land of racial justice. If one recognizes this vital urge that has engulfed the Negro community, one should readily understand why public demonstrations are taking place. The Negro has many pent-up resentments and latent frustrations, and he must release them. So let him march; let him make prayer pilgrimages to the city hall; let him go on freedom rides—and try to understand why he must do so. If his repressed emotions are not released in nonviolent ways, they will seek expression through violence; this is not a threat but a fact of history. So I have not said to my people: "Get rid of your discontent." Rather, I have tried to say that this normal and healthy discontent can be channeled into the creative outlet of nonviolent direct action. And now this approach is being termed extremist.

But though I was initially disappointed at being categorized as an extremist, as I continued to think about the matter I gradually gained a measure of satisfaction from the label. Was not Jesus an extremist for love: "Love your enemies, bless them that curse you, do good to them that hate you, and pray for them which despitefully use you, and persecute you." Was not Amos an extremist for justice: "Let justice roll down like waters and righteousness like an ever-flowing stream." Was not Paul an extremist for the Christian gospel: "I bear in my body the marks of the Lord Jesus." Was not Martin Luther an extremist: "Here I stand; I cannot do otherwise, so help me God." And John Bunyan: "I will stay in jail to the end of my days before I make a butchery of my conscience." And Abraham Lincoln: "This nation cannot survive half slave and half free." And Thomas Jefferson: "We hold these truths to be self-evident, that all men are created equal. . . ." So the question is not whether we will be extremists, but what kind of extremists we will be. Will we be extremists for hate or for love? Will we be extremists for the preservation of injustice or for the extension of justice? In that dramatic scene on Calvary's hill three men were crucified. We must never forget that all three were crucified for the same crime—the crime of extremism. Two were extremists for immorality, and thus fell below their environment. The other, Jesus Christ, was an extremist for love, truth and goodness, and thereby rose above his environment. Perhaps the South, the nation and the world are in dire need of creative extremists.

I had hoped that the white moderate would see this need. Perhaps I was too optimistic; perhaps I expected too much. I suppose I should have realized that few members of the oppressor race can understand the deep groans and passionate yearnings of the oppressed race, and still fewer have the vision to see that injustice must be rooted out by strong, persistent, and determined action. I am thankful, however, that some of our white brothers in the South have grasped the meaning of this social revolution and committed themselves to it. They are still all too few in quantity, but they are big in quality. Some—such as Ralph McGill, Lillian Smith, Harry Golden, James McBride Dabbs, Ann Braden, and Sarah Patton Boyle—have written about our struggle in eloquent and prophetic terms. Others have marched with us down nameless streets of the South. They have languished in filthy, roach-infested jails, suffering the abuse and brutality of policemen who view them as "dirty nigger-lovers." Unlike so many of their moderate brothers and sisters, they have recognized the urgency of the moment and sensed the need for powerful "action" antidotes to combat the disease of segregation.

Let me take note of my other major disappointment. I have been so greatly disappointed with the white church and its leadership. Of course, there are some notable exceptions. I am not unmindful of the fact that each of you has taken some significant stands on this issue. I commend you, Reverend Stallings, for your Christian stand on this past Sunday, in welcoming Negroes to your worship service on a nonsegregated basis. I commend the Catholic leaders of this state for integrating Spring Hill College several years ago.

But despite these notable exceptions, I must honestly reiterate that I have been disappointed with the church. I do not say this as one of those negative critics who can always find something wrong with the church. I say this as a minister of the gospel, who loves the church; who was nurtured in its bosom; who has been sustained by its spiritual blessings and who will remain true to it as long as the cord of life shall lengthen.

When I was suddenly catapulted into the leadership of the bus protest in 35
Montgomery, Alabama, a few years ago, I felt we would be supported by the white church. I felt that the white ministers, priests, and rabbis of the South

would be among our strongest allies. Instead, some have been outright opponents, refusing to understand the freedom movement and misrepresenting its leaders; all too many others have been more cautious than courageous and have remained silent behind the anesthetizing security of stained-glass windows.

In spite of my shattered dreams, I came to Birmingham with the hope that the white religious leadership of this community would see the justice of our cause and, with deep moral concern, would serve as the channel through which our just grievances could reach the power structure. I had hoped that each of you would understand. But again I have been disappointed.

I have heard numerous southern religious leaders admonish their worshipers to comply with a desegregation decision because it is the law, but I have longed to hear white ministers declare: "Follow this decree because integration is morally right and because the Negro is your brother." In the midst of blatant injustices inflicted upon the Negro, I have watched white churchmen stand on the sideline and mouth pious irrelevancies and sanctimonious trivialities. In the midst of a mighty struggle to rid our nation of racial and economic injustice, I have heard many ministers say: "Those are social issues, with which the gospel has no real concern." And I have watched many churches commit themselves to a completely otherworldly religion which makes a strange, un-Biblical distinction between body and soul, between the sacred and the secular.

I have traveled the length and breadth of Alabama, Mississippi, and all the other southern states. On sweltering summer days and crisp autumn mornings I have looked at the South's beautiful churches with their lofty spires pointing heavenward. I have beheld the impressive outlines of her massive religious-education buildings. Over and over I have found myself asking: "What kind of people worship here? Who is their God? Where were their voices when the lips of Governor Barnett dripped with words of interposition and nullification? Where were they when Governor Wallace gave a clarion call for defiance and hatred? Where were their voices of support when bruised and weary Negro men and women decided to rise from the dark dungeons of complacency to the bright hills of creative protest?"

Yes, these questions are still in my mind. In deep disappointment I have wept over the laxity of the church. But be assured that my tears have been tears of love. There can be no deep disappointment where there is not deep love. Yes, I love the church. How could I do otherwise? I am in the rather unique position of being the son, the grandson, and the great-grandson of preachers. Yes, I see the church as the body of Christ. But, oh! How we have blemished and scarred that body through social neglect and through fear of being nonconformists.

There was a time when the church was very powerful—in the time 40
when the early Christians rejoiced at being deemed worthy to suffer for what they believed. In those days the church was not merely a thermometer that recorded the ideas and principles of popular opinion; it was a thermostat that

transformed the mores of society. Whenever the early Christians entered a town, the people in power became disturbed and immediately sought to convict the Christians for being "disturbers of the peace" and "outside agitators." But the Christians pressed on, in the conviction that they were "a colony of heaven," called to obey God rather than man. Small in number, they were big in commitment. They were too God-intoxicated to be "astronomically intimidated." By their effort and example they brought an end to such ancient evils as infanticide and gladiatorial contests.

Things are different now. So often the contemporary church is a weak, ineffectual voice with an uncertain sound. So often it is an archdefender of the status quo. Far from being disturbed by the presence of the church, the power structure of the average community is consoled by the church's silent—and often even vocal—sanction of things as they are.

But the judgment of God is upon the church as never before. If today's church does not recapture the sacrificial spirit of the early church, it will lose its authenticity, forfeit the loyalty of millions, and be dismissed as an irrelevant social club with no meaning for the twentieth century. Every day I meet young people whose disappointment with the church has turned into outright disgust.

Perhaps I have once again been too optimistic. Is organized religion too inextricably bound to the status quo to save our nation and the world? Perhaps I must turn my faith to the inner spiritual church, the church within the church, as the true *ekklesia* and the hope of the world. But again I am thankful to God that some noble souls from the ranks of organized religion have broken loose from the paralyzing chains of conformity and joined us as active partners in the struggle for freedom. They have left their secure congregations and walked the streets of Albany, Georgia, with us. They have gone down the highways of the South on tortuous rides for freedom. Yes, they have gone to jail with us. Some have been dismissed from their churches, have lost the support of their bishops and fellow ministers. But they have acted in the faith that right defeated is stronger than evil triumphant. Their witness has been the spiritual salt that has preserved the true meaning of the gospel in these troubled times. They have carved a tunnel of hope through the dark mountain of disappointment.

I hope the church as a whole will meet the challenge of this decisive hour. But even if the church does not come to the aid of justice, I have no despair about the future. I have no fear about the outcome of our struggle in Birmingham, even if our motives are at present misunderstood. We will reach the goal of freedom in Birmingham and all over the nation, because the goal of America is freedom. Abused and scorned though we may be, our destiny is tied up with America's destiny. Before the pilgrims landed at Plymouth, we were here. Before the pen of Jefferson etched the majestic words of the Declaration of Independence across the pages of history, we were here. For more than two centuries our forebears labored in this country without wages; they made cotton king; they built the homes of their masters while suffering gross injustice and shameful humiliation—and yet out of a bottomless vitality they continued to thrive and develop. If the inexpressible cruelties of slavery could not stop us, the opposition we now face will surely fail. We will win our freedom because the sacred heritage of our nation and the eternal will of God are embodied in our echoing demands.

Before closing I feel impelled to mention one other point in your state- 45
ment that has troubled me profoundly. You warmly commended the Birmingham police force for keeping "order" and "preventing violence." I doubt that you would have so warmly commended the police force if you had seen its dogs sinking their teeth into unarmed, nonviolent Negroes. I doubt that you would so quickly commend the policemen if you were to observe their ugly and inhumane treatment of Negroes here in the city jail; if you were to watch them push and curse old Negro women and young Negro girls; if you were to see them slap and kick old Negro men and young boys; if you were to observe them, as they did on two occasions, refuse to give us food because we wanted to sing our grace together. I cannot join you in your praise of the Birmingham police department.

It is true that police have exercised a degree of discipline in handling the demonstrators. In this sense they have conducted themselves rather "nonviolently" in public. But for what purpose? To preserve the evil system of segregation. Over the past few years I have consistently preached that nonviolence demands that the means we use must be as pure as the ends we seek. I have tried to make clear that it is wrong to use immoral means to attain moral ends. But now I must affirm that it is just as wrong, or perhaps even more so, to use moral means to preserve immoral ends. Perhaps Mr. Connor and his policemen have been rather nonviolent in public, as was Chief Pritchett in Albany, Georgia, but they have used the moral means of nonviolence to maintain the immoral end of racial injustice. As T. S. Eliot has said: "The last temptation is the greatest treason: To do the right deed for the wrong reason."

I wish you had commended the Negro sit-inners and demonstrators of Birmingham for their sublime courage, their willingness to suffer and their amazing discipline in the midst of great provocation. One day the South will recognize its real heroes. They will be the James Merediths, with the noble sense of purpose that enables them to face jeering and hostile mobs, and with the agonizing loneliness that characterizes the life of the pioneer. They will be old, oppressed, battered Negro women, symbolized in a seventy-two-year-old woman in Montgomery, Alabama, who rose up with a sense of dignity and with her people decided not to ride segregated buses, and who responded with ungrammatical profundity to one who inquired about her weariness: "My feets is tired, but my soul is at rest." They will be the young high school and college students, the young ministers of the gospel and a host of their elders, courageously and nonviolently sitting in at lunch counters and willingly going to jail for conscience' sake. One day the South will know that when these disinherited children of God sat down at lunch counters, they were in reality standing up for what is best in the American dream and for the most sacred values in our Judaeo-Christian heritage, thereby bringing our nation back to those great wells of democracy which were dug deep by the founding fathers in their formulation of the Constitution and the Declaration of Independence.

Never before have I written so long a letter. I'm afraid it is much too long to take your precious time. I can assure you that it would have been much shorter if I had been writing from a comfortable desk, but what else can one do when he is alone in a narrow jail cell, other than write long letters, think long thoughts, and pray long prayers?

If I have said anything in this letter that overstates the truth and indicates an unreasonable impatience, I beg you to forgive me. If I have said anything that understates the truth and indicates my having a patience that allows me to settle for anything less than brotherhood, I beg God to forgive me.

I hope this letter finds you strong in faith. I also hope that circumstances 50
will soon make it possible for me to meet each of you, not as an integrationist or a civil-rights leader but as a fellow clergyman and a Christian brother. Let us all hope that the dark clouds of racial prejudice will soon pass away and the deep fog of misunderstanding will be lifted from our fear-drenched communities, and in some not too distant tomorrow the radiant stars of love and brotherhood will shine over our great nation with all their scintillating beauty.

Yours for the cause of Peace and Brotherhood
MARTIN LUTHER KING, JR.

King's Analysis of His Audience: Identification and Overcoming Difference

King's letter is worth studying for his use of the resources of identification alone. For example, he appeals in his salutation to "My Dear Fellow Clergymen," which emphasizes at the outset that he and his readers share a similar role. Elsewhere he calls them "my friends" (paragraph 12) and "my Christian and Jewish brothers" (paragraph 23). In many other places King alludes to the Bible and to other religious figures; these references would put him on common ground with his readers.

King's letter also successfully deals with various kinds of difference between his readers and himself.

Assumptions

King's readers assumed that if black people waited long enough, their situation would naturally grow better. Therefore, they argued for patience. King, in paragraph 26, questions "the strangely irrational notion that . . . the very flow of time . . . will inevitably cure all ills." Against this common assumption that "time heals," King offers the view that "time itself is neutral," something "that can be used either destructively or constructively."

Principles

King's readers believed in the principle of always obeying the law, a principle blind to both intent and application. King substitutes another principle: Obey just laws, but disobey, openly and lovingly, unjust laws (paragraphs 15–20).

Hierarchy of Values

King's readers elevated the value of reducing racial tension over the value of securing racial justice. In paragraph 10 King's strategy is to talk about "constructive, nonviolent tension," clearly an effort to get his readers to see tension as not necessarily a bad thing but a condition for achieving social progress.

Ends and Means

King's audience seems to disagree with him not about the ends for which he was working but about the means. King, therefore, focuses not on justifying civil rights but on justifying civil disobedience.

Interpretation

King's audience interpreted extremism as always negative, never justifiable. King counters by showing, first, that he is actually a moderate, neither a "do-nothing" nor a militant (paragraph 28). But then he redefines their interpretation of extremism, arguing that extremism for good causes is justified and citing examples from history to support his point (paragraph 31).

Implications or Consequences

King's readers doubtless feared the consequences of supporting the struggle for civil rights too strongly—losing the support of more conservative members of their congregations. But as King warns, "If today's church does not recapture the sacrificial spirit of the early church, it will . . . be dismissed as an irrelevant social club" (paragraph 42). King's strategy is to turn his readers' attention away from short-term consequences and toward long-term consequences—the loss of the vitality and relevance of the church itself.

Following Through

As a class look closely at one of the essays from an earlier chapter, and consider it in terms of audience analysis. What audience did the writer attempt to reach? How did the writer connect or fail to connect with the audience's experience, knowledge, and concerns? What exactly divides the author from his or her audience, and how did the writer attempt to overcome the division? How effective were the writer's strategies for achieving identification? What can you suggest that might have worked better?

USING THE FORMS OF APPEAL

We turn now to the forms of appeal in persuasion, noting how Martin Luther King, Jr., used them in his letter.

The Appeal to Reason

Persuasion, we have said, uses the same appeal to reason that we find in convincing; that is, the foundation of a persuasive argument is the case structure of thesis, reasons, and evidence. King, however, seems to have realized that an argument organized like a case would seem too formal and public for his purposes, so he chose instead to respond to the clergymen's statement with a personal letter, organized around their criticisms of him. In fact, most of King's letter amounts to self-defense and belongs to the rhetorical form known as *apologia,* from which our word "apology" derives. An *apologia* is an effort to explain and justify what one has done, or chosen not to do, in the face of condemnation or at least widespread disapproval or misunderstanding.

Although, strictly speaking, he does not present a case, King still relies heavily on reason. He uses a series of short arguments, occupying from one to as many as eight paragraphs, in responding to his readers' criticisms. These are the more important ones, in order of appearance:

Refutation of the "outside agitator" concept (paragraphs 2–4)
Defense of nonviolent civil disobedience (paragraphs 5–11)
Definitions of "just" versus "unjust" laws (paragraphs 15–22)
Refutation and defense of the label "extremist" (paragraphs 27–31)
Rejection of the ministers' praise for the conduct of the police during the Birmingham demonstration (paragraphs 45–47)

In addition to defending himself and his cause, King pursues an offensive strategy, advancing his own criticisms, most notably of the "white moderate" (paragraphs 23–26) and the "white church and its leadership" (paragraphs 33–44). This concentration on rational appeal is both effective and appropriate: it confirms King's character as a man of reason, and it appeals to an audience of well-educated professionals.

King also cites evidence that his readers must respect. In paragraphs 15 and 16, for example, he cites the words of St. Thomas Aquinas, Martin Buber, and Paul Tillich—who represent, respectively, the Catholic, Jewish, and Protestant traditions—to defend his position on the nature of just and unjust laws. He has chosen these authorities carefully, so that each of his eight accusers has someone from his own tradition with whom to identify. The implication, of course, is that King's distinction between just and unjust laws and the course of action that follows from this distinction is consistent with Judeo-Christian thought as a whole.

Following Through

1. Look at paragraphs 2–4 of King's letter. What reasons does King give to justify his presence in Birmingham? How well does he support each reason? How do his reasons and evidence reflect a strategy aimed at his clergy audience?

2. King's argument for civil disobedience (paragraphs 15–22) is based on one main reason. What is it, and how does he support it?
3. What are the two reasons King gives to refute his audience's charge that he is an extremist (paragraphs 27–31)?
4. Think about a time in your life when you did (or did not do) something for which you were unfairly criticized. Choose one or two of the criticisms, and attempt to defend yourself in a short case of your own. Remember that your argument must be persuasive to your accusers, not just to you. Ask yourself, as King did, How can I appeal to my readers? What will they find reasonable?

The Appeal to Character

In Chapter 5 our concern was how to make a good case. We did not discuss self-presentation explicitly there; but the fact is, when you formulate a clear and plausible thesis and defend it with good reasons and sufficient evidence, you are at the same time creating a positive impression of your own character. A good argument will always reveal the writer's values, intelligence, knowledge of the subject, grasp of the reader's needs and concerns, and so on. We tend to respect and trust a person who reasons well, even when we do not assent to his or her particular case.

In terms of the appeal to character, the difference between convincing and persuading is a matter of degree. In convincing, this appeal is implicit, indirect, and diffused throughout the argument; in persuading, the appeal to character is often quite explicit, direct, and concentrated in a specific section of the essay. The effect on readers is consequently rather different: in convincing, we are seldom consciously aware of the writer's character as such; in persuading, the writer's character assumes a major role in determining how we respond to the argument.

The perception of his character was a special problem for King when he wrote his letter. He was not a national hero in 1963 but rather a controversial civil rights leader whom many viewed as a troublemaker. Furthermore, of course, he wrote this now celebrated document while in jail—hardly a condition that inspires respect and trust in readers. Self-presentation, then, was very significant for King, something he concentrated on throughout his letter and especially at the beginning and end.

In his opening paragraph King acknowledges the worst smirch on his character—that he is currently in jail. But he goes on to establish himself as a professional person like his readers, with secretaries, correspondence, and important work to do.

Just prior to his conclusion (paragraphs 48–50), King offers a strongly worded critique of the white moderate and the mainstream white church, taking the offensive in a way that his readers are certain to perceive as an attack. In paragraph 48, however, he suddenly becomes self-deprecating and almost apologetic: "Never before have I written so long a letter." As unexpected as it is, this sudden shift of tone disarms the reader. Then, with gentle irony (the letter, he says, would have been shorter "if I had been writing from a comfortable desk"), King explains the length of his letter as the result of his having no other outlet for action. What can one do in jail but "write long letters, think long thoughts, and pray long prayers?" King paradoxically turns the negative of being in jail into a positive, an opportunity rather than a limitation on his freedom.

His next move is equally surprising, especially after the confident tone of his critique of the church. He begs forgiveness—from his readers if he has overstated his case and from God if he has understated his case or shown too much patience with injustice. This daring, dramatic penultimate paragraph is just the right touch, the perfect gesture of reconciliation. Because he asks so humbly, his readers must forgive him. What else can they do? The further subordination of his own will to God's is the stance of the sufferer and martyr in both the Jewish and Christian tradition.

Finally, King sets aside that which divides him from his readers—the issue of integration and his role as a civil rights leader—in favor of that which unifies him with his audience: all are men of God and brothers in faith. Like an Old Testament prophet he envisions a time when the current conflicts will be over, when "the radiant stars of love and brotherhood will shine over our great nation." In other words, King holds out the possibility for transcendence, for rising above racial prejudice to a new age, a new America. In the end his readers are encouraged to soar with him, to hope for the future.

Here King enlists the power of identification to overcome the differences separating writer and reader, invoking his status as a "fellow clergyman and a Christian brother" as a symbol of commonality. The key to identification is to reach beyond the individual self, associating one's character with something larger—the Christian community, the history of the struggle for freedom, national values, "spaceship Earth," or any appropriate cause or movement in which readers can also participate.

Following Through

We have already seen how King associates himself with the Christian community in the essay's final paragraph. Look at the list of questions for creating audience identification on page 110. Find some examples in King's letter in which he employs some of these resources of identification. Which parts of the letter are most effective in creating a positive impression of character? Why? What methods does King use that any persuader might use?

The Appeal to Emotion

Educated people aware of the techniques of persuasion are often deeply suspicious of emotional appeal. Among college professors—those who will be reading and grading your work—this prejudice can be especially strong, because all fields of academic study claim to value reason, dispassionate inquiry, and the critical analysis of data and conclusions. Many think of emotional appeal as an impediment to sound thinking and associate it with politicians who prey on our fears, with dictators and demagogues who exploit our prejudices, and with advertisers and televangelists who claim they will satisfy our dreams and prayers.

Of course, we can all cite examples of the destructive power of emotional appeal. But to condemn it wholesale, without qualification, is to exhibit a lack of self-awareness. Most scientists will concede, for instance, that they are passionately committed to the methods of their field, and mathematicians will confess that they are moved by the elegance of certain formulas and proofs. In fact, all human activity has some emotional dimension, a strongly felt adherence to a common set of values.

Moreover, we ought to have strong feelings about certain things: revulsion at the horrors of the Holocaust, pity and anger over the abuse of children, happiness when a war is concluded or when those kidnapped by terrorists are released, and so on. We cease to be human if we are not responsive to emotional appeal.

Clearly, however, we must distinguish between legitimate and illegitimate emotional appeals, condemning the latter and learning to use the former when appropriate. Distinguishing between the two is not always easy, but answering certain questions can help us do so:

Do the emotional appeals substitute for knowledge and reason?
Do they employ stereotypes and pit one group against another?
Do they offer a simple, unthinking reaction to a complex situation?

Whenever the answer is yes, our suspicions should be aroused.

Perhaps an even better test is to ask yourself, "If I act on the basis of how I feel, who will benefit and who will suffer?" You may be saddened, for example, to see animals used in medical experiments, but an appeal showing only these animals and ignoring the benefits of experimentation for human life is pandering to the emotions.

In contrast, legitimate emotional appeal supplements argument rather than substituting for it, drawing on knowledge and often on first-hand experience. At its best it can bring alienated groups together and create empathy or sympathy where these are lacking. Many examples could be cited from Martin Luther King's letter, but the most effective passage is surely paragraph 14:

> We have waited for more than 340 years for our constitutional God-given rights. The nations of Asia and Africa are moving with jetlike speed toward gaining political independence, but we still creep at horse-and-buggy pace toward gaining a cup of coffee at a lunch counter. Perhaps it is easy for those who have never felt the stinging

> darts of segregation to say, "Wait." But when you have seen vicious mobs lynch your mothers and fathers at will and drown your sisters and brothers at whim; when you have seen hate-filled policemen curse, kick, and even kill your black brothers and sisters; when you see the vast majority of your twenty million Negro brothers smothering in an airtight cage of poverty in the midst of an affluent society; when you suddenly find your tongue twisted and your speech stammering as you seek to explain to your six-year-old daughter why she can't go to the public amusement park that has just been advertised on television, and see tears welling up in her eyes when she is told that Funtown is closed to colored children, and see ominous clouds of inferiority beginning to form in her little mental sky, and see her beginning to distort her personality by developing an unconscious bitterness toward white people; when you have to concoct an answer for a five-year-old son who is asking: "Daddy, why do white people treat colored people so mean?"; when you take a cross-country drive and find it necessary to sleep night after night in the uncomfortable corners of your automobile because no motel will accept you; when you are humiliated day in and day out by nagging signs reading "white" and "colored"; when your first name becomes "nigger," your middle name becomes "boy" (however old you are), and your last name becomes "John," and your wife and mother are never given the respected title "Mrs."; when you are harried by day and haunted by night by the fact that you are a Negro, living constantly at tiptoe stance, never quite knowing what to expect next, and are plagued with inner fears and outer resentments; when you are forever fighting a degenerating sense of "nobodiness"—then you will understand why we find it difficult to wait. There comes a time when the cup of endurance runs over, and men are no longer willing to be plunged into the abyss of despair. I hope, sirs, you can understand our legitimate and unavoidable impatience.

Just prior to this paragraph King has concluded an argument justifying the use of direct action to dramatize social inequities and to demand rights and justice denied to oppressed people. Direct-action programs are necessary, he says, because "freedom is never voluntarily given by the oppressor; it must be demanded by the oppressed." It is easy for those not oppressed to urge an underclass to wait. But "[t]his 'Wait' has almost always meant 'Never.'"

At this point King deliberately sets out to create in his readers a feeling of outrage. Having ended paragraph 13 by equating "wait" with "never," King next refers to a tragic historical fact: For 340 years, since the beginning of slavery in the American colonies, black people have been waiting for their freedom. He sharply contrasts the "jetlike speed" with which Africa is overcoming colonialism with the "horse-and-buggy pace" of integration in the United States. In African homelands black people are gaining their political independence; but here, in the land of the free, they are denied even "a cup of coffee at a lunch counter." Clearly, this is legitimate emotional appeal, based on fact and reinforcing reason.

In the long and rhythmical sentence that takes up most of the rest of the paragraph, King unleashes the full force of emotional appeal in a series of concrete images designed to make his privileged white readers feel the anger, frustration, and humiliation of the oppressed. In rapid succession King alludes to mob violence, police brutality, and economic discrimination—the more public evils of racial discrimination—and then moves to the personal, everyday experience of segregation, concentrating especially on what it does to the self-respect of innocent children. For any reader with even the least capacity for sympathy, these images must strike home, creating identification with the suffering of the oppressed and fueling impatience with the evil system that perpetuates this suffering. In short, through the use of telling detail drawn from his own experience, King succeeds in getting his audience to feel what he feels—feelings, in fact, that they ought to share, that are wholly appropriate to the problem of racial prejudice.

What have we learned from King about the available means of emotional appeal? Instead of telling his audience they should feel a particular emotion, he has brought forth that emotion using five specific rhetorical techniques:

Concrete examples
Personal experiences
Metaphors and similes
Sharp contrasts and comparisons
Sentence rhythm, particularly the use of intentional repetition

We will now consider how style contributes to a persuasive argument.

Following Through

1. We have said that emotional appeals need to be both legitimate and appropriate—that is, honest and suitable for the subject matter, the audience, and the kind of discourse being written. Find examples of arguments from various publications—books, newspapers, magazines, and professional journals—and discuss the use or avoidance of emotional appeal in each. On the basis of this study, try to generalize about what kinds of subjects, audiences, and discourse allow direct emotional appeal and what kinds do not.
2. Write an essay analyzing the tactics of emotional appeal in the editorial columns of your campus or local newspaper. Compare the strategies with those used by King. Then evaluate the appeals. How effective are they in arousing your emotions? How well do they reinforce the reasoning offered? Be sure to discuss both the way the appeals work and their legitimacy and appropriateness.

The Appeal through Style

By *style* we mean the choices a writer makes at the level of words, phrases, and sentences. It would be a mistake to think of style as a final touch, something to dress up an argument. Style actually involves all of a writer's choices about what words to use and how to arrange them. Ideas and arguments do not develop apart from style, and all of the appeals discussed so far involve stylistic choices. For example, you are concerned with style when you consider what words will state a thesis most precisely or make yourself sound knowledgeable or provide your reader with a compelling image. The appeal of style works hand-in-hand with the appeals of reason, character, and emotion.

Furthermore, style makes what we say memorable. George Bush may wish he had never said it, but his statement "Read my lips: no new taxes" was a message that generated high enthusiasm and, to the former president's dismay, remained in people's minds long after he had compromised himself on that issue. Because the persuasive effect we have on readers depends largely on what they remember, the appeal through style matters as much as the appeal to reason, character, and emotion.

Writers with effective style make conscious choices on many levels. One choice involves the degree of formality or familiarity they want to convey. You will notice that King strikes a fairly formal and professional tone throughout most of his letter, choosing words like "cognizant" (paragraph 4) rather than the more common "aware." Writers also consider the *connotation* of words (what a word implies or what we associate it with) as much as their *denotation* (a word's literal meaning). For example, King opens his letter with the phrase "While confined here in the Birmingham city jail." The word "confined" denotes the same condition as "incarcerated" but has less unfavorable connotations, because people can also be "confined" in ways that evoke our sympathy.

Memorable writing often appeals to the senses of sight and sound. Concrete words can paint a picture; in paragraph 45, for example, King tells about "dogs sinking their teeth" into the nonviolent demonstrators. Writers may also evoke images through implied and explicit comparisons (respectively, metaphor and simile). King's "the stinging darts of segregation" (paragraph 14) is an example of metaphor. In this same paragraph King refers to the "airtight cage of poverty," the "clouds of inferiority" forming in his young daughter's "mental sky," and the "cup of endurance" that has run over for his people—each a metaphor with a powerful emotional effect.

Even when read silently, language has sound. Therefore, style includes the variation of sentence length and the use of rhythmic patterns as well. For example, a writer may emphasize a short, simple sentence by placing it at the end of a series of long sentences or a single long sentence, as King does in paragraph 14. One common rhythmic pattern is the repetition of certain phrases to emphasize a point or to play up a similarity or contrast; in the fourth sentence of paragraph 14, King repeats the phrase "when you" a number of times, piling up examples of racial discrimination and creating a powerful rhythm that carries readers through this unusually long sentence. Another common rhythmic pattern is parallelism. Note the following phrases, again from the fourth sentence of paragraph 14:

> "lynch your mothers and fathers at will"
>
> "drown your sisters and brothers at whim"

Here King uses similar words in the same places, even paralleling the number of syllables in each phrase. The parallelism here is further emphasized by King's choice of another stylistic device known as *alliteration,* the repetition of consonant sounds. In another passage from paragraph 14, King achieves a sound pattern that suggests violence when he describes the actions of police who "curse, kick, and even kill" black citizens. The repetition of the hard "k" sound, especially in words of one syllable, suggests the violence of the acts themselves.

Beyond the level of words, phrases, and sentences, the overall arrangement of an essay's main points or topics can also be considered a matter of style, for such arrangement determines how one point contrasts with another, how the tone changes, how the force of the argument builds. When we discuss style, we usually look at smaller units of an essay, but actually all the choices a writer makes contribute in some way to the essay's style.

Following Through

1. Analyze King's style in paragraphs 6, 8, 23, 24, 31, and 47. Compare what King does in these paragraphs with paragraph 14. How are they similar? How are they different? Why?
2. To some extent style is a gift or talent that some people have more of than others. But it is also learned, acquired by imitating authors we admire. Use your writer's notebook to increase your stylistic options; whenever you hear or read something stated effectively, copy it down and analyze why it is effective. Try to make up a sentence of your own using the same techniques but with a different subject matter. In this way you can begin to use analogy, metaphor, repetition, alliteration, parallelism, and other stylistic devices. Begin by imitating six or so sentences or phrases that you especially liked in King's letter.
3. Write an essay analyzing your own style in a previous essay. What would you do differently now? Why?

DRAFTING A PERSUASIVE ESSAY

Outside of the classroom, persuasion begins, as Martin Luther King's letter did, with a real need to move people to action. In a writing course you may have to create the circumstances for your argument. You should begin by thinking of an issue that calls for persuasion. Your argument must go beyond merely convincing your readers to believe as you do; now you must decide what action you want them to take and move them to do it.

Conceiving a Readership

Assuming that the task you have chosen or been assigned calls for persuasion, finding and analyzing your readership is your first concern. Because instructors evaluate the writing of their students, it is probably unavoidable that college writers, to some extent, tend to write for their instructors. However, real persuasion has a genuine readership, some definite group of people with a stake in the question or issue being addressed. Whatever you say must be adapted for this audience, because moving the reader is the whole point of persuasion.

How can you go about conceiving a readership? First, you should throw out the whole notion of writing to the "general public." Such a "group" is a nearly meaningless abstraction, not defined enough to give you much guidance. Suppose, for example, you are arguing that sex education in public schools must include a moral dimension as well as the clinical facts of reproduction and venereal disease. You need to decide if you are addressing students, who may not want the moral lectures; school administrators, who may not want the added responsibility and curriculum changes; or parents, who may not want the schools to take over what they see as the responsibility of family or church.

Second, given the issue and the position you will probably take, you should ask who you would want to persuade. On the one hand, you do not need to persuade those who already agree with you; on the other, it would be futile to try to persuade those so committed to an opposing position that nothing you could say would make any difference. An argument against logging in old-growth forests, for example, would probably be aimed neither at staunch environmentalists nor at workers employed in the timber industry but rather at some readership between these extremes—say, people concerned in general about the environment but not focused specifically on the threat to mature forests.

Third, when you have a degree of choice among possible readerships, you should select your target audience based on two primary criteria. First, because persuasion is directly concerned with making decisions and taking action, seek above all to influence those readers best able to influence events. Second, when this group includes a range of readers (and it often will), also consider which of these readers you know the most about and can therefore appeal to best.

Because all appeals in persuasion are addressed to an audience, try to identify your reader early in the process. You can, of course, change your mind later on, but doing so will require considerable rethinking and rewriting.

Devoting time at the outset to thinking carefully about your intended audience can save much time and effort in the long run.

Following Through

For a persuasive argument you are about to write, determine your audience; that is, decide who can make a difference with respect to this issue and what they can do to make a difference. Be sure that you go beyond the requirements of convincing when you make these decisions. For example, you may be able to make a good case that just as heterosexuals do not "choose" their attraction to the opposite sex, so homosexuality is also not voluntary. Based on this point you could argue to a local readership of moderate-to-liberal voters that they should press state legislators to support a bill extending full citizens' rights to homosexuals. But with such a desire for action in mind, you would have to think even more about who your audience is and why they might resist such a measure or not care enough to support it strongly.

In your writer's notebook respond to the questions "Who is my audience?" and "What are our differences?" (refer to the lists of questions on pages 108–109 to help formulate answers). Use your responses to write an audience profile that is more detailed than the one you wrote for an argument to convince.

Discovering the Resources of Appeal

With an audience firmly in mind, you are ready to begin thinking about how to appeal to them. Before and during the drafting stage, you will be making choices about the following:

How to formulate a case and support it with research, as needed
How to present yourself
How to arouse your readers' emotions
How to make the style of your writing contribute to the argument's effectiveness

All of these decisions will be influenced by your understanding of your readers' needs and interests.

Appealing through Reason

In both convincing and persuading, rational appeal amounts to making a case or cases—advancing a thesis or theses and providing supporting reasons and evidence. What you learned in Chapter 5 about case-making applies here as well, so you may want to review that chapter as you work on rational appeal for a persuasive paper. Of course, inquiry into the truth (Chapter 4) and research (Chapter 9) are as relevant to persuasion as they are to convincing.

One difference between convincing and persuading, however, is that in persuasion you will devote much of your argument to defending a course of action. The steps here are basically a matter of common sense:

1. Show that there is a need for action.
2. If your audience, like that for Martin Luther King's letter, is inclined to inactivity, show urgency as well as need—we must act and act now.
3. Satisfy the need, showing that your proposal for action meets the need or will solve the problem. One way to do this is to compare your course of action with other proposals or solutions, indicating why yours is better than the others.

Sometimes your goal will be to persuade your audience *not* to act because what they want to do is wrong or inappropriate or because the time is not right. Need is still the main issue. The difference, obviously, is the goal of showing that no need exists or that it is better to await other developments before a proposed action will be appropriate or effective.

Following Through

Prepare a brief of your argument (see Chapter 5). Be ready to present an overview of your audience and to defend your brief, either before the class or in small groups. Pay special attention to how well the argument establishes a need or motivation to act (or shows that there is no need for action) for your defined audience. If some action is called for, assess the solution in the context of other, common proposals: Will the proposed action meet the need? Is it realistic—that is, can it be done?

Appealing through Character

A reader who finishes your essay should have the following impressions:

The author is well-informed about the topic.
The author is confident about his or her own position and sincere in advocating it.
The author has been fair and balanced in dealing with other positions.
The author understands my concerns and objections and has dealt with them.
The author is honest.
The author values what I value; his or her heart is in the right place.

What can you do to communicate these impressions? Basically, you must earn these impressions just as you must earn a conviction and a good argument. There are no shortcuts, and educated readers are seldom fooled.

To seem well informed, you must be well informed. This requires that you dig into the topic, thinking about it carefully, researching it thoroughly and taking good notes, discussing the topic and your research with other students, consulting campus experts, and so on. This work will provide you with the following hallmarks of being well informed:

The ability to make references in passing to relevant events and people connected with the issue now or recently

The ability to create a context or provide background information, which may include comments on the history of the question or issue

The ability to produce sufficient, high-quality evidence to back up contentions

Just as digging in will make you well informed, so inquiry (struggling to find the truth) and convincing (making a case for your conviction about the truth) will lend your argument sincerity and confidence. Draw upon personal experience when it has played a role in determining your position, and don't be reluctant to reveal your own stake in the issue. Make your case boldly, qualifying it as little as possible. If you have prepared yourself with good research, genuine inquiry, and careful case-making, you have earned authority; what remains is to claim your authority, which is essential in arguing to persuade.

Represent other positions accurately and fairly; then present evidence that refutes those positions or show that the reasoning is inadequate or inconsistent. Don't be afraid to agree with parts of other opinions when they are consistent with your own. Such partial agreements can play a major role in overcoming reader resistance to your own position.

It is generally not a good idea to subject other positions to ridicule. Some of your readers may sympathize with all or part of the position you are attacking and take offense. Even readers gratified by your attack may feel that you have gone too far. Concentrate on the merits of your own case rather than the faults of others.

Coping with your readers' concerns and objections should present no special problems, assuming that you have found an appropriate audience and thought seriously about both the common ground you share and the way their outlook differs from yours. You can ultimately handle concerns and objections in one of two ways: (1) by adjusting your case—your thesis and supporting reasons—so that the concerns or objections do not arise or (2) by taking up the more significant objections one by one and responding to them in a way that reduces reader resistance. Of course, doing one does not preclude doing the other: you can adjust your case and also raise and answer whatever objections remain. What matters is that you never ignore any likely and weighty objection to what you are advocating.

Responding to objections patiently and reasonably will also help with the last and perhaps most important impression that readers have of you—that you value what they value. Being sensitive to the reasoning and moral and emotional commitments of others is one of those values you can and must share with your readers.

If you are to have any chance of persuading at all, your readers must feel that you would not deceive them, so you must conform to the standards of honesty readers will expect. Leaving readers with the impression of your honesty requires much more than simply not lying. Rather, honesty requires (1) reporting evidence accurately and with regard for the original context; (2) acknowledging significant counterevidence to your case, pointing to its existence and explaining why it does not change your argument; and (3) pointing out areas of doubt and uncertainty that must await future events or study.

Following Through

The "Following Through" assignment on page 137 asked you to prepare an audience profile and explore your key areas of difference. Now use the results of that work to help you think through how you could appeal to these readers. Use the questions on page 110 to help establish commonality with your audience and to formulate strategies for bringing you and your readers closer together.

Appealing to Emotion

In both convincing and persuading, your case determines largely what you have to say and how you order your presentation. As in King's essay, argument is the center, the framework, while emotional appeal plays a supporting role to rational appeal, taking center stage only occasionally. Consequently, your decisions must take the following into account:

What emotions to arouse and by what means
How frequent and intense the emotional appeals should be
Where to introduce emotional appeals

The first of these decisions is usually the easiest. Try to arouse emotions that you yourself have genuinely felt; whatever moved you will probably also move your readers. If your emotions come from direct experience, draw upon that experience for concrete descriptive detail, as King did. Study whatever you heard or read that moved you; you can probably adapt your sources' tactics for your own purposes. (The best strategy for arousing emotions is often to avoid emotionalism yourself. Let the facts, the descriptive detail, the concrete examples do the work, just as King did.)

Deciding how often, at what length, and how intensely to make emotional appeals presents a more difficult challenge. Much depends on the topic, the audience, and your own range and intensity of feeling. In every case you must estimate as best you can what will be appropriate, but the following suggestions may help.

As always in persuasion, your primary consideration is your audience. What attitudes and feelings do they have already? Which of these lend emotional support to your case? Which work against your purposes? You will want to emphasize those feelings that are consistent with your position and show why any others are understandable but inappropriate.

Then ask a further question: What does my audience not feel or not feel strongly enough that they must feel or feel more strongly if I am to succeed in persuading them? King, for example, decided that his readers' greatest emotional deficit was their inability to feel what victims of racial discrimination feel—hence paragraph 14, the most intense emotional appeal in his letter. Simply put, devote space and intensity to arousing emotions central to your case that are lacking or only weakly felt by your readers.

The questions of how often and where to include emotional appeals are both worth careful consideration. Regarding frequency, the best principle is to take your shots sparingly, getting as much as you can out of each effort. Positioning emotional appeals depends on pacing: use them to lead into or to clinch a key point. So positioned, they temporarily relieve the audience of the intellectual effort required to follow your argument.

It is generally not a good idea to begin an essay with your most involved and most intense emotional appeal; you don't want to peak too early. Besides that, you need to concentrate in your introduction on establishing your tone and authority, providing needed background information, and clearly and forcefully stating your thesis. The conclusion can be an effective position for emotional appeals, because your audience is left with something memorable to carry away from the reading. In most cases, however, it is best to concentrate emotional appeals in the middle or near the end of an essay.

Following Through

After you have a first draft of your essay, reread it with an eye to emotional appeal. Highlight the places where you have deliberately sought to arouse the audience's emotions. (You might also ask a friend to read the draft or exchange drafts with another student in your class.)

Decide if you need to devote more attention to your emotional appeal through additional concrete examples, direct quotations, or something else. Consider also how you could make each appeal more effective and intense and whether each appeal is in the best possible location in the essay.

Appealing through Style

As we have seen, the style of your argument evolves with every choice you make, even in the prewriting stages. As you draft, think consciously about how stylistic choices can work for you, but don't agonize over them. In successive revisions you will be able to make refinements and experiment for different effects.

In the first draft, however, set an appropriate level of formality. Most persuasive writing is neither chatty and familiar nor stiff and distant. Rather, persuasive prose is like dignified conversation—the way people talk when they care about and respect one another but do not know each other well. We can see some of the hallmarks of persuasive prose in King's letter:

It uses *I, you,* and *we.*
It avoids both technical jargon and slang.
It inclines toward strong, action verbs.
It chooses examples and images familiar to the reader.
It connects sentence to sentence and paragraph to paragraph with transitional words and phrases like *however, moreover,* and *for instance.*

All of these and many other features characterize the *middle style* of most persuasive writing.

As we discovered in King's letter, this middle style can cover quite a range of choices. King varies his style from section to section, depending on his purpose. Notice how King sounds highly formal in his introduction (paragraphs 1–5), where he wants to establish authority, but more plainspoken when he narrates the difficulties he and other black leaders had in their efforts to negotiate with the city's leaders (paragraphs 6–9). Notice as well how his sentences and paragraphs shorten on average in the passage comparing just and unjust laws (paragraphs 15–22). And we have already noted the use of sound and imagery in the passages of highest emotional appeal, such as paragraphs 14 and 47.

Just as King matches style with function, so you need to vary your style based on what each part of your essay is doing. This variation creates pacing, or the sense of overall rhythm in your essay. Readers need places where they can relax a bit between points of higher intensity, such as lengthy arguments and passionate pleas.

As you prepare to write your first draft, then, concern yourself with matching your style to your purpose from section to section, depending on whether you are providing background information, telling a story, developing a reason in your case, mounting an emotional appeal, or doing something else. Save detailed attention to style (as explained in Appendix A) for later in the process, while editing a second or third draft.

Following Through

Once you have completed the first draft of an argument to persuade, select one paragraph in which you have consciously made stylistic choices to create images, connotations, sound patterns, and so on. It may be the introduction, the conclusion, or a body paragraph where you are striving for emotional effect. Be ready to share the paragraph with your class, describing your choices as we have done with many passages from Martin Luther King's letter.

READER'S CHECKLIST FOR REVISING A PERSUASIVE ESSAY

The following list will direct you to specific features of a good persuasive essay. You and a peer may want to exchange drafts; having someone else give your paper a critical reading often helps identify weaknesses you may have overlooked. After you have revised your draft, use the suggestions in Appendix A to edit for style and check for errors at the sentence level.

1. Read the audience profile for this essay. Then read the draft all the way through, projecting yourself as much as possible into the role of the target audience. After reading the draft, find and mark the essay's natural divisions. You may also want to number the paragraphs so that you can refer to them easily.
2. Recall that persuasive arguments must be based on careful inquiry and strategic case-making. Inspect the case first. Begin by underlining the thesis and marking the main reasons in support. You might write "Reason 1," "Reason 2," and so forth in the margins. Circle any words that need clearer definition. Also note any reasons that need more evidence or other support, such as illustrations or analogies.
3. Evaluate the plan for organizing the case. Are the reasons presented in a compelling and logical order? Does the argument build to a strong conclusion? Can you envision an alternative arrangement? Make suggestions for improvement, referring to paragraphs by number.
4. Remember that persuasion requires the writer to make an effort to present him- or herself as worthy of the reader's trust and respect. Reread the draft with a highlighter or pen in hand, marking specific places where the writer has sought the identification of the target audience. Has the writer made an effort to find common ground

---

Following Through

Read the following argument, and be ready to discuss its effectiveness as persuasion. You might build your evaluation around the suggestions listed in the box "Reader's Checklist for Revising a Persuasive Essay."

Student Sample: An Essay to Persuade

The following essay was written in response to an assignment for a first-year rhetoric course. The intended readers were other students, eighteen to twenty-two years old and for the most part middle-class, who attended the same large, private university as the writer. Within this group, Shanks was

with readers by using any of the ideas listed on page 110? Make suggestions for improvement.

5. Be aware that persuasion also requires the writer to make a conscious effort to gain the audience's emotional support through concrete examples and imagery, analogies and metaphors, first-person reporting, quotations, and so on. How many instances of conscious emotional appeal are there? Are the efforts at emotional appeal uniformly successful? What improvements can you suggest? Has the writer gone too far with emotional appeal? Or should more be done?
6. Add conscious stylistic appeals later, in the editing stage, because style involves refinements in word choice and sentence patterns. However, look now to see if the draft exhibits a middle style appropriate to the targeted audience. Mark any instances of the following:
   - Poor transitions between sentences or paragraphs
   - Wordy passages, especially those containing the passive voice (see the section "Editing for Clarity and Conciseness" in Appendix A)
   - Awkward sentences
   - Poor diction—that is, the use of incorrect or inappropriate words
7. Note any examples of effective style—good use of metaphor, repetition, or parallelism, for example.
8. Describe the general tone. Does it change from section to section? How appropriate and effective is the tone in general and in specific sections of the essay?
9. After studying the argument, ask whether you are sure what the writer wants or expects of the audience. Has the writer succeeded in persuading the audience? Why or why not?

trying to reach those who might sit in class and disagree with the opinions of more outspoken students but, for whatever reasons, fail to express their own dissenting viewpoints.

JOEY SHANKS

An Uncomfortable Position

I SAT quietly in my uncomfortable chair. Perhaps it was my position, I thought, and not the poly-wood seat that tormented me; so I sat upright, realizing then that both the chair and my position were probably responsible for my disposition. But I could do nothing to correct the problem. 1

Or maybe it was the conversation. I sat quietly, only for a lack of words. Usually I rambled on any subject, even if I knew nothing about it. No one in my rhetoric class would ever accuse me of lacking words, but today I was silent. The opinions of my classmates flew steadily across the room with occasional "I agree's" and "that's the truth's." My teacher shook her head in frustration.

She mediated the debate, if it was a debate. I could not imagine that a group of white college students angrily confessing that we all were constantly victims of reverse racism could provide much of a debate. In order for our generalizations to have formed a legitimate debate, there should have been two opposing sides, but the power of the majority had triumphed again. I sat quietly, knowing that what I heard was wrong. The little I said only fueled the ignorance and the guarded, David Duke–like articulations.

Did everyone in the class really think America had achieved equal opportunity? I could only hope that someone else in the classroom felt the same intimidation that I felt. I feared the majority. If I spoke my mind, I would only give the majority a minority to screw with.

5 But what about the young woman who sat next to me? She was Hispanic with glasses and no name or voice that I knew of. She was the visible minority in a class full of Greek letters and blonde hair. She must have been more uncomfortable than I was. She sat quietly every day.

The individual in society must possess the courage and the confidence to challenge and oppose the majority if he or she feels it necessary. In the classroom I had not seen this individualism. My classmates may have had different backgrounds and interests, but eventually in every discussion, a majority opinion dominated the debate and all personalities were lost in a mob mentality. In rhetoric class, we read and discussed material designed to stimulate a debate with many sides; however, the debate was rendered useless because the power of the majority stifled open discussion and bullied the individual to submit or stay quiet.

Tocqueville wrote of the dangerous power of the majority in his book *Democracy in America:* "The moral authority of the majority is partly based upon the notion that there is more intelligence and wisdom in a number of men united than in a single individual" (113). Tocqueville illustrated a point that I witnessed in class and that history has witnessed for ages. The majority rules through the power of numbers. No matter how wrong, an opinion with many advocates becomes the majority opinion and is difficult to oppose. The majority makes the rules; therefore, we accept that "might makes right."

The true moral authority, however, lies in the fundamental acceptance that right and wrong are universal and not relative to time and place. Thomas Nagel, a contemporary philosopher, states, "Many things that you probably think are wrong have been accepted as morally correct by large groups of people in the past" (71). The majority is not right simply because it is a large group. An individual is responsible for knowing right from wrong, no matter how large the group appears. Ancient philosophers such as Aristotle and Socrates have defied generations of majorities. They preached that morality is universal and that the majority is not always right.

In our classroom after the first week, all the students chose their chairs in particular areas. Certain mentalities aligned, acknowledging similar philosophies on politics, hunting, sports, African Americans, welfare, and women. Debate on *The Awakening* awoke the beefcake majority with confused exclamations: "She's crazy! Why did the chick kill herself?" The majority either misunderstood the book or was not willing to accept another opinion.

Mark Twain, a pioneer of American literature, fought an empire of 10
slavery with his book *The Adventures of Huckleberry Finn*. Twain saw through the cruelty of racism and spoke against a nation that treated men and women like animals because of the color of their skin. Twain possessed the confidence and individualism to fight the majority, despite its power. Mark Twain protected individualism when he opposed racism and the institution of slavery. He proved that the single individual is sometimes more intelligent than men united.

Ramsey Clark, a former attorney general and now a political activist, expressed a great deal of distress over the Persian Gulf war. He spoke for the minority, a position of peace. In an interview in *The Progressive,* Clark stated, "We really believe that might makes right, and that leads us to perpetual war" (qtd. in Dreifus 32). Clark was referring to the United States' foreign policy of peace through intimidation, but his words can be taken on a universal level. We will never accomplish anything if might makes right and humanity is in a perpetual war of opinions. Clark is an example of individualism against the majority, though he will never be considered an American hero; few may remember his words, but like Mark Twain, he fought the majority's "moral authority."

In the classroom, or in the post-slavery South, or in the deserts of the Middle East, the majority has the power, and whoever has the power controls the world and may even seem to control all the opinions in it. As a country we abuse the power of the majority. America, the spokesperson for the world majority, manipulates its position while flexing and growling, "Might makes right!" This situation is a large-scale version of a rhetoric seminar in which students too frequently align with or submit to the majority opinion. In rhetoric seminar we lack champions, individuals who see wrong and cry, "Foul!" Maybe the young Hispanic woman who quietly sits is just waiting for the right moment. Perhaps I had my chance and lost it, or maybe the majority has scared all the individuals into sitting quietly in their uncomfortable chairs.

WORKS CITED

Dreifus, Claudia. "An Interview with Ramsey Clark." *The Progressive* Apr. 1991: 32–35.

Nagel, Thomas. *What Does It All Mean?* Oxford: Oxford UP, 1987.

Tocqueville, Alexis de. *Democracy in America.* 1835. New York: Penguin, 1956.

CHAPTER SEVEN

Negotiation and Mediation: Resolving Conflict

Argument with the aims of convincing and of persuading is a healthy force within a community. Whatever the issue, people hold a range of positions, and debate among advocates of these various positions serves to inform the public and draw attention to problems that need solution. Yet, while some issues seem to be debated endlessly—the death penalty, abortion, gun control, the U.S. role in the affairs of other nations—a time comes when the conflict must be resolved and a particular course of action pursued.

But what happens after each side has made its best effort to convince and persuade yet no one position has won general assent? If the conflicting parties all have equal power, the result can be an impasse, a stalemate. More often, however, one party has greater authority and is able to impose its will, as, for example, when a university dean or president imposes a policy decision on students or faculty. But imposing power can be costly—especially in terms of the worsened relationships—and it is often temporary. Foes of abortion, for example, have been able to influence policy significantly under conservative administrations, only to see their policy gains eroded when more liberal politicians gain power. If conflicts are going to be resolved—and stay resolved—each side needs to move beyond advocating its own positions and start arguing with a new aim in mind: negotiation.

Arguing to negotiate aims to resolve—or at least reduce—conflict to the mutual satisfaction of all parties involved. But negotiation involves more than simply making a deal in which each side offers a few concessions while retaining a little of its initial demands. As this chapter will show, through the process of negotiating, opposing sides come to a greater understanding of their differing interests, backgrounds, and values; ideally, negotiation builds consensus and repairs relationships that may previously have been strained.

NEGOTIATION AND THE OTHER AIMS OF ARGUMENT

You may find it difficult to think of negotiation as argument if you see argument only as presenting a case for a particular position or persuading an audience to act in accordance with that position. Both of these aims clearly involve advocating one position and addressing the argument to those with different viewpoints. But recall that one definition of argue is "to make clear." As we discussed in Chapter 4, sometimes we argue in order to learn what we should think; that is, we argue to inquire, trying out an argument, examining it critically and with as little bias as possible with an audience of nonthreatening partners in conversation such as friends or family.

Arguing to negotiate shares many of the characteristics of arguing to inquire. Like inquiry, negotiation most often takes the form of dialogue, although writing plays an important role in the process. Also, whether a party in the conflict or an outside mediator among the various parties, the negotiator must inquire into the positions of all sides. Furthermore, anyone who agrees to enter into negotiation, especially someone who is a party to the conflict, must acknowledge his or her bias and remain open to the positions and interests of others, just as the inquirer does. Negotiation differs from inquiry, however, in that negotiation must find a mediating position that accommodates at least some of the interests of all sides. The best position in negotiation is the one all sides will accept.

As we will see in more detail, argument as negotiation draws upon the strategies of the other aims of argument as well. Like convincing, negotiation requires an understanding of case structure, as negotiators must analyze the cases each side puts forth, and mediators often need to build a case of their own for a position acceptable to all. And like persuasion, negotiation recognizes the role of human character and emotions, both in the creation of conflict and in its resolution.

To illustrate the benefits to be gained through the process of negotiation, we will concentrate in this chapter on one of the most heated conflicts in the United States today: the debate over abortion. A wide range of positions exists on this issue. Extremists for fetal rights, who sometimes engage in violent acts of civil disobedience, and extremists for the absolute rights of women, who argue that a woman should be able to terminate a pregnancy at any time and for any reason, may not be amenable to negotiation. However, between these poles lie the viewpoints of most Americans, whose differences could possibly be resolved.

Negotiation has a chance only among people who have reasoned through their own position, through inquiry, and who have attempted to defend it not through force but through convincing and persuasive argumentation. And negotiation has a chance only when people see that the divisions caused by their conflict are counterproductive. They must be ready to listen to each other. They must be willing to negotiate.

THE PROCESS OF NEGOTIATION AND MEDIATION

As a student in a writing class, you can practice the process of negotiation in at least two ways. You and several other students who have written conflicting arguments on a common topic may negotiate among yourselves to find a resolution acceptable to all, perhaps bringing in a disinterested student to serve as a mediator. Or your class as a whole may mediate a dispute among writers whose printed arguments offer conflicting viewpoints on the same issue. Here we illustrate the mediator approach, which is easily adapted to the more direct experience of face-to-face negotiation.

Understanding the Spirit of Negotiation

In arguing issues of public concern, it is a mistake to think of negotiation as the same thing as negotiating the price of a car or a house or even a collective bargaining agreement. In a dialogue between a buyer and seller, both sides typically begin by asking for much more than they seriously hope to get, and the process involves displays of will and power as each side tries to force the other to back down on its demands. Negotiation as rhetorical argument, however, is less adversarial; in fact, it is more like collaborative problem-solving, in which various opposing parties work together not to rebut one another's arguments but to understand them. Negotiation leads to the most permanent resolution of conflict when it is based on an increased understanding of difference rather than on a mere exchange of concessions. Negotiators must let go of the whole notion of proving one side right and other sides wrong. Rather, the negotiator says, "I see what you are demanding, and you see what I am demanding. Now let's sit down and find out *why* we hold these positions—What are our interests in this issue? Maybe together we can work out a solution that will address these interests." Unlike negotiators mediators are impartial, and if they have a personal viewpoint on the issue, they must suppress it and be careful not to favor either side.

Understanding the Opposing Positions

Negotiation begins with a close look at opposing views. As in inquiry, the first stage of the process is an analysis of the positions, the thesis statements, and the supporting reasons and evidence offered on all sides. It is a good idea for each party to write a brief of his or her case, as described on pages 79–95 and 163–164. These briefs should indicate how the reasons are supported, so that disputants can see where they agree or disagree about data.

The mediator also must begin by inquiring into the arguments presented by the parties in dispute. To illustrate, we will look at two reasoned arguments representing opposing views on the value of the Supreme Court's *Roe v. Wade* decision. In that decision, which was handed down in 1973, the Court ruled that the Constitution does grant to citizens a zone of personal privacy, which for women would include the decision regarding whether to terminate a pregnancy. The Court did stipulate, however, that the right to abortion was not unqualified and that states could regulate abortions to protect the fetus after viability.

The first argument, "Living with *Roe v. Wade,*" is by Margaret Liu McConnell, a writer and mother of three, who herself had an abortion while she was in college. This experience led McConnell to decide that abortion on demand should not have become a constitutional right. To those who applaud abortion rights, McConnell argues that *Roe v. Wade* has had serious social and moral consequences for our nation. She does not call for the decision to be overturned, but she does want abortion-rights supporters to take a closer look at the issue and recognize that abortion is fundamentally an immoral choice, one that should result in a sense of guilt. This essay originally appeared in 1990 in *Commentary,* a journal published by the American Jewish Committee.

The second argument is by Ellen Willis, also a mother who once had an abortion. For Willis abortion is very much a right; in fact, it is the foundation of women's equality. Willis defends *Roe v. Wade* as the "cutting edge of feminism." Her audience consists of liberals who oppose abortion—"the left wing of the right-to-life movement"—specifically, the editors of *Commonweal,* a liberal Catholic journal. Her audience could also include people like Margaret Liu McConnell, who see abortion as a moral question rather than as a political question framed in terms of equal rights. "Putting Women Back into the Abortion Debate" originally appeared in the left-leaning *Village Voice* in 1985.

MARGARET LIU McCONNELL

Living with Roe v. Wade

THERE IS something decidedly unappealing to me about the pro-life activists seen on the evening news as they are dragged away from the entrances to abortion clinics across the country. Perhaps it is that their poses remind me of sulky two-year-olds, sinking to their knees as their frazzled mothers try to haul them from the playground. Or perhaps it is because I am a little hard put to believe, when one of them cries out, often with a Southern twang, "Ma'am, don't keel your baby," that he or she could really care that deeply about a stranger's fetus. After all, there are limits to compassion and such concern seems excessive, suspect. 1

Besides, as pro-choice adherents like to point out, the fact that abortion is legal does not mean that someone who is against abortion will be forced to have one against her wishes. It is a private matter, so they say, between a woman and her doctor. From this it would follow that those opposed to abortion are no more than obnoxious busybodies animated by their own inner pathologies to interfere in the private lives of strangers.

Certainly this is the impression conveyed by those news clips of anti-abortion blockades being broken up by the police. We pity the woman, head sunk and afraid, humiliated in the ancient shame that all around her know she is carrying an unwanted child. Precisely because she is pregnant, our hearts go out to her in her vulnerability. It would seem that those workers from the abortion clinic, shielding arms around her shoulders, their identification vests giving them the benign look of school-crossing guards, are her protectors. They are guiding her through a hostile, irrational crowd to the cool and orderly safety of the clinic and the medical attention she needs.

But is it possible that this impression is mistaken? Is it possible that those who guide the woman along the path to the abortionist's table are not truly her protectors, shoring her up on the road to a dignified life in which she will best be able to exercise her intellectual and physical faculties free from any kind of oppression? Is it possible that they are serving, albeit often unwittingly, to keep her and millions of other women on a demeaning and rather lonely treadmill—a treadmill on which these women trudge through cycles of sex without commitment, unwanted pregnancy, and abortion, all in the name of equal opportunity and free choice?

Consider yet again the woman on the path to an abortion. She is already 5
a victim of many forces. She is living in a social climate in which she is expected to view sex as practically a form of recreation that all healthy women should pursue eagerly. She has been conditioned to fear having a child, particularly in her younger years, as an unthinkable threat to her standard of living and to the career through which she defines herself as a "real" person. Finally, since 1973, when the Supreme Court in *Roe v. Wade* declared access to abortion a constitutional right, she has been invited, in the event that she does become pregnant, not only to have an abortion, but to do so without sorrow and with no moral misgivings. As the highly vocal proabortion movement cheers her on with rallying cries of "Freedom of Choice," she may find herself wondering: "Is this the great freedom we've been fighting for? The freedom to sleep with men who don't care for us, the freedom to scorn the chance to raise a child? The freedom to let doctors siphon from our bodies that most precious gift which women alone are made to receive: a life to nurture?"

My goal here is not to persuade militant pro-choicers that abortion is wrong. Instead, it is to establish that abortion cannot and should not be seen as strictly a matter between a woman and her doctor. For the knowledge that the law allows free access to abortion affects all of us directly and indirectly by the way it shapes the social climate. Most directly and most easy to illustrate, the realization that any pregnancy, intended or accidental, may be aborted at will affects women in their so-called childbearing years. The indirect effects are more difficult to pinpoint. I would like tentatively to suggest that *Roe v. Wade* gives approval, at the highest level of judgment in this country, to certain attitudes which, when manifest at the lowest economic levels, have extremely destructive consequences.

But to begin with the simpler task of examining *Roe*'s questionable effect on the world women inhabit: I—who at thirty-two am of the age to have "benefited" from *Roe*'s protections for all my adult years—offer here some examples of those "benefits."

It was my first year at college, my first year away from my rather strict, first-generation American home. I had a boyfriend from high school whom I liked and admired but was not in love with, and I was perfectly satisfied with the stage of heavy-duty necking we had managed, skillfully avoiding the suspicious eyes of my mother. But once I got to college I could think of no good reason not to go farther. For far from perceiving any constraints around me, I encountered all manner of encouragement to become "sexually active"—from the health center, from newspapers, books, and magazines, from the behavior of other students, even from the approval of other students' parents of their children's "liberated" sexual conduct.

Yet the truth is that I longed for the days I knew only from old movies and novels, those pre-60's days when boyfriends visiting from other colleges stayed in hotels (!) and dates ended with a lingering kiss at the door. I lived in an apartment-style dormitory, six women sharing three bedrooms and a kitchen. Needless to say, visiting boyfriends did not stay in hotels. By the end of my freshman year three out of the six of us would have had abortions.

How did it come to pass that so many of us got pregnant? How has it 10
come to pass that more than one-and-one-half million women each year get pregnant in this country, only to have abortions? Nowadays it is impossible to go into a drugstore without bumping into the condoms on display above the checkout counters. And even when I was in college, contraception was freely available, and everyone knew that the health center, open from nine to four, was ready to equip us with the contraceptive armament we were sure to need.

Nevertheless, thanks to *Roe v. Wade,* we all understood as well that if anything went wrong, there would be no threat of a shotgun marriage, or of being sent away in shame to bear a child, or of a dangerous back-alley abortion. Perhaps the incredible number of "accidental" pregnancies, both at college and throughout the country, finds its explanation in just that understanding. Analogies are difficult to construct in arguments about abortion, for there is nothing quite analogous to terminating a pregnancy. That said, consider this one anyway. If children are sent out to play ball in a yard near a house, a responsible adult, knowing that every once in a while a window will get broken, will still tell them to be very careful not to break any. But what if the children are sent into the yard and told something like this: "Go out and play, and don't worry about breaking any windows. It's bound to happen, and when it does, no problem: it will be taken care of." How many more windows will be shattered?

There were, here and there, some women who seemed able to live outside these pressures. Within my apartment one was an Orthodox Jewish freshman from Queens, another a junior from Brooklyn, also Jewish, who was in the process of becoming Orthodox. They kept kosher as far as was possible in our common kitchen, and on Friday afternoons would cook supper for a group of friends, both men and women. As darkness fell they would light candles and sing and eat and laugh in a circle of light. I remember looking in at their evenings from the doorway to the kitchen, wishing vainly that I could belong to such a group, a group with a code of behavior that would provide shelter from the free-for-all I saw elsewhere. But the only group I felt I belonged to was, generically, "young American woman," and as far as I could see, the norm of behavior for a young American woman was to enjoy a healthy sex life, with or without commitment.

A few months later, again thanks to *Roe v. Wade,* I discovered that the logistics of having an abortion were, as promised, extremely simple. The school health center was again at my service. After a few perfunctory questions and sympathetic nods of the head I was given directions to the nearest abortion clinic.

A strange thing has happened since that great freedom-of-choice victory in 1973. Abortion has become the only viable alternative many women feel they have open to them when they become pregnant by accident. Young men no longer feel obligated to offer to "do the right thing." Pregnancy is most often confirmed in a medical setting. Even though it is a perfectly normal and healthy state, in an unwanted pregnancy a woman feels distressed. The situation thus becomes that of a distressed woman looking to trusted medical personnel for relief. Abortion presents itself as the simple, legal, medical solution to her distress. A woman may have private reservations, but she gets the distinct impression that if she does not take advantage of her right to an abortion she is of her own accord refusing a simple solution to her troubles.

That is certainly how it was for me, sitting across from the counselor at 15
the health center, clutching a wad of damp tissues, my heart in my throat. The feeling was exactly parallel to the feeling I had had at the beginning of the school year: I could be defiantly old-fashioned and refuse to behave like a normal American woman, or I could exercise my sexual liberation. Here, six weeks pregnant, I could be troublesome, perverse, and somehow manage to keep the baby, causing tremendous inconvenience to everyone, or I could take the simple route of having an abortion and not even miss a single class. The choice was already made.

Physically, also, abortion has become quite a routine procedure. As one of my grosser roommates put it, comforting me with talk of her own experiences, it was about as bad as going to the dentist. My only memory of the operation is of coming out of the general anesthesia to the sound of sobbing all around. I, too, was sobbing, without thought, hard and uncontrollably, as though somehow, deep below the conscious level, below whatever superficial concerns had layered themselves in the day-to-day mind of a busy young woman, I had come to realize what I had done, and what could never be undone.

I have since had three children, and at the beginning of each pregnancy I was presented with the opportunity to have an abortion without even having to ask. For professional reasons my husband and I have moved several times, and each of our children was born in a different city with a different set of obstetrical personnel. In every case I was offered the unsolicited luxury of "keeping my options open": of choosing whether to continue the pregnancy or end it. The polite way of posing the question, after a positive pregnancy test, seems to be for the doctor to ask noncommittally, "And how are we treating this pregnancy?"

Each one of those pregnancies, each one of those expendable bunches of tissue, has grown into a child, each one different from the other. I cannot escape the haunting fact that if I had had an abortion, one of my children would be missing. Not just a generic little bundle in swaddling clothes interchangeable with any other, but a specific child.

I still carry in my mind a picture of that other child who was never born, a picture which changes as the years go by, and I imagine him growing up. For some reason I usually do imagine a boy, tall and with dark hair and eyes. This is speculation, of course, based on my coloring and build and on that of the young man involved. Such speculation seems maudlin and morbid and I do not engage in it on purpose. But whether I like it or not, every now and then my mind returns to that ghost of a child and to the certainty that for seven weeks I carried the beginnings of a being whose coloring and build and, to a large extent, personality were already determined. Buoyant green-eyed girl or shy, dark-haired boy, I wonder. Whoever, a child would have been twelve this spring.

I am not in the habit of exposing this innermost regret, this endless 20
remorse to which I woke too late. I do so only to show that in the wake of *Roe v. Wade* abortion has become casual, commonplace, and very hard to resist as an easy way out of an unintended pregnancy, and that more unintended pregnancies are likely to occur when everyone knows there is an easy way out of them. Abortion has become an option offered to women, married as well as unmarried, including those who are financially, physically, and emotionally able to care for a child. This is what *Roe v. Wade* guarantees. For all the pro-choice lobby's talk of abortion as a deep personal moral decision, casting abortion as a right takes the weight of morality out of the balance. For, by definition, a right is something one need not feel guilty exercising.

I do not wish a return to the days when a truly desperate woman unable to get a safe legal abortion would risk her life at the hands of an illegal abortionist. Neither could I ever condemn a woman whose own grip on life is so fragile as to render her incapable of taking on the full responsibility for another life, helpless and demanding. But raising abortion to the plane of a constitutional right in order to ensure its accessibility to any woman for any reason makes abortion too easy a solution to an age-old problem.

Human beings have always coupled outside the bounds deemed proper by the societies in which they lived. But the inevitable unexpected pregnancies often served a social purpose. There was a time when many young couples found in the startling new life they had created an undeniable reason to settle down seriously to the tasks of earning a living and making a home. That might have meant taking on a nine-to-five job and assuming a mortgage, a prospect which sounds like death to many baby boomers intent on prolonging adolescence well into middle age. But everyone knows anecdotally if not from straight statistics that many of these same baby boomers owe their own lives to such happy (for them) accidents.

When I became pregnant in college, I never seriously considered getting married and trying to raise a child, although it certainly would have been possible to do so. Why should I have, when the road to an abortion was so free and unencumbered, and when the very operation itself had been presented as a step on the march to women's equality?

I know that no one forced me to do anything, that I was perfectly free to step back at any time and live by my own moral code if I chose to, much as my Orthodox Jewish acquaintances did. But this is awfully hard when the society you consider yourself part of presents abortion as a legal, morally acceptable solution. And what kind of a world would it be if all those in need of a moral structure stepped back to insulate themselves, alone or in groups—ethnic, religious, or economic—each with its own exclusive moral code, leaving behind a chaos at the center? It sounds like New York City on a bad day.

This is not, of course, to ascribe the chaos reigning in our cities directly 25
to *Roe v. Wade.* That chaos is caused by a growing and tenacious underclass defined by incredibly high rates of drug abuse, and dependence on either crime or welfare for financial support. But sometimes it does seem as though the same attitude behind abortion on demand lies behind the abandonment of parental responsibility which is the most pervasive feature of life in the underclass and the most determinative of its terrible condition.

Parental responsibility can be defined as providing one's offspring at every level of development with that which they need to grow eventually into independent beings capable of supporting themselves emotionally and financially. Different parents will, of course, have different ideas about what is best for a child, and different parents will have different resources to draw upon to provide for their children. But whatever the differences may be, responsible parents will try, to the best of their ability and in accordance with their own rights, to raise their children properly. It is tedious, expensive, and takes a long, long time. For it is not a question of fetal weeks before a human being reaches any meaningful stage of "viability" (how "viable" is a two-year-old left to his own devices? A five-year-old?). It is a question of years, somewhere in the neighborhood of eighteen.

Why does any parent take on such a long, hard task? Because life is a miracle that cannot be denied? Because it is the right thing to do? Because there is a certain kind of love a parent bears a child that does not require a calculated return on investment? Because we would hate ourselves otherwise? All these factors enter into the powerful force that compels parents to give up years of their free time and much of their money to bring up their children. Yet the cool, clinical approach *Roe v. Wade* allows all of us—men no less than women—in deciding whether or not we are "ready" to accept the responsibility of an established pregnancy seems to undermine an already weakening cultural expectation that parents simply have a duty to take care of their children.

A middle- or upper-class woman may have high expectations of what she will achieve so long as she is not saddled with a baby. When she finds herself pregnant she is guaranteed the right under *Roe v. Wade* to opt out of that long and tedious responsibility, and does so by the hundreds of thousands each year. By contrast, a woman in the underclass who finds herself pregnant is not likely to have great expectations of what life would be like were she free of the burden of her child; abortion would not broaden her horizons and is not usually her choice. Yet she often lacks the maternal will and the resources to take full responsibility for the well-being of her child until adulthood.

To be sure, these two forms of refusing parental responsibility have vastly different effects. But how can the government hope to devise policies that will encourage parental responsibility in the underclass when at the highest level of judgment, that of the Supreme Court, the freedom to opt out of parental responsibility is protected as a right? Or, to put the point another way, perhaps the weakening of the sense of duty toward one's own offspring is a systemic problem in America, present in all classes, with only its most visible manifestation in the underclass.

The federal Family Support Act of 1988 was the result of much study 30
and debate on how to reform the welfare system to correct policies which have tended to make it easier for poor families to qualify for aid if the father is not part of the household. Among other provisions intended to help keep families from breaking up, states are now required to pay cash benefits to two-parent families and to step up child-support payments from absent fathers. New York City, for example, has this year begun to provide its Department of Health with information, including Social Security numbers, on the parents of every child born in the city. Should the mother ever apply for aid, the father can be tracked down and child-support payments can be deducted from his paycheck. Such a strict enforcement of child-support obligations is a powerful and exciting legal method for society to show that it will not tolerate the willful abandonment of children by their fathers.

It is evident that there is a compelling state interest in promoting the responsibility of both parents toward their child. The compelling interest is that it takes a great deal of money to care for a child whose parents do not undertake the responsibility themselves. For whatever else we may have lost of our humanity over the last several decades, however hardened we have been by violence and by the degradation witnessed daily in the lost lives on the street, we still retain a basic decent instinct to care for innocent babies and children in need.

It is also evident that parental responsibility begins well before the child is born. Thus, the Appellate Division of the State Supreme Court of New York in May of this year ruled that a woman who uses drugs during pregnancy and whose newborn has drugs in its system may be brought before Family Court for a hearing on neglect. Yet how can we condemn a woman under law for harming her unborn child while at the same time protecting her right to destroy that child absolutely, for any reason, through abortion? Is the only difference that the first instance entails a monetary cost to society while the second does not?

There is another kind of behavior implicitly condoned by *Roe v. Wade,* which involves the value of life itself, and which also has its most frightening and threatening manifestation in the underclass. Consensus on when human life begins has yet to be established and perhaps never will be. What is clear, however, is that abortion cuts short the development of a specific human life; it wipes out the future years of a human being, years we can know nothing about. Generally we have no trouble conceiving of lost future years as real loss. Lawsuits routinely place value on lost future income and lost future enjoyment, and we consider the death of a child or a young person to be particularly tragic in lost potential, in the waste of idealized years to come. Yet under *Roe v. Wade* the value of the future years of life of the fetus is determined by an individual taking into account only her own well-being.

Back in 1965, justifying his discovery of a constitutional right to privacy which is nowhere mentioned in the Constitution itself, and which helped lay the groundwork for *Roe v. Wade,* Justice William O. Douglas invoked the concept of "penumbras, formed by emanations" of constitutional amendments. Is it far-fetched to say that there are "penumbras, formed by emanations" of *Roe v. Wade* that grant the right to consider life in relative terms and to place one's own interest above any others? This same "right" when exercised by criminals is a terrifying phenomenon: these are people who feel no guilt in taking a victim's life, who value the future years of that life as nothing compared with their own interest in the victim's property. Of course, one might argue that a fetus is not yet cognizant of its own beingness and that, further, it feels no pain. Yet if a killer creeps up behind you and blows your head off with a semi-automatic, you will feel no pain either, nor will you be cognizant of your death.

Roe v. Wade was a great victory for the women's movement. It seemed 35
to promote equality of opportunity for women in all their endeavors by freeing them from the burden of years of caring for children conceived unintentionally. But perhaps support for *Roe v. Wade* should be reconsidered in light of the damage wrought by the kind of behavior that has become common in a world in which pregnancy is no longer seen as the momentous beginning of a new life, and life, by extension, is no longer held as sacred.

At any rate, even if one rejects my speculation that *Roe v. Wade* has at least some indirect connection with the degree to which life on our streets has become so cheap, surely there can be no denying the direct connection between *Roe v. Wade* and the degree to which sex has become so casual. Surely, for example, *Roe v. Wade* will make it harder for my two daughters to grow gracefully into womanhood without being encouraged to think of sex as a kind of sport played with a partner who need feel no further responsibility toward them once the game is over.

For me, that is reason enough not to support this elevation of abortion to the status of a constitutional right.

ELLEN WILLIS

Putting Women Back into the Abortion Debate

1 SOME YEARS ago I attended a New York Institute for the Humanities seminar on the new right. We were a fairly heterogeneous group of liberals and lefties, feminists and gay activists, but on one point nearly all of us agreed: The right-to-life movement was a dangerous antifeminist crusade. At one session I argued that the attack on abortion had significance far beyond itself, that it was the linchpin of the right's social agenda. I got a lot of supporting comments and approving nods. It was too much for Peter Steinfels, a liberal Catholic, author of *The Neoconservatives,* and executive editor of *Commonweal.* Right-to-lifers were not all right-wing fanatics, he protested. "You have to understand," he said plaintively, "that many of us see abortion as a *human life issue.*" What I remember best was his air of frustrated isolation. I don't think he came back to the seminar after that.

Things are different now. I often feel isolated when I insist that abortion is, above all, a *feminist issue.* Once people took for granted that abortion was an issue of sexual politics and morality. Now, abortion is most often discussed as a question of "life" in the abstract. Public concern over abortion centers almost exclusively on fetuses; women and their bodies are merely the stage on which the drama of fetal life and death takes place. Debate about abortion—if not its reality—has become sexlessly scholastic. And the people most responsible for this turn of events are, like Peter Steinfels, on the left.

The left wing of the right-to-life movement is a small, seemingly eccentric minority in both "progressive" and antiabortion camps. Yet it has played a critical role in the movement: By arguing that opposition to abortion can be separated from the right's antifeminist program, it has given antiabortion sentiment legitimacy in left-symp and (putatively) profeminist circles.[1] While left antiabortionists are hardly alone in emphasizing fetal life, their innovation has been to claim that a consistent "pro-life" stand involves opposing capital punishment, supporting disarmament, demanding government programs to end poverty, and so on. This is of course a leap the right is neither able nor willing to make. It's been liberals—from Garry Wills to the Catholic bishops—who have supplied the mass media with the idea that prohibiting abortion is part of a "seamless garment" of respect for human life.

Having invented this countercontext for the abortion controversy, left antiabortionists are trying to impose it as the only legitimate context for debate. Those of us who won't accept their terms and persist in seeing opposition to abortion, antifeminism, sexual repression, and religious sectarianism as the real seamless garment have been accused of obscuring the issue with demagoguery. Last year *Commonweal*—perhaps the most important current forum for left antiabortion opinion—ran an editorial demanding that we shape up:

[1] *Left-symp:* sympathetic to the left.

"Those who hold that abortion is immoral believe that the biological dividing lines of birth or viability should no more determine whether a developing member of the species is denied or accorded essential rights than should the biological dividing lines of sex or race or disability or old age. This argument is open to challenge. Perhaps the dividing lines are sufficiently different. Pro-choice advocates should state their reasons for believing so. They should meet the argument on its own grounds. . . ."

In other words, the only question we're allowed to debate—or the only 5
one *Commonweal* is willing to entertain—is "Are fetuses the moral equivalent of born human beings?" And I can't meet the argument on its own grounds because I don't agree that this is the key question, whose answer determines whether one supports abortion or opposes it. I don't doubt that fetuses are alive, or that they're biologically human—what else would they be? I do consider the life of a fertilized egg less precious than the well-being of a woman with feelings, self-consciousness, a history, social ties; and I think fetuses get closer to being human in a moral sense as they come closer to birth. But to me these propositions are intuitively self-evident. I wouldn't know how to justify them to a "nonbeliever," nor do I see the point of trying.

I believe the debate has to start in a different place—with the recognition that fertilized eggs develop into infants inside the bodies of women. Pregnancy and birth are active processes in which a woman's body shelters, nourishes, and expels a new life; for nine months she is immersed in the most intimate possible relationship with another being. The growing fetus makes considerable demands on her physical and emotional resources, culminating in the cataclysmic experience of birth. And child-bearing has unpredictable consequences; it always entails some risk of injury or death.

For me all this has a new concreteness: I had a baby last year. My much-desired and relatively easy pregnancy was full of what antiabortionists like to call "inconveniences." I was always tired, short of breath; my digestion was never right; for three months I endured a state of hormonal siege; later I had pains in my fingers, swelling feet, numb spots on my legs, the dread hemorrhoids. I had to think about everything I ate. I developed borderline glucose intolerance. I gained fifty pounds and am still overweight; my shape has changed in other ways that may well be permanent. Psychologically, my pregnancy consumed me—though I'd happily bought the seat on the roller coaster, I was still terrified to be so out of control of my normally tractable body. It was all bearable, even interesting—even, at times, transcendent—because I wanted a baby. Birth was painful, exhausting, and wonderful. If I hadn't wanted a baby it would only have been painful and exhausting—or worse. I can hardly imagine what it's like to have your body and mind taken over in this way when you not only don't look forward to the result, but positively dread it. The thought appalls me. So as I see it, the key question is "Can it be moral, under any circumstances, to make a woman bear a child against her will?"

From this vantage point, *Commonweal*'s argument is irrelevant, for in a society that respects the individual, no "member of the species" in *any* stage of development has an "essential right" to make use of someone else's body, let alone in such all-encompassing fashion, without that person's consent. You can't make a case against abortion by applying a general principle about everybody's human rights; you have to show exactly the opposite—that the relationship between fetus and pregnant woman is an exception, one that justifies depriving women of their right to bodily integrity. And in fact all antiabortion ideology rests on the premise—acknowledged or simply assumed—that women's unique capacity to bring life into the world carries with it a unique obligation that women cannot be allowed to "play God" and launch only the lives they welcome.

Yet the alternative to allowing women this power is to make them impotent. Criminalizing abortion doesn't just harm individual women with unwanted pregnancies, it affects all women's sense of themselves. Without control of our fertility we can never envision ourselves as free, for our biology makes us constantly vulnerable. Simply because we are female our physical integrity can be violated, our lives disrupted and transformed, at any time. Our ability to act in the world is hopelessly compromised by our sexual being.

Ah, sex—it does have a way of coming up in these discussions, despite 10
all. When pressed, right-to-lifers of whatever political persuasion invariably point out that pregnancy doesn't happen by itself. The leftists often give patronizing lectures on contraception (though some find only "natural birth control" acceptable), but remain unmoved when reminded that contraceptives fail. Openly or implicitly they argue that people shouldn't have sex unless they're prepared to procreate. (They are quick to profess a single standard—men as well as women should be sexually "responsible." Yes, and the rich as well as the poor should be allowed to sleep under bridges.) Which amounts to saying that if women want to lead heterosexual lives they must give up any claim to self-determination, and that they have no right to sexual pleasure without fear.

Opposing abortion, then, means accepting that women must suffer sexual disempowerment and a radical loss of autonomy relative to men: If fetal life is sacred, the self-denial basic to women's oppression is also basic to the moral order. Opposing abortion means embracing a conservative sexual morality, one that subordinates pleasure to reproduction: If fetal life is sacred, there is no room for the view that sexual passion—or even sexual love—for its own sake is a human need and a human right. Opposing abortion means tolerating the inevitable double standard, by which men may accept or reject sexual restrictions in accordance with their beliefs, while women must bow to them out of fear . . . or defy them at great risk. However much *Commonweal*'s editors and those of like mind want to believe their opposition to abortion is simply about saving lives, the truth is that in the real world they are shoring up a particular sexual culture, whose rules are stacked against women. I have yet to hear any left right-to-lifers take full responsibility for that fact or deal seriously with its political implications.

Unfortunately, their fuzziness has not lessened their appeal—if anything it's done the opposite. In increasing numbers liberals and leftists, while opposing antiabortion laws, have come to view abortion as an "agonizing moral issue" with some justice on both sides, rather than an issue—however emotionally complex—of freedom versus repression, or equality versus hierarchy, that affects their political self-definition. This above-the-battle stance is attractive to leftists who want to be feminist good guys but are uneasy or ambivalent about sexual issues, not to mention those who want to ally with "progressive" factions of the Catholic church on Central America, nuclear disarmament, or populist economics without that sticky abortion question getting in the way.

Such neutrality is a way of avoiding the painful conflict over cultural issues that continually smolders on the left. It can also be a way of coping with the contradictions of personal life at a time when liberation is a dream deferred. To me the fight for abortion has always been the cutting edge of feminism, precisely because it denies that anatomy is destiny, that female biology dictates women's subordinate status. Yet recently I've found it hard to focus on the issue, let alone summon up the militance needed to stop the antiabortion tanks. In part that has to do with second-round weariness—do we really have to go through all these things twice?—in part with my life now.

Since my daughter's birth my feelings about abortion—not as a political demand but as a personal choice—have changed. In this society, the difference between the situation of a childless woman and of a mother is immense; the fear that having a child will dislodge one's tenuous hold on a nontraditional life is excruciating. This terror of being forced into the sea-change of motherhood gave a special edge to my convictions about abortion. Since I've made that plunge voluntarily, with consequences still unfolding, the terror is gone; I might not want another child, for all sorts of reasons, but I will never again feel that my identity is at stake. Different battles with the culture absorb my energy now. Besides, since I've experienced the primal, sensual passion of caring for an infant, there will always be part of me that does want another. If I had an abortion today, it would be with conflict and sadness unknown to me when I had an abortion a decade ago. And the antiabortionists' imagery of dead babies hits me with new force. Do many women—left, feminist women—have such feelings? Is this the sort of "ambivalence about abortion" that in the present atmosphere slides so easily into self-flagellating guilt?

Some left antiabortionists, mainly pacifists—Juli Loesch, Mary Meehan, 15
and other "feminists for life"; Jim Wallis and various writers for Wallis's radical evangelical journal *Sojourners*—have tried to square their position with concern for women. They blame the prevalence of abortion on oppressive conditions—economic injustice, lack of child care and other social supports for mothers, the devaluation of childrearing, men's exploitative sexual behavior and refusal to take equal responsibility for children. They disagree on whether to criminalize abortion now (since murder is intolerable no matter what the cause) or to build a long-term moral consensus (since stopping abortion requires a general social transformation), but they all regard abortion as a desperate solution to desperate problems, and the women who resort to it as more sinned against than sinning.

This analysis grasps an essential feminist truth: that in a male-supremacist society no choice a woman makes is genuinely free or entirely in her interest. Certainly many women have had abortions they didn't want or wouldn't have wanted if they had any plausible means of caring for a child; and countless others wouldn't have gotten pregnant in the first place were it not for inadequate contraception, sexual confusion and guilt, male pressure, and other stigmata of female powerlessness. Yet forcing a woman to bear a child she doesn't want can only add injury to insult, while refusing to go through with such a pregnancy can be a woman's first step toward taking hold of her life. And many women who have abortions are "victims" only of ordinary human miscalculation, technological failure, or the vagaries of passion, all bound to exist in any society, however utopian. There will always be women who, at any given moment, want sex but don't want a child; some of these women will get pregnant; some of them will have abortions. Behind the victim theory of abortion is the implicit belief that women are always ready to be mothers, if only conditions are right, and that sex for pleasure rather than procreation is not only "irresponsible" (i.e., bad) but something men impose on women, never something women actively seek. Ironically, left right-to-lifers see abortion as always coerced (it's "exploitation" and "violence against women"), yet regard motherhood—which for most women throughout history has been inescapable, and is still our most socially approved role—as a positive choice. The analogy to the feminist antipornography movement goes beyond borrowed rhetoric: the antiporners, too, see active female lust as surrender to male domination and traditionally feminine sexual attitudes as expressions of women's true nature.

This Orwellian version of feminism, which glorifies "female values" and dismisses women's struggles for freedom—particularly sexual freedom—as a male plot, has become all too familiar in recent years. But its use in the abortion debate has been especially muddleheaded. Somehow we're supposed to leap from an oppressive patriarchal society to the egalitarian one that will supposedly make abortion obsolete without ever allowing women to see themselves as people entitled to control their reproductive function rather than be controlled by it. How women who have no power in this most personal of areas can effectively fight for power in the larger society is left to our imagination. A "New Zealand feminist" quoted by Mary Meehan in a 1980 article in *The Progressive* says, "Accepting short-term solutions like abortion only delays the implementation of real reforms like decent maternity and paternity leaves, job protection, high-quality child care, community responsibility for dependent people of all ages, and recognition of the economic contribution of childminders"—as if these causes were progressing nicely before legal abortion came along. On the contrary, the fight for reproductive freedom is the foundation of all the others, which is why antifeminists resist it so fiercely.

As "pro-life" pacifists have been particularly concerned with refuting charges of misogyny, the liberal Catholics at *Commonweal* are most exercised by the claim that antiabortion laws violate religious freedom. The editorial quoted above hurled another challenge at the proabortion forces:

> It is time, finally, for the pro-choice advocates and editorial writers to abandon, once and for all, the argument that abortion is a religious "doctrine" of a single or several churches being imposed on those of other persuasions in violation of the First Amendment. . . . Catholics and their bishops are accused of imposing their "doctrine" on abortion, but not their "doctrine" on the needs of the poor, or their "doctrine" on the arms race, or their "doctrine" on human rights in Central America. . . .
>
> The briefest investigation into Catholic teaching would show that the church's case against abortion is utterly unlike, say, its belief in the Real Presence, known with the eyes of faith alone, or its insistence on a Sunday obligation, applicable only to the faithful. The church's moral teaching on abortion . . . is for the most part like its teaching on racism, warfare, and capital punishment, based on ordinary reasoning common to believers and nonbelievers. . . .

This is one more example of right-to-lifers' tendency to ignore the sexual ideology underlying their stand. Interesting, isn't it, how the editorial neglects to mention that the church's moral teaching on abortion jibes neatly with its teaching on birth control, sex, divorce, and the role of women. The traditional, patriarchal sexual morality common to these teachings is explicitly religious, and its chief defenders in modern times have been the more conservative churches. The Catholic and evangelical Christian churches are the backbone of the organized right-to-life movement and—a few Nathansons and Hentoffs notwithstanding—have provided most of the movement's activists and spokespeople.

Furthermore, the Catholic hierarchy has made opposition to abortion a 20
litmus test of loyalty to the church in a way it has done with no other political issue—witness Archbishop O'Connor's harassment of Geraldine Ferraro during her vice-presidential campaign. It's unthinkable that a Catholic bishop would publicly excoriate a Catholic officeholder or candidate for taking a hawkish position on the arms race or Central America or capital punishment. Nor do I notice anyone trying to read William F. Buckley out of the church for his views on welfare. The fact is there is no accepted Catholic "doctrine" on these matters comparable to the church's absolutist condemnation of abortion. While differing attitudes toward war, racism, and poverty cut across religious and secular lines, the sexual values that mandate opposition to abortion are the bedrock of the traditional religious world view, and the source of the most bitter conflict with secular and religious modernists. When churches devote their considerable political power, organizational resources, and money to translating those values into law, I call that imposing their religious beliefs on me—whether or not they're technically violating the First Amendment.

Statistical studies have repeatedly shown that people's views on abortion are best predicted by their opinions on sex and "family" issues, not on "life" issues like nuclear weapons or the death penalty. That's not because we're inconsistent but because we comprehend what's really at stake in the abortion fight. It's the antiabortion left that refuses to face the contradiction in its own position: you can't be wholeheartedly for "life"—or for such progressive aspirations as freedom, democracy, equality—and condone the subjugation of women. The seamless garment is full of holes.

These essays by McConnell and Willis represent the two sides on which most Americans fall regarding the issue of legalized abortion. Because abortion is likely to stay legal, what is the point of trying to reconcile these positions? One benefit is that doing so might help put to rest the controversy surrounding abortion—a controversy that rages at abortion clinics and in the media, distracting Americans from other issues of importance and causing divisiveness and distrust, and that also rages within millions of Americans who want abortion to remain legal but at the same time disapprove of it. In addition, reaching some consensus on abortion might resolve the contradiction of its being legal but unavailable to many women, as extremist opponents have caused many doctors to refuse to perform abortions and restrictions on public funding for abortion has limited the access of poor women. Finally, some consensus on abortion will be necessary to formulate decisions of public policy: What restrictions, if any, are appropriate? Should parental notification or consent be required for women under eighteen? Should public funds be available for an abortion when a woman cannot otherwise afford one?

We have said that the first step in resolving conflict is to understand what the parties in conflict are claiming and why. Using the following outline form, or brief, we can describe the positions of each side:

McConnell's position: She is against unrestricted abortion as a woman's right.

Claim (or thesis): The right to abortion has hurt the moral and social climate of our nation.

Reason: It has put pressure on young single women to adopt a "liberated" lifestyle of sex without commitment.
Evidence: Her own college experiences.

Reason: It has caused an increase in unintended pregnancies.
Evidence: The analogy of children playing ball.

Reason: It has taken questions about morality out of the decision to end a pregnancy.
Evidence: Her own experiences with doctors and clinics.

Reason: It has allowed middle- and upper-class men and women to avoid the consequences of their sex lives and to evade the responsibilities of parenthood.
Evidence: None offered.

Reason: It has reduced people's sense of duty toward their offspring, most noticeably in the lower classes.

Evidence: Legislation has become necessary to make fathers provide financial support for their children and to hold women legally culpable for harming their fetuses through drug use.

Willis's position: She is for unrestricted abortion as a woman's right.

Claim (or thesis): The right to abortion is an essential part of feminism.

Reason: Without control of their reproductive lives, women constantly fear having their lives disrupted.

Evidence: A fetus makes immense demands on a woman's physical and mental resources. Her own pregnancy is an example.

Reason: Without abortion, women must live according to a sexual double standard.

Evidence: Sex always carries the risk of pregnancy.
The fear of pregnancy puts restrictions on women's ability to enjoy sex for pleasure or passion, rather than procreation.

Following Through

If you and some of your classmates have written arguments taking opposing views on the same issue, prepare briefs of your respective positions to share with one another. (You might also create briefs of your opponents' positions to see how well you have understood one another's written arguments.)

Alternatively, write briefs summarizing the opposing positions offered in several published arguments as a first step toward mediating these viewpoints.

Locating the Areas of Disagreement

Areas of disagreement generally involve differences over facts and differences in interests.

Differences over Facts

Any parties involved in negotiation, as well as any mediator in a dispute, should consider both the reasons and evidence offered on all sides in order to locate areas of factual agreement and, particularly, disagreement. Parties genuinely interested in finding the best solution to a conflict rather than in advocating their own positions ought to be able to recognize when more evidence is needed, no matter the side. Negotiators and mediators should also consider the currency and the authority of any sources. If new or better research could help resolve factual disparities, the parties should do it collaboratively rather than independently.

Following Through

In the preceding arguments on abortion, the writers do not present much factual evidence, as their arguments are relatively abstract. Are there any facts on which they agree? Would more facts make a difference in getting either side to reconsider her position? How could you gather more solid evidence or hard data?

Differences in Interests

Experts in negotiation have found that conflicts most often result from interpretive differences rather than from factual differences; that is, people in conflict look at the same situation differently depending on their values, their beliefs, and their interests. McConnell opens her argument with this very point by showing how most women's rights advocates would interpret the scene at a typical antiabortion protest and then by offering a second perspective, affected by her view that legalized abortion has victimized women.

What kinds of subjective differences cause people to draw conflicting conclusions from the same evidence? To identify these differences, we can ask the same questions that are useful in persuasion to identify what divides us from our audience (see the box "Questions about Difference"). In negotiation and mediation, these questions can help uncover the real interests that any resolution must address. It is in identifying these interests that the dialogue of negotiation begins, because only when the interests that underlie opposing positions are identified can creative solutions be formulated. Often, uncovering each party's real interests leads to the discovery of previously ignored common ground. Finding these interests should be a collaborative project, one that negotiation experts compare to problem-solving through teamwork.

Here we apply the questions about difference to McConnell's and Willis's positions on abortion rights.

Is the Difference a Matter of Assumptions? Both arguments make the assumption that legalizing abortion removed constraints on women's sexuality. McConnell blames abortion for this presumed effect, but Willis credits abortion with enabling women to enjoy sex as men have traditionally been able to do. A mediator might begin by pointing out that this assumption itself could be wrong, that it is possible, for example, that the introduction of birth control pills and the political liberalism of the 1970s contributed more to the increased sexual activity of women. McConnell wants young women not to feel

QUESTIONS ABOUT DIFFERENCE

1. Is the difference a matter of *assumptions*? As we discussed in Chapter 3 on the Toulmin method of analysis and in Chapter 4 on inquiry, all arguments are based on some assumptions.
2. Is the difference a matter of *principle*? Are some parties to the dispute following different principles, or general rules, than others?
3. Is the difference a matter of *values* or a matter of having the same values but giving them different *priorities*?
4. Is the difference a matter of *ends* or *means*? That is, do people want to achieve different goals, or do they have the same goals in mind but disagree on the means to achieve them?
5. Is the difference a matter of *interpretation*?
6. Is the difference a matter of *implications* or *consequences*?
7. Is the difference a result of *personal background, basic human needs,* or *emotions*?

To our list of questions about difference in persuasive writing, we add this last question, because negotiation requires the parties involved to look not just at one another's arguments but also at one another as people, with histories and feelings. It is not realistic to think that human problems can be solved without taking human factors into consideration. Negotiators must be open about their emotions and such basic human needs as personal security, economic well-being, and a sense of belonging, recognition, and control over their own lives. They can be open with one another about such matters only if their dialogue up to this point has established trust between them. If you are mediating among printed texts, you must use the texts themselves as evidence of these human factors.

pressured to have sex, while Willis's interest is in freeing women from a sexual double standard.

McConnell also assumes that abortion becomes guilt-free for most women because it is legal. Willis insists that women should not feel guilty. A mediator might ask what interest McConnell has in making women feel guilty and what Willis means when she says she would now feel "conflict and sadness" (paragraph 14) over choosing an abortion. What is the difference between "conflict and sadness" and "guilt"?

The main assumption these writers do not share concerns the motives of those who cast abortion as a moral issue. Willis assumes that any question about the morality of abortion is part of an effort to repress and subordinate women. This assumption makes Willis see those who disagree with her as a threat to her chief interest—women's rights. McConnell, on the other hand, challenges the feminist assumption that abortion has liberated women. To her the legalization of abortion, rather than protecting women's rights, has actually contributed to the further exploitation of women sexually, which she sees as immoral.

Is the Difference a Matter of Principle? The principle of equal rights for all individuals is featured in both arguments but in different ways. Willis is interested in equal rights among men and women. McConnell is concerned with the equal rights of the fetus as a potential human being.

Is the Difference a Matter of Values or of Priorities? The question of priorities brings us to a key difference underlying the positions of McConnell and Willis. Willis puts the value of a woman's well-being above the value of a fetus's life (paragraph 5). In paragraph 8 she states, "in a society that respects the individual, no [fetus] in *any* stage of development has an 'essential right' to make use of someone else's body . . . without that person's consent." For Willis it is immoral to force any woman to bear a child against her will. For McConnell, however, the interests of the fetus have priority over the interests of the pregnant woman. Denying the fetus's rights in this case is denying nothing less than life itself; therefore, the woman has a duty and responsibility to bear the child, even at great sacrifice to her well-being. For McConnell it is immoral for a woman to refuse this obligation (paragraphs 4 and 33).

In addition, these two writers have very different values regarding sex. For McConnell sex for pleasure, without commitment, is demeaning to women, something that they acquiesce to only because they have been told that it is normal and healthy. For Willis sexual passion "for its own sake is a human need and a human right" (paragraph 11); she seems to be responding directly to McConnell in paragraph 16: "Behind the victim theory of abortion is the implicit belief . . . that sex for pleasure is not only 'irresponsible' (i.e., bad) but something men impose on women, never something women actively seek."

Is the Difference a Matter of Ends or Means? McConnell and Willis both claim to have the same end in mind—a society in which women are truly free and equal, able to live dignified and uncompromised lives. However, they differ over legalized abortion as a means to this end. McConnell does not argue that *Roe v. Wade* should be overturned; rather, she wants her audience to recognize that abortion has cheapened both sex and life, allowing women to be victimized by men who want sex without commitment and encouraging a society that wants rights without responsibilities. Her ultimate goal is higher moral standards for the community. Willis, on the other hand, wants to make sure that freedom and equality for women stay in the forefront of the abortion debate. She resists any compromise on the abortion issue—even the concession that women should feel guilt over having abortions—because she sees the issue of morality as a slope down which women could slide back into a subordinate societal role.

Is the Difference a Matter of Interpretation? These two writers interpret abortion from polar extremes. McConnell sees it as totally negative; to her abortion is a convenience, a way of avoiding responsibility after an act of sexual carelessness. Willis's definition of abortion stresses its positive political value; it is the "cutting edge of feminism" because it guarantees to women absolute reproductive freedom. Furthermore, as we have seen, they interpret individualism differently: for Willis individualism is positive, the autonomy and freedom to reach one's goals; for McConnell it is more negative, with connotations of selfishness and immaturity.

Is the Difference a Matter of Implications or Consequences? Both writers are concerned with consequences, but neither entertains the other's concerns. Willis sees the results of legalized abortion as a more just society. McConnell argues that the positive consequences Willis would claim for women are illusory and that women have been harmed by the easy availability of abortion.

Is the Difference a Result of Personal Background, Basic Human Needs, or Emotions? In their arguments about abortion, both writers are fairly open about some of their emotions. McConnell is quite frank about her "remorse" over her abortion in her first year of college. In her description of that experience, she suggests that she was coerced by the university's health counselors. Notice, too, that she describes herself as the child of "first-generation" Americans, with strict moral standards, a fact that surely influenced her perception of liberated sexual morals.

Willis expresses anger that the arena of debate over abortion has moved from its original focus on women's rights to a new focus on the rights of the fetus. She fears that hard-won ground on women's rights could be slipping. Yet in discussing her own child, she reveals an emotional vulnerability that could possibly make her rethink her position on the morality of abortion. Note, for example, that she mentions her own abortion only once, in paragraph 14.

In face-to-face negotiation and mediation, having a conversation about underlying differences can go a long way toward helping opposing parties understand each other. Each side must "try on" the position of those who see the issue from a different perspective. They may still not agree or let go of their positions, but at this point each side ought to be able to say to the other, "I see what your concerns are." Progress toward resolution begins when people start talking about their underlying concerns or interests rather than their positions.

As a student mediating among written texts, you must decide what you could say to help each side see other viewpoints and to loosen the commitment each has to his or her own position.

Following Through

If you are negotiating between your own position and the arguments of classmates, form groups and use the questions on page 166 to identify the interests of each party. You may ask an outside student to mediate the discussion. As a group prepare a report on your conversation: What are the main interests of each party?

If you are mediating among printed arguments, write an analysis based on applying the questions to two or more arguments. You could write out your analysis in list form, as we did in analyzing the differences between McConnell and Willis, or you could treat it as an exploratory essay (see page 56).

As a creative variation for your analysis, write a dialogue with yourself as mediator, posing questions to each of the opposing parties. Have each side respond to your questions just as we demonstrated in our sample dialogue on pages 43–47.

Defining the Problem in Terms of the Real Interests

As we have said, while it is important in negotiating to see clearly what each side is demanding, successful negotiation looks for a solution that addresses the interests that underlie the positions of each side. Uncovering those interests is the first step. The next is summing them up, recognizing the most important ones a solution must address. Meeting these underlying interests is the task that negotiators undertake collaboratively.

To illustrate, let's look at the two arguments over legalized abortion. Although McConnell criticizes abortion and those who choose it, she admits that she would keep it legal. Her real interest is in reducing what she sees as the consequences of legalized abortion: irresponsible sex and a disregard for life.

Willis is not totally unwilling to consider the moral value of the fetus as human life, admitting that it begins to acquire moral value as it comes to term; her problem with the moral question is the possibility that considering it at all will endanger women's right to choose for—or against—having an abortion. Her real interest is in equality of the sexes.

A mediator between these two positions would have to help resolve the conflict in a way that guarantees women's autonomy and control over their reproductive lives and that promotes responsibility and respect for the value of life. Any resolution here must ensure both the rights of the individual and the good of the community.

Following Through

For the conflict among classmates' positions that you have been negotiating or the conflict among written texts that you have been mediating, write a description of the problem that a resolution must solve: What are the key interests that must be addressed? If you are negotiating, come to a collaborative statement.

Inventing Creative Options

Parties can work toward solutions to a problem collaboratively, each party can brainstorm solutions alone, or an individual mediator can take on this task. Collaboration can either help or hinder the invention process, depending on the relationship of the negotiators. Because coming up with possible solutions means making some concessions, you might want to do so privately rather than state publicly what you would be willing to give up. Whether you are a mediator or a negotiator, this is the stage for exploring options, for entertaining wild ideas, for experimenting without making any judgments.

With respect to the abortion issue, Willis might be willing to consider counseling for women contemplating abortion and admit that the issue inevitably involves some ethical concerns. McConnell might be willing to take a less judgmental position and concede that it is not really fair to impose either motherhood or guilt on every woman with an unwanted pregnancy.

Following Through

1. Think about a possible compromise on the issue of legalized abortion. Your ideas should address the interests of both Willis and McConnell. How likely is it that they would accept your compromise?
2. For a class assignment on negotiating or mediating a dispute, brainstorm possible solutions either independently or collaboratively. Try to make your list of options as long as you can, initially ruling out nothing.

Gathering More Data

Once a mediator has proposed a solution or negotiators have created a tentative resolution, some or all of the parties might be thinking that they could accept it if only they had a little more information. For example, one side in the abortion issue might want to know not only that there are approximately 1.5 million abortions performed each year in the United States but also that many of them are second or third abortions for the same women. If Willis learned that many women have abortions repeatedly, she might agree that the right is being abused—and that some counseling might help. If McConnell were to find out that most women have only a single abortion, she might decide that women do not interpret the right to abortion as nonchalantly as she had imagined. Professional negotiators suggest that information-gathering at this point be done collaboratively. The trust and spirit of collaboration built so far, however, can be damaged if each side tries to gather data favorable to its own original position.

Following Through

1. If you have an idea for a compromise that would address the interests of Willis and McConnell, what additional data do you think either or both of these authors would want to have before accepting your solution?
2. If you have come up with a proposal for resolving a conflict that you and some classmates have been negotiating or that you have been mediating, decide together if additional information could help you reach consensus. What questions need to be answered? Try to answer these questions collaboratively, with a joint visit to the library.

Reaching a Solution Based on Agreed-upon Principles

The kind of negotiation we have been discussing in this chapter is not of the "I-give-a-little, you-give-a-little" sort that occurs between a buyer and seller or in a hostage situation when terrorists offer to trade a number of hostages for an equal number of released prisoners. Such a resolution involves no real principle other than that concessions ought to be of equal value. It brings the opposing sides no closer to understanding why they differed in the first place.

Instead, negotiated settlements on matters of public policy such as abortion or sexual harassment or gun control ought to involve some principles that both sides agree are fair. For example, Willis might agree that abortion ought to be a real choice, not something a woman is railroaded into as McConnell feels she was at age eighteen. Based on this principle Willis might agree that professional counseling about ethics and options ought at least to be available to women considering abortion.

Following Through

If you have been mediating or negotiating a conflict with classmates, formalize your resolution if possible. Be ready to explain what principles you have agreed on as the basis for the compromise.

THE MEDIATORY ESSAY

Arguments that appear in newspapers and popular magazines usually seek to convince or persuade an audience to accept the author's position.

Sometimes, however, the writer assumes the role of mediator and attempts to negotiate a solution acceptable to the opposing sides. This writer moves beyond the stated positions and the facts of the dispute to expose the underlying interests, values, and beliefs of those in opposition. The goal is to show what interests they may have in common, to increase each side's understanding of the other, and to propose a solution to the dispute, a new position based on interests and values that will be acceptable to both sides. The following essay by Roger Rosenblatt aims to mediate one of the most deeply entrenched conflicts of our day—the issue of legalized abortion. As you read it, keep in mind the arguments of Margaret Liu McConnell and Ellen Willis. Do you think that reading this mediatory essay might bring them closer to some consensus on the question of how to live with legalized abortion?

ROGER ROSENBLATT

How to End the Abortion War

Roger Rosenblatt is a writer who regularly contributes to the New York Times Magazine, *where this essay originally appeared.*

THE VEINS in his forehead bulged so prominently they might have been blue worms that had worked their way under the surface of his skin. His eyes bulged, too, capillaries zigzagging from the pupils in all directions. His face was pulled tight about the jaw, which thrust forward like a snowplow attachment on the grille of a truck. From the flattened O of his mouth, the word "murderer" erupted in a regular rhythm, the repetition of the r's giving the word the sound of an outboard motor that failed to catch. 1

She, for her part, paced up and down directly in front of him, saying nothing. Instead, she held high a large cardboard sign on a stick, showing the cartoonish drawing of a bloody coat hanger over the caption, "Never again." Like his, her face was taut with fury, her lips pressed together so tightly they folded under and vanished. Whenever she drew close to him, she would deliberately lower the sign and turn it toward him, so that he would be yelling his "murderer" at the picture of the coat hanger.

For nearly twenty years these two have been at each other with all the hatred they can unearth. Sometimes the man is a woman, sometimes the woman a man. They are black, white, Hispanic, Asian; they make their homes in Missouri or New Jersey; they are teenagers and pharmacists and college professors; Catholic, Baptist, Jew. They have exploded at each other on the steps of the Capitol in Washington, in front of abortion clinics, hospitals, and politicians' homes, on village greens and the avenues of cities. Their rage is tireless; at every decision of the United States Supreme Court or of the President or of the state legislatures, it rises like a missile seeking only the heat of its counterpart.

This is where America is these days on the matter of abortion, or where it seems to be. In fact, it is very hard to tell how the country really feels about abortion, because those feelings are almost always displayed in political arenas. Most ordinary people do not speak of abortion. Friends who gladly debate other volatile issues—political philosophy, war, race—shy away from the subject. It is too private, too personal, too bound up with one's faith or spiritual identity. Give abortion five seconds of thought, and it quickly spirals down in the mind to the most basic questions about human life, to the mysteries of birth and our relationship with our souls.

We simply will not talk about it. We will march in demonstrations, shout 5
and carry placards, but we will not talk about it. In the Presidential election of 1992, we will cast votes for a national leader based in part on his or her position on abortion. Still, we will not talk about it.

The oddity in this unnatural silence is that most of us actually know what we feel about abortion. But because those feelings are mixed and complicated, we have decided that they are intractable. I believe the opposite is true: that we are more prepared than we realize to reach a common, reasonable understanding on this subject, and if we were to vent our mixed feelings and begin to make use of them, a resolution would be at hand.

Seventy-three percent of Americans polled in 1990 were in favor of abortion rights. Seventy-seven percent polled also regard abortion as a kind of killing. (Forty-nine percent see abortion as outright murder, 28 percent solely as the taking of human life.) These figures represent the findings of the Harris and Gallup polls, respectively, and contain certain nuances of opinion within both attitudes. But the general conclusions are widely considered valid. In other words, most Americans are both for the choice of abortion as a principle and against abortion for themselves. One has to know nothing else to realize how conflicted a problem we have before and within us.

The fact that abortion entails conflict, however, does not mean that the country is bound to be locked in combat forever. In other contexts, living with conflict is not only normal to America, it is often the only way to function honestly. We are for both Federal assistance and states' autonomy; we are for both the First Amendment and normal standards of propriety; we are for both the rights of privacy and the needs of public health. Our most productive thinking usually contains an inner confession of mixed feelings. Our least productive thinking, a nebulous irritation resulting from a refusal to come to terms with disturbing and patently irreconcilable ideas.

Yet acknowledging and living with ambivalence is, in a way, what America was invented to do. To create a society in which abortion is permitted and its gravity appreciated is to create but another of the many useful frictions of a democratic society. Such a society does not devalue life by allowing abortion; it takes life with utmost seriousness and is, by the depth of its conflicts and by the richness of its difficulties, a reflection of life itself.

Why, then, are we stuck in political warfare on this issue? Why can we 10
not make use of our ambivalence and move on?

The answer has to do with America's peculiar place in the history of abortion, and also with the country's special defining characteristics, both ancient and modern, with which abortion has collided. In the 4,000-year-old history extending from the Greeks and Romans through the Middle Ages and into the present, every civilization has taken abortion with utmost seriousness. Yet ours seems to be the only civilization to have engaged in an emotional and intellectual civil war over the issue.

There are several reasons for this. The more obvious include the general lack of consensus in the country since the mid-60's, which has promoted bitter divisions over many social issues—race, crime, war, and abortion, too. The sexual revolution of the 60's resulted in the heightened activity of people who declared themselves "pro-choice" *and* "pro-life"—misleading terms used here principally for convenience. The pro-life movement began in 1967, six years before *Roe v. Wade.* The women's movement, also revitalized during the 60's, gave an impetus for self-assertion to women on both sides of the abortion issue.

But there are less obvious reasons, central to America's special character, which have helped to make abortion an explosive issue in this country.

Religiosity. America is, and always has been, a religious country, even though it spreads its religiosity among many different religions. Perry Miller, the great historian of American religious thought, established that the New England colonists arrived with a ready-made religious mission, which they cultivated and sustained through all its manifestations, from charity to intolerance. The Virginia settlement, too, was energized by God's glory. Nothing changed in this attitude by the time the nation was invented. If anything, the creation of the United States of America made the desire to receive redemption in the New World more intense.

Yet individuals sought something in American religion that was different, 15
more emotional than the religion practiced in England. One member of an early congregation explained that the reason he made the long journey to America was "I thought I should find feelings." This personalized sense of religion, which has endured to the present, has an odd but telling relationship with the national attitude toward religion. Officially, America is an a-religious country; the separation of church and state is so rooted in the democracy it has become a cliché. Yet that same separation has created and intensified a hidden national feeling about faith and God, a sort of secret, undercurrent religion, which, perhaps because of its subterranean nature, is often more deeply felt and volatile than that of countries with official or state religions.

The Catholic Church seems more steadily impassioned about abortion in America than anywhere else, even in a country like Poland—so agitated, in fact, that it has entered into an unlikely, if not unholy, alliance with evangelical churches in the pro-life camp. In Catholic countries like Italy, France, and Ireland, religion is often so fluidly mixed with social life that rules are bent more quietly, without our personal sort of moral upheaval.

Americans are moral worriers. We tend to treat every political dispute that arises as a test of our national soul. The smallest incident, like the burning of the flag, can bring our hidden religion to the surface. The largest and most complex moral problem, like abortion, can confound it for decades.

Individualism. Two basic and antithetical views of individualism have grown up with the country. Emerson, the evangelist of self-reliance and non-conformity, had a quasi-mystical sense of the value of the individual self.[1] He described man as a self-sufficient microcosm: "The lightning which explodes and fashions planets, maker of planets and suns, is in him." Tocqueville had a more prosaic and practical view.[2] He worried about the tendency of Americans to withdraw into themselves at the expense of the public good, confusing self-assertion with self-absorption.

Abortion hits both of these views of the individual head on, of course; but both views are open to antipodal interpretations. The Emersonian celebration of the individual may be shared by the pro-choice advocate who sees in individualism one's right to privacy. It may be seen equally by a pro-life advocate as a justification for taking an individual stance—an antiliberal stance to boot—on a matter of conscience.

The idea of the independent individual may also be embraced by the 20
pro-life position as the condition of life on which the unborn have a claim immediately after conception. Pro-life advocates see the pregnant woman as two individuals, each with an equal claim to the riches that American individualism offers.

Tocqueville's concern with individualism as selfishness is also available for adoption by both camps. The pro-life people claim that the pro-choice advocates are placing their individual rights above those of society, and one of the fundamental rights of American society is the right to life. Even the Supreme Court, when it passed *Roe v. Wade,* concluded that abortion "is not unqualified and must be considered against important state interests in regulation."

To those who believe in abortion rights, the "public good" consists of a society in which people, collectively, have the right to privacy and individual choice. Their vision of an unselfish, unself-centered America is one in which the collective sustains its strength by encouraging the independence of those who comprise it. Logically, both camps rail against the individual imposing his or her individual views on society at large, each feeling the same, if opposite, passion about both what society and the individual ought to be. Passion on this subject has led to rage.

Optimism. The American characteristic of optimism, like that of individualism, is affected by abortion in contradictory ways. People favoring the

[1]Ralph Waldo Emerson (1803–1882) was an essayist and leader of New England transcendentalism.

[2]Alexis de Tocqueville (1805–1859) was a French aristocrat and magistrate who toured the United States in 1831 to study the effects of democracy. His classic work *Democracy in America* was first published in 1835.

pro-life position see optimism exactly as they read individual rights: Every American, born or unborn, is entitled to look forward to a state of infinite hope and progress. The process of birth is itself an optimistic activity.

Taking the opposite view, those favoring abortion rights interpret the ideas of hope and progress as a consequence of one's entitlement to free choice in all things, abortion definitely included. If the individual woman wishes to pursue her manifest destiny unencumbered by children she does not want, that is not only her business but her glory. The issue is national as well as personal. The pro-choice reasoning goes: The country may only reach its ideal goals if women, along with men, are allowed to achieve their highest potential as citizens, unburdened by limitations that are not of their own choosing.

Even the element of American "can-do" ingenuity applies. The invention of abortion, like other instruments of American optimism, supports both the pro-life and pro-choice stands. Hail the procedure for allowing women to realize full control over their invented selves. Or damn the procedure for destroying forever the possibility of a new life inventing itself. As with all else pertaining to this issue, one's moral position depends on the direction in which one is looking. Yet both directions are heaving with optimism, and both see life in America as the best of choices.

Sexuality. The connection of abortion with American attitudes toward sexuality is both economic and social. The American way with sex is directly related to the country's original desire to become a society of the middle class, and thus to cast off the extremes of luxury and poverty that characterized Europe and the Old World. The structure of English society, in particular, was something the new nation sought to avoid. Not for Puritan America was the rigid English class system, which not only fixed people into economically immobile slots but allowed and encouraged free-wheeling sexual behavior at both the highest and lowest strata.

At the top of the English classes was a self-indulgent minority rich enough to ignore middle-class moral codes and idle enough to spend their time seducing servants. At the opposite end of the system, the poor also felt free to do whatever they wished with their bodies, since the world offered them so little. The masses of urban poor, created by the Industrial Revolution, had little or no hope of bettering their lot. Many of them wallowed in a kind of sexual Pandemonium, producing babies wantonly and routinely engaging in rape and incest. Between the two class extremes stood the staunch English middle class, with its hands on its hips, outraged at the behavior both above and below them, but powerless to insist on, much less enforce, bourgeois values.

This was not to be the case in America, where bourgeois values were to become the standards and the moral engine of the country. Puritanism, a mere aberrant religion to the English, who were able to get rid of it in 1660 after a brief eighteen years, was the force that dominated American social life for a century and a half. Since there has been a natural progression from Puritanism to Victorianism and from Victorianism to modern forms of fundamentalism in terms of social values, it may be said that the Puritans have really never loosened their headlock on American thinking. The Puritans offered a perfect context for America's desire to create a ruling middle class, which was to be known equally for infinite mobility (geographic, social, economic) and the severest forms of repression.

Abortion fits into such thinking more by what the issue implies than by what it is. In the 1800's and the early 1900's, Americans were able to live with abortion, even during periods of intense national prudery, as long as the practice was considered the exception that proved the rule. The rule was that abortion was legally and morally discouraged. Indeed, most every modern civilization has adopted that attitude, which, put simply, is an attitude of looking the other way in a difficult human situation, which often cannot and should not be avoided. For all its adamant middle-classedness, it was not uncomfortable for Americans to look the other way, either—at least until recently.

When abortion was no longer allowed to be a private, albeit dangerous, business, however, especially during the sexual revolution of the 60's, America's basic middle-classedness asserted itself loudly. Who was having all these abortions? The upper classes, who were behaving irresponsibly, and the lower orders, who had nothing to lose. Abortion, in other words, was a sign of careless sexuality and was thus an offense to the bourgeois dream.

The complaint was, and is, that abortion contradicts middle-class values, which dictate the rules of sexual conduct. Abortion, it is assumed, is the practice of the socially irresponsible, those who defy the solid norms that keep America intact. When *Roe v. Wade* was ruled upon, it sent the harshest message to the American middle class, including those who did not oppose abortion themselves but did oppose the disruption of conformity and stability. If they—certainly the middle-class majority—did not object to *Roe v. Wade* specifically, they did very much object to the atmosphere of lawlessness or unruliness that they felt the law encouraged. Thus the outcry; thus the warfare.

There may be one other reason for abortion's traumatic effect on the country in recent years. Since the end of the Second World War, American society, not unlike modern Western societies in general, has shifted intellectually from a humanistic to a social science culture; that is, from a culture used to dealing with contrarieties to one that demands definite, provable answers. The nature of social science is that it tends not only to identify, but to create issues that must be solved. Often these issues are the most significant to the country's future—civil rights, for example.

What social science thinking does not encourage is human sympathy. By that I do not mean the sentimental feeling that acknowledges another's pain or discomfort; I mean the intellectual sympathy that accepts another's views as both interesting and potentially valid, that deliberately goes to the heart of the thinking of the opposition and spends some time there. That sort of humanistic thinking may or may not be humane, but it does offer the opportunity to arrive at a humane understanding outside the realm and rules of politics. In a way, it is a literary sort of thinking, gone now from a post-literary age, a "reading" of events to determine layers of depth, complication, and confusion and to learn to live with them.

Everything that has happened in the abortion debate has been within the polarities that social science thinking creates. The quest to determine when life begins is a typical exercise of social science—the attempt to impose objective precision on a subjective area of speculation. Arguments over the mother's rights versus the rights of the unborn child are social science arguments, too. The social sciences are far more interested in rights than in how one arrives at what is right—that is, both their strength and weakness. Thus the abortion debate has been political from the start.

A good many pro-choice advocates, in fact, came to lament the political 35
character of the abortion debate when it first began in the 60's. At that time, political thinking in America was largely and conventionally liberal. The liberals had the numbers; therefore, they felt that they could set the national agenda without taking into account the valid feelings or objections of the conservative opposition. When, in the Presidential election of 1980, it became glaringly apparent that the feelings of the conservative opposition were not only valid but were politically ascendant, many liberals reconsidered the idea that abortion was purely a rights issue. They expressed appreciation of a more emotionally complicated attitude, one they realized that they shared themselves, however they might vote.

If the abortion debate had risen in a humanistic environment, it might never have achieved the definition and clarity of the *Roe v. Wade* decision, yet it might have moved toward a greater public consensus. One has to guess at such things through hindsight, of course. But in a world in which humanistic thought predominated, abortion might have been taken up more in its human terms and the debate might have focused more on such unscientific and apolitical components as human guilt, human choice and human mystery.

If we could find the way to retrieve this kind of conflicted thinking, and find a way to apply it to the country's needs, we might be on our way toward a common understanding on abortion, and perhaps toward a common good. Abortion requires us to think one way and another way simultaneously. Americans these days could make very good use of this bifurcated way of thinking.

This brings me back to the concern I voiced at the beginning: Americans are not speaking their true minds about abortion because their minds are in conflict. Yet living with conflict is normal in America, and our reluctance to do so openly in this matter, while understandable in an atmosphere of easy polarities, may help create a false image of our country in which we do not recognize ourselves. An America that declares abortion legal and says nothing more about it would be just as distorted as one that prohibited the practice. The ideal situation, in my view, would consist of a combination of laws, attitudes, and actions that would go toward satisfying both the rights of citizens and the doubts held by most of them.

Achieving this goal is, I believe, within reach. I know how odd that must sound when one considers the violent explosions that have occurred in places like Wichita as recently as August of last year, or when one sees the pro-life and pro-choice camps amassing ammunition for this year's Presidential campaign. But for the ordinary private citizen, the elements of a reasonably satisfying resolution are already in place. I return to the fact that the great majority of Americans both favor abortion rights and disapprove of abortion. Were that conflict of thought to be openly expressed, and were certain social remedies to come from it, we would not find a middle of the road on this issue—logically there is no middle of the road. But we might well establish a wider road, which would accommodate a broad range of beliefs and opinions and allow us to move on to more important social concerns.

What most Americans want to do with abortion is to permit but dis- 40
courage it. Even those with the most pronounced political stands on the subject reveal this duality in the things they say; while making strong defenses of their positions, they nonetheless, if given time to work out their thoughts, allow for opposing views. I discovered this in a great many interviews over the past three years.

Pro-choice advocates are often surprised to hear themselves speak of the immorality of taking a life. Pro-life people are surprised to hear themselves defend individual rights, especially women's rights. And both sides might be surprised to learn how similar are their visions of a society that makes abortion less necessary through sex education, help for unwanted babies, programs to shore up disintegrating families and moral values, and other forms of constructive community action. Such visions may appear Panglossian, but they have been realized before, and the effort is itself salutary.

If one combines that sense of social responsibility with the advocacy of individual rights, the permit-but-discourage formula could work. By "discourage," I mean the implementation of social programs that help to create an atmosphere of discouragement. I do not mean ideas like parental consent or notification, already the law in some states, which, however well-intentioned, only whittle away at individual freedoms. The "discourage" part is the easier to find agreement on, of course, but when one places the "permit" question in the realm of respect for private values, even that may become more palatable.

Already 73 percent of America finds abortion acceptable. Even more may find it so if they can tolerate living in a country in which they may exercise the individual right not to have an abortion themselves or to argue against others having one, yet still go along with the majority who want the practice continued. The key element for all is to create social conditions in which abortion will be increasingly unnecessary. It is right that we have the choice, but it would be better if we did not have to make it.

Were this balance of thought and attitude to be expressed publicly, it might serve some of the country's wider purposes as well, especially these days when there is so much anguish over how we have lost our national identity and character. The character we lost, it seems to me, was one that exalted the individual for what the individual did for the community. It honored and embodied both privacy and selflessness. A balanced attitude on abortion would also do both. It would make a splendid irony if this most painful and troublesome issue could be converted into a building block for a renewed national pride based on good will.

For that to happen, the country's leaders—Presidential candidates come 45
to mind—have to express themselves as well. As for Congress, it hardly seems too much to expect our representatives to say something representative about the issue. Should *Roe v. Wade* be overturned, as may well happen, the country could be blown apart. To leave the matter to the states would lead to mayhem, a balkanization of what ought to be standard American rights. Congress used to pass laws, remember? I think it is time for Congress to make a law like *Roe v. Wade* that fully protects abortion rights, but legislates the kind of community help, like sex education, that would diminish the practice.

Taking a stand against abortion while allowing for its existence can turn out to be a progressive philosophy. It both speaks for moral seriousness and moves in the direction of ameliorating conditions of ignorance, poverty, the social self-destruction of fragmented families, and the loss of spiritual values in general. What started as a debate as to when life begins might lead to making life better.

The effort to reduce the necessity of abortion, then, is to choose life as wholeheartedly as it is to be "pro-life." By such an effort, one is choosing life for millions who do not want to be, who do not deserve to be, forever hobbled by an accident, a mistake or by miseducation. By such an effort, one is also choosing a different sort of life for the country as a whole—a more sympathetic life in which we acknowledge, privileged and unprivileged alike, that we have the same doubts and mysteries and hopes for one another.

Earlier, I noted America's obsessive moral character, our tendency to treat every question that comes before us as a test of our national soul. The permit-but-discourage formula on abortion offers the chance to test our national soul by appealing to its basic egalitarian impulse. Were we once again to work actively toward creating a country where everyone had the same health care, the same sex education, the same opportunity for economic survival, the same sense of personal dignity and worth, we would see both fewer abortions and a more respectable America.

Analyzing a Mediatory Essay

Rosenblatt's argument poses a possible resolution of the abortion controversy and, in so doing, analyzes the opposing positions and interests, as all mediation must. The following analysis shows how Rosenblatt takes his readers through the process of mediation.

Understanding the Spirit of Negotiation

A mediator has to be concerned with his or her own ethos, as well as with helping the opposing parties achieve an attitude that will enable negotiation to begin. The mediator must sound fair and evenhanded; the opposing parties must be open-minded.

Rosenblatt, interestingly, opens his essay in a way that invites commentary. In his first two paragraphs he portrays both sides at their worst, as extremists in no frame of mind to negotiate—and, in fact, in no frame of mind even to speak to each other. In his third paragraph he relates the history of their debate, describing their emotions with words like "hatred" and "rage" and their behavior with metaphors of war and destruction. Readers who see themselves as reasonable will disassociate themselves from the people in these portraits.

Following Through

Do you think Rosenblatt's introduction is a good mediation strategy? In your writer's notebook describe your initial response to Rosenblatt's opening. Having read the whole essay, do you think it is an effective opening? Once he has presented these warriors on both sides, do you think he goes on to discuss the opposing positions and their values in an evenhanded, neutral way? Can you cite some passages where you see either fairness or bias on his part?

Understanding the Opposing Positions

Rosenblatt establishes the opposing positions, already well known, in the first two paragraphs: the "pro-life" position that abortion is murder, the "pro-choice" position that outlawing abortion violates women's rights. Interestingly, Rosenblatt does not wait until the close of the essay to suggest his compromise position. Rather, he presents it in paragraph 9, although he goes into more detail about the solution later in the essay.

Following Through

In your writer's notebook paraphrase Rosenblatt's compromise position on abortion. Do you think this essay would have been more effective if Rosenblatt had postponed presenting his solution?

Locating Areas of Disagreement over Facts

Rosenblatt points out that both sides' focus on the facts alone is what has made the issue intractable. As he points out in paragraph 34, the opposing sides have adopted the "objective precision" of the social sciences: The pro-life side has focused on establishing the precise moment of the beginning of life; the pro-choice side has focused on the absolute rights of women, ignoring the emotions of their conservative opponents.

Following Through

Reread paragraph 33. In your writer's notebook paraphrase Rosenblatt's point about humanistic thinking as opposed to social science thinking. If you have taken social science courses, what is your opinion?

Locating Areas of Disagreement in Interests

Rosenblatt perceives that the disagreement over abortion may in fact be a disagreement over certain underlying interests and emotions held by each side, involving their perceptions about what life should be like in America. His aim is to help the two sides understand how these "less obvious reasons" have kept them from reaching any agreement. At the same time, he points out that many of the differences that seem to put them at odds are tied to common values deeply rooted in American culture. Thus, Rosenblatt attempts to show each side that the other is not a threat to its interests and perceptions of the American way of life.

Rosenblatt notes that both sides share an assumption that is keeping them apart: they both assume that there is one answer to the question of abortion rights, rather than a solution that accepts ambivalence. He locates the source of this assumption in what he calls "social science thinking," which leads both sides to think that problems can be objectively studied and solved apart from human subjectivity. Thus, both sides are ignoring the very thing that is so vital to the process of negotiation and mediation.

Rosenblatt further shows how different principles underlie the arguments of each side. One side bases its argument on the right to privacy and free choice, while the other bases its argument on the right to life. Both principles are fundamental to American society—and neither is completely unqualified.

In addition, Rosenblatt shows how each side values the rights of the individual but interprets these rights differently. For example, antiabortion advocates see the fetus as an individual with the right to life, while pro-choice advocates argue for the individual right of the mother to privacy. In paragraphs 18–22 Rosenblatt shows how two perceptions or interpretations of individualism, one positive (emphasizing self-reliance) and one more critical (emphasizing selfishness), are traceable throughout American culture. In fact, he shows how both sides embrace individualism as an element of their arguments.

In addressing the main difference between the opposing parties over values, Rosenblatt shows how legalized abortion could be perceived as a threat to traditional middle-class economic and social values, and he traces middle-class sexual repression back to the Puritans. Rosenblatt may be stepping outside of the neutral stance of a mediator here, as he suggests that antiabortionists are somewhat prudish. He makes no corresponding remarks about the sexual values of the pro-choice side.

Rosenblatt points out that both sides see different consequences of legalizing abortion. Antiabortion advocates see abortion as destabilizing society and undermining the middle-class American way of life. These people worry not merely about abortion but about an "unruly" society. Pro-choice advocates, on the other hand, see abortion as the route to a better society; as Rosenblatt paraphrases their vision, "the country may only reach its ideal goals if women, along with men, are allowed to achieve their highest potential as citizens . . ." (paragraph 24).

In addressing the emotional characteristics of those involved in the dispute over abortion, Rosenblatt points to the role of religion in America. He explains that Americans historically have been more emotional about religion and morality than people of other nations, even ones where Catholicism is a state religion.

Following Through

Recall the chief areas of difference between Ellen Willis and Margaret Liu McConnell in their respective arguments on the value of abortion rights. In your writer's notebook indicate which of their stated concerns correspond to points in Rosenblatt's analysis of the differences that fuel the abortion war. Does Rosenblatt say anything that might help bring Willis and McConnell closer together?

Defining the Problem in Terms of the Real Interests

Rosenblatt finds the real issue in the abortion controversy to be not whether abortion should be legal or illegal but rather how fundamental, conflicting interests in American society can be addressed. In other words, how can we create laws and institutions that reflect the ambivalence most Americans feel on the topic of abortion? How do we permit abortion legally, in order to satisfy our traditional values for privacy and individual rights, but also discourage it morally, in order to satisfy the American religious tradition that values life, respects fetal rights, and disapproves of casual and promiscuous sex?

Following Through

In your writer's notebook give your opinion of whether Rosenblatt has defined the abortion debate in terms of the opposing sides' real interests. Would his definition of the problem affect related abortion-rights issues, such as making the "abortion pill," or RU 486, available in the United States?

Inventing Creative Options

Rosenblatt's solution is based on what he calls humanistic thinking, that is, thinking that permits conflict and rejects simple solutions to complicated human problems. He shows that many Americans think that abortion is both right and wrong but cannot even talk about their feelings because they are so contradictory. His creative option is for us to accept this ambivalence as a society and pass legislation that would satisfy both "the rights of citizens and the doubts held by most of them" (paragraph 38). In paragraph 45 Rosenblatt suggests that Congress pass a law legalizing abortion but at the same time requiring various activities, such as sex education, that over time promote respect for life and strengthen community moral standards.

Following Through

Reread paragraphs 39–48, and explore in your writer's notebook your opinion of Rosenblatt's proposed solution. Should he have made it more specific?

Gathering More Data

Before opposing sides can reach an agreement based on the real issues, they often need to get more information. Rosenblatt's mediatory argument is short on actual data. In response to his proposed solution, the antiabortion side might have severe doubts that the social programs proposed could in fact reduce the number of abortions performed.

Following Through

In your writer's notebook make suggestions as to what kind of evidence Rosenblatt might have to offer to convince the antiabortion side that sex education and other social programs could reduce the number of abortions performed.

Reaching a Solution Based on Agreed-upon Principles

Rosenblatt attempts to get those who support abortion rights and those who oppose them to reduce their differences by accepting the "permit-but-discourage" principle. This is a principle that American society applies to other areas, such as marital infidelity, which is legal but certainly discouraged through social institutions and customs.

Following Through

1. Reread, if necessary, the two arguments on abortion by McConnell and Willis. Would each writer accept the principle of "permit but discourage"?
2. Draft a letter to the editor of the *New York Times Magazine,* where Rosenblatt's argument originally appeared. In no more than three paragraphs,

evaluate the argument as an attempt at mediation. Then read the following letters to the magazine, responding to Rosenblatt's essay.

Alternatively, write a letter or letters to the editor of the *New York Times,* playing the role of either Willis or McConnell, or both, responding as you think each would.

> Roger Rosenblatt's essay on abortion is timely and welcome ("How to End the Abortion War," Jan. 19). However, his belief that Americans can coalesce on a policy that "discourages" abortion without making it illegal is probably too optimistic. The polarization of Americans on this issue results from some pretty deep differences. Differences in life style, for one thing, can dictate profound political polarization. Many American women derive their most fundamental sense of self-worth from child-rearing and care of the family; many others find theirs in lives that include participation in the larger society, particularly the work place. For women in "traditional" families (and their husbands), untrammeled access to abortion constitutes a form of permissiveness that threatens the things they hold most dear. For women whose identities are tied to work outside the home, the right to control reproductive lives is essential.
>
> So I'm afraid these wars will continue. Rosenblatt and others should not tire in their efforts to find middle ground, but it would be unrealistic to think that we will be able to occupy it together anytime soon.
>
> —PHILIP D. HARVEY, Cabin John, MD

> I don't want to "permit but discourage" abortion. I want to stop abortion the way the abolitionists wanted to stop slavery. I believe slavery is wrong: that no one has the right to assure his or her quality of life by owning another. In the same way, and for the same reasons, I believe abortion is wrong: that no one has the right to assure her quality of life by aborting another.
>
> —ANITA JANDA, Kew Gardens, Queens

> Your article states that "most of us actually know what we feel about abortion." It is true that most people have a position on abortion, but that position is seldom an informed one in this era of the 10-second sound bite and the oversimplification of issues.
>
> Few people understand that *Roe v. Wade* gives the interests of the woman precedence over those of the embryo early in the pregnancy, but allows Government to favor the fetus once it has attained viability.
>
> Were a poll to propose full freedom of choice for women during the early stages of pregnancy, and prohibition of abortion during the later stages, except in cases of fetal deformity or a threat to a woman's life, I believe that the response of the American public would be overwhelmingly positive. Rosenblatt is right on the mark in saying that the public "simply will not talk about abortion." With thoughtful

and dispassionate discussion, we might lay aside the all-or-nothing attitude that currently prevails.

—RICHARD A. KELLEY, Rumson, NJ

Following Through

Analyze the three letters to the *New York Times Magazine* critiquing Rosenblatt's article. What values does each contribute to the debate? How might Rosenblatt respond to each?

Writing a Mediatory Essay

Prewriting

If you have been mediating the positions of two or more groups of classmates or two or more authors of published arguments, you may be assigned to write a mediatory essay in which you argue for a compromise position, appealing to an audience of people on all sides. In preparing to write such an essay, you should work through the steps of negotiation and mediation, as described on pages 148–171. In your writer's notebook prepare briefs of the various conflicting positions, and note areas of disagreement; think hard about the differing interests of the conflicting parties, and respond to the questions about difference on page 166.

If possible, give some thought to each party's background—age, race, gender, and so forth—and how it might contribute to his or her viewpoint on the issue. For example, in a debate about whether *Huckleberry Finn* should be taught and read aloud in U.S. high schools, an African-American parent whose child is the only minority student in her English class might well have a different perspective from that of a white teacher. Can the white teacher be made to understand the embarrassment that a sole black child might feel when the white characters speak with derision about "niggers"?

In your writer's notebook also describe the conflict in terms of the opposing sides' real interests rather than the superficial demands each side might be stating. For example, considering the controversy over *Huckleberry Finn,* you might find some arguments in favor of teaching it anytime, others opposed to teaching it at all, others suggesting that it be an optional text for reading outside of class, and still others proposing that it be taught only in twelfth grade, when students are mature enough to understand Twain's satire. However, none of these suggestions addresses the problem in terms of the real interests involved: a desire to teach the classics of American literature for what they tell us about the human condition and our country's history and values; a desire to promote respect for African-American students; a desire to ensure a comfortable learning climate for all students; and so on. You may be able to see that people's real interests are not as far apart as they might seem. For example, those who advocate teaching *Huckleberry Finn* and those who are opposed may both have in mind the goal of eliminating racial prejudice.

At this point in the prewriting process, think of some solutions that would satisfy at least some of the real interests on all sides. It might be necessary for you to do some additional research. What do you anticipate any of the opposing parties might want to know more about in order to accept your solution?

Finally, write up a clear statement of your compromise. Can you explain what principles it is based on? In the *Huckleberry Finn* debate we might propose that the novel be taught at any grade level provided that it is presented as part of a curriculum to educate students about the African-American experience, with the involvement of African-American faculty or visiting lecturers.

Drafting

There is no set form for the mediatory essay. In fact, it is an unusual, even somewhat experimental, form of writing. The important thing, as with any argument, is that you have a plan for arranging your points and that you provide clear signals to your readers. One logical way to organize a mediatory essay is in three parts:

Overview of the conflict. You describe the conflict and the opposing positions in the introductory paragraphs.

Discussion of differences underlying the conflict. Here your goal is to make all sides more sympathetic to one another and to sort out the important real interests that must be addressed by the solution.

Proposed solution. Here you make a case for your compromise position, giving reasons that it should be acceptable to all—that is, showing that it does serve at least some of their interests.

Revising

When revising a mediatory essay, you should look for the usual problems of organization and development that you would be looking for in any essay to convince or persuade. You want to be sure that you have inquired carefully and fairly into the conflict and that you have clearly presented the cases for all sides, including your proposed solution. At this point you also need to consider how well you have used the persuasive appeals:

The appeal to character. You should think about what kind of character you have projected as a mediator. Have you maintained neutrality? Do you model open-mindedness and genuine concern for the sensitivities of all sides?

The appeal to emotions. To arouse sympathy and empathy, which are needed in negotiation, you should take into account the emotional appeals discussed on pages 139–140. Your mediatory essay should be a moving argument for understanding and overcoming difference.

The appeal through style. As in persuasion, you should put the power of language to work for you. Pay attention to concrete word choice, striking metaphors, and phrases that stand out because of repeated sounds and rhythms.

For suggestions about editing and proofreading, see Appendix A.

Student Sample: A Mediatory Essay

The following mediatory essay was written by Angi Grellhesl, a first-year student at Southern Methodist University. Her essay examines opposing written views on the institution of speech codes at various U.S. colleges and its effect on freedom of speech.

ANGI GRELLHESL

Mediating the Speech Code Controversy

THE RIGHT to free speech has raised many controversies over the years. Explicit lyrics in rap music and marches by the Ku Klux Klan are just some examples that test the power of the First Amendment. Now, students and administrators are questioning if, in fact, free speech ought to be limited on university campuses. Many schools have instituted speech codes to protect specified groups from harassing speech. 1

Both sides in the debate, the speech code advocates and the free speech advocates, have presented their cases in recent books and articles. Columnist Nat Hentoff argues strongly against the speech codes, his main reason being that the codes violate students' First Amendment rights. Hentoff links the right to free speech with the values of higher education. In support, he quotes Yale president Benno Schmidt, who says, "Freedom of thought must be Yale's central commitment. . . . [U]niversities cannot censor or suppress speech, no matter how obnoxious in content, without violating their justification for existence. . . ." (qtd. in Hentoff 223). Another reason Hentoff offers against speech codes is that universities must teach students to defend themselves in preparation for the real world, where such codes cannot shield them. Finally, he suggests that most codes are too vaguely worded; students may not even know they are violating the codes (216).

Two writers in favor of speech codes are Richard Perry and Patricia Williams. They see speech codes as a necessary and fair limitation on free speech. Perry and Williams argue that speech codes promote multicultural awareness, making students more sensitive to the differences that are out there in the real world. These authors do not think that the codes violate First Amendment rights, and they are suspicious of the motives of those who say they do. As Perry and Williams put it, those who feel free speech rights are being threatened "are apparently unable to distinguish between a liberty interest on the one hand and, on the other, a quite specific interest in being able to spout racist, sexist, and homophobic epithets completely unchallenged—without, in other words, the terrible inconvenience of feeling bad about it" (228).

Perhaps if both sides trusted each other a little more, they could see that their goals are not contradictory. Everyone agrees that students' rights should be protected. Hentoff wishes to ensure that students have the right to speak their minds. He and others on his side are concerned about freedom. Defenders of the codes argue that students have the right not to be harassed, especially while they are getting an education. They are concerned about opportunity. Would either side really deny that the other's goal had value?

Also, both sides want to create the best possible educational environ- 5
ment. Here, the difference rests on the interpretation of what benefits the students. Is the best environment one most like the real world, where prejudice and harassment occur? Or does the university have an obligation to provide an atmosphere where potential victims can thrive and participate freely without intimidation?

I think it is possible to reach a solution that everyone can agree on. Most citizens want to protect constitutional rights; but they also agree that those rights have limitations, the ultimate limit being when one person infringes on the rights of others to live in peace. All sides should agree that a person ought to be able to speak out about his or her convictions, values, and beliefs. And most people can see a difference between that protected speech and the kind that is intended to harass and intimidate. For example, there is a clear difference between expressing one's view that Jews are mistaken in not accepting Christ as the son of God, on the one hand, and yelling anti-Jewish threats at a particular person in the middle of the night, on the other. Could a code not be worded in such a way as to distinguish between these two kinds of speech?

Also, I don't believe either side would want the university to be an artificial world. Codes should not attempt to ensure that no one is criticized or even offended. Students should not be afraid to say controversial things. But universities do help to shape the future of the real world, so shouldn't they at least take a stand against harassment? Can a code be worded that would protect free speech and prevent harassment?

The current speech code at Southern Methodist University is a compromise that ought to satisfy free speech advocates and speech code advocates. It prohibits hate speech at the same time that it protects an individual's First Amendment rights.

First, it upholds the First Amendment by including a section that reads, "due to the University's commitment to freedom of speech and expression, harassment is more than mere insensitivity or offensive conduct which creates an uncomfortable situation for certain members of the community" (*Peruna* 92). The code therefore should satisfy those, like Hentoff, who place a high value on the basic rights our nation was built upon. Secondly, whether or not there is a need for protection, the current code protects potential victims from hate speech or "any words or acts deliberately designed to disregard the safety or rights of another, and which intimidate, degrade, demean, threaten, haze, or otherwise interfere with another person's rightful action" (*Peruna* 92). This part of the code should satisfy those who recognize that some hurts cannot be overcome. Finally, the current code outlines specific acts that constitute harassment: "Physical, psychological, verbal and/or written acts directed toward an individual or group of individuals which rise to the level of 'fighting words' are prohibited" (*Peruna* 92).

The SMU code protects our citizens from hurt and from unconstitu- 10
tional censorship. Those merely taking a position can express it, even if it hurts. On the other hand, those who are spreading hatred will be limited as to what harm they may inflict. Therefore, all sides should respect the code as a safeguard for those who use free speech but a limitation for those who abuse it.

WORKS CITED

Hentoff, Nat. "Speech Codes on the Campus and Problems of Free Speech." *Debating P.C.* Ed. Paul Berman. New York: Bantam, 1992. 215–24.

Perry, Richard, and Patricia Williams. "Freedom of Speech." *Debating P.C.* Ed. Paul Berman. New York: Bantam, 1992. 225–30.

Peruna Express 1993–1994. Dallas: Southern Methodist U, 1993.

CHAPTER EIGHT

Image and Argument: Visual Rhetoric

We live in a world awash in pictures. We turn on the TV and see not just performers, advertisers, and talking heads but dramatic footage of events from around the world, commercials as visually creative as works of art, and video images to accompany our popular music. We boot up our computers and surf the Net; many of the waves we ride are visual swells, enticing images created or enhanced by the very machines that take us out to sea. We drive our cars through a gallery of street art—on billboards and buildings and on the sides of buses and trucks. We go to movies, video stores, arcades, and malls and window-shop, entertained by the images of fantasy fulfillment each retailer offers. So-called print media are full of images; in our newspapers, for instance, photos, drawings, and computer graphics have gone to color and vie with print for space. Even college textbooks, once mostly blocks of uninterrupted prose with an occasional black-and-white drawing or photo, now often have colorful graphics and elaborate transparency overlays.

If a picture is indeed worth a thousand words, then perhaps our image-saturated world is all to the good. Or perhaps, as some argue, all this rapid-fire, reality-manipulating technology yields jaded people with short attention spans, who haven't the patience for the slower thinking pace of print. But no matter how we assess it, the technology rolls on, continually extending its range and reach, filling our minds and, more importantly, *forming* them. Visual images are not just "out there," clamoring for our attention, but also "in here," part of how we attend to and judge experience. Like language, visual images are rhetorical. They persuade us in obvious and not-so-obvious ways. And so we need some perspective on visual rhetoric; we need to learn how to recognize its power and how to use it effectively and responsibly.

UNDERSTANDING VISUAL RHETORIC

What is "visual rhetoric"? It's *the use of images, sometimes coupled with sound or appeals to the other senses, to make an argument or persuade us to act as the image-maker would have us act.* Probably the clearest examples are advertisements and political cartoons, a few of which we will shortly examine. But visual rhetoric is as ubiquitous and as old as human civilization. We do not ordinarily think, say, of a car's body style as "rhetoric," but clearly it is, because people are persuaded to pay tens of thousands of dollars for the sleekest new body style when they could spend a few thousand for an older car that would get them from home to work or school just as well. Consider also the billions of dollars we spend on clothes, hairstyles, cosmetics, diets, and exercise programs—all part of the rhetoric of making the right "visual statement" in a world that too often judges us solely by how we look. Clearly, we spend so much because our self-images are wrapped up in how others respond to our cars, bodies, offices, homes—to whatever makes an appearance in the world as representing "us." No doubt we all want to be liked and loved for our true selves, but distinguishing this "inside" from the "outside" we project to the world has never been easy. Because we tend to become the image we cultivate, the claim that "Image is everything" may not be as superficial as it sounds. Even if not everything, image certainly is important enough to preoccupy us, and we would be hard-pressed to name a significant human activity not entangled in visual rhetoric.

We might imagine that visual rhetoric is something peculiarly modern—that without photography, computers, and Madison Avenue it wouldn't amount to much. But we would be mistaken. The pharaohs of ancient Egypt didn't build the pyramids merely to have a place to be buried; these immense structures "proclaim" the power and status of the rulers who had them built, as well as the civilization and empire they symbolize, and they "argue" against a view of human existence as merely transitory, without connection to the eternal. Even now, millennia after Egypt's decline, we can only stand before the pyramids in awe and wonder. The impact of visual rhetoric is not always as fleeting as the clever new commercial on television.

As old as the pyramids are, visual rhetoric is still older. We will never find its origins, for it began with natural places that prehistoric people invested with sacred power, with the earliest drawings and paintings, with natural and sculpted objects used in religious rites and festivals. When a culture disappears, most visual rhetoric is lost, leaving only a few fragments that archaeologists dig up and speculate about thousands of years later. There is no way to know exactly what these artifacts meant and no way to even estimate what remains undiscovered or lost beyond any possibility of recovery.

But if there is much that we cannot know about visual rhetoric—where and why it began, or what it might be like hundreds or thousands of years in the future, in cultures we cannot imagine, using technologies we cannot envision—we can still study how it works now, in our culture and time. We can learn to appreciate the art that goes into making potent images. We can learn how to interpret them. We can learn how to evaluate them. We can reflect on the ethics of visual argumentation and persuasion. We can create visual rhetoric ourselves, in images that stand alone, without words, or in visuals combined with text. This chapter will present analysis of some common forms of visual rhetoric. The assignments will give you practice in analyzing and in creating visual rhetoric of your own.

ANALYSIS: COMMON TYPES OF VISUAL RHETORIC

"Reading" Images

Rhetorical analysis of visual rhetoric involves examining images to see how they attempt to convince or persuade an audience. We must first recognize that "reading" an image demands interpretive skills, no less than reading a written text. Pictures, even photographs, do not merely reflect reality, as many people assume. Pictures are symbols that must be read, just as language is read, and that becomes clear when we look at art from different cultures. The bodies in Egyptian paintings seem distorted to us, flattened onto a geometrical plane in a combination of full frontal and profile views, but the Egyptians understood these figures as representing a timeless and ideal human form. Also, visual symbols operate within a culture—the color white, for example, can suggest purity in one culture and death in another culture. To read an argument made through images, a critic must be able to recognize visual allusions to other aspects of the culture. For example, initially, Americans knew that the white mustaches on the celebrities in the milk commercials alluded to children's milk-drinking style; but more recently, the milk mustache has become an allusion to the ad campaign itself, which has become part of our culture.

As with inquiry into any argument, we ought to begin with questions about rhetorical context: When was the visual argument created, and by whom? To what audience was it originally aimed, and with what purpose? Then we can ask what claim a visual argument makes and what reasons it offers in support of that claim. "Reading" the claims and reasons of purely visual arguments requires greater interpretive skills than reading verbal arguments, simply because pictures are even more ambiguous than words—they mean different things to different people. Then, as with verbal texts that make a case, we can examine the visual argument for evidence, assumptions, and bias, and we can ask what values it favors and what will be the implications of accepting the argument—for instance, if we buy the Jaguar, what kind of debt will we be in?

Although it is possible to make a claim and support it with no words at all, most arguments that use images do not rest their cases entirely on the images. If the visual argument includes some verbal text, some of the reasoning usually appears in the words. Either way, if we see that an argument is being offered, we can inquire into it as we have done with verbal texts: What is the claim? the reason(s)? the evidence? the assumptions? the bias? the implications? What values are being promoted? We cannot, however, expect visual arguments to make a fully developed argument to convince.

Many visual arguments do not even attempt to persuade through reasoning; they rely instead on ethical and emotional appeals. Appeals to emotions and character are frequent and powerful in visual arguments. They are most obvious in advertising, where the aim is clearly to move a target audience to buy a service or product. In many advertisements, especially for products like beer, cigarettes, and perfume, where the differences are subjective or virtually nonexistent, emotional appeal and character identification are all there is. Although some images make us fear what will happen if we don't buy the product, vote for the candidate, or at least believe the argument's claim, most emotional appeals work by promising to reward our desires for love, status, peace of mind, or escape from the everyday responsibilities of life.

Advertisements and other forms of visual argument use ethical appeals as well, associating their claim with values the audience would approve of and want to identify with—such as images that show nature being preserved, races living in harmony, families staying in touch, and people attaining the American dream of upward mobility. However, some advertisements appeal to counterculture values through images of rebellion against conventional respectability. Such ads project an ethos of "attitude" and rule-breaking.

In evaluating the ethics of visual rhetoric, we need to consider whether the argument appeals to logic, and if so, whether the case is at least reasonable: Does the image encourage good reasoning, or does it oversimplify and even mislead? Most likely, we will want to look for the emotional and ethical appeals as well and decide if the argument panders to audience members by playing to their weaknesses and prejudices or manipulates them by playing to their fantasies and fears. We can ask what values the image seems to endorse or want the audience to identify with, and we can question the implications of widespread acceptance of such values and behavior.

In the next pages, we will analyze some specific visual arguments in various genres: advertisements, editorial cartoons, public sculpture, and news photographs. We will see how "reading" visual texts requires interpretive skills and how interpretive skills, in turn, depend on the critic's knowledge of the context in which the image appears. Practice in analyzing visual rhetoric helps us appreciate the role of culture and context in all communication.

Advertisements

In the arguments made by advertisments, the claims, if not the reasons, are usually clear. And, because advertisers aim carefully at a target audience, we can readily see how strategy comes into play in making a persuasive case and in choosing ethical and emotional appeals. Here, we examine some advertisements to see how visual images and verbal texts combine to sell products and services to specific audiences.

An advertisement for Pentax (see plate 1 in the color section) appeared originally in *Sierra* magazine, published by the environmentalist Sierra Club. *Sierra*'s readership is primarily middle-class adults who love nature and are concerned about preserving the environment. It is not a radical environmental group, however, and most of the ads and articles are of interest to parents planning family trips and wanting to ensure that wilderness will be around for their children and grandchildren to enjoy.

The logical appeal of the ad is obvious. The ad argues that readers should buy a Pentax IQZoom 140M because it is a convenient, light camera with many features that will help them take great pictures. The features of the camera are the reasons for buying it, and these are clearly indicated by the large photo of the camera itself and the text in red print. The small, tacked-on snapshot of the boys is evidence in support of the reasons. Readers who want a user-friendly camera would find the argument persuasive. They want good pictures with minimal fussing. However, rather than letting the argument rest on the technological features of the camera, the advertisers depend heavily on ethical and emotional appeals to sell it to the *Sierra* readers.

The ad features the image of a stock character in mainstream American culture—the soccer mom, although in this case she is the Badger den mother. The choice of this figure shows the strategy of ethical appeal targeted at parents: a wholesome, friendly, young mother reaches out—literally—and gives a "testimony" about how successfully she uses the camera. The advertiser expects that *Sierra* readers would trust such a character and admire her values. Her affectionate descriptions of the "scrappy champions" and her reference to the "box of bandages" show that she is loving and nurturing. The Band-Aid on her right knee shows that she is a participant in the action. She is energetic and cheerful in her bright yellow uniform as she smiles up at the readers. They would find nothing in this ad to intimidate them or challenge their ideas about traditional gender roles for women and boys. In short, she confirms middle-American values.

None of what we have said so far addresses the real appeal of the ad, however. The advertisers wanted to get the audience laughing, and the eye-catching image of the woman does just that as it plays with photographic effects. The knowledge of how to "read" a two-dimensional photograph as a realistic image of three-dimensional space is nearly universal, but this image distorts even that "reality," providing some ridiculous relationships in size, such as between the woman's head and the cap that should fit it. The camera and the woman's hand seem grossly out of proportion as they float above her tiny hiking boots. These distortions of reality are funny, not threatening or disorienting as images in serious art photography can be. Most Americans know that such distorted effects occur when a wide-angle lens is used for a close-up or when the dog decides to sniff the wide-angle lens. Like the exaggeratedly childish uniform on the woman, the wide-angle distortions are merely for fun.

The direct, friendly relationship between the woman in the ad and the viewers is supported by the angle of the camera that took her photograph. The camera angle puts the viewers above her, in the position of power. There is nothing intimidating or pretentious about this ad, which suggests through both visual images and verbal text that the Pentax IQZoom 140M is a way for ordinary people to capture fun on film.

Another example of visual rhetoric, this one in an ad for GMC cars, relies even more on ethical and emotional appeals than does the Pentax ad. This ad, which is shown in plate 2 of the color section, originally appeared in April 1999 in *Ebony,* a publication aimed at African-American readers. While most advertisements for cars make a point of showing the car—typically parked in front of an expensive restaurant or racing down a winding road—the GMC advertisers opted to forgo the usual appeals to status and power. Instead, they used an image that links their cars to values and traditions that female readers of *Ebony* would find appealing.

The picture of three generations of women is striking in its expression of happiness, love, and self-confidence. It looks like a family snapshot of a farewell embrace as the youngest woman sets out on her adult life. Like the Pentax ad, this ad includes a verbal text, in the form of a short note from the granddaughter in the picture about the qualities she inherited from the two older women and the role of GMC cars in her family's history. The text not only claims that GMC cars are "trusty" and dependable enough to be passed from generation to generation but also connects the brand name with the family's strong work ethic, independence, and sense of adventure.

These are traditional American values. Citing them is a savvy rhetorical move for an advertiser who wants to connect an American brand name with ideas America stands for. The ad suggests that GMC cars help individuals, notably African-American women in this case, make something of themselves. It associates GMC with the pursuit of the American dream. The patriotic appeal of the ad is strengthened by the prominent word "independence" connecting the picture and the text.

Automobiles are more than transportation. They are a reflection of how Americans see themselves and how they want others to see them. It is not surprising, then, that an ad could succeed by showing not the GMC cars, but an image of free and independent women who drive them.

Visual images with little or no accompanying text can be powerfully persuasive by implying an argument rather than stating it explicitly. Good examples come from the advertisements for public service organizations, which promote ideas rather than products. Consider the poster reproduced in plate 3 of the color section, created by an advertising agency for the Southampton Anti-Bias Task Force. It shows a line of five sharp new crayons, all labeled "flesh." On one level, a viewer may see the poster as an eye-catching message for racial tolerance. However, anyone old enough to recall a now-discontinued Crayola crayon called "flesh" that was the color of the center crayon will see a more complicated argument. This prior knowledge allows viewers to read the image as an argument against the cultural bias that allowed millions of children to grow up thinking that "flesh" was the color skin was supposed to be—and all other skin colors were deviations from the norm. While white people might remember thinking that this "flesh" didn't quite match their own, they knew it approximated the color of white people's skin. Children of other races or mixed races knew that "flesh" was not their flesh. For all who remember the crayon, the poster alludes to one example of bias that for too long went unseen in a common toy that shaped children's minds as they played.

Because an image invites interpretation rather than blatantly stating a message, it opens a space for contemplation, just as we may contemplate the implied message of any work of art—fiction, film, poetry, painting. Our own reading of this poster led us to wonder if other examples of bias exist in American culture, invisible to all except the victims. This thought is our own extension of the poster's message, and like all interpretation, it evolved as part of the interaction between text and reader. As we noted earlier in this chapter, studying visual rhetoric reminds us of the reader's contribution to the meaning of any text, visual or verbal.

Following Through

1. Gather an assortment of automobile advertisements, some from magazines aimed at women and some from magazines with a primarily male readership. Can you make any generalizations about what appeals are more common for each sex?
2. Although the advertisement for the Volkswagen Beetle, shown in plate 4 of the color section, features an image of the product, as is customary with car ads, the lack of background, the size of the image relative to the white space surrounding it, and the unusual wording of the text all contribute to making this an unconventional piece of visual rhetoric. Consider these elements and any other aspect of the ad as you discuss how it might appeal to a specific audience of car buyers.
3. An advertisement for Comstock, Inc., a company that stocks photographs for commercial purposes, promotes its service with a striking example of its own product. The company wishes to persuade potential clients that it can supply a visual image for any idea. Discuss how the image of the goldfish bowl, shown in plate 5 of the color section, conveys the feeling of being "stuck." Do you find the image and accompanying text persuasive? Pictures, like words, often convey multiple meanings; what other possible readings of this image can you think of?
4. The Adidas advertisement shown in plate 8 of the color section is an example of the creative effects possible with photographic techniques. How

do you "read" the image of the man in relation to the image of the shadow? How does the entire picture convey the idea of speed? How are parallel and intersecting lines used to connect the runner with the Adidas logo? Why do you think the advertisers chose to identify the celebrity athlete in such fine print?

Editorial Cartoons

Editorial cartoons comment on events and issues in the news. At times they can be riotously funny, but more often they offer serious arguments in a concise and witty form. Many political cartoons rely on captions and dialogue, spoken by characters in the picture, to make their argument, so they combine visual and verbal argument. Like advertisements, editorial cartoons are not ambiguous in their purpose; their arguments are clearly stated, or at least easily inferred. However, as they age, editorial cartoons may become harder to "read," because they usually allude to current events. But some cartoons have longer lifespans, like the one by Mike Keefe on the facing page that comments on a general condition of contemporary culture—how computers are affecting people's ideas of knowledge.

This cartoon illustrates how "reading" a visual argument depends on a shared knowledge of symbols and visual metaphors within a culture. The image of a thirsty man crawling on hands and knees through a desert is a common visual metaphor suggesting any environment that denies humans something they need to sustain themselves. Other treatments of this metaphor suggest that sustenance could be anything from love, to religion, to the music of Mozart. In Keefe's cartoon, a highway labeled "information" runs through the desert. The cartoon takes our common metaphor for the Internet, as "information superhighway," and depicts it in a literal way. The man is literally on the Internet, and he is desperate for "wisdom." To read the argument of the cartoon and appreciate its humor, the viewer has to know something about what can be found on the Internet—the advertising, the data, the opinions, and especially the overwhelming glut of information, as suggested by the size of the letters on the road. The cartoon argues that relying on the Internet for knowledge will deprive a civilization of the wisdom it needs to sustain itself.

We might question how convincing political cartoons can be. Can they change people's views on an issue? A picture may indeed be worth a thousand words, but visual arguments have to present a concise argument, not a fully reasoned case. Anthony Blair, one critic of visual arguments, has written that "visual arguments tend to be one-dimensional; they present the case for one side only, without including arguments against it. . . . Visual arguments, then, must always be suspect in this respect, and their power countered by a degree of skepticism and a range of critical questions: 'Is that the whole story?' 'Are there other points of view?' 'Is the real picture so black and white?'"

Cartoons also may fail to change people's minds because their humor comes at the expense of the side they oppose—they satirize and often exaggerate the opposition's view. In fact, political cartoons are usually arguments that "preach to the choir." Believers will applaud having their position cleverly portrayed, while nonbelievers will be more annoyed or offended than persuaded by cartoons that ridicule their position. Consider the two cartoons on the next page which use both language and visual images to make cases about what the cartoonists see as misplaced priorities in the pro-life and the pro-choice movements.

The McCloskey cartoon (top) argues that the pro-choice demonstrators are hypocritical in their protests over murdered doctors, for they ignore the death of the fetus. The lower half of the drawing emphasizes the fetus by putting it in a black background and giving it wings to symbolize its human soul. This half of the cartoon stands in stark contrast to the "noisy" upper half, in which the protesters look deranged. In the Luckovich cartoon (bottom), an example of black humor, the contrast is between the shapeless fetus and the more fully depicted corpse of the doctor, both preserved in specimen bottles. One is a person; the other clearly is not. Viewers on either side of this issue would argue that these portraits misrepresent their positions through oversimplification.

Following Through

1. The cartoon by Gary Varvel on page 201 comments on attempts in Oregon to legalize doctor-assisted suicide. This is not a funny topic, but Varvel makes a humorous comment on it by exploiting a stock situation in American comedy—the ledge-jumper and the would-be rescuer. How does the

1994 THE DAILY NEWS LEADER McCLOSKEY
WE DEPLORE THIS ACT OF SENSELESS VIOLENCE— THE ABORTION DOCTOR'S LIFE WAS TAKEN AWAY FROM HIM !!
HE WON'T HAVE THE CHANCE TO LIVE OUT HIS LIFE !!
PRO-Choice
But What about ME?

We object to this one....
DEAD ABORTION Doctor
Dead Fetus
PRO-LIFE
Mike Luckovich
ATLANTA CONSTITUTION

humor work here to poke fun at the idea of doctor-assisted suicide? What aspects of the "big picture" does the cartoon leave out?

2. Find a recent editorial cartoon on an issue of interest to you. Bring it to class, and be prepared to elaborate on its argument and explain its persuasive tactics. Do you agree or disagree with the cartoonist's perspective? Discuss the fairness of the cartoon. Does it minimize the complexity of the issue it addresses?

Public Sculpture

Public sculptures, such as war memorials, aim to teach an audience about a nation's past and to honor the values for which its citizens were willing to die. An example of a public sculpture that can be read as an argument is the Marine Corps Memorial (better known as the Iwo Jima Memorial), which was erected in 1954 on the Mall in Washington, DC (see the photograph on page 202). The memorial honors all Marines who have given their lives for their country through a literal depiction of one specific act of bravery, the planting of the American flag on Iwo Jima, a Pacific island that the United States captured from the Japanese in 1945. The claim that the sculpture makes to American audiences is clear: "Honor your country." The image of the soldiers straining every muscle to raise the American flag gives the reason: "These men made extreme sacrifices to preserve the values symbolized by this flag." Interpreting the memorial is not difficult for Americans who associate the flag with freedom and who know not only the military custom of raising

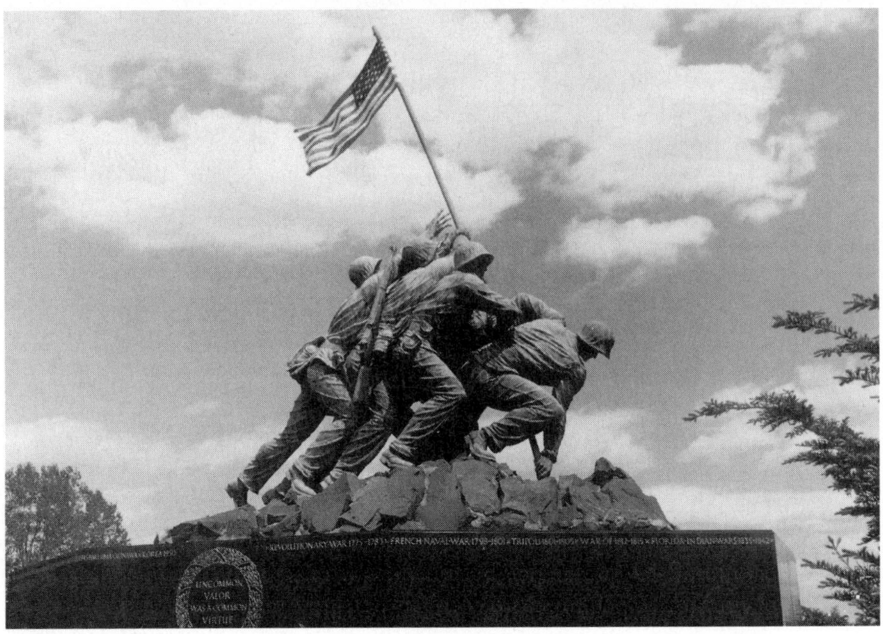

flags in victory but the history of the fierce Iwo Jima battle. But the sculpture has more to say. It communicates an emotional appeal to patriotism through details like the wind-whipped flag and the angles of the men's arms and legs, which suggest their supreme struggle.

The Iwo Jima sculpture is indeed a classic war memorial, glorifying a victory on enemy soil. We might therefore compare its argument with the argument of a very different memorial, the Vietnam War Memorial, which was dedicated in Washington in November 1982. Maya Lin designed what has come to be known simply as "the Wall" while she was an undergraduate architecture student at Yale. Her design was controversial because the monument was so untraditional in its design (see the two photographs on page 203) and in its argument, which is ambiguous and more difficult to interpret than most public sculpture. With its low, black, granite slates into which are etched the names of the war casualties, the Wall conveys a somber feeling; it honors not a victory but the individuals who died in a war that tore the nation apart.

Following Through

1. The Vietnam War Memorial invites interpretation and analysis. Because it does not portray a realistic scene or soldiers as the Iwo Jima Memorial does, readings of it may vary considerably—and this was the source of the controversy surrounding it. Look at the two photographs here, and if you have visited the Wall, try to recall your reaction to it. What specific details—the

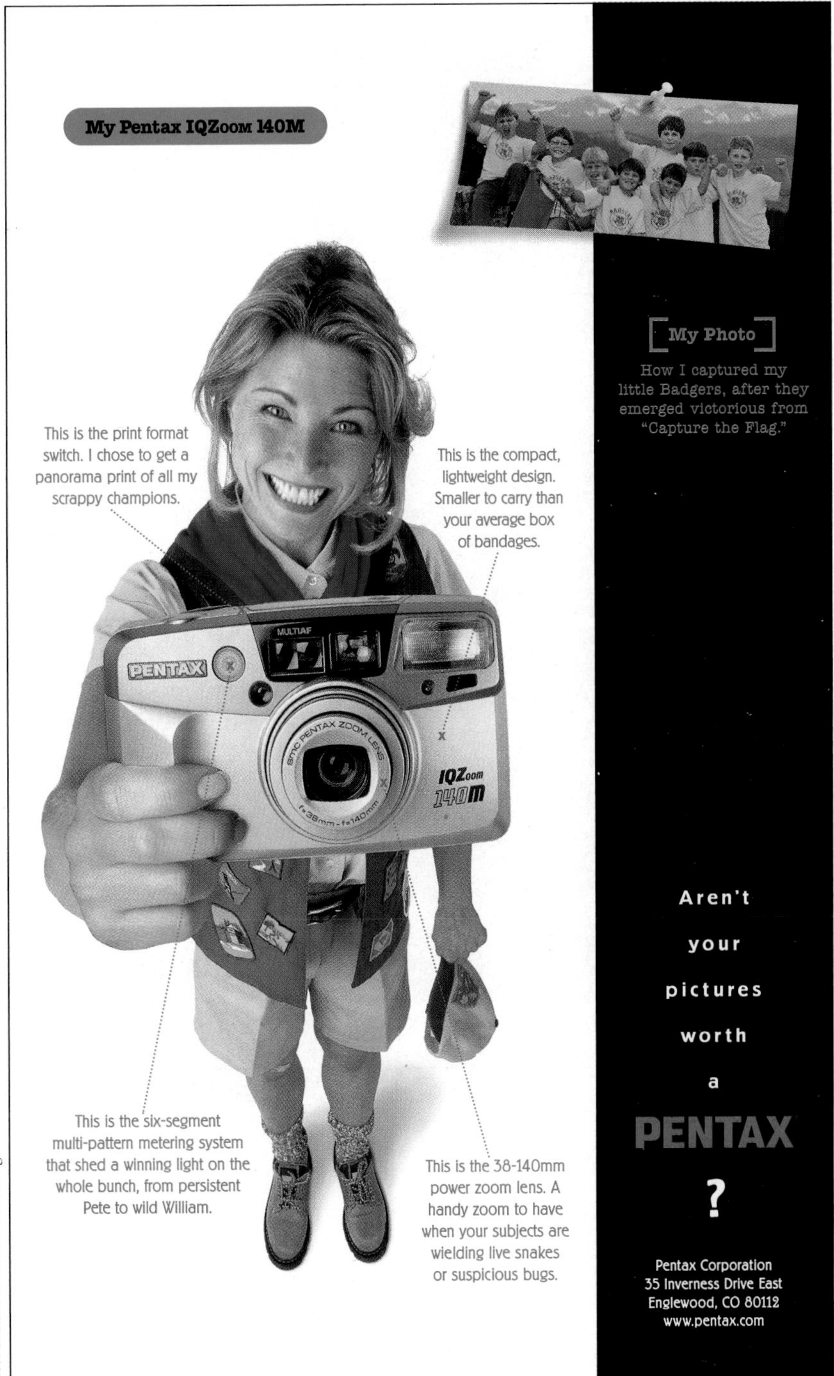

My Pentax IQZoom 140M
My Photo
How I captured my little Badgers, after they emerged victorious from "Capture the Flag."
This is the print format switch. I chose to get a panorama print of all my scrappy champions.
This is the compact, lightweight design. Smaller to carry than your average box of bandages.
This is the six-segment multi-pattern metering system that shed a winning light on the whole bunch, from persistent Pete to wild William.
This is the 38-140mm power zoom lens. A handy zoom to have when your subjects are wielding live snakes or suspicious bugs.
Aren't your pictures worth a PENTAX?
Pentax Corporation
35 Inverness Drive East
Englewood, CO 80112
www.pentax.com

Source: Thomas & Perkins Advertising

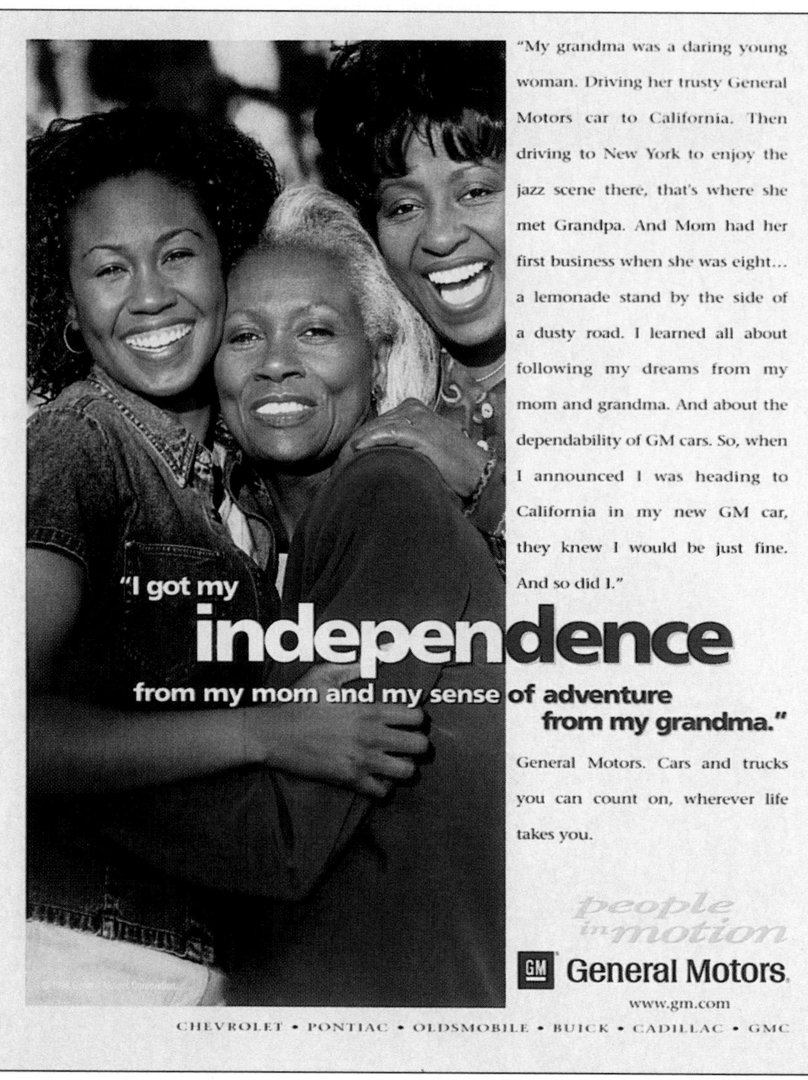

"My grandma was a daring young woman. Driving her trusty General Motors car to California. Then driving to New York to enjoy the jazz scene there, that's where she met Grandpa. And Mom had her first business when she was eight... a lemonade stand by the side of a dusty road. I learned all about following my dreams from my mom and grandma. And about the dependability of GM cars. So, when I announced I was heading to California in my new GM car, they knew I would be just fine. And so did I."
"I got my
independence
from my mom and my sense of adventure
from my grandma."
General Motors. Cars and trucks you can count on, wherever life takes you.
people in motion
GM General Motors
www.gm.com
CHEVROLET • PONTIAC • OLDSMOBILE • BUICK • CADILLAC • GMC

Source: Copyright 1998 General Motors Corp.
Used with permission of GM Media Archives.

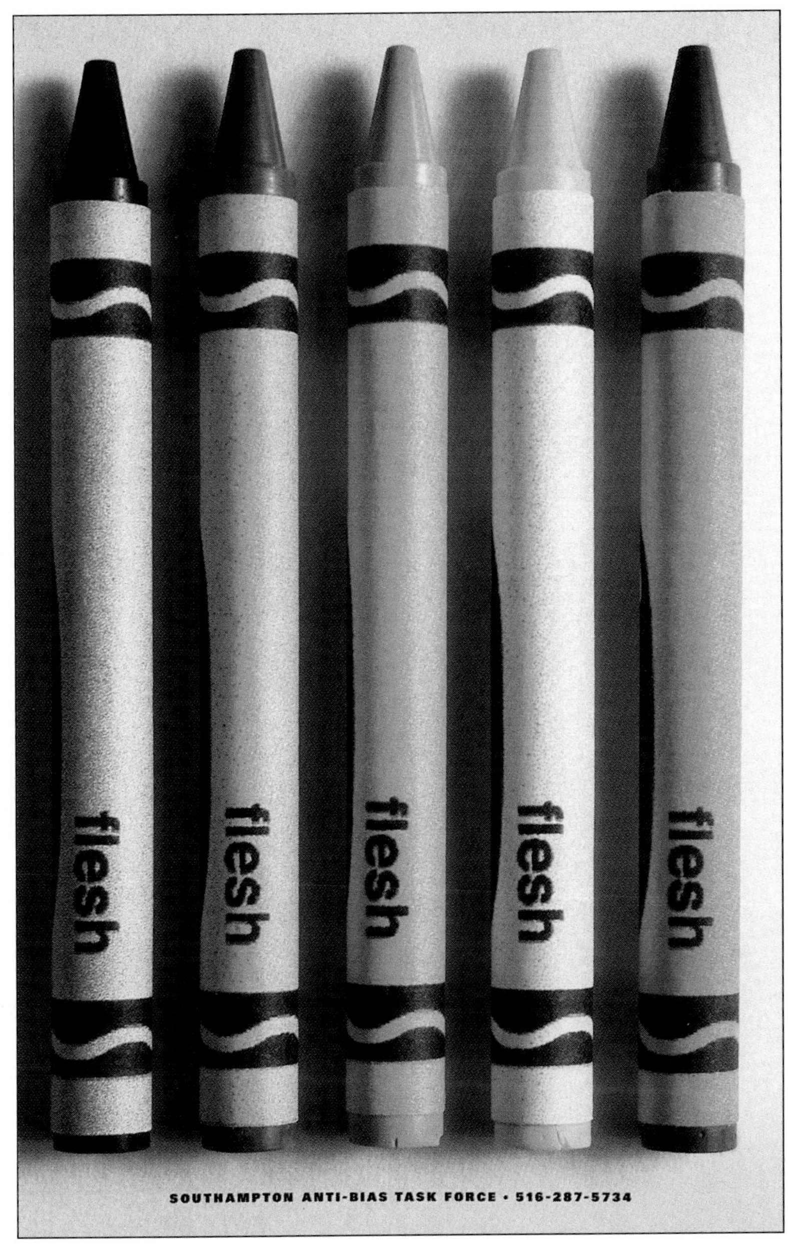

Source: Holzman & Kaplan Worldwide, Bret Wills-Photographer.

Hug it? Drive it? Hug it? Drive it?
Drivers wanted.
©1998 Volkswagen. 1-800 DRIVE VW or WWW.VW.com

Source: By permission of Volkswagen of America, Inc.

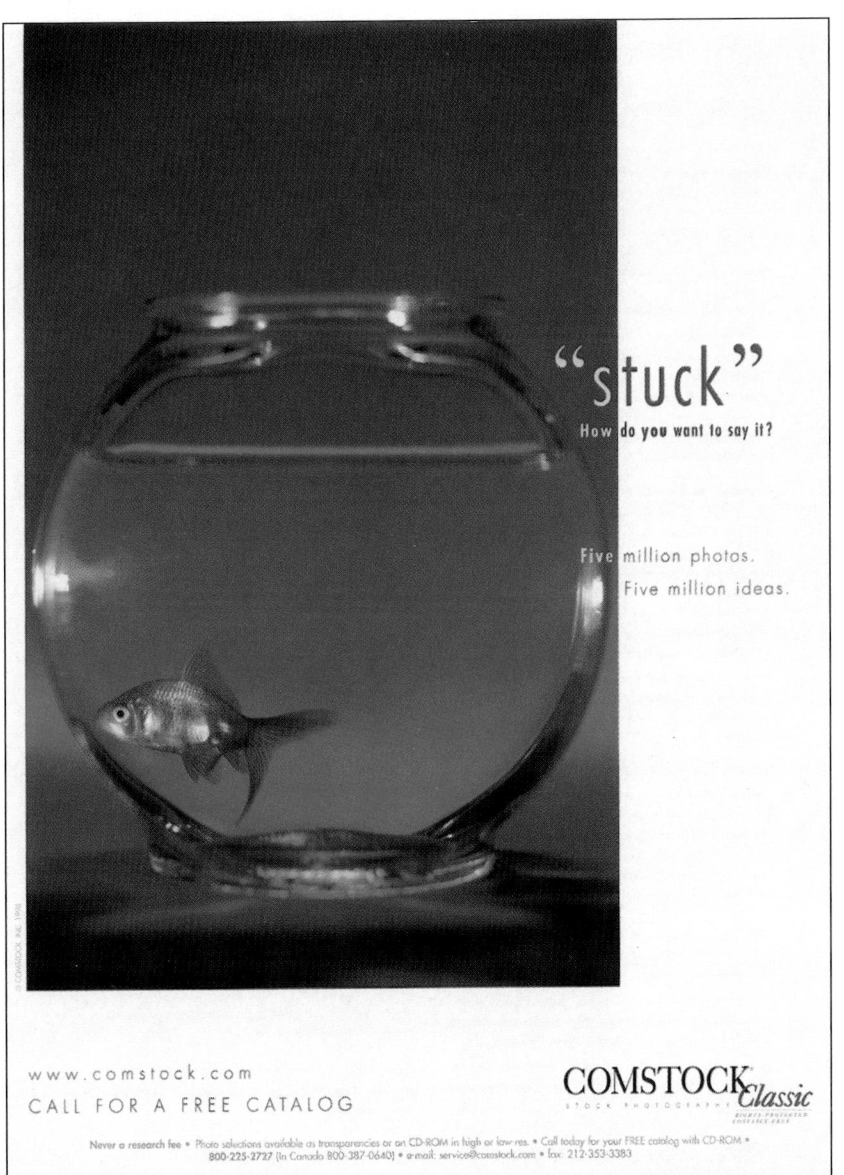

"stuck"
How do you want to say it?
Five million photos.
Five million ideas.
www.comstock.com
CALL FOR A FREE CATALOG
COMSTOCK Classic
STOCK PHOTOGRAPHY
Never a research fee • Photo selections available as transparencies or on CD-ROM in high or low-res. • Call today for your FREE catalog with CD-ROM •
800-225-2727 (In Canada 800-387-0640) • e-mail: service@comstock.com • fax: 212-353-3383

Source: By permission of Comstock, Inc.

Source: Reuters/Gregg Newton Archive Photos

The World's Fastest Man, Donovan Bailey, wears the adiStar Sprint. See our complete new line of track & field spikes at www.adidas.com.
adidas

Source: By permission of Leagas Delaney, Inc., for Adidas. Adidas has not authorized, sponsored, endorsed, or approved this publication and is not reponsible for its content.

EGINALD M THOMAS · GEORGE W STINSON Jr
IGUEL R BURRI · JOSEPH F CARROLL
ILLIAM J MADSEN · JAMES H MURPHY
COTT S WEBBER · COLEY L ANDREWS
OBERT B COWELL · WAYNE E DAWSON
OSEPH T McCREIGHT · RICHARD E POWELL
UGENE W BURKHART · JIMMY D GOLMON
ICHARD A KOSKY · WILLIAM A KUPREVICH
UGUST G MANNION Jr · GREGORY L MILLER
AMES C THOMAS · BOBBY LEE WADDELL
MOTHY E CLARK · SPOTSWOOD DEWITT
OHN H JOYCE · RICHARD V LINDE
AMES C McINTOSH · LUIS OLMOS
AMES F WENDOLOWSKI · ROBERT C WILKIE
OBERT C BOYD · DARIUS L D BROWN
HILLIP H HESS · JAMES S HOLLIS
OHN L SCHMECKER · MAX E SLOAN
TEPHEN E DUKEHART · BROWNIE HALL
OBERT R MARTINEZ · BARRY M MOUNCE
OHN H REEVES · TERRY W SHALHOOB
LYSSES WHITE · ALBERTO I JARA-VERANO
ILLIAM D CARSON · GIACOMO J CINTINEO
OBERT M KLEVENOWSKI · EARL W KNUTSON Jr

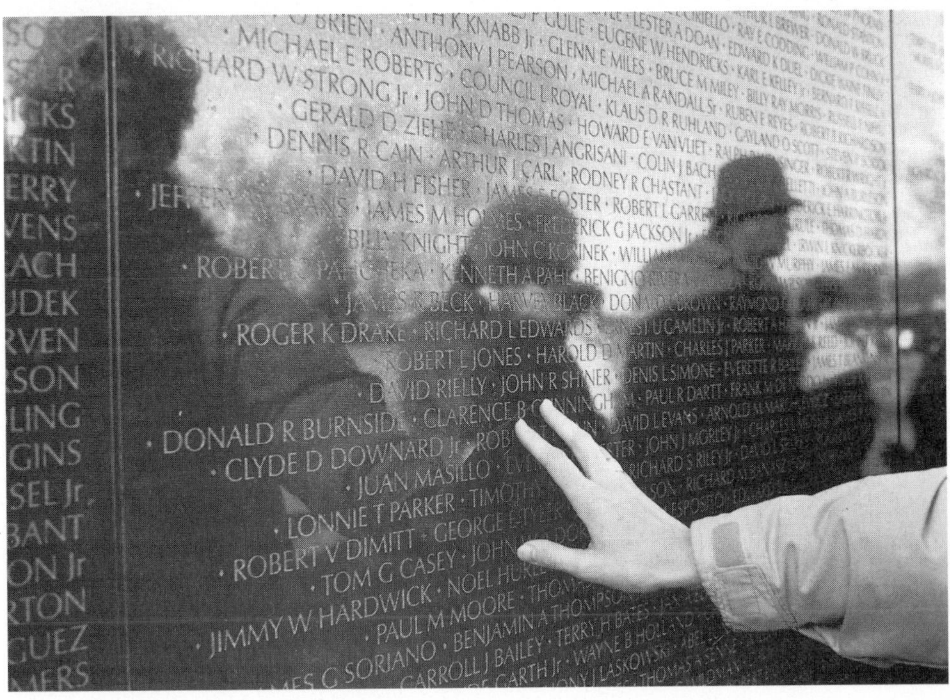
MICHAEL E ROBERTS · COUNCIL L ROYAL · MICHAEL A RANDALL Sr
DENNIS R CAIN · ARTHUR J CARL · RODNEY R CHASTANT
ROGER K DRAKE · RICHARD L EDWARDS
ROBERT L JONES · HAROLD D MARTIN · CHARLES J PARKER
DAVID RIELLY · JOHN R SHINER · DENIS L SIMONE
DONALD R BURNSIDE · CLARENCE B CUNNINGHAM
CLYDE D DOWNARD Jr
JUAN MASILLO
LONNIE T PARKER
TOM G CASEY
JIMMY W HARDWICK
PAUL M MOORE · BENJAMIN A THOMPSON

low black wall, its shape, its surfaces—lead to your interpretation? Could you characterize the Wall as having logical, ethical, and emotional appeals?

2. Even if you do not live in Washington, DC, or New York City, where the Statue of Liberty serves as another outstanding example of visual rhetoric, you can probably find public sculpture or monuments to visit and analyze. Alone or with some classmates, take notes and photographs. Then develop your interpretation of the sculpture's argument, specifying how visual details contribute to the case, and present your analysis to the class. Compare your interpretation with those of your classmates.

News Photographs

While some news photographs seem merely to record an event, the camera is not an objective machine. The photographer makes many "editorial" decisions—whether to snap a picture, when to snap it, what to include and exclude from the image—and artistic decisions about light, depth of field, and so on. The photograph below, which appeared in the *New York Times,* shows one scene photographer Bruce Young encountered when covering a snowstorm that hit Washington, DC, in January 1994. The storm was severe enough to shut down the city and all government operations. Without the caption supplied by the *New York Times,* readers might not have recognized

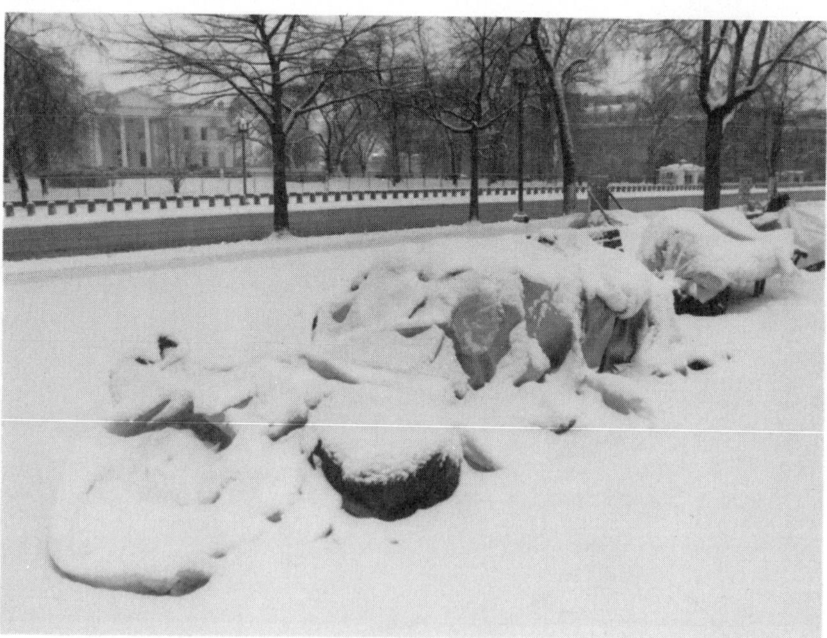

the objects in the foreground as human beings, homeless people huddled on benches, covered by undisturbed snow.

The picture argues that homelessness in America is a national disgrace, a problem that must be solved. The composition of the picture supports this claim. The White House in the background is our nation's "home," a grand and lavishly decorated residence symbolic of our national wealth. In juxtaposition in the foreground, the homeless people look like bags of garbage; they mar the beautiful picture of the snow-covered landscape. Viewers are unlikely to find in this picture evidence to blame the homeless for their condition: they are simply too pathetic, freezing under their blankets of snow. True, there is no in-depth argument here, taking into account causes for the problem, such as unemployment or mental illness, or solutions, such as shelters. The picture simply shows that homelessness is a fact of life in our cities, tarnishing the idealized image of our nation.

Following Through

1. A color news photograph of the October 1998 launch of the space shuttle *Discovery* is reproduced in plates 6 and 7 of the color section. This was the flight that carried John Glenn into space for the second time. Photographer Gregg Newton captured this image well into the launch, when the plume of smoke was all that was visible. Although some Americans were skeptical that Glenn's flight was merely a clever public relations ploy by NASA, most people celebrated Glenn's accomplishment. Media images such as this contributed to Americans' perspective on the launch. How do you "read" the photo's argument?
2. In a recent newspaper or news magazine, find a photograph related to an issue in the news, something people may have differing opinions about. What perspective or point of view does the photograph offer? Explain your "reading" of the photograph through an analysis of the content, composition, and any other details that contribute to your interpretation.

Graphics

Visual supplements to a longer text, such as an essay, article, or manual, are known as *graphics.* Given the ubiquity of visual appeals in almost everything we read and the widespread use of them in business and industry, it is odd how few school writing assignments require graphics or multimedia support. When students want to use photos, drawings, graphs, and the like in a paper, they tend to ask permission, as if they fear violating some unspoken rule. We believe that the pictorial should not be out of bounds in English papers or other undergraduate writing. Many texts could be more rhetorically effective with visual supplements, and we encourage you to use them whenever they are appropriate and helpful.

Most graphics fall into one of the following categories:

Tables and charts (typically an arrangement of data in columns and rows that summarizes the results of research)
Graphs (including bar, line, and pie graphs)
Photographs
Drawings (including maps and cartoons)

Although charts and tables are not technically images or figures, they present data in the form of visual arrangement rather than linear prose. Tables are used to display data economically in one place so that readers can find the information easily both as they read and afterward if they want to refer to the table again. Consider the example on the facing page, which combines a table with bar graphs. It comes from a study of poverty in the United States. Note how much information is "packed" into this single visual. Note also how easy it is to read, moving from top to bottom and left to right through the categories. Finally, consider how many long and boring paragraphs it would take to say the same thing in prose.

Graphs are usually no more than tables transformed into visuals we can "read" and interpret more easily. Bar graphs are one example. They allow us to compare subcategories within the major categories almost at a glance. Making the comparisons would be much more difficult if we had only the percentages listed in a table. Bar graphs are best at showing comparisons at some single point in time. In contrast, line graphs allow us to see trends—for example, the performance of the stock market. Pie graphs highlight relative proportions well. When newspapers or news magazines want to show us how the federal budget is spent, for example, they typically use pie graphs with the pieces labeled in some way to represent categories such as national defense, welfare, entitlement programs, and the like. Who gets the biggest pieces of the pie becomes instantly clear and easier to remember, the two major purposes all graphs try to achieve. Graphs in themselves may not make arguments, but they are powerful deliverers of evidence, and in that sense fall into the category of visual rhetoric.

As graphics, photographs represent people, objects, and scenes realistically and concretely. They give us a "human's eye" view of something as nothing else can. Thus, for instance, owner's manuals for cars often have a shot of the engine compartment that shows where fluid reservoirs are located. Clearly, such photos serve highly practical purposes, such as helping us locate the dipstick. But they're also used, for example, in biographies; we get a better sense of, say, Abraham Lincoln's life and times when pictures of him, his family, his home, and so on are included. But photographs can do much more than merely inform. They can also be highly dramatic and powerfully emotional in ways that only the best writers can manage with prose—hence their inclusion to generate interest and excitement or to communicate an overall impression of a subject matter or theme. Photos are powerful persuaders.

But photogaphs are not very analytical—by their nature they give us the surface of things, only what the camera can "see." A different type of graphic,

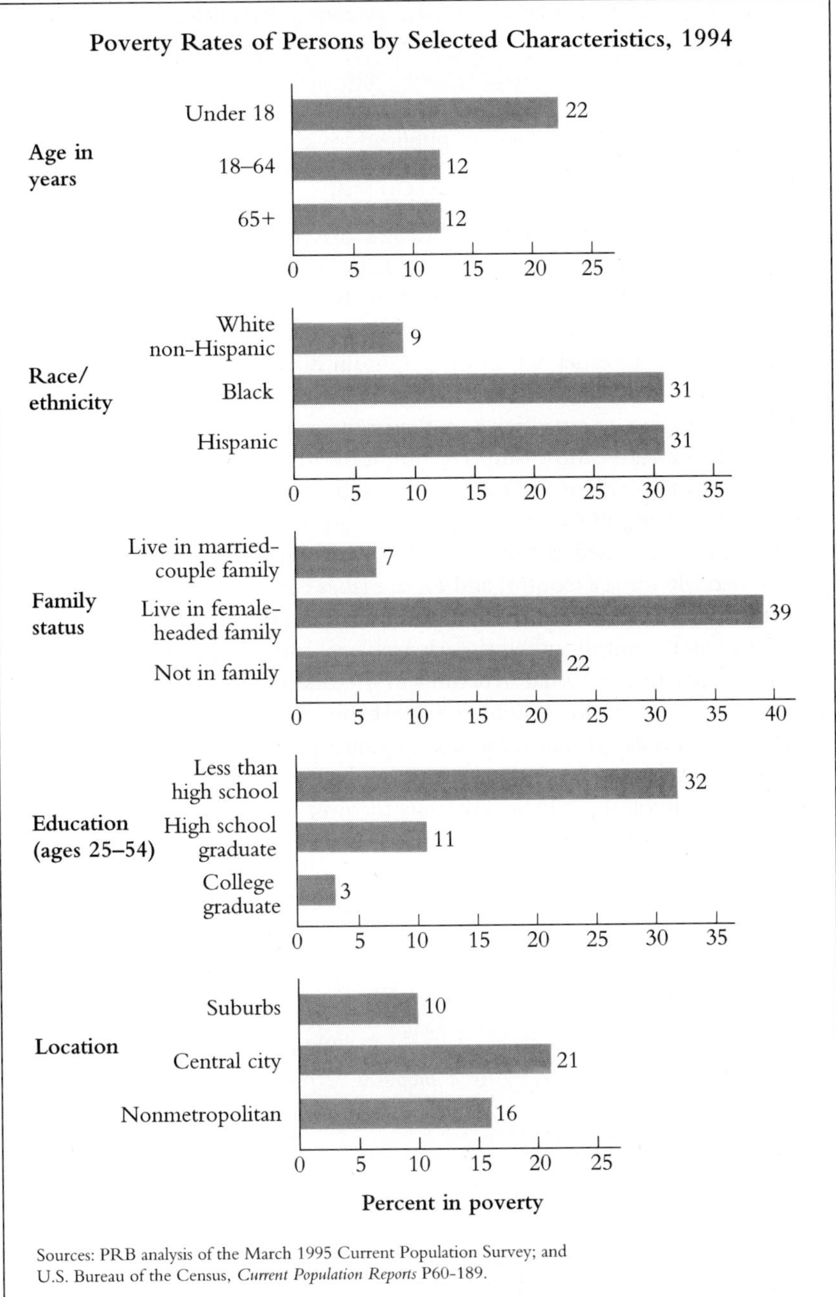

Sources: PRB analysis of the March 1995 Current Population Survey; and U.S. Bureau of the Census, *Current Population Reports* P60-189.

drawings, are preferable when we want to depict how something is put together or structured. For instance, instructions for assembling and installing a ceiling fan or a light fixture usually have many diagrams—one large one showing how all the parts fit together and smaller ones that depict steps in the process in more detail. Corporate publications often include diagrams of the company's organizational hierarchy or chain of command. Scientific articles and textbooks are often full of drawings or drawinglike images created with computer graphics; these publications use drawings because science writers want us to understand structures, particularly internal structures, that often are difficult to capture on film and difficult to interpret when they are. For example, our sense of how DNA "looks" and our understanding of its "spiral staircase" structure comes almost entirely from diagrams.

The following article illustrates how a variety of graphics can contribute to the effectiveness of a written text that informs readers about a complicated and often misunderstood subject, attention-deficit hyperactivity disorder (ADHD). ADHD afflicts millions of people the world over, most seriously in their youth, during the years of formal education. We have taught many college students diagnosed with ADHD, and you probably have friends whose intense struggle for self-control and focus makes coping with college especially difficult. This article both informs us about ADHD and argues two theses about it: (1) self-control is the primary problem, and (2) the disorder is genetic, related to smaller-than-usual structures in the brain that regulate attention. As you read, notice how the graphics support the author's informative and argumentative purposes. (In our textbook's reproduction of the article, the original page layout has been changed. You may wish to consult a copy of the magazine or access it via the Net at www.sciam.com.)

RUSSELL A. BARKLEY

Attention-Deficit Hyperactivity Disorder

This article appeared in the September 1998 issue of Scientific American; *its author, Russell Barkley, is a professor of psychiatry and neurology at the University of Massachusetts Medical Center in Worcester and an internationally recognized expert on ADHD.*

AS I watched five-year-old Keith in the waiting room of my office, I could see why his parents said he was having such a tough time in kindergarten. He hopped from chair to chair, swinging his arms and legs restlessly, and then began to fiddle with the light switches, turning the lights on and off again to everyone's annoyance—all the while talking nonstop. When his mother 1

Children with ADHD cannot control their responses to their environment. This lack of control makes them hyperactive, inattentive and impulsive.

encouraged him to join a group of other children busy in the playroom, Keith butted into a game that was already in progress and took over, causing the other children to complain of his bossiness and drift away to other activities. Even when Keith had the toys to himself, he fidgeted aimlessly with them and seemed unable to entertain himself quietly. Once I examined him more fully, my initial suspicions were confirmed: Keith had attention-deficit hyperactivity disorder (ADHD).

Since the 1940s, psychiatrists have applied various labels to children who are hyperactive and inordinately inattentive and impulsive. Such youngsters have been considered to have "minimal brain dysfunction," "brain-injured child syndrome," "hyperkinetic reaction of childhood," "hyperactive child syndrome" and, most recently, "attention-deficit disorder." The frequent name changes reflect how uncertain researchers have been about the underlying causes of, and even the precise diagnostic criteria for, the disorder.

Within the past several years, however, those of us who study ADHD have begun to clarify its symptoms and causes and have found that it may have a genetic underpinning. Today's view of the basis of the condition is strikingly different from that of just a few years ago. We are finding that ADHD is not a disorder of attention per se, as had long been assumed. Rather it arises as a developmental failure in the brain circuitry that underlies inhibition and self-control. This loss of self-control in turn impairs other important brain functions crucial for maintaining attention, including the ability to defer immediate rewards for later, greater gain.

ADHD involves two sets of symptoms: inattention and a combination of hyperactive and impulsive behaviors (see table on page 211). Most children are more active, distractible and impulsive than adults. And they are more inconsistent, affected by momentary events and dominated by objects in their immediate environment. The younger the children, the less able they are to be aware of time or to give priority to future events over more immediate wants. Such behaviors are signs of a problem, however, when children display them significantly more than their peers do.

Boys are at least three times as likely as girls to develop the disorder; 5
indeed, some studies have found that boys with ADHD outnumber girls with the condition by nine to one, possibly because boys are genetically more prone to disorders of the nervous system. The behavior patterns that typify ADHD usually arise between the ages of three and five. Even so, the age of onset can vary widely: some children do not develop symptoms until late childhood or even early adolescence. Why their symptoms are delayed remains unclear.

Huge numbers of people are affected. Many studies estimate that between 2 and 9.5 percent of all school-age children worldwide have ADHD; researchers have identified it in every nation and culture they have studied. What is more, the condition, which was once thought to ease with age, can persist into adulthood. For example, roughly two thirds of 158 children with ADHD my colleagues and I evaluated in the 1970s still had the disorder in their twenties. And many of those who no longer fit the clinical description of ADHD were still having significant adjustment problems at work, in school or in other social settings.

To help children (and adults) with ADHD, psychiatrists and psychologists must better understand the causes of the disorder. Because researchers have traditionally viewed ADHD as a problem in the realm of attention, some have suggested that it stems from an inability of the brain to filter competing sensory inputs, such as sights and sounds. But recently scientists led by Joseph A. Sergeant of the University of Amsterdam have shown that children with ADHD do not have difficulty in that area; instead they cannot inhibit their impulsive motor responses to such input. Other researchers have found that children with ADHD are less capable of preparing motor responses in anticipation of events and are insensitive to feedback about errors made in those

Diagnosing ADHD

Psychiatrists diagnose attention-deficit hyperactivity disorder (ADHD) if the individual displays six or more of the following symptoms of inattention or six or more symptoms of hyperactivity and impulsivity. The signs must occur often and be present for at least six months to a degree that is maladaptive and inconsistent with the person's developmental level. In addition, some of the symptoms must have caused impairment before the age of seven and must now be causing impairment in two or more settings. Some must also be leading to significant impairment in social, academic or occupational functioning; none should occur exclusively as part of another disorder.

INATTENTION	HYPERACTIVITY AND IMPULSIVITY
Fails to give close attention to details or makes careless mistakes in schoolwork, work or other activities	Fidgets with hands or feet or squirms in seat
Has difficulty sustaining attention in tasks or play activities	Leaves seat in classroom or in other situations in which remaining seated is expected
Does not seem to listen when spoken to directly	Runs about or climbs excessively in situations in which it is inappropriate (in adolescents or adults, subjective feelings of restlessness)
Does not follow through on instructions and fails to finish schoolwork, chores or duties in the workplace	Has difficulty playing or engaging in leisure activities quietly
Has difficulty organizing tasks and activities	Is "on the go" or acts as if "driven by a motor"
Avoids, dislikes or is reluctant to engage in tasks that require sustained mental effort (such as schoolwork)	Talks excessively
Loses things necessary for tasks or activities (such as toys, school assignments, pencils, books or tools)	Blurts out answers before questions have been completed
Is easily distracted by extraneous stimuli	Has difficulty awaiting turns
Is forgetful in daily activities	Interrupts or intrudes on others

Source: Adapted with permission from the fourth edition of the *Diagnostic and Statistical Manual of Mental Disorders.* © 1994 American Psychiatric Association.

responses. For example, in a commonly used test of reaction time, children with ADHD are less able than other children to ready themselves to press one of several keys when they see a warning light. They also do not slow down after making mistakes in such tests in order to improve their accuracy.

The Search for a Cause

No one knows the direct and immediate causes of the difficulties experienced by children with ADHD, although advances in neurological imaging techniques and genetics promise to clarify this issue over the next five years. Already they have yielded clues, albeit ones that do not yet fit together into a coherent picture.

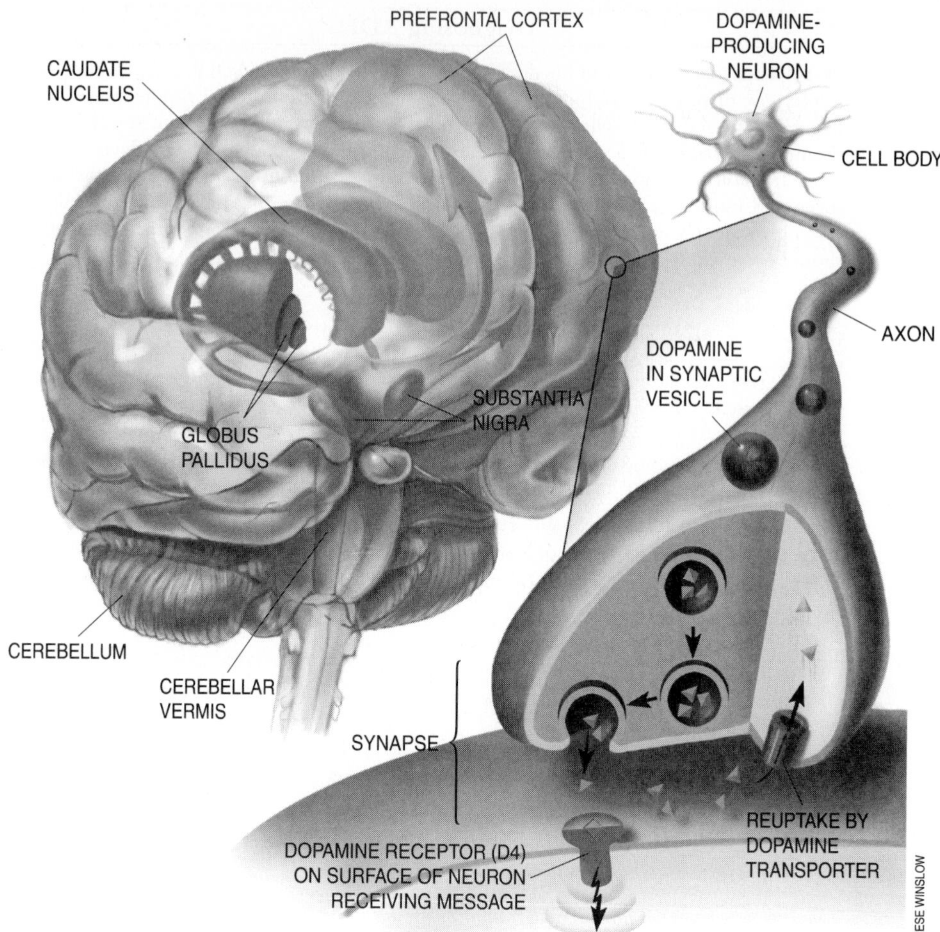

Brain structures affected in ADHD use dopamine to communicate with one another. Genetic studies suggest that people with ADHD might have alterations in genes encoding either the D4 dopamine receptor, which receives incoming signals, or the dopamine transporter, which scavenges released dopamine for reuse. The substantia nigra, where the death of dopamine-producing neurons causes Parkinson's disease, is not affected in ADHD.

Imaging studies over the past decade have indicated which brain regions might malfunction in patients with ADHD and thus account for the symptoms of the condition. That work suggests the involvement of the prefrontal cortex, part of the cerebellum, and at least two of the clusters of nerve cells deep in the brain that are collectively known as the basal ganglia (see illustration above). In a 1996 study F. Xavier Castellanos, Judith L. Rapoport and their colleagues at the National Institute of Mental Health found that the right prefrontal cortex and two basal ganglia called the caudate nucleus and the globus pallidus are significantly smaller than normal in children with ADHD. Earlier this year Castellanos's group found that the vermis region of the cerebellum is also smaller in ADHD children.

10 The imaging findings make sense because the brain areas that are reduced in size in children with ADHD are the very ones that regulate attention. The right prefrontal cortex, for example, is involved in "editing" one's behavior, resisting distractions and developing an awareness of self and time. The caudate nucleus and the globus pallidus help to switch off automatic responses to allow more careful deliberation by the cortex and to coordinate neurological input among various regions of the cortex. The exact role of the cerebellar vermis is unclear, but early studies suggest it may play a role in regulating motivation.

What causes the structures to shrink in the brains of those with ADHD? No one knows, but many studies have suggested that mutations in several genes that are normally very active in the prefrontal cortex and basal ganglia might play a role. Most researchers now believe that ADHD is a polygenic disorder—that is, that more than one gene contributes to it.

Early tips that faulty genetics underlie ADHD came from studies of the relatives of children with the disorder. For instance, the siblings of children with ADHD are between five and seven times more likely to develop the syndrome than children from unaffected families. And the children of a parent who has ADHD have up to a 50 percent chance of experiencing the same difficulties.

The most conclusive evidence that genetics can contribute to ADHD, however, comes from studies of twins. Jacquelyn J. Gillis, then at the University of Colorado, and her colleagues reported in 1992 that the ADHD risk of a child whose identical twin has the disorder is between 11 and 18 times greater than that of a nontwin sibling of a child with ADHD; between 55 and 92 percent of the identical twins of children with ADHD eventually develop the condition.

One of the largest twin studies of ADHD was conducted by Helene Gjone and Jon M. Sundet of the University of Oslo with Jim Stevenson of the University of Southampton in England. It involved 526 identical twins, who inherit exactly the same genes, and 389 fraternal twins, who are no more alike genetically than siblings born years apart. The team found that ADHD has a heritability approaching 80 percent, meaning that up to 80 percent of the differences in attention, hyperactivity and impulsivity between people with ADHD and those without the disorder can be explained by genetic factors.

15 Nongenetic factors that have been linked to ADHD include premature birth, maternal alcohol and tobacco use, exposure to high levels of lead in early childhood and brain injuries—especially those that involve the prefrontal cortex. But even together, these factors can account for only between 20 and 30 percent of ADHD cases among boys; among girls, they account for an even smaller percentage. (Contrary to popular belief, neither dietary factors, such as

the amount of sugar a child consumes, nor poor child-rearing methods have been consistently shown to contribute to ADHD.)

Which genes are defective? Perhaps those that dictate the way in which the brain uses dopamine, one of the chemicals known as neurotransmitters that convey messages from one nerve cell, or neuron, to another. Dopamine is secreted by neurons in specific parts of the brain to inhibit or modulate the activity of other neurons, particularly those involved in emotion and movement. The movement disorders of Parkinson's disease, for example, are caused by the death of dopamine-secreting neurons in a region of the brain underneath the basal ganglia called the substantia nigra.

Some impressive studies specifically implicate genes that encode, or serve as the blueprint for, dopamine receptors and transporters; these genes are very active in the prefrontal cortex and basal ganglia. Dopamine receptors sit on the surface of certain neurons. Dopamine delivers its message to those neurons by binding to the receptors. Dopamine transporters protrude from neurons that secrete the neurotransmitter; they take up unused dopamine so that it can be used again. Mutations in the dopamine receptor gene can render receptors less sensitive to dopamine. Conversely, mutations in the dopamine transporter gene can yield overly effective transporters that scavenge secreted dopamine before it has a chance to bind to dopamine receptors on a neighboring neuron.

In 1995 Edwin H. Cook and his colleagues at the University of Chicago reported that children with ADHD were more likely than others to have a particular variation in the dopamine transporter gene *DAT1*. Similarly, in 1996 Gerald J. LaHoste of the University of California at Irvine and his co-workers found that a variant of the dopamine receptor gene *D4* is more common among children with ADHD. But each of these studies involved 40 or 50 children—a relatively small number—so their findings are now being confirmed in larger studies.

From Genes to Behavior

How do the brain-structure and genetic defects observed in children with ADHD lead to the characteristic behaviors of the disorder? Ultimately, they might be found to underlie impaired behavioral inhibition and self-control, which I have concluded are the central deficits in ADHD.

Self-control—or the capacity to inhibit or delay one's initial motor (and 20
perhaps emotional) responses to an event—is a critical foundation for the performance of any task. As most children grow up, they gain the ability to engage in mental activities, known as executive functions, that help them deflect distractions, recall goals and take the steps needed to reach them. To achieve a goal in work or play, for instance, people need to be able to remember their aim (use hindsight), prompt themselves about what they need to do to reach that goal (use forethought), keep their emotions reined in and motivate themselves. Unless a person can inhibit interfering thoughts and impulses, none of these functions can be carried out successfully.

A Psychological Model of ADHD

A loss of behavioral inhibition and self-control leads to the following disruptions in brain functioning:

IMPAIRED FUNCTION	CONSEQUENCE	EXAMPLE
Nonverbal working memory	Diminished sense of time Inability to hold events in mind Defective hindsight Defective forethought	Nine-year-old Jeff routinely forgets important responsibilities, such as deadlines for book reports or an after-school appointment with the principal
Internalization of self-directed speech	Deficient rule-governed behavior Poor self-guidance and self-questioning	Five-year-old Audrey talks too much and cannot give herself useful directions silently on how to perform a task
Self-regulation of mood, motivation and level of arousal	Displays all emotions publicly; cannot censor them Diminished self-regulation of drive and motivation	Eight-year-old Adam cannot maintain the persistent effort required to read a story appropriate for his age level and is quick to display his anger when frustrated by assigned schoolwork
Reconstitution (ability to break down observed behaviors into component parts that can be recombined into new behaviors in pursuit of a goal)	Limited ability to analyze behaviors and synthesize new behaviors Inability to solve problems	Fourteen-year-old Ben stops doing a homework assignment when he realizes that he has only two of the five assigned questions; he does not think of a way to solve the problem, such as calling a friend to get the other three questions

Source: Lisa Burnett

In the early years, the executive functions are performed externally: children might talk out loud to themselves while remembering a task or puzzling out a problem. As children mature, they internalize, or make private, such executive functions, which prevents others from knowing their thoughts. Children with ADHD, in contrast, seem to lack the restraint needed to inhibit the public performance of these executive functions.

The executve functions can be grouped into four mental activities. One is the operation of working memory—holding information in the mind while working on a task, even if the original stimulus that provided the information is gone. Such remembering is crucial to timeliness and goal-directed behavior: it provides the means for hindsight, forethought, preparation and the ability to imitate the complex, novel behavior of others—all of which are impaired in people with ADHD.

The internalization of self-directed speech is another executive function. Before the age of six, most children speak out loud to themselves frequently, reminding themselves how to perform a particular task or trying to cope with a problem, for example. ("Where did I put that book? Oh, I left it under the desk.") In elementary school, such private speech evolves into inaudible muttering; it usually disappears by age 10 [see "Why Children Talk to Themselves," by Laura E. Berk; *Scientific American,* November 1994]. Internalized, self-directed speech allows one to reflect to oneself, to follow rules and instructions, to use self-questioning as a form of problem solving and to construct "meta-rules," the basis for understanding the rules for using rules—all quickly and without tipping one's hand to others. Laura E. Berk and her colleagues at Illinois State University reported in 1991 that the internalization of self-directed speech is delayed in boys with ADHD.

A third executive mental function consists of controlling emotions, motivation and state of arousal. Such control helps individuals achieve goals by enabling them to delay or alter potentially distracting emotional reactions to a particular event and to generate private emotions and motivation. Those who rein in their immediate passions can also behave in more socially acceptable ways.

The final executive function, reconstitution, actually encompasses two 25
separate processes: breaking down observed behaviors and combining the parts into new actions not previously learned from experience. The capacity for reconstitution gives humans a great degree of fluency, flexibility and creativity; it allows individuals to propel themselves toward a goal without having to learn all the needed steps by rote. It permits children as they mature to direct their behavior across increasingly longer intervals by combining behaviors into ever longer chains to attain a goal. Initial studies imply that children with ADHD are less capable of reconstitution than are other children.

I suggest that like self-directed speech, the other three executive functions become internalized during typical neural development in early childhood. Such privatization is essential for creating visual imagery and verbal thought. As children grow up, they develop the capacity to behave covertly, to mask some of their behaviors or feelings from others. Perhaps because of faulty genetics or embryonic development, children with ADHD have not attained this ability and therefore display too much public behavior and speech. It is my assertion that the inattention, hyperactivity and impulsivity of children with ADHD are caused by their failure to be guided by internal instructions and by their inability to curb their own inappropriate behaviors.

Prescribing Self-Control

If, as I have outlined, ADHD is a failure of behavioral inhibition that delays the ability to privatize and execute the four executive mental functions I have described, the finding supports the theory that children with ADHD might be helped by a more structured environment. Greater structure can be an important complement to any drug therapy the children might receive. Currently children (and adults) with ADHD often receive drugs such as Rit-

Psychological tests used in ADHD research include the four depicted here. The tower-building test (upper left), *in which the subject is asked to assemble balls into a tower to mimic an illustration, measures forethought, planning and persistence. The math test* (upper right) *assesses working memory and problem-solving ability. In the auditory attention test* (lower left), *the subject must select the appropriate colored tile according to taped instructions, despite distracting words. The time estimation test* (lower right) *measures visual attention and subjective sense of time intervals. The subject is asked to hold down a key to illuminate a lightbulb on a computer screen for the same length of time that another bulb was illuminated previously.*

alin that boost their capacity to inhibit and regulate impulsive behaviors. These drugs act by inhibiting the dopamine transporter, increasing the time that dopamine has to bind to its receptors on other neurons.

Such compounds (which, despite their inhibitory effects, are known as psychostimulants) have been found to improve the behavior of between 70 and 90 percent of children with ADHD older than five years. Children with ADHD who take such medication not only are less impulsive, restless and distractible but are also better able to hold important information in mind, to be more productive academically, and to have more internalized speech and better self-control. As a result, they tend to be liked better by other children and to experience less punishment for their actions, which improves their self-image.

My model suggests that in addition to psychostimulants—and perhaps antidepressants, for some children—treatment for ADHD should include training parents and teachers in specific and more effective methods for managing the behavioral problems of children with the disorder. Such methods involve making the consequences of a child's actions more frequent and immediate and increasing the external use of prompts and cues about rules and time intervals. Parents and teachers must aid children with ADHD by anticipating events for them, breaking future tasks down into smaller and more immediate steps, and using artificial immediate rewards. All these steps serve to externalize time, rules and consequences as a replacement for the weak internal forms of information, rules and motivation of children with ADHD.

In some instances, the problems of ADHD children may be severe 30
enough to warrant their placement in special education programs. Although such programs are not intended as a cure for the child's difficulties, they typically do provide a smaller, less competitive and more supportive environment in which the child can receive individual instruction. The hope is that once children learn techniques to overcome their deficits in self-control, they will be able to function outside such programs.

There is no cure for ADHD, but much more is now known about effectively coping with and managing this persistent and troubling developmental disorder. The day is not far off when genetic testing for ADHD may become available and more specialized medications may be designed to counter the specific genetic deficits of the children who suffer from it.

Analyzing Barkley's Graphics

Barkley's article contains the following graphics, listed in order of appearance:

A cartoon depicting the whirling, chaotic world of the ADHD sufferer
A chart of the symptoms of the disorder entitled "Diagnosing ADHD"
A computer-generated, three-dimensional graphic depicting the brain and processes having to do with neural activity
Another chart entitled "A Psychological Model of ADHD"
A set of photographs showing tests used in ADHD research

Thus, in a relatively short article, we have a wide range of graphics, each one of which we could comment on at far greater length than we do here. The following comments are designed to stimulate thinking about how graphics function rhetorically in a text, not to exhaust what could be said about any of the graphics.

Turning to the first graphic on page 209, we should notice what it "says" about the intended audience. *Scientific American*'s readership is mixed; it is not limited to scientists, but it includes scientists who enjoy reading about the work of other scientists in other fields. Thus, the articles must be "real science" but must also have broad appeal. The cartoonlike image we first encounter would almost certainly not appear in a "hard-core" science journal, written by specialists for specialists. We might also consider how well the graphic works to "predict" the content of the article and to represent the problem of ADHD.

We might compare the opening graphic with the drawing of the brain on page 212. Clearly, the cartoon is intended for the more "pop" side of *Scientific American*'s readership, whereas the drawing targets those who want a more detailed understanding of the "hard science" involved in ADHD research. The article itself moves from knowledge that can be widely shared to information more specialized and harder to grasp, returning at the end to its broader audience's interests. The movement from the cartoon to the drawing mirrors the text's development from the relatively accessible to the more specialized. The drawing assists Barkley in presenting essential information about the disorder itself.

The four photos near the end of the article (page 217) reflect a turn 35
from brain structures and neural processes to a humanistic concern for the welfare of ADHD children. The role of these photographs is less informative than it is persuasive. Because this article from *Scientific American* seems more informative than argumentative, we need to consider how it fits into the general context of debate about ADHD. Although less controversial than it once was, when even its existence was in dispute, ADHD remains a disputed topic. Some contend that the syndrome is diagnosed too often and too easily, perhaps in part at the urging of parents who know that laws mandate special treatment for ADHD cases in schools, such as more time to complete tests. Others argue that the disorder is more environmental than genetic and trace its source to a chaotic family life, too much TV, bad eating habits, and factors other than (or in addition to) brain abnormalities. Finally, among other doubts and criticism, are questions often raised by teachers: When a child is properly treated for ADHD, just how impaired is he or she? Is special treatment really warranted? up to what age?

Barkley's article hardly alludes to the controversies surrounding ADHD, probably because the view he develops represents an emerging consensus among researchers. But if we read the article with its unspoken context in mind, we see much in it intended to refute dissenters and skeptics. Clearly, the genetic hypothesis is advanced by both text and graphics, and the concluding four photos claim, in effect, that actual and reliable testing is part of the diagnostic process.

We turn now to another graphic, the charts. Surely the chart entitled "Diagnosing ADHD" on page 211 is included to confirm the existence of definite criteria for diagnosis and to insist that diagnosis should be neither hasty nor uncertain once made. Note especially the sentence "The signs must occur often and be present for at least six months to a degree that is maladaptive and inconsistent with the person's developmental level." A similar implicit argument can be found in the second chart, "A Psychological Model of ADHD."

It "says" that the disorder is thoroughly conceived, that we know much about it, and that we can be concrete about how the symptoms manifest themselves. These charts, then, while they may appear to be merely information to a casual reader, are actually arguments—claims about the solid "objective thereness," the reality, of the syndrome we call ADHD. They are definitely not merely decorative throw-ins, but rather serve complex rhetorical purposes that become especially clear in the larger context of debate about ADHD.

Following Through

1. Discuss the first graphic in the article as an introduction to the article's topic and argument. What function does this graphic serve? What message is conveyed by the assortment of items swirling around the child? Into what categories do the items fall? Why is the child male? How would you characterize his expression? What attitude about his plight does this image suggest that readers will find in the article?
2. Consider these questions as you examine the drawing of the brain on page 212 and the enlarged drawing of the connections between nerve cells, or neurons. What purposes do these visuals serve? For what part of the audience are they intended? Do they help you to understand the physiology of the disorder? Can you explain how perspective comes into play in the drawing of the two neurons? Without these graphics how much would you understand about the complex brain and neural processes discussed?
3. Discuss the four concluding photographs in the article as persuasion. How much information about psychological testing is conveyed by the photos themselves? Why are the adult figures women? How are they dressed? (Suppose they were men in white lab coats. What different impression would this create?) How would you characterize the office or clinical environment in which the child performs the tests? What messages are sent by the child's gender, age, race, clothes, hair, and cast on his left arm? by his body language and facial expressions? What might the persuasive intent be? If there is an implicit argument, what would it be, and why is it necessary?
4. Discuss why Barkley decided to present the material in the two charts in this tabulated form, rather than incorporating it into the body of the article.
5. As an exercise in considering the role of graphics, bring to class a paper you have written recently for a college or high school assignment. If you didn't use graphics, ask yourself the following questions: Could the paper be improved with graphic support? If so, given your audience and purpose(s), what graphic types would you use, and why? How would you go about securing or creating the graphics? If you did use graphics, be prepared to discuss them—what you did and why, how you went about creating the visuals, and so on. If you now see ways to improve the graphics, discuss your revision strategies as well.

WRITING ASSIGNMENTS

Assignment 1: Analyzing an Advertisement or Editorial Cartoon

Choose an ad or cartoon from a current magazine or newspaper. First, inquire into its rhetorical context: What situation prompted its creation? What purpose does it aim to achieve? Where did it originally appear? Who is its intended audience? What would they know or believe about the product or issue? Then inquire into the argument being made. To do this, you should consult the questions for inquiry on pages 39–40 to the extent that they apply to visual rhetoric. You should also consider some of the points we have made in this chapter that pertain to visual images in particular: What visual metaphors or allusions appear in the ad or cartoon? What prior cultural knowledge and experiences would the audience have to have to "read" the image? Consider how the visual argument might limit the scope of the issue or how it might play to the audience's biases, stereotypes, or fears. After thorough inquiry, reach some conclusion about the effectiveness or ethics of this particular visual argument. Write up your conclusion as a thesis, or claim. Write up your analysis as an argument to convince, using the evidence gathered during the inquiry as material to support and develop your claim. Be sure to be specific about the visual details of the ad or cartoon.

Student Sample: Analysis of Visual Rhetoric

The following student essay, by Kelly Williams, serves as an example of the above assignment. Before you begin your own essay, you might want to read the essay and discuss the conclusions she reached about an advertisement for Eagle Brand condensed milk. Unfortunately, we were unable to obtain permission to reprint the advertisement itself, but the descriptions of the ad's text and visual images should make Kelly's analysis easy to follow.

KELLY WILLIAMS

A Mother's Treat

ADVERTISEMENTS ARE effective only if they connect with their audiences. Advertisers must therefore study the group of people they hope to reach and know what such groups value and what image they like to have of themselves. Often these images come from societal expectations that tell businessmen, mothers, fathers, teens that they should look or act a certain way. Most people have a hard time deviating from these images, or stereotypes, because adhering to them gives social status. Advertisers tend to look to these stereotypes as a way to sell their products. For example, an ad depicts a man in an expensive suit driving a luxury car, and readers assume he is a lawyer, 1 physician, or business executive. Therefore, doctors, lawyers, and businessmen will buy this car because they associate it with the image of status that they would like to project. Likewise, some advertisements try to manipulate women with children by associating a product with the ideal maternal image that society places on mothers.

An advertisement for Eagle Brand condensed milk typifies the effort to persuade mothers to buy a product to perform the ideal maternal role. The advertisement appeared in magazines aimed at homemakers and in *People Magazine*'s "Best and Worst Dressed" issue of September 1998. The readers of this issue are predominantly young females; those with children are probably second-income producers or maybe even single mothers. These readers are struggling to raise a family, and they have many demands on their time. They may feel enormous pressure to fulfill ideal corporate and domestic roles. These readers may be susceptible to pressure to invest in an image that is expected of them.

The advertisement itself creates a strong connection with a maternal audience. It depicts a black-and-white photograph of a young girl about kindergarten age. The little girl's facial expression connotes hesitation and sadness. In the background is a school yard. Other children are walking toward the school, their heads facing down, creating a feeling of gloom. All readers will recognize the situation taking place. The little girl is about to attend her first day of school. One could easily guess that she is looking back to her mother with a sense of abandonment, pleading for support. Without a mother pictured, the audience assumes the maternal perspective. The girl's eyes stare at the reader. Her expression evokes protectiveness, especially in an audience of young mothers.

The wording of the text adds some comic relief to the situation. The ad is not intended to make the readers sad. The words seem to come from the mind of the child's mother: "For not insisting bunny slippers for shoes, for leaving Blankie behind, for actually getting out of the car . . ." These words also show that the mother is a good mother, very empathetic to her daughter's situation. Even the type of print for these words is part of an effective marketing strategy. The font mimics a "proper" mother's handwriting. The calligraphy contains no sharp edges, which reinforces the generalization that mothers are soft, feminine, and gentle.

The intent of the advertisement is to persuade mothers that if they buy 5
Eagle Brand milk and make the chocolate bar treat, they will be good mothers like the speaker in the ad. It tells women that cooking such treats helps to alleviate stressful situations that occur in everyday family life. The little girl in the ad is especially effective in reminding maternal figures of their duty to care for and comfort their kids. She evokes the ideal maternal qualities of compassion, empathy and protection. Indirectly, the girl is testing her mother's maternal qualities. The expectations for her mother (and the reader) to deliver on all of these needs are intense. Happily, there is an easy way to do it. By making these treats, she can fulfill the role of a genuine mother figure.

The ad also suggests that good mothers reward good behavior. The statements listing the girl's good behavior suggest that it would be heartless not to reward her for her willingness to relinquish her childhood bonds. As the ad says, "It's time for a treat." But good mothers would also know that "Welcome Home Chocolate Bars" are very sweet and rich, so this mother has to say, "I'll risk spoiling your dinner." The invisible mother in the ad is still ideal because she does care about her child's nutrition, but in this case, she will make an exception out of her concern for the emotional state of her child. The ad succeeds in selling the product by triggering mothers' maternal instincts to respond to their children's needs.

In many ways this ad is unethical. It pressures women to fit certain ideals so that Eagle Brand can sell more condensed milk. The ideal "mommy" makes the home a warm, safe, comforting place, and the ad suggests that using Eagle Brand is the way to do it. While the ad looks harmless and cute, it actually reinforces social pressures on women to make baked goods as part of their maternal duties. If you don't bake a treat to welcome your child back to the home after school, you are failing as a mother. The recipe includes preparation time, showing that the treat can be made with minimal effort. It gives mothers no excuse for not making it. Moreover, the advertisement exploits children to sell their product. All children have anxieties about new situations, but putting this into the ad just makes women feel guilty about unavoidable stresses their children have to deal with. The ad works by manipulating negative emotions in the readers.

Desserts do not have much nutritional value. It would be hard to make a logical case for making the Welcome Home Bars, so Eagle Brand used an emotional approach and an appeal to the image of the nurturing mother. There is nothing wrong with spoiling a child with a treat once in a while, but it is wrong to use guilt and social pressures to persuade mothers to buy a product.

Assignment 2: Using Visual Rhetoric as Promotion for Your School

Colleges and universities compete fiercely for students and are therefore as concerned about their image as any corporation or politician. As a class project, collect all the images your school uses to promote itself, including brochures for prospective students, catalogues, class lists, and Web home pages. Choose three or four of the best ones, and in class discussions subject them to careful scrutiny as we did in the previous section with ads and cartoons. Then, working in groups of three or four students or individually, do one or all of the following:

1. Find a side or aspect of your college or university that has been overlooked in the publications put out by the admissions office but that you believe is a strong selling point. Employing photographs, drawings, paintings, or some other visual medium, create an image appropriate for one of the school publications you collected. Join the image to an appropriate and

appealing short text. In a page or two, explain why you think your promotional image would work as well as or better than some of the ones presently in circulation.

2. If someone in the class has the computer knowledge to do so, create an alternative to your school's home page or make changes that would make it more appealing to prospective students, their parents, and other people who might use the Web.
3. Imagine that, for fun or for purposes of parody or protest, you wanted to call attention to aspects of your school that the official images deliberately omit. Proceed as in item 1. In a one- or two-page statement, explain why you chose the image you did and what purpose(s) you want it to serve.
4. Select a school organization (a fraternity or sorority, a club, etc.) whose image you think could be improved. Create a promotional image for it either for the Web or for some other existing or desirable publication.
5. As in item 3, create a visual parody of the official image of a school organization, perhaps as an inside joke intended for other participants in the organization.

No matter which of the preceding you or your group chooses, be sure to consult with other class members as you create and discuss the final results, including how revision or editing might enhance the impact. Remember that visual rhetoric can be altered in many ways; photos, for instance, can be taken from different angles and in different lighting conditions, processed in different ways, enlarged, reduced, trimmed, and so on.

Assignment 3: Analyzing Your Own Visual Rhetoric

Study all the images your class created as argument and/or persuasion in the previous assignment. Select an image to analyze in depth. Write an essay that addresses the following questions:

What audience does the image intend to reach?
What goal did the creator of the image seek to accomplish?

If something is being argued, ask:

What thesis is advanced by the image or its accompanying text?
Are there aspects of the image or text functioning as reasons for holding the thesis?

If an image persuades more than it argues, attempt to discover and understand its major source or sources of appeal. Persuasion appeals to the whole person in an effort to create *identification,* a strong linking of the reader's interests and values with the image that represents something desired or potentially desirable. Hence, we can ask:

How do the images your class created appeal to the audience's interests and values?
Do the images embody emotional appeals? How?

READER'S CHECKLIST FOR USING GRAPHICS

Graphics come in a variety of useful forms: as tables to display numerical data economically, as graphs to depict data in a way that permits easy comparison of proportions or trends, as photographs to convey realism and drama, and as drawings to depict structures. Whatever graphics you use, be sure to do the following:

1. Make sure every graphic has a definite function. Graphics are not decorative and should never be "thrown" into an essay.
2. Choose the kind or form best suited to convey the point you are trying to make.
3. Design graphics so that they are easy to "read" and interpret. That is, keep them simple, make them large enough to be read without strain, and use clear labeling.
4. Place graphics as close as possible to the text they explain or illustrate. Remember, graphics should be easier to understand than the text they supplement.
5. Refer to all your graphics in the text. Readers usually need both the graphic and a text discussion for full understanding.
6. Acknowledge the creator or source of each graphic next to the graphic itself. As long as you acknowledge the source or creator, you can borrow freely, just as you can with quotations from texts. Of course, if you wish to publish an essay that includes borrowed graphics, you must obtain written permission.

Assignment 4: Writing to Convince

Newspapers have been criticized for printing pictures that used to be considered too personal or gruesome for publication. The famous picture of the fireman carrying the baby killed in the Oklahoma City bombing is an example, as are pictures of victims of war atrocities in Kosovo and elsewhere. Highly respected newspapers like the *New York Times* have offered defenses for their decisions on this issue. Look into what publishers, readers, and critics have to say on this topic. What issues and questions come up in these debates? Draw a conclusion of your own on this topic, and write an essay supporting it.

Assignment 5: Using Graphics to Supplement Your Own Writing or Other Texts

Select an essay from the preceding assignment that could be improved either by adding graphics or by revising the graphics used. (If none of the papers seem appropriate for visual supplementation or revision, you may want to use one provided by your instructor.) Working alone or collaboratively with a writing group, rewrite/revise one of the papers. Pay attention to purpose and audience. Graphics should be efficient and memorable, designed to achieve a definite purpose and to have impact on a definite audience. The box on page 225 labeled "Reader's Checklist for Using Graphics" contains some general guidelines.

Recall that the best way to learn how to use graphics is by studying how others use them in respected publications. After reading and analyzing the graphics in the article from *Scientific American,* you might want to examine other examples of graphics in news magazines, scholarly books and articles, technical journals, institutional or business reports, and so on. You have many options: besides adding visuals, you can cut unneeded ones, redesign existing ones, change mediums (for example, from a photo to a drawing), change types (for example, from a table to a graph), and so on. Working with graphics always means working over the text as well. Expect changes in one to require changes in the other.

If more than one group works with the same paper, do not consult until rewriting or revising is complete. Then compare the results and discuss the strategies used. Which changes seem to improve the paper most? Why?

CHAPTER NINE

Researching Arguments

This chapter is intended to help you with any argument you write. Research, which simply means "careful study," is essential to serious inquiry and most well-constructed cases. Before you write, you need to investigate the ongoing conversation regarding your issue. As you construct your argument, you will need specific evidence and the support of authorities to make a convincing case to a skeptical audience.

Your high school experience may have led you to regard the "research paper" as different from other papers, but this distinction between researched and nonresearched writing does not usually apply to argumentation. An argument with no research behind it is generally a weak one indeed. Many of the arguments you read may not appear to be "researched" because the writers have not cited their sources—most likely because they were writing for the general public rather than for an academic or professional audience. In college writing, however, students are usually required to document all sources of ideas, as we will demonstrate later in this chapter.

Research for argumentation usually begins not as a search for evidence but rather as inquiry into an issue you have chosen or been assigned. Your task in inquiry is to discover information about the issue and, more importantly, to find arguments that address the issue and to familiarize yourself with the range of positions and the cases people make for them. You should inquire into these arguments using your critical reading skills and entering into dialogues with the authors until you feel satisfied with and confident about the position you take.

Sometimes, however, research must begin at an even earlier stage—when, for example, your instructor asks you to select an issue to write about. So we begin with suggestions on how to find an issue.

FINDING AN ISSUE

Let's say you have been assigned an essay on any issue of current public concern, ranging from one debated on your campus to one rooted in international affairs. If you have no ideas about what to write, what should you do?

Understand That an Issue Is More Than Merely a Topic

You must look for a subject over which people genuinely disagree. For example, homelessness is a *topic:* you could report on many different aspects of it—from the number of homeless people in our country to profiles of individual homeless people. But homelessness in itself is not really an issue because virtually everyone agrees that the problem exists. However, once you start considering solutions to the problem of homelessness, you are dealing with an *issue,* because people will disagree about how to solve the problem.

Keep Abreast of Current Events

Develop the habit of reading newspapers and magazines in print or online regularly to keep informed of debates on current issues. It has become easy to browse the day's news stories when you first turn on your computer. Many newspapers are available online. Major daily newspapers, such as the *New York Times* and the *Wall Street Journal,* maintain commercial Web sites. Here are several:

New York Times <http://www.nytimes.com>
Wall Street Journal <http://www.wsj.com>
Washington Post <http://washingtonpost.com>

Another site, *Newslibrary,* <http://www.newslibrary.com>, allows you to search around thirty-five different newspapers. It is best to write on issues of genuine concern to you rather than to manufacture concern at the last minute because a paper is due. Keep a record of your responses to your reading in your writer's notebook so that you have a readily available source of ideas.

Research the News

Visit the current periodicals shelves of your library or local newsstand. Consult the front page and the editorial/opinion columns of your city's daily paper. In addition, most newsstands and libraries carry the *New York Times* and other large-city dailies that offer thorough coverage of national and international events. Remember that you are looking for an issue, so if you find an article on the front page that interests you, think about how people might disagree over some question it raises. For example, an article announcing that health care costs rose a record fourteen percent in the past year might suggest the issue of government control over the medical profession; a campus newspaper article about a traditionally African-American fraternity could raise the issue of colleges tolerating racial segregation in the Greek system. In addition to newspapers, such magazines as *Time, Newsweek,* and *U.S. News & World Report* cover current events; and others, such as *Harper's, Atlantic Monthly, New Republic, National Review,* and *Utne Reader* offer essays, articles, and arguments on important current issues. With the growth of the Internet, new avenues are now available that allow quick and easy access to a broad range of information sources.

Research Your Library's Periodicals Indexes

Indexes are lists of articles in specific publications or groups of publications. You are most likely familiar with one index, the *Readers' Guide to Periodical Literature.* (For names of other indexes, see the section "Finding Sources" later in the chapter.) If you have a vague subject in mind, such as gender discrimination, consulting an index for articles and arguments on the topic can help you narrow your focus to a more concrete issue. Of course, if you don't have an issue in mind, looking through the *Readers' Guide* won't be very helpful, so we offer some suggestions for using indexes more efficiently.

You can, for example, look in a newspaper index (some are printed and bound while others are computerized) under "editorial" for a list of topics on which the editors have stated positions, or you can look under the name of a columnist—such as William F. Buckley, Anna Quindlen, or A. M. Rosenthal—whose views on current issues regularly appear in that paper. The bonus to using a newspaper index in this way is that it will lead you directly to arguments on an issue.

Another resource for finding arguments on an issue when you have a topic in mind is *InfoTrac,* a computerized index to magazines, journals, and selected current articles in the *New York Times.* After you type in an appropriate subject word or key word, *InfoTrac* allows you to narrow your search further. If you type in the key word of your subject followed by "and editorial" or "and opinion," only argumentative columns and editorials will appear on your screen. *InfoTrac* now also includes many full texts of articles online.

A further possibility is to browse through an index dedicated solely to periodicals that specialize in social issues topics, such as the *Journal of Social Issues* and *Vital Speeches of the Day.* Finally, *Speech Index* will help you find speeches that have been printed in books.

Inquire into the Issue

Once you have determined an issue, you can begin your inquiry into the positions already articulated in the public conversation. You may already hold a position of your own, but during inquiry you should be as open as possible to the full range of viewpoints on the issue; you should look for informative articles and for arguments about the issue.

Inquiring into an issue also involves evaluating sources. Remember that research means "careful study," and being careful as you perform these initial steps will make all the difference in the quality of the argument you eventually write. And, the more care you take now, the more time you'll save in the long run.

FINDING SOURCES

Sources for developing an argument can be found through several kinds of research. Library research is usually essential, but don't overlook what social scientists call *field research*. Also, the Internet and electronic mail offer rapidly expanding avenues for researching almost any topic. All research requires time and patience, as well as a knowledge of tools and techniques.

Field Research

Research "in the field" means studying the world directly through observations, questionnaires, and interviews.

Observations

Do not discount the value of your own personal experiences as evidence in making a case. You will notice that many writers of arguments offer as evidence what they themselves have seen, heard, and done. Such experiences may be from the past. For example, Sidney Hook's account of his own suffering after a nearly fatal stroke, told in sharp detail on pages 59–61, makes a compelling case for euthanasia.

Alternatively, you may seek out a specific personal experience as you inquire into your topic. For example, one student writing about the homeless in Dallas decided to visit a shelter. She called ahead to get permission and schedule the visit. Her paper was memorable because she was able to include the stories and physical descriptions of several homeless women, with details of their conversations.

Questionnaires and Surveys

You may be able to get information on some topics, especially if they are campus related, by doing surveys or questionnaires. This can be done very efficiently in electronic versions (Web-based or e-mail). Be forewarned, however, that it is very difficult to conduct a reliable survey.

First, there is the problem of designing a clear and unbiased instrument. If you have ever filled out an evaluation form for an instructor or a course, you will know what we mean about the problem of clarity. For example, one evaluation might ask whether an instructor returns papers "in a reasonable length of time"; however, what is "reasonable" to some students may be far too long for others. As for bias, consider the question "Have you ever had trouble getting assistance from the library's reference desk?" To get a fair response, this questionnaire had better also ask how many requests for help were handled promptly and well. If you do decide to draft a questionnaire, we suggest you do it as a class project, so that students on all sides of the issue can contribute and troubleshoot for areas of ambiguity.

Second, there is the problem of getting a representative response. For the same reasons we doubt the results of certain magazine-sponsored surveys of people's sex lives, we should be skeptical about the statistical accuracy of surveys targeting a group that may not be representative of the whole. For example, it might be difficult to generalize about all first-year college students in the United States based on a survey of only your English class—or even the entire first-year class at your college. Consider, too, that those who respond to a survey often have an ax to grind on the topic.

We don't rule out the value of surveys here, but we caution you to consider the difficulties of designing, administering, and interpreting such research tools.

Interviews

You can get a great deal of current information about an issue, as well as informed opinions, by talking to experts. As with any kind of research, the first step in conducting an interview is to decide exactly what you want to find out. Write down your questions, whether you plan to conduct the interview over the telephone, in person, or through e-mail.

The next step, which can take some effort and imagination, is to find the right person to interview. As you read about an issue, note the names (and the possible biases) of any organizations mentioned; these may have local offices, whose telephone numbers you could find in the directory. In addition, institutions such as hospitals, universities, and large corporations have information and public relations offices whose staff are responsible for providing information to those who seek it. An excellent source of over 30,000 names and phone numbers of experts in almost any field is a book by Matthew Lesko, *Lesko's Info-Power.* Finally, do not overlook the expertise available from faculty members at your own school.

Once you have determined possible sources for interviews, you must begin a patient and courteous round of telephone calls until you are connected with the right person; according to Lesko, this may take up to seven calls. Remain cheerful and clear in your pursuit. If you have a subject's e-mail address, you might write to introduce yourself and to schedule an appointment for a telephone interview.

Whether your interview is face-to-face or over the telephone, begin by being sociable but also by acknowledging that the interviewee's time is valuable. Tell the person something about the project you are working on, but withhold your own position on any controversial matters. Try to sound neutral, and be specific about what you want to know. Take notes, and include the title and background of the person being interviewed and the date of the interview, which you will need when citing this source in the finished paper. If you want to tape the interview, be sure to ask permission. Finally, if you have the individual's mailing address, it is thoughtful to send a follow-up note thanking him or her for the assistance.

If everyone in your class is researching a single topic and it is likely that more than one person would contact a particular expert on campus or in your community, avoid flooding that person with requests for his or her time. Perhaps one or two students could be designated to interview the subject and report to the class, or, if convenient, the expert could be invited to visit the class.

Library and Online Research

University libraries are vast repositories of information in print and electronic form. To use them most efficiently, consult with professional librarians. Do not hesitate to ask for help. Even college faculty can discover new sources of information by talking with librarians about current research projects.

The Internet, and its most popular component element, the World Wide Web, offers immediate access to thousands and thousands of documents on almost any subject. It provides currency and convenience, but it does not offer the reliability of the library. Care must be taken not to overrely on the Internet. It is not a shortcut to the research process. We begin with a discussion of the resources available in your library.

Library of Congress Subject Headings

Finding library sources will involve using the card or computerized catalog, reference books, and indexes to periodicals. Before using these, however, it makes sense to look first through a set of books every library locates near its catalog—the *Library of Congress Subject Headings.* This multivolume set will help you know what terms to look under when you move on to catalogs and indexes. The Library of Congress catalog is also available on the Internet at <http://lcweb.loc.gov/catalog/browse>. Consulting these subject headings first will save you time in the long run: it will help you narrow your search and keep you from overlooking potentially good sources because it also suggests related terms to look under. For example, if you look under the term "mercy killing," you will be directed to "euthanasia," where you can find the following helpful information:

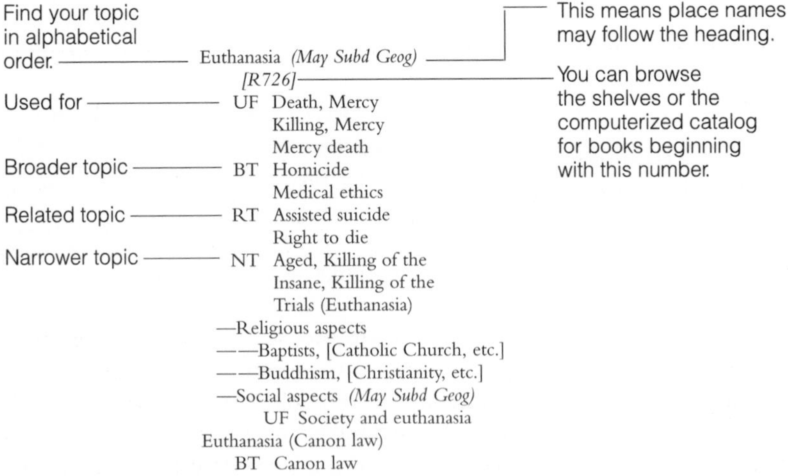

The Card or Computerized Catalog

Use your library's catalog primarily to find books or government documents. (For arguments and information on very current issues, however, keep in mind that the card or computer catalog is not the best source; because books take years to write and publish, they quickly become outdated.) Library catalogs list all holdings and are referenced according to author, title, and subject. With a computerized catalog it is also possible to find works according to key words and by Library of Congress number. Look under the subject headings you find in the *Library of Congress Subject Headings.* Moreover, because the Library of Congress system groups books according to subject matter, you may want to browse in the catalog (or on the shelves) for other books in the same range of call numbers.

Typically, the library's catalog card or screen will appear as illustrated here.

```
Search Request: A=FALUDI SUSAN
BOOK - Record 2 of 3 Entries Found                                    Brief View
------------------------------ Screen 1 of 1 ------------------------------
       TITLE:  Backlash : the undeclared war against American women
     EDITION:  1st ed.
      AUTHOR:  Faludi, Susan.

   PUBLISHER:  New York : Crown, c1991.
 DESCRIPTION:  xxiii, 552 p. : 25 cm.

    SUBJECTS:  Feminism--United States.
               Women--United States--Social conditions.
               Women--Psychology.
------------------------------------------------------------------------------
         LOCATION:              CALL NUMBER:                   STATUS:
 1. Fondren Browsing        HQ1426 .F35 1991          Charged, Due: 04/02/93
      Coll.

------------------------------------------------------------------------------
 COMMANDS:               LO Long View          I Index
                         N  Next Record        H Help
 O  Other Options        P  Previous Record

NEXT COMMAND:
```

Indexes to Periodicals

Good libraries contain many indexes that list articles in newspapers, magazines, and journals. Some of these are printed and bound; others are online and on CD-ROM. Once again, the *Library of Congress Subject Headings* can help you determine the best words to search in these indexes.

Newspaper Indexes The *New York Times Index* is printed and bound in volumes. Each volume indexes articles for one year, grouped according to subject and listed according to the month and day of publication. The subject headings in the *New York Times Index* tend to be very general. For example, we could not find the heading "euthanasia," the term for mercy killing used in the

Library of Congress Subject Headings. We had to think of a more general term, so we tried "medicine." There, we found the following:

MEDICINE AND HEALTH. See also
Abortion
Accidents and Safety
Acupuncture
Aged
Anatomy and Physiology
Anesthesia and Anesthetics
Antibiotics
Autopsies
Bacteria
Birth Control and Family Planning
Birth Defects
Blood
Death — The subject heading most likely to lead to articles on euthanasia
Environment
Epidemics
Exercise
Faith Healers
First Aid
Food Contamination and Poisoning
Handicapped
Hormones
Immunization and Immunity
Implants
Industrial and Occupational Hazards
Malpractice Insurance
Mental Health and Disorders
Nursing Homes
Pesticides and Pests
Population
Radiation
Smoking
Spas
Surgery and Surgeons
Teeth and Dentistry
Transplants
Vaccination and Vaccines
Veterinary Medicine
Viruses
Vitamins
Water Pollution
Workmen's Compensation Insurance
X-Rays

We decided the term "death" on this list seemed most likely to lead us to articles on euthanasia, and we were correct. Following is a small selection of what we found.

Topic headings are listed in alphabetical order.

DEATH. See also
Deaths

Several laws enacted in New York State in 1990 are set to take effect, including measure that will allow New Yorkers to designate another person to make health-care decisions on their behalf if they become unable to do so (M). Ja 1.1. 32:1

Articles are listed in chronological order.

Each entry contains an abstract.

Another right-to-die case emerges in Missouri, where Christine Busalacchi has been in persistent vegetative state as result of auto accident on May 29, 1987, when she was 17-year-old high school junior: her father, Pete Busalacchi, who has been seeking unsuccessfully to have his daughter transferred to Minnesota, where feeding tube may possibly be removed, says that Christine never discussed matters of life or death; Nancy Cruzan case recalled; photo (M). Ja 2. A.12:1

Missouri state court dismisses order preventing Pete Busalacchi from moving his comatose daughter Christine to another state where less strict rules might allow removal of feeding tube (S). Ja S.A.16:1

(S), (M), or (L) before the date indicates whether an article is short, medium, or long.

In a case that medical ethicists and legal experts say is apparently a first, Minneapolis-based Hennapin County Medical Center plans to go to court for permission to turn off 37-year-old Helga Wanglie's life support system against her family's wishes; photos (L). Ja 10.A.1:1

Each entry concludes with the month, day, section, page, and column.

Probate Judge Louis Kohn of St. Louis County rules that Pete Busalacchi may move his daughter, Christine, from Missouri hospital where she has lain for more than three years with severe brain damage and take her to Minnesota where law might allow removal of her feeding tube (S). Ja 17.3.5:1

People wishing to avoid heroic medical treatment in event they become hopelessly ill and unable to speak for themselves are often poorly served by so-called "living wills" to achieve that end: many health care experts recommend a newer document, health care proxy, in which patients designate surrogate who has legal authority to make medical decisions if they are too sick to offer an opinion; others recommend combining living will with health care proxy; drawing (M). Ja 17.3.9:1

Missouri Judge Louis Kohn rules Pete Busalacchi has right to determine medical care of his daughter Christine, who has been severely brain-damaged for more than three years; gives him authority to have feeding tube removed (S). Ja 18.A.16:4

Missouri appeals court bars Pete Busalacchi from moving his comatose 20-year-old daughter Christine to Minnesota where laws governing removal of life-support systems are less restrictive (S). Ja 19.1.17:2

Editorial Notebook commentary by Fred M. Hechinger says his 94-year-old mother's last days were filled with needless suffering and fear because doctors ignored her, and her family's wish that no heroic efforts be taken to prolong her life; says inhumane legal restrictions have made doctors accomplices in torture, and medical profession has shown little courage in fighting them (M). Ja 24.A.22:1

As mentioned, you will also find a limited number of *New York Times* articles listed in the computerized periodicals index known as *InfoTrac.* Another excellent source of online articles from magazines and newspapers is *Lexis-Nexis.*

Other printed and bound newspaper indexes carried by most libraries are the *Christian Science Monitor Index,* the *Times Index* (to the London *Times,* a good source for international issues), the *Wall Street Journal Index,* and the *Washington Post Index* (good for federal government issues).

Newsbank offers computerized indexes for hundreds of local and state newspapers. Your library is likely to subscribe to *Newsbank* for indexes of only one or two regional papers in your area. *Newsbank*'s CD-ROMs contain the entire text of each article indexed.

Indexes to Magazines, Journals, and Other Materials Many libraries have CD-ROM databases indexing journals in business and academic fields. *InfoTrac,* one such database, indexes current articles from the *New York Times* and many other periodicals, so you may want to begin your search here rather than with the printed and bound indexes discussed previously. Be aware, however, that *InfoTrac* is a very selective index, far less comprehensive than the printed and bound indexes, which also go back much further in time. In addition, *InfoTrac* will not include many articles that can be found in the specialized indexes that follow. *InfoTrac* is, however, constantly being upgraded, so check with your reference librarian to see how this database can help you research your issue.

1. General interest indexes:

   Readers' Guide to Periodical Literature
   Public Affairs Information Service (PAIS)
   Essay and General Literature Index
   Speech Index

2. Arts and humanities indexes:

   Art Index
   Film Literature Index
   Humanities Index
   Music Index
   Philosopher's Index
   Popular Music Periodical Index

3. Social science, business, and law indexes:

   Business Periodicals Index
   Criminology Index
   Education Index
   Index to Legal Periodicals
   Psychological Abstracts
   Social Sciences Index
   Sociological Abstracts
   Women's Studies Abstracts

4. Science and engineering indexes:

    Applied Science and Technology Index
    Biological and Agricultural Index
    Current Contents
    Environmental Index
    General Science Index

Reference Books

Students tend to overlook many helpful reference books, often because they are unaware of their existence. You may find reference books useful early in the process of inquiring into your issue, but they are also useful for locating supporting evidence as you develop your own argument. The following are some reference books you might find helpful:

First Stop: The Master Index to Subject Encyclopedias (a subject index to 430 specialized encyclopedias—a good source of general background information)
Demographic Yearbook
Facts on File
Guide to American Law (a reference work that explains legal principles and concepts in plain English)
Statistical Abstract of the United States
World Almanac and Book of Facts

Bibliographies

Books and articles sometimes include a works-cited list or bibliography, which can reveal numerous additional sources. Library catalog entries and many indexes indicate whether a book or article contains a bibliography.

Internet Research

The *Internet* is a global network that links computers, and the files stored on them, to one another. It is a valuable research tool because it provides access to information in the computers of educational institutions, businesses, government bureaus, and nonprofit organizations all over the world. Most people now use the World Wide Web for access to the Internet. The Web is that portion of the Internet that uses HTML (hypertext mark-up language) to present information in the form of Web sites that contain individual Web pages.

The Internet also provides the connections for e-mail and real-time communications, such as ongoing discussions among groups with common areas of interest; the communication functions of the Internet can also be useful for researching a topic. Because nearly all college computer networks are linked to the Internet, as a student you will have access to it (even if you do not own a computer). Most schools have a department of computer and educational technology that can tell you where and how to get connected.

Just as we advise you to seek help from a librarian when beginning your library research, so we also suggest that you begin electronic, or online, research by consulting one of the librarians at your school who has specialized training in navigating the information superhighway. Because the Internet is so large and complex and—like most real highways—is perpetually "under construction," we will offer only general advice about what Internet resources would be most useful for undergraduate research on comtemporary public issues. One of the best online sources for help with the Internet is the Library of Congress Resource Page, at <http://lcweb.loc.gov/global/search.html>. Once you are connected to this page, you can link to any number of the following resources.

The World Wide Web

Of all the networks on the Internet, the *World Wide Web* is the friendliest and the most fun because it links files from various "host" computers around the world; from one site on the Web, you can click on highlighted words known as *hypertext links* that will take you to other sites on the Web where related information is stored. For example, an online article on euthanasia may highlight the words "Hippocratic oath"; clicking on the highlighted words will allow you to see a copy of the oath and learn a little more about it.

Although the Web continues to expand, finding useful sites is not always as easy as finding books and articles in the library, because as material is posted, there is no system that neatly catalogs all the information. However, technology to help users navigate the Internet is constantly improving. The Web does support a number of *search engines,* which index existing and newly posted information, usually through the use of key words. Once you connect to your school's Internet browser (such as Netscape or Microsoft Internet Explorer), you can type in the address of one of these engines, or you may be able to load the engine by simply clicking on an icon. Addresses on the Internet are known as *uniform resource locators (URLs).* Below are the URLs for some popular search engines. Note that World Wide Web URLs begin with "http," which stands for "hypertext transfer protocol."

AltaVista <http://altavista.com>
Excite <http://www.excite.com>
Hotbot <http://www.hotbot.com>
Infoseek <http://infoseek.go.com>
Lycos <http://lycos.com>
Metacrawler <http://www.go2net.com>
Webcrawler <http://webcrawler.com>
Yahoo! <http://www.yahoo.com> (Yahoo! searches by subject, not by a key word.)

Once you access the search engine, enter key words describing the information you want. For example, by typing in "search engine," you can find the addresses of other search engines. We recommend that you try this, because new search engines are being created all the time. In fact, that is how we discovered Metacrawler, which, as its name suggests, searches all the other search engines.

We want to caution you that surfing the Web is not always a quick and easy way to do research. Be prepared to spend some time and to try a variety of search engines. Web searches can often take more time than library research because you will encounter so much irrelevant information. You will also find much information that is not suitable for use in academic writing. Because anyone can post a document on the Web, you need to check the author's credentials carefully. (The section "Evaluating Sources" will discuss this further.) The Internet is a tool that can provide new avenues for your research, but it will not replace the library as your primary research venue.

GopherSpace

Gopher, a program for accessing Internet information through hierarchical menus, is named for the Golden Gopher mascot at the University of Minnesota, where this software was developed. Gopher is an older system than the World Wide Web. Like other protocols such as FTP and telnet, Gopher looks different because it lacks a hypertext format. However, many documents are stored in *GopherSpace.* Once Gopher has retrieved a document for you, you can read it on your screen, save it to a disk, or even print out a copy of it. Instead of hypertext links, Gopher organizes hierarchical menus based on topic areas. For example, you may open a menu that lists major subject areas such as "government and politics." If you select this category, you will get another menu that may have the item "Supreme Court cases." Selecting that, you will find another list, and so on. Many of the Web search engines previously described include GopherSpace in their searches, so you may happen to find Gopher documents while you are searching the World Wide Web.

Listservs and Usenet Newsgroups

The Internet allows groups of people to communicate with one another on topics of common interest; observing and participating in such groups is another way to learn about a topic and find out what issues are being debated. *Listservs* are like electronic bulletin boards or discussion groups, where people with a shared interest can post or ask for information, and simply converse about a topic. Listservs are supported by e-mail, so if you have an e-mail account, it will cost you nothing to join a group. You may find an appropriate Listserv group by e-mailing <listserv@listserve.net> with a message specifying your area of interest, such as "list environmentalism" or "list euthanasia." You can also find listserv groups on the World Wide Web at <http://tile.net/lists/>. *Usenet newsgroups* also act like electronic bulletin boards, which your college's system administrator may or may not make available on your school's server. To find lists of active newsgroups, type in "newsgroups" as a search term in one of the Web search engines, such as Yahoo! Newsgroups and listservs are often composed of highly specialized professionals who expect other participants to have followed their discussions for weeks and months before participating. They even post lists of *frequently asked questions (FAQs)* to avoid having to cover the same topics repeatedly. Finding the exact information you need in the transcripts of their discussions is like looking for the proverbial needle in a haystack, so Usenet is not likely to be as useful as the Web as a general research tool. However, while searching the Web, you may encounter links to some discussions relevant to your topic that have been archived on the Web. You may want to cite information gathered from these groups, but you need to be very careful about what you choose to use as a source because anyone can join in, regardless of his or her credentials and expertise. Most correspondents who have professional affiliations list them along with their name and "snail mail" (U.S. postal service) address. In addition to credentials, be sure to note the name of the group, the name of the individual posting the message, the date and time it was posted, and the URL if you have found it on the Web. (See the section "Creating a Works-Cited or Reference List" for more information on citing electronic sources.)

EVALUATING SOURCES

Before you begin to read and evaluate your sources, you may need to reevaluate your issue. If you have been unable to find many sources that address the question you are raising, step back and consider changing the focus of your argument or at least expanding its focus.

For example, one student had the choice of any issue under the broad category of the relationship between humans and other animals. Michelle decided to focus on the mistreatment of circus animals, based on claims made in leaflets handed out at the circus by animal rights protestors. Even with a librarian's help, however, Michelle could find no subject headings that led to even one source in her university's library. She then called and visited animal rights activists in her city, who provided her with more materials written and published by the animal rights movement. She realized, however, that researching the truth of their claims was more than she could undertake, so she had to acknowledge that her entire argument was based on inadequate inquiry and heavily biased sources.

Once you have reevaluated your topic, use the following method to record and evaluate sources.

Eliminate Inappropriate Sources

If you are a first-year college student, you may find that some books and articles are intended for audiences with more specialized knowledge of the subject than you have. If you have trouble using a source—if it confuses you or shakes your confidence in your reading comprehension—put it aside, at least temporarily.

Also, carefully review any electronic sources you are using. While search engines make it easy to find source material on the Web, online documents often have met no professional standards for scholarship. Material can be "published" electronically without the rigorous review by experts, scholars, and editors that must occur in traditional publishing. Nevertheless, you will find legitimate scholarship on the Internet—many news reports, encyclopedias, government documents, and even scholarly journals appear online. While the freedom of electronic publishing creates an exciting and democratic arena for discussion, it also puts a much heavier burden on students to ensure that the sources they use are worthy of readers' respect. You must exercise caution whenever you use a Web source as part of your research paper.

Carefully Record Complete Bibliographic Information

For every source you are even considering using, be sure to record full bibliographic information. You should take this information from the source itself, not from an index, which may be incomplete or even inaccurate. If you make a record of this information immediately, you will not have to go back later to fill in careless omissions. We recommend that you use a separate index card for each source, but whatever you write on, you must record the following:

1. For a book:

    Author's full name (or names)
    Title of book
    City where published
    Name of publisher
    Year published

    For an article or essay in a book, record all of the information for the book, including the names of the book's author or editor and the title and the author(s) of the article; also record the inclusive page numbers of the article or chapter (for example, "pp. 100–150").

2. For a periodical:

    Author's full name (or names)
    Title of the article
    Title of the periodical
    Date of the issue
    Volume number, if given
    Inclusive page numbers

3. For a document found on the World Wide Web:

    Author's full name (or names)
    Title of the work
    Original print publication data, if applicable
    Title of the database
    Full http address
    Date you accessed the document

4. For a document found through Gopher:

   Author's full name (or names)
   Title of the work
   Original print publication data, if applicable
   Title of the database
   Full Gopher search path that accessed the document
   Date you accessed the document

5. For material found through listservs and Usenet newsgroups:

   Author's full name (or names)
   Author's e-mail address
   Subject line from the posting
   Date of the posting
   Address of the listserv or newsgroups
   Date you accessed the document

Read the Source Critically

As discussed in Chapter 2, critical reading depends on having some prior knowledge of the subject and the ability to see a text in its rhetorical context. As you research a topic, your knowledge naturally becomes deeper with each article you read. But your sources are not simply windows onto your topic, giving you a clear view; whether argumentative or informative, they present a bias. Before looking through them, you must look *at* your sources. Therefore, it is essential that you devote conscious attention to the rhetorical context of the sources you find. As you read, keep these questions in mind.

Who Is the Writer and What Is His or Her Bias?

Is there a note that tells you anything about the writer's professional title or university or institutional affiliation? If not, a quick look in the *Dictionary of American Biographies* might help; or you can consult the *Biography and Genealogy Master Index,* which will send you to numerous specialized biographical sketches. If you are going to cite the writer as an authority in your argument, you need to be able to convince your audience of his or her credibility.

How Reliable Is the Source?

Again, checking for credibility is particularly important when you are working with electronic sources. For example, one student found two sites on the Web, both through a key word search on "euthanasia." One, entitled "Stop the Epidemic of Assisted Suicide," was posted by a person identified only by name, the letters MD, and the affiliation "Association for Control of Assisted Suicide." There was no biographical information, and the "snail mail" address was a post office box. The other Web site, entitled "Ethics Update: Euthanasia," was posted by a professor of philosophy at the University of San Diego whose home page included a complete professional biography detailing his educational background and the titles and publishers of his many other books and articles. The author gave his address at USD in the Department of Philosophy. The student decided that while the first source had some interesting information—including examples of individual patients who were living with pain rather than choosing suicide—it was not a source that skeptical readers would find credible. Search engines often land you deep within a Web site, and you have to visit the site's home page to get any background information about the source and its author. Be suspicious of sites that do not contain adequate source information. They may not be reliable.

When Was This Source Written?

If you are researching a very current issue, you need to decide what sources may be too dated. Keep in mind, though, that arguments on current issues often benefit from earlier perspectives.

Where Did This Source Appear?

If you are using an article from a periodical, be aware of the periodical's readership and any editorial bias. For example, *National Review* has a conservative bent, while *The Nation* is liberal; an article in the *Journal of the American Medical Association* will usually defend the medical profession. Looking at the table of contents and scanning any editorial statements will help give you a feel for the periodical's political leanings. Also look at the page that lists the publisher and the editorial board. You would find, for example, that *New American* is published by the ultra-right-wing John Birch Society. If you need help determining political bias, ask a librarian. A reference book that lists periodicals by subject matter and explains their bias is *Magazines for Libraries.*

Why Was the Book or Article Written?

While some articles are occasioned by events in the news, most books and arguments are written as part of an ongoing debate or conversation among scholars or journalists. Being aware of the issues and the participants in this conversation is essential, as you will be joining it with your own researched argument. You can check *Book Review Index* to find where a book has been reviewed and then consult some reviews to see how the book was received.

What Is the Author's Aim?

Be aware, first, of whether the source is intended to inform or whether it is an argument with a claim to support. Both informative and argumentative sources are useful, and even informative works will have some bias. When your source is an argument, note whether it aims primarily to inquire, to convince, to persuade, or to mediate.

How Is the Source Organized?

If the writer does not employ subheadings or chapter titles, try to break the text into its various parts, and note what function each part plays in the whole.

Inquire into the Source

Because we devote so much attention to inquiry in Chapters 3 and 4, we will not go into detail about this process here. However, you should identify any author's claim and evaluate the support offered for it. Look especially closely at arguments that support your own position; seeing weaknesses in such "friendly" arguments has caused many students to experience an epiphany, or a moment of enlightenment, in which they change their whole stance on an issue. The box "Suggestions for Evaluating Sources" will help you evaluate Web sources for reliability.

Consider How You Might Use the Source

If you are fortunate, your research will uncover many authoritative and well-crafted arguments on your issue. The challenge you now face is to work out a way to use them in an argument of your own, built on your own structure and strategy and suited to your own aim and audience.

A good argument results from synthesizing, or blending together, the results of your research. Your sources should help you come up with strong reasons and evidence, as well as ideas about opposing views. But it is unlikely that all your reasons will come from one source or that each part of your argument will draw primarily upon a single source, and you don't want to create an argument that reads like a patchwork of other people's ideas. Thus, you must organize your sources according to your own argumentative strategy and integrate material from a variety of sources into each part of your argument.

SUGGESTIONS FOR EVALUATING SOURCES

1. Look at the last segment of the domain name, which will tell you who developed the site. The most reliable sites are those developed by colleges and universities (*.edu*) or by the government (*.gov*). Remember that businesses (*.bus*) are profit-minded.
2. Check whether the name of the creator of the Web page or its Webmaster, complete with an e-mail address and the date of the last update, appears—near either the top or the bottom of the page.
3. Check whether the source includes a bibliography, which indicates a scholarly page.
4. Ask yourself whether the links are credible.
5. Remember that a tilde (~) indicates a personal page; these must be evaluated carefully.

We suggest that you review Chapter 5, where we discuss developing and refining a thesis (or claim) and constructing a brief of your argument. As you make your brief, identify those sources that will help you offer reasons or support, such as expert opinion or specific data.

USING SOURCES

How you use a source depends on what you need it for. After you have drafted an argument, you may simply need to consult an almanac for some additional evidence or, say, look up John F. Kennedy's inaugural address to find a stirring quotation. But at earlier stages of the writing process, you may be unsure of your own position and even in need of general background information on the issue. What follows is some advice for those early stages, when you will be encountering a great deal of information and opposing viewpoints. As you research, remember to write down all of the bibliographical information for every source you might use.

Taking Notes

Just as you can check out books from the library for your own use at home or in your dormitory, so you can photocopy entire articles for your personal use away from the library. Likewise, if you are working with electronic sources, you can print out the entire text of many online documents. These various methods of gathering materials are helpful for doing research, but when it comes time to use the sources in a paper of your own, the traditional writing skills of note-taking, paraphrasing, and summarizing will help you work efficiently and avoid plagiarism.

Whether you are working with a book, a photocopied article, or a document retrieved from the Internet, you will save time in the long run if you write down—preferably on a large notecard—anything that strikes you as important or useful. By taking notes, you will avoid having to sort through the entire text of your research materials to find the idea you thought would work in your paper two weeks ago. The box "Suggestions for Taking Notes" summarizes the process.

Paraphrasing

Paraphrasing, which means restating a passage in your own words, improves reading comprehension. When you put an idea, especially a complex one, into your own words, you are actually explaining the idea to yourself. When you have a firm grasp of an idea, you can write more confidently, with a sense of owning the idea rather than simply borrowing it. The box "Suggestions for Paraphrasing" summarizes the technique.

We will illustrate paraphrasing with an excerpt from a source selected by one student, Patrick Pugh, who was researching the topic of euthanasia and planning to defend active euthanasia, or assisted suicide. In the university

SUGGESTIONS FOR TAKING NOTES

1. Note your source. Use the author's last name or an abbreviated title, or devise a code, such as "A," "B," "C," and so forth.
2. Note the exact page or pages where the information or quotation appears.
3. When you quote, be exact and put quotation marks around the writer's words, to avoid plagiarism if you use them later in your paper.
4. Paraphrase and summarize whenever possible; reserve quotations for passages in which the writer's words are strongly opinionated or especially memorable.

library Patrick found a book entitled *Suicide and Euthanasia: The Rights of Personhood,* a collection of essays written by doctors, philosophers, theologians, and legal experts. Published in 1981, the book was somewhat dated in 1991, when Patrick was doing his research, but he felt that the question of whether suicide is moral or immoral was a timeless one. He read an essay entitled "In Defense of Suicide" by Joseph Fletcher, a former professor at the Episcopal Divinity School and president of the Society for the Right to Die. Before

SUGGESTIONS FOR PARAPHRASING

1. Use a dictionary if any words in the original are not completely familiar to you.
2. Work with whole ideas—that is, remember that paraphrasing involves more than keeping the original word order and just plugging in synonyms. Don't be afraid to make your paraphrase longer than the original. Try to break a complex sentence into several simpler ones of your own; take apart a difficult idea and rebuild it, step-by-step. Don't just echo the original passage thoughtlessly.
3. Don't be a slave to the original—or to the thesaurus. Read the passage until you think you understand it, or a part of it. Then write your version, without looking back at the original. Rearrange the order of ideas if doing so makes the passage more accessible.
4. Don't strain to find substitutes for words that are essential to the meaning of a passage.

taking notes on Fletcher's essay, Patrick made a bibliography card recording all the necessary information about this source, as follows:

Fletcher, Joseph. "In Defense of Suicide." In Suicide and Euthanasia: The Rights of Personhood. Eds. Samuel E. Wallace and Albin Eser. Knoxville: U of Tennessee P 1981

Fletcher's article: pp. 38–50.

The following passage from Fletcher's essay offers a crucial definition; it is the kind of passage that a researcher should paraphrase on a notecard rather than quote, so that the idea becomes part of one's own store of knowledge.

> We must begin with the postulate that no action is intrinsically right or wrong, that nothing is inherently good or evil. Right and wrong, good and evil, desirable and undesirable—all are ethical terms and all are predicates, not properties. The moral "value" of any human act is always contingent, depending on the shape of the action in the situation. . . . The variables and factors in each set of circumstances are the determinants of what ought to be done—not prefabricated generalizations or prescriptive rules. . . . No "law" of conduct is always obliging; what we ought to do is whatever maximizes human well-being.
>
> —JOSEPH FLETCHER, "In Defense of Suicide"

Patrick paraphrased this passage on the following notecard. Note that he names the author of the essay, the editors of the book, and the exact pages on which the idea was found.

Fletcher's definition of ethical action:

The ethical value of any human action is not a quality inherent in the act itself. It is a judgment that we make about the act after examining the entire situation in which it takes place. Rather than relying on general rules about what is moral and immoral, we should make our decision on the basis of what is best for human well-being in any given set of circumstances.

Fletcher, pp. 38-39, in Wallace/Eser.

Following Through

From your own research, select a passage of approximately one paragraph that presents a complicated idea. Write a paraphrase of the passage.

Alternatively, you may write a paraphrase of the following paragraph, also from Joseph Fletcher's "In Defense of Suicide":

> What is called positive euthanasia—doing something to shorten or end life deliberately—is the form [of euthanasia] in which suicide is the question, as a voluntary, direct choice of death. For a long time the Christian moralists have distinguished between negative or indirectly willed suicide, like not taking a place in one of the *Titanic*'s lifeboats, and positive or directly willed suicide, like jumping out of a lifeboat to make room for a fellow victim of a shipwreck. The moralists mean that we may choose to allow an evil by acts of omission but not to do an evil by acts of comission. The moralists contend that since all suicide is evil, we may only "allow" it; we may not "do" it. (47)

Your instructor may ask you to compare your paraphrase with that of a classmate before revising it and handing it in.

Summarizing

While a paraphrase may be longer or shorter than the original passage, a summary is always considerably shorter. It ought to be at least one-third the length of the original and is often considerably less: you may, for example, reduce an entire article to one or two paragraphs.

A summary of an argument must contain the main idea or claim and the main points of support or development. The amount of evidence and detail you include depends on your purpose for summarizing: if you merely want to give your audience (or remind yourself of) the gist of the original, a bare-bones summary is enough; but if you plan to use the summary as part of making your case, you had better include the original's evidence as well. The box "Suggestions for Summarizing" outlines the process.

For an example of using a summary as part of an argument, we return to Patrick Pugh's investigation of euthanasia. In another book, *The End of Life: Euthanasia and Morality* by James Rachels, Patrick found what Rachels describes as the chief religious objections to euthanasia, with Rachels' rebuttals for each. Patrick decided to include this material, in summary, in his paper. First read the passage from Rachels's book; then read Patrick's summarized version that follows immediately after.

SUGGESTIONS FOR SUMMARIZING

1. Read and reread the original text until you have identified the thesis and main points. You ought to be able to state these in your own words without looking back at the source.
2. Make it clear at the start whose ideas you are summarizing. Refer to the writer again only as necessary for clarity.
3. If you are summarizing a long passage, break it down into subsections and work on summarizing each one at a time.
4. As with paraphrasing, work as independently as you can—from memory—as you attack each part. Then go back to the text to check your version for accuracy.
5. Try to maintain the original order of points, with this exception: if the author delayed presenting the thesis, you may want to refer to it earlier in your summary.
6. Use your own words as much as possible.
7. Avoid quoting entire sentences. If you want to quote key words and phrases, try to incorporate them into sentences of your own, using quotation marks around the borrowed words.
8. Write a draft summary; then summarize your draft.
9. Revise for conciseness and coherence; look for ways to combine sentences, using connecting words to show how ideas relate. (See the section in Appendix A entitled "Use Transitions to Show Relationships between Ideas.")

JAMES RACHELS

from The End of Life

Religious Arguments

SOCIAL OBSERVERS are fond of remarking that we live in a secular age, and there is surely something in this. The power of religious conceptions was due, in some considerable measure, to their usefulness in explaining things. In earlier times, religious ideas were used to explain everything from the origins of the universe to the nature of human beings. So long as we had no other way of understanding the world, the hold of religion on us was powerful indeed. Now, however, these explanatory functions have largely been taken over by the sciences: physics, chemistry, and their allies explain physical nature, while evolutionary biology and psychology combine to tell us about ourselves. As there is less and less work for religious hypotheses to do, the grip of religious ideas on us weakens, and appeals to theological conceptions are heard only on Sunday mornings. Hence, the "secular age." 1

However, most people continue to hold religious beliefs, and they especially appeal to those beliefs when morality is at issue. Any discussion of mercy-killing quickly leads to objections based on theological grounds, and "secular" arguments for euthanasia are rejected because they leave out the crucial element of God's directions on the matter.

Considering the traditional religious opposition to euthanasia, it is tempting to say: If one is not a Christian (or if one does not have some similar religious orientation), then perhaps euthanasia is an option; but for people who do have such a religious orientation, euthanasia cannot be acceptable. And the discussion might be ended there. But this is too quick a conclusion; for it is possible that the religious arguments against euthanasia are not valid *even for religious people.* Perhaps a religious perspective, even a conventional Christian one, does *not* lead automatically to the rejection of mercy-killing. With this possibility in mind, let us examine three variations of the religious objection.

What God Commands

It is sometimes said that euthanasia is not permissible simply because God forbids it, and we know that God forbids it by the authority of either scripture or Church tradition. Thus, one eighteenth-century minister, Humphrey Primatt, wrote ironically that, in the case of aged and infirm animals,

> God, the Father of Mercies, hath ordained Beasts and Birds of Prey to do that distressed creature the kindness to relieve him his misery, by putting him to death. A kindness which *We* dare not show to our own species. If thy father, thy brother, or thy child should suffer the utmost pains of a long and agonizing sickness, though his groans should pierce through thy heart, and with strong crying and tears he

> should beg thy relief, yet thou must be deaf unto him; he must wait his appointed time till his charge cometh, till he sinks and is crushed with the weight of his own misery.

When this argument is advanced, it is usually advanced with great con- 5
fidence, as though it were *obvious* what God requires. Yet we may well wonder whether such confidence is justified. The sixth commandment does not say, literally, "Thou shalt not *kill*"—that is a bad translation. A better translation is "Thou shalt not commit *murder,*" which is different, and which does not obviously prohibit mercy-killing. Murder is by definition *wrongful* killing; so, if you do not think that a given kind of killing is wrong, you will not call it murder. That is why the sixth commandment is not normally taken to forbid killing in a just war; since such killing is (allegedly) justified, it is not called murder. Similarly, if euthanasia is justified, it is not murder, and so it is not prohibited by the commandment. At the very least, it is clear that we cannot infer that euthanasia is wrong *because* it is prohibited by the commandment.

If we look elsewhere in the Christian Bible for a condemnation of euthanasia, we cannot find it. These scriptures are silent on the question. We do find numerous affirmations of the sanctity of human life and the fatherhood of God, and some theologians have tried to infer a prohibition on euthanasia from these general precepts. (The persistence of the attempts, in the face of logical difficulties, is a reminder that people insist on reading their moral prejudices *into* religious texts much more often than they derive their moral views *from* the texts.) But we also find exhortations to kindness and mercy, and the Golden Rule proclaimed as the sum of all morality; and these principles, as we have seen, support euthanasia rather than condemn it.

We *do* find a clear condemnation of euthanasia in Church tradition. Regardless of whether there is scriptural authority for it, the Church has historically opposed mercy-killing. It should be emphasized, however, that this is a matter of history. Today, many religious leaders favour euthanasia and think the historical position of the Church has been mistaken. It was an Episcopal minister, Joseph Fletcher, who in his book *Morals and Medicine* formulated the classic modern defence of euthanasia. Fletcher does not stand alone among his fellow churchmen. The Euthanasia Society of America, which he heads, includes many other religious leaders; and the recent "Plea for Beneficent Euthanasia," sponsored by the American Humanist Association, was signed by more religious leaders than people in any other category. So it certainly cannot be claimed that *contemporary* religious forces stand uniformly opposed to euthanasia.

It is noteworthy that even Roman Catholic thinkers are today reassessing the Church's traditional ban on mercy-killing. The Catholic philosopher Daniel Maguire has written one of the best books on the subject, *Death by Choice.* Maguire maintains that "it may be moral and should be legal to accelerate the death process by taking direct action, such as overdosing with morphine or injecting potassium"; and moreover, he proposes to demonstrate that this view is "*compatible with historical Catholic ethical theory,*" contrary to what most opponents of euthanasia assume. Historical Catholic ethical theory, he says, grants individuals permission to act on views that are supported by "good and serious reasons," even when a different view is supported by a majority of authorities. Since the morality of euthanasia *is* supported by "good and serious reasons," Maguire concludes that Catholics are permitted to accept that morality and act on it.

Thus, the positions of both scripture and Church authorities are (at least) ambiguous enough so that the believer is not bound, on these grounds, to reject mercy-killing. The argument from "what God commands" should be inconclusive, even for the staunchest believer.

The Idea of God's Dominion

10 Our second theological argument starts from the principle that "The life of man is solely under the dominion of God." It is for God alone to decide when a person shall live and when he shall die; we have no right to "play God" and arrogate this decision unto ourselves. So euthanasia is forbidden.

This is perhaps the most familiar of all the theological objections to euthanasia; one hears it constantly when the matter is discussed. However, it is remarkable that people still advance this argument today, considering that it was decisively refuted over 200 years ago, when Hume made the simple but devastating point that *if it is for God alone to decide when we shall live and when we shall die, then we "play God" just as much when we cure people as when we kill them.* Suppose a person is sick and we have the means to cure him or her. If we do so, then we are interfering with God's "right to decide" how long the life shall last! Hume put it this way:

> Were the disposal of human life so much reserved as the peculiar providence of the Almighty that it were an encroachment on his right, for men to dispose of their own lives; it would be equally criminal to act for the preservation of life as for its destruction. If I turn aside a stone which is falling upon my head, I disturb this course of nature, and I invade the peculiar providence of the Almighty by lengthening out my life beyond the period which by the general laws of matter and motion he had assigned it.

We alter the length of a person's life when we save it just as much as when we take it. Therefore, if the taking of life is to be forbidden on the grounds that only God has the right to determine how long a person shall live, then the saving of life should be prohibited on the same grounds. We would then have to abolish the practice of medicine. But everyone (except, perhaps, Christian Scientists) concedes that this would be absurd. Therefore, we may *not* prohibit euthanasia on the grounds that only God has the right to determine how long a life shall last. This seems to be a complete refutation of this argument, and if refuted arguments were decently discarded, as they should be, we would hear no more of it.

Suffering and God's Plan

The last religious argument we shall consider is based on the idea that suffering is a part of God's plan for us. God has ordained that people should suffer; he never intended that life should be continually pleasurable. (If he had intended this, presumably he would have created a very different world.) Therefore, if we were to kill people to "put them out of their misery," we would be interfering with God's plan. Bishop Joseph Sullivan, a prominent Catholic opponent of euthanasia, expresses the argument in a passage from his essay "The Immorality of Euthanasia":

> If the suffering patient is of sound mind and capable of making an act of divine resignation, then his sufferings become a great means of merit whereby he can gain reward for himself and also win great favors for the souls in Purgatory, perhaps even release them from their suffering. Likewise the sufferer may give good example to his family and friends and teach them how to bear a heavy cross in a Christlike manner.
>
> As regard those that must live in the same house with the incurable sufferer, they have a great opportunity to practice Christian charity. They can learn to see Christ in the sufferer and win the reward promised in the Beatitudes. This opportunity for charity would hold true even when the incurable sufferer is deprived of the use of reason. It may well be that the incurable sufferer in a particular case may be of greater value to society than when he was of some material value to himself and his community.

This argument may strike some readers as simply grotesque. Can we imagine this being said, seriously, in the presence of suffering such as that experienced by Stewart Alsop's roommate? "We know it hurts, Jack, and that your wife is being torn apart just having to watch it, but think what a good opportunity this is for you to set an example. You can give us a lesson in how to bear it." In addition, some might think that euthanasia is exactly what *is* required by the "charity" that bystanders have the opportunity to practise.

But, these reactions aside, there is a more fundamental difficulty with the argument. For if the argument were sound, it would lead not only to the condemnation of euthanasia but of *any* measures to reduce suffering. If God decrees that we suffer, why aren't we obstructing God's plan when we give drugs to relieve pain? A girl breaks her arm; if only God knows how much pain is right for her, who are we to mend it? The point is similar to Hume's refutation of the previous argument. This argument, like the previous one, cannot be right because it leads to consequences that no one, not even the most conservative religious thinker, is willing to accept.

We have now looked at three arguments that depend on religious assump- 15
tions. They are all unsound, but I have *not* criticized them simply by rejecting their religious presuppositions. Instead, I have criticized them on their own terms, showing that these arguments should not be accepted even by religious

people. As Daniel Maguire emphasizes, the ethics of theists, like the ethics of all responsible people, should be determined by "good and serious reasons," and these arguments are not good no matter what world-view one has.

The upshot is that religious people are in the same position as everyone else. There is nothing in religious belief in general, or in Christian belief in particular, to preclude the acceptance of mercy-killing as a humane response to some awful situations. So, as far as these arguments are concerned, it appears that Christians may be free, after all, to accept the Golden Rule.

PATRICK PUGH

Summary of Excerpt from The End of Life

(The numbers in parentheses indicate the original pages where material appeared. We will explain this method of documentation later in this chapter.)

ACCORDING TO James Rachels, in spite of the fact that we live in a secular age, many objections to active euthanasia focus on religion, and particularly Christianity. However, even religious people ought to be able see that these arguments may not be valid. For example, one of the most often-stated objections is that, in the Ten Commandments, God forbids killing. Rachels counters by pointing out that the Sixth Commandment is more accurately translated as "Thou shalt not commit murder." Since we define murder as "wrongful killing," we will not call some killing murder if we do not see it as wrong. Thus, the Sixth Commandment "is not normally taken to forbid killing in a just war . . . since such killing is (allegedly) justified" (161–62). Rachels points out that while the scriptures do not mention euthanasia, and in fact affirm the "sanctity of human life," one also finds "exhortations to kindness and mercy" for fellow humans, principles which "support active euthanasia rather than condemn it" (162).

To those who claim that "[i]t is for God alone to decide when a person shall live and when he shall die," Rachels responds that "if it is for God alone to decide when we shall live and when we shall die, then we 'play God' just as much when we cure people as when we kill them" (163). He notes that philosopher David Hume made this argument over two hundred years ago.

A third common Christian argument is that since suffering is a part of God's plan for humans, we should not interrupt it by euthanasia. Rachels responds to this with the question, How can we then justify the use of any pain-relieving drugs and procedures? (165). He concludes that "[t]here is nothing in religious belief in general, or in Christian belief in particular, to preclude the acceptance of mercy-killing as a humane response to some awful situations" (165).

Following Through

Write a summary of the argument opposing euthanasia entitled "Rising to the Occasion of Our Death" by William F. May, on pages 57–58. Or summarize any other argument that you are considering using as a source for a project you are currently working on.

Creating an Annotated Bibliography

To get an overview of the sources they have compiled, many writers find it useful to create an annotated bibliography. A *bibliography* is simply a list of works on a particular topic; it can include any kind of source—from newspaper articles to books to government documents. The basic information of a bibliography is identical to that of a works-cited list: author, title, publisher, date, and, in the case of articles, periodical name, volume, and page numbers. (See the section "Creating a Works-Cited or Reference List" for examples.) Like a works-cited list, a bibliography is arranged in alphabetical order, based on each author's last name.

To annotate a bibliography means to include critical commentary about each work on the list, usually in one or two short paragraphs. Each annotation should contain the following:

A sentence or two about the rhetorical context of the source. Is it an informative news article? an opinion column? a scholarly essay? Is it intended for lawyers? the public? students? the elderly? What is the bias?

A capsule summary of the content.

A note about why this source seems valuable and how you might use it.

Sample Annotated Bibliography Entry

Ames, Katrine. "Last Rights." *Newsweek* 26 Aug. 1991: 40–41.

This is a news article for the general public about the popularity of a book called *Final Exit,* on how to commit suicide. Ames explains the interest in the book as resulting from people's perception that doctors, technology, and hospital bureaucrats are making it harder and harder to die with dignity in this country. The article documents with statistics the direction of public opinion on this topic and also outlines some options, besides suicide, that are becoming available to ensure people of the right to die. Ames shows a bias against prolonging life through technology, but she includes quotations from authorities on both sides. This is a good source of evidence about public and professional opinion.

Following Through

Write an annotated bibliography of the sources you are using for a researched argument of your own.

INCORPORATING AND DOCUMENTING SOURCE MATERIAL IN THE TEXT OF YOUR ARGUMENT

We turn now to the more technical matter of how to incorporate source material into your own writing and how to document the material you include. You incorporate material through direct quotation or through summary or paraphrase; you document material by naming the writer and providing full publication details of the source—a two-step process. In academic writing, documenting sources is essential, even for indirect references, with one exception: you do not need to document your source for factual information that could easily be found in many readily available sources, such as the current number of women in the U.S. Senate or a Supreme Court decision.

Different Styles of Documentation

Different disciplines have specific formal conventions for documenting sources in scholarly writing. In the humanities the most common style is that of the Modern Language Association (MLA). In the physical, natural, and social sciences the American Psychological Association (APA) style is most often used. We will illustrate both in the examples that follow. Unlike the footnote style of documentation, MLA and APA use parenthetical citations in the text and simple, alphabetical bibliographies at the end of the text, making revision and typing much easier. (For a detailed explanation of these two styles, refer to the following manuals: *MLA Handbook for Writers of Research Papers*. 5th ed. New York: MLA, 1999; and *Publication Manual of the American Psychological Association*. 4th ed. Washington, DC: APA, 1994. You may also visit Web sites for the MLA at <http://www.mla.org> and the APA at <http://apa.org>.)

In both MLA and APA formats, you provide some information in the body of your paper and the rest of the information under the heading *Works Cited* (MLA) or *References* (APA) at the end of your paper. The box "Guidelines for Using MLA and APA Style" summarizes the essentials of both systems.

GUIDELINES FOR USING MLA AND APA STYLE

Avoid plagiarism by being conscious of whether you are quoting or paraphrasing. Any time you take exact words from a source, even if it is only a phrase or a significant word that expresses an author's opinion, you are quoting. You must use quotation marks in addition to documenting your source. If you make any change at all in the wording of a quotation, you must indicate the change with ellipses or brackets. Even if you use your own words to summarize or paraphrase any portions of a source, you must still name that source in your text and document it fully. Be careful about using your own words when paraphrasing and summarizing.

1. At the very least, use an attributive tag such as "According to . . ." to introduce quotations, both direct and indirect. Don't just drop them in to stand on their own.
2. Name the person whose words or idea you are using. Give the person's full name on first mention.
3. Identify the author(s) of your source by profession or affiliation so readers will understand the significance of what he or she has to say. Omit this if the speaker is someone readers would recognize without your help.
4. Use transitions into and out of quotations to link the ideas they express to whatever point you are making—that is, to the context of your essay.
5. If your lead-in to a quotation is a simple phrase, follow it with a comma. But if your lead-in can stand alone as a sentence, follow it with a colon.
6. Place the period at the end of a quotation or paraphrase after the parenthetical citation, except with block quotations.

MLA Style

1. In parentheses at the end of both direct and indirect quotations, supply the last name of the author of the source and the exact page number(s) where the quoted or paraphrased words appear. If the name of the author appears in your sentence that leads into the quotation, you can omit it in the parentheses.

    A San Jose State University professor who is black argues that affirmative action "does not teach skills, or educate, or instill motivation" (Steele 121).

Shelby Steele, a Black professor of English at San Jose State University, argues that the disadvantages of affirmative action for blacks are greater than the advantages (117).

2. In a works-cited list at the end of the paper, provide complete bibliographical information in MLA style, as explained and illustrated later in this chapter.

APA Style

1. In parentheses at the end of the directly or indirectly quoted material, place the author's last name, the date of the cited source, and the exact page number(s) where the material appears. If the author's name appears in the sentence, the date of publication should follow the name directly, in parentheses; the page number still comes in parentheses at the end of the sentence. Unlike MLA the APA style uses commas between the parts of the citation, and "p." or "pp." before the page numbers.

A San Jose State University professor who is black argues that affirmative action "does not teach skills, or educate, or instill motivation" (Steele, 1990, p. 121).

Shelby Steele (1990), a Black professor of English at San Jose State University, argues that the disadvantages of affirmative action for blacks are greater than the advantages (p. 117).

2. In a reference list at the end of the paper, provide complete bibliographical information in APA style, as explained and illustrated later in this chapter.

Direct Quotations

Direct quotations are exact words taken from a source. The simplest direct quotations are whole sentences, worked into your text, as illustrated in the following excerpt from a student essay.

MLA Style

In a passage that echos Seneca, <u>Newsweek</u> writer Katrine Ames describes the modern viewpoint: "Most of us have some choices in how we live, certainly in how we conduct our lives" (40).

This source is listed in the works-cited list as follows:

Ames, Katrine. "Last Rights." <u>Newsweek</u> 26 Aug. 1991: 40–41.

APA Style

> In a passage that echos Seneca, Newsweek writer Katrine Ames (1991) describes the modern viewpoint: "Most of us have some choices in how we live, certainly in how we conduct our lives" (p. 40).

This source is listed in the reference list as follows:

> Ames, K. (1991, August 26). Last rights. Newsweek, pp. 40–41.

Altering Direct Quotations with Ellipses and Brackets

While there is nothing wrong with quoting whole sentences, it is often more economical to quote selectively, working some words or parts of sentences from the original into sentences of your own. When you do this, use *ellipses* (three evenly spaced periods) to signify the omission of words from the original; use brackets to substitute words, to add words for purposes of clarification, and to change the wording of a quotation so that it fits gracefully into your own sentence.

The following passage from a student paper illustrates quoted words integrated into the student's own sentence, using both ellipses and brackets. The citation is in MLA style.

> Robert Wennberg, a philosopher and Presbyterian minister, explains that "euthanasia is not an exclusively modern development, for it was widely endorsed in the ancient world. [It was] approved by such respected ancients as . . . Plato, Sophocles, . . . and Cicero" (1).

The source appears in the works-cited list as follows:

> Wennberg, Robert N. Terminal Choices: Euthanasia, Suicide, and the Right to Die. Grand Rapids: Eerdmans, 1989.

Using Block Quotations

If a quoted passage takes up more than four lines of text in your essay, you should indent it one inch (or ten spaces if typewritten) from the left margin, double-space it as you do the whole paper, and omit quotation marks. In block quotations, a period is placed at the end of the final sentence, followed by one space and the parenthetical citation.

The idea of death as release from suffering was expressed by Seneca, a Stoic philosopher of Rome, who lived during the first century C.E.:

> Against all the injuries of life, I have the refuge of death. If I can choose between a death of torture and one that is simple and easy, why should I not select the latter? As I chose the ship in which I sail and the house which I inhabit, so will I choose the death by which I leave life. . . . Why should I endure the agonies of disease . . . when I can emancipate myself from all my torments? (qtd. in Wennberg 42–43)

Note that the source of the Seneca quotation is the book by Wennberg. In the parenthetical citation, "qtd." is an abbreviation for "quoted." The entry on the works-cited page would be the same as for the previous example.

Indirect Quotations

Indirect quotations are paraphrases or summaries of material, either fact or opinion, taken from a source. Following is an example of a direct quotation on a student notecard.

Expert's opinion — pro:

"It is time to rethink many of our attitudes toward death and dying. . . . I feel that society is ready to take a giant step toward a better understanding of the dignity of death, and in the attainment of that dignity, if necessary, through the acceptance of euthanasia."

— Barnard in Barnard, p.8

Here is how this quotation might be incorporated into a paper as an indirect quotation. Note that the author of the book is the same as the person indirectly quoted, so it is not necessary to repeat his name in parentheses.

MLA Style

> One cannot help but agree with pioneer heart-transplant surgeon Christiaan Barnard that death should involve dignity and that society may have to accept the practice of euthanasia as a means to death with dignity (8).

The entry on the works-cited list would appear as follows:

> Barnard, Christiaan. Good Life, Good Death. Englewood Cliffs: Prentice, 1980.

APA Style

> One cannot help but agree with pioneer heart-transplant surgeon Christiaan Barnard (1980) that death should involve dignity and that society may have to accept the practice of euthanasia as a means to death with dignity (p. 8).

The entry in the reference list would appear as follows:

> Barnard, C. (1980). Good life, good death. Englewood Cliffs, NJ: Prentice-Hall.

In-Text References to Electronic Sources

Obviously, the conventions just described apply to print sources, but you should adapt the examples given, being as specific as you can, when you are using sources drawn from the Internet and other electronic communications. Because you will be including the electronic sources in your works-cited or reference list at the end of your paper, your in-text citations should help your readers make the connection between the material you are quoting or paraphrasing in your text and the matching citation on the list. Therefore, your in-text citation, whether parenthetical or not, should begin with the author's name or, in the absence of an author, the title of the work or posting. The APA format would require that you also include the date of the posting.

CREATING A WORKS-CITED OR REFERENCE LIST

At the end of your paper, include a bibliography of all sources that you quoted, paraphrased, or summarized. If you are using MLA style, your heading for this list will read *Works Cited;* if you are using APA style, your heading will read *References.* In either case the list is in alphabetical order based on either the author's (or editor's) last name or—in the case of anonymously written works—the first word of the title, not counting articles (*a, an, the*). The entire list is double-spaced, both within and between entries. See the works-cited page of the sample student paper at the end of this chapter for the correct indentation and spacing. Note that MLA format requires that the first line of each entry be typed flush with the left margin; subsequent lines of each entry are indented half an inch (or five spaces on a typewriter). The APA recommends that papers that are submitted in final form, such as student papers, also format references with a hanging indent.

The following examples illustrate the correct form for the types of sources you will most commonly use.

Books

Book by One Author

MLA: Crusius, Timothy W. Discourse: A Critique & Synthesis of Major Theories. New York: MLA, 1989.

APA: Crusius, T. W. (1989). Discourse: A critique & synthesis of major theories. New York: Modern Language Association.

(Note that APA uses initials rather than the author's first name and capitalizes only the first word and proper nouns in the titles and subtitles of books and articles.)

Two or More Works by the Same Author

MLA: Crusius, Timothy W. Discourse: A Critique & Synthesis of Major Theories. New York: MLA, 1989.

---. A Teacher's Introduction to Philosophical Hermeneutics. Urbana: NCTE, 1991.

(Note that MLA arranges works alphabetically by title and uses three hyphens to show that the name is the same as the one directly above.)

APA: Crusius, T. W. (1989). Discourse: A critique & synthesis of major theories. New York: Modern Language Association.

Crusius, T. W. (1991). A teacher's introduction to philosophical hermeneutics. Urbana, IL: National Council of Teachers of English.

(Note that APA repeats the author's name and arranges works in chronological order.)

Book by Two or Three Authors

MLA: Deleuze, Gilles, and Felix Guattari. Anti-Oedipus: Capitalism and Schizophrenia. New York: Viking, 1977.

APA: Deleuze, G., & Guattari, F . (1977). Anti-Oedipus: Capitalism and schizophrenia. New York: Viking.

(Note that MLA style inverts only the first author's name. APA style, however, inverts both authors' names and uses an ampersand (&) instead of the word "and.")

Book by Four or More Authors

MLA: Bellah, Robert N., et al. Habits of the Heart: Individualism and Commitment in American Life. New York: Harper, 1985.

(Note that the Latin abbreviation *et al.,* meaning "and others," stands in for all subsequent authors' names. MLA style also accepts spelling out all authors' names instead of using *et al.*)

APA: Bellah, R., Madsen, R., Sullivan, W., Swidler, A., & Tipton, S. (1985). Habits of the heart: Individualism and commitment in American life. New York: Harper & Row.

(Note that APA does not use *et al.,* regardless of the number of authors.)

Book Prepared by an Editor or Editors

MLA: Connors, Robert J., ed. Selected Essays of Edward P.J. Corbett. Dallas: Southern Methodist UP , 1989.

APA: Connors, R. J. (Ed.). (1989). Selected essays of Edward P.J. Corbett. Dallas: Southern Methodist University Press.

Work in an Edited Collection

MLA: Jackson, Jesse. "Common Ground: Speech to the Democratic National Convention." The American Reader. Ed. Diane Ravitch. New York: Harper, 1991. 367–71.

APA: Jackson, J. (1991). Common ground: Speech to the Democratic National Convention. In D. Ravitch (Ed.), The American reader (pp. 367–371). New York: HarperCollins.

Translated Book

MLA: Vattimo, Gianni. The End of Modernity: Nihilism and Hermeneutics in Postmodern Culture. Trans. Jon R. Snyder. Baltimore: Johns Hopkins UP , 1988.

APA: Vattimo, G. (1988). The end of modernity: Nihilism and hermeneutics in postmodern culture. (J. R. Snyder, Trans.). Baltimore: Johns Hopkins University Press.

Periodicals

Article in a Journal with Continuous Pagination

MLA: Herron, Jerry. "Writing for My Father." College English 54 (1992): 928–37.

APA: Herron, J. (1992). Writing for my father. College English, 54, 928–937.

(Note that in APA style the article title is not fully capitalized, but the journal title is. Note also that the volume number is italicized in APA style.)

Article in a Journal Paginated by Issue

MLA: McConnell, Margaret Liu. "Living with Roe v. Wade." Commentary 90.5 (1990): 34–38.

APA: McConnell, M. L. (1990). Living with Roe v. Wade. Commentary, 90(5), 34–38.

(In both these examples, "90" is the volume number, and "5" is the number of the issue.)

Article in a Magazine

MLA: D'Souza, Dinesh. "Illiberal Education." Atlantic Mar. 1990: 51+.

(Note that the plus sign indicates that the article runs on nonconsecutive pages.)

APA: D'Souza, D. (1990, March). Illiberal education. Atlantic, pp. 51–58, 62–65, 67, 70–74, 76, 78–79.

(Note that APA requires all page numbers to be listed.)

Anonymous Article in a Newspaper

MLA: "Clinton Warns of Sacrifice." Dallas Morning News 7 Feb. 1993: A4.

APA: Clinton warns of sacrifice. (1993, February 7). The Dallas Morning News, p. A4.

(In both these examples the "A" refers to the newspaper section in which the article appeared.)

Editorial in a Newspaper

MLA: Lewis, Flora. "Civil Society, the Police and Abortion." Editorial. New York Times 12 Sept. 1992: A14.

APA: Lewis, F . (1992, September 12). Civil society, the police and abortion [Editorial]. The New York Times, p. A14.

Nonprint Sources

Interview

MLA: May, William. Personal interview. 24 Apr. 1990.

(Note that APA style documents personal interviews only parenthetically within the text: "According to W. May (personal interview, April 24, 1990), . . ." Personal interviews are not included on the reference list.)

Sound Recording

MLA: Glass, Philip. Glassworks. CBS Sony, MK 37265, 1982.

APA: Glass, P . (1982). Glassworks [CD Recording No. MK 37265]. Tokyo: CBS Sony.

Film

MLA: Scott, Ridley, dir. Thelma and Louise. Perf. Susan Sarandon, Geena Davis, and Harvey Keitel. MGM/ UA Home Video, 1991.

APA: Scott, R. (Director). (1991). Thelma and Louise [Film]. Culver City, CA: MGM/UA Home Video.

(Note that with nonprint media, APA asks you to identify the medium—CD, cassette, film, and so forth. MLA includes the principal actors, but APA does not. APA specifies the place of production, but MLA does not.)

Electronic Sources

While the documentation requirements for MLA and APA citations contain much of the same information, there are subtle format differences between the two styles. Use the following lists as general guides when you cite Internet sources.

MLA Style: Citing Internet Sources

1. Author or editor name, followed by a period
2. The title of the article or short work (such as a short story or poem) enclosed by quotation marks
3. The name of the book, journal, or other longer work in italics
4. Publication information, followed by a period:

   City, publisher, and date for books
   Volume and year for journals
   Date for magazines
   Date for and description of government documents

5. The date on which you accessed the information (no period)
6. The URL, placed inside angle brackets, followed by a period

APA Style: Citing Internet Sources

1. Author or editor last name, followed by a comma and the initials
2. The year of publication, followed by a comma, with the month and day for magazine and newspaper articles, within parentheses and followed by a period
3. The title of the article, book, or journal (follow APA conventions for titles of works)
4. The volume number
5. Page numbers
6. The word "Retrieved," followed by the date of access, followed by the source (such as the World Wide Web) and a colon
7. The URL, without a period

An Online Book

MLA: Strunk, William. The Elements of Style. 1st ed. Geneva: Humphrey, 1918. May 1995. Columbia U Academic Information Systems, Bartleby Lib. 12 Apr. 1999. <http://www.Columbia.edu/acis/bartleby/strunk/strunk100.html>.

APA: Strunk, W. (1918). The elements of style (1st ed.). [Online]. Retrieved April 12, 1999, from the World Wide Web: http://www.Columbia.edu/acis/bartleby/strunk/strunk100.html

(Note that MLA requires that the original publication data be included if it is available for works that originally appeared in print. The APA, however, requires only an online availability statement.)

World Wide Web Site

MLA: Victorian Women Writers Project. Ed. Perry Willett. Apr. 1999. Indiana U. 12 Apr. 1999 <http://www.indiana.edu/~letrs/vwwp/>.

APA: Willett, P . (1999, April). Victorian women writers project [Web page]. Retrieved April 12, 1999, from the World Wide Web: http://www.indiana.edu/~letrs/vwwp/

Article in an Electronic Journal

MLA: Harnack, Andrew, and Gene Kleppinger. "Beyond the MLA Handbook: Documenting Sources on the Internet." Kairos. 1.2 (Summer 1996). 7 Jan. 1997 <http://english.ttu.edu/Kairos/1.2/index.html>.

APA: Harnack, A., & Kleppinger, G. (1996). Beyond the MLA Handbook: Documenting sources on the Internet. Kairos [Online], 1(2). Retrieved January 7, 1997, from the World Wide Web: http://english.ttu.edu/ Kairos/1.2/index.html

Encyclopedia Article on CD-ROM

MLA: Duckworth, George. "Rhetoric." Microsoft Encarta '95. CD-ROM. Redmond: Microsoft, 1995.

APA: Duckworth. G. (1995). Rhetoric. In Microsoft encarta '95 [CD-ROM]. Redmond, WA: Microsoft.

Encyclopedia Article Online

MLA: "Toni Morrison." Encyclopaedia Britannica Online. 1994–1999. Encyclopaedia Britannica. 4 Mar. 1999 <http: //members.eb.com/bol/topic?eu=55183&sctn=#s_ top>.

APA: (1994–1999). Toni Morrison. In Encyclopaedia Britannica Online [Online]. Retrieved March 4, 1999, from the World Wide Web: http://members.eb.com/bol/ topic?eu=55183&sctn=#s_top

E-Mail, Listserv, and Newsgroup Citations

For MLA give, in this order, the author's name, the title of the document (in quotation marks), followed by the description *Online posting,* the date when the material was posted, the name of the forum (if known), the date of access, and, in angle brackets, the online address of the list's Internet site or, if unknown, the e-mail address of the list's moderator.

MLA: Stockwell, Stephen. "Rhetoric and Democracy." Online posting. 13 Jan. 1997. 22 Jan. 1997 <H-Rhetor@msu.edu>.

For APA, the custom is to not include e-mail, listservs, and newsgroups in a reference list but rather to give a detailed in-text citation as follows: (S. Stockwell, posting to H-Rhetor@msu.edu, January 13, 1997).

However, if the content of the message is scholarly, many researchers do include messages in the references:

Stockwell, S. (1997, January 13). Rhetoric and democracy. Retrieved January 22, 1997, from e-mail: H-Rhetor@ msu.edu

A STUDENT RESEARCH PAPER (MLA STYLE)

Following is student Patrick Pugh's research paper in MLA style.

Patrick Pugh
English 1302
October 21, 1992
Professor Smith

Legalizing Euthanasia: A Means
to a More Comfortable Dying Process

All people are linked by one indisputable fact: Every human being dies. For some, death comes early, seeming to cut off life before many of its mysteries have even begun to unfold. For others, death is the conclusion to a lengthy and experience-filled existence. Death is life's one absolute certainty.

At issue, however, is the desire by some men and women, many of the most vocal of whom are in the medical profession, to intervene in what they describe as a heartless extension of the dying process. The term "euthanasia," a Greek word whose literal translation is "good death," has been adopted by those who advocate legalizing certain measures to ensure a transition from life to death which is as comfortable and dignified as possible. One cannot help but agree with pioneer heart-transplant surgeon Dr. Christiaan Barnard that death should involve dignity, and that society may have to accept the practice of euthanasia as a means to death with dignity (8).

To me, having watched both my grandfather and my aunt spend months dying slow, torturous deaths from incurable lung cancer, there can be little doubt that

Pugh 2

euthanasia would have provided a far more humane close to their lives than the painful and prolonged dying that the ultimately futile regimens of chemotherapy and radiation caused them to suffer. My family members' experiences were far too common, for "80 percent of Americans who die in hospitals are likely to meet their end . . . in a sedated or comatose state; betubed nasally, abdominally, and intravenously, far more like manipulated objects than moral subjects" (Minow 124).

Advocates of euthanasia can turn to history for support of their arguments. Robert Wennberg, a philosopher and Presbyterian minister, explains that "euthanasia is not an exclusively modern development, for it was widely endorsed in the ancient world. [It was] approved by such respected ancients as . . . Plato, Sophocles, . . . and Cicero" (1). The idea that we have a right to choose death was expressed by Seneca, a Stoic philosopher of Rome, who lived in the first century C.E.:

> Against all the injuries of life, I have the refuge of death. If I can choose between a death of torture and one that is simple and easy, why should I not select the latter? As I chose the ship in which I sail and the house which I inhabit, so will I choose the death by which I leave life. In no matter more than death should we act according to our desire. . . . Why should I endure the agonies of disease . . . when I can

> emancipate myself from all my torments? (qtd. in Wennberg 42–43)

In a passage that echos Seneca, Newsweek writer Katrine Ames describes the modern viewpoint: "Most of us have some choices in how we live, certainly in how we conduct our lives. How we die is an equally profound choice, and, in the exhilarating and terrifying new world of medical technology, perhaps almost as important" (40).

Regardless of historical precedents and humane implications, euthanasia in both of its forms remains a controversial issue for many. In the first kind, known as passive, or indirect, euthanasia, death results from such measures as withholding or withdrawing life-support systems or life-sustaining medications. Passive euthanasia is often equated with simply "letting someone die," in contrast to the far more controversial active, or direct, euthanasia in which life is ended by direct intervention, such as giving a patient a lethal dose of a drug or assisting a patient in his or her suicide.

During the past two decades, the so-called Right to Die movement has made great strides in the promotion of passive euthanasia as an acceptable alternative to the extension of impending death.

> There seems to be a clear consensus that the competent adult has the right to refuse treatments. . . . This legal recognition of the right to reject medical treatment is grounded

Pugh 4

> in a respect for the bodily integrity of the individual, for the right of each person to determine when bodily invasions will take place. (Wennberg 116)

Passive euthanasia, as an extension of the stated wishes of the dying patient, has become a widely accepted practice, a fact confirmed by medical ethicist and theologian Joseph Fletcher:

> What is called passive euthanasia, letting the patient die . . . is a daily event in hospitals. Hundreds of thousands of Living Wills have been recorded, appealing to doctors, families, pastors, and lawyers to stop treatment at some balance point of the pro-life, pro-death assessment. (47)

The case for passive euthanasia has withstood, for the most part, the arguments of those who claim that life must be preserved and extended at all costs.

The euthanasia debate that is currently being waged focuses on active, or direct, euthanasia, where another person, notably a physician, assists a terminally ill patient in dying by lethal injection or provides the dying patient with the means to commit suicide. The case for active euthanasia is strong. For example, active euthanasia is preferable to passive euthanasia in cases of chronic and incurable diseases which promise the patient pain and suffering for the duration of his or her life. As Robert K. Landers explains, with the advance of AIDS and diseases such as Alzheimer's affecting our aging population, Americans are paying more attention to the idea of "giving death a hand" (555). Surely, many terminally ill patients, whose only hope for release from agonizing pain or humiliating helplessness is death, would welcome the more comfortable and dignified death that physician-assisted suicide can bring.

Still, there are those who argue that while passive euthanasia is moral, the active type is not. Ethically, is there a difference between passive and active euthanasia? Christiaan Barnard thinks not:

> Passive euthanasia is accepted in general by the medical profession, the major religions, and society at large. Therefore, when it is permissible for treatment to be stopped or not instituted in order to allow the patient to die, it makes for small mercy and less sense when the logical step of actively terminating life, and hence suffering, is not taken. Why, at that point, can life not be brought to an end, instead of extending the suffering of the patient by hours or days, or even weeks? . . . Procedurally, there is a difference between direct and indirect euthanasia, but ethically, they are the same. (68–69)

Barnard's ethics are supported by Joseph Fletcher's definition of ethical action, which holds that the ethical value of any

Pugh 6

human action is not a quality inherent in the act itself, but rather a judgment that we make about the act after examining the entire situation in which it takes place. We should decide what is moral and immoral on the basis of what is best for human well-being in any given set of circumstances (38–39).

While Fletcher is an Episcopal theologian, many other Christians do make arguments against active euthanasia on religious grounds. However, according to ethicist James Rachels, even religious people ought to be able to see that these arguments may not be valid. For example, one of the most often-stated objections is that, in the Ten Commandments, God forbids killing. Rachels counters by pointing out that the Sixth Commandment is more accurately translated as "Thou shalt not commit murder." Since we define murder as "wrongful killing," we will not call some killing murder if we do not see it as wrong. Thus, the Sixth Commandment "is not normally taken to forbid killing in a just war . . . since such killing is (allegedly) justified" (161–162). Rachels points out that while the scriptures do not mention euthanasia, and in fact affirm the "sanctity of human life," one also finds "exhortations to kindness and mercy" for fellow humans, principles which "support active euthanasia rather than condemn it" (162).

To those who claim that "[i]t is for God alone to decide when a person shall live and when he shall die," Rachels responds that "if it is for God alone to decide when we shall live and when we shall die, then we 'play God' just as much when we cure people as when we kill them" (163). He notes that philosopher David Hume made this argument over two hundred years ago.

A third common Christian argument is that since suffering is a part of God's plan for humans, we should not interrupt it by euthanasia. Rachels responds to this with the question, How can we then justify the use of any pain-relieving drugs and procedures? (165). He concludes that "[t]here is nothing in religious belief in general, or in Christian belief in particular, to preclude the acceptance of mercy-killing as a humane response to some awful situations" (165).

In fact, there is increasing support for the legalization of active euthanasia, specifically physician-assisted euthanasia, as an alternative to a lingering death for terminal patients. Landers reports that a July 1990 poll showed half the respondents believed someone suffering from incurable disease had a "moral right to commit suicide" (560). In October 1991, a poll sponsored by the Boston Globe and the Harvard School of Public Health found that 64 percent of Americans sampled favor the legalization of physician-assisted suicide, and 52 percent think they would actually consider it themselves. The public interest in suicide as a way out of suffering is also evident in the popularity of Final Exit, a detailed guide on how to commit suicide, published in March 1991. By August, that book was at the top of the New York Times' best-seller list in the category of how-to books.

Some states have put the question of legalizing active euthanasia before their voters. For example, the issue was placed on the Washington state ballot, as Initiative 119, in November of 1991 after 223,000 people signed petitions to place it there. The most controversial section of Initiative 119 stated that a conscious adult patient, who had been diagnosed with a terminal disease and who was deemed to have no more than six months to live, could ask a doctor to hasten death. The doctor had no obligation to comply, nor must the hospital allow it. But if the doctor and/or the hospital refused the patient's request, the patient had the right to be referred to a doctor or a hospital which would honor the request. Although voters in Washington rejected Initiative 119 by a 54 to 46 percent margin, the issue is far from decided. Citizens in Oregon, Florida, California, and Washington, D.C., will soon vote on similar initiatives.

At this point, there is no way to predict whether active euthanasia will be legalized in the near future. One thing is reasonably certain, however. Any compassionate person, who has sat helplessly by as a fellow human being has spent his or her final days thrashing around on a sweat-soaked bed, or who has observed a once-alert mind that has become darkened by the agony of inescapable pain, will give consideration to the eventual fate that awaits him or her. In times like these, frightened humans are united in the universal prayer, "God, spare me from this when my time comes," and even the most stubborn anti-euthanasia minds are opened to the option of an easier journey between life and death, an option that can be made a reality by the legalization of physician-assisted euthanasia.

Pugh 10

Works Cited

Ames, Katrine. "Last Rights." Newsweek 26 Aug. 1991: 40–41.

Barnard, Christiaan. Good Life, Good Death. Englewood Cliffs: Prentice, 1980.

Fletcher, Joseph. "In Defense of Suicide." Suicide and Euthanasia: The Rights of Personhood. Ed. Samuel E. Wallace and Albin Eser. Knoxville: U of Tennessee P, 1981. 38–50.

Landers, Robert. "Right to Die: Medical, Legal, and Moral Issues." Editorial Research Reports 1.36 (1990): 554–64.

Minow, Newton. "Communications in Medicine." Vital Speeches of the Day. 1 Dec. 1990: 121–25.

Rachels, James. The End of Life. Oxford: Oxford UP, 1987.

Wennberg, Robert N. Terminal Choices: Euthanasia, Suicide, and the Right to Die. Grand Rapids: Eerdmans, 1989.

Part Two

READINGS: ISSUES AND ARGUMENTS

CHAPTER TEN

Immigration

At various periods in U.S. history, policies regulating immigration have been the focus of debate. Not surprisingly, the debate heats up when the newcomers are perceived by some as too poor, too numerous, or too different. In 1882 Congress shut the door to Chinese immigration by passing the Chinese Exclusion Act. In this century the Quota Act of 1921 and the Immigration Act of 1924 banned immigration from the rest of Asia and sharply restricted it from the countries of southern and eastern Europe, with their large Jewish and Catholic populations. The debate also heated up in the 1960s, when in the climate of the civil rights movement critics denounced these immigration policies as being prejudiced against nations whose populations are not primarily white and Protestant. The 1965 Immigration and Nationality Act eliminated all national distinctions. It allowed a maximum of 20,000 people to enter from each nation of the globe; but completely aside from these numerical restrictions, it allowed entry to the parents, spouse, siblings, and any minor children of any adult American citizen. Now, as the twenty-first century dawns, the United States is again experiencing a period of high immigration, with almost one million people yearly, eighty percent of whom come from Latin America and Asia. And once more, many Americans are calling for a reexamination of our nation's immigration policies.

The topic of immigration raises many issues, one of which is illegal immigration. Most people agree that it should be reduced or stopped, but how? Is the answer more INS (Immigration and Naturalization Services) agents? more patrols? higher fences? And even if the border could be sealed, would that solve the problem? Of the approximately four million illegal aliens residing in the United States, the vast majority came here legally but overstayed the limit on their visas. Besides the questions of cost and effectiveness, Americans debate the social cost of militarizing our country's borders. In this chapter Leslie Silko, a Native American, questions the validity of political boundaries and the morality of the police power required to enforce them.

Other issues concerning both legal and illegal immigration have to do with changes in the immigrant population since the 1965 Immigration and Nationality Act went into effect, as well as with changing economic and social conditions in the United States. We ask, Are immigrants a burden or a benefit economically? Because the 1965 policy puts a higher priority on reuniting families than on immigrants' being skilled and educated, the pool of immigrants includes vast numbers of poor and unskilled people. This is not a new feature of immigration—the same can be said for the Irish Catholics who came in the mid nineteenth century. But today, our country does not have as many employment opportunities for such laborers, at least at wages that would keep them out of poverty and off of welfare. And what effect does the immigrant labor force have on the prospects for native workers who are also unskilled? Some experts argue that immigrants, both legal and illegal, cost the United States over $42.5 billion in public assistance and take jobs away from American workers; however, others claim that immigrant workers' taxes provide the nation with a net benefit of at least $10 billion per year. Furthermore, the ease and comfort of upper-middle-class life in this country depends partly on immigrant workers' performing agricultural, domestic, and janitorial tasks at wages most native workers would find unacceptable. Finally, there is debate over the economic effects of giving preferential treatment to skilled workers: an increase in immigrants with college degrees and high-level technical skills would help business but create more competition for the kinds of jobs many Americans want.

Aside from economic considerations, the immigration debate poses another question: How are the most recent immigrants affecting American culture and identity? Immigrants in the past have always been expected to give up their old ways and assimilate to the "American" way of life. In 1782 a settler from France, St. Jean de Crèvecoeur, described America as a place where settlers from different homelands would melt together into a "new race of men." Because the settlers who made up the colonial melting pot were predominantly from northern and western Europe, the "American culture" was white, middle-class, and Protestant.

Today some people question the assumptions of the melting-pot metaphor. They see America as a mosaic, in which immigrants value and preserve their unique ethnic customs while at the same time becoming part of the evolving pattern of America. Therefore, one part of the culture debate is whether American policy should promote a multicultural society or do more to ensure assimilation, such as making English the only language for public life and public schools.

Other, more extreme voices in the culture debate say that the United States must preserve its identity by cutting off the flow of immigrants who differ from the traditional ethnic makeup of the country. "Nativists" like Peter Brimelow argue that nations must be based on people with a shared history and heredity. In his controversial anti-immigration book *Alien Nation,* Brimelow offers the nativist argument that the United States has "always had a specific ethnic core. And that core has been white." In response, others, such as Anna Quindlen (see pages 14–15), argue that our national identity is based on an idea—the belief in freedom and the opportunity to succeed. From this point of view, shutting down immigration would be un-American.

While the issues we have surveyed here seem to suggest that immigration is a domestic issue, a final question suggests that it is not: Why do people leave their homes and try to start a new life in a new place? Some of these people are seeking refuge from human rights abuses, but most are fleeing poverty. As Yale political science professor Roger Smith observes, immigration will continue in spite of all our laws and fences as long as "we remain an extremely privileged and affluent country in a world of suffering." One way to reduce the tide of immigrants would be for the United States to make foreign policy decisions that would contribute to stable political and economic conditions in the parts of the world from which the greatest number of poor immigrants originate. Americans are proud of their country's reputation as a land of opportunity, but even the most compassionate among us might question how long America can keep out the welcome mat.

DAVID KENNEDY

Can We Still Afford to Be a Nation of Immigrants?

In this essay that was originally published in the Atlantic Monthly *in 1996, David Kennedy, a professor of American history at Stanford University, sets today's immigration debate in historical context. Kennedy compares the immigrants since 1965 to the immigrants who came to America in the other large wave between 1890 and 1914. Kennedy's purpose, however, is not simply to inform his readers about the past and the present. Rather, he argues that history can help us understand contemporary issues and respond wisely to contemporary events. In presenting his case, he uses historical evidence to correct popular misconceptions about the causes and effects of past immigration and then suggests how the "lamp of history" can help us understand how current immigration both resembles and differs from that of the past.*

THE QUESTION in my title implies a premise: that historically the United States has well afforded to be a nation of immigrants—indeed, has benefited handsomely from its good fortune as an immigrant destination. That proposition was once so deeply embedded in our national mythology as to be axiomatic. More than a century ago, for example, in the proclamation that made Thanksgiving Day a national holiday, Abraham Lincoln gave thanks to God for having "largely augmented our free population by emancipation and by immigration." 1

Lincoln spoke those words when there were but 34 million Americans and half a continent remained to be settled. Today, however, the United States is a nation of some 264 million souls on a continent developed beyond Lincoln's imagination. It is also a nation experiencing immigration on a scale never before seen. In the past three decades, since the passage of the Immigration and Nationality Act of 1965, the first major revision in American immigration statutes since the historic closure of immigration in the 1920s, some 20 million immigrants have entered the United States. To put those numbers in perspective: prior to 1965 the period of heaviest immigration to the United States was the quarter century preceding the First World War, when some 17 million people entered the country—roughly half the total number of Europeans who migrated to the United States in the century after 1820 (along with several hundred thousand Asians). The last pre-war census, in 1910, counted about 13.5 million foreign-born people in the American population, in contrast to about 22.5 million in 1994. Historians know a great deal about those earlier immigrants—why they came, how they ended up, what their impact was on the America of their day. Whether America's historical experience with immigration provides a useful guide to thinking about the present case is the principal question I want to address. I want not only to explore the substantive issue of immigration but also to test the proposition that the discipline of history has some value as a way of knowing and thinking about the world.

With respect to immigration itself, I intend to explore two sets of questions.

- Why did people migrate to America in the past, and what were the consequences, for them and for American society, once they landed?
- Why are people migrating to America today, and what might be the consequences, for them and for American society, of their presence in such numbers?

The Pull of America

A generation or two ago upbeat answers to the first pair of questions so pervaded the culture that they cropped up in the most exotic places—in Tunisia, for example, on July 9, 1943. The occasion was the eve of the invasion of Sicily, and General George S. Patton Jr. was addressing his troops, who were about to embark for the battle. He urged, "When we land, we will meet German and Italian soldiers whom it is our honor and privilege to attack and destroy. Many of you have in your veins German and Italian blood, but remember that these ancestors of yours so loved freedom that they gave up home and country to cross the ocean in search of liberty. The ancestors of the people we shall kill lacked the courage to make such a sacrifice and continued as slaves."

5 In his own inimitable idiom Patton was invoking what for most Americans was—and still is—the standard explanation of who their immigrant forebears were, why they left their old countries, and what was their effect on American society. In this explanation immigrants were the main-chance-seeking and most energetic, entrepreneurial, and freedom-loving members of their Old World societies. They were drawn out of Europe by the irresistible magnet of American opportunity and liberty, and their galvanizing influence on American society made this country the greatest in the world.

A radically different explanation of immigration has also historically been at work in the American mind. As the noted social scientist Edward Alsworth Ross put it in 1914:

> Observe immigrants not as they come travel-wan up the gang-plank, nor as they issue toil-begrimed from pit's mouth or mill-gate, but in their gatherings, washed, combed, and in their Sunday best. . . . [They] are hirsute, low-browed, big-faced persons of obviously low mentality. . . . They simply look out of place in black clothes and stiff collar, since clearly they belong in skins, in wattled huts at the close of the Great Ice Age. These ox-like men are descendants of those who always stayed behind.

Ross was describing in these invidious terms what he and his turn-of-the-century contemporaries called the "new" immigrants—new because they came predominantly from eastern and southern Europe, as distinct from the "old," early-and-mid-nineteenth-century immigrants, who had come mainly from northern and western Europe. Ironically, Ross was also talking about the parents of those very troops (at least the Italian-American troops) whom Patton addressed in 1943.

Between those two poles of explanation American views of immigration have oscillated. On the one hand, as Patton reminds us, immigrants were judged to be noble souls, tugged by the lodestone of American opportunity, whose talents and genius and love of liberty account for the magnificent American character. On the other hand, as in Ross's view, especially if they had the misfortune to arrive on a more recent boat, immigrants were thought to be degraded, freeloading louts, a blight on the national character and a drain on the economy—the kind of people described all too literally, so the argument goes, by Emma Lazarus's famous inscription on the base of the Statue of Liberty: "your tired, your poor . . . the wretched refuse of your teeming shore."

Yet for all their differences, the two views have several things in common. Both explain immigration in terms of the moral character of immigrants. Both understand immigration as a matter of individual choice. And both implicitly invoke the American magnet as the irresistible force that put people in motion, drawing them either to opportunity or to dependency.

Those concepts do not bear close analysis as adequate explanations for *10*
the movement of some 35 million human beings over the course of a century. This was a historical phenomenon too huge and too specific in time to be sufficiently accounted for by summing 35 million decisions supposedly stimulated by the suddenly irresistible gravitational attraction of a far-off continent.

THE PUSH OF EUROPE

For the first three centuries or so after the European discovery of the New World the principal source of immigrants to the two American continents and the Caribbean was not Europe but Africa. Only in the early nineteenth century did the accumulated total of European settlers in the New World exceed the approximately 10 million Africans who had made the trans-Atlantic voyage in the years since 1492. To explain the African diaspora by citing entrepreneurial instincts, the love of democracy, or the freely chosen decisions of migrants to follow the lodestar of American promise would be mockery. Clearly, the involuntary movement of those 10 million Africans is best explained not in terms of their individual characters and choices but in terms of the catastrophically disruptive expansion of large-scale plantation agriculture and its accursed corollary, large-scale commercial slavery.

A comparable—though, to be sure, not identical—element of involuntariness characterized emigration from nineteenth-century Europe. Any generalization about what prompted a phenomenon as long-lived and complicated as the great European migration must, of course, be subject to many qualifications. All discussions of the migration process recognize both push and pull factors. But at bottom the evidence convincingly supports the argument that *disruption* is essential to the movement of people on such a scale. And, as in the African case, the best, most comprehensive explanation for a process that eventually put some 35 million people in motion is to be found in two convulsively disruptive developments that lay far beyond the control of individual Europeans. Those developments had their historical dynamic within the context of European, not American, history.

The first of these needs little elaboration. It was, quite simply, population growth. In the nineteenth century the population of Europe more than doubled, from some 200 million to more than 400 million, even after about 70 million people had left Europe altogether. (Only half of these, it should be noted, went to the United States—one among many clues that the American-magnet explanation is inadequate.) That population boom was the indispensable precondition for Europe to export people on the scale that it did. And the boom owed little to American stimulus; rather, it was a product of aspects of European historical evolution, especially improvements in diet, sanitation, and disease control.

The second development was more complex, but we know it by a familiar name: the Industrial Revolution. It includes the closely associated revolution in agricultural productivity. Wherever it occurred, the Industrial Revolution shook people loose from traditional ways of life. It made factory workers out of artisans and, even more dramatically, turned millions of rural farmers into urban wage-laborers. Most of those migrants from countryside to city, from agriculture to industry, remained within their country of origin, or at least within Europe. But in the early stages of industrialization the movement of people, like the investment of capital during the unbridled early days of industrialism, was often more than what the market could bear. In time most European societies reached a kind of equilibrium, absorbing their own workers into their own wage markets. But in the typical transitional phase some workers who had left artisanal or agricultural employments could not be reabsorbed domestically in European cities. They thus migrated overseas.

The large scholarly literature documenting this process might be sum- 15
marized as follows: Imagine a map of Europe. Across this map a time line traces the evolution of the Industrial Revolution. From a point in the British Isles in the late eighteenth century the line crosses to the Low Countries and Germany in the early and mid nineteenth century and to eastern and southern Europe in the late nineteenth and early twentieth centuries. Across the same map a second line traces the chronological evolution of migration to the United States. As it happens, the two lines are almost precisely congruent—migration came principally from the British Isles in the eighteenth and early nineteenth centuries, then mainly from Germany, and finally from the great watersheds of the Vistula and the Danube and the mountain ranges of the Apennines and Carpathians to the south and east.

The congruence of those lines is not coincidental. Industrialization, in this view, is *the* root cause and the most powerful single variable explaining the timing, the scale, the geographic evolution, and the composition of the great European migration.

For another perspective on the importance of understanding the European migration from a European point of view, consider the lyrics of a nineteenth-century Italian folk song called "The Wives of the Americans." In this case, the "Americans" were men who had gone off to America and left their wives behind in Italy—specifically, the southern region of Campania. In fact, men, young men in particular, predominated in the nineteenth-century migratory stream, and their predominance constitutes a reliable indicator of their purposes. Many of them never intended to settle permanently elsewhere but hoped to work abroad for a time and eventually return to the old country. Repatriation rates for European immigrants averaged nearly 40 percent. Only the Jews and the Irish did not go home again in significant numbers. For some later, "new" immigrant groups, especially from the southern Danube regions, repatriation rates ran as high as 80 percent.

The song describes the wives of the Americans going to church and praying, "Send money, my husband. Send more money. The money you sent earlier I have already spent. I spent it on my lover. I spent it with pleasure. Send more money, you *cornuto fottuto* [damnable cuckold]." Those lyrics conjure an image of immigration quite different from the one General Patton urged on his Italian-American troops in 1943. Together with the figures on repatriation, they offer a strong corrective to uncritical reliance on the American-magnet explanation for the past century's European migration.

The Immigrants in America

What happened to European immigrants, and to American society, once they arrived? Much historical inquiry on this point focuses on immigrant hardship and on recurrent episodes of nativism, anti-Semitism, anti-Catholicism, and anti-foreign-radicalism, from the Know-Nothing movement of the 1850s to the American Protective Association of the late nineteenth century and the revived Ku Klux Klan of the early twentieth century, culminating in the highly restrictive immigration legislation of the 1920s. Those are important elements in the history of American immigration, and we would forget them at our peril. But getting the question right is the most challenging part of any historical investigation, and there is an analytically richer question to be asked than Why did immigrants meet sometimes nasty difficulties?

An even more intriguing question is How did tens of millions of new- 20
comers manage to accommodate themselves to America, and America to them, without more social disruption? How can we explain this society's relative success—and success I believe it was—in making space so rapidly for so many people?

The explanation is surely not wise social policy. Beyond minimal monitoring at the ports of entry, no public policy addressed the condition of immigrants once they were cleared off Castle Garden or Ellis Island. But three specific historical circumstances, taken together, go a long way toward composing an answer to the question.

First, somewhat surprisingly, for all their numbers, immigrants—even the 17 million who arrived from 1890 to 1914—never made up a very large component of the already enormous society that was turn-of-the-century America. The census of 1910 records the highest percentage of foreign-born people ever resident in the United States: 14.7 percent. Now, 14.7 percent is not a trivial proportion, but it is a decided minority, and relative to other societies that have received large numbers of immigrants, a small minority. The comparable figures in Australia and Canada at approximately the same time were 17 percent and more than 20 percent, and even higher in Argentina. So here is one circumstance accounting for the relative lack of social conflict surrounding immigration a century ago: at any given moment immigrants were a relatively small presence in the larger society.

A second circumstance was economic. Immigrants supplied the labor that a growing economy urgently demanded. What is more, economic growth allowed the accommodation of newcomers without forcing thorny questions of redistribution—always the occasion for social contest and upheaval. Here, as so often in American history, especially during the period of heavy immigration before the First World War, economic growth worked as a pre-emptive solution to potential social conflict.

The third circumstance was more complicated than sheer numbers or economic growth. I call this circumstance "pluralism"—by which I mean simply that the European immigrant stream was remarkably variegated in its cultural, religious, national, and linguistic origins. These many subcurrents also distributed themselves over an enormous geographic region—virtually the entire northeastern quadrant of the United States—and through several political jurisdictions. By the 1920s immigrants were distributed widely across the great industrial belt that stretched from New England through New York, New Jersey, Pennsylvania, and beyond: Ohio, Indiana, Illinois, Michigan, Wisconsin, and Minnesota. The states with the most immigrants, not incidentally, also had per capita incomes higher than the national average—an important fact pertinent to understanding the relationship between immigration and economic vitality.

The varied composition and broad dispersal of the immigrant stream 25
carried certain crucial implications, one being that no immigrant group could realistically aspire to preserve its Old World culture intact for more than a few generations at best. To be sure, many groups made strenuous efforts to do just that. Legend to the contrary, last century's immigrants did not cast their Old World habits and languages overboard before their ship steamed into New York Harbor. In fact, many groups heroically exerted themselves to sustain their religions, tongues, and ways of life. The Catholic school system, which for a generation or two in some American cities educated nearly as many students as the public school system, eloquently testified to the commitment of some immigrant communities to resist assimilation. But circumstances weighed heavily

against the success of such efforts. The virtual extinction of the parochial school system in the past generation—the empty schools and dilapidated parish buildings that litter the inner cores of the old immigrant cities—bears mute witness both to the ambition and to the ultimate failure of those efforts to maintain cultural distinctiveness.

A second and no less important implication of pluralism was that neither any single immigrant group nor immigrants as a whole could realistically mount any kind of effective challenge to the existing society's way of doing things. No single group had sufficient weight in any jurisdiction larger than a municipality to dictate a new political order. And there was little likelihood that Polish Jews and Italian Catholics and Orthodox Greeks could find a common language, much less common ground for political action.

To recapitulate: The most comprehensive explanation of the causes of immigration a century ago is to be found in the disruptions visited on European society by population growth and the Industrial Revolution. The United States was, to use the language of the law, the incidental beneficiary of that upheaval. The swelling immigrant neighborhoods in turn-of-the-century American cities were, in effect, by-products of the urbanization of Europe. And once landed in America, immigrants accommodated themselves to the larger society—not always easily assimilating, but at least working out a modus vivendi—without the kinds of conflicts that have afflicted other multinational societies. That mostly peaceful process of accommodation came about because of the relatively small numbers of immigrants at any given time, because of the health of the economy, and because of the constraints on alternatives to accommodation inherent in the plural and dispersed character of the immigrant stream.

Having lit this little lamp of historical learning, I would like to carry it forward and see if it can illuminate the present.

Today's Immigration

The biggest apparent novelty in current immigration is its source, or sources. Well over half of the immigration of the past thirty years has come from just seven countries: Mexico, the Philippines, China (I am including Taiwan), Vietnam, Korea, India, and the Dominican Republic.

Not a single European country is on that list. Here, it would seem, is 30
something new under the historical sun. Europe has dried up as a source of immigration and been replaced by new sources in Latin America and Asia.

And yet if we remember what caused the great European migration, the novelty of the current immigration stream is significantly diminished. Though particular circumstances vary, most of the countries now sending large numbers of immigrants to the United States are undergoing the same convulsive demographic and economic disruptions that made migrants out of so many nineteenth-century Europeans: population growth and the relatively early stages of their own industrial revolutions.

Mexico, by far the leading supplier of immigrants to the United States, conforms precisely to that pattern. Since the Second World War the Mexican population has more than tripled—a rate of growth that recollects, indeed exceeds, that of nineteenth-century Europe. And as in Europe a century ago, population explosion has touched off heavy internal migration, from rural to urban areas. By some reckonings, Mexico City has become the largest city in the world, with 20 million inhabitants and an in-migration from the Mexican countryside estimated at 1,000 people a day.

Also since the Second World War the Mexican economy, despite periodic problems, has grown at double the average rate of the U.S. economy. Rapid industrialization has been accompanied by the swift and widespread commercialization of Mexican agriculture. A Mexican "green revolution," flowing from improvements in mechanical processing, fertilizers, and insecticides, has in fact exacerbated the usual disruptions attendant on rapid industrialization: depopulation of the countryside, urban in-migration, and movement across the national border. But as in nineteenth-century Europe, most of the movement has been within Mexico itself. Since 1970 some five million Mexicans have entered the United States to stay; probably more than 10 million have moved to Mexico City alone.

Thus we are in the presence of a familiar historical phenomenon, impelled by developments that are for all practical purposes identical to those that ignited the great European migration of a century ago.

What Does the Future Hold?

If the causes of present-day immigration are familiar, what will be the *35*
consequences for today's immigrants and tomorrow's America?

I have suggested that three historical circumstances eased the accommodation between immigrants and the American society of a century ago—the relatively small number of immigrants present at any given time, the needs and vitality of the economy, and the plural and distributed character of the immigrant stream. How do those factors weigh in an analysis of immigration today?

With respect to numbers, the historical comparison gives a basis for confidence that the answer to our original question—Can we still afford to be a nation of immigrants?—is yes. The U.S. Census Bureau reports that as of 1994 foreign-born people represented 8.7 percent of the American population, or just a bit more than half the proportion they made up in the census of 1910. (Comparable recent numbers for Canada and Australia, incidentally, are approximately 16 percent and 22 percent.) So, with reference to both American historical experience and contemporary experience in other countries, the *relative* incidence of current immigration to the United States is rather modest. Surely the United States at the end of the twentieth century is resourceful enough to deal with an immigrant inflow proportionally half what American society managed to deal with quite successfully in the early years of this century.

With reference to the needs and vitality of the economy, the historical comparison is more complicated. Economic theory suggests that immigration is a bargain for any receiving society, because it augments the labor supply, one of the three principal factors of production (along with land and capital), essentially free of cost. The sending society bears the burden of feeding and raising a worker to the age when he or she can enter the labor market. If at that point the person emigrates and finds productive employment elsewhere, the source society has in effect subsidized the economy of the host society. That scenario essentially describes the historical American case, in which fresh supplies of immigrant labor underwrote the nation's phenomenal industrial surge in the half century after the Civil War.

The theory is subject to many qualifications. Unskilled immigrant workers may indeed increase gross economic output, as they did from the Pittsburgh blast furnaces to the Chicago packinghouses a century ago, and as they do today in garment shops and electronic assembly plants from Los Angeles to Houston. But as productivity has become more dependent on knowledge and skill, the net value of unskilled immigrant labor has decreased, a point that informs much of the current case for restricting immigration. Yet it is important to note that argument on this point turns on the *relative* contribution of low-skill workers to overall output; the theory is still unimpeachable in its insistence on the *absolute* value of an additional worker, from whatever source, immigrant or native. Nevertheless, large numbers of unskilled immigrants may in the long run retard still higher potential outputs, because the inexpensive labor supply that they provide diminishes incentives to substitute capital and improved technology for labor, and thus inhibits productivity gains. On the other hand, just to complicate the calculation further, insofar as the host society continues to need a certain amount of low-skill work done, the availability of unskilled immigrants may *increase* the economy's overall efficiency by freeing significant numbers of better-educated native workers to pursue higher-productivity employment. And overhanging all this part of the immigration debate is the question of whose ox is gored. Low-skill immigrants may benefit the economy as a whole, but may at the same time impose substantial hardships on the low-skill native workers with whom they are in direct competition for jobs and wages.

Of course, the theory that immigration subsidizes the host economy is true only insofar as the immigrant in question is indeed a worker, a positive contributor to the productive apparatus of the destination society. Even the crude American immigration-control system of the nineteenth century recognized that fact, when it barred people likely to become social dependents, such as the chronically ill or known criminals. The issue of dependency is particularly vexatious in the United States today for two reasons. First, the 1965 legislation contained generous clauses providing for "family reunification," under the terms of which a significant portion of current immigrants are admitted not as workers but as the spouses, children, parents, and siblings of citizens or legally resident aliens. In 1993, a typical year, fewer than 20 percent of immigrants entered under "employment-based" criteria.

Because of family-reunification provisions, the current immigration population differs from previous immigrant groups in at least two ways: it is no longer predominantly male and even more strikingly, it is older. The percentage of immigrants over sixty-five exceeds the percentage of natives in that age group, and immigrants over sixty-five are two and a half times as likely as natives to be dependent on Supplemental Security Income, the principal federal program making cash payments to the indigent elderly. Newspaper accounts suggest that some families have brought their relatives here under the family-reunification provisions in the law expressly for the purpose of gaining access to SSI. Thus it appears that the availability of welfare programs—programs that did not exist a century ago—has combined with the family-reunification provisions to create new incentives for immigration that complicate comparisons of the economics of immigration today with that in the nineteenth century.

But on balance, though today's low-skill immigrants may not contribute as weightily to the economy as did their European counterparts a hundred years ago, and though some do indeed end up dependent on public assistance, as a group they make a positive economic contribution nevertheless. It is no accident that today's immigrants are concentrated in the richest states, among them California (home to fully one third of the country's immigrant population), just as those of the 1920s were. And just as in that earlier era, immigrants are not parasitic on the "native" economy but productive participants in it. The principal motivation for immigration remains what it was in the past: the search for productive employment. Most immigrants come in search of work, and most find it. Among working-age males, immigrant labor-force-participation rates and unemployment rates are statistically indistinguishable from those for native workers. The ancient wisdom still holds: *Ubi est pane, ibi est patria* ("Where there is bread, there is my country"). Not simply geography but also that powerful economic logic explains why Mexico is the principal contributor of immigrants to the United States today: the income gap between the United States and Mexico is the largest between any two contiguous countries in the world.

One study, by the Stanford economist Clark W. Reynolds, estimated the future labor-market characteristics and prospects for economic growth in Mexico and the United States. For Mexico to absorb all the new potential entrants into its own labor markets, Reynolds concluded, its economy would have to grow at the improbably high rate of some seven percent a year. The United States, in contrast, if its economy is to grow at a rate of three percent a year, must find somewhere between five million and 15 million more workers than can be supplied by domestic sources. Reynolds's conclusion was obvious: Mexico and the United States need each other, the one to ease pressure on its employment markets, the other to find sufficient labor to sustain acceptable levels of economic growth. If Reynolds is right, the question with which I began—Can we still afford to be a nation of immigrants?—may be wrongly put. The proper question may be Can we afford *not* to be?

THE RECONQUISTA

But if economic necessity requires that the United States be a nation of immigrants into the indefinite future, as it has been for so much of its past, some important questions remain. Neither men nor societies live by bread alone, and present-day immigration raises historically unprecedented issues in the cultural and political realms.

Pluralism—the variety and dispersal of the immigrant stream—made it 45
easier for millions of European immigrants to accommodate themselves to American society. Today, however, one large immigrant stream is flowing into a defined region from a single cultural, linguistic, religious, and national source: Mexico. Mexican immigration is concentrated heavily in the Southwest, particularly in the two largest and most economically and politically influential states—California and Texas. Hispanics, including Central and South Americans but predominantly Mexicans, today compose 28 percent of the population of Texas and about 31 percent of the population of California. More than a million Texans and more than three million Californians were born in Mexico. California alone holds nearly half of the Hispanic population, and well over half of the Mexican-origin population, of the entire country.

This Hispanicization of the American Southwest is sometimes called the Reconquista, a poetic reminder that the territory in question was, after all, incorporated into the United States in the first place by force of arms, in the Mexican War of the 1840s. There is a certain charm in this turn of the wheel of history, with its reminder that in the long term the drama of armed conquest may be less consequential than the prosaic effects of human migration and birth rates and wage differentials. But the sobering fact is that the United States has had no experience comparable to what is now taking shape in the Southwest.

Mexican-Americans will have open to them possibilities closed to previous immigrant groups. They will have sufficient coherence and critical mass in a defined region so that, if they choose, they can preserve their distinctive culture indefinitely. They could also eventually undertake to do what no previous immigrant group could have dreamed of doing: challenge the existing cultural, political, legal, commercial, and educational systems to change fundamentally not only the language but also the very institutions in which they do business. They could even precipitate a debate over a "special relationship" with Mexico that would make the controversy over the North American Free Trade Agreement look like a college bull session. In the process, Americans could be pitched into a soul-searching redefinition of fundamental ideas such as the meaning of citizenship and national identity.

All prognostications about these possibilities are complicated by another circumstance that has no precedent in American immigration history: the region of Mexican immigrant settlement in the southwestern United States is contiguous with Mexico itself. That proximity may continuously replenish the immigrant community, sustaining its distinctiveness and encouraging its assertiveness. Alternatively, the nearness of Mexico may weaken the community's coherence and limit its political and cultural clout by chronically attenuating its members' permanence in the United States, as the accessibility of the mother country makes for a kind of perpetual repatriation process.

In any case, there is no precedent in American history for these possibilities. No previous immigrant group had the size and concentration and easy access to its original culture that the Mexican immigrant group in the Southwest has today. If we seek historical guidance, the closest example we have to hand is in the diagonally opposite corner of the North American continent, in Quebec. The possibility looms that in the next generation or so we will see a kind of Chicano Quebec take shape in the American Southwest, as a group emerges with strong cultural cohesiveness and sufficient economic and political strength to insist on changes in the overall society's ways of organizing itself and conducting its affairs.

50 Public debate over immigration has already registered this prospect, however faintly. How else to explain the drive in Congress, and in several states, to make English the "official" language for conducting civil business? In previous eras no such legislative muscle was thought necessary to expedite the process of immigrant acculturation, because alternatives to eventual acculturation were simply unimaginable. Less certain now that the traditional incentives are likely to do the work of assimilation, we seem bent on trying a *ukase*—a ham-handed and provocative device that may prove to be the opening chapter of a script for prolonged cultural warfare. Surely our goal should be to help our newest immigrants, those from Mexico especially, to become as well integrated in the larger American society as were those European "new" immigrants whom E. A. Ross scorned but whose children's patriotism George Patton could take for granted. To reach that goal we will have to be not only more clever than our ancestors were but also less confrontational, more generous, and more welcoming than our current anxieties sometimes incline us to be.

The present may echo the past, but will not replicate it. Yet the fact that events have moved us into *terra nova et incognita* does not mean that history is useless as a way of coming to grips with our situation. To the contrary, the only way we can know with certainty as we move along time's path that we have come to a genuinely new place is to know something of where we have been. "What's new in the starry sky, dear Argelander?" Kaiser Wilhelm I is said to have asked his state astronomer, to which Argelander replied, "And does Your Majesty already know the old?" Knowing the old is the project of historical scholarship, and only that knowledge can reliably point us toward the new. As Lincoln also said, "As our case is new, so we must think anew, and act anew. We must disenthrall ourselves, and then we shall save our country."

Questions for Discussion

1. Like a good history lecture or oral presentation, Kennedy's essay is carefully structured. In paragraph 2 Kennedy explains his purpose for writing, and in paragraph 3 he lays out a plan for accomplishing that purpose. Using paragraph 3 as a guide, group the essay's paragraphs into major subdivisions. Which groupings answer each of the questions posed in paragraph 3? Also, find some specific places, such as transitional phrases and summary paragraphs, where Kennedy tries to remind readers of his plan.

2. According to Kennedy, the commonly held view is that America has been a magnet for individuals in search of freedom and opportunity. What evidence does Kennedy give to show that immigrants in the past were pushed here rather than pulled? Is there anything in paragraphs 12–18 that changed your conceptions about earlier immigrant groups?
3. What evidence does Kennedy give to show that similar "pushing" occurs today?
4. According to Kennedy, what are the three "historical circumstances" that helped the earlier waves of immigrants fit into the American economy and culture with minimal disruption? With respect to these three conditions, what similarities and differences does Kennedy find in the wave of immigrants today? Which struck you as the most significant?
5. Kennedy seems less concerned about the economic impact of today's immigrants than he is about their impact on American culture and politics, especially in the Southwest. He would like to see the new immigrants there integrate into our society, but he opposes forced assimilation, such as making English the "official" language. He argues that we will have to become more clever and more generous in our treatment of these immigrants than our ancestors were. He quotes Lincoln: "we must think anew, and act anew." Why is this so? How would you suggest America ease the process of accommodation?

For Research and Convincing

Kennedy observes that in the past, because of "the varied composition and broad dispersal of the immigrant stream . . . no immigrant group could realistically aspire to preserve its Old World culture intact for more than a few generations at best" (paragraph 25). Look into the history of your hometown or another community that you know well. What immigrant groups settled there generations ago? What evidence of their native culture remains? If much of the culture remains, do you see this as a benefit to the community or a divisive presence? If much of the culture has disappeared, what has the community gained or lost?

For Persuasion

In her essay "Making the Mosaic" on pages 14–15, Anna Quindlen says that many people today think an authentic American is one whose "ethnic origins [are] lost in an amorphous past, not visible in accent, appearance, or allegiance" (paragraph 4). As Kennedy points out, this is what happened to many immigrants, in spite of their efforts "to sustain their religions, tongues, and ways of life" (paragraph 25). If you yourself have immigrant relatives, would you argue that their cultural identity should be preserved? Could you persuade others to join you in celebrating your ethnic traditions? Could you persuade others that it is possible to observe ethnic traditions and still be an "authentic American"?

PETER BRIMELOW

Time to Rethink Immigration?

A senior editor at Forbes *(a conservative business magazine), Peter Brimelow is best known as the author of the book* Alien Nation, *which argues that current trends in immigration will destroy the national identity of the United States. A recent immigrant himself from Britain, Brimelow speaks eloquently for many Anglos who consider themselves "authentic Americans," people whose ancestors came to the United States from Britain or northern Europe generations ago.*

Critics charge that Brimelow's views are a sophisticated example of the long history of nativist racism and ethnic bias. But no thoughtful person can dismiss the serious questions Brimelow raises (for example, "What is a nation?") nor ignore his warning that Americans may be reaching the limits of tolerance for the current wave of immigrants. The following excerpt is from an article in the National Review *(22 June 1992) that summarizes his stance in* Alien Nation.

DANTE WOULD have been delighted by the Immigration and Nat- 1
uralization Service waiting rooms. They would have provided him with a tenth Circle of Hell. There is something distinctly infernal about the spectacle of so many lost souls waiting around so hopelessly, mutually incomprehensible in virtually every language under the sun, each clutching a number from one of those ticket-issuing machines which may or may not be honored by the INS clerks before the end of the Civil Service working day.

The danger of damnation is perhaps low—although a Scottish friend of mine once found himself flung into the deportation holding tank because the INS misunderstood its own rules. And toward the end of my own ten-year trek through the system, I whiled away a lot of time watching confrontations between suspicious INSers and agitated Iranians, apparently hauled in because the Iran hostage crisis had inspired the Carter Administration to ask how many of them were enrolled in U.S. universities. (The INS was unable to provide an answer during the 444 days of the hostage crisis—or, as it turned out, at all.)

Nevertheless, you can still get a pretty good blast of brimstone if you dare suggest that it might be another of those misunderstandings when, having finally reached the head of the line, you are ordered by the clerk to go away and come back another day with a previously unmentioned Form XYZ.

Your fellow huddled masses accept this treatment with a horrible passivity. Perhaps it is imbued in them by eons of arbitrary government in their native lands. Only rarely is there a flurry of protest. At its center, almost invariably, is an indignant American spouse.

Just as New York City's government can't stop muggers but does a great 5
job ticketing young women on Park Avenue for failing to scoop up after their lapdogs, current U.S. immigration policy in effect enforces the law only against those who obey it. Annual legal immigration of some 950,000—counting the

140,000 refugees and the 100,000 granted political asylum—is overwhelmed by the 2 to 3 million illegal entries into the country every year, which result in a net annual increase of perhaps 250,000 illegal aliens. (A cautious estimate—again, no one really knows.)

The INS bureaucracy still grinds through its rituals. But meanwhile the U.S. has lost control of its borders. As it turned out, I could have avoided my INS decade by the simple expedient of staying here after I graduated from Stanford in 1972 and waiting to be amnestied, along with some 3.2 million other illegal immigrants, by the 1986 Immigration Act.

There is another parallel with New York: Just as when you leave Park Avenue and descend into the subway, on entering the INS waiting rooms you find yourself in an underworld that is almost entirely colored. In 1990, for example, only 8 percent of 1.5 million legal immigrants, including amnestied illegals, came from Europe. . . .

Only the incurious could fail to wonder: Where do all these people get off and come to the surface? That is: What impact will they have on America?

"A Nation of Immigrants"

Everyone has seen a speeded-up film of the cloudscape. What appears to the naked eye to be a panorama of almost immobile grandeur writhes into wild life. Vast patterns of soaring, swooping movement are suddenly discernible. Great towering cumulo-nimbus formations boil up out of nowhere, dominating the sky in a way that would be terrifying if it were not, in real life, so gradual that we are barely aware that anything is going on.

This is a perfect metaphor for the development of the American nation. 10
America, of course, is exceptional. What is exceptional about it, however, is not the way in which it was created, but the speed.

"We are a nation of immigrants." No discussion of U.S. immigration policy gets far without someone making this helpful remark. As an immigrant myself, I always pause respectfully. You never know. Maybe this is what they're taught to chant in schools nowadays, a sort of multicultural Pledge of Allegiance.

But it secretly amuses me. Do they really think other nations sprouted up out of the ground? ("Autochthonous" is the classical Greek word.) The truth is that *all* nations are nations of immigrants. But the process is usually so slow and historic that people overlook it. They mistake for mountains what are merely clouds.

This is obvious in the case of the British Isles, from which the largest single proportion of Americans are still derived. You can see it in the place-names. Within a few miles of my parents' home in the north of England, the names are Roman (Chester, derived from the Latin for camp), Saxon (anything ending in *-ton,* town, like Oxton), Viking (*-by,* farm, like Irby), and Norman French (Delamere). At times, these successive waves of peoples were clearly living cheek by jowl. Thus among these place-names is Wallesey, Anglo-Saxon for "Island of the Welsh"—Welsh being derived from the word used by low-

German speakers for foreigners wherever they met them, from Wallonia to Wallachia. This corner of the English coast continued as home to some of the pre-Roman Celtic stock, not all of whom were driven west into Wales proper as was once supposed.

The English language that America speaks today (or at least spoke until the post-1965 fashion for bilingual education) reflects the fact that the peoples of Britain merged, eventually; their separate contributions can still be traced in it. Every nation in Europe went through the same process. Even the famously homogeneous Japanese show the signs of ethnically distinct waves of prehistoric immigration.

But merging takes time. After the Norman Conquest in 1066, it was 15
nearly three hundred years before the invaders were assimilated to the point where court proceedings in London were again heard in English. And it was nearly nine centuries before there was any further large-scale immigration into the British Isles—the Caribbean and Asian influx after World War II.

Except in America. Here the process of merging has been uniquely rapid. Thus about 7 million Germans have immigrated to the U.S. since the beginning of the nineteenth century. Their influence has been profound—to my British eye it accounts for the odd American habit of getting up in the morning and starting work. About 50 million Americans told the 1980 Census that they were wholly or partly of German descent. But only 1.6 million spoke German in their homes.

What Is a Nation?

So all nations are made up of immigrants. But what is a nation—the end-product of all this merging? This brings us into a territory where words are weapons, exactly as George Orwell pointed out years ago. "Nation"—as suggested by its Latin root *nascere,* to be born—intrinsically implies a link by blood. A nation is an extended family. The merging process through which all nations pass is not merely cultural, but to a considerable extent biological, through intermarriage.

Liberal commentators, for various reasons, find this deeply distressing. They regularly denounce appeals to common ethnicity as "nativism" or "tribalism." Ironically, when I studied African history in college, my politically correct tutor deprecated any reference to "tribes." These small, primitive, and incoherent groupings should, he said, be dignified as "nations." Which suggests a useful definition: tribalism/nativism is nationalism of which liberals disapprove.

American political debate on this point is hampered by a peculiar difficulty. American editors are convinced that the term "state" will confuse readers unless reserved exclusively for the component parts of the United States—New York, California, etc. So when talking about sovereign political structures, where the British would use "state," the Germans "*Staat,*" and the French "*l'état,*" journalists here are compelled to use the word "nation." Thus in the late 1980s it was common to see references to "the nation of Yugoslavia," when Yugoslavia's problem was precisely that it was not a nation at all, but a state that contained several different small but fierce nations—Croats, Serbs, etc. (In my constructive way, I've been trying to introduce, as an alternative to "state," the word "polity"—defined by Webster as "a politically organized unit." But it's quite hopeless. Editors always confuse it with "policy.")

This definitional difficulty explains one of the regular entertainments of 20
U.S. politics: uproar because someone has unguardedly described America as a "Christian nation." Of course, in the sense that the vast majority of Americans are Christians, this is nothing less than the plain truth. It is not in the least incompatible with a secular *state* (polity).

But the difficulty over the N-word has a more serious consequence: it means that American commentators are losing sight of the concept of the "nation-state"—a sovereign structure that is the political expression of a specific ethno-cultural group. Yet the nation-state was one of the crucial inventions of the modern age. Mass literacy, education, and mobility put a premium on the unifying effect of cultural and ethnic homogeneity. None of the great premodern multinational empires have survived. (The Brussels bureaucracy may be trying to create another, but it has a long way to go.)

This is why Ben Wattenberg is able to get away with talking about a "Universal Nation." On its face, this is a contradiction in terms. It's possible, as Wattenberg variously implies, that he means the diverse immigrant groups will eventually intermarry, producing what he calls, quoting the English poet John Masefield, a "wondrous race." Or that they will at least be assimilated by American culture, which, while globally dominant, is hardly "universal." But meanwhile there are hard questions. What language is this "universal nation" going to speak? How is it going to avoid ethnic strife? dual loyalties? collapsing like the Tower of Babel? Wattenberg is not asked to reconcile these questions, although he is not unaware of them, because in American political discourse the ideal of an American nation-state is in eclipse.

Ironically, the same weaknesses were apparent in the rather similar concept of "cultural pluralism" invented by Horace M. Kallen at the height of the last great immigration debate, before the Quota Acts of the 1920s. Kallen, like many of today's pro-immigration enthusiasts, reacted emotionally against the calls for "Americanization" that the 1880-to-1920 immigrant wave provoked. He argued that any unitary American nationality had already been dissipated by immigration (sound familiar?). Instead, he said, the U.S. had become merely a political state (polity) containing a number of different nationalities.

Kallen left the practical implications of this vision "woefully undeveloped" (in the words of the *Harvard Encyclopedia of American Ethnic Groups*). It eventually evolved into a vague approval of tolerance, which was basically how Americans had always treated immigrant groups anyway—an extension, not coincidentally, of how the English built the British nation.

But in one respect, Kallenism is very much alive: he argued that authen- 25
tic Americanism was what he called "the American Idea." This amounted to an almost religious idealization of "democracy," which again was left

undeveloped but which appeared to have as much to do with nondiscrimination and equal protection under the law as with elections. Today, a messianic concern for global "democracy" is being suggested to conservatives as an appropriate objective for U.S. foreign policy.

And Kallenism underlies the second helpful remark that someone always makes in any discussion of U.S. immigration policy: *"America isn't a nation like the other nations—it's an idea."*

Once more, this American exceptionalism is really more a matter of degree than of kind. Many other nations have some sort of ideational reinforcement. Quite often it is religious, such as Poland's Roman Catholicism; sometimes cultural, such as France's ineffable Frenchness. And occasionally it is political. Thus—again not coincidentally—the English used to talk about what might be described as the "English Idea": English liberties, their rights as Englishmen, and so on. Americans used to know immediately what this meant. As Jesse Chickering wrote in 1848 of his diverse fellow-Americans: "English laws and institutions, adapted to the circumstances of the country, have been adopted here. . . . The tendency of things is to mold the whole into one people, whose leading characteristics are English, formed on American soil."

What is unusual in the present debate, however, is that Americans are now being urged to abandon the bonds of a common ethnicity and instead to trust entirely to ideology to hold together their state (polity). This is an extraordinary experiment, like suddenly replacing all the blood in a patient's body. History suggests little reason to suppose it will succeed. Christendom and Islam have long ago been sundered by national quarrels. More recently, the much-touted "Soviet Man," the creation of much tougher ideologists using much rougher methods than anything yet seen in the U.S., has turned out to be a Russian, Ukrainian, or Kazakh after all.

Which is why Shakespeare has King Henry V say, before the battle of Agincourt, not "we defenders of international law and the dynastic principle as it applies to my right to inherit the throne of France," but

> *We few, we happy few, we band of brothers.*

However, although intellectuals may have decided that America is not a nation but an idea, the news has not reached the American people—especially that significant minority who sternly tell the Census Bureau their ethnicity is "American." (They seem mostly to be of British origin, many generations back.) And it would have been considered absurd throughout most of American history.

John Jay in *The Federalist Papers* wrote that Americans were "one united 30
people, a people descended from the same ancestors, speaking the same language, professing the same religion, attached to the same principles of government, very similar in their manners and customs." Some hundred years later, Theodore Roosevelt in his *Winning the West* traced the "perfectly continuous history" of the Anglo-Saxons from King Alfred to George Washington. He presented the settling of the lands beyond the Alleghenies as "the crowning

and greatest achievement" of "the spread of the English-speaking peoples," which—though personally a liberal on racial matters—he saw in explicit terms: "it is of incalculable importance that America, Australia, and Siberia should pass out of the hands of their red, black, and yellow aboriginal owners, and become the heritage of the dominant world races."

Roosevelt himself was an example of ethnicities merging to produce this new nation. He thanked God—he teased his friend Rudyard Kipling—that there was "not a drop of British blood" in him. But that did not stop him from identifying with Anglo-Saxons or from becoming a passionate advocate of an assimilationist Americanism, which crossed ethnic lines and was ultimately to cross racial lines.

And it is important to note that, at the height of the last great immigration wave, Kallen and his allies totally failed to persuade Americans that they were no longer a nation. Quite the contrary: once convinced that their nationhood was threatened by continued massive immigration, Americans changed the public policies that made it possible. While the national-origins quotas were being legislated, President Calvin Coolidge put it unflinchingly: "America must be kept American."

Everyone knew what he meant.

"Pulling Up the Ladder"

Another of these helpful lines exactly describes what Americans did in the 1920s: *"Pulling up the ladder."* But pulling up the ladder may be necessary—if the lifeboat is about to capsize.

And the American lifeboat undeniably did stabilize after the 1920s. It took 35
time. As late as 1963, when Nathan Glazer and Daniel Patrick Moynihan published *Beyond the Melting Pot,* the ethnic groups that had arrived in the 1880-to-1920 wave appeared not to be assimilating into the American mainstream. At best, as Will Herberg argued in *Protestant, Catholic, Jew,* there was a "triple melting pot" working within the major religious communities—for example, Irish Catholics marrying Italian Catholics; German Jews marrying Russian Jews.

But then, just when the media-academic complex had tooled up an entire industry based on the "unmeltable ethnics," they started to melt. The figures are dramatic. According to Robert C. Christopher in his 1989 *Crashing the Gates: The De-Wasping of America's Power Elite,* half of all Italian-Americans born since World War II married non-Catholics, mainly Protestants; some 40 percent of Jews marrying in the 1980s chose Gentile spouses, a phenomenon rare if not unknown only twenty years earlier.

Christopher, a former *Newsweek* writer and political liberal, naturally saw this development as an emerging cultural synthesis free (at last!) of any nasty ethnic connotations at all. But there is a simpler interpretation: the American nation was just swallowing, and then digesting—Wasping, to adapt Christopher's terminology—an unusually large and spicy immigrant meal.

This pattern of swallowing and digesting has recurred throughout American history. Waves of immigration have been followed by lulls right back into colonial times. After the turmoil of the Revolutionary War, there was a Great Lull remarkably similar to the one earlier this century. For nearly fifty years, there was practically no immigration at all. The U.S. grew rapidly through natural increase. But the make-up of the white population remained about what it had been in the 1790 Census: largely (60 percent) English, heavily (80 percent) British, and overwhelmingly (98 percent) Protestant. This was the nation Alexis de Tocqueville described in *Democracy in America* (1835)—an irony, since his name has now been adopted by Gregory Fossedal's pro-immigration lobby. That Tocqueville's analysis still has relevance is a tribute to that nation's powers of assimilation and cultural transmission.

Thereafter, immigration relative to U.S. population peaked about every fifteen or twenty years: in 1851–54, 1866–73, 1881–83, 1905–07, and 1921–24. In between it plunged, by as much as three-quarters or more. And the ethnic composition continuously changed. Earlier in the century, the largest element was Irish; in the middle, German; by the end, from Southern and Eastern Europe. After 1924, immigration was reduced to a trickle—but that trickle was from Northern and Western Europe. These variations in the magnitude and make-up of immigration were vital to the process of digestion.

And this pattern of variation puts a different perspective on the immi- 40
gration debate. For example, it is conventional to dismiss all concerns about immigration with the argument that such fears have proved groundless in the past. Of course, this is illogical. Just because a danger has been averted in the past does not mean it cannot happen in the future. Many passengers might have climbed aboard the lifeboat safely; one more may still capsize it.

But in fact these concerns, which have been expressed by the most eminent Americans going right back to colonial times, were perfectly reasonable. They were rendered moot only by changing circumstances. Thus Benjamin Franklin worried about German immigration in 1751: "Why should Pennsylvania, founded by the English, become a Colony of *Aliens,* who will shortly be so numerous as to Germanize us instead of our Anglifying them . . . ?" Franklin was not proved wrong: instead, German immigration was halted—in the short run, by the Seven Years' War (1756–63); in the longer run, by the post-Revolution Great Lull.

Similarly, the nativist anti-Catholic "Know-Nothing" insurrection, which had seized six state governments and elected 75 congressmen by 1855, was the reaction, harsh but human, of a Protestant nation that had forgotten immigration to its apparently imminent inundation by Irish Catholics fleeing the 1846 potato famine. Subsequently, Know-Nothingism receded, partly because of the Civil War, but also because the supply of Irish Catholics turned out to be finite after all. The Irish made up nearly half of the 1851–54 wave. They were perhaps a fifth or less of the subsequent trough.

The public policies that excluded Asian immigration for nearly a hundred years also appear rather different in this historical perspective. The California Legislature's 1876 report on immigration complained that the Chinese "have never adapted themselves to our habits, mode of dress, or our educational system. . . . Impregnable to all the influences of our Anglo-Saxon life, they remain the same stolid Asiatics that have floated on the rivers and slaved in the fields of China for thirty centuries of time." Whatever its dark motive, this is on its face a very specific complaint about the difficulty of assimilating immigrants from a pre-modern society. In the interim, the Orient has modernized. Today, immigrants from the area are often viewed (perhaps naïvely) as the most, well, "Anglo-Saxon," of the current wave.

Ask a Stupid Question . . .

Historical perspective also discredits another conventional ploy in the immigration debate: *"How can X be against immigration when the nativists wanted to keep his own great-grandfather out?"* This, of course, is like arguing that a passenger already on board the lifeboat should refrain from pointing out that taking on more will cause it to capsize.

But let's assume, for the sake of argument, that X is Irish-American. 45
Disqualifying him from the debate overlooks the long and painful adjustment to America that the Irish, like every immigrant group, had to make. The Irish too came to the U.S. from what was still basically a pre-modern agricultural society. Throughout the nineteenth century, they displayed social pathologies strikingly similar to those of the current black ghetto: disease, violence, family breakdown, drug addiction (alcohol in those days), and, perhaps not surprisingly, virtually no intermarriage.

Slowly, over generations, America changed the Irish—and they changed themselves. Today, in terms of measures like income, education, and political affiliation, Irish-Americans are more or less indistinguishable from the mainstream, with which they have extensively intermarried. (Well . . . alcoholism is a little higher. But so are incomes.) In his book *The Economics and Politics of Race: An International Perspective,* the Hoover Institution economist Thomas Sowell describes this as "historically . . . one of the great social transformations of a people." Irish-Americans have earned the hard way their right to opinions about who and how many their country can absorb.

The Irish changed themselves with a great deal of encouragement from a notably stern clergy. But the Roman Catholic Church itself made an adjustment to America. Indeed, the word "Americanization" was invented in the 1850s by a Vermont Yankee convert to Catholicism, Orestes A. Brownson, who argued in his *Brownson's Quarterly Review* that the nativists had a point: the Irish should assimilate to the American nation that had already been formed; the Church should not identify itself with Old World autocracy—as Pius IX, after the 1848 Revolutions in Europe, was inclined to do. Brownson provoked a ferocious controversy. But, today, his view can be seen to have prevailed.

In politics as elsewhere, if you ask a stupid question, you get a stupid answer—or at any rate a terse answer. And asking people if they want their communities to be overwhelmed by weird aliens with dubious habits is a stupid question. The answer is inevitable. Until now in America, chance circumstances and changes in public policy have always combined to change this question before the inevitable answer became too embarrassing. But the greater the number of immigrants, and the greater their difference from the American mainstream, the louder and ruder the answer will be.

Questions for Discussion

1. Brimelow's writing style deserves attention. It is hardly dry, but what makes it colorful also makes it difficult. For example, Brimelow relies heavily on allusions—references to art, literature, and historical events. The first paragraph alludes to Dante's medieval allegory *The Divine Comedy,* in which hell is seen as a funnel-shaped pit descending to the center of the earth. Find other examples of allusions, and discuss how they help Brimelow make his case. How well do they work? For whom are they likely to be most persuasive?
2. Consider other stylistic devices in Brimelow's writing: his use of metaphors, images, humor, and irony (as in paragraphs 11 and 26, where he refers to "helpful" remarks Americans often make). What impression do you form of Brimelow himself from his use of these stylistic devices?
3. Brimelow emphasizes a fact about all nations, not just the United States—that all are composed of immigrants. This is true even of the people we call "Native Americans," whose ancestors started coming to North America from Asia tens of thousands of years ago. How might this long view of history influence our current attitudes toward immigration?
4. Brimelow's view rests fundamentally on one contention: that nations are bound together more powerfully by shared ethnicity than by shared ideas. What evidence does he offer as support? Is his contention true of nations generally? Is it true in the case of the United States?

For Inquiry and Convincing

In the section "Pulling Up the Ladder," Brimelow offers his own interpretation of the history of U.S. immigration. Compare his interpretation with Kennedy's in the first selection in this chapter. How are their views alike? How are they different?

Write an essay defending either Brimelow's interpretation or Kennedy's—or some combination of both. Be sure to relate your discussion to current patterns of both legal and illegal immigration.

For Persuasion

Whereas Brimelow warns that Americans will not tolerate current immigration patterns and that therefore the patterns themselves must change, Kennedy contends that the patterns are not likely to change and that therefore Americans must learn to be more tolerant than ever before. In an essay addressed to students on your campus, advocate one view or the other.

LINDA CHAVEZ

What to Do about Immigration

Views of immigration defy neat categories such as "liberal" and "conservative." A former member of the Reagan administration and current president of the Center for Equal Opportunity, Linda Chavez—like Peter Brimelow—is certainly a conservative. But her attitude toward immigration is generally positive, as Reagan's was, and she argues that the so-called nativist viewpoint is fundamentally mistaken. Yet she also shares common ground with Brimelow and other nativists in her strong opposition to multiculturalism.

The following article, first published in Commentary *(March 1995), offers guidelines for controlling both legal and illegal immigration. Whether we are sympathetic with her proposals or not, Chavez challenges us to translate our attitudes into policy objectives.*

LIKE SO much American social policy, immigration policy is a monument to the law of unintended consequences. Although assurances to the contrary were offered by the legislators responsible for the last major overhaul of the nation's immigration law, the 1965 Immigration and Nationality Act, that law profoundly altered both the makeup and the size of the immigrant flow. Until 1965, most immigrants came from Europe; today, some 80 percent of those legally admitted are from Asia or Latin America. The new law also significantly increased the pool of eligible applicants by giving preference to family members of immigrants already here. 1

But these changes might not have had such striking effects had they not coincided with dramatic developments in civil-rights law and with the expansion of the welfare state. As it is, immigration now intersects with two of the most troubling issues of our time: race and entitlements.

In 1993 (the last year for which figures are available), over 800,000 legal immigrants were admitted to the United States and an estimated 300,000 illegal aliens settled here, more or less permanently. Over the last decade, as many as ten million legal and illegal immigrants established permanent residence—a number higher than at any period in our history, including the peak immigration decade of 1900–10.

To be sure, these numbers are somewhat misleading: because our population is so much larger now than it was at the beginning of the century, the rate of immigration is much lower, barely one-third of what it was then. And while the proportion of persons living in the U.S. who are foreign-born is high by recent standards—about 8 percent in the last census—it is still lower than it was for every decade between 1850 and 1950.

The numbers alone, however, do not fully describe the dimensions of the immigration issue. Americans are not just concerned about the size of the immigrant population; they are worried about the kind of people who are 5 coming, how they got here, and whether they are likely to become a benefit or a burden to our society. There is deep suspicion that today's immigrants are fundamentally different from earlier waves. In recent polls, 59 percent of Americans say that immigration was good for the country in the past, but only 29 percent think it is a good thing now. Former Colorado Governor Richard Lamm, who favors restricting immigration, summed up this national ambivalence: "I know that earlier large waves of immigrants didn't 'overturn' America, but there are . . . reasons to believe that today's migration is different from earlier flows."

Immigration enthusiasts (among whom I count myself, albeit with some important reservations) like to point out that Americans have never been eager to accept new arrivals, for all our rhetoric about being an "immigrant nation." As Rita Simon of the American University law school noted recently, "We view immigrants with rose-colored glasses, turned backward." Perhaps, then, there is nothing much new in the worries so many people express about whether this generation of immigrants will indeed assimilate to American norms. But comforting as the thought may be that today's Mexicans, Vietnamese, Pakistanis, and Filipinos are the equivalent of yesterday's Italians, Jews, Poles, and Irish, it fails to take into account the tremendous transformation America itself has undergone in the last half-century.

The America to which Europeans immigrated—first northern Europeans in the 19th century and then southern and eastern Europeans in the first quarter of the 20th—was a self-confident, culturally homogeneous nation. There was never any question that immigrants would be expected to learn English and to conform to the laws, customs, and traditions of their new country (although even then, some immigration restrictionists questioned whether certain groups were capable of such conformity). And immigrants themselves—especially their children—eagerly wanted to adapt. Public schools taught newcomers not only a new language, but new dress, manners, history, myths, and even hygiene to transform them into Americans who sounded, looked, acted, thought, and smelled the part.

In those days there were no advocates insisting that America must accommodate itself to the immigrants; the burden of change rested solely with the new arrivals. To be sure, by their sheer numbers they managed subtly to alter certain features of their new country. Because of them the U.S. is less Protestant then it would otherwise have been; no doubt American cuisine and art are richer; and the pantheon of American heroes from Christopher Columbus to Joe DiMaggio to Albert Einstein is more diverse. Still, until fairly recently, Americans—native-stock or of later lineage—understood what it meant to be American, and it meant roughly the same thing regardless of where one's ancestors came from.

We are far less sure what it means to be American today. Thus the question, "What to do about immigration?" is inextricably wound up with how we define our national identity.

Some critics of immigration—most notably John O'Sullivan, the editor 10
of *National Review,* and Peter Brimelow, author of the forthcoming *Alien Nation*—believe that national identity must be defined in explicitly racial and ethnic terms and that the current high levels of nonwhite immigration will drastically alter that identity. O'Sullivan argues:

> A nation is an ethno-cultural unit—a body that begins its life as a cultural in-gathering but, by dint of common history, habits, tastes, shared experiences, tales, songs, memories, and above all, intermarriage, becomes progressively more like an extended family—that is, more ethnic—over time.

As long as America's core remained overwhelmingly Wasp, so this argument goes, it was possible for Italian Catholics or Russian Jews or Japanese Buddhists to become American. Both O'Sullivan and Brimelow fear, however, that the large numbers of nonwhites who are now coming in will undermine the assimilative capacity of the nation; they both cite Census Bureau projections that the majority of the U.S. population will become non-white (or more accurately, non-Hispanic white) by the year 2050; and they both blame current immigration policy for this portentous outcome.

But is race or ethnicity really the issue? If so, O'Sullivan and Brimelow can relax. Yes, the majority of immigrants admitted to the U.S. in the last twenty years have been relatively dark-skinned Mexicans, Filipinos, Vietnamese, Chinese, Koreans, etc. Yet by the year 2050, their great-grandchildren are unlikely to look much like them. Intermarriage rates in the U.S. have never been higher; nor have mixed-race births. The Population Reference Bureau (PRB) recently touted this development in its monthly newsletter in a front-page article, "Interracial Baby Boomlet in Progress?" Births to mixed Japanese/white couples now exceed those to all-Japanese couples. There are now so many ethnically mixed persons in the U.S. that the Census Bureau is debating whether to create a special classification for them. (Perhaps it should consider calling the category "American.") Not even groups with strong traditions or religious prohibitions against intermarriage seem exempt from the trend. About half of all American Jews, for example, marry non-Jews.

Nor is the inclination to intermarry diminishing among more recent immigrant groups. One-third of young, U.S.-born Hispanics marry non-Hispanics; and perhaps more significantly, nearly half of all Hispanics consider themselves white. Peter Brimelow dismisses this phenomenon, noting that those of Mexican origin, who make up nearly two-thirds of the entire group, are predominantly Indian. But he misses the point. By defining themselves as white, Hispanics are identifying with the majority. In a recent survey, a majority of Hispanics said the group with which they felt they had most in common was whites, and so did Asians.

In short, the problem of national identity is not primarily connected with heredity or ethnicity. It is, rather, a function of culture. But on this score, the evidence is decidedly less reassuring.

From the White House to Madison Avenue to Main Street, the idea has 15
taken hold that the United States is a multicultural society. Many doubt that such a thing as American culture even exists. When I recently told a university audience that American blacks, Hispanics, Asians, and whites have more in common with one another than they do with their contemporaries in any of their ancestral homelands, the students literally gasped in disbelief. "I don't know what you mean by 'American culture,'" one young Puerto Rican woman told me. "I have a right to my own culture and language." She said this, however, in perfect English, leaving me wondering just what culture and language she might be referring to.

But if the irony of her situation escaped this particular student—whose coloring and features suggested predominantly Spanish ancestry—her political statement was clear. A European-looking, English-speaking Hispanic who chooses to reject American culture, she represents the flip side of the large number of brown-skinned Hispanics who see themselves as white. It is hard to know how many such persons there are, but their numbers are surely growing as ethnicity becomes increasingly politicized.

Into this confusing mix come immigrants who, unlike these *ersatz* ethnics, truly are culturally different from those around them. And such are the misgivings of the rest of us that we no longer seem able or willing to help these newcomers become Americans. Public schools, which worked to acculturate previous immigrant groups, now see it as their mission to preserve immigrant languages and culture. The Los Angeles school system, which educates more Latino immigrant children than any in the nation, prides itself on teaching these youngsters primarily in Spanish for three years or more. Denver public-school officials recently ordered one local high school to stop teaching 450 Hispanic youngsters in English, and transferred out 51 Asian students so that the school could concentrate on its Spanish bilingual program. The demand for Spanish-speaking teachers is so great that districts from Los Angeles to Chicago have begun importing instructors from Mexico, Spain, and Puerto Rico; in 1993, Mexico signed an agreement with California to provide both teachers and 40,000 textbooks for the state's Spanish-language classrooms.

Yet bilingual education did not originally grow out of the pressures of immigration. It started as a small, federally funded program to help Mexican-American children (largely native-born) in the Southwest, and it was already in place years before the large influx of Spanish-speaking immigrants in the 1970's and 80's. Its chief sponsor, former Senator Ralph Yarborough (D-Tex), declared that the purpose of his bilingual-education bill was not "to create pockets of different languages throughout the country . . . but just to try to make [Mexican-American] children fully literate in English." By 1975, however, civil-rights enforcement agencies in Washington were insisting (on the basis of a Supreme Court ruling involving the Civil Rights Act of 1964) that school districts teach "language-minority" youngsters, mostly Mexican-Americans and Puerto Ricans, in Spanish or face a cut-off of all federal funds.

In the early stages of the program, the overwhelming majority of students in bilingual classes were U.S.-born; today, nearly 60 percent still are. What is more, many of these children are more fluent in English than Spanish—no one knows exactly how many, because most states use an arbitrary cut-off score (usually the 30th or 40th percentile) on a standardized English test to place Hispanic youngsters in Spanish-language programs, rather than testing to see whether they are more fluent in English or in Spanish. . . .

One solution, favored by those who want to restrict immigration for 20
other reasons, is to cut off the flow of immigrants. Yet while this might diminish the clientele for ethnic entitlements, the programs would continue to serve the native-born populations for whom they were originally created. For it is not immigrants who clamor for these programs. Asian immigrants, for one, have largely eschewed bilingual education in favor of English-immersion programs. Even some Latino immigrant parents have staged protests in California, New York, and New Jersey upon discovering that their children were being taught in Spanish; others simply withdraw their children, sending them to parochial schools that teach all students in English.

The other solution to the problem of ethnic entitlements, of course, would be simply to end them for everyone. There are many good reasons for doing this, even if immigration were to cease altogether. Race- and ethnic-based entitlements have been a bane of American social policy for the last quarter-century. They have divided Americans, increased group hostility, and perverted the whole notion of color-blind justice. Furthermore, they are the foundation on which the entire edifice of multiculturalism is built. Without the enticement of racial and ethnic preferences in education, employment, voting, and elsewhere, group identity, instead of intensifying in recent years, might have diminished.

Multicultural education has become the main instrument to help preserve group identity. But multicultural education is no more a byproduct of increased Latin and Asian immigration than are bilingual education and ballots, ethnic voting districts, and affirmative action. In fact, multicultural education first came into being largely to address the demands of blacks for proportional representation in the curriculum—though by now it has spread (some would say, metastasized) to the point where all students are encouraged to think of themselves primarily as members of groups rather than as Americans.

Thus, when California recently adopted a new textbook series for kindergarten through eighth grade, ethnic protestors turned out at school-board hearings in San Francisco, Los Angeles, San Diego, Oakland, and other cities, insisting upon changes not only in the treatment of blacks but also in the way the series dealt with Indians, Hispanics, Jews, Muslims, and even conservative Christians.

Critics of immigration like O'Sullivan and Brimelow believe that multiculturalism would, in O'Sullivan's words, "be easier to dismantle if immigration were reduced." But the California story suggests that, if anything, it is ethnic diversity itself that might actually hasten the demise of multiculturalism. Like a house of cards that has grown too unwieldy, multicultural education may collapse of its own weight if it is required to include the distinct stories of each of the hundreds of different groups now in the schools.

But the unraveling of multicultural education, salutary a prospect as it may 25
be, is hardly a good reason for maintaining our current immigration policy. Clearly, that policy needs changing in ways that are consistent with our national interests and values. I would argue, indeed, that our immigration policy should *reinforce* our national identity—which is not necessarily the same thing as our racial or ethnic composition.

What then, should we do? Let me deal with legal immigration first.

Change the System to One that Favors Skills. The basis of the current system is the principle of family reunification, adopted in 1965 with the expectation that this would maintain the ethnic balance of the U.S. population as it existed at the time. Of course things have not worked out that way. But questions of ethnic balance aside, there is nothing sacrosanct about family reunification as a guiding principle of immigration policy, and we should not be deterred from changing it out of fear that such a move might be interpreted as racist.

In any case, the problem with the current immigrant pool is not that there are too many Latinos and Asians *per se,* but that too many of the people we now admit are low-skilled. Mexicans come with only about seven years of schooling on average, and less than a quarter have obtained high-school diplomas. Such newcomers face a much more difficult period of adjustment and bring fewer benefits to the U.S. economy than would more highly skilled immigrants.

It is true that under current criteria, which include only 140,000 slots for skills-based admissions, immigrants are twice as likely to hold Ph.D.'s as are U.S.-born persons. But they are also more likely to be high-school drop-outs. We ought to admit more of the former and fewer of the latter, and regardless of their country of origin. As it turns out, immigrants from Africa and Asia have among the highest average levels of education. Nearly 90 percent of all African immigrants are high-school graduates—a figure 15-percent higher than that for Canadian immigrants. And Indians, Taiwanese, and Iranians have among the highest proportions of college or graduate degrees.

Encourage Immigrants to Assimilate. Immigration policy entails 30
more than laws regulating who gets admitted and under what criteria. It also involves—or at least should involve—how we incorporate immigrants into our society. On that score, we are doing much more poorly now than we did in the past, in part because we have given up on the notion that we have an obligation to assimilate immigrants. Regardless of what other changes we make in immigration policy, we must reverse course on this issue. If immigration to the U.S. ceased tomorrow, we would still have twenty million foreign-born persons living here, plus their children. Assimilation is essential for them, as well as for the rest of us, if we are to stop the further fragmenting of our society.

First and foremost, this means encouraging immigrants and their children to learn English, which in practical terms means abolishing bilingual education in favor of English-immersion programs in the public schools. By now we have nearly thirty years of experience demonstrating that bilingual education helps children neither to learn English nor to do better in school. Latino immigrants in particular have been badly served by bilingual education—and by their putative leaders, usually U.S.-born, who are the main lobby behind this expensive, ineffective, and wasteful program.

But bilingual education is not the only culprit. With so many services available in their native languages, immigrants have fewer incentives today to learn English than they did in the past. Private services—native-language newspapers, advertising, etc.—fall outside the scope of public policy. But *government* services ought to be provided only in English. A common language has been critical to our success in forging a sense of national identity. Our public policies should preserve and protect that heritage. If the courts continue to obstruct local and state efforts to make English the official language of government, we should pass a federal constitutional amendment to ensure it.

Limit Welfare Benefits. Although immigrants as a whole are somewhat more likely than natives to receive welfare, the opposite is true of those of working age (15–64). In addition, immigrants have higher labor-force-participation rates than natives, with Hispanic men having among the highest—83.4 percent compared with 75 percent for non-Hispanic whites. If we modify our admission criteria to favor more highly skilled immigrants, welfare among working-age immigrants should drop below even the current rate of about 3 percent, alleviating much of the concern about immigrants and welfare.

The problem is high dependency rates among refugees and elderly immigrants. Among the former, this is a direct result of U.S. policy, which guarantees cash and medical assistance to all persons admitted under the refugee-resettlement program. Having been admitted, they are then attracted to states with relatively high benefits, and this tends to encourage long-term dependency. Thus, in California, some two-thirds of Laotian and Cambodian refugees and more than one-third of Vietnamese refugees remain on welfare after more than five years in the U.S.

While dealing comprehensively with this situation entails the much 35
larger issue of welfare reform, it is possible to make a dent in it by redesigning programs to limit the number of months refugees can receive assistance. One of the most promising possibilities would be to turn over responsibility for such assistance to private agencies, such as Catholic Charities, Lutheran Immigration and Refugee Service, and the Council of Jewish Federations, which have proved more successful at moving refugees off welfare. In Chicago, 74 percent of refugees in an experimental private resettlement project found work within six months of arrival, and only 2 percent remained on welfare after thirteen months, compared with more than 40 percent in the state-administered program.

The problem of elderly immigrants is more complicated. In 1990, 55 percent of elderly Chinese immigrants in California who had arrived between 1980 and 1987 were on welfare, as were 21 percent of elderly Mexican immigrants. Because they have worked too few years or at insufficient wages to qualify for adequate Social Security benefits, most such recipients obtain Supplemental Security Income (SSI).

But many of these immigrants are the parents of resident aliens who brought them here under family-reunification provisions. Anyone who sponsors an immigrant must guarantee that he will not become a public burden, and is required to accept full financial responsibility for up to five years. Simply enforcing these provisions would greatly alleviate the problem of welfare dependency among elderly immigrants. (Among recipients in California that should not pose a problem, since 50 percent of their children's households in 1990 had incomes over $50,000, and 11 percent over $100,000.) We might also consider lengthening the number of years sponsors are required to provide support to family members; Canada currently requires a ten-year commitment.

All these reforms are addressed to the policies governing legal immigration. What about illegal immigration?

Like welfare dependency among immigrants, illegal immigration is not so big a problem as many people imagine (in one recent poll, two-thirds said they thought most immigrants are illegal aliens). Estimates of overall numbers vary widely, with some commentators hysterically claiming more than ten million illegal aliens. But the more reliable Census Bureau estimates about four million, with (as noted earlier) another 300,000 or so added each year.

In theory, no amount of illegal immigration is acceptable, since the 40
phenomenon represents our failure to maintain secure borders, a prerequisite of national sovereignty. In practice, however, it is unlikely that we will ever completely eradicate illegal immigration; our borders are too long and porous and our society too free and prosperous. But there are steps we can take that would significantly reduce the current flow.

Stop Illegal Aliens at the Border. There is no mainstream support for mass round-ups and deportations of the type used in the 1930's and 50's to roust illegal aliens; nor could such a program withstand legal challenge. Therefore, the only way to reduce the flow is to contain it at the border. The frontier between Mexico and the U.S. is 2,000 miles long, but only about 250 miles of it are traversable. Most illegal aliens enter in a handful of places near metropolitan areas—about 65 percent around San Diego and El Paso.

We know that it is possible to reduce the flow significantly, with more Immigration and Naturalization Service (INS) personnel and better equipment and technology. A recent two-month, $25-million experiment in beefed-up border control near San Diego halved the number of illegal crossings; similar experiments in El Paso produced comparable results. While the most determined may seek alternative routes of entry, for the large majority rough terrain will limit the opportunity.

Deport Alien Criminals. Apprehending and deporting illegal aliens who have successfully gotten past the border requires more resources and more draconian enforcement measures than most Americans would be willing to endorse; but there is overwhelming support for deporting those arrested for criminal acts in the U.S. In order to do this, however, local law-enforcement officials must be able to ascertain the status of persons in their custody, which they cannot now do easily. A pilot program in Phoenix, which allows police officers 24-hour access to INS records, might prove an effective model for enhancing local police efforts and making more deportations feasible.

Outlaw Sanctuaries. Several cities, including San Francisco, Sacramento, and Chicago, have enacted ordinances banning city employees from contacting the INS if they know someone is in the country illegally. These ordinances are an outrage and show utter disregard for the rule of law. Any city that chooses to obstruct immigration enforcement should lose all federal funds.

Deny Welfare Benefits to Illegal Aliens. This is what California voters 45
thought they were enacting with Proposition 187. In fact, in most states illegal aliens are already prohibited from receiving welfare and any but emergency medical treatment, but the authorities lack adequate means to verify the legal status of recipients. Consequently, a pilot program instituted in the early 1980's, the Alien Status Verification Index, should be expanded and upgraded with access to on-line INS data bases so that the status of welfare recipients can be checked.

A potentially more intractable problem is that U.S.-born children of illegal aliens are eligible, as citizens, for AFDC and other welfare benefits. Indeed, one out of four new AFDC recipients in California is a child of illegal-alien parents. The only way to prevent them from receiving benefits is to deny them citizenship in the first place, which would probably require a constitutional amendment. I would not suggest that we travel this route, at least not until we have exhausted all other means of keeping illegal aliens out. But neither should we consider the mere discussion of the issue taboo, as it is in most public-policy circles today. Especially now, when U.S. citizenship entails many more rights and benefits than responsibilities, it should not be beyond the pale to reconsider what entitles a person to obtain it.

Repeal Employer Sanctions. While we are looking at ways to prevent illegal immigration, we ought to acknowledge that the linchpin of our current policy—punishing the employers of illegal aliens—has been a miserable failure. The Immigration Reform and Control Act of 1986, which established such sanctions, did virtually nothing to reduce the flow into the country. If anything, it probably contributed to the problem of welfare dependency among the four million illegal aliens already here, by making it more difficult for them to support themselves.

In typical fashion, those who falsely promised that employer sanctions would fix the illegal-alien problem now think they can tinker with the existing provisions to make it work. Senator Alan Simpson proposes a national identity card; the U.S. Commission on Immigration Reform thinks a national computerized work registry will do the trick.

But the purpose of both would be to enable employers to become better policemen for the immigration system, when they should never have been put in that position in the first place. Nor should the rest of us have to put up with more regulations and infringements on our privacy. It is simply wrong to burden the 98.5 percent of persons who are legally in the country with cumbersome and probably ineffective new requirements in order to try to punish the 1.5 percent of persons who have no right to be here.

These recommendations probably will not satisfy the most ardent foes of 50
immigration, like the Federation of American Immigration Reform (FAIR), the most influential restrictionist organization now operating. But many restrictionists are confused or just plain wrong about the nature of the immigration problem.

FAIR, for example, focuses almost exclusively on two issues: the size of current immigration, and its economic consequences. But neither of these is the heart of the matter.

FAIR's roots are in the population-control and environmentalist movements: this explains its preoccupation with numbers. Its founder, John Tanton, is a past president of Zero Population Growth and chairman of the National Sierra Club Population Committee. FAIR's two most prominent demographer-gurus are Garrett Hardin and Leon Bouvier, both of whom have been actively involved with population-control groups. Their primary concern is that immigrants—no matter where they are from or what their social and economic characteristics—add to the size of the population. (Bouvier has actually said that he believes the ideal U.S. population would be 150 million persons, though he has not clearly spelled out what he would do with the other 100 million of us who are already here.)

It is true that immigrants account for about half of current population growth in the U.S. Nonetheless, U.S. population growth as a whole is relatively modest, at 1 percent per year. Even with immigrants, including the more fecund Latins, we are in no danger of a Malthusian population explosion. . . .

As Francis Fukuyama[1] and others have argued, most immigrants still seem to personify the very traits we think of as typically American: optimism, ambition, perseverance—the qualities that have made this country great. The ranks of successful immigrant entrepreneurs are legion; in Silicon Valley alone, recent immigrants have built many of the major technology companies, including Sun Microsystems, AST, and Borland International.

Immigrants have also transformed urban America over the last decade, 55
from Korean grocers in New York to Salvadoran busboys and janitors in Washington, Mexican babysitters and construction workers in Los Angeles, Cambodian doughnut-shop owners in Long Beach, Haitian cooks in Miami, Russian taxi drivers in Philadelphia, and Filipino nurses and Indian doctors in

[1] "Immigrants and Family Values," *Commentary,* May 1993. [Author's note]

public hospitals practically everywhere. As they always have done, immigrants still take the difficult, often dirty, low-paying, thankless jobs that other Americans shun. When they open their own businesses, these are frequently located in blighted, crime-ridden neighborhoods long since abandoned by American enterprise. And their children often outperform those who have been here for generations. This year, as in the last several, more than one-third of the finalists in the Westinghouse high-school science competition bore names like Chen, Yeu, Dasgupta, Khazanov, Bunyavanich, and Hattangadi.

The contrast between the immigrant poor and the American underclass is especially striking. As the sociologist William Julius Wilson and others have observed, Mexican immigrants in Chicago, despite their relative poverty and much lower levels of education, show few of the dysfunctional characteristics of unemployment, crime, welfare dependency, and drug use common among the city's black and Puerto Rican underclass. In cities like Los Angeles and Washington, where American blacks and Latino immigrants inhabit the same poor neighborhoods, the despair of the former seems all the more intense by contrast to the striving of the latter—as if one group had given up on America even as the other was proving the continued existence of opportunity.

For all our anxiety about immigrants, then, in the end it is Americans of all classes who are caught in the middle of a national identity crisis. It is still possible to turn immigrants into what St. John de Crèvecoeur called "a new race of men," provided the rest of us still want to do this. But if we, the affluent no less than the poor among us, cease to believe that being an American has any worth or meaning, we should not blame immigrants, most of whom entertain no such doubts.

Questions for Discussion

1. Arguing against the nativist position, Chavez claims that "the problem of national identity is not primarily connected with heredity or ethnicity. It is, rather, a function of culture" (paragraph 14). What is culture? What does Chavez seem to have in mind when she uses the word? What is ethnicity? To what extent can ethnicity and culture be separated?
2. According to Chavez, immigration policy should strive to "*reinforce* our national identity" (her emphasis), which should not be confused with "our racial or ethnic composition" (paragraph 25). How could immigration policy strengthen our national identity without favoring our current racial and ethnic composition? Are all of her proposals consistent with her overall aim? Why or why not?
3. Thinking especially of the 1965 Immigration and Nationality Act, Chavez depicts immigration policy as "a monument to the law of unintended consequences" (paragraph 1). What does she mean? What unintended consequences might her proposals have?
4. Clearly, Chavez favors the traditional goal of assimilation: new immigrants, regardless of background, should become "good Americans" in some sense.

Supposing that assimilation is a good thing, or at least to some extent necessary, how much assimilation is enough? That is, what changes must an immigrant make to function in American society and be acceptable to most Americans? What changes would be desirable—that is, helpful but not mandatory? What changes would be more or less optional, free of social pressure for conformity?

For Research, Inquiry, and Persuasion

Chavez is sharply critical of bilingual education, one of the many issues connected with immigration. Find out all you can about bilingual education—its history, goals, methods, and results. Question the claims of both its advocates and detractors. Then write an essay to an appropriate audience proposing and defending whatever course of action you think best with regard to bilingual education.

For Inquiry and Analysis

Chavez claims that the Federation for American Immigration Reform (FAIR) is "the most influential restrictionist organization" (paragraph 50). See what you can find out about FAIR—through library materials, the Internet, and anything you can get FAIR to send you.

What is their position on immigration? What reasons do they offer as justification? What aspects of their viewpoint appeal to you? What aspects do not? Why?

Based on any of the readings in this chapter or any additional research you have done on immigration, write a response to FAIR's position.

NICOLAUS MILLS

Lifeboat Ethics and Immigration Fears

Although not for the same reasons, the liberals of thirty years ago supported immigration as strongly as did Reaganite conservatives. The so-called new liberals are not so positive. Like Nicolaus Mills in the following article, they deplore nativist racism, past and present, but they also fear that immigrants' demands for social services will undermine public support for the welfare state itself and weaken or destroy other programs they strongly favor, such as affirmative action. Pro-immigration conservatives, they argue, are only interested in an uninterrupted flow of cheap labor—something that may be good for profit margins but, as the new liberals see it, bad for the wage levels of poorer Americans and for organized labor. In short, the liberal position is caught between its pro-immigration tradition and current political and economic conditions that threaten its social agenda. "Lifeboat Ethics and Immigration Fears" was first published in Dissent *(Winter 1996).*

IN *The Great Gatsby* F. Scott Fitzgerald introduces us to the nativism that was so much a part of the 1920s culture. "The idea is if we don't look out the white race will be—will be utterly submerged," Tom Buchanan tells the narrator, Nick Carraway. "It's all scientific stuff, it's been proved." 1

An embarrassed Nick says nothing. But Fitzgerald doesn't let Tom's remarks (which parallel Calvin Coolidge's 1921 observation, "Biological laws tell us . . . Nordics propagate themselves successfully. With other races, the outcome shows deterioration on both sides") go unchallenged. As soon as Tom stops speaking, his wife, Daisy, Nick's cousin, answers him back. "Tom's getting very profound," she observes sarcastically. "We've got to beat them down," she adds with a wink that summarizes her opinion of Tom's fears.

It is a putdown that works in *The Great Gatsby.* Tom Buchanan doesn't talk about race or immigration again. But seventy years later his fears are alive and well in America. To see them in action, we need look no further than Peter Brimelow's 1995 polemic *Alien Nation: Common Sense about America's Immigration Disaster.* For the English-born Brimelow, a senior editor at *Forbes,* the current mass immigration from predominantly non-European countries threatens not only "the racial hegemony of white Americans" but the ethnic balance responsible for our social cohesion as a nation. Continued unchecked immigration, Brimelow argues, promises to put America in the same position the Western Roman Empire faced during the fifth century when it was overrun by the Germanic tribes of Europe.

If he were no more than a lone voice defending the WASP values Tom Buchanan and Calvin Coolidge saw threatened in the 1920s, Peter Brimelow would be an interesting case. But in his belief that the time has come for a halt in immigration to America, Brimelow is no mere holdover from the Gatsby era, when nativist tracts like Madison Grant's *The Passing of the Great Race* and Lothrop Stoddard's *The Rising Tide of Color* were respectable reading. Brimelow speaks for an America that has become increasingly worried about the arrival of a million-plus immigrants annually to its shores and increasingly cynical about the arguments for continuing immigration at that rate.

The surveys in which a majority of the public speaks favorably about 5
past immigration and critically about current immigration (4.5 million between 1990 and 1994) only begin to tell the story. What is really at work these days in the immigration backlash and the culture of meanness it has helped foster is more than a fear of newcomers. It is a lifeboat ethics that says we aren't making it as a nation and that taking on even more people can only make our problems worse. The opponents of immigration now include trade unionists who see their collective bargaining power being weakened still further, archconservatives who want to put troops on our border with Mexico, congressional representatives who favor a computer registry with the names of everyone eligible to work in the United States, Zero-Population Growth advocates frightened by Census Bureau estimates that our population in 2050 will be eighty-two million greater than it would have been if immigration had ended in 1991, and black workers—73 percent of whom believe, according to a 1992 *Business Week*/Harris poll, that businesses would rather hire immigrants than African Americans.

The most dramatic example of such anti-immigrant fears overwhelming all other considerations and changing the political climate occurred in California during the 1994 midterm elections, when voters were presented with Proposition 187, an initiative designed to cut virtually all state aid, except emergency hospital care, to illegal aliens. In a state in which government officials put the cost to taxpayers of illegal aliens and their U.S.-born children at $3 billion annually—$1.1 billion in education, $950 million in health care, and $500 million each in welfare and prison costs—the questions raised by Proposition 187 were in themselves crucial. But as the debate over Proposition 187 heated up, the distinctions it drew between legal and illegal immigrants became increasingly marginal. Long before the November elections, what Proposition 187 was really about was signaled by its supporters when they began calling it the S.O.S. (Save Our State) initiative.

The literature handed out along with the initiative was even blunter in its appeals to resentment and its reluctance to concede that immigrants coming to California were driven by a sense of desperation and a willingness to take almost any job. "While our own citizens and legal residents go wanting, those who choose to enter our country ILLEGALLY get royal treatment at the expense of the California taxpayer," one ballot description read. Another hammered home the laziness of the newcomers. "Welfare, medical, and educational benefits are the magnets that draw ILLEGAL ALIENS," it declared. "WE CAN STOP THE ILLEGAL ALIEN INVASION NOW." Missing was any notion that today's immigrants might resemble those of the past in their character and ambition. As a television commercial argued, the only proper way for a struggling Californian to look on an illegal immigrant was as a leech: "Three hundred thousand illegal immigrant children in public schools . . . and they keep coming. It's unfair when people like you are working hard," the voiceover in one of the governor's ads reminded voters.

For Governor Pete Wilson, seemingly headed for defeat when the election began, a pro–Proposition 187 stance (combined with a recommendation that all Californians be required to carry I.D. cards when applying for a job or a government benefit) was enough to provide the basis for a come-from-behind victory over popular Secretary of State Kathleen Brown. But in a state that voted for Proposition 187 by a 3-to-2 margin, it was not just anxious white voters who took Wilson seriously. As a *Los Angeles Times* exit poll showed, Proposition 187 got 47 percent of the black vote, 47 percent of the Asian vote, and 23 percent of the Latino vote.

Wilson was not, moreover, alone among California politicians. Long before the 1994 elections, California officials at all levels made a point of calling for tougher sanctions on immigrants. Senator Dianne Feinstein argued for more Border Patrol agents and a $1-per-person border-crossing fee to pay for them. Senator Barbara Boxer advocated using the National Guard to help with Border Patrol work and increasing the penalties for the forgery of immigration documents. Even liberal politicians understood that in the California of the 1990s, being called soft on immigration was the equivalent of being called soft on communism during the cold war.

As the 1990s have progressed, California's mood has become the nation's. 10
A 1993 Yankelovich poll reflects the depth of the resentment. Sixty-four percent of those polled think most immigrants enter the United States illegally, 64 percent believe they take jobs from Americans, and 59 percent believe they add to the crime problem. Equally important, voters want the government to take steps to combat immigration. Seventy-three percent of the nation want strict limits on immigration, 50 percent want all U.S. citizens to be required to carry a national I.D. card, and 65 percent want the government to spend more money to tighten the border between the United States and Mexico. . . .

Such a backlash was unforeseen by those responsible for liberalizing America's immigration laws three decades ago. In 1965, when the Immigration and Nationality Act Amendments that led to the mass immigration of the last decade and a half were enacted, the amendments' supporters assumed that a new era of social justice was beginning. For the previous forty-one years, immigration to America had been reduced dramatically by the Johnson-Reed Act of 1924. Passed at a time when anti-immigration fever was running high, the Immigration Act of 1924 set a yearly limit of 150,000 on immigrants from outside the Western Hemisphere and then divided the 150,000 into quotas based on a country's share of the total American population of 1920. The national-origins system favored the descendants of those who had been here the longest—the British and the Northern Europeans. . . .

The amendments of 1965 were designed to undo this pattern. Enacted at the peak of the civil rights revolution, they reflected the optimism of the Great Society and the views of the coalition of Jews, Catholics, and liberals who had fought for years against the biases of the 1924 law. The new amendments put a limit on immigration from the Western Hemisphere for the first time, but in every other respect they were revolutionary. The new law abandoned all efforts to distinguish among immigrants on the basis of their race or their historical links to America. Up to twenty thousand people could come in any year from a single nation. The dominating principle was now family reunification. Eighty percent of the numerically limited visas were for close relatives of American citizens or residents.

In proposing the new legislation, President John F. Kennedy emphasized the importance of doing away with the old quota system. "It neither satisfies a national need nor accomplishes an international purpose," he declared. "In an age of interdependence among nations, such a system is an anachronism, for it discriminates among applicants for admission to the United States on the basis of accident of birth."

Two years later at the Liberty Island signing ceremony for the bill, Lyndon Johnson returned to the same themes in language reminiscent of that which he had used in signing it. The new immigration bill, the President said, repairs "a deep and painful flaw in the fabric of American justice. It corrects a cruel and enduring wrong in the conduct of the American nation.". . .

The Johnson administration and the Kennedys failed to anticipate the 15
consequences that would follow from a loophole in the 1965 law, which allowed the parents, spouse, and minor children of any adult American citizen to enter the country *without* being subject to numerical restrictions. As Asian and Latin immigrants with large extended families replaced European immigrants, the immigration multiplier—the number of admittances attributable to one immigrant—began to rise dramatically. The fifth preference of the new law, one that placed brothers and sisters high on the quota list, accelerated the process still more. Between 1971 and 1980, 4.5 million immigrants were admitted to the United States. Then in the 1980s the numbers climbed to a peak they had not reached since the turn of the century, and since then, our current immigration pattern of a million or more immigrants per year has become the norm.

It was not, however, only the size and scope of contemporary immigration that the supporters of the 1965 amendments failed to anticipate. They also failed to anticipate the problems that immigration would pose for an America no longer shaped by the prosperity of the 1960s.

In no area has this difference been more dramatic than that of affirmative action. In 1965, the year the Immigration and Nationality Amendments became law, there was no sense that newcomers to America might qualify for affirmative action. The aim of the Civil Rights Act of 1964 and the Voting Rights Act of 1965 was to undo legalized racism. The aim of affirmative action as it was understood in 1965 was to make sure that those who had been hurt by Jim Crow were in a position to compete on the new level playing field that had been created. . . .

In the 1990s all that has changed. It is not only the historic victims of racial and sexual discrimination who qualify for affirmative action. So do recent immigrants. The question is, should they? In a tight economy in which affirmative action is increasingly a zero-sum game, the competition for affirmative action slots has become fierce—especially among blacks and Latinos—and with the Supreme Court narrowing the scope of affirmative action still further with its 1995 *Adarand* decision, the immigrant question isn't only a practical one. It is also one of principle. It is not clear on what basis recent minority immigrants have a claim on benefits designed for those who have been the historic victims of American injustice. But as the law now operates, its message is that membership in a designated group, rather than actual victimization, entitles any entrant to America to special benefits.

Similar concerns arise with regard to citizenship and birth on American soil. A classic case emerged in 1995 when Immigration and Naturalization Service agents arrested a group of midwives along the Rio Grande border in Texas for a birth-certificate scam in which they charged Mexican mothers $800 to $1,200 for making up documents saying that their children were born in America and were therefore American citizens, eligible for a variety of benefits from AFDC payments to the eventual right to obtain legal residency for their parents. The scam itself gave the INS the basis for a clear line of prosecution, but what it also revealed was how easily U.S. immigration law can be circumvented.

Under U.S. law Mexican residents can easily obtain temporary visas 20
for shopping or visiting family provided they do not travel more than twenty-five miles across the border. All a pregnant Mexican woman need do is take a taxi across the international bridge and legally give birth in Texas to a U.S. citizen. If the mother is indigent, the government will even pay for her hospitalization and medical care. In the Rio Grande area of Texas as well as in California, this has meant thousands of such "American" babies being born each year.

A generous law has become an invitation for exploitation. Even a mother who is here illegally is rewarded with citizenship for her child and residence for herself and her family if she gives birth on American soil.

At the other end of the age scale, the problems are just as great. The Supplemental Security Income program was established in 1972 to help elderly retirees who did not in their lifetimes earn enough under Social Security to support themselves after they stopped working. With elderly immigrants, particularly those brought over by their children at an advanced age, SSI has taken on a very different quality. It has become a basic, rather than a supplemental, retirement program for men and women who never worked or worked for only a year or two in America. Just 10 percent of elderly United States citizens are enrolled in SSI. By contrast more than a quarter of all immigrants over the age of sixty-five now receive SSI, at a cost of $2 billion annually, and their numbers are growing. In just a decade they have increased fivefold, from 91,900 in 1982 to 440,000 today.

At what point does it make sense to say that these elderly new arrivals should not receive SSI? For the 20 percent living in families with incomes of $50,000 a year, the cutoff is clear. But there are grounds for being concerned about others as well and fearing that taxpayers are being asked to compensate for a lifetime of substandard income in a foreign counry.

Finally, there is the question of illegal immigrants and the education of their children. Under the terms of the Supreme Court's 1982 decision in *Plyer v. Doe,* the individual states are obliged to pay for the education of these children. Speaking for the Court's 5-to-4 majority, Justice William Brennan held, "There is no evidence in the record suggesting that illegal entrants pose any significant burden on the State's economy. To the contrary, the available evidence suggests that illegal aliens underutilize public services, while contributing their labor to the local economy, and tax money to the state." A decade later, Justice Brennan's economic analysis no longer applies. In 1994 the Urban Institute estimated that it cost the seven states with the highest number of immigrants $3.1 billion to educate 641,000 undocumented children, and in California the numbers were particularly high, with the state being forced to educate an estimated 300,000.

But equally problematic these days is the larger issue of whether there 25
are constitutional grounds for insisting, as the Court did, that educating the children of illegal aliens is required so as to avoid penalizing minors for the wrongdoing of the adults responsible for them. If such logic is to be the standard, why, as legal scholar Jeffrey Rosen argues, stop at education? Does not any limit on benefits for children of illegal aliens penalize them for the sins of their parents? In turn does not *Plyer v. Doe* as it stands invite wholesale violation of the law by illegal immigrant parents concerned with helping their children get a better start in life?

The result is that thirty years after the passage of the Immigration and Nationality Act Amendments of 1965 it has become very difficult, once one moves beyond the realm of scapegoating, to distinguish between the opponents of immigration whose arguments deserve to be heard and those whose objections are rooted in nativism. The former often provide for the latter.

To make matters worse, there is the stance taken on behalf of immigration by its conservative defenders. In the 1990s they have become its most influential proponents, and they have ensured that the immigration debate will continue to be a divisive one for years to come. At the core of their arguments is not a concern for those the poet Emma Lazarus described as "huddled masses yearning to be free" but the very opposite—a belief that by turning to immigrants we can bypass the worst problems the underclass poses to the economy.

This view is epitomized by Linda Chavez's 1995 *Commentary* essay "What to Do about Immigration." Chavez, the head of the U.S. Commission on Civil Rights during the Reagan years and currently president of the Center for Equal Opportunity, begins her essay by celebrating the accomplishments of recent immigrants. They have "transformed urban America over the last decade, from Korean grocers in New York, to Salvadoran busboys and janitors in Washington, Mexican babysitters and construction workers in Los Angeles, Cambodian doughnut shop owners in Long Beach, Haitian cooks in Miami, Russian taxi drivers in Philadelphia, and Filipino nurses and Indian doctors in public hospitals practically everywhere," Chavez writes. But for Chavez and the conservatives, it is not just the immigrants' successes that are important. It is that they have triumphed while long-term inner-city residents continue to fail. As Peter Salins of the Manhattan Institute for Policy Research puts it, "Wherever they have settled, immigrants have reclaimed inner-city neighborhoods that had fallen into a state of advanced decay."

For the conservatives, this comparison suggests that the revival of our inner cities now depends on immigrants. "The contrast between the immigrant poor and the American underclass is especially striking," Chavez goes on to argue. "In cities like Los Angeles and Washington, where American blacks and Latino immigrants inhabit the same poor neighborhoods, the despair of the former seems all the more intense by comparison to the striving of the latter—as if one group had given up on America even as the other was proving the continued existence of opportunity."

Missing from Chavez's essay and the conservative defense of immigration 30
is any sense that something is wrong when newcomers can find the wherewithal and energy to revitalize a neighborhood that those born into it have given up on. What is the future of an "American underclass" unable to come up with the cash or credit to open stores of their own? Are they to be pushed to still more neglected neighborhoods? Is there any obligation to help them? Chavez and the pro-immigration conservatives of the nineties never say. But at a time when they are doing their best to keep down the minimum wage and reduce welfare, their silence speaks volumes. It assumes that we are collectively better off if an inner-city neighborhood is "reclaimed"—even if that means its native-born inhabitants are made still more irrelevant to the economy around them.

Among pro-immigration conservatives, the same kind of thinking is true on an even grander scale when it comes to jobs. Michael Lind is not guilty of hyperbole when he charges, "From the point of view of business-class conservatives, the labor supply can never be too large and wages too low." "We propose a five-word constitutional amendment: There shall be open borders," the *Wall Street Journal* has declared. Immigrants, the conservative argument goes, promise a virtually painless cure for everything from the aging of our work force to our short-term labor shortages.

For high-tech industries what this means, Ron K. Unz, the CEO of Wall Street Analytics, writes in the Heritage Foundation's *Policy Review,* is skilled labor they don't have to train. "Silicon Valley, home to my own software company, is absolutely dependent upon immigrant professionals to maintain its technical edge," Unz notes. "A third of all the engineers and microchip designers here are foreign born, and if they left or their future inflow were cut off, America's computer industry would probably go with them."

But what really rouses Unz's enthusiasm and that of most pro-immigration conservatives is the idea that newcomers will do—cheaply and efficiently—what native American workers will not. Chavez puts the matter very delicately when she writes, "As they have always done, immigrants still take the difficult, often dirty, low-paying, thankless jobs that other Americans shun." Unz and most pro-immigration conservatives are more candid in talking about the kind of work immigrants will do. "In Los Angeles, the vast majority of hotel and restaurant employees are hardworking Hispanic immigrants, most here illegally, and anyone who believes that these unpleasant jobs would otherwise be filled by native-born blacks or whites is living in a fantasy world," Unz writes. "The same applies to nearly all the traditional lower-rung working-class jobs in Southern California, including nannies and gardeners whose widespread employment occasionally embarrasses the upper-middle-class Zoë Bairds of this world, even as it enables their professional careers by freeing them from domestic chores. The only means of making a job as a restaurant busboy even remotely attractive to a native-born American would be to raise the wage to $10 or $12 an hour, at which level the job would cease to exist. This is Economics 101."

Again, what the pro-immigration conservatives won't say is instructive. What is really being celebrated by them is the rebirth of an urban peasant economy, filled by legal and illegal immigrants willing to work for wages that can barely keep body and soul together. They dismiss as utopian the idea that hotels and restaurants ought to pay their workers a living wage, just as they ignore the devastating impact the presence of large numbers of immigrants has had on unskilled native-born workers, particularly high school dropouts. According to the economist George Borjas, a third of their decline in wages during the 1980s was a result of immigration.

Unz stops short of celebrating the return of the sweatshop, and he never 35
goes as far as University of Maryland economist Julian Simon, who calls for an updated version of the old *bracero* or guest worker program that from 1942 to 1964 supplied most of the labor for California agriculture. But the difference between Unz's position and that of the more radical pro-immigration conservatives is purely technical. What neither Unz nor they are interested in asking is, What happens after those working at substandard wages become sufficiently Americanized to want more? Do we send them back to the countries from which they came? Or do we keep them here and simply replace them with newer, more desperate immigrants?

For the pro-immigration conservatives, such questions don't in the long run matter. They see themselves as immune from the day-to-day chaos mass immigration can cause. But for the rest of the country, especially anyone who can't find an entry-level job, such questions *do* matter, and more often than not the response they elicit is a brutal and self-serving one. How could it be otherwise? At a time when wages are falling and welfare is being cut to the bone, the traditional justifications for immigration—America is a land of opportunity, a place of asylum—ring hollow. There is no credible way to talk about compassion for those living beyond our borders when we have so little regard for the needs of our own poor.

Questions for Discussion

1. Mills disparages what he calls a "lifeboat ethics" (paragraph 5). What does the lifeboat metaphor imply about the United States and the people who want to immigrate here? What determines right and wrong in a lifeboat situation? Look at Peter Brimelow's repeated use of the metaphor in his article. Is it apt or misleading?
2. According to Mills, what conditions have changed since 1965 that warrant new immigration policies? In what significant ways are our current laws being circumvented and exploited? How could we change our laws and policies to reduce the problems and abuses Mills points to?
3. Mills criticizes Chavez at length near the end of his essay. Reread the previous selection, and decide if Mills is fair to Chavez. Does he represent her position accurately? Are you persuaded by his critique? Why or why not?
4. We said in the headnote to this selection that liberalism is now caught between its historical support for immigration and its concern to preserve social services for poor Americans. Does Mills cope convincingly with the bind liberalism faces? Do you agree with Mills that conservatives want to exploit immigrant labor and avoid facing the problems of our underclass?

For Dialogue

Divide your class into three groups. Have one group carefully study Chavez's essay and the other Mills's essay; each group should then represent the respective author's position. The third group should draw up questions to ask the first two groups. Appoint a spokesperson for each of the three groups, and engage in a discussion. Your teacher or a student can serve as moderator.

In your writer's notebook assess how the dialogue went. Which position stood up best under questioning? Whose views did you find more convincing before the dialogue? Whose seemed more convincing following the dialogue? Why?

For Negotiation

Extreme positions, especially those held by people who are hardened in their viewpoints, can seldom be negotiated. On immigration, for example, there is too much room for disagreement between the "close our borders" position and the "open our borders" position.

But are Chavez and Mills as far apart as they might seem to be? On what exactly and to what degree do they differ? What common ground do they share?

Construct a position that mediates between Chavez's and Mills's viewpoints. Use the material and suggestions in Chapter 7 as a guide. Test your position by presenting it to the class. Did it work? If so, why? If not, how could you adjust it to appeal better to both sides?

DAVID MAUNG

Photograph

In some places along the border between San Diego and Tijuana, a steel wall has been constructed. In the photograph below, a U.S. border patrol agent stands in a doorway of the wall.

For Discussion

How do you "read" the photograph? Do you think the photographer is expressing a point of view about the wall? Does the photograph suggest that this wall will be effective in keeping out illegal immigrants? What evidence supports your conclusions?

What other borders between nations have been marked with walls? To what extent have they been successful?

LESLIE MARMON SILKO

The Border Patrol State

Whenever illegal immigration is discussed, someone asserts, "We have lost control of our borders." The contention is rarely questioned, and its implication is clear: We must increase our efforts to retain control.

A celebrated Native American writer, Leslie Marmon Silko, questions this whole line of thought. For her the border is no more than a legal fiction, and "we" have never really "controlled" it anyway. Furthermore, there are forces at work that render it beyond anyone's control. Many have called attention to the suffering and death among illegals that result from efforts to enforce U.S. immigration laws, but Silko highlights a lesser-known consequence—violation of the civil rights of American citizens, in particular citizens of color. "The Border Patrol State" was first published in The Nation *(17 October 1994).*

I USED to travel the highways of New Mexico and Arizona with a wonderful sensation of absolute freedom as I cruised down the open road and across the vast desert plateaus. On the Laguna Pueblo reservation, where I was raised, the people were patriotic despite the way the U.S. government had treated Native Americans. As proud citizens, we grew up believing the freedom to travel was our inalienable right, a right that some Native Americans had been denied in the early twentieth century. Our cousin, old Bill Pratt, used to ride his horse 300 miles overland from Laguna, New Mexico, to Prescott, Arizona, every summer to work as a fire lookout. 1

In school in the 1950s, we were taught that our right to travel from state to state without special papers or threat of detainment was a right that citizens under communist and totalitarian governments did not possess. That wide open highway told us we were U.S. citizens; we were free. . . .

Not so long ago, my companion Gus and I were driving south from Albuquerque, returning to Tucson after a book promotion for the paperback edition of my novel *Almanac of the Dead*. I had settled back and gone to sleep while Gus drove, but I was awakened when I felt the car slowing to a stop. It was nearly midnight on New Mexico State Road 26, a dark, lonely stretch of two-lane highway between Hatch and Deming. When I sat up, I saw the headlights and emergency flashers of six vehicles—Border Patrol cars and a van were blocking both lanes of the highway. Gus stopped the car and rolled down the window to ask what was wrong. But the closest Border Patrolman and his companion did not reply; instead, the first agent ordered us to "step out of the car." Gus asked why, but his question seemed to set them off. Two more Border Patrol agents immediately approached our car, and one of them snapped, "Are you looking for trouble?" as if he would relish it.

I will never forget that night beside the highway. There was an awful feeling of menace and violence straining to break loose. It was clear that the uniformed men would be only too happy to drag us out of the car if we did not speedily comply with their request (asking a question is tantamount to resistance, it seems). So we stepped out of the car and they motioned for us to stand on the shoulder of the road. The night was very dark, and no other traffic had come down the road since we had been stopped. All I could think about was a book I had read—*Nunca Mas*—the official report of a human rights commission that investigated and certified more than 12,000 "disappearances" during Argentina's "dirty war" in the late 1970s.

5 The weird anger of these Border Patrolmen made me think about descriptions in the report of Argentine police and military officers who became addicted to interrogation, torture and the murder that followed. When the military and police ran out of political suspects to torture and kill, they resorted to the random abduction of citizens off the streets. I thought how easy it would be for the Border Patrol to shoot us and leave our bodies and car beside the highway, like so many bodies found in these parts and ascribed to "drug runners."

Two other Border Patrolmen stood by the white van. The one who had asked if we were looking for trouble ordered his partner to "get the dog," and from the back of the van another patrolman brought a small female German shepherd on a leash. The dog apparently did not heel well enough to suit him, and the handler jerked the leash. They opened the doors of our car and pulled the dog's head into it, but I saw immediately from the expression in her eyes that the dog hated them, and that she would not serve them. When she showed no interest in the inside of the car, they brought her around back to the trunk, near where we were standing. They half-dragged her up into the trunk, but still she did not indicate any stowed-away human beings or illegal drugs.

The mood got uglier; the officers seemed outraged that the dog could not find any contraband, and they dragged her over to us and commanded her to sniff our legs and feet. To my relief, the strange violence the Border Patrol agents had focused on us now seemed shifted to the dog. I no longer felt so strongly that we would be murdered. We exchanged looks—the dog and I. She was afraid of what they might do, just as I was. The dog's handler jerked the leash sharply as she sniffed us, as if to make her perform better, but the dog refused to accuse us: She had an innate dignity that did not permit her to serve the murderous impulses of those men. I can't forget the expression in the dog's eyes; it was as if she were embarrassed to be associated with them. I had a small amount of medicinal marijuana in my purse that night, but she refused to expose me. I am not partial to dogs, but I will always remember the small German shepherd that night.

Unfortunately, what happened to me is an everyday occurrence here now. Since the 1980s, on top of greatly expanding border checkpoints, the Immigration and Naturalization Service and the Border Patrol have implemented policies that interfere with the rights of U.S. citizens to travel freely within our borders. I.N.S. agents now patrol all interstate highways and roads that lead to or from the U.S.-Mexico border in Texas, New Mexico, Arizona and California. Now, when you drive east from Tucson on Interstate 10 toward El Paso, you encounter an I.N.S. check station outside Las Cruces, New Mexico. When you drive north from Las Cruces up Interstate 25, two miles north of the town of Truth or Consequences, the highway is blocked with orange emergency barriers, and all traffic is diverted into a two-lane Border Patrol checkpoint—ninety-five miles north of the U.S.-Mexico border.

I was detained once at Truth or Consequences, despite my and my companion's Arizona driver's licenses. Two men, both Chicanos, were detained at the same time, despite the fact that they too presented ID and spoke English without the thick Texas accents of the Border Patrol agents. While we were stopped, we watched as other vehicles—whose occupants were white—were waved through the checkpoint. White people traveling with brown people, however, can expect to be stopped on suspicion they work with the sanctuary movement, which shelters refugees. White people who appear to be clergy, those who wear ethnic clothing or jewelry and women with very long hair or very short hair (they could be nuns) are also frequently detained; white men with beards or men with long hair are likely to be detained, too, because Border Patrol agents have "profiles" of "those sorts" of white people who may help political refugees. (Most of the political refugees from Guatemala and El Salvador are Native American or mestizo because the indigenous people of the Americas have continued to resist efforts by invaders to displace them from their ancestral lands.) Alleged increases in illegal immigration by people of Asian ancestry means that the Border Patrol now routinely detains anyone who appears to be Asian or part Asian, as well.

10 Once your car is diverted from the Interstate Highway into the checkpoint area, you are under the control of the Border Patrol, which in practical terms exercises a power that no highway patrol or city patrolman possesses: They are willing to detain anyone, for no apparent reason. Other law-enforcement officers need a shred of probable cause in order to detain someone. On the books, so does the Border Patrol; but on the road, it's another matter. They'll order you to stop your car and step out; then they'll ask you to open the trunk. If you ask why or request a search warrant, you'll be told that they'll have to have a dog sniff the car before they can request a search warrant, and the dog might not get there for two or three hours. The search warrant might require an hour or two past that. They make it clear that if you force them to obtain a search warrant for the car, they will make you submit to a strip search as well.

Traveling in the open, though, the sense of violation can be even worse. Never mind high-profile cases like that of former Border Patrol agent Michael Elmer, acquitted of murder by claiming self-defense, despite admitting that as an officer he shot an "illegal" immigrant in the back and then hid the body, which remained undiscovered until another Border Patrolman reported the event. (Last month, Elmer was convicted of reckless endangerment in a separate incident, for shooting at least ten rounds from his M-16 too close to a group of immigrants as they were crossing illegally into Nogales in March 1992.) Or that in El Paso a high school football coach driving a vanload of players in full uniform was pulled over on the freeway and a Border Patrol agent put a cocked revolver to his head. (The football coach was Mexican-American, as were most of the players in his van; the incident eventually caused a federal judge to issue a restraining order against the Border Patrol.) We've a mountain of personal experiences like that which never make the newspapers. A history professor at U.C.L.A. told me she had been traveling by train from Los Angeles to Albuquerque twice a month doing research. On each of her trips, she had noticed that the Border Patrol agents were at the station in Albuquerque scrutinizing the passengers. Since she is six feet tall and of Irish and German ancestry, she was not particularly concerned. Then one day when she stepped off the train in Albuquerque, two Border Patrolmen accosted her, wanting to know what she was doing, and why she was traveling between Los Angeles and Albuquerque twice a month. She presented identification and an explanation deemed "suitable" by the agents, and was allowed to go about her business.

Just the other day, I mentioned to a friend that I was writing this article and he told me about his 73-year-old father, who is half Chinese and had set out alone by car from Tucson to Albuquerque the week before. His father had become confused by road construction and missed a turnoff from Interstate 10 to Interstate 25; when he turned around and circled back, he missed the turnoff a second time. But when he looped back for yet another try, Border Patrol agents stopped him and forced him to open his trunk. After they satisfied themselves that he was not smuggling Chinese immigrants, they sent him on his way. He was so rattled by the event that he had to be driven home by his daughter.

This is the police state that has developed in the southwestern United States since the 1980s. No person, no citizen, is free to travel without the scrutiny of the Border Patrol. In the city of South Tucson, where 80 percent of the respondents were Chicano or Mexicano, a joint research project by the University of Wisconsin and the University of Arizona recently concluded that one out of every five people there had been detained, mistreated verbally or nonverbally, or questioned by I.N.S. agents in the past two years.

Manifest Destiny may lack its old grandeur of theft and blood—"lock the door" is what it means now, with racism a trump card to be played again and again, shamelessly, by both major political parties. "Immigration," like "street crime" and "welfare fraud," is a political euphemism that refers to people of color. Politicians and media people talk about "illegal aliens" to dehumanize and demonize undocumented immigrants, who are for the most part people of color. Even in the days of Spanish and Mexican rule, no attempts were made to interfere with the flow of people and goods from south to north and north to south. It is the U.S. government that has continually attempted to sever contact between the tribal people north of the border and those to the south.[1]

Now that the "Iron Curtain" is gone, it is ironic that the U.S. govern- 15
ment and its Border Patrol are constructing a steel wall ten feet high to span sections of the border with Mexico. While politicians and multinational corporations extol the virtues of NAFTA and "free trade" (in goods, not flesh), the ominous curtain is already up in a six-mile section at the border crossing at Mexicali; two miles are being erected but are not yet finished at Naco; and at Nogales, sixty miles south of Tucson, the steel wall has been all rubber-stamped and awaits construction likely to begin in March. Like the pathetic multimillion-dollar "antidrug" border surveillance balloons that were continually deflated by high winds and made only a couple of meager interceptions before they blew away, the fence along the border is a theatrical prop, a bit of pork for contractors. Border entrepreneurs have already used blowtorches to cut passageways through the fence to collect "tolls," and are doing a brisk business. Back in Washington, the I.N.S. announces a $300 million computer contract to modernize its record-keeping and Congress passes a crime bill that shunts $255 million to the I.N.S. for 1995, $181 million earmarked for border control, which is to include 700 new partners for the men who stopped Gus and me in our travels, and the history professor, and my friend's father, and as many as they could from South Tucson.

It is no use; borders haven't worked, and they won't work, not now, as the indigenous people of the Americas reassert their kinship and solidarity with one another. A mass migration is already under way; its roots are not simply economic. The Uto-Aztecan languages are spoken as far north as Taos Pueblo near the Colorado border, all the way south to Mexico City. Before the arrival of the Europeans, the indigenous communities throughout this region not only conducted commerce, the people shared cosmologies, and oral narratives about the Maize Mothers, the Twin Brothers and their Grandmother, Spider Woman, as well as Quetzalcoatl the benevolent snake. The great human migration within the Americas cannot be stopped; human beings are natural forces of the Earth, just as rivers and winds are natural forces.

Deep down the issue is simple: The so-called "Indian Wars" from the days of Sitting Bull and Red Cloud have never really ended in the Americas. The Indian people of southern Mexico, of Guatemala and those left in El Salvador, too, are still fighting for their lives and for their land against the "cavalry" patrols sent out by the governments of those lands. The Americas are Indian country, and the "Indian problem" is not about to go away.

One evening at sundown, we were stopped in traffic at a railroad crossing in downtown Tucson while a freight train passed us, slowly gaining speed as it

[1]The Treaty of Guadalupe Hidalgo, signed in 1848, recognizes the right of the Tohano O'Odom (Papago) people to move freely across the U.S.-Mexico border without documents. A treaty with Canada guarantees similar rights to those of the Iroquois nation in traversing the U.S.-Canada border. [Author's note]

headed north to Phoenix. In the twilight I saw the most amazing sight: Dozens of human beings, mostly young men, were riding the train; everywhere, on flat cars, inside open boxcars, perched on top of boxcars, hanging off ladders on tank cars and between boxcars. I couldn't count fast enough, but I saw fifty or sixty people headed north. They were dark young men, Indian and mestizo; they were smiling and a few of them waved at us in our cars. I was reminded of the ancient story of Aztlán, told by the Aztecs but known in other Uto-Aztecan communities as well. Aztlán is the beautiful land to the north, the origin place of the Aztec people. I don't remember how or why the people left Aztlán to journey farther south, but the old story says that one day, they will return.

Questions for Discussion

1. Silko refers to the "weird anger" (paragraph 4) of the border patrol officers. Why does she call it "weird"? Why are they angry?
2. Silko contends that the border patrol "exercises a power that no highway patrol or city patrol possesses: They are willing to detain anyone, for no apparent reason" (paragraph 9). What kinds of evidence does she offer as support? Do you find her case convincing? Why or why not?
3. "'Immigration,' like 'street crime' and 'welfare fraud,'" Silko claims, "is a political euphemism that refers to people of color" (paragraph 13). Is she right? What do these terms make you think of? How do such associations distort clear thinking about immigration, legal or illegal?
4. Originally "The Border Patrol State" appeared under the caption or rubric "America's Iron Curtain." Silko herself refers to the irony of building a steel wall between Mexico and the United States after the destruction of that great symbol of tyranny, the Berlin Wall. How apt is the analogy? What does it imply about the present and the future of efforts to control our borders?

For Research, Discussion, and Persuasion

What would happen if we eliminated the border patrol or reduced it to a token presence? Do some research to find out what the best informed opinions are.

Share the information you find with your class. Then address the following questions: What do such estimates assume? What data do they use to support their projections? Given what you know about illegal immigration, which opinion seems most plausible?

Write an essay addressed to your congressperson or state senator arguing for or against the present level of resources devoted to the border patrol.

For Analysis

Kennedy closes his essay ("Can We Still Afford to Be a Nation of Immigrants?") with a discussion of Mexican immigration to the states of the

Southwest. He says the "Hispanicization of the American Southwest is sometimes called the Reconquista" because that land was at one time Mexican and was taken by U.S. conquest in the Mexican War of the 1840s. Silko also closes her essay with a discussion of the migration of people from Mexico into the land that belonged to their ancestors. However, as a Native American, she takes an even longer historical view than does Kennedy. Discuss the similarities and differences in their perspectives, their attitudes toward this migration, and their understanding of the immigrants' motives.

For Further Research and Discussion

1. Many of the selections in this chapter refer to particular anti-immigration legislation and anti-immigration movements, such as the "Know Nothings" of the 1850s. Also, Anna Quindlen's essay on immigration in Chapter 2 (pages 14–15) reveals that telegraph inventor Samuel Morse was involved in an anti-immigration movement. Research the specifics of one of these historical topics. What led to the anti-immigration position? Were any of the fears and motives similar to any of the criticisms voiced today by those who would like to limit our current immigration policy?
2. Brimelow worries about the consequences of not having enough "native Americans" to "digest" the continuing flow of immigrants of different ethnicities, that is, to absorb them through intermarriage into the white, Anglo-Saxon, Protestant culture. He argues that past immigrant waves have become "WASP'ed." In paragraphs 35 and 36 Brimelow contrasts his perspective with that of Robert Christopher in his 1989 book *Crashing the Gates: The De-Wasping of America's Power Structure,* in which Christopher argues that the opposite has happened: past waves of immigrants have made America less dominated by one ethnic group as Jews have married Gentiles and Catholics have married Protestants. Look into both viewpoints, beginning with both Brimelow's *Alien Nation* and Christopher's *Crashing the Gates.* In your view, who is more nearly right, Brimelow or Christopher?

Additional Suggestions for Writing

1. *Inquiry and convincing.* In his book *Alien Nation* Brimelow is concerned about demographic studies that project that in the year 2050, Anglo-Saxon whites will compose 52.7 percent of the U.S. population, down from just over 75 percent in 1990. Inquire into the question of why the racial composition of a nation's citizens should be an issue of concern. You might begin by inquiring into the definition of race: What is the basis for the racial classification system we use today? Is it meaningful? One good source is the collection of essays by Stephen Jay Gould and others in the November 1994 issue of *Discover.* Take a position on why race matters, and defend it in an essay to convince.
2. *Inquiry and persuasion.* Various metaphors have been used to describe the immigrant experience in America: immigrants have been described as

entering a melting pot (either melting or failing to melt), as composing a mosaic, as climbing aboard a lifeboat, and as being digested like a meal. You may have heard of others. As we said in Chapter 2 (pages 17–18), metaphors are very persuasive arguments; in a few words they present a whole way of seeing something, with all the implications largely going unexamined. Examine one of the common metaphors associated with immigration, and persuade those who accept it to see its full implications. Does it argue for accommodation or assimilation? You may argue that your audience should discard a particular metaphor, or you may argue for a different metaphor as a replacement.

CHAPTER ELEVEN

Feminism

In the United States the women's rights movement dates back to the nineteenth century, when the main issues were achieving full rights of citizenship and access to higher education. The women's movement was highly visible during the early part of the twentieth century, leading up to the 1920 achievement of voting rights. By that time some women and men had realized that the fight for particular rights must be part of a larger revolution in society's attitudes toward the relationship between the sexes. Those who wanted to eliminate the long-standing oppressive and patriarchal attitudes that held women subordinate to men became known as feminists. The classic definition of feminism is simply the doctrine that women should enjoy all the rights—political, social, and economic—that men enjoy.

What became known as the "second wave" of feminism began in the 1960s and received its greatest impetus from the success of Betty Friedan's 1963 book *The Feminine Mystique.* Friedan argued that a myth prevailed in American society, telling women they could be happy and fulfilled only by accepting their "feminine" role as sexually passive, nurturing homemakers, content to live under male protection and domination. Second-wave feminism therefore advocated independence from men, liberation from the sexual double standard, and achievement in the world outside of the home.

As the twentieth century moved to a close and the twenty-first century opened, debate increased about the nature of feminism. Some argue that feminism is dead, that it is no longer needed, that we have entered the "post-feminist" era and the battles are over. Others say feminism has entered a "third wave," but if so, it is a wave that defies easy definitions. One thing is clear: Feminism is fragmented. We often see the term modified, as in "gender" feminists or "power" feminists or "traditional" feminists. Some divisions in the movement fall along the lines of conservative and liberal politics. On the right, feminists argue that women have won their equality. They reject the view that patriarchal institutions and attitudes continue to hold women back. All that is needed is for individual women to take control and responsibility for their lives as individuals. On the left, feminists argue that women still need the efforts of groups like the National Organization for Women to overcome lingering attitudes and policies harmful to women and children. Gloria Steinem, founder of *Ms.* magazine, identifies some projects for the women's movement in the twenty-first century: restructuring the workplace with child care, parental leaves, and flexible hours so that work and parenting are possible for both men and women; passing legislation to ensure shelter, adequate nutrition, and health care for children; and changing stereotypical gender roles to make "men fully equal inside the home."

In this chapter we do not attempt to cover all the arguments that currently divide feminists and their critics—debates about pornography, abortion, and so on. Nor do we address the media-hyped stereotype of feminists as man-haters. We do, however, consider the effects of traditional gender roles on equality of the sexes and examine the challenges feminism has posed to traditional ideas of gender. All of our readings touch upon issues of gender identity, the roles and behavior a society deems appropriate for each sex. The first reading offers an overview of the history of the women's movement, while the second addresses criticisms of both women's and men's movements in the last decade. The readings by Faludi, Wolf, and Sommers take us into the thick of the battle over what some have called "victim" or "gender" feminism. These essays debate this question: As women have gained equality in politics and the workplace, has a male-dominated society exerted pressure urging more traditionally "feminine" roles and behavior?

The last two essays are both reflections on personal identity. Katie Roiphe muses about traditional ideas of femininity, noting that her independent self is at odds with another side of her self that equates femininity with dependence and masculinity with protection. Her essay illustrates Deborah Rhode's assessment of a dilemma: "Most [Americans] want neither to relinquish all sense of sexual identity nor to restrict each sex to stereotypical patterns. Yet it is by no means clear that we can have it both ways." Finally, Elizabeth Mitchell finds herself at odds with traditional ideas of feminism, which she feels would restrict her to living for a common cause rather than for herself alone. Thus, the readings end by raising the question, Does feminism itself need to break from traditional ideas about gender roles?

CASSANDRA L. LANGER

What Is Feminism?

This selection comes from the first chapter of Cassandra Langer's A Feminist Critique: How Feminism Has Changed American Society, Culture and How We Live from the 1940's to the Present. *Here Langer attempts to define feminism by showing how events since colonial times have influenced the evolution of the concept. Her purpose, however, is not merely to present a historical narrative from a feminist perspective. She believes that reminders of the movement's historical accomplishments will help modern feminists get beyond the current polarizations that are weakening the movement.*

TODAY WE are still grappling with Sigmund Freud's question, "What do women want?" This is a fascinating, poorly understood, time-consuming, and often disheartening topic to explore.[1] It's hard to make sense of the ever-shifting points of view and developments within a social movement, as well as the many academic controversies found in the popular presentations of it. The interests of feminism are varied, and the balancing of rights against responsibilities still challenges us. The feminist critique is a way of asking questions and searching for answers based on women's experience. Although not all women want the same things, feminism has had an unparalleled influence on American life and culture. . . . 1

The central goal of feminism is to reorganize the world on the basis of equality between the sexes in all human relations. To advance their cause, feminists have focused on a variety of problems, including patriarchy, gender modeling, individual freedom, social justice, equal educational opportunity, equal pay for equal work, sexual harassment, and human rights. Unfortunately, woman's power in shaping governmental policy to her own needs has been severely limited by the politics of gender. The revolutionary fathers did not heed Abigail Adams's advice to her husband, John (who was sitting as a delegate to the Continental Congress in Philadelphia in 1777), when she wrote:

> In the new code of laws which I suppose will be necessary for you to make, I desire you would remember the ladies and be more generous and favorable to them than your ancestors. Do not put such unlimited power into the hands of the husbands. Remember, all men would be tyrants if they could. If particular care and attention is not paid to the ladies, we are determined to foment a rebellion, and will not hold ourselves bound by any laws in which we have no voice or representation.[2]

Among the mothers of the American Revolution, Abigail Adams is particularly prominent. Her strength of character and her patriotism stood the severest test, and she realized that she could not simply surrender to the legislative process created by her husband and the Sons of Liberty. Unfortunately, she could not enforce her womanly sentiments, so they went unheeded.

Higher education for women became a primary goal of the reform movement. In the United States change came at a snail's pace. Only as women emerged from the home as public speakers and abolitionists could they effect any meaningful change in their conditions. Only by breaking the bondage of the home and the handicap of silence imposed on them by patriarchy, did women begin to transcend their condition. The term *patriarchy* means a system of male authority that oppresses women through its social, political, and economic institutions. In all the historical forms that patriarchal society takes, whether feudal, capitalist, or socialist, a sex-gender system and a system of economic discrimination operate simultaneously. Patriarchy results from men's greater access to, and control of, the resources and rewards of the social system. Furthermore, specifically male values are expressed through a system of sanctions that reward the upholders and punish the transgressors.[3] In the socioeconomic sphere, women are disadvantaged by a system that favors men through legal rights, religion, education, business, and access to sex.

This imbalance led analytic feminists to coin the word *sexism,* a social situation in which men exert a dominant role over women and express in a variety of ways, both private and institutional, the notion that women are inferior to men. The terms *patriarchy* and *sexism* reflect women's rising awareness of the oppression women suffer under this system.[4] The British writer Virginia Woolf showed that she understood the circumstances that gave rise to these terms (long before the 1970s) when she argued that a woman needs financial independence and "a room of her own" to become herself. Woolf's 1929 essay "A Room of One's Own" is applicable today.[5] For the vast majority of women workers, finding a way to obtain better wages and working conditions is still a priority. Although the number of women who were "gainfully employed" increased rapidly during the nineteenth century, they were unable to control their own wages, legally manage their own property, or sign legal papers. The American writer Lydia Maria Child was outraged when she was not allowed to sign her own will; her husband, David, had to do it for her.

For these and other reasons, most feminists agree that poverty is not 5
gender neutral. During the nineteenth century, inequities were worse for working-class women who could be forced to hand over all their earnings to an irresponsible husband, even if they were left with nothing for their own survival or the maintenance of their children. If a woman tried to divorce such a husband, he was legally entitled to sole guardianship of the children. In this system, a woman had no right to her own children, and male lawmakers customarily gave custody of the babies even to an alcoholic father. Women were subordinate to men on the basis of discriminatory legislation, as well as men's exclusive ability to participate in public life.

Many men, as well as women, rebelled against this unjust system, considering the marriage laws unfair and iniquitous because they gave men control over the rights of women. Between 1839 and 1850, most states passed some kind of legislation recognizing the right of married women to own property. Women continued to struggle against the perception that they were unfit to participate in government because of their physical circumstances. Since the founding of our nation, the politics of reproduction has dominated social and economic relations between the sexes. Because of gender manipulations, it becomes very difficult to see and understand the realities of women's experience and how it affected them. . . .

Organized feminism . . . began with the Seneca Falls Convention of 1848, an event that articulated what some American women wanted in the mid-nineteenth century.[6] On July 19 and 20 of that year, five women decided to call a Women's Rights Convention at Seneca Falls, New York, to discuss the social, civil, and religious rights of women. During this period, Elizabeth Cady Stanton and Lucretia Mott reviewed the Declaration of Independence in light of their own experiences and those of other women. Their Declaration of Principles, which fueled generations of women in their bid for equality, declared: "The history of mankind is a history of repeated injuries and usurpations on the part of man toward woman, having in direct object the establishment of an absolute tyranny over her. To prove this, let facts be submitted to a candid world."[7]

In a manner similar to the current presentation of facts offered by the contemporary women's movement, these foremothers and others introduced a range of issues that implicated men and showed how their self-serving acts affected woman's status in society. These reforming women had no illusions about the gender system and knew that their views would be distorted. The declaration asserted, "In entering upon the great work before us, we anticipate no small amount of misconception, misrepresentation, and ridicule; but we shall use every instrumentality within our power to effect our object."[8]

The struggle was on. Margaret Fuller's brave book, *Woman in the Nineteenth Century,* put it bluntly:

> We would have every arbitrary barrier thrown down. We would have every path laid open to Woman as freely as Man . . . then and then only will mankind be ripe for this, when inward and outward freedom for Women as much as for Man shall be acknowledged as a *right,* not yielded as a concession. As the friend of the Negro assumes that one man cannot by right hold another in bondage, so would the friend of Woman assume that Man cannot by right lay even well-meant restrictions on Woman.[9]

Indeed, women have been answering Freud's question for a long time. The main problem is that they still are not being heard.

The Civil War of 1861 helped bring women into national politics. After 10
the victory, the intersection of the women's liberation movement and the emancipation of the slaves underscored the issue of enlarging the electorate. Since the blacks were now free citizens, they were entitled to the suffrage rights of citizens. Women saw this development as one that might bring them

the vote as well. They were totally unprepared for the opposition of the Republican politicians and the desertion of their cause by the abolitionists, who had been their staunch allies. Appalled at the appearance of the word *male* in the proposed Fourteenth Amendment to the Constitution, Elizabeth Cady Stanton, Susan B. Anthony, and Lucy Stone, leaders of the liberation movement, raised the issue of whether women were actually citizens of the United States. The advocacy of "manhood" suffrage, as Stanton warned, "creates an antagonism between black men and all women that will culminate in fearful outrages on womanhood."[10] Men, including large numbers of white men, were concerned with ensuring the vote for black men, but they were little interested in how such a measure would affect women.

From a historical vantage point, Stanton's misgivings seem prophetic. Racism and the condition of women have continued to be explosive national issues since the Civil War. These twin injustices ignited the revolution of the 1960s and sparked the heated debates surrounding the Anita Hill and Clarence Thomas Senate hearings of the 1990s.[11]

The growing chasm between men and women, regardless of race, was thrown into sharp relief by the Fourteenth Amendment, which was passed in July 1868. Although Senator Cowan of Pennsylvania offered to strike the word *male* from the legislation, and Senator Williams of Oregon argued that the interests of men and women were one, their views were ignored. Williams understood that putting women in an adversarial, rather than a complementary, position in relation to men would eventually create a state of war and "make every home a hell on earth."

On the other side of the divide, Senator Frelinghuysen of New Jersey argued that women had a "holier mission" in the home, which was to assuage the passions of men as "they come in from the battles of life." When all was said and done, the hand that rocked the cradle still had no say in the process.

The beginning of the twentieth century saw American women still fighting for the right to vote. Inequities continued in education, marriage, property rights, legal rights, religion, and the realm of divorce. The years between 1910 and 1915 were a period of confusion and growth, during which a growing number of female workers were providing fresh arguments for women's suffrage. The foundation of the Women's Party in 1916 brought new energy into the political sphere. Twelve states had finally given women the vote, so that women now constituted a new force in the presidential election.

By this time, it was clear to all parties that the group that opposed 15
national suffrage for women would lose women's support in twelve states that controlled nearly a hundred electoral votes. Even though the female vote did not sway the election of 1916, women were able to win presidential support and reorganize their party. By 1918, after years of dogged effort, the suffrage amendment passed by a vote of 274 to 136, exactly the two-thirds majority required to accomplish it. After fifty-three years of progressive effort, women finally had won the right to vote. This was the wedge women would need in

the coming years to force their way past what Carrie Chapman Catt warned suffragists would be "locked doors."

Women's greatest challenge, however, was not to gain the vote, but to change patriarchal values. Their efforts were based on two assumptions: (1) that a man claiming to be sensitive to what women want must first recognize, as Fuller pointed out, that "Man cannot by right lay even well-meant restrictions on Woman" and (2) that men who are humanists can be persuaded to give up their unfair advantages voluntarily. These assumptions bring forth an underlying assumption that feminism is both a movement that strives for equal rights for women and an ideology of social transformation whose aim is to create a better world for women beyond simple social equity. In fact, feminism urges such men to question the whole idea that an unfair advantage is really an "advantage." . . .

There are many different views and factions within feminism. The movement encompasses major differences of opinion about how its goals can best be achieved and how they should be defined. This situation is not unusual, since in all the major movements in the history of ideas and social reform, the participants have had such differences. What unites all feminists, what they all have in common that makes them "feminists," is the belief that they must question and challenge sexual stereotypes and that opportunity should not be denied to either men or women on the grounds of gender. Friedan, who is often called the mother of contemporary feminism, defined it as a conviction "that women are people in the fullest sense of the word, who must be free to move in society with all the privileges and opportunities and responsibilities that are their human and American right."[12] This is a major aspect of "classical feminism." Its mission is to achieve full equality for women of every race, religion, ethnic group, age, and sexual orientation. . . .

A major premise of feminist theory is that sexual politics supports patriarchy in its politicization of personal life.[13] In such a system, the majority of men view women first and foremost as child bearers. So the female body and how it is represented is continually and inevitably caught up in any discussion of women's liberation. Most men imagine that women's chief concerns, because of their reproductive biology, center on home and family. Thus, a patriarchal system locks women into roles that are based on their bodies' capacity to reproduce. Most men think of the home as the physical space in which women do their work: housekeeping, cooking, serving, taking care of the children, and other tasks associated with the domestic sphere. It is in this frame of reference that feminist theorists work.

The "myth of motherhood" and the cult of the nineteenth-century "true woman" persist. They categorize all women as mothers and caregivers even when they do not wish to perform these roles, or as Mary Wollstonecraft put it, "All women are to be levelled, by meekness and docility, into one character of yielding softness and gentle compliance." Under patriarchy, differences between men's and women's "true" natures have been based on a conviction that women have softer emotions than do men and that their job is to marry, produce children, and strengthen family life. According to this implied contract, as long as a woman sticks to the program, she is entitled to certain compensations and privileges. Thus, traditional marriage ensures a wedded woman's use of her husband's name and his protection and financial support. . . .

20 Although the 1950s were seen as a golden age of marriage and domesticity by many, Friedan's groundbreaking study of "The Happy Housewife Heroine," in *The Feminine Mystique* (1963), exposed the frustration of the unhappy, educated, middle-class, mostly white housewives between what they were supposed to feel and what they actually felt. Each one believed that "the problem that has no name" was hers alone—such was women's isolation from each other. At home, these women tried to make themselves beautiful, cultured, and respectable, but they were never really away from their children; they went marketing with their children, changed their children's diapers, talked about their children, and played mahjong or bridge.

"Raising three small children in suburbia," artist and writer Phyllis Rosser explained, "was the most depressing work I've ever done." Surrounded by baby bottles, cereal boxes, and dirty dishes, married women found that child rearing consumed most of their day. This was the "American Dream" that Rosser and millions of other intelligent American women were living, and for many it was a nightmare. Friedan's comparison of housewives' lives to conditions in Nazi concentration camps may seem extreme to many women (although many women viewed their mothers' lives this way), but during the 1960s, it struck a resounding chord for a generation of middle-class white women whose self-respect had been systematically destroyed by their inferior status as unpaid home workers and consumers.

The "mystique of feminine fulfillment" that Friedan chronicled emerged after World War II, when suburban housewives like my mother became the "dream image" of women all over the world. Behind it, as Friedan demonstrated, was anger and mental anguish—even insanity, brought about by the fact that they had no public careers. The loss of identity that came from being relegated to and isolated in the home created the psychic distress that many of these women experienced—"the problem with no name." It contributed to the depression and rage that many middle-class women of that generation felt because their contributions to society were belittled and child rearing was not considered intellectually challenging. Friedan rejected the biological determinism of Freudian theory. Her view of women as a weaker social group led her to argue for a massive self-help program to help women reenter the labor market.

Inspired by Friedan's book, women began to form consciousness-raising groups. In the absence of psychological experts, women's own thoughts and feelings about marriage, motherhood, and their bodies began to emerge. They discovered that women were treated like children. In essence, they felt they had no identity of their own, which led them to sail boldly into the unknown in search of themselves. . . .

From the late 1960s to the mid-1980s, feminism was a clear force for progress and against alienation. Feminism's effects on gender issues, business, government, the military, education, religion, families, and dating and sexuality—in short, all aspects of life—was felt throughout the society and culture. But Friedan's book established a framework that was hostile to the traditional nuclear family and conventional female roles, and it seemed to exclude the homemaker from feminism's brave new world. The idea of staying home, raising a family, and doing housework was so negatively portrayed that it left no place for many women who wanted to do so.

During this stage, Kate Millett's *Sexual Politics* became a best-seller, and 25
it was by far the most demanding feminist book of the 1970s. The author charged that throughout history, the interaction between men and women was one of domination and subordination. On the basis of this premise, Millett isolated "patriarchy," a pattern of male domination based on gender, as the chief institution of women's oppression. From this vantage point, it was reasonable to see the nuclear family as a "feudal institution that reduces women to chattel status." In such a system, there is no possibility of an honest disagreement among equals. In Millett's view, patriarchy authorizes the relative dominance of male domains over female ones. This dominance disadvantages women and puts them at the mercy of those who control the resources. In fact, women themselves are resources, like water or pastureland, to be traded among men. If a woman belongs to a man, she is like a slave; for example, a father may marry a daughter off against her will to further his own ambitions. The woman has no rights, and her offspring are her husband's property to do with as he likes. Millett's appraisal simply reiterated the judgments of nineteenth-century feminists, who saw a connection between the sexual division of labor in the home and in the workplace and women's oppression in modern industrial society.

According to Millett's reasoning, marriage is a financial arrangement—an exchange of goods and services in which men benefit and women lose. In this pooling of resources and sharing of responsibilities, one party, the man, retains everything he came into the marriage with, whereas in many cases, the woman brings a dowry with her, contributes free domestic and child care services, and serves her husband and his career. If she has an education and aspirations of her own, they are sacrificed to the needs of her husband and family. . . .

Coming out of the first stage of the contemporary women's movement, Millett believed that her main concern was to find an explanatory theory for the subordination of women to men. In the United States, an alliance of conservative women and clergymen insists that woman's role is to be a homemaker and caretaker. Modernism and sexism view gender in terms of occupational specialties: Man is the hardworking provider who has liberated his woman from the burdens of production. Contrary to this model, Millett and many socialist feminists of the period believed that most women would be better off if they did not have to choose between their offspring and meaningful work. They argued for professional care of the young because it would allow women to . . . choose both. In short, they were attempting to change the prevailing idea that the domestic sphere was the sole appropriate domain of women. . . .

The 1960s and 1970s saw the emergence of many spokespersons for feminism, which led to the establishment of courses that introduced women into history. It was not surprising that with a discipline as new, as unusual, and as speculative as contemporary women's studies, dissension soon emerged. I think dissension arose for two reasons. First, some of the major feminist thinkers, such as Friedan, Millett, and Gloria Steinem, were inflexible about their initial theories—Steinem's notion of women's moral superiority, for example. Many people were put off, especially, by these women's views on the nature of men and women and on women's oppression in marriage, home, and bed. Second, and, in the long run, more important, was the natural growth and continuing outreach of the liberation movement itself. Changes in occupations, day care centers, dual earning capacity, and family leave have all contributed to a more egalitarian and less conventional contemporary lifestyle in the United States.

Despite these factional disputes about the actual conditions of women's lives, despite the hardships that the antifeminist backlash of the 1980s, with its attempts to scare women back into the home, imposed on those struggling for women's liberation, feminism has impelled all types of people to construct and reconstruct their respective roles in this society and culture. The current unrest and mood of apprehension that seems to pervade the women's movement arose from the fact that many people don't really understand the double bind that women are in. Moreover, women generally fail to see their own position within the private and public domains. Caught between their own lives and political ideologies, they are only beginning to gain some insight into how policy decisions are directed at them. The ongoing debates about welfare, for example, demonstrate how laws manage women and children. "Each time we talk about things that can be experienced only in privacy or intimacy," explained political scientist Hannah Arendt, "we bring them out into a sphere where they will assume a kind of reality, which, their intensity notwithstanding, they never could have had before."[13]

30 Nowhere is this situation more evident than in attempts to deal with women's experience in the world. Foes of feminism argue that contrary to what Friedan said, what happens in the home has an impact on society and the public sphere. Their relatively recent attempts to police the womb in order to protect the life of the unborn have collapsed the private into the public. The medical control of birth has given new meaning to the expression "the personal is the political." But what does this phrase really mean? As author Mary Gordon explained, "We have to examine the definition of the personal. . . . The personal and the private have long been the hiding place of scandals. As long as the personal is defined by men, and until men listen to what women consider the personal, neither side knows what the other is talking about."[14]

So it is imperative to examine individual women's experiences to provide a framework of meaning: to understand women's experiences from the standpoint of how we actually live our lives, rather than through theoretical investigations. It is crucial to ask how we arrived at where we are now. This is far more important than knowing the political cataclysms that occurred along the way. Only by striving to transcend the unproductive polarization that has grown out of questions of private and public, identity and value, masculine and feminine, can we move beyond the play of politics and get closer to the true meaning of the movement to liberate women. . . .

. . . Between 1963 and the present, ideas stemming from the movement to liberate women have permeated psychology, sociology, anthropology, literature, art, and politics, and gained measurable influence over educational theory. Many people now recognize that inequality limits women's participation in public life and perpetuates the social emphasis on male values.

Feminism, for all its faults, has given birth to one of the few compelling visions of our era. It is a vision that attempts to deal compassionately not only with women's inequality, but with the pressing problems in the world.

The struggle for knowledge, for training, and for opportunity was first articulated by American women because of their discontent with women's status. This discontent gave birth to a reform movement on behalf of women. It was women's general belief that they were treated as mere chattel, having no rights whatsoever, existing merely to serve a father, husband, brother, or some other man. Such a picture contains partial truths. The stories of feminist networks, individual courageous acts, and collective pioneering exploits offer touchstones on the long road to answering Freud's question, "What do women want?"

NOTES

1. For instance, Gloria Steinem's books make the best-seller list; Susan Faludi's blockbuster *Backlash* exposed an undeclared war against American women; Naomi Wolf's *Fire with Fire* urged women to seize the day; and in *Who Stole Feminism?,* Christina Huff Sommers accused feminist extremists of promoting a dangerous new agenda.
2. *Familiar Letters of John Adams and His Wife Abigail Adams during the Revolution* (New York, 1876) 286–87, letter dated March 31, 1776.
3. Maggie Humm, ed., *Modern Feminisms: Political Literary Cultural* (New York: Columbia UP, 1992) 408.
4. Marilyn French, *The War Against Women* (New York: Summit, 1992).
5. Virginia Woolf, *A Room of One's Own* (New York: Harcourt, 1929).
6. For an excellent overview of these women and the events that shaped the women's rights movement, see Eleanor Flexner, *Century of Struggle: The Woman's Rights Movement in the United States* (New York: Atheneum, 1970).
7. Flexner 75.
8. Flexner 75.

9. Flexner 67.
10. Flexner 144.
11. Anna Quindlen, "Apologies to Anita" in the *New York Times* Nov. 1994: Op-Ed 5. See Jane Mayer and Jill Abramson, *Strange Justice* (New York: Hougton, 1994) regarding the many confusions about this historic case of sexual harassment and sexual politics.
12. Betty Friedan, *It Changed My Life: Writings on the Women's Movement* (New York: Random, 1976) 127.
13. Hannah Arendt, *The Human Condition* (Chicago: U of Chicago P, 1958) 50.
14. See "Mary Gordon and Robert Stone Talk about Sexual Harassment," in *Pen Newsletter* 85 (Fall 1994): 27.

Questions for Discussion

1. To what extent were you already familiar with some of the people and events described in this reading? Did you know about the property laws, the contributions of women to the Seneca Falls Convention, or the attitudes of Abigail Adams? If you have been taught about the women's movement, was it part of a women's studies course or part of a course in U.S. history? If you have had little exposure to the subject, can you explain why that might be?
2. From this account, what seems to be the explanation of why black males were able to achieve voting rights before any women did, even though white women had more money and more education?
3. Langer states in paragraph 16 that feminists assume that "men who are humanists can be persuaded to give up their unfair advantages voluntarily." Is this what happened in the case of women gaining the right to vote, to be paid the same as men, or to serve alongside men in the military? Substitute "people" for "men" in this sentence, and discuss whether it holds true in general. Do problems come from the word "unfair"?
4. In paragraph 27 Langer presents Millett's argument that state-supported, professional child care would enable women to choose both raising children and engaging in "meaningful work." Does such language suggest that childrearing is not meaningful work? Does our society as a whole regard it as meaningful work? How does our society reward those in occupations that we respect?

For Research and Analysis

As examples of persuasion, some of the writings and speeches from female abolitionists are outstanding. Angeline Grimke's speech "Bearing Witness Against Slavery" is particularly moving. Find one of these speeches or writings, and assess its rhetorical context: speaker, audience, occasion, purpose. Write an essay in which you describe the key persuasive strategies, such as identification, emotional appeals, and stylistic devices.

For Inquiry and Persuasion

Look at at least two or three contemporary U.S. history textbooks, for either high school or college, and compare their treatment of the women's movement. (Even high school texts are often found in your college library.) You might consider the amount of space allotted to the topic, the types of evidence included (for example, are there primary texts such as the portion of the letter from Abigail Adams?), and the perspective of the authors. Write an essay persuading an audience of teachers to adopt the textbook you think provides the best treatment of the issue, being very clear about what "best" means to you.

DEBORAH L. RHODE

Women's Movements, Men's Movements

Deborah Rhode is professor of law and director of the Keck Center on Legal Ethics at Stanford University. The following two selections come from a single chapter in her 1997 book Speaking of Sex: The Denial of Gender Inequality. *The purpose of the book is to correct what she perceives as the "no-problem problem"—the belief that gender inequality is no longer a problem in American society. In the first reading she examines the problems that give "feminism" a bad image and lead to quarreling factions. In the second she examines the "men's movement" and the problems facing men as they respond to our society's changing ideas about gender roles. Rhode wants men and women to stop "trashing and bashing" and to consider the real dilemma they must face together as they try to maintain their sexual identities while at the same time overturning sexual stereotypes that are harmful to both genders.*

The Women's Movement and Its Critics

THROUGHOUT THE past quarter-century, commentators on feminism have been popping the same question. As *Time* put it to Gloria Steinem, "Since most women today embrace the goals of the women's movement, why are so many of them reluctant to embrace the feminist label?" Steinem responded: "Women have two problems with the label. The first is that people don't know what it means. . . . The second is that people do know what it means."[1] 1

She is right on both counts. Many individuals who largely agree with the feminist agenda are alienated by its image. Others are uninformed, ambivalent, or unsympathetic concerning its objectives. Yet who is responsible for these attitudes remains open to dispute. According to many critics, the central problem lies with leaders of the women's movement. They are to blame for the refusal of most American women to consider themselves feminists.[2]

Leaders of the women's movement see the problem differently. Some fault the self-professed feminists who gain celebrity by sniping at their sisters, and who appear more interested in promoting themselves than a social movement. Others blame right-wing commentators who caricature the "feminazi position" and perpetuate the very image problem that they delight in criticizing. To most movement leaders, the real issue is not feminism's image but its objectives, and the threat that full gender equality poses to entrenched interests. When asked whether feminists should do more to tone down their message and counteract its negative stereotypes, Steinem responded, "This is a revolution, not a public relations movement."[3]

In fact, however, it is both. And that combination is inherently difficult to pull off. Until we gain a clearer sense of what drives resistance to the women's movement, we are unlikely to achieve its objectives.

A critical first step in understanding the challenges facing feminism is to put them in historical perspective. Women's willingness to identify themselves as feminists has bobbed up and down, partly in response to shifting media images. But public acceptance of feminist values has maintained a relatively steady upward climb. Since the 1960s, the proportion of women who perceive sex discrimination to be a serious problem has increased from less than 5 percent to more than 75 percent. The vast majority of Americans believe that the women's movement has improved women's lives, and all but a tiny percentage share its basic commitment to equal opportunity.[4]

Even people who reject the movement's label endorse many of its objectives. Polls find higher levels of agreement with statements about women's issues when the term "feminism" does not appear. Seventy to 80 percent of surveyed women agree with the objectives that dictionary definitions associate with "feminist": someone who supports political, economic, and social rights for women.[5]

Such polls should be a source of reassurance but not of rationalization. Rejection of the F-word is symptomatic of deeper difficulties. Most American women fail not only to identify themselves as feminists but also to provide active support for feminist causes. Although a majority of women see a need for a strong women's movement, they deny any responsibility for becoming involved with it personally. Three-fourths of those surveyed report paying no attention to feminism, and well under 10 percent belong to organizations that focus on women's issues. Despite some recent increases in funding, feminist causes and candidates still attract relatively little financial support. The National Organization for Women has about 280,000 members—fewer than the National Association of Garden Clubs.[6]

Moreover, most men remain at best ambivalent about feminist efforts. In principle, about 70 percent support efforts to improve women's social and economic status. In practice their response has been less enthusiastic. The majority of men appear even more resistant to the changes in their own roles and status that true equality for women would require.[7]

To understand the anxiety and animosity that feminism provokes, we need to look both beneath and beyond popular diagnoses. Most critics blame feminist leaders, although for inconsistent reasons. As the discussion below notes, activists are faulted for being too radical and not radical enough; for hating men and wanting to be just like them; for ignoring and romanticizing gender difference. This is, of course, a no-win situation, but almost no one talks about that. Nor do most critics focus on men—except to blame feminism for impersonating or demonizing them. The American public gets endless accounts of what is wrong with the women's movement. But rarely do we hear about what is wrong with the men's movement, or what might encourage more males to break free from traditional gender roles.

One of the most pervasive and persistent critiques of the women's move- 10
ment inspired a *Ms.* cartoon from the early 1990s. It featured a man watching television coverage of feminist issues. "After more than two decades of advances," reports a woman newscaster, "the American female continues to occupy a position of inferiority . . ." "Manhater," he mutters. She continues: "Women workers still earn [substantially less than] men . . ." "Castrator," he responds. By the fourth frame, as she reports on women's underrepresentation in the legislature, he is on his feet, shouting "Shrew! Nag! Witch! Lesbo!" In the closing frame, while she calmly recites statistics on rape and domestic violence, he concludes: "That's what I hate about feminists—they're so hostile."[8]

This perception is widely shared. "Feminists hate men—that's the problem" is Jerry Falwell's widely accepted diagnosis. Many Americans believe that such hostility is at least partly responsible for our inadequate progress on gender issues. Commentators frequently charge that feminist fabrications of "sinister sexism" are poisoning male-female relationships, and that "male bashing" is a problem that Americans "constantly encounter." In their more intense versions, these critiques seem slightly unhinged, and considerably shriller than their targets. According to former presidential speechwriter Mary Matalin, the women's movement has alienated mainstream America—and no wonder, given its "sensationalized tales of endless, inescapable oppression at the hands of testosterone-mad, women-loathing, capitalist-pig, Cro-Magnon brutish men." And these are the folks telling feminists to get a grip. Even if the caricatures are meant to be tongue-in-cheek, their effect is not simply to amuse. It is also to taint the struggle for equality by millions of individuals who hold no such views.[9]

Programs in women's studies attract similar complaints. In one representative account, a female student analogized her classroom experience to a satirical skit from Monty Python. The skit had featured a quiz show where the answer to every question was "pork." And, the student recalled, "whatever the quiz show host asks—for example, 'What's the capital of Pennsylvania?'—the answer was 'pork.'" Similarly, in the student's class, "the answer was always 'men' . . . 'Who contributes to all the violence in the world?' 'Men.' 'Who's responsible for everything that we endure?' 'Men.'"[10]

Although these critics have a point, they vastly overstate it. Granted, some feminists paint with broad strokes, and a tiny but vocal minority do seem to hate men. But there also are men who hate women. Tarring either sex with the excesses of a vengeful faction makes little sense. To link all feminists with man-hating is no more reasonable than to link all men with misogyny.

Contrary to popular assertions, few feminists deny their debts to men, and prominent women's-studies texts feature no shortage of male heros. After all, many men have actively supported the women's-rights movement, and its legal foundations are the product of predominantly male legislatures and judiciaries. Judging from the introductions to feminist publications, most advocates of women's rights are deeply grateful for the contributions of male partners, colleagues, editors, and research assistants. Few of these women seem to believe that they are sleeping with the enemy, metaphorically or otherwise.

15 What they do believe, however, is that American society institutionalizes gender inequality. This is also the claim that critics consistently misrepresent. To point out that men as a group are advantaged by sex-based hierarchies is not to claim that all men oppress women. And to note that male dominance often yields male sexual violence is not to imply that men in general are "Cro-Magnon brutes." Although feminist analysis often would be stronger without indiscriminate reliance on terms like "patriarchy," they do not carry the implications that critics denounce. Except in critics' caricatures, "patriarchal theory" does not present women as "powerless victims in every aspect of their lives." Nor does it cast men as the enemy. Its aim, like that of feminist analysis more generally, is to understand and challenge gender roles that systematically disadvantage women.[11]

The flip side of claims that feminists demonize men are claims that feminists act just like them, and encourage other women to do the same. In essence, this objection is that feminism preaches male values and male strategies; it has enabled more women to play by men's rules but not to live by their own. Versions of this complaint come from all points on the political spectrum. Critics from the right blame the women's movement for devaluing traditional feminine roles. According to one anti-abortion activist, "Women's lib is on the wrong track. . . . Women have [always] been the superior people. They're more civilized, they're more unselfish by nature, but now they want to compete with men at being selfish."[12]

Critics from the left also fault feminism for encouraging selfishness, although for different reasons. In *Women Together, Women Alone,* Anita Shreve notes that "one of the ironies of the Women's Movement is that in preparing the ground for greater career opportunity for women, it sowed the seeds of its own demise. . . . Women who combine career and family life simply don't have any time left to devote to . . . activist issues." Moreover, "supposedly liberated progressive *feminist* women [now exploit] other women" by delegating childcare and housework to them. "It's as though the fruits of liberation were only for a certain class of women."[13]

Other commentators join in the claim that feminism's preoccupation with success measured by men's standards has sabotaged the movement's broader objectives. In a cover article for the *New York Times Magazine,* "When Feminism Failed," former newspaper editor Mary Ann Dolan describes her disillusionment with women's workplace conduct. At her own paper, when her female colleagues achieved equal representation on the masthead, their "power grab" began. Rather than working to transform the newsroom into a "warm" and "nurturing" environment, they courted male superiors in order to pursue their own advancement. In generalizing from this experience, Dolan quotes a prominent Los Angeles executive who lambastes the new breed of female MBAs for similar reasons: these women reportedly have lost touch with their "instinctive skills." They have been "trained like men" and they act accordingly.[14] . . .

Such claims tend to overstate women's "difference," as well as understate the barriers to preserving it. Many indictments of feminism build on a romanticized view of female virtue and an inattentiveness to its cultural underpinnings. We have no convincing basis for believing that women are by nature significantly more unselfish, cooperative, or nurturing than men. To the extent that American women are especially likely to have these characteristics, it is because cultural forces reinforce such gender patterns. Where the reward structures for male and female workers are similar, it is naive not to expect similarities in their behavior.

It is even more naive to blame feminism when women adapt to current 20
workplace values. Well before the rise of the contemporary women's movement, American culture produced its share of "Queen Bees"—female leaders who made it under male rules and failed to see why others couldn't do the same. So too, only historical amnesia permits claims that feminism is responsible for women's difficulties in balancing work and family or for their reliance on poorer women to provide domestic help. It is not feminists who have opposed paid parental leave, flexible schedules, and subsidized childcare. Yet as one reviewer noted, books like *Women Together, Women Alone* "end up blaming feminism for the faults of the system feminism is trying to change."[15]

This tendency to shoot the messenger has deeper roots. For well over a century, critics have presented the women's movement as an assault on traditional homemaking roles. Unsurprisingly, these attacks strike responsive chords in women whose primary sense of status and identity depends on family relationships. Feminist critiques of the restrictive and unequal aspects of traditional gender roles have left some women feeling embattled and embittered. Blaming the movement has been a way to vent their frustration and affirm their sense of importance in a changing social order. Once family and feminism were fixed as the symbolic poles of debate, many women rallied around the values by which they ordered their own priorities. The popularity of books like *The Rules,* with mid-Victorian courtship advice, suggests the continuing appeal of traditional scripts. If women have had trouble luring men to the altar, the problem, according to author Sherrie Schneider, is that "feminism was inadvertently applied to dating."[16]

Of course, scapegoating feminists, individually or collectively, has other advantages. The media always love a catfight, and it is more diverting to hear women snarling at each other than droning on about sexist oppression. So too, if feminists are to blame, that lets men off the hook. This is no small virtue, particularly when males control all major media channels. A simplistic diagnosis of the problem also produces conveniently simplistic solutions. If women only would get their act together politically and personally, everyone could live happily ever after without any costly social adjustments.

Similar advantages are available from a second pair of complaints: that the contemporary women's movement is either too radical or not radical enough. The first of these complaints is that feminism has surrendered to extremist factions and has lost touch with the needs and values of the average woman: the "feminist fringe . . . [has become] the feminist mainstream." Some indictments of this sort, which inveigh against "cultural crackpots," are not without their own crackpot qualities. In 1992, presidential candidate Pat Robertson attracted considerable attention for his account of the Equal Rights Amendment campaign in Iowa: "[This fight] is about a socialist, anti-family political movement that encourages women to leave their husbands, kill their children, practice witchcraft, destroy capitalism and become lesbians." Anti-abortion leader Randall Terry similarly warns that the women's movement has been captured by "radical feminism," which has "vowed to destroy the traditional family unit, hates children for the most part, and promotes lesbian activity." No names are named.[17]

These caricatures do not come only from conservative men. Camille Paglia has received substantial airtime for her snarling denunciations of "crazed" and "clingy sob sisters" who control the women's movement. Mary Matalin, Katie Roiphe, Christina Hoff Sommers, Naomi Wolf, and even Betty Friedan also have weighed in against extremist feminists whose victim mythologies misrepresent the facts, exaggerate sexual oppression, and disempower women. By encouraging whiners to wallow in their subordination, contemporary feminism reportedly "burdens women with . . . the [very] status they have been struggling to escape." Rene Denfeld's *The New Victorians* offers a comprehensive catalogue of feminists' looniest theories on witchcraft, goddess worship, and matriarchal utopias. Generalizing from these examples, she sees a women's movement "bogged down in an extremist . . . crusade that has little to do with women's lives." It's a world that speaks to the very few, while alienating the many.[18]

To most of these critics, the solution is a more mainstream movement 25
that is open to all who care about gender equality. But not too openly open. Otherwise, feminism would remain identified with what Betty Friedan once labeled the "lavender menace." The trump card in many contemporary critiques of the women's movement is still lesbianism. "I don't want to make too much of this," claims Rush Limbaugh (who obviously does), but an estimated "30 percent to 40 percent of NOW's membership is lesbian or bisexual." According to the editor of the most popular men's-movement newspaper, feminism is "largely driven by lesbians and that is why most women aren't feminists." For other critics, the issue is one of priorities: the women's movement "first and foremost" should be fighting gender discrimination, and in their view, discrimination on the basis of sexual orientation is something quite different.[19]

Of course, not all critics of feminist extremism explicitly target lesbians. But the label frequently lurks in the subtext, reminding women of the consequences of falling in with the feminist fringe. And some self-identified feminists indirectly underscore that point by taking pains to establish their own heterosexual credentials. "Male sexual attention is the sun in which I bloom," Wolf informs her readers. In the mid 1990s, *Esquire* ran an entire cover story on "do me" feminists, who similarly basked in such attention.[20]

The most obvious difficulty with the extremism critique is that it compounds the problems it claims only to describe. When critics project an image of feminists as delusional, whiny, and sexually "deviant" crusaders, many women understandably will keep their distance. Yet these caricatures that pass for critique hardly represent significant feminist constituencies. Not every sloppy use of statistics or exaggerated claim in women's-conference flyers reflects a position attributable to the movement as a whole. Moreover, in any enterprise with so many self-proclaimed followers, someone occasionally will get some facts wrong. So will their critics. Indeed, commentators like Christina Hoff Sommers, who gleefully chronicles feminists' faux pas, commit similar evidentiary indiscretions. Sommers' assertions about the frequency of rape do not correspond to the findings of respected experts.[21]

Feminism, of course, needs thoughtful criticism and factual correction. What it does not need are potshot polemics strung together as evidence of some radical conspiracy to capture the women's movement. Nor does it benefit from proposals to broaden its appeal by marginalizing those who most need public support.

For every claim that feminism has lost touch with mainstream middle-class women comes a counterclaim that it has instead placed the concerns of these women over the concerns of other, less privileged constituencies. From this perspective, the women's movement looks too preoccupied with the needs of white middle-class heterosexuals and too disconnected from its original transformative vision. Unlike many other criticisms, this one rests on solid factual footing. The women's movement has a history of inadequate attention to issues of race, ethnicity, class, and sexual orientation. Despite recent improvements, the most popular contemporary feminist publications generally do not focus on the most vulnerable women. Commentators fault author-activists like Susan Faludi for "staying up late trying to figure out why women aren't anchoring the CBS Evening News" while ignoring the plight of single mothers coping with "rats in the hamper." Naomi Wolf's preoccupation with beauty rituals and eating disorders among relatively well-off women has sparked similar concerns.[22]

Yet while it is fair to ask feminists to give more attention to those who 30
suffer most from gender inequalities, it surely is unfair to dismiss the problems that Faludi and Wolf identify. The underrepresentation of women in prominent media positions and America's unhealthy standards of female attractiveness do not affect only privileged groups. Nor is it reasonable to fault prominent feminists because their work attracts wider audiences than the growing number of less celebrated authors who focus on needs of low-income women, women of color, disabled women, older women, and other particularly disadvantaged

groups. It is the mainstream public that is leaving those books off its shopping list. . . .

. . . Feminist leaders are faulted for both undervaluing and overstating gender differences, and also for focusing too much or too little on formal equality. Commentators from the right complain that the movement has strayed too far from its original commitment to equal rights. Commentators from the left maintain that activists have pursued individual rights at the expense of societal responsibilities, and have neglected the socioeconomic conditions that prevent women from exercising rights which are theoretically available.[23]

Throughout its history, the American women's movement has confronted what law professor Martha Minow labels "dilemmas of difference." Insisting on equality in formal treatment for men and women will not yield equality in actual experience as long as they face different social expectations and constraints. Yet recognizing women's "differences" risks perpetuating the stereotypes that perpetuate injustice. So too, an emphasis on achieving equal rights often diverts attention from the socioeconomic structure that limits their effectiveness. A wide gap persists between what the law promises and what it delivers regarding reproductive choice, workplace opportunities, and freedom from sexual violence.[24]

These gaps and tradeoffs are not, however, news to feminist leaders. The problem is less that the women's movement has placed too much faith in formal rights than that it has been unable to marshal sufficient societal support for their exercise. Nor have feminist efforts been insensitive to the difference dilemma. For example, the women's movement has long sought workplace policies that accommodate family responsibilities, which women still disproportionately shoulder. But activists also have worked to make such policies equally available to men, not just in theory but in practice. To understand why these efforts have had such limited success, we need to focus on more than feminist failings. We need also to confront the deeper sources of popular resistance.

Cutting across all these varied, often opposing critiques is one common tendency: to magnify feminist faults and to overlook the less visible roots of antifeminist attitudes. Many commentators assume that women's unwillingness to identify themselves as feminists is itself a central problem, and is attributable to the movement's radical agenda and man-hating image. Implicit in this claim is the further assumption that individuals who are sympathetic to feminist objectives but are put off by the label would enlist in the struggle if only activists would clean up their act.

Yet most in-depth research challenges these assumptions. Negative attitudes toward feminists are likely to be more a result than a cause of negative attitudes toward feminist objectives. Those who are uncomfortable with changes in traditional gender roles tend to project unfavorable traits and radical positions onto supporters of the women's movement. By invoking extremist images, opponents of change then discourage potential sympathizers. Men of color can increase the stakes by adding race to the equation. As bell hooks notes, young black women repeatedly hear that feminism "only serves white women and that 'dissin' it will win them points with just about anybody, particularly sexist black men."[25]

To understand these deeper sources of resistance, we need to reach more broadly and more deeply than popular criticisms suggest. Opposition to feminism involves the same selective perceptions that enable Americans to deny gender inequality as a serious problem: a reluctance to see ourselves as victims or perpetrators of injustice; our desire for roles that provide power, status, security, and a comfortable way of life; and our anxiety about alternatives. For many of us, feminism seems to put too many issues up for renegotiation.

Feminists should, of course, remain open to criticism about the way they are packaging their message. But critics, and the public generally, need to pay more attention to the other forces that encourage potshots at the wrong target. If, as both common sense and recent research suggest, most of the resistance comes from men, why aren't critics paying more attention to men's attitudes? On other issues of social inequality, we do not focus solely on the failure of the subordinate group to make change happen. When the subject is race, few commentators let white Americans off the hook. Yet in popular diagnoses of gender issues, the men's movement is nowhere to be found.

Conventional accounts of the "feminist mistake" mirror a classic vaudeville act. It features a drunk searching futilely for his lost change under a lamppost. As he acknowledges to a passerby, that isn't where he dropped the money, but it's the only place with any light. So too, when questions of gender move center stage, it is feminist fumbles that catch all the glare. But if we're truly hoping to find solutions, or even to get an accurate picture of the problem, we need better lighting. . . .

NOTES

1. Gloria Steinem, quoted in Nancy Gibbs and Jeanne McDowell Berkeley, "How to Revive a Revolution," *Time* 9 Mar. 1992: 56.
2. Nancy Gibbs, "The War against Feminists," *Time* 9 Mar. 1992: 50 (37 percent); Feminist Majority Foundation, *Women's Equality Poll,* fact sheet (New York: Feminist Majority Foundation, Apr. 1995) (30 percent); but see 1995 Harris Poll, cited in Susan Faludi, "Feminism Is Not the Story of My Life," *The Nation* 15 Jan. 1996: 28 (51 percent).
3. See Susan Faludi, "I'm Not a Feminist but I Play One on TV," *Ms.* Mar.–Apr. 1995: 31; Anthony Flint, "New Breed of Feminist Challenges Old Guard," *Boston Globe* 29 May 1994: 1; Gloria Steinem, quoted in Dierdre English, "Fear of Feminism," *Washington Post* 4 Sept. 1994: X7. For discussion of such conflicts, see Wendy Kaminer, *True Love Waits* (Reading: Addison, 1996) 39–42.
4. For perceptions of discrimination, see Faye Crosby, "Male Sympathy with the Situation of Women: Does Personal Experience Make a Difference?" *Journal of Social Issues* 42 (1986): 55; Judith H. Dobrzynski,

"Women Less Optimistic about Work, Poll Says," *New York Times,* 12 Sept. 1995: D5 (77 percent in 1995). For acknowledgments of improvement, see Susan Basow, *Gender Stereotypes and Roles* (Pacific Grove: Brooks, 1992) 335 (85 percent); Naomi Wolf, *Fire with Fire* (New York: Random, 1993) 58 (77 percent). For equality, see Rene Denfeld, *The New Victorians* (New York: Warner, 1995) 4 (between 90 and 98 percent of Americans believe that men and women should have the same education and employment opportunities).

5. Feminist Majority Foundation, *Women's Equality Poll;* 1995 Harris Poll, cited in Faludi, "Feminism" 28; Roper Starch Worldwide, *1995 Virginia Slims Opinion Poll* (Storrs: Roper Center, 1995) 9; Martha Burk and Heidi Hartmann, "Beyond the Gender Gap," *The Nation* 10 June 1996: 19.
6. For support without responsibility, see Gibbs 52; Christina Hoff Sommers, *Who Stole Feminism?* (New York: Simon, 1994) 18; Roberta A. Sigel, *Ambition and Accommodation: How Women View Gender Relations* (Chicago: U of Chicago P, 1996) 75–82, 173–75. For lack of attention and membership, see Wolf 58; Feminist Majority Foundation. For financial support, see Rick Wartzman, "Power of the Purse: Women Are Becoming Big Spenders in Politics and on Social Causes," *Wall Street Journal* 17 Oct. 1994: A1. For membership, see Dennis Boyles, *The Modern Man's Guide to Modern Women* (New York: Harper, 1993) 128.
7. Roper 9.
8. Marian Henley, *Ms.* Jan. 1992: 59.
9. Jerry Falwell, quoted in Jody L. Rohlena, ed., *Sounds like a New Woman* (New York: Penguin, 1993) 19; Karen Lehrman, "The Feminist Mystique," *The New Republic* 16 Mar. 1992: 30; Christina Hoff Sommers, "Hard-Line Feminists Guilty of Ms.-Representation," *Wall Street Journal* 7 Nov. 1991: A14; Denfeld 28; Mary Matalin, "Stop Whining!" *Newsweek* 25 Oct. 1993: 62.
10. Daphne Patai and Noretta Koertge, *Professing Feminism: Cautionary Tales from the Strange World of Women's Studies* (New York: Basic, 1994) 83. See also Lehrman 30; Sommers A14.
11. Denfeld 162.
12. Kristin Luker, *Abortion and the Politics of Motherhood* (Berkeley: U of California P, 1984) 163.
13. Anita Shreve, quoted in Gayle Greene Fawcett, "Women Together" (book review), *The Nation* 29 Apr. 1991: 564.
14. Mary Ann Dolan, "When Feminism Failed," *New York Times Magazine* 26 June 1988: 20.
15. See Carolyn G. Heilbrun, *Reinventing Womanhood* (New York: Norton, 1979) 42 (discussing Queen Bees); Fawcett 563 (book review).
16. For discussion of these themes in the context of the failed campaign for the Equal Rights Amendment, see Deborah L. Rhode, *Justice and Gender* (Cambridge: Harvard UP, 1989) 68–70. See also Ellen Fein and Sherrie

Schneider, *The Rules: Time-Tested Secrets for Capturing the Heart of Mr. Right* (New York: Warner, 1996); Schneider, quoted in Mike Littwin, "Retro Feminism," *Pittsburgh Post-Gazette* 18 Sept. 1996: D5.

17. Denfeld 9 ("feminist fringe"); Matalin 62 ("crackpots"); Pat Robertson, quoted in "Robertson Letter Attacks Feminists," *New York Times* 26 Aug. 1992: A16; Randall Terry, quoted in Rohlena 53.
18. Camille Paglia, quoted in Daniel Harris, "Nietzsche Does Downtown," *The Nation* 21 Nov. 1994: 615; Matalin 62; Katie Roiphe, *The Morning After: Sex, Fear, and Feminism on Campus* (Boston: Little, 1993) 10; Wolf 136; Kate Saunder, "Winning Not Whining," *Sunday Times* (London) 7 Nov. 1993: 36; Sarah Chrichton, "Sexual Correctness," *Newsweek* 25 Oct. 1993: 52 (quoting Friedan's statement that she is "sick of women wallowing in the victim status"); Denfeld 5.
19. Wolf 126 (advocating inclusive feminism); Rush Limbaugh, *The Way Things Ought to Be* (New York: Pocket, 1992) 192; Chris Harding, quoted in E. Anthony Rotundo, *American Manhood* (New York: Basic, 1993) 288; Denfeld 41.
20. Wolf 185–86; Tad Friend, "The Rise of 'Do Me' Feminism," *Esquire* Feb. 1994: 47.
21. Paula Kamen, "Acquaintance Rape: Revolution and Reaction," in Nan Bauer Maglin and Donna Perry, eds., *"Bad Girls"/"Good Girls"* (New Brunswick: Rutgers UP, 1996) 142–43.
22. See Nancie Caraway, *Segregated Sisterhood: Racism and the Politics of American Feminism* (Knoxville: U of Tennessee P, 1991); bell hooks, "Black Students Who Reject Feminism," *Chronicle of Higher Education* 13 July 1991; bell hooks, "All the Men Are White," in Marita Golden and Susan Richards Shreve, eds., *Skin Deep: Black Women and White Women Write about Race* (New York: Doubleday, 1995). For criticisms of Faludi, see Boyles 131. For criticisms of Wolf, see bell hooks, *Outlaw Culture: Resisting Representations* (New York: Routledge, 1994) 96, 102; Susan Vogel, "A Feminist Revisits Feminism," *The Recorder* 8 Mar. 1995: 7.
23. For critiques from the right, see Denfeld 5–20; Sommers 22–24; Sarah Bryan Miller, "Why I Quit NOW," *Wall Street Journal* 10 Aug. 1995: A8. For critiques from the left, see sources cited in Deborah L. Rhode, "Feminist Critical Theories," *Stanford Law Review* 42 (1990): 617, 633–35. For a general critique of the rights focus, see Mary Ann Glendon, *Rights Talk: The Impoverishment of Political Discourse* (New York: Free, 1991).
24. Martha Minow, *Making All the Difference: Inclusion, Exclusion and American Law* (Ithaca: Cornell UP, 1990) 49.
25. For antifeminist attitudes, see Gloria Cowan, Monja Mestlin, and Julie Masek, "Predictors of Feminist Self-Labeling," *Sex Roles* 27 (1992): 321, 329; Jennifer Crocker and Rïa Luhtanen, "Collective Self-Esteem and Ingroup Bias," *Journal of Personality and Social Psychology* 58 (1990): 60.

For the use of extremist images, see Cynthia Cockburn, *In the Way of Women: Men's Resistance to Sex Equality in Organizations* (Ithaca: ILR, 1991) 167; Greta Gaard, "Anti-Lesbian Intellectual Harassment in the Academy," in VeVe Clark, Shirley Nelson Garner, Margaret Higonnet, and Ketu H. Katrak, *Antifeminism in the Academy* (New York: Routledge, 1996) 115; hooks, "Black Students Who Reject Feminism" A44.

Questions for Discussion

1. What does the term *feminism* denote and connote to members of your class? Share your viewpoint with classmates, and explain what you feel has led you to hold the perspective you do. Are any members of your class actively involved in a feminist organization or political movement?
2. How does Rhode's assessment of men's role in the inequality problem compare with that of Langer? Find specific passages in each that sound either accusatory or conciliatory.
3. What kind of binds have women found themselves in as they assumed traditionally "male" behavior in the public sphere of work? Have women in your class found themselves caught between two gender identities, one for school and career, and another for family and romance?

For Inquiry and Convincing

Is gender inequality a problem? If you think it is, what evidence have you encountered in your life? If you do not think it is, what evidence supports your view? As you inquire, think about Rhode's point about our tendency toward "selective perception" (paragraph 36). Reflect on whether you might be biased by any of the items on her list. Then, extend your inquiry into library and Internet sources, deciding what the evidence about gender roles leads you to conclude. Good sources would be almanacs and government documents about income, employment, educational levels, and political offices. The October 1997 issue of *Ms.* magazine published many statistics comparing women's situation in the late 1990s with their situation in 1973, when the magazine was founded. Some of the topics covered include sports, politics, religion, health, family, arts, and culture. Write up your findings as an argument to convince someone who would disagree with you.

The Men's Movement and Its Critics

O, the trouble, the trouble with women,
I repeat it again and again
From Kalamazoo to Kamchatka
The trouble with women is—men.

—OGDEN NASH AND KURT WEILL[1]

1 In one of Nicole Hollander's "Sylvia" cartoons, the heroine listens to a television report on the men's movement: "During the Seventies women bonded with each other, explored their feelings. . . . Now men are getting a chance to have those things." "So," muses Sylvia, "now can we have the stuff they have?"[2]

The men's movement lends itself to this kind of parody. "Ain't they still running the world?" asks one piece in a women's humor collection. "What [do] they need a movement for?" "White men don't need a support group because they already have one," claims civil-rights leader Julian Bond. "It's called the United States of America."[3]

The most popular texts by male activists, Robert Bly's *Iron John* and Sam Keen's *Fire in the Belly,* have inspired caricatures of their own. The parodies in Alfred Gingold's *Fire in the John* don't need to depart much from the originals to produce the desired comic effect. These texts have, after all, lured mostly middle-class, middle-aged men to wilderness campfires, where they beat on tom-toms and search for the Wild Man within. Yet seldom do Americans acknowledge that underlying these seemingly eccentric rituals is a message that we urgently need to hear.[4]

It is, to be sure, misleading even to speak of *a* men's movement. No shared objectives or prominent national organizations unite the groups focusing on men's issues. Rather, there are multiple factions, often with competing concerns. Although relatively few American men are participants in these groups or knowledgeable about their agendas, activists' ideas are gaining a toehold in the culture.

5 One wing of the men's movement is an outgrowth and ally of feminist struggles. Its aim is to transform masculinity—to eliminate sex-based stereotypes that perpetuate sex-based inequalities, encourage homophobia, and restrict men's opportunities. This part of the movement, which draws on an increasingly rich body of men's-studies scholarship, has the strongest theoretical foundations but the weakest political appeal. At last count, groups like the National Organization for Men against Sexism numbered well under a thousand members. A related and to some extent overlapping constituency includes gay-rights scholars and activists, who also seek to challenge traditional gender roles.[5]

By contrast, men's-rights organizations have a quite different political base and social agenda. Members of these organizations generally see themselves as victims rather than allies of feminists. Many male activists are embittered survivors of hostile divorces. Their objective, according to the Men's Rights Association (MRA) newsletter, is "to marshall manpower in defense of men, masculinity, and the family. Our definition of men's liberation is freedom to be (not from being) men." Where the women's movement fits in all this is equally clear. A riddle from one MRA newsletter asks: "What's the difference between a terrorist and women's lib?" The answer: "You can negotiate with a terrorist."[6]

These groups complain mainly about how men are penalized by courts, "sucked dry" by lawyers, and "nabbed" for sexual "abuses" that only radical libbers see as abusive. Activists often draw on a broad literature of victimization that makes feminist "whining" look mild by comparison. *Playboy* columnist Asa Babar complains that men have had "twenty-five years of sexists calling us sexists" and it's time to stop the "sexual inquisition." Efforts to do just that are creating a new constituency of aggrieved activists, "diligently rolling their ball of pain" from one media event to another.[7]

On one level, as men's-studies scholars Michael Kimmel and Michael Kaufman note, these claims of oppression seem grossly exaggerated. Most participants in such organizations are middle-class, middle-aged, white heterosexual men—"among the most privileged groups in the history of the world." But somehow the collective "power of that group does not translate into an individual sense of feeling empowered." Many men of color, who view themselves as targets of the greatest societal prejudice, have particular difficulty with white feminists' claims.[8]

While conceding that "some men run the world," movement leaders emphasize that "most men don't." As Warren Farrell puts it: What's so great about earning more money when wives are the ones who get to spend it? According to Aaron Kipnis, author of *Knights without Armor,* "the conventional notion that men are somehow more privileged than women is starting to look like a bad joke. . . . Many of us have, at various times, felt victimized, scapegoated, manipulated, dominated, or abused by women."[9]

Andrew Kimbrell's *Masculine Mystique* offers a representative parade of 10
horrors. Compared with women, men die sooner, commit suicide more often, die on the job more frequently, drop out of high school in greater numbers, abuse drugs and alcohol at higher rates, are more often victims of violent crime, receive longer criminal sentences, and have greater risks of lung, liver, and heart disease. More African American men are in jail than in college, and in higher education, African American women outnumber their male classmates by 40 precent.[10]

Although these are serious problems, men's-rights literature contributes little toward solutions. These publications read like entries in an oppression sweepstakes: the apparent aim is to put men's grievances on equal footing with those of women. Yet not only are most such descriptions of gender inequality highly selective—they also deny men's responsibility for their own disadvantages. For example, men die sooner in large part because they engage in more risky behavior. They are less likely to receive physical custody of children after divorce because they are less likely to be primary caretakers during marriage. Males not only account for most of the victims of violent crime, but they also account for 90 percent of the perpetrators. They serve longer prison sentences largely because they have longer criminal records and fewer mitigating circumstances. For most disadvantages that men experience, it is difficult to hold women responsible. A similar point cannot be made about many of the inequalities that women experience.[11]

Men's-rights activists also deny the deeper ideological and structural causes of the problems they describe. For example, understanding men's disproportionate rates of violence, substance abuse, and other risk-taking behavior requires a much more complicated analysis than is currently in vogue. Racism, poverty, and inadequate governmental policies deserve more than walk-on roles. So do conventional understandings of masculinity, which are part of men's problems, not their solutions.

Similar criticisms apply to another prominent branch of the men's movement, which uses "mythopoetic" literature, rituals, and retreats to assist spiritual healing. According to popular leaders like Robert Bly, American manhood confronts a crisis rooted in the structures of modern industrial society. In Bly's view, these structures deprive male children of strong father figures and encourage domination by overpowering mothers. The result is a "feminized masculinity" and the remedy is for men to relive their adolescent struggle. They need finally to break free from their mothers and to reclaim their absent fathers. Other activists broaden the number of women accountable for men's problems. The fault, they say, lies not only with domineering mothers but also with emasculating wives and partners.[12]

By contrast, leaders like Sam Keen place primary blame for men's problems on other societal structures, such as the "corporate industrial warfare system." However, these activists, like Bly, focus on individual growth rather than societal transformation—on self-help strategies rather than political struggle. Through retreats and workshop rituals, the American male should get in touch with his genetically programmed warrior instincts. This will, in turn, create a stronger masculine identity. The beating of drums, literally and symbolically, creates a safe space in which a man can "shout and say what he wants" in a society that has repressed those desires.[13]

The use of male bonding rituals is, of course, by no means unique. Many 15
fraternal organizations and men's recovery groups rely on such strategies. Even an elite all-male association such as California's Bohemian Club sends its members—including cabinet officials and Fortune 500 executives—off on mythic retreats at "Cave Man Camp." What is, however, distinctive about men's-movement gatherings is the premise that they are the answer to the current crisis of masculinity.[14]

There are multiple problems with this solution, largely because male leaders deny the true dynamics of the crisis. Even if their causal diagnoses were correct, these activists have offered no evidence that weekend retreats and mythic rituals can compensate men for the prolonged absence of their fathers or produce sustained personality changes. Virtually all respected psychological research suggests the contrary. In any event, if, as Bly and other leaders maintain, the root of the difficulty lies in cultural values that minimize men's parental role or encourage destructive corporate priorities, then self-help approaches hardly supply an adequate response.[15]

This wing of the men's movement also offers no analysis of why women are left with the vast majority of child-rearing responsibilities, or why male decisionmakers perpetuate socially dysfunctional policies. Nor do activists make any effort to place men's restricted family role in the larger context of men's power. Male leaders present themselves as the tragic figures of paternal neglect and corporate greed, while ignoring the social transformation necessary to prevent those patterns from recurring.[16]

Not only does the men's movement offer an impoverished analysis of solutions, but it also denies the full dimensions of the problem. Issues of class and race are largely absent, and the omissions cause little concern among predominantly white and economically comfortable audiences. As feminist critics note, leaders like Bly never even "mention the epidemic of male violence against women." Strengthening masculinity so that men can "shout [out their] wants" is not a helpful prescription for reducing abuse. Ann Jones, an expert on domestic violence, makes that point directly: "Battered women, who could use some *ironing* Johns, report that . . . the bedrooms of the nation are already filled with hairy men shouting relentlessly about what they want."[17]

This is not to suggest that the impulse behind these bonding rituals is entirely misguided. Men need more opportunities to express emotion and to establish intimacy with other men. At least the participants in such retreats and workshops realize that something is missing from their lives. But as men's-studies experts point out, these individuals "are not looking in even the approximately right direction for the cause of their wounds." And the prescriptions that they are getting cannot begin to treat even their symptoms.[18]

The same is true of the solutions offered by religiously affiliated men's 20
organizations. Male dominance and the legitimacy of gender hierarchy is a shared premise of groups ranging from the religious right's "Promise Keepers" and "Jocks for Jesus" to Louis Farrakhan's "Million-Man Marchers." The message to men is "take your role back," become "leaders" of your family, church, and community. The message to women is to accept being followers.[19]

Promise Keepers is the inspiration of Bill McCartney, a born-again Christian and former football coach. What began in 1970 as a prayer meeting with some 70 participants now holds mass rallies with an annual attendance of over 700,000. According to McCartney, the group speaks to "godly men" who "recognize that [they] have fumbled the ball." Promise Keeper rallies extend the metaphor. They offer a kind of evangelical sporting event in which fans on one side of the stadium challenge the other with chants like "I love

Jesus—How about you?" Although heralded as "spiritual revivals," these gatherings are not without commercial appeal. Each event typically grosses several million dollars through sales of shirts, caps, jackets, and instructional material.[20]

At the core of Promise Keepers' religious mission are seven commitments. These include requirements that members honor Christ; support the church; practice spiritual, moral, ethical, and sexual purity; reach beyond racial and denominational barriers; and build strong families through love, protection, and traditional biblical values. It is this last mandate that gives feminists pause, along with other values that do not appear among the core commitments. *Seven Promises of a Promise Keeper* advises men to insist on asserting the leadership role in their family: "If you're going to lead, you must lead. . . . Treat the lady gently and lovingly. But lead." Promise Keepers' leaders are virulently anti-gay (McCartney is on record describing homosexuality as an "abomination against almighty God"), and its magazines include vitriolic messages concerning abortion, AIDS, and the American Civil Liberties Union.[21]

Moreover, the right wing of the men's movement has no monopoly on prejudice. Louis Farrakhan has an extended record of sexist, racist, anti-Semitic, and homophobic pronouncements, and his initial plan for a Million-Man March in Washington offered more of the same. African American men were to come together to atone for past misconduct, and to chart their future "as responsible heads of [their] families . . . [and] neighborhoods." Women were to stay at home, care for children, organize teach-ins, and pray from the sidelines. Although other black leaders sought to distance the occasion from Farrakhan's agenda, they did not lift the ban on female marchers. And that ban assumed added significance in the context of women's longstanding exclusion from leadership positions in the African American community. Why, asked columnist Julianne Malveaux, should "I stand by my man when he's trying to step over me?"[22]

For many women, however, that question is not rhetorical, and the answer is not self-evident. As historian Ruth Rosen notes, the religious wing of the men's movement is offering variations on an "age-old bargain"—one that "promises support and loyalty in exchange for power and control." To women straining under the double burden of breadwinning and caretaking, it may not seem like an unreasonable trade, especially if they don't have all that much power and control to begin with. And in poor black communities, ravaged by crime, violence, drugs, and unemployment, any mobilization around family values holds obvious appeal. Not surprisingly, many women support events like the Million-Man March and Promise Keepers' rallies.[23] . . .

At its most fundamental level, the problem for American men parallels 25
the problem for American women: both groups face widespread denial that there *is* a serious problem. But the task of building a coherent men's movement also bumps up against unique obstacles, because even those who acknowledge the need for change are deeply divided about the direction it should take. And

men themselves seem profoundly ambivalent about whether reviving traditional understandings of masculinity would address or merely amplify the problem.

Part of the difficulty is that the upheaval in gender roles since the 1970s has supplemented, but by no means supplanted, traditional values. The once-dominant ideal was elusive enough: few if any men felt confident that they were sufficiently powerful, strong, economically secure, and sexually attractive. But today's demands are even harder to meet because they are internally inconsistent.[24]

Competing ideals play out in media images and social expectations. Americans vacillate: Do they want men to be ambitious breadwinners or involved fathers? "Macho seducers" or "sensitive new-age guys"? Traditional understandings of masculinity are no longer the norm, but nontraditional ones have yet to be accepted. American society tells working mothers they can "have it all," at least in theory. But the same message isn't going out to working fathers. Except in occasional Hollywood fantasies, Mr. Mom is not a cultural hero, and neither private employers nor government decisionmakers are doing much to accommodate his needs. If, as social theorist Lynn Segal argues, the men's movement is stuck in "slow motion," it is partly because we provide little institutional support for changes in men's roles.[25]

Our society's schizophrenia about masculine ideals comes at a price and it is one we can ill afford. Men are "being asked to take on roles and show care in ways that violate the traditional male code and require skills that they do not have." The result is confusion and frustration. Some men also feel "hung out to dry" by feminists, who blame them for a structure of inequality that isn't their fault and who seem to be after their jobs, status, power, and even their magazines. From this perspective, even sex is becoming a chore, now that assertive women are "trying to supervise all the time. 'Now do this, No, not like that, like this.' " Many men are deeply resentful and resent not feeling free to say so. The problems men experience in the home are compounded by the problems they face in the world outside it. Their recent losses in real income and job security have taken a toll. Many men end up "nostalgic about the past, embattled in the present, and worried about the future."[26]

The challenge remaining is to channel disaffection into constructive strategies for change. This is not a hopeless task, but the most popularized wings of the men's movement are pushing in the wrong direction. The problems these groups identify will not be solved by symbolic rallies or self-help retreats. Nor will we find answers in newer versions of older hierarchies, with kinder, gentler dominance repackaged as responsible leadership. What women need from the men's movement is a substantial revision in traditional ideals of masculinity. And in the long run, that is what men need as well.

Western industrialized societies conventionally define masculinity in op- 30
position to femininity. The roles and characteristics that we value for women we devalue for men. Psychological research consistently finds that people give

lower ratings to men who display traits or perform work that departs from gender stereotypes. One consequence is that many men lose access to crucial experiences, emotions, and relationships. Prevailing images of masculinity encourage toughness, aggression, competitiveness, sexual conquest, and workplace achievement. Other values, such as tenderness, intimacy, and nurturance, fall outside our conventional vision of the "manly" man.[27]

Gender stereotypes discourage many men from taking an equal part in child-rearing, from forming close personal friendships, from working in nontraditional occupations, from accepting homosexuality, and from adequately controlling aggression. In low-income communities, the celebration of male power, coupled with the absence of other opportunities for achievement and self-esteem, has fostered some particularly destructive patterns. The prevailing rigidity of gender roles imposes substantial costs on both sexes, and both have much to gain from change.[28]

Why, then, have so few men been active in the struggle to achieve it? During the early days of the feminist movement, it was common to hear that "women's liberation is men's liberation too." Long lists of male benefits emerged, such as the twenty-one itemized examples in Warren Farrell's *The Liberated Man*. Feminism was supposed to free men from some of the pressure of breadwinning and to expand their choices at home and in the workplace. Men also would have more control over their own lives once women had more opportunities in theirs.[29]

That message met with only partial acceptance. While many men were prepared, at least in principle, to support equal rights for women, they were more ambivalent about changes in their own roles, status, and self-image. Often their initial tendency was to "sit tight, keep their heads down and wait it out, hoping that when the storm passes and the sociological dust settles, nothing fundamental will have changed."[30]

Now, some three decades later, the dust is still unsettled but it is clear that fundamental transformations are inevitable. The structural foundations for traditional gender patterns are eroding. Recent employment patterns are curtailing men's opportunities for economic independence and domestic dominance. Most families depend on women's wages and most Americans share, at least in principle, some commitment to gender equality. That commitment is, in turn, altering cultural expectations about everything from sexual behavior to parental responsibility. These transformations cannot be readily reversed. Changes in women's lives necessarily imply changes in men's. What is less clear is how long that process will take, where it will end, and how much resistance it will meet along the way. . . .

35 Yet defining masculinity in opposition to femininity remains problematic if gender equality is our goal. Historical and cross-cultural experience suggest that no culture is likely to provide equal respect for qualities associated with women as long as men devalue those qualities in themselves. That insight underlies an increasingly rich body of work in men's studies. One of its core objectives is to offer new visions of masculinity that better express the full

range of human potential, including characteristics historically viewed as feminine.[31] . . .

The precise shape that these images should assume is, of course, still open to debate. For some commentators, the goal is to dismantle all gender stereotypes. From this perspective, we should try to make a full spectrum of traits and roles equally available to both men and women. Implicit in this vision is a commitment to individual self-determination unconstrained by gender.

For other commentators, such a homogenized vision seems neither plausible nor desirable. All societies institutionalize sex-appropriate roles and traits. Although what constitutes appropriate behavior varies over time and across cultures, it is questionable whether we can dispense with culturally constructed differences altogether. Many Americans believe it is unwise even to try.

Prominent men's-studies theorists often reject any "androgynous blurring of masculinity and femininity into a melange of some vaguely defined human qualities." They prefer a vision that combines virtues traditionally associated with masculinity, such as strength, self-reliance, courage, and dependability, with other virtues that should also become associated with masculinity, such as compassion and nurturance.[32]

Each of these competing visions holds some appeal and, at this juncture, few Americans seem ready to choose between them. Most individuals want neither to relinquish all sense of sexual identity nor to restrict each sex to stereotypical patterns. Yet it is by no means clear that we can have it both ways. Most of what we know about personality development suggests that as long as sex-linked traits remain, the pressures for conformity will limit individual choice.

We need not, however, reach consensus about the role of gender in an 40
ideal society before we can address problems in the one we have. Although there are obvious limits to the cultural changes that we can consciously direct, we have by no means tested the boundaries of what is possible. On issues of gender, the personal is the political, but it is not always political enough. The challenge remaining is to direct some of the energy that is fueling the men's self-help movement into strategies for broader social change.

The trashing and bashing that characterize much of contemporary gender politics make good reading but bad policy. The recent polarization around gender issues has done more to obscure than to address the most pressing concerns of both sexes. Our current stalemates on key policy questions should remind us of what we already know. Men and women really are all in this together, and the reconstruction of gender roles requires our shared commitment.

NOTES

1. Reprinted in Matt Ridley, *The Red Queen: Sex and the Evolution of Human Nature* (New York: Macmillan, 1994) 245.

2. Nicole Hollander, "Sylvia," reprinted in Kay Leigh Hagan, ed., *Women Respond to the Men's Movement* (San Francisco: Harper, 1992) 149.
3. Hattie Gossett, "Mins Movement?" in Ross Warren, ed., *The Best Contemporary Women's Humor* (New York: Crossing, 1994) 149; Julian Bond, quoted in Sally Jacobs, "The Put Upon Privileged Ones," *Boston Globe* 22 Nov. 1992: 1.
4. Robert Bly, *Iron John* (New York: Vintage, 1992); Sam Keen, *Fire in the Belly* (New York: Bantam, 1991); Alfred Gingold, *Fire in the John* (New York: St. Martin's, 1991).
5. Susan Basow, *Gender Stereotypes* (Pacific Grove: Brooks, 1992) 336 (describing organizations). For a fuller description of different wings of the men's movement, see William G. Doty, *Myths of Masculinity* (New York: Crossroad, 1993) 57–63.
6. *The Liberator,* quoted in Diane Mason, "National Men's Rights Group Has It All Wrong," *St. Petersburg Times* 15 June 1990: D1.
7. Mason D1; Asa Babar, quoted in Michael Kimmel, *Manhood in America: A Cultural History* (New York: Free, 1996) 302. See also James L. Wilks, "Fathers Have Rights, Too," *Essence* June 1995: 134; Richard Doyle, *The Rape of the Male* (St. Paul: Poor Richard's, 1986). For the description of activists, see Jerry Adler, with Karen Springen, Daniel Glick, and Jeanne Gordon, "Drums, Sweat, and Tears," *Newsweek* 24 June 1991: 46.
8. Michael S. Kimmel and Michael Kaufman, "Weekend Warriors: The New Men's Movement," in Michael S. Kimmel, ed., *The Politics of Manhood: Profeminist Men Respond to the Mythopoetic Men's Movement* (Philadelphia: Temple UP, 1995) 15, 18; Christopher McLean, "The Politics of Men's Pain," in Christopher McLean, Maggie Carey, and Cheryl White, eds., *Men's Ways of Being* (Boulder: Westview, 1996) 11. For men of color, see bell hooks, *Black Looks: Race and Representation* (Boston: South End, 1992) 99–113.
9. Mel Feit, quoted in Ellis Cose, *A Man's World: How Real Is Male Privilege and How High Is Its Price?* (New York: Harper, 1995) 29; Warren Farrell, *The Myth of Male Power* (New York: Simon 1993) 33–34; Andrew Kipnis, quoted in Cose 36.
10. Andrew Kimbrell, *The Masculine Mystique* (New York: Ballantine, 1995) 4–12; idem, "A Time for Men to Pull Together," *Utne Reader* May–June 1991: 67.
11. For crime, see Myriam Miedzian, *Boys Will Be Boys* (New York: Doubleday, 1991) 11, 20–22; Kathleen Daly, *Gender, Crime and Punishment* (New Haven: Yale UP, 1994).
12. Bly 189–90; Hans Sebald, *Momism: The Silent Disease of America* (Chicago: Nelson, 1976); Herb Goldberg, *Inner Male* (New York: New American Library, 1987); Herb Goldberg, *What Men Really Want* (New York: Signet, 1991). For a critical review, see Fred Pfeil, *White Guys: Studies in Post-Modern Domination and Difference* (New York: Kerso, 1995) 171–72.

13. Keen 39–67, 233–46; Bly 8, 26. For critical discussion of assumptions, see R. W. Connell, *Masculinities* (Berkeley: U of California P, 1995) 6.
14. Kimmel, *Manhood in America* 315–16.
15. Ronald F. Levant, "Toward the Reconstruction of Masculinity," *Journal of Family Psychology* 5 (1992): 384.
16. Rosemary Radford Ruether, "Patriarchy and the Men's Movement: Part of the Problem or Part of the Solution," in Kay Leigh Hagan, ed., *Women Respond to the Men's Movement* (San Francisco: Harper, 1992) 16; Myriam Miedzian, "'Father Hunger': Why 'Soup Kitchen' Fathers Are Not Good Enough," in Hagan 127.
17. Elizabeth Dodson Gray, "Beauty and the Beast: A Parable for Our Time," in Hagan 159, 165; Ann Jones, *Next Time She'll Be Dead: Battering and How to Stop It* (Boston: Beacon, 1994) 98.
18. Ken Clatterbaugh, "Mythopoetic Founders and New Age Patriarchy," in Kimmel, *Politics of Manhood* 44, 59; McLean 16–19.
19. *Promise Keepers Handbook,* quoted in Ellen Goodman, "What Role Will Black Women Play in the 'New' Family?" *Chicago Tribune* 24 Oct. 1995: 17.
20. Richard Wolf, "Men at Work," *USA Today* 8 Aug. 1995: A9; David Briggs, "The New Rugged Cross: The Burgeoning Christian Men's Movement," *Buffalo News* 16 Aug. 1995: B7.
21. Louis Sahagun, "For Men Only: Spiritual Drive Fills Stadiums—Group Targets Male Identity Crisis," *New Orleans Times-Picayune* 9 July 1995: A2; Joe Conason, Alfred Ross, and Lee Cokorinos, "The Promise Keepers Are Coming: The Third Wave of the Religious Right," *The Nation* 7 Oct. 1996: 14; James D. Davis, "Rooted in Christianity: Movement Rallies Men to Pledge a New Approach to Family and Society," *Sun-Sentinel* (Fort Lauderdale) 30 July 1995: 1E.
22. Donna Britt, "Black Women, Loyalty, Pride and the March," *Washington Post* 22 Sept. 1995: B1; Julianne Malveaux, "A Woman's Place Is in the March: Why Should I Stand by My Man When He's Trying to Step over Me?" *Washington Post* 8 Oct. 1995: C3. See also Kristal Brent Zook, "A Manifesto of Sorts for a Black Feminist Movement," *New York Times Magazine* 12 Nov. 1995: 86.
23. Ruth Rosen, "A Feminist Send-Off for a Million Men," *Los Angeles Times* 12 Oct. 1995: B9; Britt; Briggs.
24. Kimmel, *Manhood in America* 7; McLean 16.
25. Basow 337; Lynn Segal, *Slow Motion: Changing Masculinities, Changing Men* (New Brunswick: Rutgers UP, 1990).
26. Levant 381 ("male code"); Kimmel and Kaufman 40–41 ("hung out to dry"); Eric Skjei and Richard Rabkin, *The Male Ordeal: Role Crisis in a Changing World* (New York: Putnam, 1981) 119 (sex); Kathleen Gerson, *No Man's Land* (New York: Basic, 1993) 277 ("embattled and nostalgic").

27. Rhoda Unger and Mary Crawford, *Women and Gender: A Feminist Psychology* (Philadelphia: Temple UP, 1992) 137. For images, see Rotundo 291; Miedzian 11, 101.
28. Robert A. Strikwerda and Larry May, "Male Friendship and Intimacy," in May and Strikwerda, eds., *Rethinking Masculinity* (Lanham: Rowman, 1992) 95; Larry May and Robert A. Strikwerda, "Fatherhood and Nurturance," in May and Strikwerda 75; Patrick D. Hopkin, "Gender Treachery, Homophobia, Masculinity, and Threatened Identity," in May and Strikwerda 111, 119; Michael S. Kimmel, "Rethinking Masculinity" in Kimmel, ed., *Changing Men: New Directions in Research on Men and Masculinity* (Newbury Park: Sage, 1987) 9; Robert Staples, *Black Masculinity: The Black Male's Role in American Society* (San Francisco: Black Scholar, 1982).
29. Warren Farrell, *The Liberated Man* (New York: Random, 1994) 182; Connell 24.
30. Skjei and Rabkin 100.
31. For historical and cross-cultural experience, see Skjei and Rabkin 318; Peggy Sanday, *Female Power and Male Dominance: On the Origins of Sexual Inequality* (New York: Cambridge UP, 1991). For men's studies, see Connell; David D. Gilmore, *Manhood in the Making: Cultural Concepts of Masculinity* (New Haven: Yale UP, 1990); Kimmel, *Manhood in America;* Pfeil; Nancy Levit, "Feminism for Men: Legal Ideology and the Construction of Maleness," *University of California Law Review* 43 (1996): 1038.
32. Kimmel, *Manhood in America* 333.

Questions for Discussion

1. Rhode feels that men's studies experts offer more fruitful solutions to men's problems than do men's rights activists. Explain what she sees as the difference in perspective between them. Does your school offer any courses in men's studies? Use the Internet to find out how common such courses are at other universities. What arguments might be made for and against such courses?
2. If you have been involved in any of the men's rights movements described here or have read *Iron John* or other self-help books for men, do you think that Rhode's characterization of these movements and authors is accurate? Promise Keepers was popular in the late 1990s. If that group remains in existence, how popular is it today? How do you account for its current level of popularity?
3. What are some of the problems men face today, as described in Rhode's essay? Do you agree with her that men themselves are responsible for many of their physical and emotional problems, as well as some of their complaints about rights violations? To what extent do you feel "prevailing images of masculinity" as described in paragraph 30 also bring about these

problems? Are conflicting messages, as described in paragraphs 27 and 28, part of the problem as well?

For Inquiry and Convincing

In the next reading Susan Faludi gives her view of the causes of "crises of masculinity," which she says have happened at many points in history. Compare her diagnosis of men's perceived problems with Rhode's diagnosis. On what points would they agree? How do they differ? Do additional research and write an essay to convince, addressed to other readers of both Faludi and Rhode, on the issue of why men might be having an identity crisis. You could decide, of course, that there is no male identity problem in our culture.

SUSAN FALUDI

The Backlash against Feminism

In 1991 Susan Faludi published a widely discussed book assessing the climate of opinion about feminism in America. In Backlash: The Undeclared War against American Women, *she offers evidence of many attempts to reverse the gains of feminism: from the media's reports of burned-out career women and frustrated husband-hunters; from the beauty industry's silicone implants and diet-plan mania; from films like* Baby Boom *and television shows like* thirtysomething *that glorified motherhood over career; and particularly from the politics of the New Right, which coupled "family values" with women's return to the domestic sphere. Unlike Christina Hoff Sommers and others who blame extremist ideology and hypocritical leadership for the "backlash" against feminism, Faludi sees the reaction as a struggle to regain power by interests who feel threatened by the tremendous gains women made in the 1970s and 1980s. In the following excerpt from* Backlash, *Faludi argues that masculine opposition to feminism, especially among certain socioeconomic groups, is responsible for a counterassault on women's rights.*

And when women do not need to live through their husbands and children, men will not fear the love and strength of women, nor need another's weakness to prove their own masculinity.

—BETTY FRIEDAN, *The Feminine Mystique*

THIS STIRRING proclamation, offered in the final page of Friedan's classic work, is one prediction that never came to pass. Feminists have always optimistically figured that once they demonstrated the merits of their cause, male hostility to women's rights would evaporate. They have always been disappointed. "I am sure the emancipated man is a myth sprung from our hope and eternal aspiration," feminist Doris Stevens wrote wearily in the early 1900s (qtd. in Cott 45). "There has been much accomplishment," Margaret Culkin Banning wrote of women's rights in 1935, ". . . and more than a few years have passed. But the resentment of men has not disappeared. Quietly it has grown and deepened" (358). 1

When author Anthony Astrachan completed his seven-year study of American male attitudes in the 1980s, he found that no more than 5 to 10 percent of the men he surveyed "genuinely support women's demands for independence and equality" (402). In 1988, the American Male Opinion Index, a poll of three thousand men conducted for *Gentlemen's Quarterly,* found that less than one fourth of men supported the women's movement, while the majority favored traditional roles for women. Sixty percent said wives with small children should stay home (1:2). Other studies examining male attitudes toward the women's movement—of which, regrettably, there are few—suggest that the most substantial share of the growth in men's support for feminism may have occurred in the first half of the '70s, in that brief period when women's "lib" was fashionable, and slowed since. As the American Male Opinion Index observed, while men in the '80s continued to give lip service to such abstract matters of "fair play" as the right to equal pay, "when the issues change from social justice to personal applications, the consensus crumbles" (1:26). By the '80s, as the poll results made evident, men were interpreting small advances in women's rights as big, and complete, ones; they believed women had made major progress toward equality—while women believed the struggle was just beginning. This his-and-hers experience of the equal rights campaign would soon generate a gulf between the sexes.

At the same time that men were losing interest in feminist concerns, women were gaining and deepening theirs. During much of the '70s, there had been little divergence between men and women in polling questions about changing sex roles, and men had even given slightly more support than women to such issues as the Equal Rights Amendment. But as women began to challenge their own internalized views of a woman's proper place, their desire and demand for equal status and free choice began to grow exponentially. By the '80s, as the polls showed, they outpaced men in their support for virtually every feminist position.

The pressures of the backlash only served to reinforce and broaden the divide. As basic rights and opportunities for women became increasingly threatened, especially for female heads of households, the ranks of women favoring not just a feminist but a social-justice agenda swelled. Whether the question was affirmative action, the military buildup, or federal aid for health care, women were becoming more radical, men more conservative. This was especially apparent among younger women and men; it was younger men who gave the most support to Reagan. (Contrary to conventional wisdom, the rise of "the conservative youth" in the early '80s was largely a one-gender phenomenon.) Even in the most liberal baby-boom populations, male and female attitudes were polarizing dramatically. A national survey of "progressive" baby boomers (defined as the 12 million who support social-change groups) found 60 percent of the women called themselves "radical" to "very liberal," while 60 percent of the men titled themselves "moderate" to "conservative." The pollsters identified one prime cause for this chasm: The majority of women surveyed said they felt the '80s had been a "bad decade" for them (while the majority of men disagreed)—and they feared the next decade would be even worse (Craver).

5 The divergence in men's and women's attitudes passed several benchmarks in 1980. For the first time in American history, a gender voting gap emerged over women's rights issues (Klein 6). For the first time, polls found men less likely than women to support equal roles for the sexes in business and government, less likely to support the Equal Rights Amendment—and more likely to say they preferred the "traditional" family where the wife stayed home

(Klein 158–159; Walsh 60). Moreover, some signs began to surface that men's support for women's rights issues was not only lagging but might actually be eroding. A national poll found that men who "strongly agreed" that the family should be "traditional"—with the man as the breadwinner and the woman as the housewife—suddenly jumped four percentage points between 1986 and 1988, the first rise in nearly a decade (Niemi et al.). (The same year, it fell for women.) The American Male Opinion Index found that the proportion of men who fell into the group opposing changes in sex roles and other feminist objectives had risen from 48 percent in 1988 to 60 percent in 1990—and the group willing to adapt to these changes had shrunk from 52 percent to 40 percent (2:5).

By the end of the decade, the National Opinion Research poll was finding that nearly twice the proportion of women as men thought a working mother could be just as good a parent as a mother who stayed home. In 1989, while a majority of women in the *New York Times* poll believed American society had not changed enough to grant women equality, only a minority of men agreed. A majority of the men *were* saying, however, that the women's movement had "made things harder for men at home" (Belkin A1). Just as in previous backlashes, American men's discomfort with the feminist cause in the last decade has endured—and even "quietly grown and deepened."

While pollsters can try to gauge the level of male resistance, they can't explain it. And unfortunately our social investigators have not tackled "the man question" with one-tenth the enterprise that they have always applied to "the woman problem." The works on masculinity would barely fill a bookshelf. We might deduce from the lack of literature that manhood is less complex and burdensome, and that it requires less maintenance than femininity. But the studies that are available on the male condition offer no such assurance. Quite the contrary, they find masculinity a fragile flower—a hothouse orchid in constant need of trellising and nourishment. "Violating sex roles has more severe consequences for males than females," social researcher Joseph Pleck concluded (9). "[M]aleness in America," as Margaret Mead wrote, "is not absolutely defined; it has to be kept and reearned every day, and one essential element in the definition is beating women in every game that both sexes play" (318). Nothing seems to crush the masculine petals more than a bit of feminist rain—a few drops are perceived as a downpour. "Men view even small losses of deference, advantages, or opportunities as large threats," wrote William Goode, one of many sociologists to puzzle over the peculiarly hyperbolic male reaction to minuscule improvements in women's rights (137).

"Women have become so powerful that our independence has been lost in our own homes and is now being trampled and stamped underfoot in public." So Cato wailed in 195 B.C., after a few Roman women sought to repeal a law that forbade their sex from riding in chariots and wearing multicolored dresses. In the 16th century, just the possibility that two royal women might occupy thrones in Europe at the same time provoked John Knox to issue his famous diatribe, "The First Blast of the Trumpet Against the Monstrous Regiment of Women."

By the 19th century, the spokesmen of male fears had mostly learned to hide their anxiety over female independence behind masks of paternalism and pity. As Edward Bok, the legendary Victorian editor of the *Ladies' Home Journal* and guardian of women's morals, explained it to his many female readers, the weaker sex must not venture beyond the family sphere because their "rebellious nerves instantly and rightly cry out, 'Thus far shalt thou go, but no farther'" (qtd. in Kinnard 308). But it wasn't female nerves that were rebelling against feminist efforts, not then and not now.

10 A "crisis of masculinity" has erupted in every period of backlash in the last century, a faithful quiet companion to the loudly voiced call for a "return to femininity." In the late 1800s, a blizzard of literature decrying the "soft male" rolled off the presses. "The whole generation is womanized," Henry James's protagonist Basil Ransom lamented in *The Bostonians.* "The masculine tone is passing out of the world; it's a feminine, a nervous, hysterical, chattering, canting age. . . . The masculine character . . . that is what I want to preserve, or rather, as I may say, to recover; and I must tell you that I don't in the least care what becomes of you ladies while I make the attempt!" (290). Child-rearing manuals urged parents to toughen up their sons with hard mattresses and vigorous athletic regimens. Billy Sunday led the clerical attack on "feminized" religion, promoting a "muscular Christianity" and a Jesus who was "no dough-faced, lickspittle-proposition" but "the greatest scrapper that ever lived" (qtd. in Douglas 397). Theodore Roosevelt warned of the national peril of losing the "fiber of vigorous hardiness and masculinity" and hardened his own fiber with the Rough Riders (Kimmel 243). Martial swaggering prevailed on the political platform; indeed, as sociologist Theodore Roszak writes of the "compulsive masculinity" era that culminated in World War I, "The period leading up to 1914 reads in the history books like one long drunken stag party" (92).

The masculinity crisis would return with each backlash. The fledgling Boy Scouts of America claimed one-fifth of all American boys by 1920; its founder's explicit aim was to staunch the feminization of the American male by removing young men from the too powerful female orbit. Chief Scout Ernest Thompson Seton feared that boys were degenerating into "a lot of flat-chested cigarette-smokers, with shaky nerves and doubtful vitality" (qtd. in Hantover 294). Again, in the years following World War II, male commentators and literary figures were panicking over reduced masculine powers. At home, "momism" was siphoning virile juices. Philip Wylie's best-selling *Generation of Vipers* advised, "We must face the dynasty of the dames at once, deprive them of our pocketbooks," before the American man degenerated into "the Abdicating Male" (qtd. in Lynn 60). In what was supposed to be a special issue on "The American Woman," *Life* magazine fixated on the weak-kneed American man. Because women had failed to live up to their feminine duties, the 1956 article charged, "the emerging American man tends to be passive and irresponsible" (qtd. in Lynn 72). In the business world, the *Wall Street Journal* warned in 1949 that "women are taking over" (qtd. in Chafe 182). *Look* decried the rise of "female dominance": First, women had grabbed control of the stock market, the magazine complained, and now they were advancing on "authority-wielding executive jobs" (qtd. in Ehrenreich, *Hearts* 37).

In the '80s, male nerves rebelled once more, as "a decline in American manhood" became the obsession of male clergy, writers, politicians, and scholars all along the political spectrum, from the right-wing Reverend Jerry Falwell to the leftist poet and lecturer Robert Bly. Antiabortion leaders such as Randall Terry rallied thousands of men with their visions of a Christ who was a muscle-bound "soldier," not a girlish "sheep." A new "men's movement" drew tens of thousands of followers to all-male retreats, where they rooted out "feminized" tendencies and roused "the wild man within." In the press, male columnists bemoaned the rise of the "sensitive man." *Harper's* editor Lewis Lapham advocated all-male clubs to tone sagging masculinity: "Let the lines of balanced tension go slack and the structure dissolves into the ooze of androgyny," he predicted (qtd. in Kimmel). In films and television, all-male macho action shows so swamped the screen and set that the number of female roles in this era markedly declined. In fiction, violent macho action books were flying off the shelves, in a renaissance for this genre that Bantam Books' male-action-adventure editor equated with the "blood-and-thunder pulp dime novels of the nineteenth century" (Mehren). In apparel, the masculinity crisis was the one bright spot in this otherwise depressed industry: sales boomed in safari outfits, combat gear, and the other varieties of what *Newsweek* aptly dubbed "predatory fashion" (Conant). In national politics, the '88 presidential campaign turned into a testosterone contest. "I'm not squishy soft," Michael Dukakis fretted, and leapt into a tank. "I'm very tough" (qtd. in McManus and Drogin). George Bush, whose "wimpiness" preoccupied the press, announced, "I'm the pitbull of SDI." He stocked his wardrobe with enough rugged togs to adorn an infantry, and turned jogging into a daily photo opportunity. Two years into his presidency, George Bush's metaphorical martial bravado had taken a literal and bloody turn as his administration took the nation to war; it might be said that Bush began by boasting about "kicking a little ass" in his debate with Geraldine Ferraro and ended by, as he himself put it, "kicking ass" in the Persian Gulf (Warner).

Under this backlash, like its predecessors, an often ludicrous overreaction to women's modest progress has prevailed. "The women are taking over" is again a refrain many working women heard from their male colleagues—after one or two women are promoted at their company, but while top management is still solidly male. In newsrooms, white male reporters routinely complain that only women and minorities can get jobs—often at publications where women's and minorities' numbers are actually shrinking. "At Columbia," literature professor Carolyn Heilbrun has observed, "I have heard men say, with perfect sincerity, that a few women seeking equal pay are trying to overturn the university, to ruin it" (203). At Boston University, president John Silber fumed that his English department had turned into a "damn matriarchy"—when only six of its twenty faculty members were women ("Tenure"). Feminists have "complete control" of the Pentagon, a brigadier general complained (qtd. in Falwell)—

when women, much less feminists, represented barely 10 percent of the armed services and were mostly relegated to the forces' lowest levels.

But what exactly is it about women's equality that even its slightest shadow threatens to erase male identity? What is it about the way we frame manhood that, even today, it still depends so on "feminine" dependence for its survival? A little-noted finding by the Yankelovich Monitor survey, a large nationwide poll that has tracked social attitudes for the last two decades, takes us a good way toward a possible answer. For twenty years, the Monitor's pollsters have asked its subjects to define masculinity. And for twenty years, the leading definition, ahead by a huge margin, has never changed. It isn't being a leader, athlete, lothario, decision-maker, or even just being "born male." It is simply this: being a "good provider for his family" (Hayward).

If establishing masculinity depends most of all on succeeding as the 15
prime breadwinner, then it is hard to imagine a force more directly threatening to fragile American manhood than the feminist drive for economic equality. And if supporting a family epitomizes what it means to be a man, then it is little wonder that the backlash erupted when it did—against the backdrop of the '80s economy. In this period, the "traditional" man's real wages shrank dramatically (a 22 percent free-fall in households where white men were the sole breadwinners), and the traditional male breadwinner himself became an endangered species (representing less than 8 percent of all households) (Phillips 18). That the ruling definition of masculinity remains so economically based helps to explain, too, why the backlash has been voiced most bitterly by two groups of men: blue-collar workers, devastated by the shift to a service economy, and younger baby boomers, denied the comparative riches their fathers and elder brothers enjoyed. The '80s was the decade in which plant closings put blue-collar men out of work by the millions, and only 60 percent found new jobs—about half at lower pay (Ehrenreich, *Fear* 207). It was a time when, of all men losing earning power, younger baby-boom men were losing the most. The average man under thirty was earning 25 to 30 percent less than his counterpart in the early '70s. Worst off was the average young man with only a high-school education: He was making only $18,000, half the earnings of his counterpart a decade earlier (Phillips 19, 204). Inevitably, these losses in earning power would breed other losses. As pollster Louis Harris observed, economic polarization spawned the most dramatic attitudinal change recorded in the last decade and a half: a spectacular doubling in the proportion of Americans who describe themselves as feeling "powerless" (33–37).

When analysts at Yankelovich reviewed the Monitor survey's annual attitudinal data in 1986, they had to create a new category to describe a large segment of the population that had suddenly emerged, espousing a distinct set of values. This segment, now representing a remarkable one-fifth of the study's national sample, was dominated by young men, median age thirty-three, disproportionately single, who were slipping down the income ladder—and furious about it. They were the younger, poorer brothers of the baby boom, the ones who weren't so celebrated in '80s media and advertising tributes to that generation. The Yankelovich report assigned the angry young men the euphemistic label of "the Contenders" (Hayward).

The men who belonged to this group had one other distinguishing trait: They feared and reviled feminism. "It's these downscale men, the ones who can't earn as much as their fathers, who we find are the most threatened by the women's movement," Susan Hayward, senior vice president at Yankelovich, observes. "They represent 20 percent of the population that cannot handle the changes in women's roles. They were not well employed, they were the first ones laid off, they had no savings and not very much in the way of prospects for the future." Other surveys would reinforce this observation. By the late '80s, the American Male Opinion Index found that the *largest* of its seven demographic groups was now the "Change Resisters," a 24 percent segment of the population that was disproportionately underemployed, "resentful," convinced that they were "being left behind" by a changing society, and most hostile to feminism (1:17–29). . . .

To some of the men falling back, it certainly has looked as if women have done the pushing. If there has been a "price to pay" for women's equality, then it seems to these men that they are paying it. The man in the White House during much of the '80s did little to discourage this view. "Part of the unemployment is not as much recession," Ronald Reagan said in a 1982 address on the economy, "as it is the great increase of the people going into the job market, and—ladies, I'm not picking on anyone but . . .—because of the increase in women who are working today.". . .

The '80s economy thinned the ranks of middle-income earners and polarized the classes to the greatest extreme since the government began keeping such records in 1946. In this climate, the only way a middle-class family maintained its shaky grip on the income ladder was with two paychecks. Household income would have shrunk three times as much in the decade if women hadn't worked in mass numbers (Phillips 202). And this fact dealt the final blow to masculine pride and identity: not only could the middle-class man no longer provide for his family, the person who bailed him out was the wife he believed he was meant to support.

20 To the men who were suffering, the true origins of economic polarization seemed remote or intangible: leveraged buyouts that larded up debt and spat out jobs; a speculative boom that collapsed in the 1987 Black Monday stock market crash; a shift to offshore manufacturing and office automation; a loss of union power; the massive Reagan spending cuts for the poor and tax breaks for the rich; a minimum wage that placed a family of four at the poverty level; the impossible cost of housing that consumed almost half an average worker's income. These are also conditions, it's worth noting, that to a large degree reprise economic circumstances confronting American workers in previous backlash eras: Mass financial speculation led to the panic of 1893 and

the 1929 crash; under the late-19th-century and Depression-era backlashes, wage earners also reeled under waves of corporate mergers, unions lost their clout, and wealth was consolidated in the hands of the very few.

When the enemy has no face, society will invent one. All that free-floating anxiety over declining wages, insecure employment, and overpriced housing needs a place to light, and in the '80s, much of it fixed itself on women. "There had to be a deeper cause [for the decade's materialism] than the Reagan era and Wall Street," a former newspaper editor wrote in the *New York Times Magazine*—then concluded, "The women's movement had to have played a key role" (Dolan). Seeking effigies to hang for the '80s excesses of Wall Street, the American press and public hoisted highest a few female MBAs in this largely white male profession. "FATS" ("Female Arbitrageurs Traders and Short Sellers") was what a particularly vindictive 1987 column in *Barron's* labeled them (Schwartz). When the *New York Times Magazine* got around to decrying the avidity of contemporary brokers and investment bankers, the publication reserved its fiercest attack for a minor female player: Karen Valenstein, an E. F. Hutton vice president who was one of Wall Street's "preeminent" women (Gross 16). (In fact, she wasn't even high enough to run a division.) The magazine article, which was most critical of her supposed failings in the wife-and-motherhood department, unleashed a torrent of rage against her on Wall Street and in other newspapers (the *New York Daily News* even ran an un-popularity poll on her), and she was ultimately fired, blacklisted on Wall Street, and had to leave town. She eventually opened a more lady-like sweater store in Wyoming (Hopkins 70). Still later, when it came time to vent public wrath on the haves of the decade, Leona Helmsley was the figure most viciously tarred and feathered. She was dubbed "the Wicked Witch of the West" and a "whore" by politicians and screaming mobs, scalded in a *Newsweek* cover story (entitled "Rhymes with Rich"), and declared "a disgrace to humanity" (by, of all people, real-estate king Donald Trump). On the other hand, Michael Milken, whose multibillion-dollar manipulations dwarf Helmsley's comparatively petty tax evasions, enjoyed fawning full-page ads from many admirers, kid-gloves treatment in national magazines such as *Vanity Fair,* and even plaudits from civil rights leader Jesse Jackson.

For some high-profile men in trouble, women, especially feminist women, became the all-purpose scapegoats—charged with crimes that often descended into the absurd. Beset by corruption and awash in weaponry boondoggles, military brass blamed the Defense Department's troubles on feminists who were trying "to reduce combat effectiveness" and on "the feminization of the American military" (Mitchell); commanding officers advised the Pentagon that pregnancy among female officers—a condition affecting less than 1 percent of the total enlisted force at any one time—was the armed services' "single biggest readiness problem" (Evans). Mayor Marion Barry blamed a "bitch" for his cocaine-laced fall from grace—and one of his more vocal defenders, writer Ishmael Reed, went further, recasting the whole episode later in a play as a *feminist* conspiracy. Joel Steinberg's attorney claimed that the notorious batterer and child beater had been destroyed by "hysterical feminists" (qtd. in Munk). And even errant Colonel Oliver North blamed his legal troubles in the Iran-Contra affair on "an arrogant army of ultramilitant feminists" (qtd. in Jaroslavsky).

Once a society projects its fears onto a female form, it can try to cordon off those fears by controlling women—pushing them to conform to comfortingly nostalgic norms and shrinking them in the cultural imagination to a manageable size. The demand that women "return to femininity" is a demand that the cultural gears shift into reverse, that we back up to a fabled time when everyone was richer, younger, more powerful. The "feminine" woman is forever static and childlike. She is like the ballerina in an old-fashioned music box, her unchanging features tiny and girlish, her voice tinkly, her body stuck on a pin, rotating in a spiral that will never grow.

In times of backlash, images of the restrained woman line the walls of the popular culture's gallery. We see her silenced, infantilized, immobilized, or, the ultimate restraining order, killed. She is a frozen homebound figure, a bedridden patient, an anonymous still body. She is "the Quiet Woman," the name on an '80s-vintage wine label that depicted a decapitated woman. She is the comatose woman on display in perfume ads for Opium and many other '80s scents. She is Laura Palmer, the dead girl of "Twin Peaks," whom *Esquire* picked for the cover of its "Women We Love" issue. While there have been a few cases—Murphy Brown on TV, or, to some degree, Madonna in music—where a female figure who is loud and self-determined has successfully challenged the popular consensus, they are the exceptions. More commonly, outspoken women on screen and stage have been hushed or, in a case like Roseanne Barr's, publicly shamed—and applause reserved for their more compliant and whispery sisters. In this past decade, the media, the movies, the fashion and beauty industries, have all honored most the demure and retiring child-woman—a neo-Victorian "lady" with a pallid visage, a birdlike creature who stays indoors, speaks in a chirpy small voice, and clips her wings in restrictive clothing. Her circumstances are, at least in mainstream culture, almost always portrayed as her "choice"; it is important not only that she wear rib-crushing garments but that she lace them up herself.

25 The restrained woman of the current backlash distinguishes herself from her predecessors in earlier American backlashes by appearing to choose her condition twice—first as a woman and second as a feminist. Victorian culture peddled "femininity" as what "a true woman" wants; in the marketing strategy of contemporary culture, it's what a "liberated" woman craves, too. Just as Reagan appropriated populism to sell a political program that favored the rich, politicians, and the mass media, and advertising adopted feminist rhetoric to market policies that hurt women or to peddle the same old sexist products or to conceal antifeminist views. Bush promised "empowerment" for poor women—as a substitute for the many social-service programs he was slashing (Murray and Wessel). Even *Playboy* claimed to ally itself with female progress.

Women have made such strides, the magazine's spokeswoman assured the press, "there's no longer a stigma attached to posing" (Carter).

The '80s culture stifled women's political speech and then redirected self-expression to the shopping mall. The passive consumer was reissued as an ersatz feminist, exercising her "right" to buy products, making her own "choices" at the checkout counter. "You *can* have it all," a Michelob ad promised a nubile woman in a bodysuit—but by "all," the brewing company meant only a less-filling beer. Criticized for targeting young women in its ads, an indignant Philip Morris vice president claimed that such criticism was "sexist," because it suggested that "adult women are not capable of making their own decisions about whether or not to smoke" (Waldman). The feminist entreaty to follow one's own instincts became a merchandising appeal to obey the call of the market—an appeal that diluted and degraded women's quest for true self-determination. By returning women to a view of themselves as devoted shoppers, the consumption-obsessed decade succeeded in undercutting one of the guiding principles of feminism: that women must think for themselves. As Christopher Lasch (who would himself soon be lobbing his own verbal grenades at feminists) observed in *The Culture of Narcissism,* consumerism undermines women's progress most perniciously when it "seems to side with women against male oppression."

> The advertising industry thus encourages the pseudo-emancipation of women, flattering them with its insinuating reminder, "You've come a long way, baby" and disguising the freedom to consume as genuine autonomy. . . . It emancipates women and children from patriarchal authority, however, only to subject them to the new paternalism of the advertising industry, the industrial corporation, and the state. (139–40)

The contemporary counterassault on women's rights contributes still another unique tactic to the old backlash strategy books: the pose of a "sophisticated" ironic distance from its own destructive ends. To the backlash's list of faked emotions—pity for single women, worry over the fatigue level of career women, concern for the family—the current onslaught adds a sneering "hip" cynicism toward those who dare point out discrimination or anti-female messages. In the era's entertainment and advertising, aimed at and designed by baby boomers, the self-conscious cast of characters constantly let us know that *they* know their presentation of women is retrograde and demeaning, but what of it? "Guess we're reliving 'Father Knows Best,'" television figures ironically chuckle to each other, as if women's secondary status has become no more than a long-running inside joke. To make a fuss about sexual injustice is more than unfeminine; it is now uncool. Feminist anger, or any form of social outrage, is dismissed breezily—not because it lacks substance but because it lacks "style."

It is hard enough to expose antifeminist sentiments when they are dressed up in feminist clothes. But it is far tougher to confront a foe that professes not to care. Even the unmitigated furor of an antiabortion "soldier" may be preferable to the jaundiced eye of the sitcom spokesmen. Feminism is "so '70s," the pop culture's ironists say, stifling a yawn. We're "postfeminist" now, they assert, meaning not that women have arrived at equal justice and moved beyond it, but simply that they themselves are beyond even pretending to care. It is an affectlessness that may, finally, deal the most devastating blow to American women's rights.

WORKS CITED

The American Male Opinion Index. 2 vols. New York: Conde, 1988.

Astrachan, Anthony. *How Men Feel: Their Response to Women's Demand for Equality and Power.* Garden City: Anchor, 1986.

Banning, Margaret Culkin. "Raise Their Hats." *Harper's* Aug. 1935: 354–58.

Belkin, Lisa. "Bars to Equality Seen as Eroding, Slowly." *New York Times* 20 Aug. 1989: A1+.

Carter, Alan. "Transformer." *TV Guide* 27 Aug. 1988: 20.

Chafe, William H. *The American Woman: Her Changing Social, Economic, and Political Roles, 1920–1970.* New York: Oxford UP, 1972.

Conant, Jennet. "The High-Priced Call of the Wild." *Newsweek* 1 Feb. 1988: 56.

Cott, Nancy F. *The Grounding of Modern Feminism.* New Haven: Yale UP, 1987.

Craver, Roger. Personal interview, 1991, reporting results of 1990 Craver Matthews Smith Donor Survey.

Dolan, Mary Anne. "When Feminism Failed." *New York Times Magazine* 26 June 1988: 23.

Douglas, Ann. *The Feminization of American Culture.* New York: Avon, 1977.

Ehrenreich, Barbara. *Fear of Falling: The Inner Life of the Middle Class.* New York: Pantheon, 1989.

———. *The Hearts of Men: The American Dream and the Flight from Commitment.* Garden City: Anchor, 1983.

Evans, David. "The Navy's 5000 Pregnant Sailors." *San Francisco Examiner* 15 Aug. 1989: A19.

Falwell, Jerry. *Listen, America!* Garden City: Doubleday-Galilee, 1980.

Friedan, Betty. *The Feminine Mystique.* 1963. New York: Dell-Laurel, 1983.

Goode, William J. "Why Men Resist." *Rethinking the Family.* Ed. Barrie Thorne with Marilyn Yalom. New York: Longman, 1982.

Gross, Jane. "Against the Odds: A Woman's Ascent on Wall Street." *New York Times Magazine* 6 Jan. 1985: 16.

Hantover, Jeffrey P. "The Boy Scouts and the Validation of Masculinity." *The American Man.* Eds. Elizabeth and Joseph H. Pleck. Englewood Cliffs: Prentice, 1980.

Harris, Louis. *Inside America.* New York: Vintage, 1987.

Hayward, Susan [senior vice president, Yankelovich Clancy Shulman]. Personal interview, Sept. 1989.

Heilbrun, Carolyn. *Reinventing Womanhood.* New York: Norton, 1979.

Hopkins, Ellen. "The Media Murder of Karen Valenstein's Career." *Working Woman* March 1991: 70.

James, Henry. *The Bostonians.* 1886. Middlesex: Penguin, 1979.

Jaroslavsky, Rich. "Washington Wire." *Wall Street Journal* 2 Feb. 1990: A1.

Kimmel, Michael S. "Men's Responses to Feminism at the Turn of the Century." *Gender & Society* 1.3 (1987).

Kinnard, Cynthia D., ed. *Antifeminism in American Thought: An Annotated Bibliography.* Boston: Hall, 1986.

Klein, Ethel. *Gender Politics.* Cambridge: Harvard UP, 1984.

Lasch, Christopher. *The Culture of Narcissism.* New York: Norton, 1979.

Lynn, Mary C., ed. *Women's Liberation in the Twentieth Century.* New York: Wiley, 1975.

McManus, Doyle, and Bob Drogin. "Democrats and Foreign Policy: Test of Toughness." *Los Angeles Times* 28 Feb. 1988, sec. 1: 1.

Mead, Margaret. *Male and Female.* New York: William & Morrow, 1949.

Mehren, Elizabeth. "Macho Books: Flip Side of Romances." *San Francisco Chronicle* 2 Aug. 1988: B4.

Mitchell, Brian. *The Weak Link: The Feminization of the American Military.* Washington: Regnery, 1989.

Munk, Erika. "Short Eyes: The Joel Steinberg We Never Saw." *Village Voice* 21 Feb. 1989: 20.

Murray, Alan, and David Wessel. "Modest Proposals: Faced with the Gulf War, Bush's Budget Avoids Bold Moves at Home." *Wall Street Journal* 5 Feb. 1991: A1.

Niemi, Richard G., John Mueller, and Tom W. Smith. *Trends in Public Opinion: A Compendium of Survey Data.* New York: Greenwood, 1989.

Phillips, Kevin. *The Politics of Rich and Poor.* New York: Random, 1990.

Pleck, Joseph H. *The Myth of Masculinity.* Cambridge: MIT P, 1981.

Roszak, Theodore. "The Hard and the Soft: The Force of Feminism in Modern Times." *Masculine/Feminine: Readings in Sexual Mythology and the Liberation of Women.* Eds. Betty and Theodore Roszak. New York: Harper, 1969.

Schwartz, Steven F. "FATS and Happy." *Barron's* 6 July 1987: 27.

"Tenure and Loose Talk." *Washington Post* 26 June 1990: A20.

Waldman, Peter. "Tobacco Firms Try Soft, Feminine Sell." *Wall Street Journal* 19 Dec. 1989: B1.

Walsh, Doris L. "What Women Want." *American Demographics* June 1986.

Warner, Margaret Garrard. "Fighting the Wimp Factor." *Newsweek* 19 Oct. 1987: 28.

Questions for Discussion

1. Does Faludi offer sufficient hard evidence in paragraphs 2–6 to convince you that the majority of American men do not support feminist objectives? Were you surprised by these statistics? Why or why not? Do you think it would be possible to find other statistics that would indicate more male support for women's equality? Update the data to reflect today's attitudes in men.
2. What does Faludi mean by "masculinity crisis" (paragraph 11)? What is her strategy in presenting so many historical examples in paragraphs 8–12?
3. In paragraph 14 Faludi cites a survey claiming that American society defines masculinity in terms of a person's ability to be a "good provider for his family." Does this mean that women as well as men tend to think of masculinity in economic terms? What social values are revealed by this definition? How would you define the terms *masculinity* and *femininity*?
4. In paragraphs 15–20 Faludi attempts to link some of the backlash against feminism with economic conditions in the 1980s. Do you find this cause-and-effect argument convincing? Why or why not? Can you think of analogous situations in which economic insecurity might contribute to a group's attempt to oppress minorities?
5. What images of women do you find in popular culture today? Is it common for magazines, television, and film to portray women as being male-dependent, frivolous, even childlike? Do you see any examples of advertisements that promote "sexist products" as feminist choices?

For Inquiry and Convincing

Consider how the terms *masculine* and *feminine* are commonly defined. Does our society define them in ways that assign greater power to men than to women? Do men, in Betty Friedan's words, "need another's weakness to prove their own masculinity"? Does our use of these terms enhance relationships between the sexes or make them more problematic? or both? Should we try to even out the differences by playing up androgyny and playing down masculinity and femininity, or does playing up the differences between the sexes make life more interesting? Should we try to change our definitions of "masculine" and "feminine"? Take a position on one of these related issues, refine your thesis, and make a case in support of it.

For Persuasion

Equal rights imply equal access to power. Do gains in power for women necessarily mean a loss in power for men? Regardless of your answer, but keeping your answer in mind, make a case persuading men why they should support feminism. Be specific. For example, you might focus on why men should support the women's movement even though many claim it has "made things harder for men at home" (paragraph 6).

KIRK ANDERSON

Cartoon

The following cartoon appeared in Ms. *magazine in 1993. How commonly do your friends and acquaintances share the attitudes expressed by these characters?*

THE INCREDIBLE SHRINKING WOMAN

For Discussion

What is the point of the cartoon's title? What definition of "feminism" is being expressed? Evaluate the effectiveness of the cartoon as persuasion.

NAOMI WOLF

The Beauty Myth

Feminist writer Naomi Wolf, a 1984 graduate of Yale, sees a backlash against feminism in our culture's promotion of female beauty. Her controversial book The Beauty Myth: How Images of Beauty Are Used against Women *(1991) charges that as women's material opportunities have expanded, an insidious psychological force has begun to undermine their sense of self-worth. Constantly dissatisfied with their real faces and bodies, women devote inordinate attention, time, and money to pursuing the slender, youthful, unchanging female image dictated by our society as the ideal, some even risking their health to do so through surgery or starvation. Wolf argues that the beauty myth is political, not aesthetic; it is imposed by a society threatened by women's rise in power. The following excerpt is Wolf's introduction to her book. As you read, decide to what extent Wolf seems to be anti-beauty: Does she seem to oppose all efforts to "look good"?*

AT LAST, after a long silence, women took to the streets. In the two decades of radical action that followed the rebirth of feminism in the early 1970s, Western women gained legal and reproductive rights, pursued higher education, entered the trades and the professions, and overturned ancient and revered beliefs about their social role. A generation on, do women feel free? 1

The affluent, educated, liberated women of the First World, who can enjoy freedoms unavailable to any women ever before, do not feel as free as they want to. And they can no longer restrict to the subconscious their sense that this lack of freedom has something to do with—with apparently frivolous issues, things that really should not matter. Many are ashamed to admit that such trivial concerns—to do with physical appearance, bodies, faces, hair, clothes—matter so much. But in spite of shame, guilt, and denial, more and more women are wondering if it isn't that they are entirely neurotic and alone but rather that something important is indeed at stake that has to do with the relationship between female liberation and female beauty.

The more legal and material hindrances women have broken through, the more strictly and heavily and cruelly images of female beauty have come to weigh upon us. Many women sense that women's collective progress has stalled; compared with the heady momentum of earlier days, there is a dispiriting climate of confusion, division, cynicism, and above all, exhaustion. After years of much struggle and little recognition, many older women feel burned out; after years of taking its light for granted, many younger women show little interest in touching new fire to the torch.

During the past decade, women breached the power structure; meanwhile, eating disorders rose exponentially and cosmetic surgery became the fastest-growing medical specialty. During the past five years, consumer spending doubled, pornography became the main media category, ahead of legitimate films and records combined, and thirty-three thousand American women told researchers that they would rather lose ten to fifteen pounds than achieve any other goal (Wooley and Wooley). More women have more money and power and scope and legal recognition than we have ever had before; but in terms of how we feel about ourselves *physically,* we may actually be worse off than our unliberated grandmothers. Recent research consistently shows that inside the majority of the West's controlled, attractive, successful working women, there is a secret "underlife" poisoning our freedom; infused with notions of beauty, it is a dark vein of self-hatred, physical obsessions, terror of aging, and dread of lost control (Cash et al.).[1]

It is no accident that so many potentially powerful women feel this way. 5
We are in the midst of a violent backlash against feminism that uses images of female beauty as a political weapon against women's advancement: the beauty myth. It is the modern version of a social reflex that has been in force since the Industrial Revolution. As women released themselves from the feminine mystique of domesticity, the beauty myth took over its lost ground, expanding as it waned to carry on its work of social control.

The contemporary backlash is so violent because the ideology of beauty is the last one remaining of the old feminine ideologies that still has the power to control those women whom second wave feminism would have otherwise made relatively uncontrollable: It has grown stronger to take over the work of social coercion that myths about motherhood, domesticity, chastity, and passivity, no longer can manage. It is seeking right now to undo psychologically and covertly all the good things that feminism did for women materially and overtly.

This counterforce is operating to checkmate the inheritance of feminism on every level in the lives of Western women. Feminism gave us laws against job discrimination based on gender; immediately case law evolved in Britain and the United States that institutionalized job discrimination based on women's appearances. Patriarchal religion declined; new religious dogma, using some of the mind-altering techniques of older cults and sects, arose around age and weight to functionally supplant traditional ritual. Feminists, inspired by Friedan, broke the stranglehold on the women's popular press of advertisers for household products, who were promoting the feminine mystique; at once, the diet and skin care industries became the new cultural censors of women's intellectual space, and because of their pressure, the gaunt, youthful model supplanted the happy housewife as the arbiter of successful womanhood. The sexual revolution promoted the discovery of female sexuality; "beauty pornography"—which for the first time in women's history artificially links a commodified "beauty" directly and explicitly to sexuality—invaded the mainstream to undermine women's new and vulnerable sense of sexual self-

[1] Dr. Cash's research shows very little connection between "how attractive women are" and "how attractive they feel themselves to be." All the women he treated were, in his terms, "extremely attractive," but his patients compare themselves only to models, not to other women. [Author's note]

worth. Reproductive rights gave Western women control over our own bodies; the weight of fashion models plummeted to 23 percent below that of ordinary women, eating disorders rose exponentially, and a mass neurosis was promoted that used food and weight to strip women of that sense of control. Women insisted on politicizing health; new technologies of invasive, potentially deadly "cosmetic" surgeries developed apace to re-exert old forms of medical control of women.

Every generation since about 1830 has had to fight its version of the beauty myth. "It is very little to me," said the suffragist Lucy Stone in 1855, "to have the right to vote, to own property, etcetera, if I may not keep my body, and its uses, in my absolute right" (qtd. in Dworkin 11). Eighty years later, after women had won the vote, and the first wave of the organized women's movement had subsided, Virginia Woolf wrote that it would still be decades before women could tell the truth about their bodies. In 1962, Betty Friedan quoted a young woman trapped in the Feminine Mystique: "Lately, I look in the mirror, and I'm so afraid I'm going to look like my mother." Eight years after that, heralding the cataclysmic second wave of feminism, Germaine Greer described "the Stereotype": "To her belongs all that is beautiful, even the very word beauty itself . . . she is a doll . . . I'm sick of the masquerade" (55, 60). In spite of the great revolution of the second wave, we are not exempt. Now we can look out over ruined barricades: A revolution has come upon us and changed everything in its path, enough time has passed since then for babies to have grown into women, but there still remains a final right not fully claimed.

The beauty myth tells a story: The quality called "beauty" objectively and universally exists. Women must want to embody it and men must want to possess women who embody it. This embodiment is an imperative for women and not for men, which situation is necessary and natural because it is biological, sexual, and evolutionary: Strong men battle for beautiful women, and beautiful women are more reproductively successful. Women's beauty must correlate to their fertility, and since this system is based on sexual selection, it is inevitable and changeless.

None of this is true. "Beauty" is a currency system like the gold standard. 10
Like any economy, it is determined by politics, and in the modern age in the West it is the last, best belief system that keeps male dominance intact. In assigning value to women in a vertical hierarchy according to a culturally imposed physical standard, it is an expression of power relations in which women must unnaturally compete for resources that men have appropriated for themselves.

"Beauty" is not universal or changeless, though the West pretends that all ideals of female beauty stem from one Platonic Ideal Woman; the Maori admire a fat vulva, and the Padung, droopy breasts. Nor is "beauty" a function of evolution: Its ideals change at a pace far more rapid than that of the evolution of species, and Charles Darwin was himself unconvinced by his own explanation that "beauty" resulted from a "sexual selection" that deviated from the rule of natural selection; for women to compete with women through "beauty" is a reversal of the way in which natural selection affects all other mammals.[1] Anthropology has overturned the notion that females must be "beautiful" to be selected to mate: Evelyn Reed, Elaine Morgan, and others have dismissed sociobiological assertions of innate male polygamy and female monogamy. Female higher primates are the sexual initiators; not only do they seek out and enjoy sex with many partners, but "every nonpregnant female takes her turn at being the most desirable of all her troop. And that cycle keeps turning as long as she lives." The inflamed pink sexual organs of primates are often cited by male sociobiologists as analogous to human arrangements relating to female "beauty," when in fact that is a universal, nonhierarchical female primate characteristic.

Nor has the beauty myth always been this way. Though the pairing of the older rich men with young, "beautiful" women is taken to be somehow inevitable, in the matriarchal Goddess religions that dominated the Mediterranean from about 25,000 B.C.E. to about 700 B.C.E., the situation was reversed: "In every culture, the Goddess has many lovers. . . . The clear pattern is of an older woman with a beautiful but expendable youth—Ishtar and Tammuz, Venus and Adonis, Cybele and Attis, Isis and Osiris . . . their only function the service of the divine 'womb'" (Miles 43). Nor is it something only women do and only men watch: Among the Nigerian Wodaabes, the women hold economic power and the tribe is obsessed with male beauty; Wodaabe men spend hours together in elaborate makeup sessions, and compete—provocatively painted and dressed, with swaying hips and seductive expressions—in beauty contests judged by women (Woodhead). There is no legitimate historical or biological justification for the beauty myth; what it is doing to women today is a result of nothing more exalted than the need of today's power structure, economy, and culture to mount a counteroffensive against women.

[1]See Cynthia Eagle Russett, "Hairy Men and Beautiful Women," *Sexual Science: The Victorian Construction of Womanhood* (Cambridge: Harvard UP, 1989) 78–103.

On page 84 Russett quotes Darwin: "Man is more powerful in body and mind than woman, and in the savage state he keeps her in a much more abject state of bondage, than does the male of any other animal; therefore it is not surprising that he should have gained the power of selection. . . . As women have long been selected for beauty, it is not surprising that some of their successive variations should have been transmitted exclusively to the same sex; consequently that they should have transmitted beauty in a somewhat higher degree to their female than to their male offspring, and thus have become more beautiful, according to general opinion, than men." Darwin himself noticed the evolutionary inconsistency of this idea that, as Russett puts it, "a funny thing happened on the way up the ladder: Among humans, the female no longer chose but was chosen." This theory "implied an awkward break in evolutionary continuity," she observes: "In Darwin's own terms it marked a rather startling reversal in the trend of evolution."

See also Natalie Angier, "Hard-to-Please Females May Be Neglected Evolutionary Force," *New York Times* 8 May 1990, and Natalie Angier, "Mating for Life? It's Not for the Birds or the Bees," *New York Times* 21 Aug. 1990. [Author's note]

If the beauty myth is not based on evolution, sex, gender, aesthetics, or God, on what is it based? It claims to be about intimacy and sex and life, a celebration of women. It is actually composed of emotional distance, politics, finance, and sexual repression. The beauty myth is not about women at all. It is about men's institutions and institutional power.

The qualities that a given period calls beautiful in women are merely symbols of the female behavior that that period considers desirable: *The beauty myth is always actually prescribing behavior and not appearance.* Competition between women has been made part of the myth so that women will be divided from one another. Youth and (until recently) virginity have been "beautiful" in women since they stand for experiential and sexual ignorance. Aging in women is "unbeautiful" since women grow more powerful with time, and since the links between generations of women must always be newly broken: Older women fear young ones, young women fear old, and the beauty myth truncates for all the female life span. Most urgently, women's identity must be premised upon our "beauty" so that we will remain vulnerable to outside approval, carrying the vital sensitive organ of self-esteem exposed to the air.

Though there has, of course, been a beauty myth in some form for as 15
long as there has been patriarchy, the beauty myth in its modern form is a fairly recent invention. The myth flourishes when material constraints on women are dangerously loosened. Before the Industrial Revolution, the average woman could not have had the same feelings about "beauty" that modern women do who experience the myth as continual comparison to a mass-disseminated physical ideal. Before the development of technologies of mass production—daguerreotypes, photographs, etc.—an ordinary woman was exposed to few such images outside the Church. Since the family was a productive unit and women's work complemented men's, the value of women who were not aristocrats or prostitutes lay in their work skills, economic shrewdness, physical strength, and fertility. Physical attraction, obviously, played its part; but "beauty" as we understand it was not, for ordinary women, a serious issue in the marriage marketplace. The beauty myth in its modern form gained ground after the upheavals of industrialization, as the work unit of the family was destroyed, and urbanization and the emerging factory system demanded what social engineers of the time termed the "separate sphere" of domesticity, which supported the new labor category of the "breadwinner" who left home for the workplace during the day. The middle class expanded, the standards of living and of literacy rose, the size of families shrank; a new class of literate, idle women developed, on whose submission to enforced domesticity the evolving system of industrial capitalism depended. Most of our assumptions about the way women have always thought about "beauty" date from no earlier than the 1830s, when the cult of domesticity was first consolidated and the beauty index invented.

For the first time new technologies could reproduce—in fashion plates, daguerreotypes, tintypes, and rotogravures—images of how women should look. In the 1840s the first nude photographs of prostitutes were taken; advertisements using images of "beautiful" women first appeared in mid-century. Copies of classical artworks, postcards of society beauties and royal mistresses, Currier and Ives prints, and porcelain figurines flooded the separate sphere to which middle-class women were confined.

Since the Industrial Revolution, middle-class Western women have been controlled by ideals and stereotypes as much as by material constraints. This situation, unique to this group, means that analyses that trace "cultural conspiracies" are uniquely plausible in relation to them. The rise of the beauty myth was just one of several emerging social fictions that masqueraded as natural components of the feminine sphere, the better to enclose those women inside it. Other such fictions arose contemporaneously: a version of childhood that required continual maternal supervision; a concept of female biology that required middle-class women to act out the roles of hysterics and hypochondriacs; a conviction that respectable women were sexually anesthetic; and a definition of women's work that occupied them with repetitive, time-consuming, and painstaking tasks such as needlepoint and lacemaking. All such Victorian inventions as these served a double function—that is, though they were encouraged as a means to expend female energy and intelligence in harmless ways, women often used them to express genuine creativity and passion.

But in spite of middle-class women's creativity with fashion and embroidery and child rearing, and, a century later, with the role of the suburban housewife that devolved from these social fictions, the fictions' main purpose was served: During a century and a half of unprecedented feminist agitation, they effectively counteracted middle-class women's dangerous new leisure, literacy, and relative freedom from material constraints.

Though these time- and mind-consuming fictions about women's natural role adapted themselves to resurface in the post-war Feminine Mystique, when the second wave of the women's movement took apart what women's magazines had portrayed as the "romance," "science," and "adventure" of homemaking and suburban family life, they temporarily failed. The cloying domestic fiction of "togetherness" lost its meaning and middle-class women walked out of their front doors in masses.

So the fictions simply transformed themselves once more: Since the 20
women's movement had successfully taken apart most other necessary fictions of femininity, all the work of social control once spread out over the whole network of these fictions had to be reassigned to the only strand left intact, which action consequently strengthened it a hundredfold. This reimposed onto liberated women's faces and bodies all the limitations, taboos, and punishments of the repressive laws, religious injunctions, and reproductive enslavement that no longer carried sufficient force. Inexhaustible but ephemeral beauty work took over from inexhaustible but ephemeral housework. As the economy, law, religion, sexual mores, education, and culture were forcibly opened up to include women more fairly, a private reality colonized female consciousness. By using ideas about "beauty," it reconstructed an alternative female world with its own laws, economy, religion, sexuality, education, and culture, each element as repressive as any that had gone before.

Since middle-class Western women can best be weakened psychologically now that we are stronger materially, the beauty myth, as it has resurfaced in the last generation, has had to draw on more technological sophistication and reactionary fervor than ever before. The modern arsenal of the myth is a dissemination of millions of images of the current ideal; although this barrage is generally seen as a collective sexual fantasy, there is in fact little that is sexual about it. It is summoned out of political fear on the part of male-dominated institutions threatened by women's freedom, and it exploits female guilt and apprehension about our own liberation—latent fears that we might be going too far. This frantic aggregation of imagery is a collective reactionary hallucination willed into being by both men and women stunned and disoriented by the rapidity with which gender relations have been transformed: a bulwark of reassurance against the flood of change. The mass depiction of the modern woman as a "beauty" is a contradiction: Where modern women are growing, moving, and expressing their individuality, as the myth has it, "beauty" is by definition inert, timeless, and generic. That this hallucination is necessary and deliberate is evident in the way "beauty" so directly contradicts women's real situation.

And the unconscious hallucination grows ever more influential and pervasive because of what is now conscious market manipulation: powerful industries—the $33-billion-a-year diet industry (O'Neill), the $20-billion cosmetics industry, the $300-million cosmetic surgery industry (*Standard and Poor's*), and the $7-billion pornography industry ("Crackdown")—have arisen from the capital made out of unconscious anxieties, and are in turn able, through their influence on mass culture, to use, stimulate, and reinforce the hallucination in a rising economic spiral.

This is not a conspiracy theory; it doesn't have to be. Societies tell themselves necessary fictions in the same way that individuals and families do. Henrik Ibsen called them "vital lies," and psychologist Daniel Goleman describes them working the same way on the social level that they do within families: "The collusion is maintained by directing attention away from the fearsome fact, or by repackaging its meaning in an acceptable format" (16–17). The costs of these social blind spots, he writes, are destructive communal illusions. Possibilities for women have become so open-ended that they threaten to destabilize the institutions on which a male-dominated culture has depended, and a collective panic reaction on the part of both sexes has forced a demand for counterimages.

The resulting hallucination materializes, for women, as something all too real. No longer just an idea, it becomes three-dimensional, incorporating within itself how women live and how they do not live: It becomes the Iron Maiden. The original Iron Maiden was a medieval German instrument of torture, a body-shaped casket painted with the limbs and features of a lovely, smiling young woman. The unlucky victim was slowly enclosed inside her; the lid fell shut to immobilize the victim, who died either of starvation or, less cruelly, of the metal spikes embedded in her interior. The modern hallucination in which women are trapped or trap themselves is similarly rigid, cruel, and euphemistically painted. Contemporary culture directs attention to imagery of the Iron Maiden, while censoring real women's faces and bodies.

25 Why does the social order feel the need to defend itself by evading the fact of real women, our faces and voices and bodies, and reducing the meaning of women to these formulaic and endlessly reproduced "beautiful" images? Though unconscious personal anxieties can be a powerful force in the creation of a vital lie, economic necessity practically guarantees it. An economy that depends on slavery needs to promote images of slaves that "justify" the institution of slavery. Western economies are absolutely dependent now on the continued underpayment of women. An ideology that makes women feel "worth less" was urgently needed to counteract the way feminism had begun to make us feel worth more. This does not require a conspiracy; merely an atmosphere. The contemporary economy depends right now on the representation of women within the beauty myth. Economist John Kenneth Galbraith offers an economic explanation for "the persistence of the view of homemaking as a 'higher calling'": the concept of women as naturally trapped within the Feminine Mystique, he feels, "has been forced on us by popular sociology, by magazines, and by fiction to disguise the fact that woman in her role of consumer has been essential to the development of our industrial society. . . . Behavior that is essential for economic reasons is transformed into a social virtue" (qtd. in Minton). As soon as a woman's primary social value could no longer be defined as the attainment of virtuous domesticity, the beauty myth redefined it as the attainment of virtuous beauty. It did so to substitute both a new consumer imperative and a new justification for economic unfairness in the workplace where the old ones had lost their hold over newly liberated women.

Another hallucination arose to accompany that of the Iron Maiden: The caricature of the Ugly Feminist was resurrected to dog the steps of the women's movement. The caricature is unoriginal; it was coined to ridicule the feminists of the nineteenth century. Lucy Stone herself, whom supporters saw as "a prototype of womanly grace . . . fresh and fair as the morning," was derided by detractors with "the usual report" about Victorian feminists: "a big masculine woman, wearing boots, smoking a cigar, swearing like a trooper" (qtd. in Friedan 79). As Betty Friedan put it presciently in 1960, even before the savage revamping of that old caricature: "The unpleasant image of feminists today resembles less the feminists themselves than the image fostered by the interests who so bitterly opposed the vote for women in state after state" (87). Thirty years on, her conclusion is more true than ever: That resurrected caricature, which sought to punish women for their public acts by going after their private sense of self, became the paradigm for new limits placed on aspiring women everywhere. After the success of the women's movement's second wave, the beauty myth was perfected to checkmate power at every level in individual women's lives. The modern neuroses of life in the female body spread to woman after woman at epidemic rates. The myth is undermining—slowly, imperceptibly, without our being aware of the real forces of erosion—the ground women have gained through long, hard, honorable struggle.

The beauty myth of the present is more insidious than any mystique of femininity yet: A century ago, Nora slammed the door of the doll's house; a generation ago, women turned their backs on the consumer heaven of the isolated multiapplianced home; but where women are trapped today, there is no door to slam. The contemporary ravages of the beauty backlash are destroying women physically and depleting us psychologically. If we are to free ourselves from the dead weight that has once again been made out of femaleness, it is not ballots or lobbyists or placards that women will need first; it is a new way to see.

WORKS CITED

"Crackdown on Pornography: A No-Win Battle." *U.S. News & World Report* 4 June 1984.

Cash, Thomas, Diane Cash, and Jonathan Butters. "Mirror-Mirror on the Wall: Contrast Effects and Self-Evaluation of Physical Attractiveness." *Personality and Social Psychology Bulletin* 9.3 (1983).

Dworkin, Andrea. *Pornography: Men Possessing Women.* New York: Putnam, 1981.

Friedan, Betty. *The Feminine Mystique.* 1963. London: Penguin, 1982.

Goleman, Daniel. *Vital Lies, Simple Truths: The Psychology of Self-Deception.* New York: Simon, 1983.

Greer, Germaine. *The Female Eunuch.* London: Paladin Grafton, 1970.

Miles, Rosalind. *The Women's History of the World.* London: Paladin Grafton, 1988.

Minton, Michael H., with Jean Libman Block. *What Is a Life Worth?* New York: McGraw, 1984.

Morgan, Elaine. *The Descent of Woman.* New York: Bantam, 1979.

O'Neill, Mollie. "Congress Looking into the Diet Business." *New York Times* 25 July 1988.

Standard and Poor's Industry Survey. New York: Standard and Poor's, 1988.

Reed, Evelyn. *Woman's Evolution: From Matriarchal Clan to Patriarchal Family.* New York: Pathfinder, 1986.

Woodhead, Linda. "Desert Dandies." *The Guardian* July 1988.

Wooley, S. C., and O. W. Wooley. "Obesity and Women: A Closer Look at the Facts." *Women's Studies International Quarterly* 2 (1979): 69–79.

Questions for Discussion

1. Wolf seeks to convince her readers that the beauty myth is just that—a myth. What reasons and evidence does she offer to make them see that beauty is not an aesthetic absolute? Do you find her case convincing?
2. What reasons and evidence does Wolf offer to convince her readers that in creating the beauty myth, society is motivated by politics and economics? (To be sure you understand this part of her argument, write a paraphrase of paragraph 25.) Explain her analogy between the beauty myth and the medieval Iron Maiden (paragraph 24). How does this analogy reinforce Wolf's argument that the myth is politically motivated?
3. Wolf says in paragraph 14, "The qualities that a given period calls beautiful in women are merely symbols of the female behavior that that period considers desirable: *The beauty myth is always actually prescribing behavior and not appearance.*" For example, the quality of thinness might symbolize that our society wants women to deny themselves the pleasures of food, even to exist on the daily calorie rations of a person in the Third World or in a prison camp. What other behavior might the beauty myth prescribe?
4. In a preface to a later edition of *The Beauty Myth,* Wolf wrote that she was misunderstood by many critics as being anti-beauty and that she would like to make clear to readers that women should be free to adorn and show off their bodies if they want, celebrating their real beauty. She says it is fine to wear lipstick but not to feel guilty about not conforming to the ideal image of beauty. Do you find any evidence in the excerpt to suggest that Wolf is not against makeup and fashion? Do you find any evidence to suggest that she is against them? Could you write a new first paragraph to introduce Wolf's argument more clearly?

For Convincing

Women know that achieving "beauty" is often painful and expensive, in terms of both time and money. Wolf charges that entire industries have formed to profit from women's anxieties about their appearance. However, a glance at men's magazines in most newsstands shows a proliferation of reading material devoted to men's fashion, grooming, and physique—the "masculine" term for "figure." The advertisements here suggest that a similar industry exists for men. Do men have their own masculine version of the "beauty myth" that causes them to suffer, to spend time and money for the sake of their appearance? If so, how widely is it subscribed to? Do you think any motives other than simple vanity underlie it? Write an argument, perhaps addressed to Naomi Wolf, to make the case that excessive concern for one's appearance is not limited to the female sex. If you don't think this is a significant concern for men, write an argument addressed to women, to convince them that they should or should not be more like men in this respect.

For Research and Persuasion

In "Sex," a later chapter of *The Beauty Myth,* Wolf attempts to persuade her readers that men would prefer women to accept themselves as they are. She writes, "At least one major study proves that men are as exasperated with the beauty myth as women are. 'Preoccupation with her appearance, concern about face and hair' ranked among the top four qualities that most annoyed men about women" (171). However, she does admit that "some men get a sexual charge from a woman's objective beauty," an attraction that is often a form of "exhibitionism" as a man "[imagines] his buddies imagining him doing what he is doing while he does it" (175). You may want to look at the entire chapter in which Wolf discusses love and the beauty myth. Do additional research, both in the field and in the library, to draw some conclusions of your own about how images of "ideal" beauty affect sexual relationships. Depending upon your conclusions, write an essay in which you attempt to change the behavior of men, women, or both sexes.

CHRISTINA HOFF SOMMERS

The Backlash Myth

Christina Hoff Sommers is the W. H. Brady Fellow at the American Enterprise Institute whose commentaries on contemporary life and morals have appeared in a variety of journals. She angered most of the feminist movement with her 1994 book Who Stole Feminism: How Women Have Betrayed Women, *in which she charges that feminists destroyed their own movement by taking positions that mainstream American women found too extreme, such as the rejection of traditional family roles and hostility toward men. In this selection she argues that claims of victimhood by Naomi Wolf in* The Beauty Myth *and Susan Faludi in* Backlash *are ill-founded, even paranoid. Read the excerpts from their works preceding this selection and then Sommers's response.*

When regard for truth has been broken down or even slightly weakened, all things will remain doubtful.

—ST. AUGUSTINE

A COUPLE of years ago, American publishing was enlivened by the release of Susan Faludi's *Backlash* and Naomi Wolf's *The Beauty Myth,* two impassioned feminist screeds uncovering and denouncing the schemes that have prevented women from enjoying the fruits of the women's movement.[1] For our purposes, what these books have in common is more interesting and important than what distinguishes them. Both reported a widespread conspiracy against women. In both, the putative conspiracy has the same goal: to prevent today's women from making use of their hard-won freedoms—to punish them, in other words, for liberating themselves. As Ms. Wolf informs us: "After the success of the women's movement's second wave, the beauty myth was perfected to checkmate power at every level in individual women's lives."[2] 1

Conspiracy theories are always popular, but in this case the authors, writing primarily for middle-class readers, faced a tricky problem. No reasonable person in this day and age could be expected to believe that somewhere in America a group of male "elders" has sat down to plot ways to perpetuate the subjugation of women. How, then, could they persuade anyone of the existence of a widespread effort to control women for the good of men?

The solution that they hit upon made it possible for them to have their conspiracy while disavowing it. Faludi and Wolf argued that the conspiracy against women is being carried out by malevolent but invisible backlash forces or beauty-myth forces that act in purposeful ways. The forces in question are subtle, powerful, and insidiously efficient, and women are largely unconscious of them. What is more, the primary enforcers of the conspiracy are not a group of sequestered males plotting and planning their next backlash maneuvers: it is women themselves who "internalize" the aims of the backlash, who, unwittingly, do its bidding. In other words, the backlash is Us. Or, as Wolf puts it, "many women internalize Big Brother's eye."[3]

Faludi's scope is wider than Wolf's; she argues that the media and the political system have been co-opted by the backlash, as well:

> The backlash is not a conspiracy, with a council dispatching agents from some central control room, nor are the people who serve its ends often aware of their role; some even consider themselves feminists. For the most part, its workings are encoded and internalized, diffuse and chameleonic . . . generated by a culture machine that is always scrounging for a "fresh" angle. Taken as a whole, however, these codes and cajolings, these whispers and threats and myths, move overwhelmingly in one direction: they try to push women back into their "acceptable" roles.[4]

Wolf focuses more narrowly on the "beauty backlash," which pressures women to diet, dress up, make up, and work out in ways that are "destroying women physically and depleting us psychologically":[5] "The beauty backlash against feminism is no conspiracy, but a million separate individual reflexes . . . that coalesce into a national mood weighing women down; the backlash is all the more oppressive because the source of the suffocation is so diffuse as to be almost invisible."[6]

Having thus skirted a claim of outright conspiracy, Faludi and Wolf 5
nevertheless freely use the *language* of subterfuge to arouse anger and bitterness. In their systems, the backlash and the beauty myth become malevolent personified forces behind plot after plot against women.

They incite unscrupulous stooges in the media to write articles that make "single and childless women feel like circus freaks." Cosmetics saleswomen are backlash agents, "trained," Wolf says, "with techniques akin to those used by professional cult converters and hypnotists." She calls Weight Watchers a "cult" and compares its disciplines to those of the Unification Church, Scientology, est, and Lifespring. In aerobics classes, "robotic" women do the "same bouncing dance . . . practiced by the Hare Krishnas for the same effect."[7]

What the backlash "wants" is clear to both Faludi and Wolf. By the seventies, women had been granted a great deal of equality. The primary aim of the backlash is to retake lost ground, to put women to rout.[8] The subtitle of Faludi's book is *The Undeclared War against American Women. Backlash* itself may be regarded as a feminist counterattack in this supposed war. As Patricia Schroeder noted in a review of the book, women are not "riled up enough," and Faludi "may be able to do what political activists have tried to do for years."[9] Indeed, she and Wolf together succeeded in moving countless women to anger and dismay.

Where did Faludi and Wolf get the idea that masses of seemingly free women were being mysteriously manipulated from within? A look at their source of inspiration illustrates the workings of a law of intellectual fashion that the journalist Paul Berman calls "Parisian determinism"—that is, whatever is the rage in Paris will be fashionable in America fifteen years later.[10]

Michel Foucault, a professor of philosophy at the distinguished Collège de France and an irreverent social thinker who felt deeply alienated from the society in which he lived, introduced his theory of interior disciplines in 1975. His book *Discipline and Punish,* with its novel explanation of how large groups of people could be controlled without the need of exterior controllers, took intellectual Paris by storm. Foucault had little love for the modern democratic state. Like Marx, he was interested in the forces that keep citizens of democracies law-abiding and obedient.

According to Foucault, the individual subjects of contemporary democ- 10
racies are not free at all. Instead, democratic societies turn out to be even more rigidly authoritarian than the tyrannies they replaced. Modern citizens find themselves subject to the rules (he calls them "disciplines") of modern bureaucratic institutions: schools, factories, hospitals, the military, the prisons. In premodern societies, where power was overtly authoritarian, enforcement was inconsistent, haphazard, and inefficient: the king's minions could not be everywhere all the time. In contemporary societies, control is pervasive and unceasing: the modern citizen, having internalized the disciplines of the institutions, polices himself. This results in a "disciplinary society" of "docile" subjects who keep themselves in line with what is expected. According to the philosopher Richard Rorty, Foucault believed he was exposing "a vast organization of repression and injustice."[11] He regarded the multitude of self-disciplined individuals as constituting a "microfascism" that is even more efficiently constraining than the macrofascism of totalitarian states.

How seriously can one take Foucault's theory? Not very, says Princeton political philosopher Michael Walzer, who characterizes Foucault's politics as "infantile leftism."[12] Foucault was aware that he was equating modern democracies with repressively brutal systems like the Soviet prison camps in the Gulag. In a 1977 interview, he showed some concern about how his ideas might be interpreted: "I am indeed worried by a certain use . . . which consists in saying, 'Everyone has their own Gulag, the Gulag is here at our door, in our cities, our hospitals, our prisons, it's here in our heads.'"[13] But, as Walzer points out, so long as Foucault rejected the possibility of individual freedom, which is the moral basis for liberal democracy, it was unclear how he could sustain the distinction between the real Gulag and the one inside the heads of bourgeois citizens.

Foucault's theory has few adherents among social philosophers, but it is nonetheless highly popular among gender feminist theorists, who find his critique of liberal democracy useful for their purposes. Foucault has given them an all-purpose weapon to be used against traditional-minded feminists.

Equity feminists believe that American women have made great progress and that our system of government allows them to expect more. They do not believe that women are "socially subordinate." By contrast, the gender feminists believe that modern women are still in thrall to patriarchy, and Foucault helps them to make their case. When equity feminists point to the gains made by women in recent decades, gender feminists consider them naive. Applying Foucault, they insist that male power *remains* all-pervasive, only now it has become "interiorized" and therefore even more efficient; force is no longer necessary. In effect, they have adopted Foucault's "discourses" to argue that "femininity" itself is really a discipline that continues to degrade and oppress women, even those in the so-called free democracies. As Sandra Lee Bartky puts it:

> No one is marched off for electrolysis at the end of a rifle. . . . Nevertheless . . . the disciplinary practices of femininity . . . must be understood as aspects of a far larger discipline, an oppressive and inegalitarian system of sexual subordination. This system aims at turning women into the docile and compliant companions of men just as surely as the army aims to turn its raw recruits into soldiers.[14]

For Bartky, contemporary American women live in a kind of sexual prison, subject to disciplines that ordain much of their daily lives:

> The woman who checks her make-up half a dozen times a day to see if her foundation has caked or her mascara run, who worries that the wind or rain may spoil her hairdo, who looks frequently to see if her stockings have bagged at the ankle, or who, feeling fat, monitors everything she eats, has become, just as surely as the inmate [under constant surveillance], a self-policing subject, a self committed to a relentless self-surveillance. *This self-surveillance is a form of obedience to patriarchy* [my emphasis].[15]

Catharine MacKinnon presents her own, sexier version of how contemporary women have "interiorized" a self-destructive, self-sustaining, despairing, craven identity that serves men very well and continues to humiliate women:

> Sexual desire in women, at least in this culture, is socially constructed as that by which we come to want our own self-annihilation; that is, our subordination is eroticized; . . . we get off on it, to a degree. This is our stake in this system that is not in our interest, our stake in this system that is killing us. I'm saying that femininity as we know it is how we come to want male dominance, which most emphatically is not in our interest.[16]

MacKinnon rejects "femininity as we know it" because it has come to mean accepting and even desiring male domination. Her militant, gynocentric feminism would teach women to see how deeply, craftily, and deceptively the male culture has socialized them to compliance: "Male dominance is perhaps the most pervasive and tenacious system of power in history. . . . Its force is exercised as consent, its authority as participation."[17]. . .

The assumption that women must defend themselves against an enemy who is waging an undeclared war against them has by now achieved the status of conventional feminist wisdom. In large part, this has happened because seemingly reasonable and highly placed feminists have not seen fit to challenge it. Whether they have been silent because they agree or because they have found it politic to refrain from criticism, I do not know.

Foucault promulgated his doctrine of self-surveillance in the midseventies. By the mideighties, it had turned up in the books of feminist theorists; by the nineties, it had become thematic in feminist best-sellers. Wolf mentions Foucault in her bibliography. Faludi offers him no acknowledgment, but her characterization of the backlash bespeaks his influence:

> The lack of orchestration, the absence of a single string-puller, only makes it harder to see—and perhaps more effective. A backlash against women's rights succeeds to the degree that it appears *not* to be political, that it appears not to be a struggle at all. It is most powerful when it goes private, when it lodges inside a woman's mind and turns her vision inward, until she imagines the pressure is all in her head, until she begins to enforce the backlash too—on herself.[18]

Wolf and Faludi tend to portray the "disciplined" and docile women in the grip of the backlash as Stepford wives—helpless, possessed, and robotic. Wolf sometimes speaks of women as victims of "mass hypnosis." "This is not a conspiracy theory," she reminds us. "It doesn't have to be."[19] Faludi explains how the backlash managed to "infiltrate the thoughts of women, broadcasting on these private channels its sound-waves of shame and reproach."[20]

In addition to Foucauldian theory, Faludi and Wolf have appropriated masses of statistics and studies that "consistently show" the workings of the backlash and the beauty myth and their effects on American women. But although their books are massively footnoted, reliable statistical evidence for the backlash hypothesis is in terribly short supply. According to Wolf, "Recent research consistently shows that inside the majority of the West's controlled, attractive, successful working women, there is a secret 'underlife' poisoning our freedom; infused with notions of beauty, it is a dark vein of self-hatred, physical obsessions, terror of aging, and dread of lost control."[21] The research she cites was done in 1983 at Old Dominion University. She claims that the researchers found that attractive women "compare themselves only to models, not to other women," and feel unattractive. This kind of claim is central to Wolf's contention that images of beautiful, willowy women in fashion magazines demoralize real women. In fact, the study she cited suggested the opposite. The Old Dominion researchers compared the self-reports of three groups of college-age women: one group evaluated themselves after looking at photos of fashion models, another group after looking at pictures of unattractive peers, and a third group after looking at pictures of very attractive peers. The researchers were careful not to exaggerate the significance of this small experiment, but they (tentatively) concluded that although reactions to attractive *peers* negatively influenced women's self-evaluation, exposure to the models had no such effect:

> Perhaps in the eyes of most of our subjects, peer beauty qualified as a more appropriate standard for social comparison than professional beauty. . . . Viewed in a practical sense, our results further suggest that thumbing through popular magazines filled with beautiful models may have little immediate effect on the self-images of most women.[22]

I called the principal author of the study, Thomas Cash, a psychologist 20
at Old Dominion, and asked him what he thought about Ms. Wolf's use of his research. "It had nothing to do with what we found. It made no sense. What I reported was just the opposite of what Wolf claimed. . . . She grabbed it, ran with it, and got it backward."[23] We have already discussed her sensational disclosure that the beauty backlash is wreaking havoc with young women by leading them into a lethal epidemic of anorexia with annual fatalities of 150,000. The actual fatalities appear to be considerably fewer than 100 per year.

Much of the support Wolf brings for her beauty-myth theory consists of merely labeling an activity insidious rather than showing it to be so—exercising, dieting, and buying Lancôme products at the cosmetics counter in Bloomingdale's all come under attack. Characterizing Weight Watchers as a cult does not constitute evidence that it is one. In her zeal to construe every effort of American women to lose weight as a symptom of a male-induced anxiety, she overlooks the fact that many people—men as well as women—suffer from obesity and are threatened by diseases that do not affect people who are fit. Stressing the importance of diet and fitness can hardly be considered as an insidious attempt by the male establishment to disempower women. The desire to achieve greater fitness is perhaps the main motive inspiring both men and women to exercise and to monitor their diets. . . .

Faludi's approach is that of the muckraking reporter bent on saving women by exposing the lies, half-truths, and deceits that the male-oriented media have created to demoralize women and keep them out of the workplace. Her readers might naturally assume that she herself has taken care to be truthful. However, not a few astonished reviewers discovered that *Backlash* relies for its impact on many untruths—some far more serious than any it exposes. In her *New York Times* review, the journalist and feminist Ellen Goodman gently chastised Faludi for overlooking evidence that did not fit her puzzle. But Goodman's tone was so enthusiastic—she praised the book for its "sharp style" and thoroughness—that few heeded her criticisms.[24] Within weeks *Backlash* jumped to the top of the best-seller lists, becoming the hottest feminist book in decades. Faludi was in demand—on the lecture circuit, on talk shows, in book stores, and in print. The more serious criticism came a few months later.

In a letter to the *New York Times Book Review,* Barbara Lovenheim, author of *Beating the Marriage Odds,* reported that she had looked into some of

Faludi's major claims and found them to be erroneous. Her letter presented some egregious examples and concluded that Faludi "skews data, misquotes primary sources, and makes serious errors of omission."[25] Although Lovenheim is a respected and responsible journalist, the review editors of the *Times* have a policy of fact-checking controversial material, and they asked Lovenheim to provide detailed proof that her criticisms of Faludi were well-grounded. She complied, and the *Times* devoted half a page to the publication of Lovenheim's letter. . . .

One of Faludi's more sensational claims—it opens her book—is that there is a concerted effort under way to demoralize successful women by spooking them about a man shortage. Faludi denies that there is a shortage, but Lovenheim shows that the facts do not support her. Though there is no man shortage for women in their twenties and early thirties, things change by the time women reach their midthirties. The census data indicate that between the ages of thirty-five and forty-four, there are 84 single men for every 100 women.[26] There are as many as one million more single women than single men between ages thirty-five and fifty-four. Lovenheim points out that Faludi made it look otherwise by leaving out all divorced and widowed singles.

Faludi responded to Lovenheim's letter two weeks later. She said she 25
"welcomed" attempts to correct "minor inaccuracies." But she could not "help wondering at the possible motives of the letter writer, who is the author of a book called *Beating the Marriage Odds.*" She made an attempt to explain her bizarre claim that older women have a lower incidence of Down's births. The claim was poorly worded, she conceded: she really meant to say that since women over thirty-five tend to be screened for birth defects, many abort their defective fetuses, lowering their rate of live births to babies with this abnormality. She neglected to add that this concession undercuts her larger argument.

After Lovenheim's letter was published, reviewers in several journals began to turn up other serious errors in Faludi's arguments. She had cited, for example, a 1986 article in *Fortune* magazine reporting that many successful women were finding demanding careers unsatisfying and were "bailing out" to accommodate marriage and children. According to Faludi, "The *Fortune* story left an especially deep and troubled impression on young women aspiring to business and management careers. . . . The year after *Fortune* launched the 'bailing out' trend, the proportion of women applying to business schools suddenly began to shrink—for the first time in a decade."

In a review, Gretchen Morgenson of *Forbes* magazine called this thesis "interesting but wrong." She wrote, "There was no shrinkage following the *Fortune* story. According to the American Assembly of Collegiate Schools of Business, which reports on business school graduates, the proportion of women graduates increased every year from 1967 through 1989, the most recent figures available."[27]

Morgenson also deflated Faludi's claim that in the eighties, "women were pouring into many low-paid female work ghettos." United States Bureau of Labor statistics, she pointed out, show that "the percentage of women executives, administrators, and managers among all managers in the American work force has risen from 32.4 percent in 1983 to 41 percent in 1991." Morgenson judged Faludi's book "a labyrinth of nonsense followed by eighty pages of footnotes."[28]. . .

The fact that most women *reject* the divisive radical feminism she has been promoting appears finally to have impressed Ms. Wolf, whose new book, *Fire with Fire*,[29] trumpets a shift from what she calls "victim feminism" to a new "power feminism." Wolf's power feminism turns out to be a version of the classically liberal mainstream feminism with the addition of some contemporary "feel good" themes. To the dismay of many who admired the heated claims of her first book, Wolf now seems to regard American women as individuals who must be encouraged to take charge of their lives rather than whine about mass hypnosis and male conspiracies. The victim feminism whose able spokesperson she had hitherto been she now regards as "obsolete": "It no longer matches up with what women see happening in their lives. And, if feminism, locked for years in the siege mentality that once was necessary, fails to see this change, it may fail to embrace this new era's opportunities."[30]

The new Wolf calls for a feminism that "is tolerant about other women's choices about equality and appearance," a feminism that "does not attack men on the basis of gender," one that "knows that making social change does not contradict the principle that girls just want to have fun."[31]

When I read this, I felt like calling Ms. Wolf to tell her, "All is forgiven!" But I probably would have been unable to refrain from adding, "Well, almost all: was the siege mentality to which you so cleverly contributed in *The Beauty Myth* really necessary?" In the end I'm inclined to chalk up her earlier extremism to the effective indoctrination she got in women's studies at Yale.

Her former allies are not so forgiving. After all, it was only just yesterday that they had been cheering Wolf's descriptions of how women are in mass hypnosis and in thrall to the men who exploit them. On the academic feminist e-mail network, one now sees Wolf reviled and attacked. A typical reaction comes from e-mailer Suzanna Walters, a sociology professor at Georgetown University: "Wolf's book is trash and backlash and everything nasty (including homophobic and racist)."[32]

Get used to this, Ms. Wolf. You'll soon be finding out how it feels to be called antifeminist simply because you refuse to regard men as the enemy and women as their hapless victims. You speak of "the principle that girls just want to have fun." That will doubly offend your erstwhile sisters in arms. First, they prefer all female Americans above the age of fourteen to be referred to as "women." Second, they find the idea that women want to have fun, frivolous and retrograde. You'll be monitored for more such breaches of doctrine. And, in particular, Susan Faludi will now classify you as just another backlasher. . . .

NOTES

1. Susan Faludi, *Backlash: The Undeclared War against American Women* (New York: Crown, 1991); Naomi Wolf, *The Beauty Myth: How Images of Beauty Are Used against Women* (New York: Doubleday, 1992).

2. Wolf 19.
3. Wolf 99.
4. Faludi xxii.
5. Wolf 19.
6. Wolf 4.
7. Wolf 124.
8. According to Faludi, "Just when women's quest for equal rights seemed closest to achieving its objectives, the backlash struck it down. . . . The Republican party elevated Ronald Reagan and both political parties began to shunt women's rights off their platforms" xix.
9. Rep. Patricia Schroeder reviewed *Backlash* for Knight-Ridder Newspapers. I am quoting from the version that appeared in the *Austin American Statesmen* 24 Nov. 1991: E6.
10. Paul Berman mentioned "Parisian determinism" during a discussion at an academic conference. He had good news for those worried about what may be coming next out of Paris: today fashionable French intellectuals are interested in liberalism and human rights, with special attention to writings of James Madison and Thomas Jefferson.
11. Richard Rorty, "Foucault and Epistemology," in David Couzens Hoy, ed., *Foucault: A Critical Reader* (Oxford: Basil, 1986) 47.
12. Michael Walzer, "The Politics of Michel Foucault," in Hoy 51.
13. Michel Foucault, *Power/Knowledge: Selected Interviews and Other Writings, 1972–1977,* ed. Colin Gordon (New York: Random, 1980) 134.
14. Sandra Lee Bartky, *Femininity and Domination: Studies in the Phenomenology of Oppression* (New York: Routledge, 1990), p. 75.
15. Bartky 80.
16. Catharine MacKinnon, "Desire and Power: A Feminist Perspective," in Cary Nelson and Lawrence Grossberg, eds., *Marxism and the Interpretation of Culture* (Chicago: U of Illinois P, 1988) 110.
17. Catharine MacKinnon, *Toward a Feminist Theory of the State* (Cambridge: Harvard UP, 1989) 116–17.
18. Faludi xii.
19. Wolf 17.
20. Faludi 455.
21. Wolf 10.
22. Thomas F. Cash, Diane Walker Cash, and Jonathan W. Butters, " 'Mirror, Mirror on the Wall . . . ?' Contrast Effects and Self-Evaluations of Physical Attractiveness," *Personality and Social Psychology Bulletin* 9.3 (1983): 354–55.
23. Ms. Wolf did not speak to the principal author at Old Dominion, Thomas Cash, and there is some doubt that she ever saw the article she cites. She says, for example, that Cash arrived at his conclusions by studying some of his patients, who, he said, were "extremely attractive." But Cash did not study his patients. At the beginning of the article, he and his coauthors clearly state that they used "a sample of fifty-one female

college students . . . recruited from introductory psychology classes." Dr. Cash told me, "I remember thinking she must be confusing my study with another. I never mentioned anything about my patients, and did not study them."

24. Ellen Goodman, " 'The Man Shortage' and Other Big Lies," *New York Times Book Review* 27 Oct. 1991: 1.
25. Barbara Lovenheim, letter to the *New York Times Book Review* 9 Feb. 1992.
26. Bureau of Census, Current Population Reports, Series P 23, no. 162, June 1989. Cited in Barbara Lovenheim, *Beating the Marriage Odds* (New York: Morrow, 1990) 34.
27. Gretchen Morgenson, "A Whiner's Bible," *Forbes* 16 Mar. 1992: 153.
28. Morgenson 152.
29. Naomi Wolf, *Fire with Fire* (New York: Random, 1993).
30. *Glamour,* Nov. 1993: 224.
31. *Glamour,* 277.
32. S. Walters, Women's Studies Network (Internet: LISTSERV@UMDD.UMD.EDU.), 2 Feb. 1994.

Questions for Discussion

1. What is Sommers's main reason for saying that Wolf and Faludi are mistaken in their arguments? What evidence does Sommers present to deflate their claims?
2. Does reading Sommers's critique of these two works alter your own response to them? Does Sommers offer valid criticism, or would you agree with Deborah Rhode that Sommers engages in "potshot polemics" (see page 358, paragraph 28)? Note that in paragraph 27 Rhode points to an error in Sommers's own reporting of data. Discuss what you might learn from this volley of charges regarding accuracy of the facts in published research.
3. Sommers's tone is angry. What is she angry about? How does her choice of quoted material contribute to the tone? What do you think of Sommers's praise in paragraphs 29–33 for Wolf's later book, *Fire with Fire*? What does she like about it?
4. Reread Sommers's description of Foucault's theory about interior disciplines (paragraphs 9–11). Sommers's summary is hardly unbiased, and you might note what choices she has made as a writer to discredit it as she describes it. Can you explain Foucault's idea in your own words? Would you totally reject this idea? You might also discuss Sommers's argument that calling Foucault's theory into question also calls into question Wolf's and Faludi's arguments.
5. What is Sommers's purpose in attacking the arguments of these two other feminists?

For Inquiry and Convincing/Mediation

Sommers, Wolf, and Faludi address the question of free will versus social control. Inquire into Sommers's argument that women are not victims of social forces and either Wolf's or Faludi's arguments that they are. In each case consider the claim made, the reasons in support, and the evidence offered. How does each writer make her case? How does Sommers show that women freely choose to do things that Wolf would label as self-limiting? How does she show that men have not resisted women's career advances? Does Sommers represent Wolf's or Faludi's claims accurately? Do you think there might be some truth to both perspectives, or are they mutually exclusive ways of explaining social behavior? Decide which case is more convincing to you, and write an argument supporting your view. Or write a mediatory essay that attempts to bring the two viewpoints onto some common ground.

KATIE ROIPHE

The Independent Woman (and Other Lies)

Katie Roiphe is a controversial figure among feminists. Her well-known book The Morning After: Sex, Fear, and Feminism on Campus *(1993) attempted to prove that concern over "date rape" on college campuses was inflated, the result of women's refusal to take responsibility for their own sexual behavior. In this reading, which was originally printed in a men's magazine,* Esquire, *in 1997, she reflects on a recurring fantasy that she knows is politically incorrect in "our liberated, postfeminist world."*

I WAS out to drinks with a man I'd recently met. "I'll take care of that," he said, sweeping up the check, and as he said it, I felt a warm glow of security, as if everything in my life was suddenly going to be taken care of. As the pink cosmopolitans glided smoothly across the bar, I thought for a moment of how nice it would be to live in an era when men always took care of the cosmopolitans. I pictured a lawyer with a creamy leather briefcase going off to work in the mornings and coming back home in the evenings to the townhouse he has bought for me, where I have been ordering flowers, soaking in the bath, reading a nineteenth-century novel, and working idly on my next book. This fantasy of a Man in a Gray Flannel Suit is one that independent, strong-minded women of the nineties are distinctly not supposed to have, but I find myself having it all the same. And many of the women I know are having it also. 1

Seen from the outside, my life is the model of modern female independence. I live alone, pay my own bills, and fix my stereo when it breaks down. But it sometimes seems like my independence is in part an elaborately constructed facade that hides a more traditional feminine desire to be protected and provided for. I admitted this once to my mother, an ardent seventies feminist, over Caesar salads at lunch, and she was shocked. I saw it on her face: How could a daughter of mine say something like this? I rushed to reassure her that I wouldn't dream of giving up my career, and it's true that I wouldn't. But when I think about marriage, somewhere deep in the irrational layers of my psyche, I still think of the man as the breadwinner. I feel as though I am working for "fulfillment," for "reward," for the richness of life promised by feminism, and that mundane things such as rent and mortgages and college tuitions are, ultimately, the man's responsibility—even though I know that they shouldn't be. "I just don't want to have to think about money," one of my most competent female friends said to me recently, and I knew exactly what she meant. Our liberated, postfeminist world seems to be filled with women who don't want to think about money and men who feel that they have to.

There are plenty of well-adjusted, independent women who never fantasize about the Man in the Gray Flannel suit, but there are also a surprising number who do. Of course, there is a well-established tradition of women looking for men to provide for them that spans from Edith Wharton's *The House of Mirth* to Helen Gurley Brown's *Sex and the Single Girl* to Mona Simpson's *A Regular Guy.* You could almost say that this is the American dream for women: Find a man who can lift you out of your circumstances, whisk you away to Venice, and give you a new life.

In my mother's generation, a woman felt she had to marry a man with a successful career, whereas today she is supposed to focus on her own. Consider that in 1990, women received 42 percent of law degrees (up from 2.5 percent in 1960) and that as of 1992, women held 47 percent of lucrative jobs in the professions and management. And now that American women are more economically independent than ever before, now that we don't need to attach ourselves to successful men, many of us still seem to want to. I don't think, in the end, that this attraction is about bank accounts or trips to Paris or hundred dollar haircuts, I think it's about the reassuring feeling of being protected and provided for, a feeling that mingles with love and attraction on the deepest level. It's strange to think of professional women in the nineties drinking cafe lattes and talking about men in the same way as characters in Jane Austen novels, appraising their prospects and fortunes, but many of us actually do.

A friend of mine, an editor at a women's magazine, said about a recent 5
breakup, "I just hated having to say, 'My boyfriend is a dog walker.' I hated the fact that he didn't have a real job." And then immediately afterward, she said, "I feel really awful admitting all of this." It was as if she had just told me something shameful, as if she had confessed to some terrible perversion. And I understand why she felt guilty. She was admitting to a sort of 1950s worldview that seemed as odd and unfashionable as walking down the street in a poodle skirt. But she is struggling with what defines masculinity and femininity in a supposedly equal society, with what draws us to men, what attracts us, what keeps us interested. She has no more reason to feel guilty than a man who says he likes tall blonds.

I've heard many women say that they wouldn't want to go out with a man who is much less successful than they are because "he would feel uncomfortable." But, of course, he's not the only one who would feel uncomfortable. What most of these women are really saying is that they themselves would feel uncomfortable. What most of these women are really saying is that they themselves would feel uncomfortable. But why? Why can't the magazine editor be happy with the dog walker? Why does the woman at Salomon Brothers feel unhappy with the banker who isn't doing as well as she is? Part of it may have to do with the way we were raised. Even though I grew up in a liberal household in the seventies, I perceived early on that my father was the one who actually paid for things. As a little girl, I watched my father put his credit card down in restaurants and write checks and go to work every morning in a suit and tie, and it may be that this model of masculinity is still imprinted in my mind. It may be that there is a picture of our fathers that many of us carry like silver lockets around our necks: Why shouldn't we find a man who will take care of us the way our fathers did?

I've seen the various destructive ways in which this expectation can affect people's lives. Sam and Anna met at Brown. After they graduated, Anna went to Hollywood and started making nearly a million dollars a year in television production, and Sam became an aspiring novelist who has never even filed a tax return. At first, the disparity in their styles of life manifested itself in trivial ways. "She would want to go to an expensive bistro," Sam, who is now twenty-seven, remembers, "and I would want to get a burrito for $4.25. We would go to the bistro, and either she'd pay, which was bad, or I'd just eat salad and lots of bread, which was also bad." In college, they had been the kind of couple who stayed up until three in the morning talking about art and beauty and *The Brothers Karamazov,* but now they seemed to be spending a lot of time arguing about money and burritos. One night, when they went out with some of Anna's Hollywood friends, she slipped him eighty dollars under the table so that he could pretend to pay for dinner. Anna felt guilty. Sam was confused. He had grown up with a feminist mother who'd drummed the ideal of strong, independent women into his head, but now that he'd fallen in love with Anna, probably the strongest and most independent woman he'd ever met, she wanted him to pay for her dinner so badly she gave him money to do it. Anna, I should say, is not a particularly materialistic person, she is not someone who cares about Chanel suits and Prada bags. It's just that to her, money had become a luminous symbol of functionality and power.

The five-year relationship began to fall apart. Sam was not fulfilling the role of romantic lead in the script Anna had in her head. In a moment of desperation, Sam blurted out that he had made a lot of money on the stock market. He hadn't. Shortly afterward, they broke up. Anna started dating her boss, and she and Sam had agonizing long-distance phone calls about what had happened. "She kept telling me that she wanted me to be more of a man," Sam says. "She kept saying that she wanted to be taken care of." There was a certain irony to this situation, to this woman who was making almost a million dollars a year, sitting in her Santa Monica house, looking out at the ocean, saying that she just wanted a man who could take care of her.

There is also something appalling in this story, something cruel and hard and infinitely understandable. The strain of Anna's success and Sam's as of yet unrewarded talent was too much for the relationship. When Anna told Sam that she wanted him to be more masculine, part of what she was saying was that she wanted to feel more feminine. It's like the plight of the too-tall teenage girl who's anxiously scanning the dance floor for a fifteen-year-old boy who is taller than she is. A romantic might say, What about love? Love isn't supposed to be about dollars and cents and who puts their Visa card down at an expensive Beverly Hills restaurant. But this is a story about love in its more tarnished, worldly forms, it's about the balance of power, what men and women really want from one another, and the hidden mechanics of romance and attraction. In a way, what happened between my friends Sam and Anna is a parable of the times, of a generation of strong women who are looking for even stronger men.

10 I've said the same thing as Anna—"I need a man who can take care of me"—to more than one boyfriend, and I hear how it sounds. I recognize how shallow and unreasonable it seems. But I say it anyway. And, even worse, I actually feel it.

The mood passes. I realize that I can take care of myself. The relationship returns to normal, the boyfriend jokes that I should go to the bar at the plaza to meet bankers, and we both laugh because we know that I don't really want to, but there is an undercurrent of resentment, eddies of tension and disappointment that remain between us. This is a secret refrain that runs through conversations in bedrooms late at night, through phone wires, and in restaurants over drinks. One has to wonder, why, at a moment in history when women can so patently take care of themselves, do so many of us want so much to be taken care of?

The fantasy of a man who pays the bills, who works when you want to take time off to be with your kids or read *War and Peace,* who is in the end responsible, is one that many women have but fairly few admit to. It is one of those fantasies, like rape fantasies, that have been forbidden to us by our politics. But it's also deeply ingrained in our imaginations. All of girl culture tells us to find a man who will provide for us, a Prince Charming, a Mr. Rochester, a Mr. Darcy, a Rhett Butler. These are the objects of our earliest romantic yearnings, the private desires of a whole country of little girls, the fairy tales that actually end up affecting our real lives. As the feminist film critic Molly Haskell says, "We never really escape the old-fashioned roles. They get inside our heads. Dependence has always been eroticized."

Many of the men I know seem understandably bewildered by the fact that women want to be independent only sometimes, only sort of, and only selectively. The same women who give eloquent speeches at dinner parties on the subject of "glass ceilings" still want men to pay for first dates, and this can be sort of perplexing for the men around them who are still trying to fit into the puzzle that the feminism of the seventies has created for them. For a long time, women have been saying that we don't want a double standard, but it sometimes seems that what many women want is simply a more subtle and refined version of a double standard: We want men to be the providers and to regard us as equals. This slightly unreasonable expectation is not exactly new. In 1963, a reporter asked Mary McCarthy what women really wanted, and she answered, "They want everything. That's the trouble—they can't have everything. They can't possibly have all the prerogatives of being a woman and the privileges of being a man at the same time."

"We're spoiled," says Helen Gurley Brown, one of the world's foremost theorists on dating. "We just don't want to give up any of the good stuff." And she may have a point. In a world in which women compete with men, in which all of us are feeling the same drive to succeed, there is something reassuring about falling—if only for the length of a dinner—into traditional sex roles. You can just relax. You can take a rest from yourself. You can let the pressures and ambitions melt away and give in to the archaic fantasy: For just half an hour, you are just a pretty girl smiling at a man over a drink. I think that old-fashioned rituals, such as men paying for dates, endure precisely because of how much has actually changed; they cover up the fact that men and women are equal and that equality is not always, in all contexts and situations, comfortable or even desirable.

This may explain why I have been so ungratefully day-dreaming about 15
the Man in the Gray Flannel Suit thirty years after Betty Friedan published *The Feminine Mystique.* The truth is, the knowledge that I can take care of myself, that I don't really need a man, is not without its own accompanying terrors. The idea that I could make myself into a sleek, self-sufficient androgyne is not all that appealing. Now that we have all of the rooms of our own that we need, we begin to look for that shared and crowded space. And it is this fear of independence, this fear of not needing a man, that explains the voices of more competent, accomplished corporate types than me saying to the men around them, "Provide for me, protect me." It may be one of the bad jokes that history occasionally plays on us: that the independence my mother's generation wanted so much for their daughters was something we could not entirely appreciate or want. It was like a birthday present from a distant relative—wrong size, wrong color, wrong style. And so women are left struggling with the desire to submit and not submit, to be dependent and independent, to take care of ourselves and be taken care of, and it's in the confusion of this struggle that most of us love and are loved.

For myself, I continue to go out with poets and novelists and writers, with men who don't pay for dates or buy me dresses at Bergdorf's or go off to their offices in the morning, but the Man in the Gray Flannel Suit lives on in my imagination, perplexing, irrational, revealing of some dark and unsettling truth.

Questions for Discussion

1. Do you agree with Roiphe that "marrying up" is the woman's version of the American Dream? What is the man's version? Are the genders blurring in their views of achieving success? Are men likely to aspire to "marry up"—or does that violate social definitions of masculinity?
2. While this seems to be a personal essay, Roiphe is making an argument here. What is her claim? What is her evidence? What are some key terms—for example, what does she mean by "need" when she speaks of her fear of "not needing a man" (paragraphs 10 and 16)? What assumptions is she making about men? What assumptions about working women? (You might consider what she means by "androgyne" in paragraph 16.) What are the

implications of her argument? Is it realistic, given today's economy? today's divorce rates? Finally, do you think she is serious about this argument, or is she merely sharing an escapist daydream?

3. In paragraphs 4 and 9 Roiphe says that women's attraction to successful men is not just about financial security. What else is it about, as you interpret these paragraphs?

For Convincing

Roiphe quotes Molly Haskell as saying, "We never really escape the old-fashioned roles. They get inside our heads. Dependence has always been eroticized" (paragraph 13). Roiphe gives examples of how our culture romanticizes female dependence in works like *Gone with the Wind* and characters like Prince Charming. She does not complain that such messages do harm to women, but rather she complains that women must now reject these, along with rape fantasies, as politically incorrect. What do you think? Do you agree that our culture sends girls and women messages that associate women's sexuality with domination by men? Consider film, fiction, fashion promotions, and music. What conclusions do you draw? Are these messages harmful to women? Decide on an appropriate audience, and write to convince them of your conclusions.

For Inquiry

Roiphe argues that our culture ingrains in women the idea that domination by men is romantic and protective. Compare Roiphe's view with Christina Sommers's rejection of Foucault's theory of internal discipline. Note Sommers's insistence that Catherine MacKinnon is wrong when she says, "Sexual desire in women, at least in this culture, is socially constructed; . . . our subordination is eroticized; . . . we get off on it, to a degree. . . . [F]emininity as we know it is how we come to want male dominance, which most emphatically is not in our interest." Is it possible that women could be led to prefer a gender identity that keeps them subordinate and repressed? You might consider looking at studies of adolescent girls that examine whether they suffer a loss of self-confidence when they enter puberty. The book *Reviving Ophelia* by Mary Pipher offers case studies and analyses of girls' problems. Pipher argues that girls receive strong messages to give up androgynous qualities and "shrink their souls down to petite size."

ELIZABETH MITCHELL

An Odd Break with the Human Heart

The following essay appeared in a collection entitled To Be Real: Telling the Truth and Changing the Face of Feminism, *edited by Rebecca Walker. Walker, cofounder of a feminist group called Third Wave, writes in the preface that the authors, all young women, see their mothers' brand of feminism as conforming to an "identity and way of living that doesn't allow for individuality [and] complexity." In this essay Mitchell reflects upon the traditional "feminine" gender role of nurturing and selflessness but argues that a "break with the human heart" ought to free women from the community obligations of sisterhood and identity politics that she sees as characteristic of second-wave feminists.*

MUDDY, WILD-EYED, some of them hairless, all of them shoeless, my dolls must be somewhere waiting for me. They're probably in my parents' attic, slumped against each other, my distinct levels of affection for each of them written on their bodies. Missing limbs indicate a favorite; smooth hair marks one received too late for me to care. 1

If I had as much free time now as I had during childhood, when I could devote half the afternoon to reading and riding my bike, and the other half to staring at the ceiling and imagining it flooded, I'm sure I would collapse under the weight of my guilt. It's not that I did my dolls wrong, but that I secretly resented them. They made me a mother too soon.

As a child, dolls were my children. Empathy came easily then, and adults fostered it with their encouragement of maternal gestures. Is the baby tired? Is it sick? Does it want to go outside? The classic picture books that were read to me undercut my annoyance with my orphanage of stuffed playthings and exaggerated my guilt: a toy bear on a store shelf is heartsick until a little girl finally sees beyond his frailties and brings him home. A despondent velveteen rabbit is abandoned by a child who did the unspeakable: he grew up. I would take these tales to heart and then spend the afternoon silently batting a vacant-eyed doll in a shoebox swing.

My brothers, in contrast, could be entertained by their toys, educated at whatever minor level by their racetracks and craft kits and mechanical gadgets. The world was new to me too, the strength of my arms and legs untested, but I was given the responsibility of caring for another object that contained only what I invested in it. How would I now work out the politics of who would sleep in my bed? How would I talk to my toy? I would have wished for a magnifying glass; instead I was coached to play with a mirror. What could I possibly learn? That my primary responsibility was to others, that I should shower love on something that gives me nothing in return?

My three-year-old niece often worries over a fluffy white rabbit. She tends to a number of other dolls and animals, too, but when she invited me 5 out for a walk on the day she received her first tricycle, it was the rabbit that came along, packed into the front basket so that it could get some air. Every time we approached a buckle in the sidewalk, my niece would dismount the tricycle and wheel it over, explaining to me that she didn't want the rabbit to get too violently jarred. She had made the doll a voodoo icon of herself. Clearly, she was too scared to negotiate these obstacles her first time out, but the feeling was better projected on to some other entity—as if, already, it would be unseemly for her to elicit concern about her own worries. She had made her empathy total. Watching her efforts, I, like a traitor, felt overwhelmed by how sweet she was in her compassion, but I felt troubled too, by how prepared she was for the life of a girl. Through dolls, the heart muscles of females are strengthened, ensuring that they will be ruled by compassion and, through that compassion, by others, for the rest of their lives.

Like it or not, we women are community-oriented. We are easy marks, for example, for high-powered peer pressure. Madison Avenue bombards us with messages about acceptable appearance, and we respond with astronomical spending on skin and hair. And if you look at the most antisocial behavior—violent crime—you'll find that we play a correspondingly minimal role: women account for only 6 percent of the national total. It would be impossible to say whether our instinct to serve and preserve communities is essential (i.e., biological) or simply socialized, but it is undeniably powerful.

I find it telling that even many of the most militant feminists are unable to act selfishly. Eileen MacDonald's book on female guerrillas, *Shoot the Women First,* derives its title from a warning supposedly issued in the last few decades to antiterrorist squad recruits in Germany. Intelligence-gathering networks found that once women had crossed over into the guerrilla life, they became more dangerous than their male counterparts. They would not hesitate to begin an exchange of fire; they persisted more passionately in the struggle; and they were more willing to take chances. Most of these women based their beliefs on feminism. And they were drawn to the rebel's pose. Astrid Proll, an early member of the anticapitalist Red Army Faction, which first bloomed in Germany in the seventies and continued its advocacy of violence into the early nineties, told MacDonald: "You must understand that then the most fantastic thing in the world was not to be a rock star, but a revolutionary."

MacDonald found that these women were impelled to transgress their traditional roles as peacekeepers because they felt doubly oppressed—both politically (because of ethnicity, ideology, or religious belief) and socially (because they were women). What allowed them to move from internalizing their protest to projecting it to the public realm, one could argue, was their sense that there was no true community to protect in the first place. Nothing of worth could be destroyed in the violence because the very foundations of society were so dangerously fissured. Their violence was loaded with ideological meaning, the culmination of a political diatribe. But even among these women, who had risked everything and broken every taboo, they persisted in seeing themselves as servants of a principle. Their cause was frequently referred to as a surrogate, a child, even a "son." The women were acting on his behalf.

The women of my mother's generation seemed given to this same sort of communal effort, winning victories for the feminist movement, for their sisters, for their daughters. They had the comfort of knowing that what they fought for was needed by all members of their gender; sexual freedom, equal opportunity in the workplace, access to all the institutions of power. They also had more clear-cut antagonists to act against: people, usually men, whose goal it seemed was to siphon off their strength, experience, and knowledge. The world has by no means become perfect for women, but the troubles, at least for middle- and upper-class women in the United States, have grown less glaring. What values do we all seek as a gender, we have to wonder, and how do we fight for them? Who is now the enemy?

Lately, I have felt the need for a new type of female rebel because I *10*
recognize that the limitations that tether me may be both harder to identify and to sever than the ones that my mother and her generation fought against. Now that we've broken the barriers that once kept us out of law schools and board rooms, we have unearthed another, more hidden source of many of our limitations: the human heart. Suddenly, as the curtain parts, we see a deeper and more beguiling force at work in constructing a self for ourselves. These are the commitments to our loved ones and friends, and their dreams for us of a self that fits into their lives neatly and cozily, like a puzzle piece. These are the wishes of a parent or the sway of feminism on our career choices.

To overcome these forces, and to look at our lives autonomously, we need to shrug off what we women have been trained to care about above all else: other people, their thoughts, feelings, and concerns. We need to put the training we received when we cared for dolls into perspective. Or we will be compelled to experience only shadow lives.

This is not to say that everyone I know is held back by ties to their community. Many women I know have identified their own ambitions and—more importantly—their own desires, and have dared to be self-interested. But many others have not. None of us would question our abilities to do a job as well as a man, but too often we don't risk leaving our ministering roles to pursue our own vision. While we are able to focus on what we know would make us feel satisfied, we remain addicted to institutions—to schools, workplaces, and other symbols of accomplishment. The rules of our lives have been changed by the women's movement, but for many women, these rules have brought with them a new set of limits, not a new sense of freedom.

Obviously, many factors influence the degree to which one's life is dictated by others. Financial need can limit certain freedoms, as can a family that is close and protective. The people I know who have traveled the farthest, taken the biggest risks, and spoken with the most freedom have often felt ostracized from society or their families. This is not to say that a terrible mother or father will make you ultimately happy; but family troubles may lead you to feel liberated.

I personally have never been away for very long from my hometown in Connecticut—probably ten months at most. Nor have I returned there for more than a few weeks at a time in the last decade. I go back for short visits, my eye selecting the fragments of landscape that seem most evocative of my youth: the thin clapboard houses, the clean yards, the sandy roads, the gray bark of trees, a sky that seems stained a perpetual, petulant dun color. It probably is not. The state has a reputation for quaint and verdant scenery; I'm sure I am just imagining the bleakness.

15 The weight I feel settling fully in my heart as the car races toward home is neither sentimentality, nostalgia, nor hostility. This is where the entire clan on my mother's side was born, raised, and currently lives. Down the street from my parents' house is my elementary school; ten blocks away is the publishing company where I held my first job, breaking the gender barrier as their first office girl. At the bottom of the hill is the Catholic church where my parents were married, I was confirmed, and where, as a teenager, my anger reverberated with the organ pipes. The similarity of each day in these towns seems to blend toward eternity. When I wander around here, life doesn't look empty; it seems uncomfortably full of meaning, and a pervasive solemnity tends to wash away my hope for a self-realized future.

I was not born into sisterhood: I closed a line of sons. And so my search for a feminist self is most naturally not a communal enterprise but one against, and for, my mother and her generation. My mother keeps me on a long leash. To some extent, she seems to use me as a proxy to fight her demons of self-doubt and insecurity, and to battle the sexism and limitations that she has seen but would hate to name as discrimination. I move away from home, traveling farther, earning more, putting off motherhood. She's very proud. Then I hear the soft swish of the chain through the dust. I am not exactly towed back in, but held at the run of my tether. I hear that she's been asking my brothers, "Has she talked yet of children?"

That anxiousness for me to give birth, I know, is a cipher for another desire. Now that I am in my late twenties, everyone wants to extol to me the glory of babies. My uncle reminds me frequently that he has a carriage waiting for my use. My four-year-old nephew asks me why I don't have a child yet, since after all they're fun and you can play with their toys. Even my chatty cab driver tells me I should breed soon.

In our society, babies have come to represent everything but unmaturated human beings. They function as the nexus for debate and discussion in a world changed by feminism. Few people expect women's love relationships to resemble those of our grandmothers or our mothers, but most still wonder how anyone could reject children. For my mother and many in her generation, babies are our safety net. If everything goes wrong in this wild new world of female emancipation, at least I can say that I bore children. For some, a baby provides the guarantee of domesticity; a child will anchor me at home, where my loved ones or family can find me. For my nephew, it is the doll that I need to qualify as a real girl.

For me and most of my female peers, having children lies down the road, like a can we keep kicking and catching up to. But I don't want all the hope of life to reside in the beginning of a new human being. I want that anticipation to reside in an unborn part of myself, whether it be intellectual, spiritual, or emotional. I want to push myself toward this self-realization, but I am hounded by anxieties, among which three are particularly powerful: one, that the notion of self-realization is an illusion, ultimately indistinguishable from self-aggrandizement. Two, that because my self-interest is hazy to me, my movement toward what I think I want will actually lead me on a path to what I dread; that my dreams of complete freedom, like my childhood fantasies of being a back-up dancer for the Beatles, will expose themselves as wrongheaded with the years. And three, that the sobriety of the community where I was born, or rather, of which I was born, will call me back. With only a touch of grim humor, my elders repeatedly espoused certain scraps of advice: "Always remember, no job is fun. Working a 'dumb job' is better than pursuing a less secure, desired job. Life isn't going to be exciting every minute." None of these are outrageously dark in and of themselves. But together, they compose a drumbeat of resignation. Nathaniel Hawthorne would be proud that the old New England spirit lives on.

Feminism enters this world like a life raft. Its message, in stark contrast, 20
seems to be wholly optimistic. If you remain strong, self-reliant, angry at the right times, supportive, and, when given the opportunity, ambitious to break new ground for the gender, then everything will work out well. You will feel at peace with yourself. But whether intended or not, feminism usually celebrates power; it holds up politically motivated women to idolize: the founder of a feminist journal or the leader of a local uprising. Simultaneously, it encourages a suppression of the ego in homage to the greater good of sisterhood. And those images are infectious, especially to those of us who have not given up on feminism yet, who want it not just to change institutions but the quality of all women's lives. To be a great woman, I should prioritize the common good, whether that involves a communal task or merely rising higher in my profession, functioning as a symbol of my gender in the social hierarchy.

I should place my life on the altar of our continued struggle, but in my heart I only want to be an explorer of the world, free to move where I want. I am less concerned with making enough money to buy beauty than in finding beauty in the Badlands or the frozen Baltic Sea.

Back when I was in third grade, our teacher would run a column in the class-produced newsletter, listing each child's dreams for the future. Veterinarians were in abundance, as were mothers and race-car drivers. At that age, such visions of an imaginary future are considered adorable. Parents like to look at the lists and chuckle at how bold, how perfect, or perhaps how prescient their children's choices are. By high school, no one seems to care much about what teenagers aspire to; they'd rather judge "Most Popular" or predict "Most Likely to Succeed." At that point, society has asserted its interest, clearly letting us know what is expected of us. By young adulthood, we've usually come up with new visions of a fulfilling life—and learned to keep those fantasies to ourselves.

By the time we're adults, feminism has given us confidence, but oddly only within the context of competition with men—and primarily within social constructs that already exist. When, for example, I am offered the opportunity of power in the workplace, no matter how minor, I feel urged to take it, like an addict, to demonstrate the talents of my gender, to stand as a marker for the shifting demographics in the white-collar workplace, to take the path my mother's generation hewed for me: to a desk, a regular paycheck, a Rolodex.

I am well aware that I could perform in a job as well as a man, but can I achieve autonomous, personal excellence? Without clear markers for this kind of success, many women in my generation, including myself, feel ill at ease. If one can refer to a graduate degree, a title of employment, a project involving many other people, then one's efforts are taken seriously. We are differentiated from our mother's generation or the generation before that. We feel secure with the definitions of success that have always existed in this country.

When I consider these definitions, these traditions, these constraints, I 25
feel the urge to call upon women to rebel, but I struggle to define what the benefit of rebellion would be. The old rewards seem too empty. I suspect the true goal would be the perpetual pursuit of joy. In seeking joy, the agonies would not disappear—perhaps, in fact, happiness would rarely materialize—but the human gesture would be toward delight, and that pursuit, I believe, must begin with the individual. Groups or movements can bring equality. Only individuals can achieve ecstasy.

Part of the challenge of living out one's own vision is that it demands an odd break with the hyperactivity of the human heart. We women have the profound ability to see ourselves everywhere—in every person, in virtually every role, in the way that my niece could see her own fears reflected in a stuffed rabbit.

Compassion, love, and empathy are all important values, and extremely attractive. But in women, they can become debilitating, even dangerous. Why do women stay in threatening relationships, for example? I don't want to simplify this. There are obviously a zillion reasons, among them financial dependency, the fear of being alone, and the terror of retribution. But also, I believe, is that flicker of compassion that forfeits all self-preservation. And why does that empathy spark? Because the other person had austere parents, a hard day at work; because he or she breathes, because he or she merely exists. In love, as an adult, I challenge myself not to give away my heart like a pacifier. I try to stop the hair trigger of my empathy, to keep myself from offering my affection purely as the salve that will restore peace to a troubled soul. It's necessary to offer compassion, but love should not be confused with pity.

We need to identify where our own passions lie and isolate them from what we think other people want for us. What do *we* want to do with our lives? Whom do *we* choose to love? These questions are not easy to sort out, nor can anyone predict what is right for another person. In fact, to do so would be antithetical to this call to action. But we should give each other respect and leeway, recognizing that the true pursuit of a fully realized self, when it is in process, is often less automatically attractive or valued than the empty exercise of power.

Of course the process will never cease, I recognize that my life will not be easily partitioned into the before and after of an epiphany inspired by a life led by true desire. Perhaps my veil of anxiety will never lift. I will await myself the way I linger for a friend on a mountain lookout, allowing them the moment when they will recognize the mysterious cue that allows them to leave. Am I done yet? Am I ready to go back and sort through the aspirations and ambitions that my loved ones bequeathed me, as they did the dolls, and figure out which ones are worth my respect, my time, my effort?

To some extent, I suppose I have already begun this process. Despite the 30
fact that there are many influences from my community I have put off, part of what I am taking on in at least temporarily rejecting the demands of my family, my friends, my gender, is an option my mother—who loves to travel but rarely does, who adores journalism but gave it up for marriage and children—has always wanted me to have: the exquisite agony of being an individual and the awful luxury of feeling unsettled.

Questions for Discussion

1. What is Mitchell's argument against dolls? Do you agree with her comparison of the way girls and boys are encouraged to interact with their toys?
2. Mitchell is the child of an active second-wave feminist. What pressures does she feel her mother in particular and the feminist movement in general have placed upon her? Do these sound like reasonable complaints, or does Mitchell sound ungrateful? Why does she not want to join the "sisterhood" of feminists?
3. Mitchell wants to be an independent woman. Compare her views of independence with those of Katie Roiphe in the preceding essay. Do they both admit to some fears? Compare the two authors' versions of safety nets for women who want to retreat from "the exquisite agony of being an individual."
4. There are plenty of arguments in our culture holding that true happiness and success come only when we do not put ourselves and our ambitions first. We certainly hear this from religion and from some areas of popular culture, such as films like *Mr. Holland's Opus*. How do students in your class respond to these arguments? Are they realistic career advice?

For Inquiry

In this essay Mitchell explores the tensions between what she wants for herself and what others want for her. She discusses the arguments made by feminists, the arguments made by family and friends, and the arguments of her own heart, which she fears may be foolish and selfish. Do you feel pulled in different directions about your future and your ideas of success? If so, write an essay exploring the arguments on various sides. Whether you are male or female, consider if you are pulled toward community, compassion, and self-sacrifice on the one hand and more individualistic values on the other. If you feel no dilemmas about self versus community, why do you think that is so?

For Persuasion

If you are involved in a campus or community service organization or activist group, make an argument for joining a group effort. What do you feel the group is accomplishing that would otherwise not get done? Why do you feel the sacrifice of your time and effort is worthwhile? Write an editorial for your local or campus paper aimed at persuading others to join.

An Ad for Women's Jeans

The following advertisement for women's jeans originally appeared in fashion magazines such as Elle *and* Vogue. *What persuasive techniques does it use?*

Created for men.

lingerie catalogs

hair coloring

string bikini

breast implants

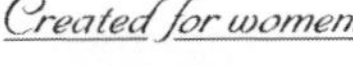
Created for women.

LAWMAN
JEANS
They fit who you are.

For Discussion

The ad for Lawman jeans uses both text and images to make an argument for buying the jeans that "fit who you are." Who is "you"? What do you infer about the audience that Lawman is trying to reach? How would you explicitly state the argument for the jeans? What is it suggesting about its competitors' jeans? Do you agree with the implication that women buy the items "created for men" in order to make themselves into something they are not?

For Further Research and Discussion

1. Research Elizabeth Cady Stanton's nineteenth-century arguments for communal living and child-rearing arrangements. What were her objections to traditional marriage and family?
2. One factor that makes it difficult for American women to have a career and a family is that the United States is one of the few countries that does not have some type of government-supported day care. Look into the arrangements that other countries have made that assist working mothers.
3. Cassandra Langer's account stresses the feminist assertion that "the personal is political," but she has omitted from her history a discussion of women's struggle to acquire knowledge and means of birth control. Reread paragraphs 18 and 19. Look into Margaret Sanger's efforts to win this right for women and the resistance she met from men of her day. How might Langer have used this information in her explanation of sexual politics?
4. Since writing *The Beauty Myth,* Naomi Wolf has published another book, *Fire with Fire* (1993), in which she argues for a version of feminism that would make women the equals of men but would not deny them their sexuality. Read both Friedan's *The Second Stage* and Wolf's *Fire with Fire,* and compare their suggested revisions to feminism.

Additional Suggestions for Writing

1. *Convincing.* Those who support same-sex education for girls argue that females achieve more when males are not in the academic environment. Look into the arguments for and against sexually segregated education for women. One argument in favor is that women have different learning styles from men; for example, some proponents say that women learn better in less competitive, more collaborative environments. Recent studies have shown that girls' sense of identity and self-confidence is as strong as that of boys until they reach the age of twelve or thirteen. Do girls become less self-assured as they enter puberty? What theories explain this change? Could anxieties about their femininity be behind the problem? You probably have experiences and observations of your own pertaining to these questions. After you have inquired into the subject, make a case for your position on sexually segregated education.

2. *Persuasion.* After considering the goals of feminism and the possible definitions of "femininity," decide if it is possible to be feminine and a feminist. As you inquire, think about who decides what is feminine—men or women or both sexes? Research the biographies of some leading feminists: Would they serve as examples to support your position? Why do so many people have an image (Naomi Wolf calls it a "hallucination") of the Ugly Feminist? Write a persuasive argument aimed at college women, taking either the position that they can be feminists without losing their femininity *or* the position that, at least in our society today, being a feminist necessarily makes a woman appear less feminine.
3. *Analysis persuasion.* The consumer culture is very persuasive—toward men, women, and children. Inquire into how advertising might be contributing to some common form of behavior in American society today. Is this behavior in the self-interest of the group targeted by the advertising? Is it in the best interest of society as a whole? Or is it merely in the interest of the business or organization sponsoring the advertisement? Consider how visual images contribute to the persuasion. You might want to look at student Kelly Williams's essay on pages 221–223 to see how one student looked at one advertisement that she believes aimed to make mothers conform to a stereotyped image. Write an essay, with or without graphic support, aimed at persuading the target audience to resist the arguments you have selected.

CHAPTER TWELVE

Marriage and Family

Strictly speaking, a *family* is a group of people bound by blood or law. But a technical definition does not come close to explaining the meaning of family. The obligations and responsibilities that family members have for one another and the relation of young to old, of present to past generations, of individual to family, of husband to wife (or in some cultures, husband to wives)—all are examples of ways "family" may differ if we look at it across time and culture. In the United States today we commonly think of family as the "nuclear family"—that is, a man and a woman, a marriage based on their love for each other, children born to them or adopted, and a sharing of responsibilities based on traditional roles for men and women. But we know that in reality, families can be childless couples, unwed mothers or divorced parents and their children, blended families of multiple marriages or partnerships, and even a child with five parents. We also know that some fathers and mothers reverse the traditional roles of male breadwinner and female homemaker, or they share equally in both roles.

With all of these departures from the stereotypical model, many today claim that the family is in crisis, owing mainly to changes in traditional gender roles and in traditional attitudes toward marriage. The main concern is: What are the effects of these changes on America's children? A society is justified in placing such topics on the table of public discourse because problems created in the home become the problems of the society as a whole. When we look at children today, we cannot deny that we find behavior problems in school, drug and alcohol use, and crimes that we used to think children were incapable of committing.

But can we point to changes in the family as the source of these problems? And if we can find a correlation between these trends and broken or fatherless homes, what can be done to restore the family? Proponents of "family values" claim that premarital sex, uncommitted spouses, and unwed motherhood indicate a need for traditional values. They offer a range of suggestions for restoring such values, including government policies, education, and moral exhortation. But liberals respond that changes in the family represent responses to broad social and economic forces that would be hard to turn back, and ask what policies and values can best support the families that exist, as they exist.

The readings in this section provide arguments from a variety of viewpoints on divorce, working mothers, single parents, and other departures from the traditional model. The first reading, "The Paradox of Perfection" by Arlene Skolnick, holds our stereotypical ideal of the "traditional" family up to the light of history to show that our model of the family may be unrealistic and even destructive. The selections by Midge Decter and Betty Holcomb focus on changing ideas about gender roles and the sacrifices involved in raising children. Do mothers and fathers make different kinds of sacrifices? David Popenoe argues that fathers perform vital and unique roles in child-rearing.

Popenoe's, Stephanie Coontz's, and Barbara Whitehead's essays all look at marriage as an institution feeling the pressures of change. Coontz shows how forces in American society—economic, social, even scientific—have lessened the role of marriage in organizing our relationships, making it more of an option than a necessity. Whitehead argues against the attitudes and policies that she believes have encouraged a "culture" of divorce in the United States. Finally, Popenoe makes an urgent plea that we return to traditional ideas about marriage in order to restore the role of fathers, whose disappearance from the family, owing mainly to divorce, he sees as disastrous for our nation's children.

As you read these essays, from the left and the right, on the fragility or durability of the family, keep in mind that Americans have not only one of the highest divorce rates in the world but also the highest marriage rate. Furthermore, according to Arlene Skolnick, "We are the most traditionalist of Western nations in our family values."[1] And she reminds us that Americans are ambivalent, cherishing the ideal of the family but accepting the reality of individual families and their problems.

[1] Arlene Skolnick, "Family Values: The Sequel," *The American Prospect* May–June 1997: 86–94.

ARLENE SKOLNICK

The Paradox of Perfection

Arlene Skolnick, a psychologist at the University of California, Berkeley, has written many works on the family, the most recent of which is Family in Transition *(1998). "The Paradox of Perfection" is an earlier work, originally published in 1980 in the* Wilson Quarterly, *but it continues to be reprinted because it offers a history of the American family prior to World War II that is both concise and interestingly detailed. Skolnick argues that modern discussions of the family "lack ballast" because they focus on a post–World War II model of the nuclear family. If we don't look back further in time, we can have no understanding of how that model became entrenched in our collective consciousness. As you read, notice how Skolnick uses evidence from history to support her argument that the ideal is not only mythical but harmful to the family.*

THE AMERICAN Family, as even readers of *Popular Mechanics* must know by now, is in what Sean O'Casey would have called "a terrible state of chassis." Yet, there are certain ironies about the much-publicized crisis that give one pause. 1

True, the statistics seem alarming. The U.S. divorce rate, though it has reached something of a plateau in recent years, remains the highest in American history. The number of births out-of-wedlock among all races and ethnic groups continues to climb. The plight of many elderly Americans subsisting on low fixed incomes is well known.

What puzzles me is an ambiguity, not in the facts, but in what we are asked to make of them. A series of opinion polls conducted in 1978 by Yankelovich, Skelley, and White, for example, found that 38 percent of those surveyed had recently witnessed one or more "destructive activities" (e.g., a divorce, a separation, a custody battle) within their own families or those of their parents or siblings. At the same time, 92 percent of the respondents said the family was highly important to them as a "personal value."

Can the family be at once a cherished "value" and a troubled institution? I am inclined to think, in fact, that they go hand in hand. A recent "Talk of the Town" report in *The New Yorker* illustrates what I mean:

> A few months ago word was heard from Billy Gray, who used to play brother Bud in "Father Knows Best," the 1950s television show about the nice Anderson family who lived in the white frame house on a side street in some mythical Springfield—the house at which the father arrived each night swinging open the front door and singing out "Margaret, I'm home!" Gray said he felt "ashamed" that he had ever had anything to do with the show. It was all "totally false," he

> said, and had caused many Americans to feel inadequate, because they thought that was the way life was supposed to be and that their own lives failed to measure up.

As Susan Sontag has noted in *On Photography,* mass-produced images 5
have "extraordinary powers to determine our demands upon reality." The family is especially vulnerable to confusion between truth and illusion. What, after all, is "normal"? All of us have a backstairs view of our own families, but we know The Family, in the aggregate, only vicariously.

Like politics or athletics, the family has become a media event. Television offers nightly portrayals of lump-in-the-throat family "normalcy" ("The Waltons," "Little House on the Prairie") and, nowadays, even humorous "deviance" ("One Day at a Time," "The Odd Couple"). Family advisers sally forth in syndicated newspaper columns to uphold standards, mend relationships, suggest counseling, and otherwise lead their readers back to the True Path. For commercial purposes, advertisers spend millions of dollars to create stirring vignettes of glamorous-but-ordinary families, the kind of family most 11-year-olds wish they had.

All Americans do not, of course, live in such a family, but most share an intuitive sense of what the "ideal" family should be—reflected in the precepts of religion, the conventions of etiquette, and the assumptions of law. And, characteristically, Americans tend to project the ideal back into the past, the time when virtues of all sorts are thought to have flourished.

We do not come off well by comparison with that golden age, nor could we, for it is as elusive and mythical as Brigadoon. If Billy Gray shames too easily, he has a valid point: While Americans view the family as the proper context for their own lives—9 out of 10 people live in one—they have no realistic context in which to view the family. Family history, until recently, was as neglected in academe as it still is in the press. The familiar, depressing charts of "leading family indicators"—marriage, divorce, illegitimacy—in newspapers and newsmagazines rarely survey the trends before World War II. The discussion, in short, lacks ballast.

Let us go back to before the American Revolution.

Perhaps what distinguishes the modern family most from its colonial 10
counterpart is its newfound privacy. Throughout the 17th and 18th centuries, well over 90 percent of the American population lived in small rural communities. Unusual behavior rarely went unnoticed, and neighbors often intervened directly in a family's affairs, to help or to chastise.

The most dramatic example was the rural "charivari," prevalent in both Europe and the United States until the early 19th century. The purpose of these noisy gatherings was to censure community members for familial transgressions—unusual sexual behavior, marriages between persons of grossly discrepant ages, or "household disorder," to name but a few. As historian Edward Shorter describes it in *The Making of the Modern Family:*

> Sometimes the demonstration would consist of masked individuals circling somebody's house at night, screaming, beating on pans, and blowing cow horns . . . on other occasions, the offender would be seized and marched through the streets, seated perhaps backwards on a donkey or forced to wear a placard describing his sins.

The state itself had no qualms about intruding into a family's affairs by statute, if necessary. Consider 17th-century New England's "stubborn child" laws that, though never actually enforced, sanctioned the death penalty for chronic disobedience to one's parents.

If the boundaries between home and society seem blurred during the colonial era, it is because they were. People were neither very emotional nor very self-conscious about family life, and, as historian John Demos points out, family and community were "joined in a relation of profound reciprocity." In his *Of Domesticall Duties,* William Gouge, a 17th-century Puritan preacher, called the family "a little community." The home, like the larger community, was as much an economic as a social unit; all members of the family worked, be it on the farm, or in a shop, or in the home.

There was not much to idealize. Love was not considered the basis for marriage but one possible result of it. According to historian Carl Degler, it was easier to obtain a divorce in colonial New England than anywhere else in the Western world, and the divorce rate climbed steadily throughout the 18th century, though it remained low by contemporary standards. Romantic images to the contrary, it was rare for more than two generations (parents and children) to share a household, for the simple reason that very few people lived beyond the age of 60. It is ironic that our nostalgia for the extended family—including grandparents and grandchildren—comes at a time when, thanks to improvements in health care, its existence is less threatened than ever before.

Infant mortality was high in colonial days, though not as high as we are 15
accustomed to believe, since food was plentiful and epidemics, owing to generally low population density, were few. In the mid-1700s, the average age of marriage was about 24 for men, 21 for women—not much different from what it is now. Households, on average, were larger, but not startlingly so: A typical household in 1790 included about 5.6 members, versus about 3.5 today. Illegitimacy was widespread. Premarital pregnancies reached a high in 18th-century America (10 percent of all first births) that was not equalled until the 1950s.

In simple demographic terms, then, the differences between the American family in colonial times and today are not all that stark; the similarities are sometimes striking.

The chief contrast is psychological. While Western societies have always idealized the family to some degree, the *most vivid* literary portrayals of family life before the 19th century were negative or, at best, ambivalent. In what might be called the "high tragic" tradition—including Sophocles, Shakespeare, and the Bible, as well as fairy tales and novels—the family was portrayed as a high-voltage emotional setting, laden with dark passions, sibling rivalries, and violence. There was also the "low comic" tradition—the world of hen-pecked husbands and tyrannical mothers-in-law.

It is unlikely that our 18th-century ancestors ever left the book of Genesis or *Tom Jones* with the feeling that their own family lives were seriously flawed.

By the time of the Civil War, however, American attitudes toward the family had changed profoundly. The early decades of the 19th century marked the beginnings of America's gradual transformation into an urban, industrial society. In 1820, less than 8 percent of the U.S. population lived in cities; by 1860, the urban concentration approached 20 percent, and by 1900 that proportion had doubled.

Structurally, the American family did not immediately undergo a com- 20
parable transformation. Despite the large families of many immigrants and farmers, the size of the *average* family declined—slowly but steadily—as it had been doing since the 17th century. Infant mortality remained about the same, and may even have increased somewhat, owing to poor sanitation in crowded cities. Legal divorces were easier to obtain than they had been in colonial times. Indeed, the rise in the divorce rate was a matter of some concern during the 19th century, though death, not divorce, was the prime cause of one-parent families, as it was up to 1965.

Functionally, however, America's industrial revolution had a lasting effect on the family. No longer was the household typically a group of interdependent workers. Now, men went to offices and factories and became breadwinners; wives stayed home to mind the hearth; children went off to the new public schools. The home was set apart from the dog-eat-dog arena of economic life; it came to be viewed as a utopian retreat or, in historian Christopher Lasch's phrase, a "haven in a heartless world." Marriage was now valued primarily for its emotional attractions. Above all, the family became something to worry about.

The earliest and most saccharine "sentimental model" of the family appeared in the new mass media that proliferated during the second quarter of the 19th century. Novels, tracts, newspaper articles, and ladies' magazines—there were variations for each class of society—elaborated a "Cult of True Womanhood" in which piety, submissiveness, and domesticity dominated the pantheon of desirable feminine qualities. This quotation from *The Ladies Book* (1830) is typical:

> See, she sits, she walks, she speaks, she looks—unutterable things! Inspiration springs up in her very paths—it follows her footsteps. A halo of glory encircles her, and illuminates her whole orbit. With her, man not only feels safe, but actually renovated.

In the late 1800s, science came into the picture. The "professionalization" of the housewife took two different forms. One involved motherhood and childrearing, according to the latest scientific understanding of children's special physical and emotional needs. (It is no accident that the publishing of children's books became a major industry during this period.) The other was the domestic science movement—“home economics,” basically—which focused on the woman as full-time homemaker, applying “scientific” and “industrial” rationality to shopping, making meals, and housework.

The new ideal of the family prompted a cultural split that has endured, one that Tocqueville had glimpsed (and rather liked) in 1835. Society was divided more sharply into man's sphere and woman's sphere. Toughness, competition, and practicality were the masculine values that ruled the outside world. The softer values—affection, tranquility, piety—were worshiped in the home and the church. In contrast to the colonial view, the ideology of the “modern” family implied a critique of everything beyond the front door.

What is striking as one looks at the writings of the 19th-century “ex- 25
perts”—the physicians, clergymen, phrenologists, and “scribbling ladies”—is how little their essential message differs from that of the sociologists, psychiatrists, pediatricians, and women's magazine writers of the 20th century, particularly since World War II.

Instead of men's and women's spheres, of course, sociologists speak of “instrumental” and “expressive” roles. The notion of the family as a retreat from the harsh realities of the outside world crops up as “functional differentiation.” And, like the 19th-century utopians who believed society could be regenerated through the perfection of family life, 20th-century social scientists have looked at the failed family as the source of most American social problems.

None of those who promoted the sentimental model of the family—neither the popular writers nor the academics—considered the paradox of perfectionism: the ironic possibility that it would lead to trouble. Yet it has. The image of the perfect, happy family makes ordinary families seem like failures. Small problems loom as big problems if the “normal” family is thought to be one where there are no real problems at all.

One sees this phenomenon at work on the generation of Americans born and reared during the late 19th century, the first generation reared on the mother's milk of sentimental imagery. Between 1900 and 1920, the U.S. divorce rate doubled, from four to eight divorces annually per 1,000 married couples. The jump—comparable to the 100 percent increase in the divorce rate between 1960 and 1980—is not attributable to changes in divorce laws, which were not greatly liberalized. Rather, it would appear that, as historian Thomas O'Neill believes, Americans were simply more willing to dissolve marriages that did not conform to their ideal of domestic bliss—and perhaps try again.

If anything, family standards became even more demanding as the 20th century progressed. The new fields of psychology and sociology opened up whole new definitions of familial perfection. “Feelings”—fun, love, warmth, good orgasm—acquired heightened popular significance as the invisible glue of successful families.

Psychologist Martha Wolfenstein, in an analysis of several decades of government-sponsored infant care manuals, has documented the emergence of a "fun morality." In former days, being a good parent meant carrying out certain tasks with punctilio; if your child was clean and reasonably obedient, you had no cause to probe his psyche. Now, we are told, parents must commune with their own feelings and those of their children—an edict which has seeped into the ethos of education as well. The distinction is rather like that between religions of deed and religions of faith. It is one thing to make your child brush his teeth; it is quite another to transform the whole process into a joyous "learning experience." 30

The task of 20th-century parents has been further complicated by the advice offered them. The experts disagree with each other and often contradict themselves. The kindly Dr. Benjamin Spock, for example, is full of contradictions. In a detailed analysis of *Baby and Child Care,* historian Michael Zuckerman observes that Spock tells mothers to relax ("trust yourself") yet warns them that they have an "ominous power" to destroy their children's innocence and make them discontented "for years" or even "forever."

Since the mid-1960s, there has been a youth rebellion of sorts, a new "sexual revolution," a revival of feminism, and the emergence of the two-worker family. The huge postwar Baby-Boom generation is pairing off, accounting in part for the upsurge in the divorce rate (half of all divorces occur within seven years of a first marriage). Media images of the family have become more "realistic," reflecting new patterns of family life that are emerging (and old patterns that are re-emerging).

Among social scientists, "realism" is becoming something of an ideal in itself. For some of them, realism translates as pluralism: All forms of the family, by virtue of the fact that they happen to exist, are equally acceptable—from communes and cohabitation to one-parent households, homosexual marriages, and, come to think of it, the nuclear family. What was once labeled "deviant" is now merely "variant." In some college texts, "the family" has been replaced by "family systems." Yet, this new approach does not seem to have squelched perfectionist standards. Indeed, a palpable strain of perfectionism runs through the pop literature on "alternative" family lifestyles.

For the majority of scholars, realism means a more down-to-earth view of the American household. Rather than seeing the family as a haven of peace and tranquility, they have begun to recognize that even "normal" families are less than ideal, that intimate relations of any sort inevitably involve antagonism as well as love. Conflict and change are inherent in social life. If the family is now in a state of flux, such is the nature of resilient institutions; if it is beset by problems, so is life. The family will survive.

Questions for Discussion

1. Skolnick refers to the power of the photograph to cause us to see illusion as reality. Observe some images of the family in advertisements, commer-

cials, movies, and TV shows. What do they suggest that the family is like today? How do some of these images compare with your own family?

2. Politicians' moral transgressions have become fair game for public scrutiny, with the media behaving today like the "charivari" of colonial times. However, for the most part, what goes on in the homes of private citizens is considered their own business. What are some of the positive and negative consequences of establishing boundaries between family and community?
3. How did the Industrial Revolution contribute to the development of a sentimental model of the home and family? How did this model change the roles of both men and women? Why did the basis for marriage change from practical considerations to romantic love?
4. Does Skolnick convince you that this model of perfection is counterproductive for actual American families? What are some of the effects, according to Skolnick?
5. Were you surprised by Skolnick's statistic about premarital pregnancies in paragraph 15? (Another historian, David Popenoe, estimates that as many as forty percent of eighteenth-century brides were pregnant.) Why do you suppose that people tend to think the past was less troubled, morally, than the present?

For Research and Convincing

The traditional nuclear family, the "haven in a heartless world," developed along with the Industrial Revolution, mass communication, and advertising. Look at images of the ideal family in film, advertising, and TV. Is this model one way that we keep a healthy economy running by stimulating demand for goods and services? Or does the "ideal family" in our culture promote nonmaterial values? If you find that images suggest that "perfect" family happiness can be bought, write an argument to convince your readers of the harm these images might do.

For Persuading

Skolnick looks only at the evolution of white, middle-class ideas of the family. Look into the history of the family in another cultural tradition, such as African-American or Native American or one of the many immigrant cultures. What differences in family models do you find? If you find that these cultures have different values and practices, argue for or against preserving them rather than assimilating to the dominant model of the "typical/ideal" American family. What conflicts might arise for family members as they negotiate between competing models of "family"?

For Inquiry and Analysis

It's hard to believe that women could have been persuaded toward "feminine" behavior by the inflated and melodramatic rhetoric of the passage from *The Ladies Book* of 1830. Of course, it is always easier in hindsight to distinguish between manipulation and ethical persuasion and to howl and groan over bad style, but this specimen almost defies parody. Find some current advice in popular culture, such as newspaper columns or magazines, for men or for women about their roles as parents and husbands or wives. Does this advice promote the model of perfection? Evaluate the text as rhetoric: What appeals does it use to reach its intended audience? Who is the author, and what motives and perceived benefits might lie behind the creation of the text? How does style contribute? If you feel the advice is manipulative, could you convince the readers to see it as such?

MIDGE DECTER

The Madness of the American Family

This selection was given as a speech to members of The Heritage Foundation in July 1998 by author and social critic Midge Decter. The Heritage Foundation, according to the editors of its journal, Policy Review, *which printed Decter's speech, is a "research and educational institute that formulates and promotes conservative public policies based on the principles of free enterprise, limited government, traditional American values, and a strong national defense." Keep in mind that Decter, a trustee of the foundation, was speaking not to convince a group of opponents but to rally a friendly audience.*

THE IDEA of talking about the subject called "family" always puts 1
me in mind of a line from the ancient Greek playwright Euripides. "Whom the Gods would destroy," he said, "they first make mad." Now, to be sure, there are no gods—there is only God—and even if there were, you would have to think that, far from destroying us, they are busily arranging things very nicely for us. Nor do I think that American society has gone mad, exactly. Look around you at this magnificent country: You would have to say that somebody is surely doing something right.

Nevertheless, the ghost of that ancient Greek keeps whispering his words of ageless experience in my ear. If we Americans cannot be said to have gone mad, we have certainly been getting nuttier by the day.

Take one example of our nuttiness. We are healthier than people have ever been in all of human history. Just to list the possibly debilitating diseases that American children need never again experience—measles, whooping cough, diphtheria, smallpox, scarlet fever, polio—is to understand why we have begun to confront the issue of how to provide proper amenities to the fast-growing number of people who are being blessed with a vigorous old age.

And yet, as it seems, from morning until night we think of nothing but our health and all the potential threats to it. We measure and count and think about everything we put into our mouths. While we are speculating about which of the many beautiful places there will be for us to retire to, we are at the same time obsessed with all the substances and foodstuffs that are lying in wait to kill us, and try out each new magical prescription for the diet that will keep us ever young and beautiful. This has gone so far that, for example, not long ago a group of pediatricians had to issue a warning to new mothers that, far from beneficial, a low-fat diet was in fact quite injurious to infants and toddlers.

And as if an obsession with nutrition were not enough, every day mil- 5
lions upon millions of us whom life has seen fit to save from hard labor find ourselves instead, like so many blinded horses of olden times, daily enchained to our exercise treadmills.

So we treat our health as if it were a disease and the benign conditions of our lives as if they were so many obstacles to our well-being.

And if that is nutty, what shall we say about finding ourselves engaged in discussing something called the family? How on earth, if the gods are not out to destroy us, have we got ourselves into *this* fix? Talking about the family should be like talking about the earth itself: interesting to observe in all its various details—after all, what else are many if not most great novels about?—but hardly up for debate. And yet people just like you and me nowadays find themselves doing precisely that: Is it good for you? Is it necessary, especially for children? And—craziest of all—what is it?

In our everyday private lives, of course, we drive around in, or fly around in, and otherwise make household use of the products of various technologies of a complexity that is positively mind-boggling without giving it a second thought. Yet at the same time, millions among us who have attended, or who now attend, universities find it useful to take formal courses in something called "family relations," as if this were a subject requiring the most expert kind of technical training. And in our lives as a national community we call conferences, engage in public programs, create new organizations, and beyond that publish and read several libraries of books devoted entirely to questions about the family—not to speak of the fact that here I am as well this evening, offering you some further conversation on the subject.

I look around this room and wonder, how on earth have we come to this place, you and I? How did the wealthiest, healthiest, and luckiest people who have ever lived get to such a point? It is as if, in payment for our good fortune, we had been struck by some kind of slow-acting but in the long run lethal plague. This plague is a malady we must diagnose and put a name to if we are ever as a nation to return to our God-given senses.

Where did the idea that the family might somehow be an object of 10
debate and choice come from? It is never easy, as epidemiologists will tell you, to trace the exact origin of a plague. Who exactly is our Typhoid Mary?

I can't say I know, precisely, but I knew we were in trouble back in the late 1950s when I picked up *Esquire* magazine one day and read an essay about his generation written by a young man still in university. The writer concluded with the impassioned assertion that if he thought he might end up some day like his own father, working hard every day to make a nice home for the wife and kids, he would slit his throat. *Slit his throat.* Those were his exact words.

Now, I might not have paid close attention to the sentiment expressed by this obviously spoiled and objectionable brat were it not for two things: First, we were in those days hearing a lot from their teachers about just how brilliant and marvelous was the new generation of students in the universities, and second, *Esquire* was in those days known for its claim to have its finger on the cultural pulse. Thus, this was a young man whose mountainous ingratitude was worth paying a little attention to.

And sure enough, not too much later, what we know as the 1960s began to happen. Enough said. Should it, then, have come as a surprise that in short order that young author's female counterparts began in their own way to declare that throat-cutting would be the proper response to the prospect of ending up like their mothers? Well, surprise or no, the plague was now upon us for fair.

The End of Responsibility

Am I trying to suggest that the only course of social health is to live exactly as one's parents did? Of course not. The United States is a country whose character and achievements have depended precisely on people's striking out for new territories—actual territories and territories of the mind as well. We have not lived as our parents did, and we do not expect our children—or, anyway, our grandchildren—to live as we do.

Several years ago I was privileged to attend my grandfather's hundredth 15
birthday party. When we asked him what, looking back, was the most important thing that had ever happened to him, without a moment's hesitation he astonished us by answering that the most important thing that ever happened to him was being privileged to witness the introduction of the use of electricity into people's homes. And now I see my own grandchildren, even the youngest of them, sitting hunched over their keyboards, fingers flying, communing with unseen new-found friends in far-flung places and giving this new possibility not a second thought.

So of course we do not live as our parents lived, but that young man writing in *Esquire* was saying something else: Underneath the posturing, he was saying that he did not wish ever to become a husband and father. And the raging young women who came along soon after him were saying they, for their part, would be all too happy to be getting along without him.

And what, finally, when the dust of all these newfound declarations of independence began to settle, was the result of this new turmoil? The young men began to cut out—cut out of responsibility, cut out of service to their country, and cut out of the terms of everyday, ordinary life. They said they were against something they called "the system." But what, in the end, did they mean by that? Insofar as the system was represented by business and professional life, most of them after a brief fling as make-believe outcasts cut back into that aspect of the system very nicely; but insofar as it meant accepting the terms of ordinary daily life, of building and supporting a home and family, they may no longer have been prepared to slit their throats, but they would for a long time prove to be at best pretty skittish about this last act of becoming grown men.

And their girlfriends and lovers? They, on their side, were falling under the influence of a movement that was equating marriage and motherhood with chattel slavery. "We want," said Gloria Steinem, one of this movement's most celebrated spokeswomen ("a saint" is what *Newsweek* magazine once called her), "to be the husbands we used to marry."

Let us ponder that remark for a moment: "We want to be the husbands we used to marry." Underlying the real ideology of the women's movement, sometimes couched in softer language and sometimes in uglier, is the proposition that the differences between men and women are merely culturally imposed—culturally imposed, moreover, for nefarious purposes. That single proposition underlies what claims to be no more than the movement's demands for equal treatment, and it constitutes the gravamen of the teaching of women's studies in all our universities.

20 And need I say that it has been consequential throughout our society? I don't, I think, have to go through the whole litany of the women's complaints. Nor do I have to go into detail about their huge political success in convincing the powers that be that they represented half the country's population, and thus obtaining many truly disruptive legislative remedies for their would-be sorrows.

Among the remedies that follow from the proposition that the differences between men and women are merely culturally imposed has been that of letting women in on the strong-man action. Why, it was successfully argued, should they not be firemen, policemen, coal miners, sports reporters—in many ways most significant of all—combat soldiers?

The Soldier and the Baby-Tender

At the outset of the Gulf War, early in that first phase of it called Desert Shield, the *New York Post* carried on its front page a newsphoto—it may have appeared in many papers, or at least it should have—illustrating a story about the departure for Saudi Arabia of a group of reservists. The picture was of a young woman in full military regalia, including helmet, planting a farewell kiss on the brow of an infant at most three months old being held in the arms of its father. The photo spoke volumes about where this society has allowed itself to get dragged to and was in its way as obscene as anything that has appeared in that cesspool known as *Hustler* magazine. It should have been framed and placed on the desk of the president, the secretary of defense, the chairman of the Joint Chiefs, and every liberal senator in the United States Congress.

That photo was not about the achievement of women's equality; it was about the nuttiness—in this case, perhaps the proper word *is* madness—that has overtaken all too many American families. For the household in which—let's use the social scientists' pompous term for it—"the sexual differentiation of roles" has grown so blurry that you can't tell the soldier from the baby-tender without a scorecard is a place of profound disorder. No wonder we are a country with a low birthrate and a high divorce rate.

We see milder forms of this disorder all over the place, especially in cases where young mothers have decreed that mothers and fathers are to be indistinguishable as to their—my favorite word—roles. Again, you cannot tell—or rather, you are not supposed to be able to tell—the mommy from the daddy. The child, of course, knows who is what. No baby or little kid who is hungry or frightened or hurting ever calls for his daddy in the middle of the night. He might *get* his daddy, but it is unlikely that that would have been his intention.

25 Everybody has always known such things: What is a husband, what is a wife; what is a mother, what is a father. How have we come to the place where they are open for debate? "Untune that string," says Shakespeare, "and hark what discord follows."

It is not all that remarkable, for instance, that there should have been the kind of women's movement that sprang up among us. There have from time to time throughout recorded history been little explosions of radicalism, of refusal to accept the limits of human existence, and what could be a more radical idea than that there is no natural difference between the sexes? Just to say the words is to recognize that what we have here is a rebellion not against a government or a society, but against the very constitution of our beings, we men and women.

The question is, what caused such an idea to reverberate as it did among two generations of the most fortunate women who ever lived? As for their men, what idea lay at the bottom of their response to all this we do not quite know, for they giggled nervously and for the most part remained silent. But it is not difficult to see that if the movement's ideas represented an assault on the age-old definition of their manhood, it also relieved them of a great burden of responsibility: Seeing that their services as protectors and defenders and bread-winners had been declared no longer essential, they were now free—in some cases literally, in some cases merely emotionally—to head for the hills.

Since the condition of families depends to a considerable degree on the condition of marriages, small wonder, then, that the subject of family has been put up for debate.

Most recently, we are being asked to consider whether two lesbians or two male homosexuals should not also be recognized as a family. Oftentimes the ostensible issue centers on money; that is, spousal benefits for one's homosexual mate. But actually, as we know, what is being demanded is about far more than money.

30 Money is easy to think about; that's why the homosexual-rights movement has placed such emphasis on this particular legislative campaign. But what is really being sought is that society should confer upon homosexual unions the same legitimacy as has always been conferred upon heterosexual ones.

What comes next, of course, is the legal adoption of children. Why not a family with two daddies? After all, some unfortunates among us don't even have one. (Lesbians, of course, suffer no such complications. All their babies require for a daddy is a syringe. Thus, we have that little classic of children's literature, to be found in the libraries of the nation's public schools, entitled *Heather Has Two Mommies.*)

In other words, when it comes to families, any arrangement is considered as good as any other.

People don't pick their professions that way; they don't decide where to live that way; they don't furnish their lives or their houses that way; they don't even dress themselves that way . . . but families? Why not? Aren't they, after all, no more than the result of voluntary agreements between two private individuals? And anyway, don't people have rights? Who are their fellow citizens to tell them how to live and decide that one thing is good and another is bad?

Such questions explain why it was that in the 1970s a famous White House Conference on the Family, called primarily to discuss the crisis in the inner cities and packed full of so-called family experts and advocates from all over the country, could not even begin to mount a discussion, let alone provide a report, because from the very first day they could not even reach agreement on the definition of the word "family."

You Can't Fool Mother Nature

35 The question is, how did we as a society ever come to this disordered place? For one thing, what has encouraged us to imagine that anything is possible if we merely will it to be? And for another, how have we strayed this far from the wisdom so painfully earned by all those who came before us and prepared the earth to receive us? I ask these questions in no polemical spirit, because few of us have not in one way or another been touched by them, if not in our own households, then in the lives of some of those near and dear to us.

What is it, in short, that so many Americans have forgotten, or have never learned, about the nature of human existence?

One thing they have forgotten—or perhaps never learned—is that you can't fool Mother Nature. If you try to do so, you sicken and die, spiritually speaking—like those little painted turtles that used to be a tourist novelty for children and, because their shells were covered in paint, could never live beyond a few days.

Well, we do not, like those novelty turtles, literally die: On the contrary, as I have said, we have been granted the possibility of adding years to our lives; but far too many of us, especially the young people among us, live what are at bottom unnatural lives. Too many young women, having recovered from their seizure of believing that they were required to become Masters of the Universe, cannot find men to marry them, while the men on their side cannot seem to find women to marry. Both grope around, first bewildered and then made sour by what is happening to them. And there is nothing in the culture around them—that nutty, nutty culture—to offer medicine for their distemper.

What is it Mother Nature knows that so many of us no longer do? It is that marriage and family are not a choice like, say, deciding where to go and whom to befriend and how to make a living. Together, marriage and parenthood are the rock on which human existence stands.

40 Different societies may organize their families differently—or so, at least, the anthropologists used to take great pleasure in telling us (I myself have my doubts)—and they may have this or that kinship system or live beneath this or

that kind of roof. But consider: In societies, whether primitive or advanced, that have no doubt about how to define the word "family," every child is born to two people, one of his own sex and one of the other, to whom his life is as important as their own and who undertake to instruct him in the ways of the world around him.

Consider this again for a moment: *Every child is born to two people, one of his own sex and one of the other, to whom his life is as important as their own and who undertake to instruct him in the ways of the world around him.* Can you name the social reformer who could dream of a better arrangement than that?

The Swamp of Self

Are there, then, no violations of this arrangement? Among the nature-driven families I am talking about are there no cruel fathers or selfish and uncaring mothers? Of course there are. I have said that family is a rock, not the Garden of Eden; and a rock, as we know, can sometimes be a far from comfortable place to be. Off the coast of San Francisco there used to be a prison they called "the rock," and that is not inapt imagery for some families I can think of.

But even in benign families there are, of course, stresses and strains. To cite only one example, it takes a long time, if not forever, for, say, a late-blooming child, or a child troubled or troublesome in some other way, to live down his past with his own family, even should he become the world's greatest living brain surgeon. Families are always, and often quite unforgivingly, the people Who Knew You When. So, as I said, the rock of family can sometimes have a pretty scratchy surface.

But there is one thing that living on a rock does for you: It keeps you out of the swamps. The most dangerous of these swamps is a place of limitless and willfully defined individual freedom.

The land of limitless freedom, as so many among us are now beginning 45
to discover, turns out to be nothing other than the deep muck and mire of Self. And there is no place more airless, more sunk in black boredom, than the land of Self, and no place more difficult to be extricated from. How many among us these days are stuck there, seeking for phony excitements and emotions, flailing their way from therapy to therapy, from pounding pillows to primal screaming to ingesting drugs to God knows what else, changing their faces and bodies, following the dictates first of this guru and then of that, and all the while sinking deeper and deeper into a depressing feeling of disconnection they cannot give a name to?

The only escape from the swamp of Self is the instinctual and lifelong engagement in the fate of others. Now, busying oneself with politics or charity—both of which are immensely worthy communal undertakings involving the needs and desires of others—cannot provide the escape I am talking about. For both, however outwardly directed, are voluntary. The kind of engagement I mean is the involuntary discovery that there are lives that mean as much to you as your own, and in some cases—I am referring, of course, to your children and their children and their children after them—there are lives that mean more to you than your own. In short, the discovery that comes with being an essential member of a family.

I do not think it is an exaggeration to use the word "discovery." No matter how ardently a young man and woman believe they wish to spend their lives with one another, and no matter how enthusiastically they greet the knowledge that they are to have a baby, they do not undertake either of these things in full knowledge of the commitment they are undertaking. They nod gravely at the words "for richer or poorer, in sickness and in health," but they do not know—not really, not deep down—that they are embarked upon a long, long, and sometimes arduous and even unpleasant journey.

I think this may be truer of women than of men. A woman holding her first-born in her arms, for instance, is someone who for the first time can truly understand her own mother and the meaning of the fact that she herself had been given life. This is not necessarily an easy experience, especially if her relations with her mother have been in some way painful to her; but even if they have not, this simple recognition can sometimes be quite overwhelming. That, in my opinion, is why so many first-time mothers become temporarily unbalanced.

I cannot, of course, speak for the inner life of her husband; his experience is bound to be a different one. But the panic that so often and so famously overtakes a first-time expectant father is surely related to it. To become a family is to lose some part of one's private existence and to be joined in what was so brilliantly called "the great chain of being."

In short, being the member of a family does not make you happy; it 50
makes you human.

One Choice Among Many?

All this should be a very simple matter; God knows, it's been going on long enough. So why have we fallen into such a state of confusion?

The answer, I think, lies in the question. By which I mean that we Americans living in the second half of the 20th century are living as none others have lived before. Even the poor among us enjoy amenities that were once not available to kings. We live with the expectation that the babies born to us will survive. The death of an infant or a child is an unbearable experience. Yet go visit a colonial graveyard and read the gravestones: Our forefathers upon this land lived with the experience, year after year after year, of burying an infant—lived two weeks, lived four months, lived a year. How many burials did it take to be granted a surviving offspring?

I am not speaking of prehistoric times, but of 200 years ago. Two hundred years, my friends, is but a blink of history's eye. Could any of us survive such an experience? I doubt it.

Even a hundred years ago—*half* a blink of history's eye—people lived with kinds of hardship only rarely known among us now. Read the letters of the Victorians (fortunately for our instruction in life, people used to write a lot of letters; those who come after us, with our phone calls and e-mail, will know so little about us). They were sick *all the time.* Or take a more pleasant example, provided by my husband, the music nut: We can sit down in the comfort of home every afternoon and listen to works of music their own composers may never have heard performed and that not so long ago people would travel across Europe to hear a single performance of.

So we live as no others who came before us were privileged to do. We 55
live with the bounties of the universe that have been unlocked by the scientists and engineers and then put to use by those old swashbucklers with names like Carnegie and Edison and Ford—and, yes, Gates—who were seeking their own fortunes and in the process made ours as well. Moreover, not long from now, we are told, there will be nearly one million Americans one hundred years old or more.

We live, too—and should not permit ourselves to forget it—with another kind of bounty: We are the heirs of a political system that, despite a number of threatened losses of poise and balance, has remained the most benign and just, and even the most stable, in the world.

The truth is that precisely because we are living under an endless shower of goodies, we are as a people having a profoundly difficult time staying in touch with the sources of our being. That is why so many young women were so easily hoodwinked into believing that marriage and motherhood were what they liked to call "options," just one choice among many. That is why so many young men were so easily convinced to settle for the sudden attack of distemper afflicting the women whom fate intended for them. That is why so many people of good will find it difficult to argue with the idea that homosexual mating is no different from their own—everybody to his own taste, and who's to say, especially when it comes to sex, that anything is truer, or better, or more natural than anything else?

In short, because God has permitted us to unlock so many secrets of His universe, we are in constant danger of fancying that any limits upon us are purely arbitrary and we have the power to lift them. In the past half-century, what has not been tried out, by at least some group or other in our midst, in the way of belief and ritual or—horrible word—lifestyle? We have watched the unfolding of catalogues-full of ancient and newly made-up superstitions, the spread of fad medicines and "designer" drugs (each year, it seems, produces a new one of these). Lately we have seen beautiful young children, children living in the most advanced civilization on earth, painfully and hideously mutilating their bodies in the name, they will tell you, of fashion.

All this, I believe, stems from the same profound muddle that has left us as a society groping for a definition of the word "family." Maybe people are just not constituted to be able to live with the ease and wealth and health that have been granted to us.

But this would be a terrible thing to have to believe, and I do not believe 60
it, and neither do you, or you would not be here this evening. As Albert Einstein once said, the Lord God can be subtle, but He is not malicious. What does seem to be a fair proposition, however, is that given the whole preceding

history of mankind, to live as we do takes more than a bit of getting used to. It takes, indeed, some serious spiritual discipline.

Wisdom and Gratitude

I believe that two things will help us to be restored from our current nuttiness. The first is for us, as a people and a culture, to recapture our respect for the wisdom of our forbears. That wisdom was earned in suffering and trial; we throw it away—and many of us have thrown it away—at their and our very great peril. The second is a strong and unending dose of gratitude: the kind of gratitude that people ought to feel for the experience of living in freedom; the kind of gratitude the mother of a newborn feels as she counts the fingers and toes of the tiny creature who has been handed to her; the kind of gratitude we feel when someone we care about has passed through some danger; the kind of gratitude we experience as we walk out into the sunshine of a beautiful day, which is in fact none other than gratitude for the gift of being alive.

All around us these days, especially and most fatefully among the young women in our midst, there are signs of a surrender to nature and the common sense that goes with it. The famous anthropologist Margaret Mead—a woman who in her own time managed to do quite a good deal of damage to the national ethos—did once say something very wise and prophetic. She said that the real crimp in a woman's plans for the future came not from the cries but from the smiles of her baby.

How many young women lawyers and executives have been surprised to discover, first, that they could not bear to remain childless, and second, that they actually preferred hanging around with their babies to preparing a brief or attending a high-level meeting? One could weep for the difficulty they had in discovering the true longings of their hearts. Next—who knows—they may even begin to discover that having a real husband and being a real wife in return may help to wash away all that bogus posturing rage that has been making them so miserable to themselves and others.

When that happens, we may be through debating and discussing and defining and redefining the term "family" and begin to relearn the very, very old lesson that life has limits and that only by escaping Self and becoming part of the onrushing tide of generations can we ordinary humans give our lives their intended full meaning. We have been endowed by our Creator not only with unalienable rights but with the knowledge that is etched into our very bones.

All we have to do is listen. And say thank you. And pray. 65

Questions for Discussion

1. Decter, a social critic, wants to show what is wrong with current attempts to redefine the family. What is Decter's definition of family? Where do you find it in the speech?

2. Throughout her speech Decter uses metaphors of mental and physical illness when referring to those who question her definition of family. Find several places where this metaphor recurs. What does she mean to say, literally, about those who want to change traditional family roles? You might note that she repeatedly asks what has brought Americans to this stage of "nuttiness." Where does she answer this question? What does she see as the cause of the problem?
3. What reasons does Decter offer to support her view that wanting to revise the traditional family is mad and unnatural? What evidence does she provide to support and develop her argument about what is natural and what is unnatural?
4. Based on the speech, describe the demographic profile of the audience. What does Decter assume about their socioeconomic status? about their age? Where do you see evidence of these assumptions in the text? In paragraph 57, what does she mean when she says Americans' abundance of wealth gives them a "profoundly difficult time staying in touch with the sources of [their] being"? Is she advocating a less materialistic lifestyle for her listeners?
5. Decter's speech appeared in the journal *Policy Review.* What particular policies does she advocate in her speech, either directly or implicitly?

For Convincing

Decter sees an important difference between accepting parental obligations on the one hand and doing charity work or community service on the other. Explain what that difference is, in terms of self-sacrifice, and use evidence of your own, from your experiences and observations and from library research, to support or refute her position.

For Research and Convincing

Decter argues that life has meaning only when one becomes part of "the unrushing tide of generations," in other words, by having children. Yet many women, and men, choose to remain childless. For couples, and especially for women, voluntary childlessness is often stigmatized as selfish. Look into studies of the reasons people choose to remain childless. Is it a refusal to accept limits and make sacrifices? Support or refute Decter's charge that choosing not to be a parent is a way of ducking responsibility.

BETTY HOLCOMB

Families Are Changing—For the Better

Betty Holcomb is senior editor of Working Mother *magazine. This selection is excerpted from her 1998 book* Not Guilty! The Good News about Working Mothers, *in which she argues that women can have both children and careers without guilt and stress, provided that they get support from employers and families and societal recognition that parenting and homemaking are valuable labor. In this essay she aims to persuade husbands and wives that rethinking gender-based divisions of labor in the home will lead to happier marriages and stronger families.*

1 WHEN LAURA Koenig arrives home from work in Stoughton, Wisconsin, she often finds dinner on the table, the dishwasher empty and waiting for a new load of dishes. There may even be a load of clothes already in the wash. All of this is done by her husband, Kurt, who gets home a couple hours ahead of her. "It's awesome, isn't it?" Laura says. "My marriage is better than it's ever been. I couldn't be happier."

Koenig, an occupational therapist and mother of two, still sounds a little surprised in early 1997 as she recounts this homecoming scene. "It sure beats the heck out of being angry all the time," she says, laughing. Five years ago, she thought their marriage was over, largely because Kurt did so little child care and housework. "All I used to think about was how could I screw him over. Now I look for things to make him feel good. It's so different."

Her husband, Kurt, sounds equally awed by the change in their marriage. He now uses the same words as Laura to describe it. "It's better than it's ever been," he says. "We couldn't be happier."

Not only that, but Kurt says he's much closer to his children. "It's been a gradual evolution. Taking part in the day-to-day rigors of life has helped my relationship with the kids." That means the children now turn to him for solace and support. "The kids don't go to Mom for everything now; they have confidence that I can meet their needs. My daughter will ask to do things with me, to read and draw with her. It's much more comfortable now."

5 But the road to this marital bliss was a remarkably bumpy one. It was not so long ago that Laura issued Kurt an ultimatum: "Either come to marriage counseling or move out." The issue? As for so many dual-earner couples, his lack of participation in child care and domestic chores. Kurt's new engagement at home grew directly from the insights he gained in counseling as a way to save his marriage. Both he and Laura learned that it can be far more dangerous to resist change than to embrace it.

Indeed, the Koenigs show just how much family life in America has changed over the past two decades—all in response to the growing numbers of mothers who now have jobs outside the home. Between 1975 and 1993, the number of two-paycheck families in America swelled from 43 to 63 percent of all families, making them the solid majority today. As that happens, life inside the average household is shifting, with Americans reinventing what it means to be a husband or wife, mom or dad, son or daughter.

"Having women work after having children changes everything. We now have a new family form," says Rosalind Barnett, scholar at the Murray Research Center at Radcliffe College and coauthor, with Caryl Rivers, of *She Works, He Works: How Two Income Families Are Happier, Healthier, and Better Off.* And contrary to the handwringing from social conservatives, this new kind of family turns out to be quite a vibrant one, with benefits for men, women, and children. Women's new earning power offers both men and women more flexibility about the way they pursue their careers and family life. With two incomes, families are more secure economically and better able to weather a recession or downsizing at work, which has had savage effects on family life in the past. There is also plenty of evidence that women's new economic clout has the effect of encouraging a new intimacy between men and their children, as Kurt is discovering.

To be sure, the mere fact that a woman has a job outside the home does not automatically guarantee a happy life. Marriage is one of the most complicated human relationships; so is the one between parents and children. The effects of women's employment on a marriage and family life are as various as the jobs they hold, the husbands they marry, the children they bear. Nor is the fallout from a job on family life some static phenomenon. Rather, the effects vary over time, as circumstances change both at work and at home. And there is a growing body of research that shows that the attitudes a woman or man has about male and female roles matter as much as anything.

Sociologists and psychologists also report that the best marriages today are those forged between equals, much like the one Kurt and Laura have achieved, where responsibilities for home, children, and breadwinning are shared. Such a union breeds a sense of reciprocity, empathy, and affirmation for both mates that deepens intimacy, trust, and respect in a marriage. "People are more willing to be direct, to reveal themselves and be themselves when they feel like equals," says Janice Steil, professor of psychology at Adelphi University's Derner Institute of Advanced Psychological Studies and author of *His and Her Marriage from the 1970's to the 1990's.*

10 That this message is still a faint one in American culture, that there is still a deep ambivalence about mothers working, is not surprising to researchers, however. The truth is that American families are caught in the cross fire of change as society moves ever so slowly to accept the new family roles. Today men and women live in what sociologists call a "transitional" phase; that is, the daily realities of individual families have changed, but the nation's institutions and social expectations lag behind. Most still follow rules created for families of another era. "We're in the middle of an evolution," says James Levine, head of the Fatherhood Project at the Families and Work Institute. "These patterns just don't change overnight, because gender roles are so over-

determined. The scripts that women and men have internalized growing up, the economic realities, the continuing differential between men's and women's earning power, all conspire to keep men and women in the old roles."

Nonetheless, there is a louder call than ever from social conservatives for a return to old-fashioned "family values," when men earned a living and women stayed home with the kids. "One Breadwinner Should Be Enough," conservative economist Jude Wanniski headlined in the *Wall Street Journal* in early 1996. "When both husband and wife must work full-time to make ends meet," he insisted, "children are more likely to become unruly, communication between the spouses breaks down . . . the divorce rate increases and so does abortion." At about the same time, the right-wing Rockford Institute featured a picture of the 1950s Cleaver family, from the sitcom *Leave It to Beaver,* under the headline "Ward and June Were Right" on the cover of one of its 1996 monthly newsletters. Social conservative David Blankenhorn at the Institute for American Values asserts that "marriage is the most fragile institution in society today," and calls for a return to the old ways. "Feminists are constantly talking about wanting to reengineer sex roles, that men should do more nurturing. But it would be better to accept the premise that fathers are different from mothers. Men still see their primary responsibility as breadwinning and protection. And both men and women like it that way."

Certainly, there are some men and women who prefer those roles. But the evidence shows that many families are thriving today as they adapt to a changing way of life. Men want more expansive roles, more involvement with kids. And what Blankenhorn and other social conservatives miss is that the core problem in many marriages today is not that men's and women's roles are changing. Rather, the real threat to marriage and family life often lies in the inability or resistance to change those roles. Further, it is not some feminist plot or liberal ideology that inspires men and women to reinvent their family life. Rather, it is the day-to-day realities of home life today, transformed by women's new earning power, that drives couples to alter the terms of marriage and parenthood.

For Laura Koenig, it took a full five years after the birth of her first child, Danny, for the tension in her marriage to build to a crisis. By then, she had had a second child, Alexandra, who was eight months old. And by then, fights over housework and child care had become the stuff of daily life. "I felt such a lack of support and appreciation. I began to feel it would be easier to be with my children by myself. It would mean one less person to clean up after."

That truth came hard to her. "I went into marriage thinking I'd be married for the rest of my life," she says. When she found herself pregnant at twenty-two, she knew raising a child would be demanding. But she trusted that she and Kurt could do a good job. She never expected to be overwhelmed by the duties of raising the kids and keeping the house running.

But at twenty-six, with a job and two kids, housework and child care 15
were foremost on her mind. Because of their different work schedules, Kurt

generally arrived home a few hours ahead of her, with the two children. Back then, she recalls, "I'd typically arrive home and the kids' stuff would be all over the floor in front of the door. The kids would be hollering for something to eat. And Kurt was there reading the paper, hanging out and watching TV. I always wondered how he could do that," she recalls.

After dinner, the scenario was no less frustrating to Laura. Kurt would again retreat into his own world with a newspaper or watching television, while she cleaned the kitchen, gave the kids a bath, and got them into bed. "Kurt never used to take responsibility for the kids. He saw it as my job and only helped if I asked him to. If he gave them a bath, he'd tell me it was for me. If he put on their pajamas, he'd say he did it for me."

His attitude infuriated her. "I blew up. I asked him, 'Why is it always my job? Don't you enjoy these children? Aren't they your children, too?'"

At the time, this was hardly a new question in the Koenig household. Over the years since the birth of their first child and then their second, she had tried to get Kurt to take more responsibility for the kids. "We went through stages of trying to negotiate this. I remember sitting down and saying, 'These are all the things that need to get done around the house above and beyond my job. We have to get meals, clean up, give the kids baths,' and so on," she recalls. "I'd ask him, 'Which items will you do, will I do? Which do you never want to do?' These talks would change things for a while." But, she recalls, "it was never a sustained effort. It would work for a couple of weeks or a couple of months. Then it reverted back to the old scenario. He always paid the bills and took care of the cars. But otherwise, I did everything else. It was like I had two full-time jobs."

And this, she came to see, was corrosive to the marriage. "My anger was biting his head off. I'd swear and stomp my feet," she says, to prompt the talks about chores. Otherwise, she retreated into her anger, withdrawing from Kurt. "The anger went into every depth of our life. I remember feeling he didn't do this and didn't do that, then I'd be damned if I'd cuddle with him. I would just be cold," she says. "If he was watching TV, I'd just find anything to do besides go down and watch TV with him."

20 Such a situation is a familiar one to psychologists who deal with two-career couples. While the external trappings of their lives are dramatically different from those of earlier generations, many still inhabit the psychic landscape of the past. Kurt, for example, says that he didn't sense there was a truly serious problem in the marriage, even after the repeated talks about housework and child care. He'd grown up as an only child; his mom took care of all the household chores. The stress that Laura was experiencing was invisible to him. "I was off in my little world, assuming things were fine," he says. That is, until Laura gave him the ultimatum to get out or go into marriage counseling.

Such a situation is also a common one to family counselors. With few role models and no real system for assigning duties in the marriage, many couples wage war over the minutiae of daily life. "It's a new structure for marriage, so questions arise all the time about the extent to which expectations match in the marriage. Who's going to stay home with a sick child? Who's going to do the housework?" says Lisa Silberstein, a clinical psychologist in New Haven, Connecticut, and author of *Dual-Career Marriage: A System in Transition*. "The success in the marriage and marital satisfaction depend on how much a couple can keep those issues on the table and talking about them."

The conversations the Koenigs had in marriage counseling over the course of a year helped them arrive at new roles at home. Kurt began to take more initiative with the children and household chores. Not only that, but Kurt says he now views his wife as his true equal. "It was never an issue what my wife earns. I've never been the type to have a wife who sits home and takes care of the nest. I just never felt real strongly about that, that I needed a stay-at-home wife taking care of my kids," he says. On the other hand, he adds that "there maybe was a time when I was working and Laura was still in school, when I didn't see her as equal. But now we split everything fifty-fifty and there are a lot of benefits from that."

And that is exactly what the research on marriage shows. Dual-career couples who manage to share child care and housework tend to describe their marriages as far more satisfying than others. Such give-and-take in all aspects of family life makes both men and women feel valued and supported, and allows an intimacy that is otherwise hard to achieve, according to sociologist Pepper Schwartz, who has conducted broad surveys of marriage in America. The "mutual friendship"—the shared values and shared sense of responsibility for all aspects of family life—is the most gratifying aspect of their lives, Schwartz asserted in her book *Peer Marriage*. . . .

Still, marriage counselors and sociologists who study dual-career couples concede that such easygoing acceptance of the new expectations, roles, and responsibilities in marriage is far from a simple task for many couples. The questions that Laura Koenig put to her husband, Kurt, at the flash point in their marriage—Why was child care always her job? Didn't he enjoy their children? Weren't they his children, too?—reverberate through American culture. "Who Takes Care of the House and the Kids?" asked the headline of the *Newark Star-Ledger* in February 1997. That story covered a survey by *American Baby* magazine that found a majority of moms wished their spouses would do more around the house. By now, no one has to explain what is meant by the term "second shift." Survey after survey shows that women still put in far more hours than men do at home. Women managers at the nation's major corporations put in thirty-three hours a week on housework and child care, compared with eighteen hours a week for men, according to a study by Rodgers and Associates, the research arm of Work/Family Directions. That means the average woman manager puts in a total of eighty hours a week between duties at home and on the job, compared with sixty-seven hours for a man. It also means that a man is typically putting in a couple extra hours a week on the job, a powerful reinforcement of traditional roles for men and women. Strategies for getting men to share housework and child care are now regular topics for women's and parenting magazines.

Why, then, is it so hard to arrive at equity on the home front, given the 25
benefits for both men and women? More than anything, the answer seems to lie in a deep-rooted cultural allegiance to old-fashioned gender roles. Although family life is clearly changing, the cultural attachment to the old ways is deeply internalized and hard to shake.

When Ellen Galinsky and Dana Friedman, then copresidents of the Families and Work Institute, released their research in mid-1995 showing that married women were now true breadwinners, bringing in half or more of the income in the majority of American families, their research made news for weeks, reaching millions of Americans.

But even before the findings were released, there was one inconsistency in the raw data that intrigued Friedman. While the new numbers left no doubt that women were now true providers, women still insisted that men's careers were more important than women's. Almost two-thirds of the married women polled said their husbands' jobs provided more financial security for their families. "Their opinions just didn't jibe with reality; they didn't reflect what women were bringing into the family," Friedman recalls. Unfortunately, neither she nor Galinsky had anticipated the response, so they had no way to explain the inconsistency. Still curious, Friedman decided to pursue the issue in small focus groups. What she found was illuminating. "Women are in a sort of collusion with men in making men feel that their work is more important than women's."

Women confided, for example, that they understood the need to "preserve the natural order" between the sexes. "Women told me men would just be too threatened if women said their careers were as important as men's," says Friedman. "They said maybe women devalue what they do to make men feel more important."

This finding comes as no surprise to Janice Steil, professor of psychology at Adelphi University, who has devoted her career to exploring how men and women work out equality in the context of intimate relationships. And increasingly, she has come to see that the psychic reality of men and women, the way they define what it means to be a good husband and father or a good wife and mother, is key in predicting marital happiness. "The more I looked at the research, the more it led me to think about the importance of the way men and women internalize their gender roles," says Steil. Indeed, many social scientists now describe "sex role ideology" as a key factor in predicting how well or how poorly people will fare in modern marriage. Such beliefs are among the most powerful and most deeply held ideas people have, since gender is such an important part of a person's sense of self. And the notion of femaleness, of what it means to be a woman, is very closely bound up with being a mother. "When you listen to the stereotypes of what you say a mother is and what a woman is, they're very, very similar," says psychologist Kay Deaux, who pioneered research on gender stereotypes. Words such as "nurturing," "warm," "sensitive," "caring," for example. And those ideas are so powerful because they are instilled and reinforced from birth. "Gender is something that is part of nearly every interaction we have in life, and the stereotypes are reinforced over and over again." Such ideas can be comforting in that they maintain the status quo. "Part of gender identification has to do with power issues," says Susan Fiske, the social psychologist who took her arguments about stereotypes all the way to the U.S. Supreme Court. Although Fiske has focused primarily on how gender identity plays out in the workplace, her ideas about the interplay of gender and power certainly have relevance for marriage. "People do understand the function that maintaining a certain identity has in maintaining power. It can happen without it being conscious. It's not intentional, but it's comfortable to hold a set of beliefs because it maintains things as they are." . . .

. . . [W]hile women may "collude" in saying that men's jobs are more 30
important in public survey data, economists and other social scientists note a very different phenomenon playing itself out in the privacy of American households. A woman's paycheck does play a very pivotal role in the bargaining that goes on between husbands and wives. Indeed, in the past five years, a new body of economic research has come to illuminate—and even quantify—the way a woman's paycheck, or lack of one, impacts family life. "Economists used to treat the family as a little factory run by one person," says Joan Lundberg, professor of economics at the University of Washington and a leading expert on the economics of family life. Under that model, economists assumed the "factory" was run by the male breadwinner, and family members simply pooled resources and acted in the common interest of the group. The idea that women stayed home was perceived as a simple choice, for example, based on women's lower earning power outside the home. "But we came to realize [that] that really trivialized the way family life works, especially since couples now have to contemplate the fact that they may be divorced," Lundberg says. "We have had to look at how individuals operate within the family, not just the family as a unit."

Indeed, women's economic stake in marriage is profoundly changed by their relatively new ability to earn a good living—and that changes the terms of marriage. Not only that, but most will have fewer children and live longer, and so work will play a larger role in their lives than it did in previous generations. "No young woman in her right mind today would think she could specialize in the profession of homemaking as women did in previous generations," says Lundberg. "They can't count on that as a reasonable lifetime possibility anymore."

Nor is it one that particularly appeals to most women, even after they have children. "I believe more women are working today not just because they 'have' to, but because they are choosing economic autonomy," says Heidi Hartmann, economist at the Women's Policy Institute in Washington, D.C.

"Work does change power within the family. It means that if a woman finds herself in a bad situation, it's easier to get out of it. Basically, I think it's great that women are moving toward economic self-determination. It's empowering for them." . . .

Having that sense of control is certainly one reason why women generally fare better in marriages when they earn a paycheck. But, of course, the formula for women's well-being is not quite so simple as all that. It's not the mere existence of a paycheck that empowers women. Were that the case, Americans would have reached marital bliss by now. "If chores in the home were divided on a *purely* rational basis, husbands and wives who were employed equal numbers of hours would do equal amounts of housework," wrote sociologist Catherine Ross in one of the earliest and most important studies of how couples divvy up the chores.

What she found in 1987, and other researchers have confirmed since then, was that relative earning power is often at the heart of domestic relations. It is the difference between a husband's and wife's income that is often the deciding factor in how a couple divvies up child care and housework. The larger the difference between the two paychecks, the wider the disparity between the spouses. "The more money the wife contributes to the family, the greater leverage in getting her husband to help around the house," wrote Ross. Part of the reason is related to the way that housework and child care are valued in America, of course. Ross noted that "if housework is devalued, unrewarded, onerous and menial, the spouse with more power should be able to delegate it to the other." Which is precisely the conclusion that Steil finds in a review of the literature in the mid-1990s. The economics, combined with the power of gender roles, make for a potent mix in marriage, setting the terms of work and intimacy, of power and dependency, and, most of all, of who owns which work. Once again, it is the association of certain types of work with gender that takes center stage in the relationship. "There is a sense that men shouldn't have to get stuck doing female tasks, that it's somehow denigrating to men, that doing 'women's work' will hurt their self-esteem," she says.

Conversely, some women feel driven to do "women's work" to prove 35
they are "real women," that is, good mothers. That urge can be especially acute when they earn more than their husbands, a situation that obviously upsets the usual assumptions of power between men and women. Their career success calls into question their femininity, their ability to fulfill the traditional expectations of women. One female executive and mother of two children in Fort Worth, Texas, vividly recalls the days not so long ago when she hurried home from her job to cook dinner, supervise her son's piano practice, clean up after the meal, and get him to bed. "I rushed home to make dinner, set the table. Then we'd eat, and I'd drag my son to the piano to practice. We'd spend a half hour at the piano. It was excruciating pain for both my son and me. And I was exhausted by trying to do all this after work," she says. She says she

felt compelled to keep this grueling evening schedule to maintain her own esteem. "I had to prove I was a good mother, and cooking dinner every night was part of that."

As she grew more confident in her abilities as a mother, she gave up the routine. "I can't believe I did that to myself," she says, laughing. Now that her children are nine and fourteen, she no longer needs or wants to keep up the grueling schedule. And unlike many women, she can afford to buy her way out of this situation if her husband doesn't pick up the slack. Both are professionals and live a comfortable lifestyle, and these days, she is just as likely to order takeout at a local restaurant or go to a restaurant. They also have a cleaning service to lighten the load of housework. Interestingly, the services she buys to keep her life on track also incorporate assumptions about gender. Both the housework and child care have always been done by women. . . .

. . . [However,] women's growing economic clout can only enlarge the possibilities for men, women, and their children. Freed from the shackles of old gender roles, they can explore their options in life as they see them.

Most notably, there is a new cultural expectation that men will be more involved fathers. "The idea that men will be active participants in raising children is still relatively new. But it's so evident; when you walk around any major city, you see young men carrying their babies and pushing baby carriages," says Lois Hoffman, professor of psychology at the University of Michigan and one of the nation's leading experts on how women's employment affects today's families. "You just wouldn't have seen that even a decade ago." Indeed, psychologist Faye Crosby notes that it's not so long ago that men were derided as "henpecked" when they did household chores. Now, she and others note, the men who are actively involved with their children are "heroes," making a distinct change in the culture. "Of course, we all know that women still do more than men at home," Crosby adds. "But the point is that the public dialogue is changing, and men's resistance to participating at home is less than it once was." . . .

There is also evidence the "new male," the one driven by his own desire to be a deeply involved father, does indeed exist and his ranks are growing. "Men are still as concerned as ever about providing for their families, but they are also concerned about having a close emotional relationship with their kids," Levine from the Fatherhood Project says. "They see the old role of father as provider as just too narrow. They understand that that role meant that women took care of the emotional lives of families. And that's not what they want."

40 Such a view is not yet sanctioned in the culture, he quickly adds, and what he hears most from men working in corporations is that they need a "safe place" to talk about what it means to be a father today. "Their emotional conflicts are different from women's because they don't feel as comfortable about their conflicts. They don't feel they have permission until they hear

another guy talking about it," he says. "And they have a great fear that they're going to be considered uncommitted to the company if they talk about their families and explore how to be an involved father."

When men do break through the constraints of their traditional roles, studies show, they achieve an intimacy with their children—even with tiny babies—that is very similar to what moms describe. In one breakthrough study, Kyle Pruett, a psychiatrist at Yale University, looked at the dynamics in seventeen families in which the fathers were the primary caregivers for their children. The family situations varied widely: Some of the men were unemployed; the incomes of the rest ranged from $7,000 to $125,000. Some were at home full-time for quite an extended period; in other cases, the men returned to work after a paternity leave. Yet despite all these different circumstances, virtually every one of them reported feelings that paralleled those of new moms—including a reluctance to leave their new babies in anyone else's care, even their wives'. In one case, for example, a father called home repeatedly his first day back on the job—just to make sure that his wife knew how to properly care for their infant.

Men's attachment to their children grows from those same rewards that women have always known come from caring for a child. The drudgery of diapers and whining is worth enduring once a close bond is forged with a child. Indeed, Mike Downey sounds very much like the stereotype of a proud mother as he describes his eight-month-old son. "Davis smiles with his whole face and body. His little legs kick. Nothing could be more exciting," he croons. "Right now, he's just this lump of happiness."

Downey, a technical writer at the University of Texas A&M, insists that "nothing is better or more important than being a dad." And he is true to his word. He took a six-week paternity leave after the birth of their first child, Chelsea. He remembers the days after Chelsea was born as the most special. "I had a reclining chair, and I'd sit in it with Chelsea resting on my cheek and both of us sleeping." After Davis was born, he took a three-week paternity leave. If he had his druthers, he'd cut back to part-time work to be with the kids even more. He is not overly romantic. "I don't think I could do this full-time. I think everyone needs a balance." He's had to learn how to deal with temper tantrums and days that just get plain wearing. Still, he insists, "There's no other job like this. The rewards are instant. You always know when you're doing well, and when you're not. It's hard when you're not. But there's this instant gratification when you do it right. There's nothing else like it, having your child in love with you," he says. "It definitely keeps you wanting to come back the next day."

Rebecca Downey delights in her husband's involvement with the kids. "I think he was sorry he couldn't breast-feed Chelsea," she says, laughing. "But he shared everything else. I think he changed more diapers than I did, took her to half the doctor's appointments, and knows everything about the kids that I do." Part of Mike's devotion, she concedes, is that this is his second marriage. "I think he thought a lot about what it takes to make relationships work," she says.

She believes both her children benefit from the two of them sharing the 45
care. "We both feel that it's good for the kids to have two involved parents, instead of only one or one and a half. We want them to grow up to have a good sense of themselves, that both parents care about them."

At home, the Downeys also divvy up the household chores. "He does his share of the housekeeping, his share of the laundry, and he cleans up after big meals," says Rebecca, a human resources manager. This is a conscious decision, worked out in advance of having children. "He and I chose to share it all, so I have the luxury of pursuing a career and not neglecting my children. I love going to work and coming home."

There is an important lesson in this for their children, Rebecca adds. These kids are growing up seeing that men and women need not be constrained by their gender. Many women feel especially strongly about the expanded options for their daughters. "Chelsea is bright. I want her to believe she can do anything she wants, whatever she's good at," says Rebecca. "She sees Mike doing the chores and assumes men do that. I want her to have that expectation when she gets married someday."

Thousands of miles away, in Kent, Washington, Barbara Brazil, the assistant to the chief counsel in her local school district, echoes similar hopes for her children. With two boys, however, her hopes are to instill a sense of equity on the domestic front. "In our house, our kids know both of us work. They see Dad do the wash and the cooking. I think that's very important. I want them to see men and women sharing the work and treating each other with respect," she says.

Some research bears out Brazil's belief. Kids raised in dual-earner households do tend to be more flexible about men's and women's roles when they become adults. But there are still few wide-ranging, long-term studies of how children turn out when they grow up in such new-style families. The truth is, of course, that most families are still wrestling with the practical and psychological fallout of the changing terms of marriage, making it hard to gauge just how today's kids will react to their parents as role models. Open conflict over the household chores could, for example, turn a girl off from wanting to fight for equity at home. A cultural pessimism, fanned by the conservative backlash, can undermine young women's confidence that men can and will change. As the article "The Death of Supermom" in the widely circulated Long Island newspaper *Newsday,* for example, quoted [elsewhere], shows, young women may be fearful of pressing for equality. "Young women find that after they get married, they don't want to 'poison' the atmosphere with their husbands by an 'overinsistence on equality,'" according to Teri Apter, a social psychologist.

One can only hope that such pessimism won't be allowed to take root 50
in the hearts and minds of today's children. Equality in both work and home life is clearly a winning proposition for everyone. "Women tell me that their

kids are proud of them. They feel that one of the gifts they're giving their children is a new model for a different type of life, one where women can do anything they like," says therapist Lisa Silberstein. For that to happen, Americans need to broaden their idea of possibilities for both men and women.

Questions for Discussion

1. Holcomb says in paragraph 10 that social definitions of men's and women's roles are lagging behind the daily realities of life in a two-income family. Discuss with your classmates the roles they think are appropriate for men and women, or the roles they play now if they are married or expect to play if and when they get married. Have the men seen many models of changing roles in the home for them? Do women still expect husbands' work to be more important than their own?
2. Why do you think Holcomb goes into such detail about the Koenigs? Do you think their troubles before counseling were extreme or typical?
3. How does Holcomb attempt to persuade her readers that men and women can indeed move beyond the idea that there is a "natural order" between the sexes and that upsetting it would be too great a threat to men's ideas of what is masculine and women's ideas of what is feminine? What evidence does she give to show that this "natural order" is simply imposed by stereotypes and can be overcome?
4. Holcomb's examples come from middle-class, professional families. Do you think that implementing the changes she advocates would be more difficult in working-class families, in which husband and wife work for hourly wages?

For Research and Convincing

Look into workplace attitudes toward "family-friendly" policies like flextime and paternity and maternity leaves. At issue here is whether workers, men or women, can afford to reduce their commitment to and involvement in the workplace in order to make time for parenting. What evidence do you find that asking for family leaves or flextime is detrimental to a career? If you conclude that the workplace is essentially hostile to family, try to convince employers that changes need to be made. You might look for evidence of companies that have made changes. How have these worked out? Would employers be correct in responding that choosing parenthood means accepting limits, such as limitations on one's ambitions?

For Inquiry

In paragraph 7 Holcomb speaks of the "new family form" that has arisen because women so frequently work outside the home after having children. While this reading focused on husband-wife work relationships, other relationships are changing to accommodate this new family. Inquire into the debate about the benefits and liabilities to children when both parents work outside the home. What biases do you find in debates about such issues as whether young children should be placed in day care? Write an exploratory essay that goes beyond the polemics and politics of "family values" or "women's rights" and shows how the new family form has changed the parent-child relationship.

STEPHANIE COONTZ

The Future of Marriage

Like Arlene Skolnick, Stephanie Coontz, a historian at Evergreen State College, believes that Americans too often compare families today to an ideal that is more myth than reality. Her book The Way We Never Were *(1992) explores our nostalgia for what we believe were the values of the 1950s. This selection is from her second book,* The Way We Really Are: Coming to Terms with America's Changing Families, *published in 1997. Here, Coontz looks at the declining importance of marriage in our culture and questions how realistic efforts can be that attempt to reverse this trend. Writing from a liberal perspective, she argues that it is unwise to resist the forces of change.*

Note that when Coontz refers to "new consensus" groups, she defined that group earlier in her book as conservatives who want policies favoring the two-parent, married family with traditional gender roles. The "consensus" that they advocate is approval of women working outside the home as long as they take time off from work while their children are young. As part of the compromise, they argue that husbands should help around the house. In the following selection, she argues against the consensus groups' positions on divorce and single-parenting.

MOST AMERICANS support the emergence of alternative ways of organizing parenthood and marriage. They don't want to re-establish the supremacy of the male breadwinner model or to define masculine and feminine roles in any monolithic way. Many people worry, however, about the growth of alternatives to marriage itself. They fear that in some of today's new families parents may not be devoting enough time and resources to their children. The rise of divorce and unwed motherhood is particularly worrisome, because people correctly recognize that children need more than one adult involved in their lives. 1

As a result, many people who object to the "modified male breadwinner" program of the "new consensus" crusaders are still willing to sign on to the other general goals of that movement: "to increase the proportion of children who grow up with two married parents," to "reclaim the ideal of marital permanence," to keep men "involved in family life," and to establish the principle "that every child deserves a father."[1]

Who could disagree? When we appear on panels together, leaders of "traditional values" groups often ask me if I accept the notion that, on the whole, two parents are better than one. If they would add an adjective such as two *good* parents, or even two *adequate* ones, I'd certainly agree. And of course it's better to try to make a marriage work than to walk away at the firt sign of trouble.

As a historian, however, I've learned that when truisms are touted as stunning new research, when aphorisms everyone agrees with are presented as a courageous political program, and when exceptions or complications are ignored for the sake of establishing the basic principles, it's worth taking a close look for a hidden agenda behind the cliches. And, in fact, the new consensus crowd's program for supporting the two-parent family turns out to be far more radical than the feel-good slogans might lead you to believe.

Members of groups such as the Council on Families in America claim 5
they are simply expressing a new consensus when they talk about "reinstitutionalizing enduring marriage," but in the very next breath they declare that it "is time to raise the stakes." They want nothing less than to make lifelong marriage the "primary institutional expression of commitment and obligation to others," the main mechanism for regulating sexuality, male–female relations, economic redistribution, and child rearing. Charles Murray says that the goal is "restoration of marriage as an utterly distinct, legal relationship." Since marriage must be "privileged," other family forms or child-rearing arrangements should not receive tax breaks, insurance benefits, or access to public housing and federal programs. Any reform that would make it easier for divorced parents, singles, unmarried partners, or stepfamilies to function is suspect because it removes "incentives" for people to get and stay married. Thus, these groups argue, adoption and foster care policies should "reinforce marriage as the child-rearing norm." Married couples, and only married couples, should be given special tax relief to raise their children. Some leaders of the Institute for American Values propose that we encourage both private parties and government bodies "to distinguish between married and unmarried *couples* in housing, credit, zoning, and other areas." Divorce and illegitimacy should be stigmatized.[2]

We've come quite a way from the original innocuous statements about the value of two-parent families and the importance of fathers to children. Now we find out that we must make marriage the only socially sanctioned method for organizing male–female roles and fulfilling adult obligations to the young. "There is no realistic alternative to the one we propose," claims the Council on Families in America. To assess this claim, we need to take a close look at what the consensus crusaders mean when they talk about the need to reverse the "deinstitutionalizing" of marriage.[3]

Normally, social scientists have something very specific in mind when they say that a custom or behavior is "institutionalized." They mean it comes "with a well-understood set of obligations and rights," all of which are backed up by law, customs, rituals, and social expectations. In this sense, marriage is still one of America's most important and valued institutions.[4]

But it is true that marriage has lost its former monopoly over the organization of people's major life transitions. Alongside a continuing commitment to marriage, other arrangements for regulating sexual behavior, channeling relations between men and women, and raising children now exist. Marriage was once the primary way of organizing work along lines of age and sex. It determined the roles that men and women played at home and in public. It was the main vehicle for redistributing resources to old and young, and it served as the most important marker of adulthood and respectable status.

All this is no longer the case. Marriage has become an option rather than a necessity for men and women, even during the child-raising years. Today only half of American children live in nuclear families with both biological parents present. One child in five lives in a stepfamily and one in four lives in a "single-parent" home. The number of single parents increased from 3.8 million in 1970 to 6.9 million in 1980, a rate that averages out to a truly unprecedented 6 percent increase each year. In the 1980s, the rate of increase slowed and from 1990 to 1995 it leveled off, but the total numbers have coninued to mount, reaching 12.2 million by 1996.[5]

These figures understate how many children actually have two parents in the home, because they confuse marital status with living arrangements. Approximately a quarter of all births to unmarried mothers occur in households where the father is present, so those children have two parents at home in fact if not in law. Focusing solely on the marriage license distorts our understanding of trends in children's living arrangements. For example, the rise in cohabitation between 1970 and 1984 led to more children being classified as living in single-parent families. But when researchers counted unmarried couples living together as two-parent families, they found that children were spending *more* time, not less, with both parents in 1984 than in 1970. Still, this simply confirms the fact that formal marriage no longer organizes as many life decisions and transitions as it did in the past.[6]

Divorce, cohabitation, remarriage, and single motherhood are not the only factors responsible for the eclipse of marriage as the primary institution for organizing sex roles and interpersonal obligations in America today. More people are living on their own before marriage, so that more young adults live outside a family environment than in earlier times. And the dramatic extension of life spans means that more people live alone after the death of a spouse.[7]

The growing number of people living on their own ensures that there are proportionately fewer families of *any* kind than there used to be. The Census Bureau defines families as residences with more than one householder related by blood, marriage, or adoption. In 1940, under this definition, families accounted for 90 percent of all households in the country. By 1970, they represented just 81 percent of all households, and by 1990 they represented 71 percent. The relative weight of marriage in society has decreased. Social institutions and values have adapted to the needs, buying decisions, and lifestyle choices of singles. Arrangements other than nuclear family transactions have developed to meet people's economic and interpersonal needs. Elders, for example, increasingly depend on Social Security and private pension plans, rather than the family, for their care.[8]

Part of the deinstitutionalization of marriage, then, comes from factors that few people would want to change even if they could. Who wants to shorten the life spans of the elderly, even though that means many more people are living outside the institution of marriage than formerly? Should we lower the age of marriage, even though marrying young makes people more likely to divorce?[9] Or should young people be forced to live at home until they do marry? Do we really want to try to make marriage, once again, the only path for living a productive and fulfilling adult life?

Working Women, Singlehood, and Divorce

If the family values crusaders believe they are the only people interested in preserving marriages, especially where children's well-being is involved, self-righteousness has blinded them to reality. I've watched people of every political persuasion struggle to keep their families together, and I've met very few divorced parents who hadn't tried to make their marriages work. Even the most ardent proponents of reinstitutionalizing marriage recognize that they cannot and should not force everyone to get and stay married. They do not propose outlawing divorce, and they take pains to say that single parents who were not at fault should not be blamed. Yet they still claim that moral exhortations to take marriage more seriously will reduce divorce enough to "revive a culture of enduring marriage."

15 This is where the radical right wing of the family values movement is far more realistic than most moderates: So long as women continue to make long-term commitments to the workforce, marriage is unlikely to again become the lifelong norm for the vast majority of individuals unless draconian measures are adopted to make people get and stay married. Paid work gives women the option to leave an unsatisfactory marriage. In certain instances, much as liberals may hate to admit it, wives' employment increases dissatisfaction with marriage, sometimes on the part of women, sometimes on the part of their husbands. When a wife spends long hours at work or holds a nontraditional job, the chance of divorce increases.[10]

I'm not saying we can't slow down the divorce rate, lessen emotional and economic disincentives for marriage, and foster longer-lasting commitments. But there is clearly a limit to how many people can be convinced to marry and how many marriages can be made to last when women have the option to be economically self-supporting. In this sense, the right-wing suspicion that women's work destabilizes marriage has a certain logic.

There is, however, a big problem with the conclusion that the radical right draws from this observation. To say that women's employment has *allowed* divorce and singlehood to rise in society as a whole does not mean that women's work *causes* divorce and singlehood at the level of the individual family, or that convincing women to reduce their work hours and career aspirations would reestablish more stable marriages.[11]

Trying to reverse a historical trend by asking individuals to make personal decisions opposing that trend is usually futile. When individuals try to conduct their personal lives as if broader social forces were not in play, they often end up worse off than if they adapted to the changing times. What traditional values spokesman in his right mind would counsel his own daughter not to prepare herself for higher-paid, nontraditional jobs because these might lead to marital instability down the road?

After all, even if a woman *prefers* to have a male breadwiner provide for her, the fact that people can now readily buy substitutes for what used to require a housewife's labor changes marriage dynamics in decisive ways. Most individuals and families can now survive quite easily without a full-time domestic worker. If this frees women to work outside the home, it also frees men from the necessity of supporting a full-time homemaker.

Before the advent of washing machines, frozen foods, wrinkle-resistant 20
fabrics, and 24-hour one-stop shopping, Barbara Ehrenreich has remarked, "the single life was far too strenuous for the average male." Today, though, a man does not really need a woman to take care of cooking, cleaning, decorating, and making life comfortable. Many men still choose marriage for love and companionship. But as Ehrenreich notes, short of outlawing TV dinners and drip-dry shirts, it's hard to see how we can make marriage as indispensable for men as it used to be. And short of reversing laws against job discrimination, there's no way we can force women into more dependence on marriage. Neither men nor women need marriage as much as they used to. Asking people to behave as if they do just sets them up for trouble.[12]

Wives who don't work outside the home, for instance, are at much higher economic and emotional risk if they *do* get deserted or divorced than women who have maintained jobs. They are far more likely to be impoverished by divorce, even if they are awarded child support, and they eventually recover a far lower proportion of the family income that they had during marriage than women who had been working prior to the divorce.[13]

Women who refrain from working during marriage, quit work to raise their children, or keep their career aspirations low to demonstrate that "family comes first" are taking a big gamble, because there are many factors other than female independence that produce divorce. Some of them are associated with women's decisions or expectations *not* to work or *not* to aspire to higher education. For example, couples who marry in their teens are twice as likely to divorce as those who marry in their twenties. Women who marry for the first time at age 30 or more have exceptionally low divorce rates, despite their higher likelihood of commitment to paid work. Women who don't complete high school have higher divorce rates than women who do, and high school graduates have higher divorce rates than women who go on to college. With further higher education, divorce rates go up again, but should we advise a woman to abandon any aspirations she may have developed in college because her statistical chance of staying married will rise if she quits her education now? . . .

Highly educated and high-paid women may have a greater chance of divorcing, but women with low earnings and education have lower prospects of getting married in the first place. Men increasingly choose to marry women who have good jobs and strong educational backgrounds. In the 1980s, reversing the pattern of the 1920s, "women with the most economic resources were the most likely to marry." But of course these are also the women most able to leave a bad marriage.[14]

The Issue of No-Fault Divorce

Some people believe we could stabilize families, and protect homemakers who sacrifice economic independence, by making divorce harder to get, especially in families with children. This sounds reasonable at first hearing. Divorce tends to disadvantage women economically, and to set children back in several ways. It is hardest of all on women who committed themselves and their children to the bargain implied by the 1950s marriage ideal—forgoing personal economic and educational advancement in order to raise a family, and expecting lifetime financial support from a husband in return. A 47-year-old divorced mother describes what happened to her: "Instead of starting a career for myself, I helped my husband get his business started. I had four children. I made the beds. I cooked the meals. I cleaned the house. I kept my marriage vows. Now I find myself divorced in midlife with no career. My husband makes $100,000 a year, and we're struggling to get by on a quarter of that."[15]

We could avoid such inequities, say the family values crusaders, if today's 25
marriage contract was not "considerably less binding than, for example, a contract to sell a car or a cow." "The first step is to end unilateral divorce," says Maggie Gallagher of the Institute for American Values. She advocates imposing a five- to seven-year waiting period for contested divorces.[16]

The argument that "we ought to enforce marriage just like any other contract" sounds reasonable until you take a historical and sociological perspective on the evolution of divorce law. Then a number of problems become clear. First, requiring people to stay together has nothing to do with enforcing contract law. When someone breaks a contract, the courts don't normally force the violator to go back and provide the services; they merely assign payment of money damages. If an entertainer refuses to perform a concert, for example, no matter how irresponsibly, the promoter cannot call the police to haul the performer into the theater and stand over him while he sings, or even impose a cooling-off period so he can rethink whether he wants to honor the contract. Instead, the promoter is awarded damages. The contract analogy may make a case for seeking damages, but it has no relevance to the issue of making divorce harder to get.

A woman who has sacrificed economic opportunities to do the bulk of child raising ought to get compensation for that when a marriage breaks up, no matter whose "fault" the failure is. Even full-time working wives often give up higher-paying jobs or education in order to take the lion's share of responsibility for family life. The tendency of many courts during the 1970s to reduce alimony and maintenance allowances for wives was based on the mistaken assumption that because more women were working, male–female equality had already been achieved. Maintenance awards need to be rethought, as well as separated from child support payments, a process now occurring in many states. But improving maintenance provisions for the spouse who did family caregiving is a separate question from forcing someone to remain in a marriage against his or her will—or to do *without* support for a protracted period of time while the courts sort through who was "at fault."[17]

Second, making divorces harder to get would often exacerbate the bitterness and conflict that are associated with the *worst* outcomes of divorce for kids. One of the hot new concepts of the consensus school is that we need to preserve the good-enough marriage—where there is not abuse or neglect but merely an "acceptable" amount of adult unhappiness or discontent in comparison to the benefits for children in keeping the family together. But what government agency or private morals committee will decide if a marriage is "good enough"?

One author suggests we might require parents with children under 18 to "demonstrate that the *family* was better off broken than intact. Unhappiness with one's spouse would not then be a compelling argument for divorce. Domestic violence would be." Yet what would prevent the person who wanted out of the marriage from upping the ante—for example, from threatening domestic violence to get his or her way?[18]

Furthermore, it is *women* more than men who have historically needed 30
the protection of divorce. And yes, I mean protection. Because of men's greater economic and personal power, one divorce historian points out, husbands traditionally handled marital dissatisfaction by intimidating or coercing their wives into doing what the men wanted, such as accepting an extramarital affair or living with abuse. Alternatively, the man simply walked away, taking no legal action. Women, with less social and domestic power, "turned to an external agency, the law, for assistance." Women were the majority of petitioners for divorce and legal separation in English and American history long before the emergence of a feminist movement. Access to divorce remains a critical option for women.[19]

Finally, sociological research finds little evidence that no-fault laws have been the main cause of rising divorce rates, or that, on average, women do worse with no-fault than they did in the days when spouses had to hire detectives or perjurers to prove fault. While more than half the states enacted some form of no-fault divorce legislation in the 1970s, the rates of marital dissolution in most of these states were no higher in the 1970s than would be expected from trends in states that did *not* change their laws. Researcher Larry Bumpass suggests that, in some instances, no-fault has speeded up "cases that were already coming down the pipeline," but the rise in divorce seems to be independent of any particular legal or social policy. And, of course, making divorce harder to get does nothing to prevent separation or desertion.[20]

Work on preventing unnecessary divorces, separations, and desertions needs to happen *before* a marriage gets to the point of rupture. We can experiment with numerous ways to do that, from marriage education to moral persuasion to parenting classes to counseling. We can educate young people about the dangers of our society's throwaway mentality, pointing out that it creates emotional as well as material waste. We should certainly warn people that divorce is never easy for the partners or for their children. Still, history suggests that no amount of classes, counseling, or crusades will reinstitutionalize marriage in the sense that the family values crusaders desire.

Divorce rates are the product of long-term social and economic changes, not of a breakdown in values. Individual belief systems are a comparatively minor factor in predicting divorce. Despite the Catholic Church's strong opposition to divorce, for example, practicing Catholics are as likely to divorce as non-Catholics. Studies have shown that prior disapproval of divorce has little bearing on a person's later chance of divorce, although people who do divorce are likely to modify their previous disapproval. Once again, we have a situation where many intricately related factors are involved. Neither legal compulsions nor moral exhortations are likely to wipe out historical transformations that have been building for so long.[21]

Unwed Motherhood

Many people I talk with think the place we should draw the line on family diversity is at the question of unwed motherhood. If we could just take care of this problem, they say, society could survive even a fairly large number of divorces.

The growth of unwed motherhood is an even more complicated story 35
than that of divorce, because some of it stems from expanding options for women and some from worsening constraints, especially for low-income or poorly educated women. Often, it's a messy mix, with increased sexual freedom interacting in explosive ways with decreased economic opportunities for both sexes and continuing inequities between men and women.

For example, many people consider the rise in pregnancy among very young teens a symptom of what's wrong with today's "liberated" sexuality. But men over age 20 father five times more births among junior high school girls, and two and a half times more births among senior high school girls, than do the girls' male peers. When the mother is 12 years old or younger, the father's average age is 22. These girls may be responding to new sexual options, but they are doing so within a very old pattern of unequal, exploitative power relations. Three-fourths of girls who have sex before age 14 say they were coerced, and research suggests that a majority of teens who give birth have been physically or sexually abused at some point in their past.[22]

Contrary to what you might guess, the most rapid increase in the rate of nonmarital childbearing occurred between 1940 and 1958, when the rate *tripled* from 7.1 births per 1,000 unmarried women to 21.2. The rate of unwed childbearing rose very slowly from 1958 to 1971, then declined until 1976. Then it rose steadily again until 1992, not quite doubling to reach 45.2 unwed births per 1,000 unmarried women in 1992.[23]

This timing obviously calls into question the popular perception that 1960s permissiveness started the rise in unwed childbearing. Indeed, the increase in unwed motherhood between 1960 and 1975 was *not* due to a significant increase in birth rates among unmarried women but to a combination of two other factors. One was the fact that married women's fertility fell by more than 40 percent during the period, which increased the proportion of unwed births among the total number of births. The second was that the absolute number of single women was rising, putting more women "at risk" for an out-of-wedlock birth. Only after 1975 did the *proportion* of unmarried women who gave birth begin to rise—not just their absolute numbers or their contribution to total births in comparison to married women.[24]

So it's wrong to blame the rise of unwed births on the sexual revolution of the 1960s and 1970s. While it's true that the decision to raise a child born out of wedlock is related to changing cultural values, it appears that changing economic relations between men and women are more important than is usually realized. The renewed increase in rates of unmarried childbearing after 1975 *followed* the fall in real wages for young men that began in 1973. Men with low or irregular wages are far less likely to marry a woman they impregnate than men who have a steady job and earn a family wage. Women are less likely to see such men as desirable marriage partners.

The interactions between economic, social, and cultural factors are too 40
complicated to support any single generalization about *the* cause of unwed motherhood. In a small though highly publicized number of cases, women's new economic independence has allowed them to choose to bear children out of wedlock. Contrary to conventional wisdom, this choice is more common for women in their twenties and thirties than for teens, and the proportion of such cases remains small. Unwed motherhood is seldom actively pursued by women. National statistics reveal that more than 80 percent of pregnancies among unmarried women are unplanned.

Although the consensus crowd may call for a campaign of stigmatization to prevent women from keeping an unplanned child, it is unlikely that women "of independent means" will give up their hard-earned freedom of choice. And stigmatization would not necessarily prevent unwed motherhood among impoverished women. Historically, out-of-wedlock births have often soared during times of economic stress, and the main result of stigmatization or punitive social policy has been child abandonment or even murder.[25]

Economic stress remains a critical factor in many out-of-wedlock births. The overwhelming majority of single mothers have only a high school education or less. Only one in seven unmarried mothers has a family income above $25,000 the year her child is born; 40 percent have incomes of less than $10,000.[26]

I understand why people worry about women who seem not to plan their childbearing wisely. But I also know, both from sociological research and from participating in parenting workshops across the country, that there are hundreds of paths to becoming a single mother. Some of the tales I hear would seem irresponsible to even the most ardent proponent of women's right to choose; others stem from complicated accidents or miscalculations that even the most radical right winger would probably forgive; still others flow from carefully thought-out choices. But I fail to see how we can draw a hard and fast line between the decisions of unmarried and married women. As one unwed mother said to me, "I made some stupid choices to get where I am. But my reasons for having a kid were no worse than my sister's, who had a baby she didn't want in order to save her marriage. Why should I be the one they stand up and preach against on TV?"

Take the three never-married mothers I met at a workshop in Georgia. One was a young girl who had gotten pregnant "by accident/on purpose" in hopes that her unfaithful boyfriend would marry her. It hadn't worked, and in the ensuing year she sometimes left her baby unattended while she went out on new dates. Shocked into self-examination by being reported for neglect, she concluded that going back to school and developing some job skills might be more help in escaping her own neglectful parents than chasing after a new boyfriend. Another, 25 years old at the time we met, had been 15 when she got pregnant. She considered abortion, but she would have had to drive 300 miles, by herself, to the nearest provider, and she didn't even have money for a hotel room.

Both these young mothers had gone onto welfare. The first had gotten 45
off in three years, and never expected to need it again. The second had stayed on for only a year the first time, then married and found her first job. Shortly afterward, though, her husband left her and she went back on welfare because her work didn't cover child care or medical benefits. Within a year she had found another job and left welfare again. But the company relocated. Twice more she had cycled on and off Aid to Families with Dependent Children because of layoffs or ill health.

At one low point in her welfare days, she told me, she tried prostitution, planning to accumulate some cash she could hide from the welfare agency so she'd have a small financial cushion once she landed a new job. Unfortunately, she said wryly, she hadn't anticipated the job-related expenses in that occupation. For a while she spent a lot of her extra earnings on drugs and alcohol, "to get the dirty taste out of my mouth." She was straight and sober now, and she had a job, but she wasn't willing to stand up and make any testimonials, as her minister had urged her to do during the workshop at which we met. "It's going to be one day at a time for a long time."

These two stories are quite typical. Three-fourths of welfare recipients leave welfare within two years (half get out within a year), but the scarcity and instability of the jobs they find often drive them back to welfare in a few years. Even if they keep their jobs, they seldom earn enough to rise above the poverty line. In light of the hardships facing poor and near-poor mothers, including lack of jobs, child care, and work training, the fact that such a tiny proportion of women stay on welfare continuously for five years (about 15 percent) is testimony to a work ethic and determination that many of us, more fortunately placed, have never tested so severely.[27]

The third woman, by contrast, was an older, well-paid professional who superficially fit the stereotype of the selfish, liberated woman "mocking the importance of fatherhood" by choosing to have a child on her own. But this woman had had three wedding plans fall through before she decided to go ahead on her own. She attributed her failures with men to having been caught between two value systems. Old-fashioned enough in her romantic fantasies to be attracted only to powerful, take-charge men, she was modern enough in her accomplishments that such men generally found her threatening once the early excitement of a relationship died down. At age 35, her last fiancé had walked away, leaving her pregnant. With her biological clock ticking "now or never" in her ear, she decided to have the child.

I have also met men who tell angry stories about having been tricked by a woman into thinking it was "safe" to have sex. "Why should I have to pay child support?" demanded one. "Doesn't that just encourage women to have babies outside of marriage?" It is, of course, totally unethical for a woman to assure a man that sex is "safe" when it isn't. But what is the alternative? If a man could get off the hook by claiming "she told me it was safe," no unmarried father would pay child support.

Charles Murray of the American Enterprise Institute thinks that would 50
be just fine. He advocates denying child support to any woman who bears a baby out of wedlock: Girls, he declares, need to grow up knowing that if they want any legal claims whatsoever on the father of their child, "they must marry." Answering objections that this gives men free reign to engage in irresponsible sex, Murray offers a response straight out of a Dickens novel. A man who gets a woman pregnant, he observes, "has approximately the same causal responsibility" for her condition "as a slice of chocolate cake has in determining whether a woman gains weight." It is *her* responsibility, not the cake's, to resist temptation.[28]

The analogy works nicely if you think of sexual behavior in terms of greedy women cruising an erotic dessert buffet, trying to decide which sperm-filled slice of temptation to sample. But it misses something important about the dynamics of courting. For centuries, parents have had to teach their daughters that it was ultimately their responsibility to avoid pregnancy, whatever promises a boy might make. Now we will have to teach our sons the same thing, and strict child support just might drive the lesson home.

Meanwhile, though, unwed motherhood, like divorce, is rising around the world. In places as diverse as Southern Africa and Northern Europe, more than 20 percent of all births are to unwed mothers. Part of the reason is the rise in women's economic independence. Part is the decline in society's coercive controls over personal life. And part is simply that with falling marital fertility, even comparatively low rates of unmarried childbearing create higher proportions of children born to unwed mothers.

Unwed motherhood creates tremendous hardships in some situations, while it is far less damaging in societies that pay women decent wages and make a commitment to providing parental leave and quality child care. Half of all births in Sweden and a quarter of all births in France are to unmarried women, for example, but the children do not face the same poverty and limited life options as their counterparts in the United States. We will not abolish unwed motherhood; but we can affect its outcome.[29] . . .

The Reproductive Revolution

The final obstacle to reinstitutionalizing traditional marriage is the recent revolution in reproductive techniques. The main beneficiaries of this revolution have been heterosexual married couples with infertility problems. But the methods developed to aid such couples in conceiving have shattered what we might quite literally call older "preconceptions" about the links between marriage, childbirth, and child raising. Reproduction has been separated not just from marriage but from gender, age, and even sex itself.

55 Consider the possibilities of in vitro fertilization, which involves fertilizing a woman's eggs in a Petri dish and then transferring them to the woman's womb. The eggs may come from the woman herself or from a female donor; the sperm can come from the woman's partner or another male donor. An ovum transfer involves moving a five-day-old embryo from one female to another, who then carries the embryo to term. When these are combined, it means that a "child can have at least five parents," not counting any later changes with remarriage: a donor mother, a birth mother, a social mother (the one who raises the child), a donor father, and a social father.[30]

Traditional definitions of marriage and parental rights will not resolve the issues raised by such medical and technological change. Surrogate custody disputes have pitted the claims of biological mothers against biological fathers. In one court case a woman who went through pregnancy and birth with someone else's egg was termed a "prenatal foster mother." A man who participated with his wife in freezing embryos for in vitro fertilization sued (unsuccessfully) after the divorce to prevent her from implanting them, charging that he was being forced to become a father against his will.[31]

Ethicists debate whether it is fair for older mothers and fathers to take advantage of the new technology, given that they may die before their child even reaches adolescence. Issues of privacy and obligation arise for the biological parents of embryo transplants. Social parents move into uncharted territory in explaining "the facts of life" to their children. Payments for egg donors complicate the question of what is a free and informed choice. Yet many donors speak of the joy of helping another woman have a child; and the parents of children conceived by unconventional fertilization methods are as loving and caring as those who conceive by "natural" means. Obviously, our definitions of parental rights and responsibilities must change to encompass these new possibilities and danger spots.[32]

Reality Bites

It makes little sense to whip up hysteria about an issue if you don't have any concrete solutions. Yet for people who believe we're on the verge of "cultural suicide," the measures proposed by the family values crusaders are curiously halfhearted. Amitai Etzioni urges individuals to make "supervows," voluntary premarriage contracts indicating "that they take their marriage more seriously than the law requires." One of the few concrete reforms David

Blankenhorn proposes to ensure "a father for every child" is that we forbid unmarried women access to sperm banks and artificial insemination. In addition, he asks men to take pledges that "marriage is the pathway to effective fatherhood," wants the president to issue an annual report on the "state of fatherhood," and thinks Congress should designate "Safe Zones" for male responsibility. Can anyone who looks at the historical trends in divorce, unwed motherhood, and reproductive technology seriously think such measures will bring back the married-couple–biological-parent monopoly over child rearing?[33]

Barbara Dafoe Whitehead of the Institute for American Values advocates "restigmatization" of divorce and unwed motherhood; "stigmatization," she argues, "is a powerful means of regulating behavior, as any smoker or overeater will testify." But while overeaters may now feel "a stronger sense of shame than in the past," this has hardly wiped out the problem of obesity. Indeed, the proportion of overweight Americans has increased steadily since the 1950s. As for curbing smoking, the progress here has come from stringent public regulations against smoking, combined with intensive (and expensive) interventions to help people quit. The pretended "consensus" of the new family values crusaders would quickly evaporate if they attempted to institute an equally severe campaign against single parents. After all, 90 percent of the people in a 1995 Harris poll believe society "should value all types of families."[34]

Besides, stigmatization is a blunt instrument that does not distinguish 60
between the innocent and the guilty any better than no-fault divorce. Dan Quayle's latest book, for example, includes a divorced family among five examples he gives of the "strong" families that still exist in America. He puts a divorced single mother into a book intended to prove that "intact" families are ideal because, "Though Kathy experienced divorce, she did not foresee or want it." It was not this woman's intent, Quayle explains, to pursue "a fast-track career." She "expected to play the traditional role, to raise her children and create a home for a husband of whom she was proud." Such distinctions put the consensus brokers in the tricky business of examining people's motives to decide which divorced or single parents had good intentions and therefore should be exempt from stigmatization.[35]

It would be easy to dismiss the flimsy reforms proposed by the "new consensus" proponents as fuzzy-headed wishful thinking were it not for the fact that their approach opens such a dangerous gap between practice and theory. At best, affirming lifelong marriage as a principle while issuing exceptions for people whose *intentions* were good encourages a hypocrisy that is already far too common in today's political and cultural debates. Consider Congressman Newt Gingrich, who was born into a single-parent family, made his ex-wife a single mom by divorcing her, and has a half-sister who is gay. "I'm not sitting here as someone who is unfamiliar with the late twentieth century," he has said. "I know life can be complicated." Yet that didn't stop him from blaming Susan Smith's murder of her two children in 1994 on lack of family values. . . .[36]

At worst, this approach offers right-wing extremists moderate-sounding cover for attempts to penalize or coerce families and individuals that such groups find offensive. Insisting that everyone give lip service to lifelong marriage as an ideal while recognizing in practice that life is complicated is like having a law on the books that *everyone* breaks at one time or another. Authorities can use it selectively to discipline the poor, the powerless, or the unpopular, while letting everyone else off the hook.

The family values crusade may sound appealing in the abstract. But it offers families no constructive way to resolve the new dilemmas of family life. Forbidding unmarried women access to sperm banks, for instance, is hardly going to put the package of child rearing and marriage back together. It would take a lot more repression than that to reinstitutionalize lifelong marriage in today's society.

As Katha Pollitt argues, "we'd have to bring back the whole nineteenth century: Restore the cult of virginity and the double standard, ban birth control, restrict divorce, kick women out of decent jobs, force unwed pregnant women to put their babies up for adoption on pain of social death, make out-of-wedlock children legal nonpersons. That's not going to happen."[37] If it did happen, American families would be worse off, not better, than they are right now.

NOTES

1. "Marriage in America: A Report to the Nation" (New York: Council on Families in America, Mar. 1995) 10–11, 13.
2. David Popenoe, "Modern Marriage: Revising the Cultural Script," in David Popenoe, Jean Bethke Elshtain, and David Blankenhorn, eds., *Promises to Keep: Decline and Renewal of Marriage in America* (Lanham: Rowman, 1996) 254; "Marriage in America" 4; David Popenoe, *Life without Father: Compelling New Evidence That Fatherhood and Marriage Are Indispensable for the Good of Children and Society* (New York: Free Press, 1996) 222; David Blankenhorn, *Fatherless America: Confronting Our Most Urgent Social Problem* (New York: Basic, 1995) 229; Charles Murray, "Keep It in the Family," *Times of London* 14 Nov. 1993; Maggie Gallagher, *The Abolition of Marriage: How We Destroy Lasting Love* (Washington: Regnery, 1996) 250–57; Barbara Dafoe Whitehead, "Dan Quayle Was Right," *Atlantic Monthly* 271 (April 1993): 49.
3. "Marriage in America" 4. The "deinstitutionalizing" phrase comes from Blankenhorn 224.
4. William Goode, *World Changes in Divorce Patterns* (New Haven: Yale UP, 1993) 330.
5. On the leveling off of family change, see Peter Kilborn, "Shifts in Families Reach a Plateau," *New York Times* 27 Nov. 1996. Other information in this and the following three paragraphs, unless otherwise noted, come from Steven Rawlings and Arlene Saluter, *Household and Family Characteristics: March 1994,* Current Population Reports Series P20-483 (Washington: Bureau of the Census, U.S. Department of Commerce, Sept.

1995) xviii–ix; Michael Haines, "Long-term Marriage Patterns in the United States from Colonial Times to the Present," *History of the Family* 1 (1996); Arthur Norton and Louisa Miller, *Marriage, Divorce, and Remarriage in the 1990s,* Current Population Reports Series P23-180 (Washington: Bureau of the Census, Oct. 1992); Richard Gelles, *Contemporary Families: A Sociological View* (Thousand Oaks: Sage, 1995) 116–20, 176; Shirley Zimmerman, "Family Trends: What Implications for Family Policy?" *Family Relations* 41 (1992): 424; Margaret Usdansky, "Single Motherhood: Stereotypes vs. Statistics," *New York Times* 11 Feb. 1996: 4; *New York Times* 30 Aug. 1994: A9; *New York Times* 10 Mar. 1996: A11, and 17 Mar. 1996: A8; U.S. Bureau of the Census, *Statistical Abstracts of the United States* (Washington: 1992); Sara McLanahan and Lynne Casper, "Growing Diversity and Inequality in the American Family," in Reynolds Farley, ed., *State of the Union: America in the 1990s,* vol. 1 (New York: Russell Sage, 1995).

6. Larry Bumpass, "Patterns, Causes, and Consequences of Out-of-Wedlock Childbearing: What Can Government Do?" *Focus* 17 (U of Wisconsin–Madison Institute for Research on Poverty, 1995): 42; Larry Bumpass and R. Kelly Raley, "Redefining Single-Parent Families: Cohabitation and Changing Family Reality," *Demography* 32 (1995): 98.
7. *Olympian* 26 Feb. 1996: D6.
8. Susan Watkins, Jane Menken, and John Bongaarts, "Demographic Foundations of Family Change," *American Sociological Review* 52 (1987): 346–58.
9. Barbara Wilson and Sally Clarke, "Remarriages: A Demographic Profile," *Journal of Family Issues* 13 (1992).
10. Gelles 344–45; Alan Booth, David Johnson, Lynn White, and John Edwards, "Women, Outside Employment, and Marital Instability," *American Journal of Sociology* 90 (1989): 567–83.
11. Saul Hoffman and Greg Duncan, "The Effect of Incomes, Wages, and AFDC Benefits on Marital Disruption," *Journal of Human Resources* 30 (1993): 1–41.
12. Barbara Ehrenreich, "On the Family," *Z Magazine* Nov. 1995: 10; Ailsa Burns and Cath Scott, *Mother-Headed Families and Why They Have Increased* (Hillsdale: Erlbaum, 1994) 183.
13. Terry Arendell, "Women and the Economics of Divorce in the Contemporary United States," *Signs* 13 (1987): 125.
14. Valerie Oppenheimer and Vivian Lew, "American Marriage Formation in the Eighties: How Important Was Women's Economic Independence?" in K. O. Mason and A. Jensen, eds., *Gender and Family Change in Industrialized Countries* (Oxford: Oxford UP, 1994); Aimee Dechter and Pamela Smock, "The Fading Breadwinner Role and the Economic Implications for Young Couples," Institute for Research on Poverty, Discussion Paper 1051-94, Dec. 1994: 2; Marian Wright Edelman, *Families in Peril: An Agenda for Social Change* (Cambridge: Harvard UP, 1987) 55;

Lawrence Lynn and Michael McGeary, eds., *Inner-City Poverty in the United States* (Washington: National Academy Press, 1990) 163–67; University of Michigan researcher Greg Duncan, testimony before the House Select Committee on Children, Youth and Families, 19 Feb. 1992; *New York Times* 4 Sept. 1992: A1; Daniel Lichter, Diane McLaughlin, George Kephart, and David Landry, "Race and the Retreat from Marriage: A Shortage of Marriageable Men?" *American Sociological Review* 57 (1992): 797; Kristin Luker, "Dubious Conceptions—The Controversy over Teen Pregnancy," *American Prospect* Spring 1991.

15. Dirk Johnson, "Attacking No-Fault Notion, Conservatives Try to Put Blame Back in Divorce," *New York Times* 12 Feb. 1996: A8.
16. Maggie Gallagher, "Why Make Divorce Easy?" *New York Times* 20 Feb. 1996; "Welfare Reform and Tax Incentives Can Reverse the Anti-Marriage Tilt," *Insight* 15 Apr. 1996: 24; Suzanne Fields, "The Fault-Lines of Today's Divorce Policies," *Washington Times* 22 Apr. 1996. See also Maggie Gallagher, *The Abolition of Marriage: How We Destroy Lasting Love* (Washington: Regnery, 1996).
17. Stephen Sugarman and Herma Hill Kay, eds., *Divorce Reform at the Crossroads* (New Haven: Yale UP, 1990); Cynthia Stearns, "Divorce and the Displaced Homemaker: A Discourse on Playing with Dolls, Partnership Buyouts and Dissociation under No-Fault," *University of Chicago Law Review* 60 (1993): 128–39; Ann Luquer Estin, "Maintenance, Alimony, and the Rehabilitation of Family Care," *North Carolina Law Review* 71 (1993). For my understanding of recent legal trends, I am greatly indebted to conversations with Olympia attorney Christina Meserve.
18. Maggie Gallagher, "Recreating Marriage," in Popenoe, Elshtain, and Blankenhorn 237.
19. Roderick Phillips, *Untying the Knot: A Short History of Divorce* (Cambridge: Cambridge UP, 1991) 232. The one exception to this occurs in countries where men, but not women, have the right to divorce. High divorce rates in these countries tend to be associated with low status for women; in other situations, high divorce rates are associated with women's higher status and greater amount of economic and personal autonomy. See Burns and Scott 182.
20. Larry Bumpass, "What's Happening to the Family? Interactions between Demographic and Institutional Change," *Demography* 27 (1990) 485.
21. Andrew Cherlin, *Marriage, Divorce, Remarriage* (Cambridge: Harvard UP, 1981) 49; Johnson; William Goode, *World Changes in Divorce Patterns* (New Haven: Yale UP, 1993) 318; Shirley Zimmerman, "The Welfare State and Family Breakup: The Mythical Connection," *Family Relations* 40 (1991): 141.
22. Mike Males, "Poverty, Rape, Adult/Teen Sex: Why Pregnancy Prevention Programs Don't Work," *Phi Delta Kappan* Jan. 1994: 409; Ellen Goodman, "Return to Statutory Rape Laws," *Olympian* 22 Feb. 1995: A9; Mike Males, *The Scapegoat Generation: America's War on Adolescents*

(Monroe: Common Courage, 1996) 17–18; Debra Boyer and David Fine, "Sexual Abuse as a Factor in Adolescent Pregnancy and Child Maltreatment," *Family Planning Perspectives* 24 (1992).

23. *Vital and Health Statistics: Births to Unmarried Mothers,* series 21, no. 53 (Hyattsville: National Center for Health Statistics, Department of Health and Human Services, 1995) table 1, p. 27.
24. Sara McLanahan and Lynne Casper, "Growing Diversity and Inequality in the American Family," in Reynolds Farley, ed., *State of the Union: America in the 1990s,* vol. 2 (New York: Russell Sage, 1995) 10–11; Stephanie Ventura, *Vital and Health Statistics: Births to Unmarried Mothers: United States, 1980–92,* series 21, Data on Natality, Marriage, and Divorce, no. 53 (Hyattsville: Department of Health and Human Services) no. PH5 95-1931, table 1, p. 27.
25. "More 'Murphy Brown' Moms," *Olympian* 14 July 1993; *New York Times* 14 July 1993: A1; Rachel Fuchs, *Poor and Pregnant in Paris: Strategies for Survival in the Nineteenth Century* (New Brunswick: Rutgers UP, 1992); Elizabeth Kuznesof, "Household Composition and Headship as Related to Changes in Mode of Production: Sao Paulo 1715 to 1836," *Society for Comparative Study of Society and History* 41 (1980) 100.
26. Usdansky.
27. Katherine Edin, *Welfare Myths: Fact or Fiction? Exploring the Truth about Welfare* (New York: Center on Social Welfare Policy and Law, 1996); Joel Handler, "'Ending Welfare As We Know It': Another Exercise in Symbolic Politics," U of Wisconsin–Madison Institute for Research on Poverty, Discussion Paper 1053-95, Jan. 1995: 7–9.
28. Charles Murray, "Keep It in the Family," *London Times* 14 Nov. 1993.
29. Judith Bruce, Cynthia Lloyd, and Ann Leonard, with Patrice Engle and Niev Duffy, *Families in Focus: New Perspectives on Mothers, Fathers, and Children* (New York: Population Council, 1995) 19; Tamar Lewin, "Decay of Families Is Global," *New York Times* 30 May 1995: A5; Leon Eisenberg, "Is the Family Obsolete?" *Key Reporter* 60 (1995): 1–5; Usdansky; Bumpass 42.
30. John Edwards, "New Conceptions: Biosocial Innovations and the Family," *Journal of Marriage and the Family* 53 (1991): 349–60; Andrea Bonnicksen, *In Vitro Fertilization: Building Policy from Laboratories to Legislatures* (New York: Columbia UP, 1989).
31. *Olympian* 4 July 1992: A5, 29 Oct. 1990: A8, and 1 Oct. 1989: A10; *New York Times* 8 Jan. 1996: A1, A7; *New York Times* 10 Jan. 1996: A1, B7; Lori Andrews, *Between Strangers: Surrogate Mothers, Expectant Fathers, and Brave New Babies* (New York: Harper, 1989); Elaine Hoffman Baruch, Amadeo D'Adamo, and Joni Seager, *Embryos, Ethics, and Women's Rights* (Binghamton: Haworth, 1989); John Robertson, *Children of Choice: Freedom and the New Reproductive Technologies* (Princeton: Princeton UP, 1994); Derek Morrison, "A Surrogacy Issue: Who Is the Other

Mother?" *International Journal of Law and the Family* 8 (1994); Jill Smolowe, "The Test-Tube Custody Fight," *Time* 18 Mar. 1996: 80; Janet Dolgin, "Just a Gene: Judicial Assumptions about Parenthood," *UCLA Law Review* 40 (1993); Ruth Macklin, *Surrogates and Other Mothers: The Debates over Assisted Reproduction* (Philadelphia: Temple UP, 1994).

32. Susan Chira, "Of a Certain Age, and in a Family Way," *New York Times* 2 Jan. 1994; Jan Hoffman, "Egg Donations Meet a Need and Raise Ethical Questions," *New York Times* 8 Jan. 1996; Elisabeth Rosenthal, "From Lives Begun in a Lab, Brave New Joy," *New York Times* 10 Jan. 1996; Bonnickson.
33. Ruth Shalit, "Family Mongers," *New Republic* 16 Aug. 1993: 13; Popenoe 194; David Popenoe, "American Family Decline, 1960–1990," *Journal of Marriage and the Family* 55 (1993): 539; Blankenhorn 220–33; and quoted in *Newsweek* 6 Feb. 1995: 43; "Marriage in America: A Report to the Nation," Council on Families in America, March 1995: 4.
34. Whitehead 49; Carole Sugarman, "Jack Sprat Should Eat Some Fat," *Washington Post National Weekly Edition* 2–8 May 1994; *Olympian* 5 Feb. 1996: A8; Janet Giele, "Decline of the Family: Conservative, Liberal, and Feminist Views," in Popenoe, Elshtain, and Blankenhorn 104.
35. Dan Quayle and Diane Medved, *The American Family: Discovering the Values That Make Us Strong* (New York: Harper, 1996) 2, 87, 114.
36. Katharine Seelye, "The Complications and Ideals," *New York Times* 24 Nov. 1994.
37. Katha Pollitt, "Bothered and Bewildered," *New York Times* 22 July 1993.

Questions for Discussion

1. If you have read Midge Decter's "Madness of the American Family," you may recall that she describes the ideal family as a child "born to two people, one of his own sex and one of the other, to whom his life is as important as their own and who undertake to instruct him in the ways of the world around him." Coontz's seem in total agreement with Decter. Where does their thinking part company?
2. What are some of the reasons that marriage has declined as an institution, according to Coontz? Which seem irreversible? How could any of them be reversed? Can you explain what Coontz means in paragraph 17 when she draws a distinction between women's employment as *allowing* divorce as opposed to *causing* divorce? Do you know of women who have chosen to divorce after becoming employed? What can you say about their motives?
3. Paragraphs 24–33 offer an argument on no-fault divorce. Outline Coontz's claim, reasons, and evidence. Evaluate her case in class discussion. If the breakup of a marriage is the fault of a woman who bore the burden of parenting and housekeeping, what is the reasoning for her receiving a maintenance award?

4. Explain Coontz's reason for believing that no amount of persuasion or education will change the divorce rate. What could change the divorce rate?
5. Stigmas against unwed motherhood have fallen away. How common is the "Murphy Brown" model of unwed motherhood—that is, the woman with a successful career but no husband, who decides to have a baby (paragraph 48)? What, according to Coontz, is the more common picture? What could cause numbers of unwed mothers to drop? an improvement in the economy? a fall in the economy? Compare paragraphs 42 and 52. Is there a contradiction?
6. In earlier times Americans spoke of the "shotgun" wedding, in which the pregnant bride's father or brothers held a gun to the head of the bridegroom, figuratively speaking—at least in most cases. Compare the shotgun wedding to what Charles Murray advocates in paragraph 50. Could social policies like no child support for unwed mothers encourage more responsible use of birth control or bring back abstinence until the wedding night?

For Convincing

Look into the policy suggestions Coontz offers in paragraphs 58–60 for strengthening the institution of marriage. If any of them seem more realistic than Coontz thinks, do some research and decide if a case can be made to implement the proposal. Or think of a proposal of your own that might strengthen marriage ties. In particular, you might want to look at the "supervows" marriage, also known as "covenant marriage" in Louisiana, where couples can choose between this and an ordinary marriage vow. Or you might investigate the debate over no-fault divorce or examine ways to make divorce more stigmatized and difficult so as to help keep couples together.

TOM CHENEY

Cartoon

This cartoon, which appeared in the New Yorker *magazine, gets its humor from a revision of the wording of the standard wedding vows—and the expressions of the couple at the altar, who have apparently never thought of their lifelong monogamous commitment exactly as the preacher's words describe it.*

"And do you, Rebecca, promise to make love only to Richard, month after month, year after year, and decade after decade, until one of you is dead?"

For Discussion

The cartoon invites a discussion of the role of style in persuasion. The standard wedding vows, while solemn, are romantic and poetic. With small variations in the wordings, all the standard vows aim to bind the bride and groom to fidelity for a lifetime. What is the effect of the wording in the cartoon?

BARBARA DAFOE WHITEHEAD

The Making of a Divorce Culture

Barbara Dafoe Whitehead's book The Divorce Culture *appeared in 1997, drawing praise from conservatives on the subject of family values and criticism from liberals such as Arlene Skolnick, who disagrees with Whitehead's conclusions that misplaced values, rather than social and economic changes, are the reason behind the large number of divorces and single-parent families today. After reading this excerpt, which combines most of Whitehead's introduction with part of a later chapter on ethics, you might want to consult Skolnick's response, which appeared in* The American Prospect *for May/June 1997.*

DIVORCE IS now part of everyday American life. It is embedded in our laws and institutions, our manners and mores, our movies and television shows, our novels and children's storybooks, and our closest and most important relationships. Indeed, divorce has become so pervasive that many people naturally assume it has seeped into the social and cultural mainstream over a long period of time. Yet this is not the case. Divorce has become an American way of life only as the result of recent and revolutionary change. 1

The entire history of American divorce can be divided into two periods, one evolutionary and the other revolutionary. For most of the nation's history, divorce was a rare occurrence and an insignificant feature of family and social relationships. In the first sixty years of the twentieth century, divorce became more common, but it was hardly commonplace. In 1960, the divorce rate stood at a still relatively modest level of nine per one thousand married couples. After 1960, however, the rate accelerated at a dazzling pace. It doubled in roughly a decade and continued its upward climb until the early 1980s, when it stabilized at the highest level among advanced Western societies. As a consequence of this sharp and sustained rise, divorce moved from the margins to the mainstream of American life in the space of three decades.

Ideas are important in revolutions, yet surprisingly little attention has been devoted to the ideas that gave impetus to the divorce revolution. Of the scores of books on divorce published in recent decades, most focus on its legal, demographic, economic, or (especially) psychological dimensions. Few, if any, deal fully with its intellectual origins. Yet trying to comprehend the divorce revolution and its consequences without some sense of its ideological origins, is like trying to understand the American Revolution without taking into account the thinking of John Locke, Thomas Jefferson, or Thomas Paine. This more recent revolution, like the revolution of our nation's founding, has its roots in a distinctive set of ideas and claims.

. . . The making of a divorce culture has involved three overlapping changes: first, the emergence and widespread diffusion of a historically new and distinctive set of ideas about divorce in the last third of the twentieth century; second, the migration of divorce from a minor place within a system governed by marriage to a freestanding place as a major institution governing family relationships; and third, a widespread shift in thinking about the obligations of marriage and parenthood.

5 Beginning in the late 1950s, Americans began to change their ideas about the individual's obligations to family and society. Broadly described, this change was away from an ethic of obligation to others and toward an obligation to self. I do not mean that people suddenly abandoned all responsibilities to others, but rather that they became more acutely conscious of their responsibility to attend to their own individual needs and interests. At least as important as the moral obligation to look after others, the new thinking suggested, was the moral obligation to look after oneself.

This ethical shift had a profound impact on ideas about the nature and purpose of the family. In the American tradition, the marketplace and the public square have represented the realms of life devoted to the pursuit of individual interest, choice, and freedom, while the family has been the realm defined by voluntary commitment, duty, and self-sacrifice. With the greater emphasis on individual satisfaction in family relationships, however, family well-being became subject to a new metric. More than in the past, satisfaction in this sphere came to be based on subjective judgments about the content and quality of individual happiness rather than on such objective measures as level of income, material nurture and support, or boosting children onto a higher rung on the socioeconomic ladder. People began to judge the strength and "health" of family bonds according to their capacity to promote individual fulfillment and personal growth. As a result, the conception of the family's role and place in the society began to change. The family began to lose its separate place and distinctive identity as the realm of duty, service, and sacrifice. Once the domain of the obligated self, the family was increasingly viewed as yet another domain for the expression of the unfettered self.

These broad changes figured centrally in creating a new conception of divorce which gained influential adherents and spread broadly and swiftly throughout the society—a conception that represented a radical departure from earlier notions. Once regarded mainly as a social, legal, and family event in which there were other stakeholders, divorce now became an event closely linked to the pursuit of individual satisfactions, opportunities, and growth.

The new conception of divorce drew upon some of the oldest, and most resonant, themes in the American political tradition. The nation, after all, was founded as the result of a political divorce, and revolutionary thinkers explicitly adduced a parallel between the dissolution of marital bonds and the dissolution of political bonds. In political as well as marital relationships, they argued, bonds of obligation were established voluntarily on the basis of mutual affection and regard. Once such bonds turned cold and oppressive, peoples, like individuals, had the right to dissolve them and to form more perfect unions.

In the new conception of divorce, this strain of eighteenth-century political thought mingled with a strain of twentieth-century psycho-therapeutic thought. Divorce was not only an individual right but also a psychological resource. The dissolution of marriage offered the chance to make oneself over from the inside out, to refurbish and express the inner self, and to acquire certain valuable psychological assets and competencies, such as initiative, assertiveness, and a stronger and better self-image.

The conception of divorce as both an individual right and an inner experience merged with and reinforced the new ethic of obligation to the self. In family relationships, one had an obligation to be attentive to one's own feelings and to work toward improving the quality of one's inner life. This ethical imperative completed the rationale for a sense of individual entitlement to divorce. Increasingly, mainstream America saw the legal dissolution of marriage as a matter of individual choice, in which there were no other stakeholders or larger social interests. This conception of divorce strongly argued for removing the social, legal, and moral impediments to the free exercise of the individual right to divorce. . . .

. . . The divorce ethic radically changed established ideas about the social and moral obligations associated with divorce. In the past Americans assumed that there were multiple stakeholders in the unhappy business of marital dissolution: the other spouse, the children, relatives, and the larger society. All these stakeholders held an interest in the marital partnership as the source of certain goods, goods that were put at risk each time a marriage dissolved. At particular risk were children, who were the most likely to experience severe losses as a consequence of divorce, especially the loss of the steady support and sponsorship of a father. In divorcing, spouses also jeopardized their own relationships with their children and put at risk the children's relationships with grandparents, relatives, and even family friends. Moreover, since married parents had the central social responsibility for preparing the next generation for useful lives as citizens, workers, and future family members, the dissolution of a marriage was an event in which the society claimed an interest.

However, the notion of divorce as the working out of an inner life experience cast it in far more individualistic terms than in the past. Because divorce originated in an inner sense of dissatisfaction, it acknowledged no other stakeholders. Leaving a marriage was a personal decision, prompted by a set of needs and feelings that were not subject to external interests or claims. Expressive divorce reduced the number of legitimate stakeholders in divorce to one, the individual adult.

If expressive divorce excluded the idea that there are other parties at interest in the "divorce experience," it also overturned earlier notions about one's moral responsibilities to others. An individual's right to divorce was rooted in the individual's right to have a satisfying inner life to fulfill his/her needs and desires. The entitlement to divorce was based on the individual entitlement to pursue inner happiness.

Like all entitlements, the psychological entitlement to divorce was jealously guarded and protected. No one, including the divorcing individual's children, had a "right" to intervene in this intensely private experience or to try to disrupt the course of an emotionally healthy journey toward divorce. Nor were there morally compelling arguments for considering the interests and claims of others in the marriage. If divorce was an entirely subjective and individual experience, rooted in a particular set of needs, values, and preferences, then there was no basis for making judgments about the decision to divorce. The new ethic of divorce was morally relativistic: There could be no right or wrong reasons for divorce; there were only reasons, which it was the task of therapy to elicit and affirm.

Taken together, the conception of divorce as an inner journey of the self 15
and the ethical imperative to put one's interests and needs first had one far-reaching consequence: It weakened the rationale for the legal or social regulation of divorce. If the divorce experience was an inner journey of the sovereign self, what right had anyone to place impediments in the way? . . .

The shift to a system of no-fault divorce both reflected and contributed to the new conception of divorce. For a couple who had come to a mutual decision to end a marriage, the traditional practice of finding and assigning fault to one spouse often required fabricating some offense like adultery and thereby tainting the reputation of one partner. No-fault divorce was designed to eliminate this legal playacting and thereby to make divorce more honest. California enacted the nation's first no-fault statute in 1970, and other states soon followed; by 1980, all but two states had no-fault divorce laws on the books. Fault no longer sullied divorce or tarnished reputations; in this sense, the legal dissolution of marriage had become a "cleaner" as well as an easier process.

However, no-fault divorce fully supported the single-stakeholder theory of expressive divorce. It established a disaffected spouse's right unilaterally to dissolve a marriage simply by declaring that the relationship was over. Characterizing standard legal practice in the states, legal scholar Mary Ann Glendon has observed: ". . . the virtually universal understanding . . . is that the breakdown of a marriage is irretrievable if one spouse says it is." Even more consequentially, no-fault gave one parent the unilateral power to disrupt at will and without cause the other parent's affective relationship with his or her child. . . .

. . . By the 1970s the elimination of fault in most of the states' divorce laws made the sorting out of responsibility for marital breakup a psychological rather than a legal endeavor. Considerations of fault did not disappear so much as change venue; fault was not assigned by the courts but worked out in therapy. Achieving a constructive "emotional" divorce became a dominant goal of marriage therapy.

Nonetheless, according to therapeutic precepts, the fault for marital breakup must be shared, even when one spouse unilaterally seeks a divorce. In essence, counseling established a joint-fault system aimed at persuading each individual to accept responsibility for the breakup. As one study of therapeutic opinion notes, "the strategy which most clearly differentiates divorce therapy from marital or family therapy is what we have labelled orchestrating the motivation to divorce." This may include "openly arguing for the advantages of the divorce as opposed to continuing marital unhappiness and trial separation." The goal here was to accept responsibility for the failure of the marriage and thereby to achieve a new level of self-understanding. "To view oneself as innocent victim is thus to engage in fundamental distortion," the study goes on, "the consequence of which is a high probability for an equally bad remarriage."

20 Such therapeutic reasoning defied a more commonsense view of right and wrong, however. Many husbands and wives who did not seek or want divorce were stunned to learn from their therapists that they were equally "at fault" in the dissolution of their marriages. The notion of fault apparently had a moral basis which endured even after the notion of fault had been eradicated in law and mores. . . .

One consequence of this individualistic approach was its neglect of marriage as the domain of obligation and commitment, particularly to children. Not only did marriage counseling ignore the spousal relationship, it also excluded children as stakeholders in the marital partnership. Intentionally or not, it relieved divorcing couples of their responsibilities for considering their children's well-being. . . .

. . . [D]ivorce has indeed hurt children. It has created economic insecurity and disadvantage for many children who would not otherwise be economically vulnerable. It has led to more fragile and unstable family households. It has caused a mass exodus of fathers from children's households and, all too often, from their lives. It has reduced the levels of parental time and money invested in children. In sum, it has changed the very nature of American childhood. Just as no patient would have designed today's system of health care, so no child would have chosen today's culture of divorce.

Divorce figures prominently in the altered economic fortunes of middle-class families. Although the economic crisis of the middle class is usually described as a problem caused by global economic changes, changing patterns in education and earnings, and ruthless corporate downsizing, it owes more to divorce than is commonly acknowledged. Indeed, recent data suggest that marriage may be a more important economic resource than a college degree. According to an analysis of 1994 income patterns, the median income of married-parent households whose heads have only a high school diploma is ten percent higher than the median income of college-educated single-parent households. Parents who are college graduates *and* married form the new economic elite among families with children. Consequently, those who are concerned about what the downsizing of corporations is doing to workers should also be concerned about what the downsizing of families through divorce is doing to parents and children.

Widespread divorce depletes social capital as well. Scholars tell us that strong and durable family and social bonds generate certain "goods" and services, including money, mutual assistance, information, caregiving, protection, and sponsorship. Because such bonds endure over time, they accumulate and form a pool of social capital which can be drawn down upon, when needed, over the entire course of a life. An elderly couple, married for fifty years, is likely to enjoy a substantial body of social and emotional capital, generated through their long-lasting marriage, which they can draw upon in caring for each other and for themselves as they age. Similarly, children who grow up in stable, two-parent married households are the beneficiaries of the social and emotional capital accumulated over time as a result of an enduring marriage bond. As many parents know, children continue to depend on these resources well into young adulthood. But as family bonds become increasingly fragile and vulnerable to disruption, they become less permanent and thus less capable of generating such forms of help, financial resources, and mutual support. In short, divorce consumes social capital and weakens the social fabric. At the very time that sweeping socioeconomic changes are mandating greater investment of social capital in children, widespread divorce is reducing the pool of social capital. As the new economic and social conditions raise the hurdles of child-rearing higher, divorce digs potholes in the tracks.

25 . . . The media routinely portray the debate over the family as one between nostalgists and realists, between those who want to turn back the clock to the fifties and those who want to march bravely and resolutely forward into the new century. But this is a lazy and misguided approach, driven more by the easy availability of archival photos and footage from 1950s television sitcoms than by careful consideration of the substance of competing arguments.

More fundamentally, this approach overlooks the key issue. And that issue is not how today's families might stack up against those of an earlier era; indeed, no reliable empirical data for such a comparison exist. In an age of diverse family structures, the heart of the matter is what kinds of contemporary family arrangements have the greatest capacity to promote children's well-being, and how we can ensure that more children have the advantages of growing up in such families.

In the past year or so, there has been growing recognition of the personal and social costs of three decades of widespread divorce. A public debate has finally emerged. Within this debate, there are two separate and overlapping discussions.

The first centers on a set of specific proposals that are intended to lessen the harmful impact of divorce on children: a federal system of child-support collection, tougher child-support enforcement, mandatory counseling for divorcing parents, and reform of no-fault divorce laws in the states. What is striking about this discussion is its narrow focus on public policy, particularly on changes in the system of no-fault divorce. In this, as in so many other crucial discussions involving social and moral questions, the most vocal and visible participants come from the world of government policy, electoral politics, and issue advocacy. The media, which are tongue-tied unless they can speak in the language of left-right politics, reinforce this situation. And the public is offered needlessly polarized arguments that hang on a flat yes-or-no response to this or that individual policy measure. All too often, this discussion of divorce poses what *Washington Post* columnist E. J. Dionne aptly describes as false choices.

Notably missing is a serious consideration of the broader moral assumptions and empirical claims that define our divorce culture. Divorce touches on classic questions in American public philosophy—on the nature of our most important human and social bonds, the duties and obligations imposed by bonds we voluntarily elect, the "just causes" for the dissolution of those bonds, and the differences between obligations volunteered and those that must be coerced. Without consideration of such questions, the effort to change behavior by changing a few public policies is likely to founder.

The second and complementary discussion does try to place divorce 30
within a larger philosophical framework. Its proponents have looked at the decline in the well-being of the nation's children as the occasion to call for a collective sense of commitment by all Americans to all of America's children. They pose the challenging question: "What are Americans willing to do 'for the sake of *all* children'?" But while this is surely an important question, it addresses only half of the problem of declining commitment. The other half has to do with how we answer the question: "What are individual parents obliged to do 'for the sake of their own children'?"

Renewing a *social* ethic of commitment to children is an urgent goal, but it cannot be detached from the goal of strengthening the *individual* ethic of commitment to children. The state of one affects the standing of the other. A society that protects the rights of parents to easy, unilateral divorce, and flatly rejects the idea that parents should strive to preserve a marriage "for the sake of the children," faces a problem when it comes to the question of public sacrifice "for the sake of the children." To put it plainly, many of the ideas we have come to believe and vigorously defend about adult prerogatives and freedoms in family life are undermining the foundations of altruism and support for children.

With each passing year, the culture of divorce becomes more deeply entrenched. American children are routinely schooled in divorce. Mr. Rogers teaches toddlers about divorce. An entire children's literature is devoted to divorce. Family movies and videos for children feature divorced families. *Mrs. Doubtfire,* originally a children's book about divorce and then a hit movie, is aggressively marketed as a holiday video for kids. Of course, these books and movies are designed to help children deal with the social reality and psychological trauma of divorce. But they also carry an unmistakable message about the impermanence and unreliability of family bonds. Like romantic love, the children's storybooks say, family love comes and goes. Daddies disappear. Mommies find new boyfriends. Mommies' boyfriends leave. Grandparents go away. Even pets must be left behind.

More significantly, in a society where nearly half of all children are likely to experience parental divorce, family breakup becomes a defining event of American childhood itself. Many children today know nothing but divorce in their family lives. And although children from divorced families often say they want to avoid divorce if they marry, young adults whose parents divorced are more likely to get divorced themselves and to bear children outside of marriage than young adults from stable married-parent families. . . .

. . . Divorce has spread throughout advanced Western societies at roughly the same pace and over roughly the same period of time. Yet nowhere else has divorce been so deeply imbued with the larger themes of a nation's political traditions. Nowhere has divorce so fully reflected the spirit and susceptibilities of a people who share an extravagant faith in the power of the individual and in the power of positive thinking. Divorce in America is not unique, but what we have made of divorce is uniquely American. . . .

Questions for Discussion

1. Whitehead holds that increased divorce rates stem from the 1950s, when people began to measure "family well-being" in terms of personal happiness rather than such "objective measures as level of income, material nurture and support." If you read Arlene Skolnick's history of the family (pages 432–437), discuss how the two authors' explanations for the rise in divorce rates concur and how they differ. At what point did the need for emotional satisfaction enter the family sphere, according to Skolnick? And what was her explanation, as compared with Whitehead's?
2. What does Whitehead advocate to address the problem of widespread divorce? Does she want to eliminate no-fault divorce?
3. In paragraph 24, what does Whitehead mean by "social capital"?
4. Would Whitehead be concerned about "the divorce culture" if children were not involved? Should she be? Should we?
5. Does Whitehead offer any suggestions as to how we might renew an individual "ethic of commitment to children" (paragraph 31)? What does she see as the difference between an individual ethic of commitment and a social ethic of commitment?

For Inquiry and Convincing

The themes Whitehead finds in American culture are similar to those discussed in Robert Bellah's best-seller *Habits of the Heart: Individualism and Commitment in American Life.* Bellah is a sociologist of religion at University of California, Berkeley, and his book has become a classic in sociology. Read his chapter on "Love and Marriage," which offers many examples from his research about how American couples talk in expressive and therapeutic terms about their marriages. Compare Bellah's perspective with Whitehead's, and do further research to determine if expressive individualism could be a factor in our nation's high rate of divorce. Is it fair to say that the prevalence of divorce has as much to do with values as it does with economic and social forces? Write an argument in support of your conclusions.

DAVID POPENOE

A World without Fathers

David Popenoe is a sociology professor at Rutgers—The State University of New Jersey, Brunswick. He has written several books, including Disturbing the Nest: Family Change and Decline in Modern Society *(1988) and* Life without Father *(1996), from which the following selection was adapted and printed in* The Wilson Quarterly *in Spring 1996. As these titles might suggest, Popenoe is pessimistic about the changes in the American family. Here he makes a case that fathers play a unique role in raising children and argues that the consequences are severe when fathers are not a part of their children's daily lives.*

THE DECLINE of fatherhood is one of the most basic, unexpected, 1
and extraordinary social trends of our time. Its dimensions can be captured in a single statistic: in just three decades, between 1960 and 1990, the percentage of children living apart from their biological fathers more than doubled, from 17 percent to 36 percent. By the turn of the century, nearly 50 percent of American children may be going to sleep each evening without being able to say good night to their dads.

No one predicted this trend, few researchers or government agencies have monitored it, and it is not widely discussed, even today. But the decline of fatherhood is a major force behind many of the most disturbing problems that plague American society: crime and delinquency; premature sexuality and out-of-wedlock births to teenagers; deteriorating educational achievement; depression, substance abuse, and alienation among adolescents; and the growing number of women and children in poverty.

The current generation of children and youth may be the first in our nation's history to be less well off—psychologically, socially, economically, and morally—than their parents were at the same age. The United States, observes Senator Daniel Patrick Moynihan (D.-NY), "may be the first society in history in which children are distinctly worse off than adults."

Even as this calamity unfolds, our cultural view of fatherhood itself is changing. Few people doubt the fundamental importance of mothers. But fathers? More and more, the question of whether fathers are really necessary is being raised. Many would answer no, or maybe not. And to the degree that fathers are still thought necessary, fatherhood is said by many to be merely a social role that others can play: mothers, partners, stepfathers, uncles and aunts, grandparents. Perhaps the script can even be rewritten and the role changed—or dropped.

There was a time in the past when fatherlessness was far more common 5
than it is today, but death was to blame, not divorce, desertion, and out-of-wedlock births. In early-17th-century Virginia, only an estimated 31 percent of white children reached age 18 with both parents still alive. That percentage

climbed to 50 percent by the early 18th century, to 72 percent by the turn of the present century, and close to its current level by 1940. Today, well over 90 percent of America's youngsters reach 18 with two living parents. Almost all of today's fatherless children have fathers who are alive, well, and perfectly capable of shouldering the responsibilities of fatherhood. Who would ever have thought that so many men would choose to relinquish them?

Not so long ago, the change in the cause of fatherlessness was dismissed as irrelevant in many quarters, including among social scientists. Children, it was said, are merely losing their parents in a different way than they used to. You don't hear that very much anymore. A surprising finding of recent social science research is that it is decidedly worse for a child to lose a father in the modern, voluntary way than through death. The children of divorced and never-married mothers are less successful in life by almost every measure than the children of widowed mothers. The replacement of death by divorce as the prime cause of fatherlessness, then, is a monumental setback in the history of childhood.

Until the 1960s, the falling death rate and the rising divorce rate neutralized each other. In 1900, the percentage of all American children living in single-parent families was 8.5 percent. By 1960, it had increased to just 9.1 percent. Virtually no one during those years was writing or thinking about family breakdown, disintegration, or decline.

Indeed, what is most significant about the changing family demography of the first six decades of the 20th century is this: because the death rate was dropping faster than the divorce rate was rising, by 1960 more children were living with both of their natural parents than at any other time in world history. The figure was close to 80 percent for the generation born in the late 1940s and early 1950s.

But then the decline in the death rate slowed, and the divorce rate skyrocketed. "The scale of marital breakdowns in the West since 1960 has no historical precedent that I know of, and seems unique," says Lawrence Stone, the noted Princeton University family historian. "There has been nothing like it for the last 2,000 years, and probably longer."

Consider what has happened to children. Most estimates are that only 10
about 50 percent of the children born during the 1970–84 "baby bust" period will still live with their natural parents by age 17—a staggering drop from nearly 80 percent.

One estimate paints the current scene in even starker terms and also points up the enormous difference that exists between whites and blacks. By age 17, white children born between 1950 and 1954 had spent eight percent of their lives with only one parent; black children had spent 22 percent. But among those born in 1980, by one estimate, white children will spend 31 percent of their childhood years with one parent and black children 59 percent.

In theory, divorce need not mean disconnection. In reality, it often does. One large survey in the late 1980s found that about one in five divorced fathers had not seen his children in the past year, and less than half of divorced fathers saw their children more than several times a year. A 1981 survey of adolescents who were living apart from their fathers found that 52 percent had not seen them at all in more than a year; only 16 percent saw their fathers as often as once a week. Moreover, the survey showed fathers' contact with their children dropping off sharply with the passage of time after the marital breakup.

The picture grows worse. Just as divorce has overtaken death as the leading cause of fatherlessness, out-of-wedlock births are expected to surpass divorce later in the 1990s. They accounted for 30 percent of all births by 1991; by the turn of the century they may account for 40 percent of the total (and 80 percent of minority births). And there is substantial evidence that having an unmarried father is even worse for a child than having a divorced father.

Across time and cultures, fathers have always been considered essential—and not just for their sperm. Indeed, until today, no known society ever thought of fathers as potentially unnecessary. Marriage and the nuclear family—mother, father, and children—are the most universal social institutions in existence. In no society has the birth of children out of wedlock been the cultural norm. To the contrary, a concern for the legitimacy of children is nearly universal.

At the same time, being a father is universally problematic for men. 15
While mothers the world over bear and nurture their young with an intrinsic acknowledgment and, most commonly, acceptance of their role, the process of taking on the role of father is often filled with conflict and doubt. The source of this sex-role difference can be plainly stated. Men are not biologically as attuned to being committed fathers as women are to being committed mothers. The evolutionary logic is clear. Women, who can bear only a limited number of children, have a great incentive to invest their energy in rearing children, while men, who can father many offspring, do not. Left culturally unregulated, men's sexual behavior can be promiscuous, their paternity casual, their commitment to families weak. This not to say that the role of father is foreign to male nature. Far from it. Evolutionary scientists tell us that the development of the fathering capacity and high paternal investments in offspring—features not common among our primate relatives—have been sources of enormous evolutionary advantage for human beings.

In recognition of the fatherhood problem, human cultures have used sanctions to bind men to their children, and of course the institution of marriage has been culture's chief vehicle. Marriage is society's way of signaling that the community approves and encourages sexual intercourse and the birth of children, and that the long-term relationship of the parents is socially important. Margaret Mead once said, with the fatherhood problem very much in mind, that there is no society in the world where men will stay married for very long unless culturally required to do so. Our experience in late-20th-century America shows how right she was. The results for children have been devastating.

In my many years as a sociologist, I have found few other bodies of evidence that lean so much in one direction as this one: on the whole, two parents—a father and a mother—are better for a child than one parent. There are, to be sure, many factors that complicate this simple proposition. We all know of a two-parent family that is truly dysfunctional—the proverbial family from hell. A child can certainly be raised to a fulfilling adulthood by one loving parent who is wholly devoted to the child's well-being. But such exceptions do not invalidate the rule any more than the fact that some three-pack-a-day smokers live to a ripe old age casts doubt on the dangers of cigarettes.

The collapse of children's well-being in the United States has reached breathtaking proportions. Juvenile violent crime has increased sixfold, from 16,000 arrests in 1960 to 96,000 in 1992, a period in which the total number of young people in the population remained relatively stable. Reports of child neglect and abuse have quintupled since 1976, when data were first collected. Eating disorders and rates of depression have soared among adolescent girls. Teen suicide has tripled. Alcohol and drug abuse among teenagers, although it has leveled off in recent years, continues at a very high rate. Scholastic Aptitude Test scores have declined nearly 80 points, and most of the decline cannot be accounted for by the increased academic diversity of students taking the test. Poverty has shifted from the elderly to the young. Of all the nation's poor today, 38 percent are children.

One can think of many explanations for these unhappy developments: the growth of commercialism and consumerism, the influence of television and the mass media, the decline of religion, the widespread availability of guns and addictive drugs, and the decay of social order and neighborhood relationships. None of these causes should be dismissed. But the evidence is now strong that the absence of fathers from the lives of children is one of the most important causes.

The most tangible and immediate consequence of fatherlessness for chil- *20*
dren is the loss of economic resources. By the best recent estimates, the income of the household in which a child remains after a divorce instantly declines by about 21 percent per capita on average, while expenses tend to go up. Over time, the economic situation for the child often deteriorates further. The mother usually earns considerably less than the father, and children cannot rely on their fathers to pay much in the way of child support. About half of previously married mothers receive no child support, and for those who do receive it, both the reliability and the amount of the payment drop over time.

Child poverty, once endemic in America, reached a historic low point of 14 percent in 1969 and remained relatively stable through the 1970s. Since then, it has been inching back up. Today more than 20 percent of the nation's children (and 25 percent of infants and toddlers) are growing up in poverty.

The loss of fathers' income is the most important cause of this alarming change. By one estimate, 51 percent of the increase in child poverty observed during the 1980s (65 percent for blacks) can be attributed to changes in family structure. Indeed, much of the income differential between whites and blacks today, perhaps as much as two-thirds, can be attributed to the differences in family structure. Not for nothing is it said that marriage is the best antipoverty program of all. . . .

What [else] do fathers do? Much of what they contribute to the growth of their children, of course, is simply the result of being a second adult in the home. Bringing up children is demanding, stressful, and often exhausting. Two adults can not only support and spell each other; they can offset each other's deficiencies and build on each other's strengths.

Beyond being merely a second adult or third party, fathers—men—bring an array of unique and irreplaceable qualities that women do not ordinarily bring. Some of these are familiar, if sometimes overlooked or taken for granted. The father as protector, for example, has by no means outlived his usefulness. His importance as a role model has become a familiar idea. Teenage boys without fathers are notoriously prone to trouble. The pathway to adulthood for daughters is somewhat easier, but they still must learn from their fathers, as they cannot from their mothers, how to relate to men. They learn from their fathers about heterosexual trust, intimacy, and difference. They learn to appreciate their own femininity from the one male who is most special in their lives (assuming that they love and respect their fathers). Most important, through loving and being loved by their fathers, they learn that they are love-worthy.

Recent research has given us much deeper—and more surprising—in- 25
sights into the father's role in child rearing. It shows that in almost all of their interactions with children, fathers do things a little differently from mothers. What fathers do—their special parenting style—is not only highly complementary to what mothers do but is by all indications important in its own right for optimum child rearing.

For example, an often-overlooked dimension of fathering is play. From their children's birth through adolescence, fathers tend to emphasize play more than caretaking. This may be troubling to egalitarian feminists, and it would indeed be wise for most fathers to spend more time in caretaking. Yet the father's style of play seems to have unusual significance. It is likely to be both physically stimulating and exciting. With older children it involves more physical games and teamwork requiring the competitive testing of physical and mental skills. It frequently resembles an apprenticeship or teaching relationship: come on, let me show you how.

Mothers tend to spend more time playing with their children, but theirs is a different kind of play. Mothers' play tends to take place more at the child's level. Mothers provide the child with the opportunity to direct the play, to be in charge, to proceed at the child's own pace. Kids, at least in the early years, seem to prefer to play with daddy. In one study of 2½-year-olds who were given a choice, more than two-thirds chose to play with their father.

The way fathers play has effects on everything from the management of emotions to intelligence and academic achievement. It is particularly important in promoting the essential virtue of self-control. According to one expert, "children who roughhouse with their fathers . . . usually quickly learn that biting, kicking, and other forms of physical violence are not acceptable." They learn when enough is enough and when to "shut it down." . . .

At play and in other realms, fathers tend to stress competition, challenge, initiative, risk taking, and independence. Mothers, as caretakers, stress emotional security and personal safety. On the playground, fathers will try to get the child to swing ever higher, higher than the person on the next swing, while mothers will be cautious, worrying about an accident. It's sometimes said that fathers express more concern for the child's longer-term development, while mothers focus on the child's immediate well-being (which, of course, in its own way has everything to do with a child's long-term well-being). What is clear is that children have dual needs that must be met. Becoming a mature and competent adult involves the integration of two often-contradictory human desires: for communion, or the feeling of being included, connected, and related, and for agency, which entails independence, individuality, and self-fulfillment. One without the other is a denuded and impaired humanity, an incomplete realization of human potential.

For many couples, to be sure, these functions are not rigidly divided 30
along standard female–male lines. There may even be a role reversal in some cases, with men largely assuming the female style and women the male style. But these are exceptions that prove the rule. Gender-differentiated parenting is of such importance that in child rearing by homosexual couples, either gay or lesbian, one partner commonly fills the male-instrumental role while the other fills the female-expressive role. . . .

We know, however, that fathers—and fatherlessness—have surprising impacts on children. Fathers' involvement seems to be linked to improved quantitative and verbal skills, improved problem-solving ability, and higher academic achievement. Several studies have found that the presence of the father is one of the determinants of girls' proficiency in mathematics. And one pioneering study found that the amount of time fathers spent reading was a strong predictor of their daughters' verbal ability.

For sons, who can more directly follow their fathers' example, the results have been even more striking. A number of studies have uncovered a strong relationship between father involvement and the quantitative and mathematical abilities of their sons. Other studies have found a relationship between paternal nurturing and boys' verbal intelligence.

How fathers produce these intellectual benefits is not yet clear. No doubt it is partly a matter of the time and money a man brings to his family. But it is probably also related to the unique mental and behavioral qualities of men; the male sense of play, reasoning, challenge, and problem solving, and the traditional male association with achievement and occupational advancement.

Men also have a vital role to play in promoting cooperation and other "soft" virtues. We don't often think of fathers in connection with the teaching of empathy, but involved fathers, it turns out, may be of special importance for the development of this important character trait, essential to an ordered society of law-abiding, cooperative, and compassionate adults. Examining the results of a 26-year longitudinal study, a trio of researchers reached a "quite astonishing" conclusion: the most important childhood factor of all in developing empathy is paternal involvement in child care. Fathers who spent time alone with their children more than twice a week, giving meals, baths, and other basic care, reared the most compassionate adults.

Again, it is not yet clear why fathers are so important in instilling this 35
quality. Perhaps merely by being with their children they provide a model for compassion. Perhaps it has to do with their style of play or mode of reasoning. Perhaps it is somehow related to the fact that fathers typically are the family's main arbiter with the outside world. Or perhaps it is because mothers who receive help from their mates have more time and energy to cultivate the soft virtues. Whatever the reason, it is hard to think of a more important contribution that fathers can make to their children.

Fatherlessness is directly implicated in many of our most grievous social ills. Of all the negative consequences, juvenile delinquency and violence probably loom largest in the public mind. Reported violent crime has soared 550 percent since 1960, and juveniles have the fastest-growing crime rate. Arrests of juveniles for murder, for example, rose 128 percent between 1983 and 1992.

Many people intuitively believe that fatherlessness is related to delinquency and violence, and the weight of research evidence supports this belief. Having a father at home is no guarantee that a youngster won't commit a crime, but it appears to be an excellent form of prevention. Sixty percent of America's rapists, 72 percent of its adolescent murderers, and 70 percent of its long-term prison inmates come from fatherless homes. Fathers are important to their sons as role models. They are important for maintaining authority and discipline. And they are important in helping their sons to develop both self-control and feelings of empathy toward others. . . .

Another group that has suffered in the new age of fatherlessness is, perhaps unexpectedly, women. In this new era, Gloria Steinem's oft-quoted quip that a woman without a man is like a fish without a bicycle no longer seems quite so funny. There is no doubt that many women get along very well without men in their lives and that having the wrong men in their lives can be disastrous. But just as it increases assaults on children, fatherlessness appears to generate more violence against women. . . .

. . . [M]arriage appears to be a strong safety factor for women. A satisfactory marriage between sexually faithful partners, especially when they are raising their own biological children, engenders fewer risks for violence than probably any other circumstance in which a woman could find herself. Recent surveys of violent-crime victimization have found that only 12.6 of every 1,000 married women fall victim to violence, compared with 43.9 of every 1,000 never-married women and 66.5 of every 1,000 divorced or separated women.

Men, too, suffer grievously from the growth of fatherlessness. The world 40
over, young and unattached males have always been a cause for social concern. They can be a danger to themselves and to society. Young unattached men

tend to be more aggressive, violent, promiscuous, and prone to substance abuse; they are also more likely to die prematurely through disease, accidents, or self-neglect. They make up the majority of deviants, delinquents, criminals, killers, drug users, vice lords, and miscreants of every kind. Senator Moynihan put it succinctly when he warned that a society full of unattached males "asks for and gets chaos."

Family life—marriage and child rearing—is an extremely important civilizing force for men. It encourages them to develop those habits of character, including prudence, cooperativeness, honesty, trust, and self-sacrifice, that can lead to achievement as an economic provider. Marriage also focuses male sexual energy. Having children typically impresses on men the importance of setting a good example. Who hasn't heard at least one man personally testify that he gave up certain deviant or socially irresponsible patterns of life only when he married and had children? . . .

Marriage by itself, even without the presence of children, is also a major civilizing force for men. No other institution save religion (and perhaps the military) places such moral demands on men. To be sure, there is a selection factor in marriage. Those men whom women would care to marry already have some of the civilized virtues. And those men who are morally beyond the pale have difficulty finding mates. Yet epidemiological studies and social surveys have shown that marriage has a civilizing effect independent of the selection factor. Marriage actually promotes health, competence, virtue, and personal well-being. With the continued growth of fatherlessness, we can expect to see a nation of men who are at worst morally out of control and at best unhappy, unhealthy, and unfulfilled.

Just as cultural forms can be discarded, dismantled, and declared obsolete, so can they be reinvented. In order to restore marriage and reinstate fathers in the lives of their children, we are somehow going to have to undo the cultural shift of the last few decades toward radical individualism. We are going to have to re-embrace some cultural propositions or understandings that throughout history have been universally accepted but which today are unpopular, if not rejected outright.

Marriage must be re-established as a strong social institution. The father's role must also be redefined in a way that neglects neither historical models nor the unique attributes of modern societies, the new roles for women, and the special qualities that men bring to child rearing.

Such changes are by no means impossible. Witness the transformations 45
wrought by the civil rights, women's, and environmental movements, and even the campaigns to reduce smoking and drunk driving. What is necessary is for large numbers of adults, and especially our cultural and intellectual leaders, to agree on the importance of change. . . .

. . . Current laws send the message that marriage is not a socially important relationship that involves a legally binding commitment. We should consider a two-tier system of divorce law: marriages without minor children would be relatively easy to dissolve, but marriages with such children would be dissolvable only by mutual agreement or on grounds that clearly involve a wrong by one party against the other, such as desertion or physical abuse. Longer waiting periods for divorcing couples with children might also be called for, combined with some form of mandatory marriage counseling or marital education. . . .

Today in America the social order is fraying badly. We seem, despite notable accomplishments in some areas, to be on a path of decline. The past three decades have seen steeply rising rates of crime, declining political and interpersonal trust, growing personal and corporate greed, deteriorating communities, and increasing confusion over moral issues. For most Americans, life has become more anxious, unsettled, and insecure.

In large part, this represents a failure of social values. People can no longer be counted on to conduct themselves according to the virtues of honesty, self-sacrifice, and personal responsibility. In our ever-growing pursuit of the self—self-expression, self-development, self-actualization, and self-fulfillment—we seem to have slipped off many of our larger social obligations.

At the heart of our discontent lies an erosion of personal relationships. People no longer trust others as they once did; they no longer feel the same sense of commitment and obligation to others. In part, this may be an unavoidable product of the modern condition. But it has gone much deeper than that. Some children across America now go to bed each night worrying about whether their father will be there the next morning. Some wonder whatever happened to their father. And some wonder who he is. What are these children learning at this most basic of all levels about honesty, self-sacrifice, personal responsibility, and trust?

What the decline of fatherhood and marriage in America really means, 50
then, is that slowly, insidiously, and relentlessly our society has been moving in an ominous direction. If we are to make progress toward a more just and humane society, we must reverse the tide that is pulling fathers apart from their families. Nothing is more important for our children or for our future as a nation.

Questions for Discussion

1. Popenoe argues for reestablishing marriage as "a strong social institution" (paragraph 44). What are his primary reasons for doing so? Do you find his reasons and evidence convincing? Some of his evidence is controversial. Although Popenoe is a scholar, *The Wilson Quarterly* does not publish footnotes and documentation. Which of his evidence would you like to find out more about?
2. Do you think that Popenoe is perpetuating stereotypes about masculine gender roles? About women and motherhood? For example, could the play styles he describes be formed by cultural definitions of feminine and masculine? Popenoe wants to praise men by identifying what they bring to

marriage and family, but why does he also argue that marriage and family are necessary to civilize men (paragraphs 40–42)?

3. Why have fathers disappeared? Do you see any correlation between Popenoe's argument and Midge Decter's on the question of men and responsibility? In particular, why do fathers often fade out of children's lives as Popenoe describes in paragraph 12? Does he seem to hold the fathers responsible for this loss of contact? What explanations can you offer for it?

For Inquiry and Convincing

Cause-and-effect arguments are difficult to make, especially because one must take into account all possible factors before saying that two phenomena that appear together are causally related. Also, empirical evidence must be gathered and interpreted carefully. Choose one of the cause-and-effect relationships Popenoe asserts in his essay, and investigate whether there is debate among researchers and conflict in their findings. For example, psychologists have done many studies on the effects of the death of a parent versus divorce on young children. Write a paper explaining the debate on one of these questions, and draw conclusions about which findings seem most convincing.

For Further Research and Discussion

1. How does the United States compare to other countries on the question of the stability of marriage and the nuclear family? Which cultures come off better by comparison? Which come off worse? What explanations can you find for the differences? How do these compare with the claims made by the writers in this chapter about why American families are foundering?
2. What have scientists found about biological and physiological aspects of what we call "love"? What are the various chemical changes that occur in the "infatuation" stage? Look into findings that suggest this stage has a limited term—something like seven years. Do you think Americans have unrealistic expectations about passionate love as the basis for marriage? Would a less romantic view of the basis of marriage better suit the biological reality of long-term partnerships?
3. Look into some of the claims made by these writers about the relationship between family and economic prosperity and high levels of education. Is it fair to say that as Americans increase their ability to choose, they will opt for greater freedoms rather than accepting limits and making sacrifices? Even grandparents seem to prefer their freedom to family responsibilities, as evidenced by the rise of retirement communities far from children and grandchildren and RV bumper stickers that say, "I'm spending my children's inheritance."
4. Studies have found that perhaps the greatest stress on marriage is having a baby. Compare what Decter has to say about parenting and its sacrifices with what social scientists have to say about how children affect the

relationship between husband and wife. How can Americans better cope with these stresses? Is this something outsiders can help with, such as by providing child care through employment?

Additional Suggestions for Writing

1. *Persuasion.* Look into what churches have done to stop the rise of divorce. In particular, what counseling do clergy offer for couples planning to wed? If there is evidence that greater attention to the sacredness of marriage vows and premarital counseling from a religious perspective do in fact contribute to successful marriages, write a paper encouraging couples to take advantage of such counseling.
2. *Persuasion.* Investigate the claims Barbara Whitehead makes about the effects of fathers' interaction with children. If you find more evidence for educational and psychological benefits, write an essay to fathers, urging them to increase their time spent with children. How might they do so? Can you use evidence from your own life and observations?
3. *Convincing.* David Popenoe suggests that divorce can be reduced if "cultural and intellectual leaders agree on the importance of change" (paragraph 45) and move to enact policies to bring about the needed change, as in the civil rights and environmental movements. Consider some of the policies he suggests. Weigh the analogy with these other two movements. Make a case for or against the feasibility of an antidivorce movement.

CHAPTER THIRTEEN

Gay and Lesbian Rights

Homosexuality may not have increased in recent decades, but society's awareness of it certainly has, largely because many gay men and women have become more open about their sexual orientation. Their "coming out" has brought many issues to the public's attention, most notably whether gay people should be protected against discrimination in employment, housing, and insurance and in custody cases and adoption. Indeed, many ask, Why should gay people not be able to marry? In some communities "domestic partnerships"—both homosexual and heterosexual—have recently been legally recognized as unions similar to marriage, and a small but growing number of employers extend benefits to the partners of homosexual employees. But only in Hawaii can gays and lesbians legally marry, and in many states sexual relations between members of the same sex are illegal.

While many homosexual men and women have decided to become activists, publicly pressing for protection against discrimination, others prefer to stay "in the closet," largely out of fear. According to the National Gay and Lesbian Task Force, over ninety percent of gay men and lesbians have been victims of some type of violence or harassment. One issue we take up here is *why* some heterosexuals react so strongly to homosexuality and the issues surrounding it. Homophobia is often referred to as "the last acceptable prejudice," because so many heterosexuals think that discriminating against gay people—even exhibiting open hostility toward them—is defensible on moral grounds. Those who call homosexuality immoral usually turn to religion for support. But how strong are these religious arguments? And if homosexuality is judged immoral, what bearing does that judgment have on an individual's constitutional rights?

The causes of homosexuality have been much debated, and so far researchers have yet to agree on an explanation. From the nineteenth century until 1973, the medical community regarded homosexuality as a disease or pathology, something that could be cured using treatments such as aversion and electroshock therapy and neurosurgery—none of which succeeded. While many still agree with former Vice President Dan Quayle that homosexuality is a choice, current biological research increasingly suggests that it is not. Recent work points to the role of hormones, especially hormones to which the fetus is exposed while in the womb. Research on twins reinforces the view that genetics plays a significant role in sexual orientation.

Why and how people become homosexual, however, is not the primary concern of the public debate over attitudes and policies regarding homosexuals and their rights. Five to ten percent of the American population is gay and lesbian, and because of their minority status, they face discrimination and harassment of one sort or another. The arguments in this chapter address these questions:

Why do many heterosexual people react so strongly to homosexuality?
How does homophobia affect American society as a whole? Should people who disapprove of homosexuality be able to discriminate against homosexuals?
What might both gay and straight people do about homophobia?
Should sexual orientation be protected by civil rights legislation as race, gender, and religion now are?

The issues raised in these readings are central to the debates about more specific gay rights issues such as the role of homosexuals in the military, the right of homosexuals to marry, and the need for antidiscrimination laws.

JEFFREY NICKEL

Everybody's Threatened by Homophobia

Homophobia *is a term often used to describe the attitude of those who express hostility toward homosexuals; it suggests a prejudice that is actually rooted in fear. Whatever the cause, the prejudice too often results in acts of violence against gay men and lesbian women. The following argument appeared originally in* Christopher Street, *a literary magazine whose writers and readers are primarily homosexual. In his essay Jeffrey Nickel wants to show his readers that they can make a case against homophobia that will appeal to the interests of heterosexuals.*

Do I hate my brother because he reminds me of myself, or do I hate my brother because he reminds me of someone who is "not" myself? Whom do I hate; the one who is me, or the one who is anything but me?

—ELIE WIESEL

THE ANSWER is both. But knowing that would seem to be of little help. Our brothers *are* hated; sisters, too. We're right to tell America of the horrors that hatred visits upon us; of the humiliation, the isolation, and even the killings perpetuated, all in the name of heterosexual hegemony. These should be enough to convince this country that it's been terribly wrong about who we are. But there's more to the story. We can also tell about what homophobia—perhaps surprisingly—does to *others;* those who are perceived to be gay, those who are afraid they *might* be, and everyone else who clearly isn't but is nevertheless forced to feel bigotry's nasty bite. This is a lot of people—close to everyone, really. If only they could understand *these* things, too; maybe they would see. 1

As Allen Ginsberg wrote, "They can! They can! They can!" Practically every school child in America knows that a "faggot" is the worst thing they could be. How many wonder to themselves, is that *me*? Kids do have the vague perception that there are people in the world called homosexuals, though that's about all they know. How many boys who don't yet "like" girls think homosexuality is the explanation, when in fact for them, it's not? If gay weren't "bad" in their minds, they would feel no more anguish than that experienced by a child who discovers she's left-handed. But gay *is* bad in the country's consciousness, so children *do* worry a hell of a lot about being it. The "late-bloomer" thinks constantly of what might be "wrong" with him. Because the mere *possibility* that some of our children will be gay isn't even entertained, children who, in a freer society, would be relieved by that plausible conclusion are instead shut off from even *thinking* (much less talking) about it. It is awful that so many young gay people attempt, and often succeed in, killing themselves because of who they are. It's just as awful that so many straight kids try and die for what they mistakenly *think.* How refreshing it would be for young people to be able to discover their sexuality without fear. But right now, that's only a fantasy. Kids in this country must not only be straight; they must make absolutely sure that they are *not* gay. They shouldn't *have* to make sure.

A straight friend of mine whom I came out to when I was seventeen confided in me that he occasionally had gay thoughts and dreams. I told him there was no cause to worry; that virtually all people have same-sex (and other-sex) fantasies to some degree or another. But as enlightened as he truly was about homosexuality, these thoughts *still* bothered him deeply. What would it be like for someone who believed the worst things about homosexuality? I know what it is to be gay and feel the guilt, but I have a hard time imagining what it's like to really be straight and feel it. As a gay person I've had the "coming out process" to sort out all the meanings, but what do straight people have? It doesn't lessen the pain of the gay person's coming-to-terms to admit that these feelings are probably excruciating for many heterosexuals as well. And as is true in our case too, it's all for nothing.

I remember, especially in boyhood, the amazing level of paranoia that surrounded any form of male-to-male physical contact—aside perhaps from sports—as well as any kind of inter-male emotional experience. Males can hardly touch each other in this culture, except, as always, by lashing out. Susan Trausch of the *Boston Globe* put it well when she said that many men (and boys too) are fighting desperately to continue breathing what she called "100 percent pure macho air." They wish to be super-men; super-aggressive, super-obnoxious, and super-ignorant. Their mentality has the dual disadvantage of making automatons of men, and figurines of women. A lot of this mentality is attributable to self- and other-directed homophobia. Men practically have to go to counseling just to be able to talk to each other in real ways. What a pointless chasm we've created, just to make sure that closeness isn't "misconstrued."

5 I've told before the awful story of what happened to a friend of mine while we were in grade school. This boy hung around another boy so much and so ardently that it seemed he had a crush on him. He probably did. The other kids teased him for it a great deal, as I vaguely recall. But the teacher believed this was so intolerable that she had to do something about it, immediately. It really is unbelievable, but here's what she did: A "trial" was held in the classroom, with all members of the class present, at which this boy had to "defend" his feelings toward the other boy. The teacher herself served as the prosecutor. (He had no real defense.) My understanding is that this boy (now a man) really *isn't* gay. Yet he was totally humiliated in front of all of his peers, in such a way that it took him several years to once again build up any semblance of his lost self-esteem. Dating was impossible for him for quite a long time. Some day, I would like to confront this teacher—whom theretofore I'd adored—and ask her what the hell she thought she was doing. It was child abuse of the worst kind, perpetuated against someone who didn't even possess the "demons" she most loathed.

Although I don't presume to know all of what this anxiety does to women, I imagine that it heightens an already well-inculcated sense that women are supposed to have no sexuality whatsoever. Women are taught to please men. Though they are, in a way, given more latitude to express affection for other women than men are for other men. Because women's sexuality is trivialized they're often prevented from knowing just what would constitute lesbianism and what would not. If there were no stigma to homosexuality, this stultifying paranoia just wouldn't exist. Prejudice against homosexuality sharply limits how all men and women may acceptably behave, among themselves and with each other.

I hadn't thought much about how homophobia hurts heterosexuals until I saw a piece on the TV show *20/20* about two or three years ago. They had fascinating stories about several straight people who were actually attacked—physically—because others thought they were gay. One heterosexual couple holding hands walking down the street was beaten repeatedly. It seems the woman's short hair made it seem from the back that they were two men. What an awful education in bigotry it must have been for these poor people. It's interesting to contemplate how these bigots reacted to the knowledge that they were pummeling a wife and her husband: "Oh—we're very sorry to have broken your bones, but we mistook you for someone else."

A similar event took place in Lewes, Delaware, just last year. A man walking down the street with his arm around the shoulder of his (male) friend was struck and seriously injured by a pickup truck, after the driver yelled "faggot" at him. A second man in the truck then hit him in the head with a beer bottle. Then, the driver backed the truck over a curb and onto the sidewalk where the man was standing, crushing the man's legs between the rear of the truck and three metal mailboxes. He then put the truck in reverse once again in order to run over this man a second time, apparently in order to finish him off. He was prevented from doing so only because he couldn't gain the necessary momentum in the space available to jump the curb. The man's legs were so severely injured that the doctors had to graft muscles, tendons, and skin from other parts of his body in order to repair them. During the entire incident the men on the sidewalk were pleading with their attackers: "We're just buddies; we're not gay." One of the men attacked was a married, heterosexual father. But it didn't matter.

And this year, three Pensacola teenagers who said they were out to beat up a gay person in order to get beer money, did so with a lead pipe, fatally, to a man named John Braun, who was a married (straight) father of four. It's incredible: Heterosexuals have actually *died* because of homophobia.

For John Braun and many others, it's too late to understand their stake 10
in eliminating prejudice against gay people. It's too late for him to join P-FLAG[1] and march on Gay Pride Day. But for most people, it isn't too late. Before their children kill themselves far from home; before they lie bleeding,

[1]P-FLAG is an acronym for the national organization Parents-Friends of Lesbians and Gays.

mistaken, and prone; before their brothers die slowly alone; if we talk about it, they can understand. They can! They can! They can!

Questions for Discussion

1. Nickel divides his argument into three main sections, each focusing on a different segment of the heterosexual population hurt by homophobia: young people whose sexuality is just developing (paragraphs 2–3), children and adults who do not feel comfortable expressing affection for friends of their own sex (paragraphs 4–6), and men and women who are attacked because they are mistaken for homosexuals (paragraphs 7–9). Which section provides Nickel's strongest reason? Comment on his strategy for arranging and supporting these three reasons.
2. Do you agree that "practically every school child in America knows that a 'faggot' is the worst thing they could be" (paragraph 2)? If you agree, can you say how our society conveys this idea?
3. What do you think Nickel means when he says that in our society "women's sexuality is trivialized" (paragraph 6)? Do you agree that society gives women "more latitude to express affection" for each other? Could this be related to the idea that their sexuality is not as powerful as that of men?
4. Notice that Nickel wants his readers to feel sympathetic to the problems of heterosexuals. How can you tell that his own sympathies are genuine?
5. What persuasive devices does Nickel use to urge his readers on to action?

For Inquiry

In your writer's notebook assess the truth of Nickel's argument, based on your own experiences and observations.

PETE HAMILL

Confessions of a Heterosexual

Responding to acts of discrimination and violence, some gay rights activists make a point of displaying their pride and their anger through marches, demonstrations, and civil disobedience. In this selection Esquire *columnist Pete Hamill argues that some of the protesters have gone too far and are in fact creating a backlash among people who thought they had overcome their prejudices against gay people. As you read, consider whether Hamill is writing to militant homosexuals or to other heterosexuals—and what his purpose is.*

EARLY ONE evening in the spring, I left my apartment in Green- 1
wich Village and went out to get a few things from the grocery store. The air was mild, the leaves were bursting from the trees. I paused for a moment on a corner, waiting for a light to change and the kamikaze traffic to come to a halt. Waiting beside me was a gray-haired man with a face the color of boiled ham and the thick, boxy body of an old dockwalloper. Before the light turned green, we heard distant chants, tramping feet, and suddenly, like a scene from a Chaplin movie, a small army of the night turned the corner. They came marching directly at us.

"Bash back!" they chanted. "Bash back!"

One of them looked at me and the other man and screamed: "You're fuckin' *killing* us! And we're not gonna *take it* anymore!"

Most of the members of this particular mob were young. A few were joking around, enjoying the fraternity of the march. But the faces of most of the demonstrators were contorted in fury as they raised clenched fists at the sky. While drivers leaned on auto horns and people came to their windows to watch, one wide-eyed kid spat in our direction and shouted, "Breeder shit!"

"What the hell *is* this?" the man beside me said. "Who *are* they?" 5

One marcher peeled off and explained. They were protesting gay-bashing and its most recent local manifestation, the planting of a bomb inside Uncle Charlie's, one of the more popular homosexual hangouts in the city. The marchers paraded off, and the man beside me said: "Tell ya the truth, I'd like to bash a few of these bastards myself."

With that brutal parting line, he stormed off. But as I watched him go, I felt an odd, uncomfortable solidarity with the man. He was my age, born in the Depression, raised in the '40s and '50s, and though we had probably led different lives, we almost surely came from the same roots. We were both out of the New York working class, children of immigrants, shaped by codes, geographies, and institutions now lost. We had thought the neighborhood triumvirate of church, saloon, and Tammany Hall would last forever; it didn't. We learned from our fathers and the older men (and not from television) what a man was supposed to do if he was to call himself a man: put money on the kitchen table, defend wife and children, pay his debts, refuse to inform, serve his country when called, honor picket lines, and never quit in a fight. Sexuality was crude and uncomplicated: Men fucked women. Period. So when my accidental companion had strangers curse him and spit at him, and above all, when he understood that they were gay, he reacted out of that virtually forgotten matrix. He wanted to give them a whack in the head.

But I was alarmed that a milder version of the same dark impulse rose in me. After all, I know that gay-bashing is real; homosexuals are routinely injured or murdered every day, all over the world, by people who fear or hate their version of human sexuality.

Yet what rose in me that night wasn't an instinct to hurt anyone in some homophobic spasm. It was more than simple irritation, and it was not new. In some fundamental way, I was bored by the exhibition of theatrical rage from the gay movement. I am tired of listening to people who identify themselves exclusively by what they do with their cocks. And I don't think I'm alone. Discuss the subject long enough with even the most liberal straight males of my generation, and you discover that twenty years of education, lobbying, journalism, and demonstrating by gays have had only a superficial effect; in some deep, dark pool of the psyche, homosexuals are still seen with a mixture of uneasiness and contempt.

Gay activists, of course, would laugh darkly at the above and think: *This* 10
is not news. But most of them won't even listen to the reasons for these prejudices. Sadly, the folklore of the old neighborhood is not the only cause. Much of this persistent distaste is based on personal experience. Most males of my generation first encountered homosexuals during adolescence, and those men were not exactly splendid representatives of the gay community. When I was growing up, there were four known homosexuals in the neighborhood. All were in their forties. All singled out boys in the low teens. Two paid for sex, and in a neighborhood where poverty was common, a few dollars was a lot of money.

By all accounts, gay men, in those darkest years of The Closet, lived more dangerous and vulnerable lives than they do now. They were subject to blackmail, murder, beatings, and exposure on a more ferocious scale than today. But nothing so melodramatic seemed to happen in our neighborhood. Though everybody on the street knew about three of the four gay men, I don't remember any incidents of gay-bashing. Only one suffered public disgrace. One day, the police came to his door and took him off. A few days later his weeping wife and baffled children moved away, never to be seen again.

When I understood what these men actually *did,* I was horrified. For an Irish Catholic kid in those years, sex itself was terrifying enough; the homosexual variety seemed proof of the existence of Satan. Through all my years of adolescence, I believed that homosexuals were people who preyed exclusively on the very young, a belief strengthened by later experiences on subways, in men's rooms, and in the high school that I attended (where I met one of those tortured priests of the Catholic literary tradition). That belief was shared by most of the boys I grew up with, and when we left the neighborhood for the service (the working-class version of going off to college), we saw more of the same.

In the sailor joints of Norfolk or Pensacola, homosexuals were constantly on the prowl, looking for kids who were drunk, lonesome, naive, or broken-hearted over some Dear John letter shoved in their hip pockets. Again, older men taught us the code, demonstrating how Real Men were supposed to react. It was never very pretty: There was often violence, some gay man smashed and battered into the mud outside a tough joint after midnight. There was a lot of swaggering machismo, a triumphant conviction that by stomping such people we were striking a mighty blow against predators and corrupters. I'm still ashamed of some of the things I saw and did in those years.

It never occurred to us that some of these older gay men were actually looking for—and finding—other homosexuals, as driven in their search for love and connection as we were in our pursuit of lush young women. We were all so young that we arrogantly assumed that all of us were straight and they were bent; *we* were healthy, *they* were carriers of some sickness. It took me a while to understand that the world was more complicated than it was in the *Bluejackets' Manual.*[1]

The years passed. I grew up. I worked with homosexuals. I read novels 15
and saw plays written by homosexuals about the specifics of their lives. Gradually, the stereotypes I carried were broken by experience and knowledge. At the same time, I was roaming around as a reporter, seeing riots and wars, too much poverty and too many dead bodies. The ambiguities, masks, and games of human sexuality seemed a minor issue compared with the horrors of the wider world. Even after the gay-liberation movement began, in the wake of the 1969 Stonewall Riot, in New York, the private lives of homosexuals seldom entered my imagination. I didn't care what people did in bed, as long as they didn't wake up in the morning and napalm villages, starve children, or harm the innocent.

Some of my friends "came out" in the years after Stonewall. The process was more difficult for them than it was for me. On more than a few evenings, I found myself listening to a painful account of the dreadful angst that accompanied living in The Closet, and the delirious joy that came with kicking down its door forever. I apologized for any crudities I might have uttered while they were in The Closet; they forgave me. We remained friends.

In the years after Stonewall, I met gay men living in monogamous relationships, gay men of austere moral codes, gay men with great courage. I read interviews with gay cops, soldiers, and football players. I knew that there were thousands of gay men living lives of bourgeois respectability. There were even right-wing gay Republicans. Like many men my age, I thought, What the hell, there's room for everybody.

Then came AIDS.

[1] A bluejacket is an enlisted member of the U.S. Navy.

And for people like me, everything about homosexuals changed once more. Thousands have died from this terrible disease, but for people my age, the gulf between straight and gay seems to be widening instead of closing. I find myself deploring homophobia, like any good liberal, and simultaneously understanding why it seems to be spreading among otherwise decent people. A phobia, after all, is a fear. And AIDS terrifies.

Under the combined pressures of fear and pity, I've been forced to con- 20
front my own tangled notions about gays. I cherish my gay friends, and want them to live long and productive lives. But while AIDS has made many millions even more sympathetic to and understanding of gay lives, I find myself struggling with the powerful undertow of the primitive code of my youth. I've lost all patience with much of the paranoid oratory of gay radicals. I can't abide the self-pitying aura of victimhood that permeates so much of their discussion. Their leaders irritate me with their insistence on seeing AIDS as if it were some tragic medieval plague of unknown origin instead of the result of personal behavior.

I know that AIDS cases are increasing among heterosexuals, and the virus is spreading wildly among intravenous drug users. For me, this knowledge is not abstract. I know one sweet young woman who died of the disease, picked up from her junkie husband; I was at her christening, and I'm still furious that she's dead. I also know that the rate of infection among homosexuals is down, the result of "safe sex" campaigns, education, and abstinence.

But when the gay militants in ACT UP go to St. Patrick's Cathedral and one of them crushes a Communion Host on the floor as a protest against the Church's traditional policies, I'm revolted. This is cheap blasphemy and even worse politics. I'm angered when the homosexual bedroom police force gays out of The Closet against their will while simultaneously opposing the tracing of AIDS carriers. When gay activists harass doctors, disrupt public meetings, and scream self-righteously about their "rage," my heart hardens.

I'm sure the government isn't doing enough to find a cure for AIDS. But it's also not doing enough to cure lung cancer, which kills 130,000 people every year, or acute alcoholism (57,000 every year), or to avert the ravages of cocaine addiction. Like AIDS (which has killed 81,000 Americans in a decade), these afflictions are spread, or controlled, by personal behavior. I've had more friends die of smoking, drinking, or doing dope than I have friends who died of AIDS. But I don't ever hear about the "rage" of the cigarette addict or the stone drunk or the crackhead, even though none of my stricken friends went gently into that good night. If anything, most current social rage is directed *against* such people, while the diseases continue to kill. And yet in most American cities, if you measured inches of type in newspapers, you might believe that all of the old diseases have been conquered and only AIDS remains.

I'm not among those who believe there is some all-powerful "Homintern" that manipulates the media while filling the museums with Robert Mapplethorpe photographs. But I don't feel I'm lining up with the unspeakable Jesse Helms when I say that I'm also fed up with the ranting of those gays who believe that all straights are part of some Monstrous Conspiracy to end homosexual life. One lie is not countered with another.

Certainly, as gay rhetoric becomes more apocalyptic, the entire public discussion is being reduced to a lurid cartoon, devoid of criticism, irony, nuance, and even common sense. Certainly, there is less room for tolerance. I know a few gay people who resent being told that if they don't follow the party line they are mere "self-hating gays." And as someone outside the group, I don't like being told that I must agree with the latest edition of the established creed or be dismissed as a homophobe. More than anything else, I'm angry with myself when some of the old specters come rising out of the psychic mists of my own generation. 25

In the face of the AIDS plague, gays and straights should be forging a union by cool reason. Instead, we are presented with cheap pity, romantic bullshit, or the irrational, snarling faces of haters. As in so many areas of our society, divisions are drawn in black and white; there are no shades of gray. Homophobia is countered by heterophobia; the empty answer to gay-bashing is a vow to bash back. There are sadder developments in American life, I suppose, but for the moment, I can't think of one.

Questions for Discussion

1. Using the "folklore" and experiences of his own working-class background, Hamill suggests that there was a connection between homophobia and socioeconomic class when he was growing up in the 1940s and 1950s. Do you think such a connection still exists?
2. Hamill refers to the 1940s and 1950s as "those darkest years of The Closet" (paragraph 11). Can you make any connection between homosexuals' staying in the closet and the experiences Hamill describes in paragraphs 10–13?
3. What made it possible for Hamill to overcome his prejudices? Have you had a similar experience in overcoming any form of prejudice?
4. Hamill defends his own recurring homophobia as a reaction to AIDS and the "ranting" of gay activists. What evidence does he offer to justify his new attitude? Is it all related to AIDS? How does Hamill use language as a tool to persuade readers to see the militant activity as he does?
5. In paragraph 9 Hamill says that "twenty years of education, lobbying, journalism, and demonstrating by gays have had only a superficial effect" on public perceptions. What solution is he proposing to the problem of homophobia?

For Inquiry and Persuasion

Research any recent demonstrations by gay rights activists, such as those in ACT UP. What are these groups protesting, and what methods are they using? How confrontational are their protests? How often is civil disobedience involved? Why have they taken such a militant approach? Look also at what they are saying, at what kind of language they are using. You might have to turn to periodicals aimed at the gay community, such as *The Advocate* and *Christopher Street,* which are indexed in *InfoTrac.* Your campus may have an organization for gay and lesbian students, which might also be a source for gay rights literature.

After inquiring thoroughly, if you feel Hamill's criticisms are justified, write persuasively to the militants, suggesting a cooler approach. If you think their approach is justified, write to Hamill and others like him who have lost patience with the demonstrations; try to generate understanding and sympathy.

For Mediation

After inquiring into gay rights demonstrations, write a mediatory essay aimed at both militant gays and an audience of men and women who feel as Hamill does. Before you write, create a brief of each side's position and reasons. In your mediatory essay attempt to get each side to understand the other's emotions and interests. How might militant gays and straights work together to eliminate homophobia?

GARY TRUDEAU

Cartoon

In one segment of Gary Trudeau's comic strip Doonesbury, *Mike Doonesbury's good friend Mark realizes that he is homosexual.*

Doonesbury BY GARRY TRUDEAU

For Discussion

The cartoon makes us laugh at Mike's attitude, a stereotype of heterosexual males' discomfort around homosexuals. But in spite of its humor, the strip raises many issues. Does it suggest that homosexuality is or is not a choice? If sexual preference is innate, not a choice, how could a young man or woman grow up not recognizing gay or lesbian attractions, as happened in the case of the character Mark? Is it possible that American culture, in which heterosexual eroticism pervades our advertising and entertainment, and even the literature that young people read, could lead most everyone to assume that he or she is heterosexual?

PETER J. GOMES

Homophobic? Reread Your Bible

Those who contend that homosexuality is immoral often cite the Bible for support. Although nonbelievers would find these arguments weak, the weight of biblical authority is unquestionable among many Christian audiences. During the crucial election year of 1992, fundamentalist Christians and others called upon Scripture to make their case that homosexuality is immoral and gay rights a threat to "traditional family values"; several gay rights measures were defeated in the process. In the following argument Peter Gomes, a minister and professor of Christian morals at Harvard University, challenges the fundamentalists' interpretation of the Bible.

OPPOSITION TO gays' civil rights has become one of the most visible symbols of American civic conflict this year, and religion has become the weapon of choice. The army of the discontented, eager for clear villains and simple solutions and ready for a crusade in which political self-interest and social anxiety can be cloaked in morality, has found hatred of homosexuality to be the last respectable prejudice of the century. 1

Ballot initiatives in Oregon and Maine would deny homosexuals the protection of civil rights laws. The Pentagon has steadfastly refused to allow gays into the armed forces. Vice President Dan Quayle is crusading for "traditional family values." And Pat Buchanan, who is scheduled to speak at the Republican National Convention this evening, regards homosexuality as a litmus test of moral purity.

Nothing has illuminated this crusade more effectively than a work of fiction, *The Drowning of Stephan Jones,* by Bette Greene. Preparing for her novel, Ms. Greene interviewed more than 400 young men incarcerated for gay-bashing, and scrutinized their case studies. In an interview published in *The Boston Globe* this spring, she said she found that the gay-bashers generally saw nothing wrong in what they did, and, more often than not, said their religious leaders and traditions sanctioned their behavior. One convicted teenage gay-basher told her that the pastor of his church had said, "Homosexuals represent the devil, Satan," and that the Rev. Jerry Falwell had echoed that charge.

Christians opposed to political and social equality for homosexuals nearly always appeal to the moral injunctions of the Bible, claiming that Scripture is very clear on the matter and citing verses that support their opinion. They accuse others of perverting and distorting texts contrary to their "clear" meaning. They do not, however, necessarily see quite as clear a meaning in biblical passages on economic conduct, the burdens of wealth, and the sin of greed.

Nine biblical citations are customarily invoked as relating to homosexu- 5
ality. Four (Deuteronomy 23:17, I Kings 14:24, I Kings 22:46, and II Kings 23:7) simply forbid prostitution, by men and women.

Two others (Leviticus 18:19–23 and Leviticus 20:10–16) are part of what biblical scholars call the Holiness Code. The code explicitly bans homosexual acts. But it also prohibits eating raw meat, planting two different kinds of seed in the same field, and wearing garments with two different kinds of yarn. Tattoos, adultery, and sexual intercourse during a woman's menstrual period are similarly outlawed.

There is no mention of homosexuality in the four Gospels of the New Testament. The moral teachings of Jesus are not concerned with the subject.

Three references from St. Paul are frequently cited (Romans 1:26–2:1, I Corinthians 6:9–11, and I Timothy 1:10). But St. Paul was concerned with homosexuality only because in Greco-Roman culture it represented a secular sensuality that was contrary to his Jewish-Christian spiritual idealism. He was against lust and sensuality in anyone, including heterosexuals. To say that homosexuality is bad because homosexuals are tempted to do morally doubtful things is to say that heterosexuality is bad because heterosexuals are likewise tempted. For St. Paul, anyone who puts his or her interest ahead of God's is condemned, a verdict that falls equally upon everyone.

And lest we forget Sodom and Gomorrah, recall that the story is not about sexual perversion and homosexual practice. It is about inhospitality, according to Luke 10:10–13, and failure to care for the poor, according to Ezekiel 16:49–50: "Behold, this was the iniquity of thy sister Sodom, pride, fullness of bread, and abundance of idleness was in her and in her daughters, neither did she strengthen the hand of the poor and needy." To suggest that Sodom and Gomorrah is about homosexual sex is an analysis of about as much worth as suggesting that the story of Jonah and the whale is a treatise on fishing.

Part of the problem is a question of interpretation. Fundamentalists and 10
literalists, the storm troopers of the religious right, are terrified that Scripture, "wrongly interpreted," may separate them from their values. That fear stems from their own recognition that their "values" are not derived from Scripture, as they publicly claim.

Indeed, it is through the lens of their own prejudices and personal values that they "read" Scripture and cloak their own views in its authority. We all interpret Scripture: Make no mistake. And no one truly is a literalist, despite the pious temptation. The questions are, By what principle of interpretation do we proceed, and by what means do we reconcile "what it meant then" to "what it means now"?

These matters are far too important to be left to scholars and seminarians alone. Our ability to judge ourselves and others rests on our ability to interpret Scripture intelligently. The right use of the Bible, an exercise as old as the church itself, means that we confront our prejudices rather than merely confirm them.

For Christians, the principle by which Scripture is read is nothing less than an appreciation of the work and will of God as revealed in that of Jesus. To recover a liberating and inclusive Christ is to be freed from the semantic bondage that makes us curators of a dead culture rather than creatures of a new creation.

Religious fundamentalism is dangerous because it cannot accept ambiguity and diversity and is therefore inherently intolerant. Such intolerance, in the name of virtue, is ruthless and uses political power to destroy what it cannot convert.

It is dangerous, especially in America, because it is anti-democratic 15
and is suspicious of "the other," in whatever form that "other" might appear. To maintain itself, fundamentalism must always define "the other" as deviant.

But the chief reason that fundamentalism is dangerous is that, at the hands of the Rev. Pat Robertson, the Rev. Jerry Falwell, and hundreds of lesser-known but equally worrisome clerics, preachers, and pundits, it uses Scripture and the Christian practice to encourage ordinarily good people to act upon their fears rather than their virtues.

Fortunately, those who speak for the religious right do not speak for all American Christians, and the Bible is not theirs alone to interpret. The same Bible that the advocates of slavery used to protect their wicked self-interests is the Bible that inspired slaves to revolt and their liberators to action.

The same Bible that the predecessors of Mr. Falwell and Mr. Robertson used to keep white churches white is the source of the inspiration of the Rev. Martin Luther King, Jr., and the social reformation of the 1960's.

The same Bible that antifeminists use to keep women silent in the churches is the Bible that preaches liberation to captives and says that in Christ there is neither male nor female, slave nor free.

And the same Bible that on the basis of an archaic social code of ancient 20
Israel and a tortured reading of Paul is used to condemn all homosexuals and homosexual behavior includes metaphors of redemption, renewal, inclusion, and love—principles that invite homosexuals to accept their freedom and responsibility in Christ and demands that their fellow Christians accept them as well.

The political piety of the fundamentalist religious right must not be exercised at the expense of our precious freedoms. And in this summer of our discontent, one of the most precious freedoms for which we must all fight is freedom from this last prejudice.

Questions for Discussion

1. In paragraphs 5–9 Gomes offers his interpretations of the biblical passages usually cited as showing God's condemnation of homosexuality. How well does Gomes deflate the arguments from Leviticus and from the gospels written by St. Paul? To what extent does Gomes's own authority as a

minister and Harvard theologian lend force to his view of these passages? (You may want to consult the biblical passages yourself before you respond.)

2. Gomes argues that all reading of Scripture involves interpretation (paragraph 11). What, for him, is the difference between right and wrong interpretation? How is "right" interpretation similar to inquiry, as we describe it on pages 37–41? Must a "right" interpretation be apolitical—that is, influenced by no political viewpoint?
3. What argumentative and stylistic techniques does Gomes use in paragraphs 17–20 to support his point about right and wrong interpretations of the Bible?
4. In his criticism of the rhetorical, or persuasive, strategy of the religious right, Gomes says their use of the Bible "encourage[s] ordinarily good people to act upon their fears rather than their virtues" (paragraph 16). Do you agree? Is it always bad to use fear as an emotional appeal in persuasive argumentation?
5. What other issues can you think of in which people commonly call upon the authority of the Bible for support? Do you think Gomes would argue that any of these misuse Scripture in the way he describes here?

For Analysis and Persuasion

A classic example of persuasive argumentation that calls upon the Bible as a source of authority is the "Letter from Birmingham Jail" by Martin Luther King, Jr. (pages 113–125). After you have read King's "Letter" and our analysis of King's audience and purpose (pages 110–112), go back and locate all of King's references to the Bible. Write a paper in which you discuss King's use of the Bible, noting the specific fears or virtues of his audience to which he is appealing.

JONATHAN ALTER

Degrees of Discomfort

A person who has no tolerance for others of a particular race is a racist. The following argument, originally published in Newsweek, *asks whether homophobia, or prejudice against homosexuals, is equivalent to racism. The question is important because defenders of homosexual rights argue that the two forms of discrimination are comparable, while those who oppose gay rights claim their own right to disapprove of people whose behavior is repugnant or even sinful according to their own moral standards. Note how Jonathan Alter's argument makes the case for civil rights for gay people but not for universal tolerance of homosexuality. Note, too, that Alter wrote his essay in response to an incident in which Martin Luther King's son first made and then retracted a statement critical of homosexuals.*

WHEN ANDY Rooney got in trouble last month, gay activists complained he was being publicly rebuked for his allegedly racist remarks and not for his gay-bashing.[1] They wanted to know why homophobia was viewed as less serious than racism. The case of Martin Luther King III last week brought the comparison into even sharper relief. After a speech in Poughkeepsie, NY, in which he said "something must be wrong" with homosexuals, the young Atlanta politician met with angry gay leaders and quickly apologized. His father's legacy, King said, was "the struggle to free this country of bigotry and discrimination." In that light, he added, he needed to examine his own attitudes toward homosexuals. 1

King will need to ask himself this question: Is homophobia the moral equivalent of racism? To answer yes sounds right; it conforms to commendable ideals of tolerance. But it doesn't take account of valid distinctions between the two forms of prejudice. On the other hand, to answer no—to say, homophobia is not like racism for this reason or that—risks rationalizing anti-gay bias.

Discrimination against homosex*uals* is not the same as personal distaste for homosex*uality*. The former is clearly akin to racism. There is no way to explain away the prejudice in this country against gays. People lose jobs, promotions, homes, and friends because of it. Incidents of violence against gays are up sharply in some areas. Hundreds of anti-sodomy laws remain on the books, and gays are shamelessly discriminated against in insurance and inheritance. The fact is, a lot of people are pigheaded enough to judge a person entirely on the basis of his or her sexuality. Rooney's mail—and that of practically everyone else commenting publicly on this issue—is full of ugly anti-gay invective.

[1]Rooney, a commentator on *60 Minutes*, was briefly suspended by CBS in 1990 for making remarks that offended blacks but not for comments critical of homosexuality.

But does that mean that anyone who considers the homosexual sex act sinful or repulsive is the equivalent of a racist? The answer is no. Objecting to it may be narrow-minded and invasive of privacy, but it does not convey the same complete moral vacuity as, say, arguing that blacks are born inferior. There is a defensible middle position. Recall Mario Cuomo's carefully articulated view of abortion: personally opposed, but deeply supportive of a woman's right to choose. That tracks quite closely to polls that show how the majority of Americans approach the subject of homosexuality.

Like all straddles, this one offends people on both sides: straights who 5
consider all homosexuality sinful, and gays who consider a hate-the-sin-but-not-the-sinner argument merely another form of homophobia. Moreover, the "personal opposition" idea rings more hollow on homosexuality than on abortion; after all, there is no third-party fetus—just consenting adults whose private behavior should not be judged by outsiders. Of course there are times when squeamishness is understandable. In coming of age, many gays have made a point of flaunting their sexuality, moving, as one joke puts it, from "the love that dare not speak its name" to "the love that won't shut up." Exhibitionism and promiscuity (less common in the age of AIDS) are behavioral choices that, unlike innate sexual preference, can be controlled. It's perfectly legitimate to condemn such behavior—assuming heterosexuals are held to the same standard.

Simply put, identity and behavior are not synonymous. A bigot hates blacks for what they *are;* a reasonable person can justifiably object to some things homosexuals *do.* The distinction between objecting to who someone is (unfair) and objecting to what someone does (less unfair) must be maintained. The worst comment about gays allegedly made by Rooney was that he would not like to be locked in a room with them. That would be a tolerable sentiment only if the homosexuals were *having sex* in the room. Otherwise it's a form of bigotry. Who would object to being locked in a room with cigarette smokers if they weren't smoking?

"Acting gay" often involves more than sexual behavior itself. Much of the dislike for homosexuals centers not on who they are or what they do in private, but on so-called affectations—"swishiness" in men, the "butch" look for women—not directly related to the more private sex act. Heterosexuals tend to argue that gays can downplay these characteristics and "pass" more easily in the straight world than blacks can in a white world.

This may be true, but it's also irrelevant. For many gays those traits aren't affectations but part of their identities; attacking the swishiness is the same as attacking *them.* Why the visceral vehemence, particularly among straight men? Richard Isay, a psychiatrist and author of the 1989 book *Being Homosexual,* suggests that homophobia actually has little to do with the sex act itself. "This hatred of homosexuals appears to be secondary in our society to the fear and hatred of what is perceived as being 'feminine' in other men and in oneself."

Such fears, buried deep, are reminiscent of the emotional charge of racial feelings. At its most virulent, this emotion leads to blaming the victim—for

AIDS, for instance, or for poverty. In its more modest form, the fear, when recognized, can be helpful in understanding the complexities of both homosexuality and race.

That consciousness is sometimes about language—avoiding “fag” and 10
“nigger.” But the interest groups that expend energy insisting that one use “African-American” instead of “black” or “gay and lesbian” instead of “homosexual” are missing the point. Likewise, the distinctions between racism and homophobia eventually shrivel before the larger task at hand, which is simply to look harder at ourselves.

Questions for Discussion

1. In your own words explain what Alter sees as “a defensible middle position” on the issue of discrimination against homosexuals (paragraph 4). How does he support and defend that position?
2. Evaluate Alter's argument in paragraph 6, which compares homosexuals to cigarette smokers. In context, how valid is this analogy?
3. In paragraphs 7–8 Alter points out that what many straight people call “affected” behavior in gay people is actually part of their identities, something that they may not be able to hide, even if they wanted to. Is one's sexual orientation something everyone should try to downplay in public? Should, for example, heterosexual couples be expected to avoid romantic physical contact in public, as most homosexual couples feel they must do?
4. Alter seems to conclude that homophobia, or “personal distaste for homosex*uality,*” is not as severe a character flaw as racism (paragraphs 3–4). How does he support this point? Do you agree with him?
5. Alter quotes psychiatrist Richard Isay on a possible cause for homophobia (paragraph 8). What do you think of Isay's theory? Look at Pete Hamill's description of how “Real Men were supposed to react” if approached by a homosexual (paragraph 13 in his essay earlier in this chapter). Do you think Isay's theory might help explain some of the violence committed against gay men?

For Inquiry

Alter acknowledges that his middle position would offend “people on both sides” (paragraph 5). Write a dialogue with Alter in which you examine the truth of his position, posing questions that would represent the viewpoints of both sides. See pages 39–40 for suggestions about what to ask.

JONATHAN RAUCH

Beyond Oppression

Some writers have claimed that gay men and lesbians are an oppressed class. Jonathan Rauch sets forth what he sees as criteria for claiming oppression, and he argues that gay men and lesbians in the United States do not meet these criteria. What is Rauch's purpose in denying victim status to gay people?

At 10:30 on a weeknight in the spring of 1991, Glenn Cashmore 1
was walking to his car on San Diego's University Avenue. He had just left the Soho coffee house in Hillcrest, a heavily gay neighborhood. He turned down Fourth Street and paused to look at the display in an optician's window. Someone shouted, "Hey, faggot!" He felt pain in his shoulder and turned in time to see a white Nissan speeding away. Someone had shot him, luckily only with a pellet gun. The pellet tore through the shirt and penetrated the skin. He went home and treated the wound with peroxide.

Later that year, on the night of December 13, a 17-year-old named John Wear and two other boys were headed to the Soho on University Avenue when a pair of young men set upon them, calling them "faggots." One boy escaped, another's face was gashed and Wear (who, his family said, was not gay) was stabbed. Cashmore went to the hospital to see him but, on arriving, was met with the news that Wear was dead.

This is life—not all of life, but an aspect of life—for gay people in today's America. Homosexuals are objects of scorn for teenagers and of sympathy or moral fear or hatred for adults. They grow up in confusion and bewilderment as children, then often pass into denial as young adults and sometimes remain frightened even into old age. They are persecuted by the military, are denied the sanctuary of publicly recognized marriage, occasionally are prosecuted outright for making love. If closeted, they live with fear of revelation; if open, they must daily negotiate a hundred delicate tactical issues. (Should I bring it up? Tell my boss? My co-workers? Wear a wedding band? Display my lover's picture?)

There is also AIDS and the stigma attached to it, though AIDS is not uniquely a problem of gay people. And there is the violence. One of my high school friends—an honors student at Brophy Prep, a prestigious Catholic high school in Phoenix—used to boast about his late-night exploits with a baseball bat at the "fag Denny's." I'm sure he was lying, but imagine the horror of being spoken to, and about, in that way.

If you ask gay people in America today whether homosexuals are op- 5
pressed, I think most would say yes. If you ask why, they would point to the sorts of facts that I just mentioned. The facts are not blinkable. Yet the oppression diagnosis is, for the most part, wrong.

Not wrong in the sense that life for American homosexuals is hunky-dory. It is not. But life is not terrible for most gay people, either, and it is becoming less terrible every year. The experience of gayness and the social status of homosexuals have changed rapidly in the last twenty years, largely owing to the courage of thousands who decided that they had had enough abuse and who demanded better. With change has come the time for a reassessment.

The standard political model sees homosexuals as an oppressed minority who must fight for their liberation through political action. But that model's usefulness is drawing to a close. It is ceasing to serve the interests of ordinary gay people, who ought to begin disengaging from it, even drop it. Otherwise, they will misread their position and lose their way, as too many minority groups have done already.

"Oppression" has become every minority's word for practically everything, a one-size-fits-all political designation used by anyone who feels unequal, aggrieved, or even uncomfortable. I propose a start toward restoring meaning to the notion of oppression by insisting on *objective* evidence. A sense of grievance or discomfort, however real, is not enough.

By now, human beings know a thing or two about oppression. Though it may, indeed, take many forms and work in different ways, there are objective signs you can look for. My own list would emphasize five main items. First, direct legal or governmental discrimination. Second, denial of political franchise—specifically, denial of the right to vote, organize, speak, or lobby. Third—and here we move beyond the strictly political—the systematic denial of education. Fourth, impoverishment relative to the non-oppressed population. And, fifth, a pattern of human rights violations, without recourse.

Any one or two of those five signposts may appear for reasons other than 10
oppression. There are a lot of reasons why a people may be poor, for instance. But where you see a minority that is legally barred from businesses and neighborhoods and jobs, that cannot vote, that is poor and poorly educated, and that lives in physical fear, you are looking at, for instance, the blacks of South Africa, or blacks of the American South until the 1960s; the Jews and homosexuals of Nazi Germany and Vichy France; the untouchable castes of India, the Kurds of Iraq, the women of Saudi Arabia, the women of America 100 years ago; for that matter, the entire population of the former Soviet Union and many Arab and African and Asian countries.

And gay people in America today? Criterion one—direct legal or governmental discrimination—is resoundingly met. Homosexual relations are illegal in twenty-three states, at least seven of which specifically single out acts between persons of the same sex. Gay marriage is not legally recognized anywhere. And the government hounds gay people from the military, not for what they do but for what they are.

Criterion two—denial of political franchise—is resoundingly not met. Not only do gay people vote, they are turning themselves into a constituency to be reckoned with and fought for. Otherwise, the Patrick Buchanans of the world would have sounded contemptuous of gay people at the Republican convention last year, rather than panicked by them. If gay votes didn't count, Bill Clinton would not have stuck his neck out on the military issue during the primary season (one of the bravest things any living politician has done).

Criterion three—denial of education—is also resoundingly not met. Overlooked Opinions Inc., a Chicago market-research company, has built a diverse national base of 35,000 gay men and lesbians, two-thirds of whom are either not out of the closet or are only marginally out, and has then randomly sampled them in surveys. It found that homosexuals had an average of 15.7 years of education, as against 12.7 years for the population as a whole. Obviously, the findings may be skewed if college-educated gay people are likelier to take part in surveys (though Overlooked Opinions said that results didn't follow degree of closetedness). Still, any claim that gay people are denied education appears ludicrous.

Criterion four—relative impoverishment—is also not met. In Overlooked Opinions' sample, gay men had an average household income of $51,624 and lesbians $42,755, compared with the national average of $36,800. Again, yuppie homosexuals may be more likely to answer survey questions than blue-collar ones. But, again, to call homosexuals an impoverished class would be silly.

Criterion five—human rights violations without recourse—is also, in the *15*
end, not met, though here it's worth taking a moment to see why it is not. The number of gay bashings has probably increased in recent years (though it's hard to know, what with reporting vagaries), and, of course, many gay-bashers either aren't caught or aren't jailed. What too many gay people forget, though, is that these are problems that homosexuals have in common with non-gay Americans. Though many gay-bashers go free, so do many murderers. In the District of Columbia last year, the police identified suspects in fewer than half of all murders, to say nothing of assault cases.

And the fact is that anti-gay violence is just one part of a much broader pattern. Probably not coincidentally, the killing of John Wear happened in the context of a year, 1991, that broke San Diego's all-time homicide record (1992 was runner-up). Since 1965 the homicide rate in America has doubled, the violent crime arrest rate for juveniles has more than tripled; people now kill you to get your car, they kill you to get your shoes or your potato chips, they kill you because they can do it. A particularly ghastly fact is that homicide due to gunshot is now the second leading cause of death in high school–age kids, after car crashes. No surprise, then, that gay people are afraid. So is everyone else.

Chances are, indeed, that gay people's social class makes them safer, on average, than other urban minorities. Certainly their problem is small compared with what blacks face in inner-city Los Angeles or Chicago, where young black males are likelier to be killed than a U.S. soldier was in a tour of duty in Vietnam.

If any problem unites gay people with non-gay people, it is crime. If any issue does not call for special-interest pleading, this is it. Minority advocates, including gay ones, have blundered insensitively by trying to carve out hate-crime statutes and other special-interest crime laws instead of focusing on tougher measures against violence of all kinds. In trying to sensitize people to crimes aimed specifically at minorities, they are inadvertently desensitizing them to the vastly greater threat of crime against everyone. They contribute to the routinization of murder, which has now reached the point where news of a black girl spray-painted white makes the front pages, but news of a black girl murdered runs in a round-up on page D-6 ("Oh, another killing"). Yes, gay-bashing is a problem. But, no, it isn't oppression. It is, rather, an obscenely ordinary feature of the American experience.

Of course, homosexuals face unhappiness, discrimination, and hatred. But for everyone with a horror story to tell, there are others like an academic I know, a tenured professor who is married to his lover of fourteen years in every way but legally, who owns a split-level condo in Los Angeles, drives a Miata, enjoys prestige and success and love that would be the envy of millions of straight Americans. These things did not fall in his lap. He fought personal and professional battles, was passed over for jobs and left the closet when that was much riskier than it is today. Asked if he is oppressed, he says, "You're damn straight." But a mark of oppression is that most of its victims are not allowed to succeed; they are allowed only to fail. And this man is no mere token. He is one of a growing multitude of openly gay people who have overcome the past and, in doing so, changed the present.

"I'm a gay person, so I don't live in a free country," one highly successful 20
gay writer said recently, "and I don't think most straight people really sit down and realize that for gay people this is basically a totalitarian society in which we're barely tolerated." The reason straight people don't realize this is because it obviously isn't true. As more and more homosexuals come out of hiding, the reality of gay economic and political and educational achievement becomes more evident. And as that happens, gay people who insist they are oppressed will increasingly, and not always unfairly, come off as yuppie whiners, "victims" with $50,000 incomes and vacations in Europe. They may feel they are oppressed, but they will have a harder and harder time convincing the public.

They will distort their politics, too, twisting it into strained and impotent shapes. Scouring for oppressions with which to identify, activists are driven further and further afield. They grab fistfuls of random political demands and stuff them in their pockets. The original platform for April's March on Washington[1] called for, among other things, enforced bilingual education, "an end to genocide of all the indigenous peoples and their cultures," defense budget cuts, universal health care, a national needle exchange program, free substance-abuse treatment on demand, safe and affordable abortion, more money for breast cancer "and other cancers particular to women," "unrestricted, safe and affordable alternative insemination," health care for the "differently-abled and

[1]A major gay rights demonstration was held in Washington, DC, on April 25, 1993.

physically challenged," and "an end to poverty." Here was the oppression-entitlement mentality gone haywire.

Worst of all, oppression politics distorts the face of gay America itself. It encourages people to forget that homosexuality isn't hell. As the AIDS crisis has so movingly shown, gay people have built the kind of community that evaporated for many non-gay Americans decades ago. You don't see straight volunteers queuing up to change cancer patients' bedpans and deliver their groceries. Gay people—and unmarried people generally—are at a disadvantage in the top echelons of corporate America, but, on the other hand, they have achieved dazzlingly in culture and business and much else. They lead lives of richness and competence and infinite variety, lives that are not miserable or squashed.

The insistence that gay people are oppressed is most damaging, in the end, because it implies that to be gay is to suffer. It affirms what so many straight people, even sympathetic ones, believe in their hearts: that homosexuals are pitiable. That alone is reason to junk the oppression model, preferably sooner instead of later.

If the oppression model is failing, what is the right model? Not that of an oppressed people seeking redemption through political action; rather, that of an ostracized people seeking redemption through personal action. What do you do about misguided ostracism? The most important thing is what Glenn Cashmore did. After John Wear's murder, he came out of the closet. He wrote an article in the *Los Angeles Times* denouncing his own years of silence. He stepped into the circle of people who are what used to be called known homosexuals.

25 This makes a difference. *The New York Times* conducted a poll on homosexuals this year and found that people who had a gay family member or close friend "were much more tolerant and accepting." Whereas oppression politics fails because it denies reality, positive personal example works because it demonstrates reality. "We're here, we're queer, get used to it," Queer Nation's chant,[1] is not only a brilliant slogan. It is a strategy. It is, in some ways, *the* strategy. To move away from oppression politics is not to sit quietly. It is often to hold hands in public or take a lover to the company Christmas party, sometimes to stage kiss-ins, always to be unashamed. It is to make of honesty a kind of activism.

Gay Americans should emulate Jewish Americans, who have it about right. Jews recognize that to many Americans we will always seem different (and we are, in some ways, different). We grow up being fed "their" culture in school, in daily life, even in the calendar. It never stops. For a full month of every year, every radio program and shop window reminds you that this is, culturally, a Christian nation (no, not Judeo-Christian). Jews could resent this,

[1]Queer Nation is a gay political organization—many members of which are in their twenties—that advocates a highly visible gay presence in society.

but most of us choose not to, because, by way of compensation, we think hard, we work hard, we are cohesive, we are interesting. We recognize that minorities will always face special burdens of adjustment, but we also understand that with those burdens come rewards of community and spirit and struggle. We recognize that there will always be a minority of Americans who hate us, but we also understand that, so long as we stay watchful, this hateful minority is more pathetic than threatening. We watch it; we fight it when it lashes out; but we do not organize our personal and political lives around it.

Gay people's main weapons are ones we already possess. In America, our main enemies are superstition and hate. Superstition is extinguished by public criticism and by the power of moral example. Political activists always underestimate the power of criticism and moral example to change people's minds, and they always overestimate the power of law and force. As for hate, the way to fight it is with love. And that we have in abundance.

Questions for Discussion

1. Rauch acknowledges the opposition's arguments in paragraphs 1–4, but he denies that any of the examples constitute "*objective* evidence" of oppression (paragraph 8). Would you agree?
2. Does Rauch offer enough evidence to show that homosexuals meet only one of his criteria for claiming oppression? Could you raise any questions about the five criteria he sets up? Can you think of additional criteria?
3. In paragraph 24 Rauch argues that gay people work on the model that they are ostracized, not oppressed. What is the difference?
4. Rauch suggests that gay people can improve their situation through personal rather than political action. What is he advocating? Do you think his plan will work?

For Convincing

Many of the arguments in this chapter suggest or deny that parallels exist between racism and discrimination against homosexuals. Make your own case for or against such parallels, using some of the readings here as well as additional sources and evidence.

TONI A. H. McNARON

In or Out in the Classroom

Toni A. H. McNaron is professor of English and women's studies at the University of Minnesota. Over the course of her more than thirty years of college teaching, she initially hid her identity as a lesbian but eventually decided to acknowledge it openly in her classroom. The dilemma of whether to teach from inside or outside the closet intrigued her enough to survey other gay and lesbian professors. The result of her research is her book Poisoned Ivy: Lesbian and Gay Academics Confronting Homophobia *(1997), from which this selection is excerpted.*

IF I as faculty member have a secret pertaining to my personal life, being in so public a venue as a classroom will be dangerous. On any given day, a student might ask a question that relates to the secret and threatens its exposure. My response will have to be in the nature of a cover-up or escape unless I am prepared to blow my carefully constructed cover. 1

During my years in the pedagogical closet, in the late 1960s and early 1970s, I routinely taught an advanced course in Shakespeare that was made up almost entirely of graduate students. Each time we discussed the sonnets, a bright male student asked if I saw something more than friendship going on between the poet and the young man to whom the first 127 poems are dedicated. My response was immediate and forceful: "Oh, no, but I can see what's happened here. You've misunderstood the poems in question because you are reading as a twentieth-century person. During the Renaissance, a revival of Platonic ideals was taking place; hence, platonic friendship was being practiced by many English noblemen. Within such a framework, the bond between two friends was actually superior to a sexual liaison because such relationships were susceptible to suspicion, jealousy, and anger, whereas friendships were more permanent and highly valued. The poet in the sonnets, then, is extolling the difference between the trust and harmony he can feel with his fair-haired young male friend and the consuming, destructive passion awakened by the dark-haired lady of the last twenty-seven sonnets."

My response was a flat denial of the text, because the poems to the young man describe jealousy over his youth, beauty, and the possibility that he is seeing other people. More importantly, I was misusing esoteric knowledge to protect my own identity. If I had admitted the possibilities behind the student's question, I risked saying "we" when I spoke of same-sex relationships. The danger of outing myself prevented me from being of any itellectual or potentially personal assistance to the student who had most likely taken a risk in asking such a question. Similarly, I discouraged serious discussion of the relationships between Romeo and Mercutio, Hamlet and Horatio, Bassanio and Antonio, Rosalind and Celia, Othello and Iago or Cassio, and Hermione and Paulina. I broke into a sweat even when students expressed interest in the sixteenth-century stage practice of having young men play women's parts and the cross-dressing involved in this practice or the use of gender disguise in the comedies. Lecturing about such instances of sexual ambiguity and fluidity frightened me.

Thinking about these once so-frightening moments and the impact of being closeted on pedagogical effectiveness, I am reminded of a jack-in-the-box. Once presented with this toy, a child is prompted by curiosity to unlatch the brightly decorated box. A painted face springs up and the unsuspecting child often reacts with terror before feeling pleasure or enjoyment. Once out of the box, the jack is much harder to fold back into its hiding place. The springing out is sudden, whereas the replacement is slow and tricky. Often the jack pops back up rather than settling back into its container, and the toy is not enjoyable unless someone can put the coiled figure back in place.

My immediate impulse to lecture my student about arcane matters 5
seemed at the time nothing more than a serious Renaissance scholar's intent to correct a reading of the text before us. What I see today is an attempt to fold the entire issue of homosexuality as well as my own secret life back into an academic container.

Ironically, by stuffing the issue back into what I prayed was safety, I practically ensured that students would continue to ask questions. My only real protection would have been to laugh back in the jack's face, to acknowledge the legitimate basis of this curiosity about same-sex relationships as they figured in Shakespeare's work. A second irony turns around my flying in the face of my own pedagogical philosophy. I held that by encouraging spontaneity in general, I could facilitate inquiry into the more complex and contested aspects of the Renaissance. I spoke about the pervasiveness of paradox and ambiguity during this period of English history and letters, and about the uneasiness with such ambiguity in our own culture. Yet on the subject of one of the most fundamental ambiguities of the period, sexual and gender identity, I did not allow discussion.

A gay professor of linguistics for 17 years, currently teaching on the West Coast, remarks as follows: "In the closet, I was always aware of 'neutralizing' any language marked for sexual orientation. I also felt that while straight colleagues could, in class, make reference to their personal lives to 'put a human touch' on what they were teaching and thereby develop greater rapport with their students, I could not." Similarly, a lesbian philosophy professor recalls teaching an introductory course before she was out. A student commented in a derogatory tone that if John Stuart Mill's liberty principle were "used to defend homosexuality, someone might suspect Mill of being homosexual." The professor countered by saying that such a suspicion could also lead its thinker to develop a better opinion of homosexuality, since Mill was clearly a respected thinker of his era. Once out, this same professor received several student complaints referring to her "exhibitionism" and saying they would never "advertise" their sexual orientation and wished she would have the "good taste" to keep hers to herself. She reflects on these circumstances as follows: "If I had been out, I doubt the first situation would have occurred at all; if I hadn't been, there would have been no occasion for the second."

There is no agreement among the respondents to my questionnaire about what constitutes outness, but they all speak about what it means in their own academic lives to teach and conduct research from inside or outside their own particular definitions of a closet. I myself define teaching as an out professor as being willing and even eager to integrate my lesbian perspective into my literary studies. Furthermore, I practice this willingness by introducing theoretical and interpretive remarks with a phrase like "as a lesbian-feminist scholar." For many respondents, such a stance is either not possible because of their subject matter or not preferred because of personal styles. I make no claims for my own definition. Rather I offer it to clarify my own academic perspective and to open up the whole question of what the concept means to each person involved.

Teaching as a publicly declared lesbian scholar has allowed me tremendous opportunities to challenge lesbian or gay and also heterosexual students in my classes. I no longer worry about being surprised by student questions regarding possibly coded homoerotic energy in literary works. If anything, I now must be alert to the students who find it disquieting if not annoying for me to announce that Walt Whitman and Stephen Crane or Willa Cather and Emily Dickinson were among the American writers who felt and expressed love and passion for members of their own sex. In responding to them, I try to remember how terrified I was in the past so that I do not repress whatever it may be that motivates their discomfort.

However, I also am unwilling to stop telling students the truth. Since I 10
teach literature written in England and the United States, and since many of the finest writers in and out of the canons of literary study were and are gay or lesbian, to bury this central biographical fact is to commit an injustice. To colleagues who argue that they never include biographical information of any kind, I can only point out that students, like the general population, assume heterosexuality unless invited or even forced to do otherwise. Silence about any biographical detail that has a bearing on plot, character development, tone, and language could prevent a full understanding of a text.

I have found that most students welcome the truth, even when it disturbs them. It seems only sensible to espouse a pedagogy built on the hypothesis that the more a student knows about the environment from which culture springs and within which knowledge and ideas are generated, the fuller that student's learning and understanding will be. Therefore, a fundamental principle of higher education is served if faculty of all persuasions tell students the truth about the men and women studied in courses, including their sexuality.

Many heterosexual faculty may well omit such information out of ignorance. We tend to teach what we ourselves have been taught. Others may withhold information out of anxiety over perhaps being thought to be gay or lesbian themselves. Those who are convinced that their sexual orientation is the only "normal" or "decent" one might lie about their subject matter when it comes into direct conflict with their moral beliefs or might fear that they will encourage their students to see erotic and sexual energy toward members of one's own sex as a viable option for human beings.

Gains and Risks

Lesbian and gay faculty who do choose to come out in their classrooms note both the gains and risks involved. A lesbian teaching at a midwestern graduate school describes her coming out as a process: "For years I stewed on whether I could be out in class—finally did it in one class, now do it regularly. I think it has a profound impact on my relationships with my students. I have become de facto counselor for many lesbian and gay students."

This faculty member also faced one of the more complex risks of being out, i.e., being unwilling to collude in any effort to continue burying gay or lesbian truths within their subject fields. She resigned from a lesbian graduate student's Ph.D. committee because that student was writing on secrets in Willa Cather's novels without dealing with the author's lesbianism as perhaps the most significant "secret" of all.

15 The lesbian professor mentions her relationship with the student's primary advisor, a heterosexual colleague with whom she had a mutually supportive history and who insisted that it was valid for the graduate student to ignore the author's sexual identity. The lesbian professor's response was emotional: "Young people are still dying regularly, literally dying, because they have nothing in their lives to let them know that being lesbian or gay is OK, that there are successful, healthy lesbian and gay people in the world."

This lesbian professor recalls another awkward conversation with the same colleague in which the appropriateness of her decision to come out in all her classes was questioned. Her colleague asked why she had to be a "lesbian" to her students rather than a "person." When the professor shared a letter she routinely sends to prospective students, her colleague grew more accepting. Reading a description of a person who loves the outdoors, comes from New Jersey, and is an avid gardener lessened the colleague's anxiety over the inclusion of lesbianism as a defining marker. The lesbian professor hoped through this exercise to convince her colleague of the possibility of being both a lesbian and a person.

Years of painful personal experience have taught me that a reductionistic view of sexual identity as total selfhood is entirely too prevalent among academics. These same academics would be appalled if I were to assume that their mentioning a spouse or children in class meant that they gave students only information tied to their sexual orientation. . . .

In some instances, respondents report a certain flattening of discussion of gay and lesbian issues as a result of their coming out:

> For a couple years when I was closeted I used an exercise in a sophomore level class that I really liked. When discussing Amy Lowell's love poems, identified in the text as being written to another woman, I asked the class in small groups to assume they were an editorial board of *The World's Greatest Love Poems.* Having already decided to use her poems, they now must decide if they will include information that they were written to another woman. . . . This exercise had generated good discussion on a complex topic. However, one of the first times I used it after I had come out early in the semester, there was little good discussion. I suspected then, and still do, that their knowing I was a lesbian inhibited them.

In other cases, faculty feel marked conflicts between their attempts at objectivity and their own responses to students' negative comments, as one lesbian professor who has taught for 15 years in the midAtlantic region writes:

> The semester the classroom became an unsafe place for me, I decided to go back into the closet.

While teaching a first-year writing course on "Race, Class, and Sexuality," which included work by people of color, gays, and lesbians, writers from different social classes, and heterosexuals, the professor was surprised to learn that some students thought the course was "about" lesbianism. Of her 68 texts, only 4 were written by lesbians. However, the teacher realized that for at least one male student, her identification as a lesbian had become part of the course content. When asked by him if he might write on why lesbians should not be allowed to parent, she responded professionally: Of course he had a right to argue his beliefs.

The student's initial argument turned on these points: children of gay 20
and lesbian parents would be subjected to homophobia; and lesbian and gay parenting, because subject to more planning and/or technological intervention, was a sign of selfishness rather than "natural" desire.

The class and the professor responded by pointing out that there is racism in the world but no one thinks of arguing that people of color stop having children. She continues as follows:

> We convinced him. He would have to come up with a better argument and evidence. He did. When he next presented, he had carefully researched Civil Rights law. He used the lack of civil rights to argue that legally gays and lesbians should not be allowed to parent since they were not protected. At the end of the semester, I asked myself what he had learned: to challenge his professor; to use effective argumentation as a means of voicing bigotry; he even earned an A− on the paper.

Later this professor asked herself what she had learned, and her answer is sobering: If she is to continue believing that by making students better thinkers, she helps make them better people, she cannot teach that course again. She used these words:

> Now I hide behind a text [that] is my closet. I peek out behind its pages to denounce the editors who remark that Kate O'Flaherty married Oscar Chopin while failing to mention anything about Langston Hughes' or E. M. Forster's sexual orientation. I inform my students "according to your editors, unless you are married, you have no sexuality." But I no longer teach many works I admire, enjoy, and have an investment in.

Faculty teaching in conservative areas or teaching the sciences, and some working in church-related or community colleges, often said they would lose too much of their students' respect to make it worthwhile to be out in classes. A lesbian who has worked at a community college in the Midwest for 26 years commented on the loss of credibility: "During the years I was more out in [first-year] English classes, one of my colleagues (lesbian) suggested I was trying to teach with both hands tied behind my back. She was likely correct; it's difficult to have credibility with many of our students." Whatever personal loss she may have experienced from a decision to be less out in the classroom, this faculty member has chosen to do so to teach more effectively. This dilemma was caused by a homophobic climate too deeply rooted for one teacher to combat.

Campus homophobia was often noted by faculty in this study. A gay faculty member who has been teaching for 16 years in a Catholic university reports: "Since the student body is so homophobic, I can never be a popular teacher. I can't hope for advancement based on my record with students. Only closeted gays can advance this way, so 90% stay closeted. It's a horrible set-up." This faculty member understands the pressures on his colleagues and describes a context over which neither he nor they has much control. His own decision to remain out even at the expense of his student evaluations must be taken seriously. He reflected that change is unlikely at his large private institution. "I'm really convinced of little improvement in 16 years teaching. A handful of people who are the official gay scholars can capitalize on being gay, which is OK, but it's of no help to anyone else." This context might be compared with England during the reign of Queen Elizabeth I. Though a woman was on the throne, education and opportunities for the average woman did not change. It seems that, for many, benefits do not trickle down from those enjoying advantages. . . .

For me, coming out in class took a very long time. Years after I had tenure and could no longer attribute remaining closeted to any fear of losing my job, I nonetheless held back from making this information public to students. More than one respondent notes that he or she lost a position offer or a promotion or advancement because of being openly gay or lesbian. Telling myself my heterosexual colleagues were not "ready" for my big announcement, I led a double life for several years. I was out in the local community but remained tightly closeted at the university. In the summer of 1975 I was teaching Introduction to Women's Studies. Knowing that I wanted to have a couple of class meetings focus on lesbianism, I found myself in a quandary. Finally I decided I would lecture one day about the history of lesbianism in the twentieth century; the second day I would invite a panel of women from the community to speak about being lesbians.

I got through the lecture, though my palms were sweating by the end 25
and my heartbeat racing to the finish line. The people I had asked to participate in the panel had all agreed to come, accepting my inability to speak out myself and seeming to bear me no grudge for what could easily be construed as cowardice attached to privilege. Driving to campus on the fateful morning, I rehearsed my introductory speech: "Today we are fortunate to have a panel of local lesbians who are going to talk with us about their lives and about the levels of oppression lesbians suffer." The slight awkwardness caused by my having to repeat "lesbians" twice in the same sentence was more than compensated for by my relief at finding a way to avoid using the disassociative "they."

Class assembled, the panel members seated themselves around a table on the lecture podium, and the bell rang. Nothing else stood between me and the anxiety-ridden introduction. In the back of the room were two friends with whom I was currently working at a rural feminist center for women and young children. I had asked them to come because this panel was the first time a formal class at the university had included out lesbians.

I called the class to order, reminded them of our topic, and began my introduction. Soon I was appalled and excited to hear coming from my mouth, "They are going to talk with us about their lives as lesbians and the levels of oppression we suffer." My friends stood up for a moment at the back of the room, wide grins on their faces; the panel members exchanged surprised but pleased glances; I sat down. I have no idea what the generous women who spoke to those undergraduates actually said. All I could hear were my words, which may well have gone unnoticed by most students in the room, but which echoed loudly and triumphantly in my own head. I knew change had come for me for good. . . .

Teaching Out of the Closet

In the excitement and empowerment that flowed from my tiny announcement on a summer morning in the late 1970s, I did what converts usually do: I swung the pendulum to the farthest extreme from where it had been originally. On the first day of every class, after asking students to fill out index cards on which they told me such demographic facts as name, majors, and progress toward graduation, and such narrative data as why they were taking my course, what hobbies and talents they possessed, and the last movie or book they had seen or read, I told them about myself. Always included was the fact that my major interests were lesbian literature and culture.

I have no idea how most students responded, but several vivid incidents remain in my memory. In a class on Shakespeare in which I made my stock comments on the first day, I noticed that on the second day one student sat with two books open on her desk: Shakespeare's *As You Like It* and the *Holy Bible.* Initially I thought perhaps she had found some line in the play that echoed something she knew from the Bible, but this did not seem to be the case. When she continued to bring the Bible to class, often choosing to sit right beside my own desk in the circle, I began to ponder what was going on. On a late afternoon walk, a thought came to me: Perhaps the student brought her Bible to defend herself against me as the sinning soul she undoubtedly thought me. I flashed to scenes from novels and films in which people held crosses in front of their faces to ward off some attacking vampire.

30 Rather than becoming angry or defensive as a result of this epiphany, I felt genuinely amused and then sympathetic toward the student. How difficult her position must be. She needed my course and so had to stay in it. I went to the next class determined to make the effort less frightening for her. By then we were studying *Romeo and Juliet,* so I decided to give a short talk about the place of religion in Shakespeare's day and of Christianity in particular in the plot of that play. While some of what I said was critical of the character of the Friar, that criticism came not from his practicing his Christian faith but rather from his dangerous failure to do so.

My tactic seemed to succeed. The student in question returned the next class period still in possession of her Bible but relaxed enough to leave it closed and under the text of the play. By midterm, she had stopped bringing it altogether, had begun to contribute positively to discussions, and even visited me during office hours to ask whether Shakespeare was a Christian since she kept finding veiled references to Christian beliefs. Without fudging the truth (i.e., no hard evidence can be found to label him in this way), I managed to show her that some basic Christian tenets such as forgiveness and fidelity are central to any moral or ethical system. At the end of the term, I received a course evaluation from a female student who commented that she had learned about more than Shakespeare during the term and that the instructor had heard and respected her religious views. I felt certain this had come from the student who started out so frightened of who I was and what I had to say.

If I ask myself why this story has stuck in my mind for so long, I know the answer has to do with teaching out of the closet. It is absolutely my right to come out to students; it is equally my responsibility to consider their well-being and perhaps to take some unusual measures to ensure that my desire to create a safer context for myself and the gays or lesbians in my classes does not create a dangerous or frightening context for the heterosexual students. It doesn't matter that no heterosexual teachers of mine ever seemed to have given any thought to the likes of me when they taught. I want to act more inclusively than others whom I find ignorant at best, bigoted at worst.

Many students find it empowering to study in such an open setting. This is true not only for gay and lesbian students, who naturally appreciate my public openness about my own sexual orientation, but also for many heterosexual students. In about 1980 I offered a graduate seminar on the nineteenth-century American poet Emily Dickinson. Since a great many of her poems reflect homoerotic feelings for several close women friends, I encouraged students to read for coded lesbian content. While explaining the process of reading for various codes in earlier literatures, I mentioned my own schemes for recognizing lesbian references. These approaches depend upon an erotics and aesthetics based on physical and emotional likeness, constructs that have evolved at least in part from my personal experience of lesbianism.

My frankness in the seminar opened up space for the students to discuss their own sense of the relationship between sexual expression and linguistic or poetic practice. This became apparent from in-class discussions, from students' reading journals, and in their final evaluations of the course. I was wrong in assuming that such space was presumed by heterosexual students. Several of them wrote long, eloquent comments about how emancipating the seminar had been; they said they were able for the first time to incorporate body knowledge into an intellectual setting. I was moved by this and became even more committed to coming out in classes, seeing that the benefits spread to a much larger group than I had imagined.

In 1989 I taught a course on black women writers. One of our texts was 35
Audre Lorde's *Zami,* an account of her childhood and young adulthood. Since Lorde remains one of the most outspoken African-American lesbians, much of her story concerns her early awareness of her attraction to women. Most students in my class were white undergraduates who had given relatively little serious thought to how or why they were heterosexual, though they were part of the campus feminist community and so had considered matters related to gender. In many cases, Lorde's book was their first unequivocal exposure to lesbian material in a college course.

Even though *Zami* is about nonsexual aspects of Lorde's coming of age, the lesbian scenes stuck in students' minds. Each session devoted to the book was punctuated with comments about matters such as "why" she became a lesbian.

Since the previously studied books had all been written by heterosexual black women, I had not made any reference to lesbianism. However, I did assume that everyone in class knew that I was a lesbian, and I was surprised when students began making overtly homophobic comments: "She probably became a lesbian because of her close relationship with her mother"; "I like the book except for the scenes about her being lesbian—they make me feel ishy"; "Why does she have to write so much about her sex life—the other books we've read have all sorts of other things going on in them"; "I can't relate to this book at all—not only is she black but since she's a lesbian nothing about her personal life makes any sense to me at all." During the second discussion period I felt compelled to come out directly in an effort not to squelch such remarks but to open up the discussion for me and any students who wanted to argue for a different emphasis.

Some heterosexual students felt immediately embarrassed, rushing to assure me that they were "just fine" with the subject, that some of their best friends were lesbian, that they had not meant anything negative or critical of Lorde even though they had voiced obviously negative and critical reactions to one of the central facts in Lorde's self-definition. One or two lesbian students came out, making clear to their classmates just how silenced and invisible they felt when judgmental remarks are made without any apparent concern for live lesbians who might be sitting next to the speakers.

Though the classroom atmosphere was decidedly tense for a time, the overall effect was productive. Not only was the remainder of our work on Audre Lorde truer to her text, but subsequent discussion of all books and issues was marked by a more rigorous analysis and a higher degree of self-reflection on most students' parts about their own sexual development and the ideas of the erotic in the works of such major figures as Toni Morrison and Alice Walker. On a broader scale, my intervention, together with the admission of invisibility on the part of lesbian students, encouraged many of the heterosexual women to acknowledge the limiting effects of unexamined heterosexism. They began to grasp how that system had kept them even from realizing there might be lesbians in the same room with them.

In their evaluations, students wrote movingly about the course's having 40
prompted them to begin a serious consideration of their journeys into heterosexuality. Some spoke of being inspired by Audre Lorde's brave example to begin writing their own sexual autobiographies, a process that was obviously affording them new insights into their private choices and the way in which heterosexist hegemony continues to flourish. Lorde herself said that what she wanted most from all sisters, black or white, lesbian or heterosexual, was for us to live a conscious life; these comments seemed integral to the course.

Many students thanked me for interrupting the usual class discussion to come out, telling me that everything about the class had seemed to deepen from that point. Since then, I have continued to acknowledge my lesbianism at some point during the term, no matter what the subject matter. However, I realize that my being in literature gives me an advantage; coming out in science or math or engineering classes surely depends upon a determined stance about the need to be open with one's students about this particular aspect of one's life. In such fields, a professor must make a decision about when and how to incorporate the fact of being gay or lesbian into her or his pedagogical approach. While, as one respondent told me, "Molecules aren't sexed," the learning situation is. Furthermore, at some point in almost every discipline, we are obligated to offer examples to our students. A professor who values being out in class surely has an opportunity to make lesbian or gay reality a part of his or her discourse. . . .

Some faculty feel no need to come out to students, even if their campuses are accepting of diversity. A lesbian professor of comparative literature makes no effort to hide her identity from individual students when asked direct questions. She includes lesbian and gay texts in her courses, but she has never come out in the classroom. She does not ascribe to the notion that being lesbian allows her to read differently from those who are not. Were she to teach lesbian or gay studies, she would see her identity as directly relevant and would consider it productive to come out.

However clear this individual is about not revealing her lesbianism in classroom settings, she nonetheless remembers two moments in her teaching career when she felt a need, "not acted upon in either case, to announce [her] sexuality to a class as a pertinent part of discussion." The first was in the early 1980s, when she and several other women faculty were invited to a class taught by an African-American colleague. The topic was feminism in Alice Walker's *The Color Purple.* "In the discussion, the instructor deplored the lesbianism in the novel as denigrating to ideas about black life in America in a way that I found offensive and bigoted. I challenged prescribing content because of what we 'want' from texts." The professor did not make a personal statement because doing so would have distracted from the main point of the discussion. She was highly unsatisfied with the experience.

The second instance came in 1994 during the final class meeting of a course on forms of discrimination related to the history of infectious diseases. The lesbian professor reports "less dynamic discussion and less controversy than we had hoped, less lively debate than had occurred the last time we taught the course." The class was nearly half students of color, a far higher percentage than that on campus as a whole. Several of those students commented that discussions had "walked right up to issues of race but then skirted around them," an accusation the professor felt was justified. She asked whether beginning the semester with some discussion of overlapping identities would have improved the climate so that students might have taken more risks:

> This elicited a productive conversation in which students identified aspects of their identities that complicated their classroom lives. I did not come out, largely because the students were talking about themselves in important ways and I did not want to shift attention. However, as I think about my pedagogical strategies, next time I teach [this course], I will handle the issue differently.

• • •

For me, pedagogical strength seems to be attendant upon my coming 45
out early in the term. In most undergraduate classes, I tell a favorite story on my "coming out day":

> Let's say I get to know, like, and respect someone through shared social or political activities or aims. At some point in our process, I learn that they occupy some category previously off my scale of acceptability. It's as if I had built a picture frame around what is "normal" or "good," which I assume includes the individual, who suddenly I find possesses characteristics that force me to exclude him or her from my picture. I can leave my friend or colleague outside

> the frame or I can revisit my lumberyard to purchase more wood to enlarge my frame.

This story usually works in getting students to think about the limitations inherent in prejudice against whole groups of people. On several occasions, the story has prompted notes from students who want to thank me for giving them a way to understand what happens when they find out something surprising about a friend or family member. One person wrote the following: "I just want to thank you, Toni, for your story about your picture frame. After class, I went right over to my lumberyard and bought more wood!" . . .

As more becomes known about the rich diversity of approaches to teaching as gay or lesbian faculty, I need to remember that circumstances vary widely and each individual must make his or her own decisions. I remind myself constantly that none of us ever knows the innermost processes any lesbian or gay faculty member goes through in finding the best solution. For many gay and lesbian colleagues in this country, there is no genuine solution at all. People simply must do what they can to keep body and soul intact, and this is perhaps the saddest reality shared with me during this research. I want to carry that reality close to my heart and mind as I continue to argue for the highest degree of openness possible in a given context.

Questions for Discussion

1. What are some of the pros and cons that McNaron and her colleagues have had to face following their decision to come out? Do you think that the subject matter of McNaron's teaching made her sexuality more relevant to class discussions and her students' education than if she had been teaching a course in which questions of sexual relationships would not arise? Has she convinced you that, at least in her case, coming out was a reasonable decision?
2. How did you react to the narrative about McNaron's own experience of coming out in class for the first time? Have you ever been in a class in which a professor spoke openly about his or her homosexuality? If so, what was the reaction? How would you feel as a student in that situation?
3. Paragraphs 19–21 should be of interest to students in a course emphasizing argument. If you have read the chapters in this text on arguing to inquire and arguing to convince, what do you think of the student's argument discussed here? How did he revise his thinking after the class inquired into his original argument? From what is given about his second argument, do you feel it would have been convincing? to which readers? What assumptions and values does it imply?
4. Should teachers avoid teaching texts that might bring out students' prejudices in class discussion? If students express intolerance, should their views go unchallenged?
5. What is McNaron's reasoning on the fact that some students might be profoundly uncomfortable with her announcement? Do you agree?

6. Do you think that it would be more difficult for homosexual faculty or for homosexual students to be open about their sexuality in class discussions, assuming that such discussion was relevant to the subject matter?

For Persuasion

1. Do you believe becoming a better thinker makes you a better person? Can you use examples from your own education to show that any projects, especially writing projects in which you had to reason about an issue, made you a better person? Be sure to explain what you mean by "better," and be specific about the research, thinking, and lasting influence of the experience.
2. As a student, what is your perspective on having a professor be open about his or her sexuality in the classroom, in particular in a first-year writing program? Suppose a class was reading the essays in this chapter, and the teacher was gay or lesbian. Do you feel he or she should come out as part of the inquiry into issues surrounding gay and lesbian rights? Consider some of the issues that gay and lesbian faculty have to confront and the purpose of using current issues as topics for writing, and make a case directed to the teacher from a writing student's point of view.

For Further Research and Discussion

1. One large area of debate related to homosexual rights involves marriage, or the legal benefits of marriage: tax breaks, employer-sponsored insurance coverage for spouses, inheritance rights, even the right not to be forced to testify in court against one's mate. There is, further, the symbolic statement that marriage makes about a couple's commitment to each other. In 1967 the Supreme Court called marriage "one of the basic civil rights of man," yet no state except Hawaii recognizes marriages between members of the same sex. Inquire into this issue, and be ready to report to the class on the range of opinions about marriage and domestic partnerships. (Gay people themselves are divided on the question.)
2. Inquire into the latest research on the causes of homosexuality. What interpretation do most gay people seem to accept on this matter? If a clear case could be made for biological causation, your class might want to discuss how such a conclusion would influence any of the arguments about homophobia and gay rights.

Additional Suggestions for Writing

1. *Inquiry and convincing.* Based on your inquiry into the views on gay marriage, write an exploratory essay in which you discuss areas of agreement and disagreement. Conclude with a statement of your own position on this issue, indicating which reasons uncovered in your research best support your position. Then go on to draft and revise a case for an opposing audience.
2. *Persuasion.* In this chapter's first selection Jeffrey Nickel points out that homophobia is something children learn at an early age in our society. Some

school districts have devised curriculums aimed at encouraging greater tolerance for homosexuals through, for example, the use of storybooks that depict children who have "two mommies" or "two daddies." This aspect of New York City's "Rainbow Curriculum" was quite controversial.

Do research into educational curriculums that deal with homosexuality. Find out where such curriculums have been tried and what the pro and con arguments are. If you decide such curriculums would not be effective in reducing homophobia or that reducing homophobia should not be a function of the schools, write a persuasive argument against instituting such curriculums. If you decide that they are a good idea, make a persuasive argument for some specific course of action.

3. *Mediation.* The AIDS epidemic has focused public attention on questions of rights and responsibilities. Some gay advocates argue that it is the responsibility of the government and the medical community to find a vaccine to prevent AIDS so that people need not live in terror if they fail to follow all the guidelines for safe sex. At the other extreme, people argue that because AIDS is a preventable disease, it is the responsibility of each adult to see that he or she is not exposed through risky behavior and that the government and medical community ought to give their full attention to life-threatening diseases that strike at random. Investigate these arguments about AIDS research and spending and the range of viewpoints in between. Write a mediatory essay that suggests a position all sides could find reasonable.

CHAPTER FOURTEEN

The News and Ethics

Probably no other institution is more controversial or subject to more conflicting pressures than "the press," a term we casually use to refer to all the media that give us our sense of what's going on in the world. Once the press really was *the press,* wholly a print medium; but first radio, then television, and now the Internet compete successfully with the daily newspaper for the public's loyalties. Indeed, the electronic media, especially television, compete so well that there are serious doubts about whether newspapers can survive. Those who think they won't point to the folding of many papers and the scramble of many others to maintain a circulation large enough to secure the advertising revenue that sustains all organized news operations.

A basic premise of this chapter is that our open, democratic society has a high stake not merely in the survival but in the long-term health of high-quality print journalism, especially in newspapers. As important and influential as the electronic media are, they typically do not and probably cannot offer the depth and detail, the analysis and reflection that can make news more than sound bites, sensationalism, and disconnected stories. Knowing what is happening is one thing, understanding another. And even knowing can be problematic if television is our only source for news. The more complex the issue and the less superficially "interesting" it is, the more we must depend on print journalism. That which doesn't "play" well on television gets little or no attention.

Recognizing the importance of newspapers, however, does not mean we should be uncritical of them. On the contrary, to varying degrees and in different ways, all the selections in this chapter are critical of current journalistic practices. Indeed, it is difficult to find spirited defenses of the current system, even among journalists themselves, who in the past have often proudly defended their profession against detractors. Almost everyone agrees that the daily newspaper is in crisis and that part of this crisis is ethical, concerned with norms governing how news is gathered and disseminated.

Especially when an institution is in crisis, it is always a good idea to return to fundamental questions. Nothing could be more fundamental than the question Jack Fuller poses in the first selection: What is news? Any honest answer will reveal how constrained even a "free" press is and how descriptive questions tend to merge with normative ones, for we cannot ask what the news is without at least implying what it *should* be. And, of course, both questions are worth thinking and arguing about.

We move in the next two selections deeper into what Fuller calls "news values." Everyone agrees that the news should be fair. But what is "fair"? Is fairness more important than accuracy or intellectual honesty? What exactly are the values involved in responsible journalism? Are some values more important than others? If so, why?

In the second reading Michael Schudson offers a historical perspective on fairness. What was fair in colonial America is not necessarily fair now or fair a century ago. Norms change. But Schudson clearly advocates "modern analytical and procedural fairness" as an enduring value, whereas the next writer, Jim Squires, thinks that fairness is impossible given the largely unconscious biases of reporters and the corruption of contemporary news by the demand that it be entertaining. Do any of the traditional journalistic values have much of a chance when news media are judged entirely by the numbers, TV ratings, and circulation?

Clearly, if we agree with Squires that "real news" has lost out in an "entertainment culture with no moral compass and no concern for fairness—or taste," then we must also ask, How can the news be reformed? It won't do to conclude that the press is hopelessly corrupt and the news untrustworthy and leave it at that. We simply can't afford to "write off" the news, for we depend on it for most of our knowledge about the world and for information to guide important decisions. If the news isn't doing its job, then it must be reformed. But how? in what ways exactly? and by whom? Some avenues of reform have been tried already, such as the experiments in so-called public or civic journalism, which our last author, James Fallows, finds promising. Is this the way to go? Or should we try something else?

Of course, we need not judge the press as harshly as some of its severest critics do; we could hold that the case against the press is overstated and that news coverage is actually more extensive than ever and on the whole reasonably reliable and even-handed. Perhaps only modest reforms are needed, or even none at all—and we can also question the motives of the reformers, motives that may not be as purely altruistic or as public-spirited as they are given out to be. Just as the current system has "winners" and "losers," so any reform of it will as well.

Regardless of how we assess current journalism, we need to evolve our own critical strategies for "reading"—that is, interpreting—the news. Some people are naive and believe everything they read. Others opt for extreme skepticism, avowing that they believe "only half of what they see and nothing that they read." Neither attitude—all or nothing—will do. The first approach lacks sophistication, the second discrimination. Perhaps, then, the fourth reading, by W. Lance Bennett, is the most important, for it suggests ways to take the news in without being "taken in," ways to think critically about the news without rejecting it wholesale.

The press has never been uncontroversial, and in our society it can't and shouldn't be. Precisely because it matters so much, because a free society cannot exist without a free press, we must return again and again to "news values." If the values must change, if they must be refined and redefined, the issue endures. It is something we must care about if we want informed citizens making intelligent choices.

JACK FULLER

What Is News?

A novelist, winner of the prestigious Pulitzer Prize, and publisher of the Chicago Tribune, *Jack Fuller's view of news and ethics carries special weight, the authority of an accomplished and experienced journalist. In this excerpt from his 1996 book* News Values: Ideas for an Information Age, *he advances a modest view of what "truth" in news reporting should mean, what biases the news cannot escape, and what values should inform the telling of news stories. Perhaps most interesting is his examination of the concept of fairness and his valuing of other intellectual virtues over it.*

As you read, bear in mind that certain newspapers, because of their age, prestige, and financial backing, enjoy special status as "national institutions." The Tribune *is one of these, as is the* New York Times, *the* Wall Street Journal, *and a handful of other papers. Views of journalism from such sources merit respect, but they may not be representative of "news values" found in less well-established papers.*

WHAT IS the proper standard of truth for the news? To answer that, one must first come to some clear understanding of what news is. Even at its most presumptuous, the news does not claim to be timeless or universal. It represents at most a provisional kind of truth, the best that can be said quickly. Its ascription is modest, so modest that some of the most restless and interesting journalists have had trouble making any claim of truth at all. 1

In *Let Us Now Praise Famous Men,* James Agee, then a writer for *Fortune* magazine, savaged the whole idea of journalistic truth:

> Who, what, where, when and why (or how) is the primal cliche and complacency of journalism: but I do not wish to appear to speak favorably of journalism. I have never yet seen a piece of journalism which conveyed more than the slightest fraction of what any even moderately reflective and sensitive person would mean and intend by those inachievable words, and that fraction itself I have never seen clean of one or another degree of patent, to say nothing of essential falsehood. Journalism is true in the sense that everything is true to the state of being and to what conditioned and produced it (which is also, but less so perhaps, a limitation of art and science): but that is about as far as its value goes. . . . [J]ournalism is not to be blamed for this; no more than a cow is to be blamed for not being a horse.

Even accepting that news is not the kind of truth that would meet the rigors of science or the clarity of revealed religious insight, there is still too little agreement on how to define it. Though journalists might agree the beast is a cow, they will debate what breed and how much milk it can produce. Look at one day's newspapers from a dozen cities and you will find, even correcting for local factors, no consensus.

One might be tempted to say that news is anything that news organizations report. In fact, this definition has adherents among a few journalists whose fascination with power leads them to overestimate their own. It also appeals to certain outsiders, such as those who encourage the media to do more uplifting stories in the expectation that they might revise grim reality as easily as they revise a sentence.

But the definition of news does not have to be so empty in order to 5
explain most variations in coverage. Most respectable journalists on American newspapers would, I think, roughly agree with this statement: News is a report of what a news organization has recently learned about matters of some significance or interest to the specific community that news organization serves.

This narrows the debate over the news value of any particular item but does not lead to unanimity. The *New York Times* may consider a vote in Congress on free trade to be the most important story of the day while the *New York Daily News* leads with a deadly fire in the Bronx. This is because of each newspaper's understanding of the community of readers it serves and, perhaps, because of differing judgments about what is significant.

There are some papers, to be sure, that do not seem to be concerned with the element of significance at all. Such a paper would always go with a sex scandal over a coup attempt in the Soviet Union. Most contemporary journalists would scoff at this as pandering, but the honest ones have to say that they, too, take account of the pull of basic (even base) human curiosity; the difference is whether any consideration of larger interests comes into play.

What is significant will always be a matter of debate, but in general the evaluation should turn on the foreseeable consequences. Significance and interest provide separate bases for calling an event or piece of information news, and either may be sufficient. No matter how few people were interested in reading about strategic arms limitation talks, the enormous importance of these negotiations to the future of the planet made them extremely newsworthy. And no matter how insignificant Michael Jordan's performance in minor-league baseball may have been to the history of the United States, the deep popular interest in it justified extensive coverage.

The Fundamental Biases

My proposed definition of news includes several elements that are not wholly subjective (though this does not mean they are unambiguous): timeliness, interest for a given community, significance. These look beyond the journalists' personal preferences outward to phenomena in the world that can be discussed, if not measured.

The elements of the definition also suggest some ways in which the 10
journalist's report of reality is likely to be fundamentally biased.

First, journalism emphasizes the recent event or the recently discovered fact at the expense of that which occurred before or had already been known. Journalists recognize this bias and talk about the need to put "background" information into their pieces. But commonly the internal logic of reporting puts "background" information very much in the background and tolerates little more of it than is absolutely necessary to permit the reader to make some sense of the new material. From time to time a newspaper may go back and attempt to tell about an event or issue comprehensively, but this is very special treatment. The bias of immediacy is the rule.

Second, the journalist has a bias in favor of information that interests his audience. This helps explain the favorite complaint about news—that it accentuates the negative. People's curiosity shows a tropism for misfortune. Disaster always becomes the talk of a community in a way that good fortune less commonly does. Trouble touches some people's empathy and others' sense of doom. Fear and anger operate strongly at greater distances than love, so bad news travels farther. One might delight to hear that the daughter of someone he knew had just received a prestigious scholarship, but he would shudder at the brutal murder of a stranger's child a continent away.

The bias of interest also means that the audience's blind spots will tend to be blind spots in the news. If people are generally indifferent about a particular subject—say international trade talks such as GATT—the journalist knows that it will be very difficult to make them pay attention to it, regardless of how important it may be in their lives. Whole areas of inquiry go years, decades without attention in the news until they become involved in an event that captures people's imagination. The engineering of bridges receives scant notice until a large span collapses. Human retrovirology meant nothing to the general population until the scourge of AIDS. Even disciplines that find themselves more commonly in the news—economics, law, medicine—are lit up piecemeal, depending on the fascination of the day. The Phillips curve in economics reaches public print when in defiance of it inflation and unemployment both begin to run high. Even an obscure field of law such as admiralty might get an examination in the news when something of sufficient drama happens upon the high seas. We learn everything we never wanted to know about the human colon when a president has part of his removed.

Walter Lippmann described the press as a searchlight that restlessly prowls across the expanses, never staying on any feature for very long. Actually, human curiosity is the searchlight. We journalists just go where it points.

15 Finally, there is a bias toward what occurs close to the audience's community. Often this manifests itself as a simple matter of geography. A *National Lampoon* parody of a hometown newspaper called the *Dacron Republican-Democrat* some years back had a page one headline that read: "Two Dacron Women Feared Missing in Volcanic Disaster." The drop head read: "Japan Destroyed."

Community is not always defined by physical proximity. Communities of interest have newspapers, too, and the list of publications includes more than the trade press. Consider, for example, the *Wall Street Journal* and the *New York Times.* Both have specialized audiences and are edited to satisfy their interests. *USA Today* also appeals to a distinct public—the business traveler away from home—and this explains many of the editing choices it makes, which would be foolish for a metropolitan daily newspaper with an audience that has a much different set of shared interests.

The bias of community provides an answer to a snobbish question one often hears: Why don't other newspapers pay as much attention to international affairs as the *New York Times* does? The *Times* recognizes that for much of its audience the world is the pertinent community of interest. A disproportionate part of its readership engages directly in international business and public policy. Since it is circulated nationally, the *Times* becomes a kind of local newspaper for this community (and can be as provincial about matters outside its territory as any other paper; just try to get guidance from the *Times* about the best easy-listening CDs or religious TV shows). There are not enough people in most cities who are deeply engaged in international affairs to command strong international coverage in their metropolitan dailies, though in certain centers such as Los Angeles, Washington, DC, and Chicago the audience is large enough to support a substantial foreign-news commitment by the local papers, and in others such as Miami there is enough interest in one part of the world to require the newspaper to make a large commitment of space and attention to it.

The element of significance in the definition of news does not necessarily introduce a bias. Rather it might be said to be the heading under which to group all other biases. These may arise out of the social circumstances of journalists, the imperatives of the economic market on their news organizations, the culture from which a journalist comes, or the larger intellectual currents of the times: interesting issues, but . . . they do not distinguish observational bias among journalists from the bias of any other observer. . . .

Intellectual Honesty and the Golden Rule

• • •

Intellectual honesty means that in presenting a news report a journalist may draw certain conclusions and make certain predictions about the consequences of a particular event, but it also imposes a duty to do justice to the areas of legitimate debate. This is what separates news from polemical writing. The former must attempt to represent a matter of public concern in its fullness. A polemic aims to persuade the audience that one view of the matter is undoubtedly correct.

The Golden Rule has endured through the centuries as an ethical proposition of enormous force because it offers a subjective method for determining the moral direction one's behavior should take. It asks that an individual treat others the way he would like to be treated, to turn the tables, to empathize. This is a useful way to look at the requirement of intellectual honesty. 20

In reporting a matter of legitimate debate (How big should the Pentagon budget be? Did Alderman X take a bribe?), the journalist will surely reach some conclusions. And, with some constraints described later, he should feel free to share his conclusions with his readers. But in doing so, the Golden Rule suggests that the reporter must try to put the case against his conclusions as forcefully as he would want an opponent to put the reporter's own arguments.

This, like many moral propositions, sets an extraordinarily high aspiration. If you deeply believe your own position, you will find it very difficult to express the opposite point of view with the same enthusiasm and force. But the Golden Rule is a corrective; it points the right direction. And, with discipline, it is not too much to expect reporters (freed of the impossible requirement of objectivity and the nonfunctional requirement of neutral expression) to play square with others' arguments, stating them honestly and presenting the facts and logic supporting them. The Golden Rule is a perfectionist goal, toward which to stumble in our imperfect, human way.

Even the unalloyed gold standard does not require a journalist to report every view of a subject, only those that could be held by informed, reasonable people. Of course, a journalist's bias may unduly restrict what he considers the range of reasonable, informed opinion. And illegitimate claims may need to be reported as important facts in their own right—such as the racist, antisemitic, and xenophobic views that mar the political landscape from time to time. A reporter also needs to operate within the constraints of time, space, and reader attention span that limit everything a newspaper does. But these must not become excuses for lapsing into the one-sided, polemical approach in the news columns. A journalist's reputation should turn in large part upon the quality of his judgment in wisely sorting through these difficult issues so as to produce work of genuine intellectual integrity. . . .

FAIRNESS

Journalists often use the concept of fairness to describe their discipline. Unfortunately, the idea of fairness has a rich philosophical history. This gives it implications that may be inimical to the truth discipline. Even as journalistic cliche, the idea of fairness leads in odd directions.

"Journalism," one saying goes, "should comfort the afflicted and afflict the comfortable." Taken loosely as a call for journalists to concern themselves with the suffering of the weakest members of society and to have the courage to tell unpleasant truths about the powerful, the statement makes sense. But it also can be an invitation to bias, and journalists too often accept the call. Should journalists *always* afflict the comfortable, even when the comfortable are doing no harm? Should they afflict them simply *because* of their comfort? And what about the afflicted? What if telling the truth to and about them would cause them discomfort? Should the truth be shaded or withheld in order to give them comfort instead? What if truth were the painful antidote that in the long run would cure the affliction?

25 Any deep consideration of the idea of fairness leads eventually to questions of distributive justice of the very sort raised by these tidings of comfort and affliction. In its simplest terms, the issue is whether fairness means letting everyone compete on the same terms, regardless of the advantages and disadvantages they bring to the competition, or whether fairness requires that players carry a handicap. Is it fair to say that a poor child from the urban projects and the child of wealth and privilege should be judged by the same standard when evaluating them for admission to college? What about when trying to understand the moral quality of their behavior?

John Rawls's *Theory of Justice* provides an excellent contemporary example of the idea of distributive justice. Rawls has the courage to face the whole range of social advantages and disadvantages, as well as natural abilities and disabilities (with which one may be born and for which one thus may be said to have no personal responsibility)—not only physical strength and intellectual acumen, but also creativity, ambition and indolence, beauty and ugliness. He boldly calls on people's sense of distributive fairness to compensate for them, as if to repair God's injustice. This leads him a long way from the idea of fairness as equality of opportunity.

What might fairness in its Rawlsian, distributive sense mean in journalism? Some participants in the public debate come better equipped for it than others. Distributive fairness would have to involve some form of compensation by the journalist for this disparity. He might, for example, call all close factual issues for the weaker party or shade the way he put both sides' arguments in order to give the weaker side a chance of persuading the audience. In more extreme cases, he might have to withhold information helpful to the advantaged side in order to keep the game even. All of these compensatory strategies sharply conflict with a journalist's primary duty of simple candor, and this is why fairness is a poor choice of words to describe a journalist's discipline.

The ideal of intellectual honesty, tested by the Golden Rule, offers a much surer guide. But this requires a degree of self-restraint that is not natural in people who become immersed in a subject and develop strong feelings about it. The Golden Rule must be taught, and that has been difficult in journalism because of the lack of clarity and consensus about just what the proper discipline should be.

One problem has been the shift in weight between fact and value in news reports. No journalist I know would favor lying to give the weaker party a more even chance of prevailing in the debate. Far more likely would a journalist shade his report of a valuative debate to favor an individual suffering under a disadvantage. Somebody, he might say, has to speak up for the flood victims, or the physically handicapped, or the urban underclass, or the Vietnam veteran, or the AIDS victim. And he might even overlook some strong counterarguments on the assumption that the secure, well-financed majority interests can look out for their side of the argument very well by themselves, thank you very much. This helps account, I think, for the populist streak in American journalism as well as for journalists' reputation for being more liberal than their audience. It also may be one reason journalists have seemed to many people to be getting more liberal over time. As self-restraint against expressing opinion in news reports has fallen, the compensatory impulse becomes more marked. . . .

THE LIMIT OF OPINION

30 But this is not the end of the requirements of journalism's basic disciplines. Beyond intellectual honesty, journalists reporting the news need to restrain the expression of their opinions, showing modesty in their judgments about facts and always withholding ultimate judgment on matters of value. A political writer should not include in his report on a presidential campaign his view about whom people should vote for. Nor should he write his story in a way that would lead a reasonable reader to infer his preference. A reporter covering a trial should not reveal his conclusions about who is lying or whether the defendant is guilty or innocent. In an article about the abortion controversy, the writer should not come out for or against *Roe v. Wade*. . . .

This . . . stricter approach is necessary in order to uphold the traditional distinction between news reporting and editorializing. (Editorials are polemical. They make their opinion about ultimate issues plain. And they need not recite all contrary arguments, though taking them into account makes for more persuasive editorials.) Preserving this distinction makes good sense for a number of reasons. People have grown used to it. Withholding ultimate judgment communicates the reporter's commitment to neutrality in his approach to reporting a story even as he departs from strict neutrality of expression. (It is hard to read the comments of an explicit supporter of a candidate and avoid the thought that he will not give the candidate's opponent an even break.) Modesty of opinion and holding back ultimate judgments of value produce a report that invites the audience to weigh information for itself and at the same time offer the audience some help in getting through the ambiguities and complexities. These disciplines make it easier for journalists to put all reasonable positions forcefully. (It is one thing to give all arguments their due when one does not choose between them explicitly. It is another to take an ultimate position and then have to give everyone the benefit of the Golden Rule.) Finally, withholding ultimate judgments makes pluralism in the reporting staff easier to manage.

It is hard enough under the discipline of modesty of opinion to permit writers latitude and still produce a newspaper with a sense of coherence. This would be virtually impossible if reporters were freed to express ultimate judgments. To make all the judgments in the paper consistent, editors and publishers would have to impose a political view, story by story, or else choose only those reporters whose views were essentially consistent with the paper's editorial positions. The result would be a coherent publication, on the model of the European press, but not one that reflects a large, geographic community the way American audiences have come to expect their newspapers to do. . . .

Questions for Discussion

1. In his definition of the news and his discussion of "the fundamental biases" of news coverage, Fuller stresses "the specific community [a] news organization serves"—that is, its readership. Obviously, no paper can ignore its readers and survive. But what is the difference between "writing for" one's specific community and "writing down" to it? Should newspapers both challenge their readers and accommodate them? In what ways?
2. According to Fuller, what kind of truth does responsible journalism seek? To what does he compare journalistic truth? What truth are you looking for when you read a paper? Would you describe "newspaper truth" as Fuller does? Why or why not?
3. Fuller points to an obvious tension when an editor must decide whether to print a story and how much emphasis to give it—the sometimes sharp contrast between significance and interest. No one faults a paper for covering a significant story that may not captivate the average reader. Problems arise when papers "play up" stories that interest people too much but have no real, long-term significance. Fuller justifies the latter as dictated by reader interest. But to what extent does the news *create* interest in a story by giving it more space and prominence than it deserves? Do we need more rules and norms especially for reducing the scandal-mongering so dominant in today's press?

For Discussion and Analysis

Most readers would say that Fuller's view of the news is balanced, honest, and reasonable. But to what extent does his view represent current practice?

Address this question by bringing to class several editions of a local paper or papers. As a class or in groups, assess the news according to Fuller's definition. Do you find the biases Fuller discusses? Do you find the intellectual virtues Fuller espouses? Do you like the way your paper or papers covered the news for a particular day? What changes, if any, would you like to see?

After full class discussion, assess some aspect of the coverage—say, political or international news—or some feature story at length and in detail, applying Fuller's analysis. Share your insights with other class members, and assess what they have to say. In further class discussion, address this question: On balance, how good a job is the paper doing?

MICHAEL SCHUDSON

In All Fairness

We tend to think of ethics as something unchanging and universal. But notions of right and wrong always have a history, and norms change as the economic and social conditions of ordinary life change. Lending money at interest, for example, was once considered unnatural and sinful, whereas now we condemn only loan-sharking, the taking of excessive interest by force or the threat of force.

Clearly, then, we need historical perspective to understand and assess current news ethics. We must be willing to examine whatever norms we invoke. And we cannot talk intelligently about right and wrong in news coverage without seeing the news in the general context of contemporary life. Michael Schudson's article, published in the Media Studies Journal *(Spring/Summer 1998), offers this needed historical perspective. Schudson is a professor in the communication department at the University of California, San Diego, and author of an important book relevant to our topic,* The Power of News.

EVERYBODY'S A media critic in a democracy. The news media are the chief institutions for making our public life visible, and a lot rides on how they present us to ourselves. As citizens, we have a stake in trying to make our standards theirs. So people complain that the news media are too liberal—or too conservative. The media overplay violence—or they sanitize it. They are the lapdogs of their corporate owners—or they bite the economic system that feeds them. They are insufferably prurient—or they are rigidly puritanical. They are insidiously partisan—or they are boringly neutral. And on and on. Where have you been, Monica Lewinsky? 1

American journalists, buffeted by critics from every corner and wracked by self-criticism too, have long insisted that they try to be fair. But what's fair? That has changed from one era to the next.

In colonial journalism, printers proclaimed their concern for fairness in order to shed responsibility for what appeared in their pages. Benjamin Franklin insisted in his "Apology for Printers," published in 1731, that the printer was just that—one who prints, not one who edits, exercises judgment or agrees with each opinion in his pages. "Printers are educated in the Belief that when Men differ in Opinion, both Sides ought equally to have the Advantage of being heard by the Publick; and that when Truth and Error have fair Play, the former is always an overmatch for the latter: Hence they chearfully serve all contending Writers that pay them well, without regarding on which side they are of the Question in Dispute."

At first, colonial printers did not imagine their newspapers to be either political instruments or professional agencies of news gathering. None of the early papers reached out to collect news; they printed what came to them.

Colonial printers, more than their London brethren, were public figures—running the post office, serving as clerks for the government and printing the laws. But they were also small businessmen who were careful not to offend their customers.

In the first half-century of American journalism, little indicated that the newspaper would become a central forum for political discourse. Colonial printers avoided controversy when they could, preached the printer's neutrality when they had to and printed primarily foreign news because it afforded local readers and local authorities no grounds for grumbling. Out of a sample of 1,900 items Franklin's weekly *Pennsylvania Gazette* printed from 1728 to 1765, only 34 touched on politics in Philadelphia or Pennsylvania.

As conflict with England heated up after 1765, politics entered the press and printerly "fairness" went by the board. In a time when nearly everyone felt compelled to take sides, printers found neutrality harder to maintain than partisanship. The newspaper began its long career as the mouthpiece of political parties and factions. Patriots had no tolerance for the pro-British press, and the new states passed and enforced treason and sedition statutes.

American victory in the war for independence did not bring immediate freedom for the press. During the state-by-state debates over ratification of the Constitution in 1787 and 1788, Federalists dominated the press and squeezed Antifederalists out of public debate. In Pennsylvania, leading papers tended not to report Antifederalist speeches at the ratification convention. When unusual newspapers in Philadelphia, New York and Boston sought to report views on both sides, Federalists stopped their subscriptions and forced the papers to end their attempt at evenhandedness.

Some of the nation's founders supported outspoken political criticism so long as they were fighting a monarchy for their independence but held that open critique of a duly elected republican government could be legitimately curtailed. Sam Adams, the famed Boston agitator during the struggle for independence, changed his views on political action once republican government was established. This great advocate of open talk, committees of correspondence, an outspoken press and voluntary associations of citizens now opposed all hint of public associations and public criticism that operated outside the regular channels of government. As one contemporary of Adams observed, it did no harm for writers to mislead the people when the people were powerless, but "To mislead the judgement of the people, where they have all power, must produce the greatest possible mischief."

The Sedition Act of 1798 forbade criticism of the Federalist government and as many as one in four editors of oppositional papers were brought up on charges under this law. But this went one step further than many Americans of the day could stomach. Federalist propaganda notwithstanding, Thomas Jefferson won the presidency in 1800. The Sedition Act expired, party opposition began to be grudgingly accepted and a more libertarian theory of the press gained ground.

In 19th-century journalism, editors came to take great pride in the speed and accuracy of the news they provided. With the introduction in the 1830s of the rotary press and soon the steam-powered press, amidst an expanding urban economy on the Eastern seaboard and the rush of enthusiasm for Jacksonian democracy, commercial competition heated up among city newspapers. A new breed of "penny papers" hired newsboys to hawk copies on the street; penny-press editors competed for wider readership and increasingly sought out local news—of politics, crime and high society. 10

While this newly aggressive commercialism in journalism was an important precondition for modern notions of objectivity, at first it fostered only a narrow concept of stenographic fairness. Newspapers boasted more and more about the speed and accuracy of their news gathering, but editors found this perfectly consistent with political partisanship and choosing to cover only the speeches or rallies of their favorite party. It was equally consistent, in their eyes, for reporters to go over speeches with sympathetic politicians they had covered to improve, in printed form, on the oral presentation. Into the 1870s and 1880s, Washington correspondents routinely supplemented their newspaper income by clerking for the very congressional committees they wrote about.

As late as the 1890s, when a standard Republican paper covered a presidential election, it not only deplored and derided Democratic candidates in editorials but often neglected to mention them in the news. In the days before public-opinion polling, the size of partisan rallies was taken as a proxy for likely electoral results. Republican rallies would be described as "monster meetings" while Democratic rallies were often not covered at all. In the Democratic papers, of course, it was just the reverse.

While partisanship endured, reporters came to enjoy a culture of their own independent of political parties. They developed their own mythologies (reveling in their intimacy with the urban underworld), their own clubs and watering holes and their own professional practices. Interviewing, for instance, became a common activity for reporters only in the 1870s and 1880s. No president submitted to an interview before Andrew Johnson in 1868, but by the 1880s the interview was a well-accepted and institutionalized "media event," an occasion created by journalists from which they could then craft a story. This new journalistic practice did not erase partisanship. It did, however, foreshadow reporters' emerging dedication to a sense of craft. Journalists began to locate themselves in a new occupational culture with its own rules, its own rewards and its own *esprit*.

Interviewing was a practice oriented more to pleasing an audience of news consumers than to parroting or promoting a party line. By the 1880s, newspapers had become big business. They erected towering downtown buildings, employed scores of reporters, sponsored splashy civic festivals and ran pages of advertising from the newly burgeoning department stores. The papers vastly expanded their readership in this growing marketplace. Accordingly, reporters writing news came to focus less on promoting parties and more on making stories.

15 Yet not until the 1920s was American journalism characterized by what we might call modern analytical and procedural fairness. Analytical fairness had no secure place until journalists as an occupational group developed loyalties more to their audiences and to themselves as an occupational community than to their publishers or their publishers' favored political parties. At this point journalists also came to articulate rules of the journalistic road more often and more consistently. As an Associated Press executive declared in 1925, "If you do not remember anything else that I have said, I beg of you to remember this, for it is fundamental: The Associated Press never comments on the news."

This newly articulated fairness doctrine was related to the sheer growth in news gathering: Rules of objectivity enabled editors to keep lowly reporters in check, although they had less control over high-flying foreign correspondents. Objectivity as ideology was a kind of industrial discipline. At the same time, it seemed a natural and progressive ideology for an aspiring occupational group at a moment when science was god, efficiency was cherished, and increasingly prominent elites judged partisanship a vestige of the tribal 19th century. First Mugwump reformers, led by the Anglo-Saxon patricians of the Northeast during the late 19th century, and then the Progressives, who pursued a broader reform movement in the early 20th century, argued that politics itself should be beyond partisanship. No wonder journalists picked up on their appeal.

Yet at the very moment that journalists embraced "objectivity," they also recognized its limits. In the 1930s, there was a vogue for what contemporaries called "interpretive journalism." Leading journalists and journalism educators insisted that the world had grown increasingly complex and needed not only to be reported but explained. Political columnists, like Walter Lippmann, David Lawrence, Frank Kent and Mark Sullivan, came into their own. Journalists insisted that their task was to help readers not only to know but to understand. At the same time, they now took it for granted that understanding had nothing to do with party or partisan sentiment.

Was this progress? Was a professional press taking over from party hacks? Not everyone was sure. If the change brought a new dispassionate tone to news coverage, it also opened the way to making entertainment rather than political coherence a chief criterion of journalism.

Speaker of the House "Uncle" Joe Cannon objected in 1927: "I believe we had better publicity when the party press was the rule and the so-called independent press the exception, than we have now," he said in his autobiography, *Uncle Joe Cannon*. "The correspondents in the press gallery then felt their responsibility for reporting the proceedings of Congress. Then men representing papers in sympathy with the party in power were alert to present the record their party was making so that the people would know its accomplishments, and those representing the opposition party were eager to expose any failures on the part of the Administration." In the independent press, in contrast, serious discussion of legislation gave way to entertainment: "The cut of a Congressman's whiskers or his clothes is a better subject for a human interest story than what he says in debate."

News, Cannon mourned, had replaced legislative publicity. What had 20
really happened was that journalists had become their own interpretive community, writing to one another and not to parties or partisans.

The triumph of an ethic of analytical and procedural fairness (or "objectivity" as it has presumptuously been called) was never complete. Even journalism's leaders took it for granted that fairness in journalism could be combined with active partisanship in politics. Claude Bowers proudly recalled in his autobiography, *My Life,* that, while an editorial writer for the New York *World,* he wrote speeches for Democratic senatorial candidate Robert Wagner while running daily editorials in Wagner's support. As Ronald Steel recounts in his biography *Walter Lippmann and the American Century,* Lippmann and James Reston in 1945 helped write a speech for Republican Sen. Arthur Vandenberg in which he broke from his isolationism. Lippmann then praised the turnabout in his column. Reston wrote a front page story on the speech in *The New York Times,* noting the "unusual interest" it attracted and observing that Sen. Vandenberg presented his theme "with force." President-elect John F. Kennedy shared with Lippmann a draft of his inaugural address. Lippmann proposed some modest changes that Kennedy accepted. After the new president delivered his speech, Lippmann praised it in his column as a "remarkably successful piece of self-expression." When George Will helped Ronald Reagan prepare for his television debates with Jimmy Carter in 1980 and then as an ABC commentator discussed Reagan's performance, he acted in a well-developed tradition.

With such intimate political involvement from leading lights of the journalism establishment, it is difficult to accept journalists' claims of political innocence—even the claims of journalists, like *Washington Post* editor Leonard Downie, who forswear voting for fear it could taint their scrupulous neutrality. But scrupulous accuracy and fairness are indeed the watchwords of journalistic competence today, even though the work of editorial writers, columnists and sports reporters (who are obliged to write from the viewpoint of the home team) offers countercurrents to professional ideals of detachment.

In the 1960s and again in the 1990s, some journalists have rebelled at the voicelessness of objective reporting and seek to write with an edge or an attitude that calls attention to the story as a piece of writing, not just a neutral vessel for transporting purportedly raw reality to audiences. Cutthroat competition encourages this. So does a postmodern relativism that spits at pretensions to objectivity.

At the same time, journalists, when criticized, invariably return to the old standbys. They assert their accuracy, their impartiality and their intrepid willingness to pursue the truth without fear or favor. There is safety in this. There is also honor: honor in the abnegation rather than the aggrandizement of self, and honor in the ordinary ambition to pursue a craft well rather than pursue art or influence badly. . . .

Is modern professional fairness better for democracy, on balance, than 25
the partisan press? So far as I know, no one has ever seriously studied this question. There are few studies that compare, say, party-oriented European journalism with objectivity-oriented American journalism, and none that successfully answer the tricky question of which serves democracy better. Do citizens know more about politics and vote more often where there is a party press or an independent press? In most European democracies, there is higher voter turnout and higher scores on tests of political knowledge than in the United States. But in Europe there are also stronger political parties and very different electoral institutions. What their effect might be on the values that direct the news media is simply unknown.

There is something enduring about the desire to be fair in journalism—both the writer's quest to be believed and the news institution's strong interest in maintaining its own credibility. But there is nothing at all stable across history or across national cultures about the actual rules and practices that pass for fairness. Today's journalistic fairness in the United States is a blend of high hopes, historic traditions, contemporary political culture and the expediencies journalists face in keeping audiences, owners and sources at bay. It is a shifting set of principles and practices that will be tested and reformulated by a changing informational environment whose shape will not hold still.

Questions for Discussion

1. What are the most important phases in the history of the press as Schudson tells the story? How does he explain the changes? Probably the most important recent innovation is news via the Internet—newspapers themselves now often update their own stories on Web sites. What long-term effect might Internet news have on newspapers?
2. What exactly is "modern analytical and procedural fairness"? How does Schudson explain it? Read or reread the Fuller selection in this chapter. Does Fuller shed any light on it? If so, how? Watch the evening news on one of the major networks and/or examine headline stories in your local paper. Do you detect this notion of fairness in how the stories are told? In what specific ways?
3. What is your reaction to Schudson's exposure of the double role that some journalists play—that is, on the one hand, writing speeches for politicians, and on the other, writing favorably in the news about these politicians and their speeches? Should this practice be banned or at least discouraged by news agencies and newspapers?

For Inquiry and Convincing

In the United States mainstream news journalism now strives to be non-partisan, reporting the news without apparent political bias. But this was not the case in the nineteenth century in our own papers, nor is it common practice in Europe today. Schudson asks, "Is modern professional fairness better for democracy, on balance, than the partisan press?" Another, more pointed way to phrase this question is to say: Many Americans profess to be bored by the news and alienated from politics. Would they be less bored and alienated if the press was openly partisan?

We can investigate this question in at least two ways: by comparing our papers with European ones or, more easily, by comparing papers with well-known partisan news magazines published in the United States, such as the *National Review* (conservative) or *The Nation* (liberal). Choose one or both routes, and study the coverage of one or two major stories. Write a paper that either defends current newspaper practice or argues for a more partisan press. Remember that the issue is not excitement as such, but rather *what is better for democracy.*

For Inquiry

We tend to think about news in terms of contrasting opposites—partisan versus neutral, news stories versus editorials. But Schudson mentions a third possibility, interpretive journalism, which attempts to provide more background for a story and a more extensive context or contexts for understanding and evaluating it. We can find examples of interpretive journalism in most daily newspapers, especially in efforts to cover unusually complex and confusing issues such as genetic engineering. Some papers are heavily committed to interpretive journalism; the *Christian Science Monitor* is a distinguished example.

Locate several instances of interpretive journalism from two or three different papers. Compare it to routine news reporting and to partisan writing. Are they really different? How? Write a paper exploring the differences and the role played by interpretive journalism in news coverage. Conclude by offering a tentative position on the following question: Is an interpretive press preferable to a neutral or partisan one for developing well-informed citizens?

JIM SQUIRES

The Impossibility of Fairness

"The news is subordinated to entertainment" is the gist of Jim Squires's argument, and, he claims, it is so subordinated because too many news sources are owned by huge entertainment conglomerates, like Time Warner. The result is not merely distortion of the news, he contends, but much more seriously "outright corruption of journalism." This article appeared in the same issue of Media Studies Journal *as the previous selection by Michael Schudson and represents a traditional perspective sharply critical of current journalism. Squires was once editor of the* Chicago Tribune *and a media adviser to Ross Perot. His book* Read All about It!: The Corporate Takeover of America's Newspapers *develops his case in more detail.*

1 ESTABLISHING PARAMETERS of fairness in the age of cyberspace is no different from trying to set them 50 years ago at the Chicago *Tribune* or *The New York Times.* Each case is unique, and the debate always ends the way it did in the Victorian England of author Thomas Hughes.

"He never wants anything but what's right and fair;" Hughes wrote of a character in *Tom Brown's Schooldays,* "only when you come to settle what's right and fair, it's everything that he wants, and nothing that you want."

Recollection of my own record starts with my treatment of a Nashville used-car salesman who committed suicide in the 1960s following my story of his pending indictment. *The* (Nashville) *Tennessean,* though entirely accurate, was unfair to the car dealer by singling him out for front-page notoriety. Not all those expected to be indicted by the grand jury that day were treated the same way.

I also wrote countless stories based on anonymous sources, and I was not once concerned about the racial, ethnic and gender balance of the sources I quoted. A great deal of my unfairness was rooted in my unavoidable personal profile as a Southern white male. In the broad sense that fairness by news media is now being debated in the public mind, it is possible that none of the zillion stories I wrote was fair.

5 Yet even the worst individual case of unfairness does not approach the level of injustice being perpetrated by the information industry as a whole. What could be more unfair to citizens than the outright corruption of journalism, which takes place daily in all quarters of the so-called news media?

With the exception of a few fine and committed newspapers and magazines, the professional standards and values of journalism have gone to hell in a hand-basket, cast out in favor of an entertainment culture with no moral compass and no concern for fairness—or taste.

Even at its worst and most unfair, the American brand of journalism once had as its goal a quest for accuracy and perspective that would eventually produce truth. News, which is the product of real journalism, was best defined by the Hutchins Commission on freedom of the press in 1947 as a "truthful, comprehensive, and intelligent account of the day's events in a context which gives them meaning."

Ostensibly, information was gathered, evaluated and eventually disseminated in the interest of enlightenment and education. Conversely, the consumers of journalism had good reason to believe that the purveyors of news existed to provide them a fair deal and a fair account. Journalism's value in the marketplace was its quality, of which fairness is a vital part. Like all the great products of American capitalism, brand-name integrity was its greatest asset. Shoddy, inferior news coverage invariably failed in the competitive marketplace. This is no longer true.

The broadcast industry is an entertainment industry to which news is purely incidental. It is primarily television's shoddy attempts at journalism, such as its injurious handling of the identification of the Atlanta Olympics bombing suspect, that have fueled the fairness controversy and spawned cries for press regulation. Print journalism used to routinely withhold the names of suspects until they had been charged. Even when one publication felt it necessary, others often restrained themselves, minimizing the damage. This is no longer possible when TV has a breathless correspondent, dressed like a cat burglar, camped outside the suspect's apartment, endlessly speculating live on camera about everything but the color of the man's underwear. "The bigger the lie, the louder the cry" has taken on new meaning in light of the instant global impact of a CNN bulletin or a report on the Internet.

10 Today television and movie producers, networks, cable operators and information providers of all stripes value "news" not for its importance, quality or public service contributions but for its ability to attract an audience and turn a profit. Thus, for today's press, the best story is a sex scandal such as the "bimbo eruptions" that have plagued President Clinton.

In a speech last year Harold Evans, the distinguished English author, editor and former president and publisher of Random House, quoted William S. Paley, founder of CBS, as saying that the day news becomes a profit center will be lamentable. "Well, the day has come," Evans said. "It's about dusk."

With the passing of time, the standards of journalism have been relaxed to the point of nonexistence. Yet news remains the favorite subject of the entertainment business to such an extent that the lines between news and entertainment have been forever obliterated. News provides a steady stream of programming free of creative and promotion costs. From the ABC and CNN coverage of the Iranian hostage crisis to television's obsession with O. J. Simpson nearly 20 years later, true stories have proven to be a sure ticket to ratings and profits.

Movies, television specials and even sitcoms are built around "news" situations and actual events. Celebrity personalities are most often substituted for genuine newsmakers, but sometimes the newsmakers end up getting hired by the news media and become celebrities themselves. Accuracy in the retelling of their stories is, quite naturally, less important to scripts than excitement and audience appeal. People walk out of movies like *JFK,* which purported to chronicle the conspiracy behind the assassination of President Kennedy, or last year's fictional extravaganza on the Titanic, and say in all seriousness, "I didn't know that." Guess not, it never happened.

For today's press the "best news" combines sex and crime and prominent people, like O. J. Simpson and President Clinton. The actual events become great television entertainment. Then they spawn books, which are turned into movies, which attempt to make them even more entertaining than they were originally.

News events spawn new celebrities, who show up at a later event with 15
a microphone, pretending to practice the craft of journalism. Actors, comedians, politicians, lawyers, infamous criminals—and some who fit all five categories—now regularly masquerade as reporters on newscasts and talk shows. Watergate burglar G. Gordon Liddy and Clinton White House political adviser George Stephanopoulos are both now widely considered to be journalists. Former Nixon speechwriter Patrick Buchanan and civil rights activist Jesse Jackson go from being story subject one month to storyteller the next. Lawyer Johnnie Cochran may be on television standing beside a famous defendant one day and on another interviewing the same defendant from behind an anchor desk.

Worse, many of the people signing the paychecks of these pretenders and making the programming decisions can't see any difference between real news and celebrity news programming. They think that having been celebrated in one news event qualifies someone to cover another. It never crosses their minds that their position in charge of news organizations carries with it a responsibility to protect and preserve the values of real journalism.

Sadly, through acquisition and merger much of the real journalism establishment has been swallowed up by the entertainment industry. Some of the biggest, most important and powerful news organizations in the world today are owned by companies whose main business is make believe. The Cable News Network and *Time* magazine, for example, are controlled by the entertainment giant Time Warner, cable owner, maker of HBO movies and producer of sleazy rap songs.

To grasp the implications of this for journalism and democracy, what would happen if a strong grass-roots movement for media censorship were ever mounted in this country? Its most just and likely targets would be cable television pornography, the violence-profanity-sex formula movies of HBO and Time Warner's abhorrent rap lyrics—all of which trumpet the legally obscene F-word.

It is easy to imagine that Time Warner would raise its First Amendment shield and march behind it to Washington to oppose this assault on its profit centers. So would many other major media companies with whom Time Warner has significant financial dealings and mutual interests.

But would this be fair to the watchers of CNN, the readers of *Time* and 20
the customers of other journalism organizations with ties to Time Warner? How much fairness could censorship proponents and their political leaders expect from *Time* and CNN, or from any journalist assigned to the story? No matter how ethical, scrupulous and professional these journalists might be, their freedom from the appearance of conflict of interest would be gone. How fair is that to citizens who expect and depend on a free press to educate them on matters of public policy? . . .

Throughout our history, the free press has enjoyed a right to a special place in the democracy with special privileges under law because it was a special business with a unique goal of serving the public interest.

Journalism can't make that claim anymore. Except for a few newspaper companies, news organizations have become indistinguishable from other media. Journalists' paychecks come from the same payroll as those of the movie moguls, TV execs, radio personalities and record producers; from the same corporate bank accounts as the cash for independent movies and free-lance magazine pieces.

These same coffers are the source of virtually all the big book contracts that are handed out not to real authors but to tabloid journalists, kiss-and-tell gold diggers, toe-sucking, secret-spilling presidential political advisers and tattooed, rule-breaking, in-your-face athletes whose stock in trade is incivility. . . .

A favorite phrase in the "lexicon" of the new entertainment/journalism . . . is "the smoking gun," meaning, of course, irrefutable evidence. For "the smoking gun" on what happened to the free press in America, look no further than its embarrassing performance on the most perfect of all television "news stories"—the Monica Lewinsky scandal. When two newspapers as serious and respected as *The Dallas Morning News* and *The Wall Street Journal* get so carried away with tabloidism that they both rush into print leaked phony stories using anonymous sources and then have to apologize, there's only one conclusion. With all due respect to my admired friend Harry Evans, it's past dusk. It is midnight in the garden and far too late to worry about fairness.

Questions for Discussion

1. Early in his article Squires calls attention to one source of bias in his own news reporting: his "unavoidable personal profile as a Southern white male." He concedes that, as we now understand fairness, "it is possible that none of the zillion stories I wrote was fair." Do we expect fairness in the sense Squires describes it? Is it realistic or desirable to expect reporters to

become aware of their personal backgrounds and to adjust to some degree for them?

2. Squires contends that news has fallen prey to "an entertainment culture with no moral compass and no concern for fairness—or taste." How does he back up this assertion? Do you find this central contention convincing? Why or why not? To what extent would you say his rejection of current journalism stems from a distaste for mass or popular culture generally?
3. Squires paints a very bleak picture and offers no hope for improvement, much less reform. In other words, he depicts a problem we all recognize but offers no solution. Suppose that his basic contention about the press is correct—that the news is merely entertainment—and that the root of the problem is corporate takeovers. How might the industry be reformed or the conditions conducive to what he calls "real news" be enhanced?

For Research and Persuasion

We should not be surprised when older, traditional journalists see their craft as in decline and blame it on the electronic media, especially television. Journalism *has* changed a great deal in the past three or four decades—and changed in ways that many journalists themselves find unacceptable. People who remember when television didn't exist or didn't have nearly the impact it has now will certainly tend to make it the culprit.

But before we rush to support this condemnation of TV journalism, we should at least study it. As a class make a list of as many TV news programs as you can think of. Be sure to include both new and long-running ones, as well as a broad spectrum of programs ranging from the stodgy to the sensational. Divide the list among class members, and have each watch several segments, taking careful notes about what is covered and how. Then discuss what you've found. Are the news media as hopelessly bad as Squires claims?

Write an essay in response to Squires but addressed to your peers, who have always lived in a TV-saturated world. Advocate some sort of responsible, personal approach to TV news watching, and attempt to persuade your readers to at least try your approach.

For Inquiry and Mediation

How we judge the news depends almost entirely on what we think it is or ought to be. In this chapter's first selection Jack Fuller offers a modest and realistic view of the news—"a report of what a news organization has recently learned about matters of some significance or interest to the specific community [it] serves." In contrast, Squires cites a definition that makes strong, idealistic claims for what the news should be—a "truthful, comprehensive, and intelligent account of the day's events in a context which gives them meaning."

Inquire into both definitions, paying close attention to the words used and their implications. As you consider them, bear in mind the tension in any profession between what is and what ought to be, and the difficulty of balancing standards that challenge the profession to improve against standards that demoralize, that are too high to reach and thus foster cynicism.

Then write a paper attempting to combine the best of Fuller with the best of Squires, together with your own notions of what the news is and should be. Address your paper to other students, whose expectations for the news need to be *both* demanding *and* realistic, neither too low nor too high.

MIKE TWOHY

Cartoon

In the previous essay, "The Impossibility of Fairness," Jim Squires argues that standards of honesty and accuracy erode as the news becomes more and more an entertainment industry, with each paper and news team competing for the public's attention. This cartoon from the New Yorker *magazine comments on the media obsession to be first with a story—or even the possibility of a story.*

For Discussion

Are you aware of recent examples of false reporting or news stories that have proven to be inaccurate? Do you think public perception of the media is as bad as this cartoon suggests? If, as Squires points out, "journalism's value in the marketplace was its quality," what will be the future of journalism if the public sees it as this cartoon does?

W. LANCE BENNETT

Escaping the News Prison: How People See beyond the Walls

It is fashionable to be critical of the press, but rarely do we hear critiques of the consumer, the person who reads the paper and listens to the evening news. If we simply "absorb" the news, W. Lance Bennett suggests, taking it in passively, without any critical thinking, we are doomed never to see beyond the "news prison walls," beyond what might be called the "official construction" of reality, for newspapers generally report what officials say with little or no analysis. But how can we interpret the news intelligently? This is the question Bennett, a specialist in mass communication and professor at the University of Washington, tries to answer. This selection is taken from his 1988 book News: The Politics of Illusion.

A SMALL percentage of people stand in sharp contrast to the majority who absorb and expel news information as though they were contestants in a lifelong trivia match. Some people seem to have an inside line on the politics behind news reports. . . . 1

Consider two facts that help explain who becomes liberated from the political confines of the news. First, we already know that the news consists overwhelmingly of "objective" (or at least "fair") "documentary" reports that pass along, with little analysis, the political messages of official spokespersons. Less than 1 percent of mass media coverage contains any sort of independent analysis from the reporter's perspective, while around 90 percent of the news originates from circumstances that give officials substantial control over political content. Second, consider the fact that most Americans who are politically active, system-supporting citizens have been socialized in environments (family, school, workplace) that discourage analytical or ideological political thinking. This combination of nonanalytical news with nonanalytical people does not bode well for much analytical thinking in response to political messages in the news.

A third factor further undermines the critical thinking of the public. Political actors tend to construct simplistic political messages that appeal to myths and unquestioned beliefs held by large segments of the public. Such messages are seldom brought into focus because of the absence of analysis in the news and the lack of analytical dispositions in the audience. As a result, most news messages appeal directly to unconscious myths and unquestioned beliefs. In short, the propagandistic, nonanalytical qualities of mass news mesh smoothly with the well-conditioned, nonanalytical orientation of the citizenry.

This profile of the news prisoner contains an obvious clue about those who escape. *In order to escape the news prison, people must develop some independent, analytical perspective from which to interpret the news.* So much for the obvious.

More difficult is to identify the sort of perspective that helps people understand the news more clearly. There are actually several orientations that would enable people to break through the layers of subtle persuasion in the news and think sensibly about what might be going on behind the stories. For example, *a grasp of American history would provide a perspective on the patterns of myth and rhetoric in political events.* A common technique of political propaganda is to blur the relationship between past and present. When historic disasters like foreign involvements or economic collapses seem to be on the verge of recurring, public officials can be expected to persuade the public that important differences distinguish present circumstances from the past. At other times, when the signs of change seem entirely clear, threatened elites may try to persuade the public to avoid the fearsome future and step back into the comforting shadow of the past. The repeated and successful use of these communication patterns suggests that the American people can be led easily to see differences where none exist and to ignore distinctions where they are apparent.

5 A firm grasp of political history would provide people with a more secure foundation than they now have from which to resist political pressures and with which to develop alternative understandings. Unfortunately, most school boards look with disfavor on history curricula that offer coherent interpretations of American politics. As a result, the majority of American children suffer through several years of the same history course—a course that emphasizes disconnected facts and events, reinforces basic myths that leave people vulnerable to political rhetoric, discourages people from developing a secure understanding of power and politics in American society, and, above all, emphasizes the deeds of great national heroes. This "hero history" not only brings myths to life but also encourages people to trust contemporary hero-leaders to do their thinking and acting for them. There are, to put it bluntly, few Americans with an adequate grasp of their country's history.

Another possible frame of reference for the news would be the sort provided in this book, namely, a theoretical grasp of how politicians and journalists act together to make the news. Such a perspective would help people to locate and interpret the gaps and biases in mass media coverage. When diplomatic talks are called "cordial and productive," people could assume immediately that nothing had happened and that the leaders involved had some other political reason to hold the conference. Flags would go up cautioning people to discount unverified rumors spread by "unidentified" officials. Similar skepticism would apply to "doublespeak" statements like this one in the news: "'We've made no secret of our views,' said a U.S. official who insisted on anonymity." People could recognize political manipulation in the news through the use of leaks, pseudo-events, and various image-making techniques. After hearing "both sides of an issue," people might even begin to wonder what the third side looked like and why it was not reported.

Unfortunately, people are not required to take courses on how to interpret the news. To the contrary, most people are encouraged by every trusted authority, particularly parents and teachers, to take the news seriously and at face value. The majority of us are taught to ingest large quantities of news and wait for an objective understanding of events to strike as if by revelation. Waiting for objective revelations from the news may be more satisfying than waiting for Godot, but it is surely as pointless. Children are quizzed in school on the content of classroom news supplements as though they represented the most accurate and comprehensive coverage of the known world. By memorizing the "right answers" to news quizzes, these children grow up thinking that knowing the facts in the news is equivalent to understanding something about the real world.

The news worship that begins in childhood is continued in adult life by the widespread support for the ideal of objective reporting. The notion that events can and should be presented without values or interpretation feeds the image of the good citizen as a concerned seeker of truth. At the same time, the widespread belief in objective reporting obscures the possibility that most "truths" that emerge from the news are likely to be the result of subtle political messages that appeal to subconscious beliefs and prejudices. People can hardly be blamed for thinking that they have found truth under such circumstances. After all, few things seem as objectively true as having one's deepest prejudices confirmed by respected authorities. Presenting two sides of every story with no critical "bridge" to transcend the differences between the sides only invites people to choose the version closest to their existing beliefs. Studies of newspaper readers (presumably the most critical information-seekers) have shown that newspapers primarily reinforce preexisting political attitudes.

In the absence of a grasp of newsmaking theory or political history, the only other obvious source of independent news judgment is political ideology. Ideologies are formal systems of belief about the nature, origins, and means of promoting values that people regard as important. Not only do ideologies provide people with a clear sense of life's purpose, but they provide a logic for interpreting the world by giving rules for translating real-world events into illustrations of how those values are promoted or damaged. Thus, people who view the news through the lens of an ideology are likely to spot hidden political messages and translate them into independent political statements. The trouble with ideologies is that they can become rigid and limiting frames of reference, leading people to select only the information that fits them while rejecting all other input. For example, many people in the United States continue to hold a "cold war" ideology that views the appearance of socialism or communism anywhere in the world as inherently threatening to democracy, freedom, and the American way of life. For those who cling rigidly to the "cold war" belief system, many important distinctions about world politics may be lost. The emergence of Socialist governments in Europe may seem to be a threatening step along the road to world totalitarianism. Socialism in the Western hemisphere ("our backyard") seems intolerable. Lost in this ideological view is the understanding that all Socialist and Communist governments are not alike, and that most of them do not pose threats to democracy, freedom, or the American way.

Since the news seldom explains how other political systems work from 10
the standpoint of the people who live in them, we tend to hear mostly U.S. official and expert opinion about other systems. And when it comes to Communist or Socialist systems, the chances are pretty good that equal time will be given some venerable "cold warrior" quick to predict the end of democracy and communism on our doorstep. News consumers with kindred and rigid ideological views can use these familiar pronouncements to reinforce existing beliefs rather than learn something new about the world from another viewpoint.

If people recognized this vicious circle of news and popular belief, they might be more inclined to build an imperative for learning into their belief systems, turning ideology into a dynamic rather than a static outlook. *If used constructively, ideologies could create challenging understandings of the world by enabling people to find the inconsistencies, puzzles, and paradoxes in events.* Thinking through the puzzles in political events can broaden an ideology by adapting it to resolve the puzzles. This process of adaptation simultaneously creates new ways of seeing the world. For example, Richard Nixon and Henry Kissinger were able to see beyond ideology to recognize the advantages of opening political and economic relations with once-dreaded "Communist" China. After high political authorities had pronounced China safe to think about, journalists began to cover Chinese events from a less rigid ideological viewpoint. If it is possible to do business with a one-party Communist state like China, why not a multiparty Socialist country like Nicaragua? The answer depends largely on whether one's ideology is open or closed to learning new things about the world.

In a perfect world, people would supplement their ideologies with a command of history and a theoretical grasp of news politics. Such a combination of perspectives would enable people to combat news propaganda with their own conclusions. This is not, as you probably guessed, a perfect world. It is unlikely that more than a tiny fraction of the public has an understanding of American history or news politics, and by even the most generous estimates, few people can be called self-reflective ideologues.

Even those few people who manage to construct a political worldview may find it a mixed blessing. On the one hand, they are able to understand political communication in comprehensive and personally satisfying ways. On the other hand, their ideological insights are likely to be discredited by the majority of their fellow citizens, who have been taught to wait for "objective" revelations to emerge from the news. Hence, another paradox: People who espouse a stance of objectivity toward the news are likely to accept blindly the institutional bias of the news media (if, indeed, they are able to form any political conclusions at all), while those who manage to form clear political perspectives are likely to be condemned for being "opinionated." . . .

Questions for Discussion

1. "The Associated Press never comments on the news," an executive of that organization claimed in 1925 (quoted by Michael Schudson; see the second reading in this chapter). In other words, official news sources don't, in a strong sense, *interpret* the news, but rather claim "neutral" or "objective" ground. According to Bennett, this claim is suspect. Why? In what ways do reporters interpret the news even when they don't offer commentary? In what sense does the news come to reporters already interpreted, shaped for public consumption by the very sources consulted?
2. Bennett claims that most Americans are socialized to "absorb and expel news information as though they were contestants in a lifelong trivia match." Is this an accurate description of your experience? Do you attach high value to knowing factual details about current events? Were you taught in school or at home to question the news or subject it to analysis?
3. According to Bennett, "*people must develop some independent, analytical perspective from which to interpret the news*" (his emphasis). What does "independent" mean? independent from what or from whom? Is this independence total? That is, mustn't we be dependent on *something* to have an "independent" view of anything?
4. Bennett says that waiting for "an objective understanding of events" to arise from the news is like "waiting for Godot," an illusion to a play by Samuel Beckett in which several characters stand around talking, anticipating the arrival of a character who never comes. There are some things we can understand more or less, as we say, scientifically, like the structure of an atom. Why is the news not like this? What exactly must we be able to do to *understand* human events, as opposed to merely reciting so-called facts about them?

For Analysis

Probably Bennett's most important point is that "news messages appeal directly to unconscious myths and unquestioned beliefs." In class discussion develop a list of some of these myths and beliefs, and question their basis and history. In other words, make them conscious and subject to question.

Then secure the latest edition of a daily paper, and study it with your list in mind. Write an essay analyzing the myths and beliefs appealed to in one or two news stories. Conclude your essay by addressing this question: Is there an alternative to myths and beliefs? That is, can the news work at all without appealing to myths or beliefs of some kind?

For Research and Convincing

Bennett suggests several ways to "see beyond the prison walls." With his ideas in mind, do some research into other sources that purport to help us read the news more critically. Then, taking what seems best from Bennett and your other sources, and combining it with your own ideas, write an essay for your peers to convince them, first, that the news should be read critically, and second, that you have a good way of doing it. For the second part, bear in mind that people usually read papers quickly and that a too elaborate approach won't be practical.

JAMES FALLOWS

"Public Journalism": An Attempt to Connect the Media with the Public

Attempts to reform the media are motivated primarily by two closely related perceptions: that increasingly the public is indifferent to and/or cynical about traditional news coverage and that the gap between politicians and ordinary citizens, especially between Washington and most of the rest of the country, is threatening to become unbridgeable. Both are obviously dangerous for the health of a democracy and are reflected in declining circulations for some papers and low voter turnout even in major election years.

One such reform is so-called public or civic journalism. It is designed to overcome the problem Bennett describes in the previous selection—that "around 90 percent of the news originates from circumstances that give officials substantial control over political content." Instead of going to politicians or "spin doctors" for the news, public journalism goes to the public first, asking them what they care about and want discussed, and then offers the politicians a chance to respond. The goal is to get a dialogue going between politicians and the public, with the former less in control of the agenda. James Fallows, a distinguished journalist and editor of the New Republic, *explores public journalism in the following excerpt from his important recent book,* Breaking the News: How the Media Undermine American Democracy.

DURING THE U.S. military's darkest moments just after the Vietnam War, a group of officers and analysts undertook a "military reform" movement. Rather than papering over the deep problems that the Vietnam years had revealed, and rather than searching for external sources of blame, this group attempted to locate the internal problems that had weakened the military so that the problems could be faced and solved. The "military reformers'" record of success was not perfect, but at their instigation the U.S. military coped with more of its fundamental difficulties than any other American institution has. 1

Since the early 1990s, a group of journalistic reformers has launched a similar attempt to cope with the basic weaknesses of their institution. As was the case with the military reformers, their efforts have been scorned by some of the most powerful leaders of the current establishment. As with the military reformers, they do not have the complete or satisfying answer to all of today's journalistic problems. But, like the military reformers, they are more right than wrong. At a minimum their ideas point the way to a media establishment that is less intensely scorned than today's is.

Those involved in the "public journalism" (sometimes called "civic journalism") movement stress its cooperative, collaborative nature. But several people have played large roles in developing its ideas.

One is Davis Merritt, a man in his late fifties, who since the mid-1970s has been editor of the *Wichita Eagle* in Kansas. The cover of his 1995 book *Public Journalism and Public Life* says "by Davis 'Buzz' Merritt," and he has the laconic, unrushable bearing one would associate with a test pilot or astronaut named "Buzz." . . .

People involved in the public journalism movement often talk of "epiphanies" or transforming experiences that convinced them that a different course was necessary. Merritt says that his came just after the 1988 presidential election campaign. His paper was carrying the predictable wire stories: about the Dukakis campaign's response to the Bush campaign's attacks, about Gary Hart and his girl friends, about what Willie Horton did or did not do, about what Michael Dukakis would or would not do if his wife was raped. 5

Merritt says that as he put these stories into his paper each day, he found himself asking, Why are we publishing this? What are we doing? The accepted style of political coverage, he thought, was bringing out the worst in every participant in public life. It drove out serious candidates. It rewarded gutter-fighting. It disgusted most of the public. It embarrassed even the reporters. It trivialized the election—and it made everyone feel dirty when it was done. With the election experience fresh in his mind, Merritt began thinking about how journalists could use all their traditional tools of investigation, explanation, fair-mindedness, and so on in a way that was less destructive to the society in which journalists and readers alike had to live. . . .

In 1991 the fledgling [public journalism] movement got an important boost when David Broder of the *Washington Post,* probably the best-respected political reporter of his time, gave a lecture in California implicitly endorsing their approach. His statement was seen as significant not simply because of his personal stature but also because he had had contact with the public-journalism advocates and had come to a conclusion like theirs on his own.

In a speech sponsored by the Riverside, California *Press-Enterprise* and the University of California at Riverside, Broder said that coverage of public affairs had become a cynical and pointless insiders' game. Political consultants—rather than candidates—had come to have a dominant role in politics, Broder said. And these hired guns, "these new political bosses, have become for those of us in political journalism not only our best sources but, in many cases, our best friends."

The two groups got along because they both loved the operating details of politics, Broder said. They felt a distance from the slightly comic, sweating candidates who had to give speeches and raise money and submit themselves to the voters' will. For these poor candidates, Broder said, election day really was a judgment day. But for the reporters and consultants, no matter what the results of the election, they could play the game over and over again.

There was a more disturbing similarity between the groups, Broder said. "We both disclaim any responsibility for the consequences of elections." 10

> Let me say again, for emphasis: We disclaim ANY responsibility for the consequences of elections. Consultants will tell you they are hired to produce victory on Election Day. Reporters will tell you that we are hired to cover campaigns. . . . I've often said to our White House reporters, "My job is to deliver these turkeys; after they're in office, they're your responsibility."
>
> What this means in less facetious terms is that a very large percentage of the information that the American people get about politics comes from people who disclaim any responsibility for the consequences of our politics.

After spending nearly four decades in this activity, Broder said, he felt uneasy about the consequences of his life's work. By concentrating on the operations of politics and disdaining the results, reporters "have colluded with the campaign consultants to produce the kind of politics which is turning off the American people." By the early 1970s—the time of movies like *The Candidate* and books like *The Selling of the President*—journalists began to realize that the most important part of a political campaign was the ads a candidate put on radio and television:

> So we began to focus on the ads, and we began to write about them. We began to write about the people who made the ads, the campaign consultants and media advisers and pollsters. We wrote about them so often that I think we have turned some of them into political celebrities in their own right. We have helped to make them both famous and rich.
>
> In all of this, we forgot about the people who were the consumers of these ads, those who had the message pushed at them, willingly or not, every time they turned on their radio or television set. We forgot our obligation as journalists to help them cope with this mass of political propaganda coming their way.

The line Broder had drawn—between accepting and ignoring the consequences of what reporters wrote—was to be the main dividing line between the public journalism movement and the "mainstream" press. Even before this speech, Broder had written a column issuing a similar challenge to journalists. "It is time for us in the world's freest press to become activists," he wrote in 1990, "not on behalf of a particular party or politician, but on behalf of the process of self-government."

Toward the end of advancing this kind of "activism," Broder laid out in his speech recommendations for future campaign coverage that would pay less attention to tactical maneuvers and more to the connection between the campaign and real national problems. One specific suggestion, which seems obvious now but had rarely been done before Broder proposed it, was that reporters cover campaign ads not from the candidates' point of view but from the voters'. That is, instead of emphasizing what each campaign was trying to accomplish with the ads—how they were exploiting their opponents' vulnerabilities, which interest groups they were trying to peel off, and how—the reporters should examine how truthful and realistic the advertisements were. One immediate effect of Broder's recommendation was the rapid spread of "Ad Watch"–type coverage in campaign coverage, in which correspondents examined political ads for smears and misrepresentations.

Public Journalism in Practice. Through meetings coordinated by Jay Rosen's Project on Public Life and the Press (which is based at New York University and funded by the Knight Foundation), public journalism became a "movement" by 1993. Its main base of support was in regional newspapers and some broadcast stations, usually working in partnership with the papers. . . .

The best-known project in public journalism's short history is probably 15
the *Charlotte Observer*'s approach to covering the North Carolina elections in 1992. The paper's editors, who had carefully studied Broder's proposals . . . didn't want their coverage to be driven by the issues that each candidate thought would be tactically useful in the election. Instead, they began an elaborate effort to determine what issues the state's people believed were most important, and what other issues might have the greatest impact on the state's future welfare even though the public was not yet fully aware of them. The paper commissioned a poll of more than a thousand area residents (not merely subscribers) to ask their views about the public issues that concerned them most. The poll was not a yes-or-no survey but involved extensive discussions to explore the reasons behind the respondents' views. After the initial polling, the *Observer* arranged for five hundred residents to serve as an ongoing citizens' advisory panel to the paper through the election season.

Based on the issues that emerged from the polls and panel discussions, as well as from efforts by the paper's reporters and editors to judge the trends that would affect the state, the paper drew up lists of topics about which the public expected answers from the candidates. These citizen-generated issues were not the same as the ones on which many of the candidates had planned to run. For instance, the citizen panels showed a widespread concern about environmental problems caused by Charlotte's rapid growth. Politicians had not planned to emphasize this theme, but the paper decided to push for statements on this and the other issues the citizen panels had recommended. At the same time, it ran fewer stories about advertising strategies, about horse-race-style opinion polls, and about other traditional campaign techniques.

The moment of truth for this new approach came early in the campaign season, and it involved a question that a newspaper did *not* ask. After the citizens' panel had stressed its interest in environmental issues (among other concerns), the *Observer* prepared a big grid to run in the newspaper, showing each candidate's position on the questions the panel had raised. At the time, the long-time Democratic officeholder Terry Sanford was running for the Senate. The *Observer*'s editor, Rich Opel, has described what happened next:

> Voters are intensely interested in the environment. . . . So our reporters went out to senatorial candidates and said, "Here are the voters' questions." Terry Sanford, the incumbent senator, called me up from Washington and said, "Rich, I have these questions from your reporter and I'm not going to talk about the environment until the general election." This was the primary. I said, "Well, the voters want to know about the environment now, Terry." He said, "Well, that's not the way I have my campaign structured." I said, "Fine, I will run the questions and I will leave a space under it for you to answer. If you choose not to, we will just say, 'Would not respond' or we will leave it blank." We ended the conversation. In about ten days he sent the answers down.

Most political reporters for most newspapers know how they would instinctively respond when a candidate told them he was delaying discussion of an issue. "That's interesting," they would say. "What's the thinking behind that?" Like a campaign consultant, the reporter would be instantly engaged in figuring out why the issue would be useless against other Democrats in the primaries but would be useful against Republicans in the general election. By responding as proxies for the public rather than as consultants' manqués, the reporters evoked the discussion their readers wanted to hear.

"This is not a way of being 'tough' on a candidate for its own sake, but of using toughness in service of certain public values," Jay Rosen has said of the Charlotte project. "It is also a way of adding some civility, since there are rewards to balance the penalties that dominate today's campaigns. In normal campaign coverage, candidates get praised and criticized, but on the basis of what values? In this case the paper said: *here* are the issues the public wants to hear about. We'll judge you on whether you respond to these views." Most newspapers, he said, also judge candidates by a set of values—but never lay out clearly for the reader or the candidate exactly what those values are. . . .

Complaints from the Media Establishment. There has, however, 20
been one important source of backlash against the public-journalism approach. It has come from the editors of the country's largest and most influential newspapers. Leonard Downie, executive editor of the *Washington Post,* has said the movement's basic premise is "completely wrong." Max Frankel, the former executive editor of the *New York Times,* has expressed a similar hostility—as have others, including William F. Woo, editor of the *St. Louis Post-Dispatch.*

The crux of their unhappiness lies with the concept of "objectivity." One of public journalism's basic claims is that journalists should stop kidding themselves about their ability to remain detached from and objective about public life. Journalists are not like scientists, observing the behavior of fruit flies but not influencing what the flies might do. They inescapably change the reality of whatever they are observing by whether and how they choose to write about it.

From the nearly infinite array of events, dramas, tragedies, and successes occurring in the world each day, newspaper editors and broadcast producers must define a tiny sample as "the news." The conventions of choosing "the news" are so familiar, and so much of the process happens by learned and ingrained habits, that it is easy for journalists to forget that the result reflects *decisions,* rather than some kind of neutral scientific truth.

At the national level, the daily public-affairs news concentrates heavily on what the president said and did that day; how well- or badly organized his staff seems to be; whether he is moving ahead or falling behind in his struggle against opponents from the other party; and who is using what tactics to get ready for the next presidential race. Each time the chairman of the Federal Reserve opens his mouth, he usually gets on the front page of the newspaper and on the evening network news. Each month, when the government releases its report on unemployment rates and consumer-price increases, papers and networks treat this as a genuine news event. Each summer when the leaders of industrialized nations hold their G-7 meeting, the news gives us a few minutes of prime ministers and presidents discussing their latest economic disputes. When the local school board selects a new superintendent of schools, that announcement, and the comments of the new superintendent, are played prominently in the local news.

A case could be made that some or all of these events are really the most important "news" that a broad readership needs each day. But you could just as easily make a case that most of these official, often ceremonial events should be overlooked and that a whole different category of human activity deserves coverage as "news." Instead of telling us what Newt Gingrich will do to block Bill Clinton's spending plans for education, the "news" might involve the way parochial schools work and ask whether their standard of discipline is possible in public schools. Instead of describing rivalries on the White House staff, the "news" could treat the presidency the way it does the scientific establishment, judging it mainly by public pronouncements and not looking too far behind the veil. The simplest daily reminder that the news is the result of countless judgment calls, rather than some abstract truth, is a comparison of the front page of the *Wall Street Journal* with that of almost any other major newspaper. The "news" that dominates four-fifths of most front pages is confined, in the *Journal,* to two little columns of news summary. (Here is an alarming fact: Those two columns represent more words than a half-hour TV news show would, if written out.) The rest of the front page represents the *Journal*'s attempt to explain what is interesting and important about the world, though it may not be at the top of the breaking "news." The two great journalistic organizations that illustrate how creatively the "news" could be defined are in fact the *Journal*'s news (not editorial) sections and National Public Radio's news staff. Each of them covers the breaking news but does so in a summary fashion, so it can put its energy, space, and professional pride into reports that are not driven by the latest official pronouncement.

"It's absolutely correct to say that there are objectively occurring events," 25
says Cole Campbell, of the *Virginian-Pilot.* "Speeches are made, volcanoes

erupt, trees fall. But *news* is not a scientifically observable event. News is a choice, an extraction process, saying that one event is more meaningful than another event. The very act of saying that means making judgments that are based on values and based on frames."

It might seem that in making this point, Campbell and his colleagues had "discovered" a principle that most people figure out when they are in high school. There is no such thing as "just the news," and that's why editors are both necessary and powerful. But the public-journalism advocates have pushed this obvious-seeming point toward a conclusion that has angered many other editors. They have argued that the way modern journalists *choose* to present the news increases the chance that citizens will feel unhappy, powerless, betrayed by, and angry about their political system. And because the most powerful journalistic organs are unwilling to admit that they've made this choice, Rosen says, it is almost impossible for them to change.

"I couldn't disagree more with that view of newspaper journalism," Leonard Downie of the *Washington Post* has said in discussing the public-journalism theory that reporters should be actively biased in favor of encouraging the community to be involved in politics:

> I think our job is to report the news. To come as near as we can to giving people the truth, recognizing that the truth is multifaceted and that it changes from time to time as we learn more. I know that is what we do at the *Washington Post*. I know there are times when individual feelings among reporters and editors may cause them to want to take a side. We work very hard here to try to drive that out of our work.

Downie says that this approach is hard on his reporters, who in an attempt to suppress their personal feelings about an issue must "pretend to be less fully human than they really are." (Downie himself takes this belief to such an extreme that he *refuses to vote* in elections, feeling that this would make him too involved in the political process.) He admits that the newspaper's claim of "objectivity" is not convincing to many readers, who believe that the paper has its own angle on many stories. But he says that wavering even for a moment from the pursuit of "objectivity" would be disastrous.

> Where I am most bothered is when a newspaper uses its news columns—not its editorial page or its publisher—to achieve specific outcomes in the community. That is what I think is wrong, and very wrong. That line is very bright, and very sharp, and extremely dangerous. It is being manipulated by academics who are risking the terrible prostitution of our profession. Telling political candidates that they must come to a newspaper's forum, or that they must discuss certain issues—that is very dangerous stuff. That is not our role. There are plenty of institutions in every community to do this sort of thing. If newspapers are lax in covering these activities—if we are

> guilty only of covering crime and horse-race politics, then we should do our job better. We shouldn't change our job.

This defense of pure, detached "objectivity" drives many public-journalism advocates crazy. Rosen, Merritt, Campbell, and others say that when papers and TV stations have taken a more "engaged," less "objective" approach, they virtually never receive complaints from their readers or viewers. "*All* of the resistance to public journalism has come from other journalists, not from the public or politicians," Jay Rosen has said. "The resistance is always in the name of the community, but it is hard to find anyone in the community who objects." In its several years of public-journalism projects, the *Virginian Pilot* has received one hostile letter to the editor, claiming that its new approach to the community's problems meant abandoning the old standard of objectivity. But that letter came from a retired newspaper editor; the paper says it has received no similar complaints from readers without a professional axe to grind.

"I think Len Downie is right when he says that public journalism is an 30
'ideology,'" says Cole Campbell. "There are *two* ideologies, and he is unselfconscious about the ideology that drives his kind of journalism.

> The ideology of mainstream journalism is, When there is conflict, there is news. When there is no conflict, there's no news. That is ideological. It is out of touch with how people experience life.

Buzz Merritt elaborated on this point in *Public Journalism and Public Life:* "It is interesting that journalism's binding axiom of objectivity allows, even requires, unlimited toughness as a tool as well as a credo, yet it rejects *purposefulness*—having a motivation beyond mere exposure—as unprofessional. Without purposefulness, toughness is mere self-indulgence."

The Hidden Consensus. Beneath the apparent gulf that separates the public-journalism advocates from their elite critics is a broader ground of hopeful consensus. Although Leonard Downie objects vehemently to public journalism in theory, he has said that he respects most of the actual journalistic projects that have been done in its name. "The notion that in political campaigns you should shift some of your resources away from covering consultants and toward reporting the issues voters are primarily interested in—that is simply an evolution of good political journalism," he said.

> These are not new ways of reporting. Using public opinion surveys to find out what people think about their own communities, doing solutions reporting to see what things are working in solving societal problems—this is all part of what I would see as normal newspaper reporting.

But why, Downie asks, call this "public journalism"? Why not just call it "good journalism" and try to do more of it?

Other editors who have been on the warpath against the public-journalism concept, including William Woo of the *St. Louis Post-Dispatch* and

Howard Schneider of *Newsday,* have also said there is "nothing new" in the concept of public-spirited reporting. It's what papers should have been doing all along.

35 The public-journalism advocates might take this as a sign that they are winning the battle. In the 1970s and early 1980s, the military reformers in the Pentagon knew that the tide had turned their way when their opponents began saying that there was "nothing new" in the reformers' analysis. After all, its principles had been in circulation since the time of Douglas MacArthur, or Robert E. Lee, or for that matter Genghis Khan.

The rancor surrounding the public-journalism debate actually seems to arise from two misunderstandings. One concerns the nature of journalism's "involvement" in public life. When Leonard Downie and Max Frankel hear that term, they seem to imagine drumbeating campaigns by a newspaper on behalf of a particular candidate or a specific action-plan for a community. What the editors who have put public journalism into effect mean is "just good journalism"—that is, making people care about the issues that affect their lives, and helping them see how they can play a part in resolving those issues.

And when big-paper editors hear that the public journalists want to "listen" to the public and be "guided" by its concerns, the editors imagine something that they dread. This sounds all too similar to pure "user-driven" journalism, in which the marketing department surveys readers to find out what they're interested in, and the editors give them only that. This version of public journalism sounds like an invitation to abandon all critical judgment and turn the paper into a pure "feel good" advertising sheet. It misrepresents the best conception of public journalism, which is that editors and reporters will continue to exercise their judgment about issues, as they claim to now, but will pay more attention than today's elite journalists do to the impact of their work on the health of democracy.

"I think the people who make this criticism have not looked closely enough at what public interest journalism is doing," William Kovach, of the Nieman Foundation, said in 1995. "Papers are using surveys, but they are very careful surveys; they're doing a lot of work in neighborhoods. It's not a politically designed opinion poll to take a snap judgment." The editors who have undertaken public-journalism projects say they are using their best reportorial skills to determine not what people want to hear but what issues concern them most, and then applying that knowledge in their coverage.

Leonard Downie is right: This approach is "just good journalism." The real questions it raises are not hair-splitting quarrels about what it should be called but the practical work of implementation. . . .

Questions for Discussion

1. What exactly is the point of David Broder's speech—in his own words, as Fallows cites them, and according to Fallow's interpretation? In what sense

and to what degree can reporters be held "responsible" for what they write?

2. Most thoughtful people respond positively to the notion that politics in general and political campaigns in particular ought to connect more vitally with genuine national problems. But how do we know when we are dealing with genuine national problems? How does public journalism go about determining what they are? Do you find this approach satisfactory?
3. Recent surveys of the attitudes of current college students and recent college graduates conclude that the vast majority are alienated from politics. Suppose that the goals and methods of public journalism became more common—would that make a difference? Would you take a greater interest in politics if the politicians and their "hired guns" had less control over the news? Or does the alienation from politics have deeper sources than news coverage?
4. In criticizing public journalism, Leonard Downie of the *Washington Post* contends that "telling political candidates that they must come to a newspaper's forum . . . is dangerous . . . [and] not our role. There are plenty of institutions in every community to do this sort of thing." What institutions does he have in mind? Are they doing "this sort of thing" well? How do newspapers cover, for instance, debates between political candidates sponsored by the League of Women Voters?

For Convincing

Fallows contends that there is really a "hidden consensus" on the values, goals, and methods of public journalism—that even what he calls its "elitist critics" are moving in the direction of this reform movement. Look at political coverage in several newspapers and on reputable television news sources. Can you detect the alleged hidden consensus?

Write a paper affirming, denying, or partly affirming and denying Fallows's contention.

For Research and Inquiry

Since 1993 especially, much has been written about civic or public journalism. Thus far, as Fallows indicates, the experiment has been mostly restricted to "small time" papers, not the big national ones. As a class project, find out everything you can about the movement, and discuss the results of your research in class. Write a paper exploring this apparent limitation and suggesting ways that it might be overcome.

Additional Suggestions for Writing

Many journalists first practice their craft as college students working for campus newspapers more or less run by students. Study several editions of your campus paper (or, if there isn't one, of a paper from a campus close to yours).

Compare it, if possible, to other campus papers, and consult with students working for the paper. Discuss the results of your research as a class.

Then write an essay assessing the campus newspaper. Does it represent its community? all of it? How does it represent its community? What sources do the reporters use? To what extent and in what ways do the stories interpret campus events? Could the coverage be improved? How?

CHAPTER FIFTEEN

Liberal Education and Contemporary Culture

No institution in the United States receives more attention than our educational system. Studies of it abound, and new ones seem to appear almost weekly. It is rare not to hear or read something about education in the news every day, while scholarly articles and books about it proliferate beyond anyone's ability to read them all.

Why are we so obsessed with this topic? Most Americans believe that education is the route to a better life, the foundation of democracy, and the key to a strong economy, a competitive work force, and social and moral progress. "Better education" becomes the magic solution to so many questions concerning the nation's problems. We are obsessed with it, then, because our perceived stake in it is so high. That's why the press covers it extensively and why politicians push the issue toward the top of their campaigns for office and their legislative agendas.

With ideals and expectations so high, we should not be surprised that the educational system often disappoints enough to be called "failing" or "a failure." Until the past decade or so, however, almost all the criticism was directed at the public schools, especially high schools, while our universities and colleges were extolled as among the best in the world. Now higher education comes in for as much criticism as the public schools. As the cost of a college education continues to soar, rising much faster than the rate of inflation, more and more people wonder whether we are getting our money's worth, especially when a degree may no longer lead as often as it once did to a desired first job. Industry spends millions educating their employees after college, in part because many lack even basic communication skills, and businesses increasingly resort to hiring people whose degrees were earned in other countries. There is much talk that we are losing our competitive edge and that college graduates are no longer well-informed citizens, able to provide moral and intellectual leadership. In short, whereas once it was always the public schools that were failing, now many also apply the label to higher education, public and private.

The focus of concern is undergraduate education, especially the first two years, when students traditionally receive broad exposure to the liberal arts (literature, history, philosophy, and so on) prior to concentrating on their majors. The notion of "liberal arts" comes to us from ancient Athens and Rome, where "liberal" meant "free" in the sense of not being a slave: male citizens were educated in the liberal arts, slaves in the manual or practical arts. Liberal arts education still has strong identifications with social class: Virtually all of our most prestigious (that is, selective and usually expensive) universities claim to offer a liberal arts education, as contrasted with technical and vocational schools, which supposedly do not. One problem the liberal arts face in the United States is the association with privilege in a democratic culture uneasy with class distinctions. We want to say the liberal arts are for everyone. But are they?

Another problem is that university faculties cannot agree about what an "educated person" should know and therefore what a liberal arts education should be. The typical result is a laundry list of courses that satisfy what we call "basic requirements" but that do not constitute either a coherent course of study or a shared body of knowledge required for all students. Perhaps we should resign ourselves to such disagreements in a diverse culture with universities offering courses in virtually all fields of knowledge. Who's to say what an "educated person" should know? But if we can't answer this question, does the ideal of a liberal arts education have any substance, any meaning? Or is it merely an empty ideal we cling to out of habit?

Liberal arts education faces many other problems, none of which have easy solutions. For example, the traditional liberal arts education is limited to the West, primarily to the heritage of Greece and Rome as transmitted through later European culture to those parts of the world colonized by European powers. We live, however, in a world of global commerce, communication, and politics, where knowledge of the West alone is insufficient and can foster a destructive cultural arrogance. How inclusive can a liberal arts education become without losing focus and character? Can an essentially Western educational ideal function in a global context?

No matter how we answer the questions posed thus far—and even if we think, as many critics do, that liberal arts education is dead—we should ponder this: fundamentally, the liberal arts are the study of human achievements, cultures, and institutions. Because nothing human can be created or studied without language, the liberal arts also include English, foreign languages, and mathematics. Clearly, education wouldn't amount to much without humanistic study and couldn't go on at all without knowledge of the various symbol systems that enable all study. As long as we invest in education, we'll be investing in the liberal arts.

But if there is something permanent about the liberal arts, dealing as they do with human culture, they must be responsive to the times, to cultural change and pressures. All the selections in this chapter deal with contemporary American culture. "Collegiate Life: An Obituary" offers a sketch of the undergraduate student and college life based on extensive empirical research. The two articles "on the uses of a liberal education" offer sharply contrasting personal narratives, one by a professor at the University of Virginia, whose students are relatively privileged, and the other by a researcher into poverty, who created a liberal arts course for ghetto students in New York City. For the first writer a liberal arts education is too often "lite entertainment for bored college students," and for the second "a weapon in the hands of the restless poor"—a forceful reminder that the cultural situation in which liberal arts are taught has everything to do with what they are and how they function.

No inquiry into liberal education and contemporary culture can afford to ignore university culture itself, exclusive of students—in other words, the institutional structure. Our final reading, John Tagg's "The Decline of the Knowledge Factory," exposes this structure well en route to explaining why reforming liberal arts education is so difficult.

Above all, as we think about liberal arts education and contemporary culture, we must always remember how closely tied together they are. Physics may be physics regardless of where it's taught and to whom, but literature and philosophy, to mention only two important liberal arts, assuredly are not. No curriculum will work if it is out of touch with its culture, and a culture divorced from the liberal arts will be thin and puerile. Getting them to dance together more or less harmoniously while preserving the rigor and discipline of higher education is probably the major challenge we face.

ARTHUR LEVINE and JEANETTE S. CURETON

Collegiate Life: An Obituary

Arthur Levine is president of Teacher's College at Columbia University; Jeanette Cureton was an educational researcher at Harvard during their collaboration. Their book, When Hopes and Fears Collide: A Portrait of Today's College Student *(1998), presents the results of five years (1992–1997) of research involving many universities and colleges and including extensive conversations with students and student affairs officers. This article from the journal* Change *summarizes their conclusions.*

Our institutions of higher education are almost unimaginably diverse, each having its own unique history, character, and student profile. Any discussion of general trends or treatment of the "typical" or "average" student, therefore, may only imperfectly reflect your own experience. Yet we think you will recognize the portrait and find it helpful in understanding and articulating what's happening on college campuses today.

IN 1858, John Henry Cardinal Newman wrote *The Idea of a Univer-* 1
sity. His ideal was a residential community of students and teachers devoted to the intellect. To him, a college was "an alma mater, knowing her children one by one, not a foundry, or a mint, or a treadmill." Given a choice between an institution that dispensed with "residence and tutorial superintendence and gave its degrees to any person who passed an examination in a wide range of subjects" or "a university which . . . merely brought a number of young men together for three or four years," he chose the latter.

Newman's ideal was so appealing that it has been embraced regularly over the years by higher education luminaries from Robert Hutchins and Paul Goodman to Alexander Meiklejohn and Mortimer Adler. Belief in it remains a staple of nearly every college curriculum committee in the country.

But that ideal is moribund today. Except for a relatively small number of residential liberal arts colleges, institutions of higher education and their students are moving away from it at an accelerating pace. The notion of a living-learning community is dead or dying on most campuses today.

This is a principal finding of several studies we conducted between 1992 and 1997, which involved our surveying a representative sample of 9,100 undergraduate students and 270 chief student affairs officers, as well as holding focus groups on 28 campuses. . . .

DEMOGRAPHICS

A major reason for the changes we describe is simply demographic. In 5
comparison with their counterparts of the 1960s and 1970s, undergraduates today are more racially diverse and, on average, considerably older. In fact, since 1980, the lion's share of college enrollment growth has come from stu-

dents who might be described as nontraditional. By 1993, 24 percent of all college students were working full-time, according to our Undergraduate Survey; at two-year colleges, this figure had reached 39 percent.

By 1995, 44 percent of all college students were over 25 years old; 54 percent were working; 56 percent were female; and 43 percent were attending part-time. Currently, fewer than one in six of all undergraduates fit the traditional stereotype of the American college student attending full-time, being 18 to 22 years of age, and living on campus (see U.S. Department of Education, in Resources).

What this means is that higher education is not as central to the lives of today's undergraduates as it was to previous generations. Increasingly, college is just one of a multiplicity of activities in which they are engaged every day. For many, it is not even the most important of these activities; work and family often overshadow it.

As a consequence, older, part-time, and working students—especially those with children—often told us in our surveys that they wanted a different type of relationship with their colleges from the one undergraduates historically have had. They preferred a relationship like those they already enjoyed with their bank, the telephone company, and the supermarket.

WHAT STUDENTS WANT

Think about what you want from your bank. We know what we want: an ATM on every corner. And when we get to the ATM, we want there to be no line. We also would like a parking spot right in front of the ATM, and to have our checks deposited the moment they arrive at the bank, or perhaps the day before! And we want no mistakes in processing—unless they are in our favor. We also know what we do not want from our banks. We do not want them to provide us with softball leagues, religious counseling, or health services. We can arrange all of these things for ourselves and don't wish to pay extra fees for the bank to offer them.

Students are asking roughly the same thing from their colleges. They 10
want their colleges to be nearby and to operate at the hours most useful to them—preferably around the clock. They want convenience: easy, accessible parking (at the classroom door would not be bad); no lines; and a polite, helpful, efficient staff. They also want high-quality education but are eager for low costs. For the most part, they are willing to comparison shop, and they place a premium on time and money. They do not want to pay for activities and programs they do not use.

In short, students increasingly are bringing to higher education exactly the same consumer expectations they have for every other commercial establishment with which they deal. Their focus is on convenience, quality, service, and cost.

They believe that since they are paying for their education, faculty should give them the education they want; they make larger demands on faculty than past students ever have. They are also the target audience for alternatives to traditional higher education. They are likely to be drawn to distance education, which offers the convenience of instruction at home or the office.

They are prime candidates for stripped-down versions of college, located in the suburbs and business districts of our cities, that offer low-cost instruction made possible by heavy faculty teaching loads, mostly part-time faculties, limited selections of majors, and few electives. Proprietary institutions of this type are springing up around the country.

On campus, students are behaving like consumers, too. More than nine out of 10 chief student affairs officers told us in last year's Student Affairs Survey that student power in college governance has increased during the 1990s (or at least has remained the same), but that undergraduates are less interested in being involved in campus governance than in the past.

A small minority of undergraduates continue to want voting power or 15
control over admissions decisions, faculty appointments, bachelor's degree requirements, and the content of courses; however, a decreasing percentage desire similar roles in residential regulations and undergraduate discipline, areas in which students would seem most likely to want control. Overall, the proportion of students who want voting or controlling roles in institutional governance is at its lowest level in a quarter century, according to comparisons between our 1993 Undergraduate Survey and the 1969 and 1976 Carnegie Council surveys.

This is precisely the same attitude most of us hold with regard to the commercial enterprises we patronize. We don't want to be bothered with running the bank or the supermarket; we simply want them to do their jobs and do them well—to give us what we need without hassles or headaches. That is, help the consumers and don't get in their way. Students today are saying precisely the same things about their colleges.

Social Life

From a personal perspective, students are coming to college overwhelmed and more damaged than in the past. Chief student affairs officers in 1997 reported rises in eating disorders (on 58 percent of campuses), classroom disruption (on 44 percent), drug abuse (on 42 percent), alcohol abuse (on 35 percent), gambling (on 25 percent), and suicide attempts (on 23 percent).

As a consequence, academic institutions are being forced to expand their psychological counseling services. Three out of five colleges and universities reported last year that the use of counseling services had increased. Not only are counselors seeing students in record numbers, but the severity of the students' problems and the length of time needed to treat them are greater than in the past.

Students tell us they are frightened. They're afraid of deteriorating social and environmental conditions, international conflicts and terrorism, multiculturalism and their personal relationships, financing their education and getting jobs, and the future they will face. Nearly one-third of all college freshmen (30 percent) grew up with one or no parent (see Sax et al., in Resources). As one dean of students we talked with concluded, "Students expect the [college] community to respond to their needs—to make right their personal problems and those of society at large."

The effect of these accumulated fears and hurts is to divide students and 20
isolate them from one another. Students also fear intimacy in relationships; withdrawal is easier and less dangerous than engagement.

Traditional dating is largely dead on college campuses. At institutions all over the country, students told us, in the words of a University of Colorado undergraduate, "There is no such thing as dating here." Two-person dating has been replaced by group dating, in which men and women travel in unpartnered packs. It's a practice that provides protection from deeper involvement and intimacy for a generation that regularly told us in focus group interviews that they had never witnessed a successful adult romantic relationship.

Romantic relationships are seen as a burden, as a drag or potential anchor in a difficult world. Yet sexual relationships have not declined, even in the age of AIDS. Student descriptions of sexual activity are devoid of emotional content; they use words such as "scoping," "clocking," "hooking," "scamming," "scrumping," "mashing," and "shacking" to describe intimate relations.

In general, with increasing pressures on students, collegiate social life occupies a smaller part of their lives. In the words of an undergraduate at the University of the District of Columbia, "Life is just work, school, and home." In fact, one-fifth of those queried on our campus site visits (21 percent) defined their social lives in terms of studying; for another 11 percent, sleeping was all they cared about. When we asked students at the University of Colorado for the best adjective to describe this generation, the most common choice was "tired."

But not all of the retreat from social life is time-based. Chief student affairs officers describe students as loners more often now than in the past. Requests for single rooms in residence halls have skyrocketed. The thought of having a roommate is less appealing than it once was.

Similarly, group activities that once connected students on college cam- 25
puses are losing their appeal and are becoming more individualized. For instance, the venue for television watching has moved from the lounge to the dorm room. Film viewing has shifted from the theater to the home VCR. With student rooms a virtual menagerie of electronic and food-preparation equipment, students are living their lives in ways that allow them to avoid venturing out if they so choose.

Student Organizational Mitosis

None of this is to say that collegiate social life is dead, but its profile and location have changed. On campus, there is probably a greater diversity of activities available than ever before, but each activity—in the words of the chief student affairs officer of the University of Southern Mississippi—"appeals to smaller pockets of students."

This is, in many respects, the consequence of student organizational mitosis and the proliferation of the divides between undergraduates. For instance, the business club on one college campus divided into more than a dozen groups—including women's; black; Hispanic; gay, lesbian, and bisexual; and Asian and Filipino business clubs.

Deans of students regularly told us last year that "there is less larger-group socializing" and that "more people are doing things individually and in separate groups than campus-wide." In contrast to the Carnegie Council's 1979 study, current students describe themselves in terms of their differences, not their commonalities. Increasingly, they say they associate with people who are like themselves rather than different.

In the main, when students do take time to have fun, they are leaving campus to do so. Our Campus Site Visits study indicated that drinking is the primary form of recreation for 63 percent of students, followed closely by going to clubs and bars (59 percent) and simply getting off campus (52 percent). By contrast, the latter two activities were not mentioned in the Carnegie Council's 1979 study.

Drinking was not a surprise. It was the first choice in our earlier study, 30
but there is more binge drinking today. Drinking to get drunk has become the great escape for undergraduates.

Escaping from campus is a trend that goes hand in hand with the high numbers of students living in off-campus housing—more than triple the percentage in the late 1960s. Only 30 percent of students we surveyed reported living on campus. Add to this the fact that students are also spending less time on campus because of jobs and part-time attendance, and the result is that increasingly campuses are places in which instruction is the principal activity. Living and social life occur elsewhere.

MULTICULTURALISM

Campuses are more deeply divided along lines of race, gender, ethnicity, sexuality, and other differences today than in the past. A majority of deans at four-year colleges told us last year that the climate on campus can be described as politically correct (60 percent), civility has declined (57 percent), students of different racial and ethnic groups often do not socialize together (56 percent), reports of sexual harassment have increased (55 percent), and students feel uncomfortable expressing unpopular or controversial opinions (54 percent).

Multiculturalism is a painful topic for many students. The dirty words on college campuses now are no longer four letters: they are six-letter words like "racist" and "sexist"—and "homophobic," which is even longer. Students don't want to discuss the topic. In focus group interviews, students were more willing to tell us intimate details of their sex lives than to discuss diversity on campus.

Tension regarding diversity and difference runs high all across college life. Students talked about friction in the classroom; in the residence halls; in reactions to posters placed on campus or to visiting speakers; in campus activities and the social pursuits of the day; in hiring practices; in testing; in the dining room, library, bookstore, and sports facilities; in every aspect of their campus lives. In this sense, the campus in the 1990s is a less hospitable place for all undergraduates, regardless of background, than it once was.

ACADEMICS

Although instruction remains the principal on-campus activity that 35
brings undergraduates together, the academic arena is experiencing its own form of student disengagement. Pursuit of academic goals is clearly utilitarian. It's as if students have struck a bargain with their colleges. They're going to class all right, but they're going by the book: they're doing what's necessary to fulfill degree requirements and gain skills for a job, but then they're out the door. They're focused and career-oriented, and see college as instrumental in leading to a lucrative career. "Task-oriented students who focus on jobs" is how a Georgia Tech student affairs official labeled them.

Although students do not believe that a college education provides a money-back guarantee of future success, they feel that without one, a good job—much less a lucrative or prestigious job—is impossible to obtain. At the very least, it's a kind of insurance policy to hedge bets against the future. As a student at Portland (Oregon) Community College put it, "College is the difference between white-collar and blue-collar work." Fifty-seven percent of undergraduates we surveyed in 1993 believed that the chief benefit of a college education is increasing one's earning power—an 11 percentage-point increase since 1976.

By contrast, the value placed on nonmaterial goals (that is, learning to get along with people and formulating the values and goals of one's life) has plummeted since the late 1960s, dropping from 71 and 76 percent respectively to 50 and 47 percent. Whereas in 1969 these personal and philosophic goals were cited by students as the primary reasons for attending college, in 1993, students placed them at the bottom of the list.

Although a great number of students are focused and intent on pursuing career goals, many also face a variety of academic hurdles. They are coming to college less well prepared academically. Nearly three-fourths (73 percent) of deans in 1997 reported an increase within the last decade in the proportion of students requiring remedial or developmental education at two-year (81 percent) and four-year (64 percent) colleges.

Nearly one-third (32 percent) of all undergraduates surveyed reported having taken a basic skills or remedial course in reading, writing, or math, up from 29 percent in 1976. Despite high aspirations, a rising percentage of students simply are not prepared for the rigors of academe.

Another academic hurdle for students is a growing gap between how 40
students learn best and how faculty teach. According to research by Charles

Schroeder of the University of Missouri–Columbia, published in the September/ October 1993 *Change,* more than half of today's students perform best in a learning situation characterized by "direct, concrete experience, moderate-to-high degrees of structure, and a linear approach to learning. They value the practical and the immediate, and the focus of their perception is primarily on the physical world." According to Schroeder, three-quarters of faculty, on the other hand, "prefer the global to the particular; are stimulated by the realm of concepts, ideas, and abstractions; and assume that students, like themselves, need a high degree of autonomy in their work."

Small wonder, then, that frustration results and that every year faculty believe students are less well prepared, while students increasingly think their classes are incomprehensible. On the faculty side, this is certainly the case. The 1997 Student Affairs Survey revealed that at 74 percent of campuses, faculty complaints about students are on the rise. One result is that students and faculty are spending less time on campus together. With work and part-time attendance, students increasingly are coming to campus just for their classes.

This explains, in part, why students are taking longer to complete college. Fewer than two out of five are able to graduate in four years (see Astin et al., in Resources). Twenty-eight percent now require a fifth year to earn a baccalaureate, according to U.S. Department of Education statistics from 1996. In reality, obtaining the baccalaureate degree in four years is an anomaly today, particularly at public and less selective institutions.

The Future

The overwhelming majority of college students believe they will be successful. But their fears about relationships, romance, and their future happiness were continuing themes in every focus group. Their concerns about finances were overwhelming. There was not one focus group in which students did not ask whether they would be able to repay their student loans, afford to complete college, get a good job, or avoid moving home with Mom and Dad.

The college graduate driving a cab or working at the Gap was a universal anecdote. There was more mythology here than there were concrete examples, however. College graduates being forced to drive taxis is one of the great American legends, rivaled only by the tale of George Washington and the cherry tree.

Finances were a constant topic of discussion. Students told us of the need 45
to drop out, stop out, and attend college part-time because of tuition costs. They told us of the lengths they had to go to pay tuition—even giving blood. More than one in five (21 percent) who participated in the Undergraduate Survey said that someone who helped pay their tuition had been out of work while they attended college.

At heart, undergraduates are worried about whether we can make it as a society, and whether they can actually make it personally. In our surveys, the majority did say they expected to do better than their parents. But in our focus groups, students regularly told us, "We're going to be the first generation that doesn't surpass our parents in making more money." "How will I buy a house?" "How will I send my kids to college?"

This is a generation of students desperately clinging to the American Dream. Nearly nine out of 10 (88 percent) students are optimistic about their personal futures, but their hope, though broadly professed, is fragile and gossamer-like. Their lives are being challenged at every turn: in their families, their communities, their nation, and their world. This is a generation where hope and fear collide.

Conclusion

In sum, these changes in America's undergraduates add up to a requiem for historic notions of collegiate life—the ivory tower, the living-learning community, the residential college, and all the rest. But the changes are not sudden; they began even before Cardinal Newman wrote his classic. Most are a natural consequence of the democratization of higher education. This is what happens when 65 percent of all high school graduates go on to college and higher education is open to the nation's population across the lifespan. Four years of living in residence becomes a luxury few can afford.

So how should higher education respond? Dismissing the present or recalling a golden era lost are not particularly helpful—for the most part the changes are permanent. But there are a few things colleges can do.

The first is to focus. Most colleges have less time with their students on campus than in the past. They need to be very clear about what they want to accomplish with students and dramatically reduce the laundry lists of values and goals that constitute the typical mission statement.

The second is to use all opportunities available to educate students. Required events, such as orientation, should be used to educate rather than to deal with logistics. The awards a college gives should represent the values it most wants to teach. The same is true for speakers. The in-house newsletter can be used to educate. And of course, maybe the best advice is that almost any event can be used for educational purposes if the food and music are good enough.

Third, build on the strengths unique to every generation of students. For instance, current undergraduates, as part of their off-campus activities, are involved in public service—an astounding 64 percent of them, according to the Undergraduate Survey. Service learning, then, becomes an excellent vehicle to build into the curriculum and cocurriculum of most colleges.

Fourth, work to eliminate the forces that push students off campus unnecessarily. For example, most colleges talk a great deal about multiculturalism, but in general have not translated the rhetoric into a climate that will make the campus more hospitable to current students.

In like manner, using financial aid more to meet need than to reward merit would lessen the necessity for students to work while attending college. These are steps any college with the will and commitment can take. Both campus life and our students would benefit greatly.

RESOURCES

Astin, A. W., L. Tsui, and J. Avalos. *Degree Attainment Rates at American Colleges and Universities: Effects of Race, Gender, and Institutional Type.* Los Angeles: Higher Education Research Institute, UCLA, 1996.

Sax, L. J., A. W. Astin, W. S. Korn, and K. M. Mahoney. *The American Freshman: National Norms for Fall 1997.* Los Angeles: Higher Education Research Institute, UCLA, 1997.

U.S. Department of Education. National Center for Education Statistics. *Condition of Education, 1996* (NCES 96304). Washington: GPO, 1996.

———. National Center for Education Statistics. *Digest of Education Statistics, 1997* (NCES 98-015). Washington: GPO, 1997.

Questions for Discussion

1. The article opens by recalling Newman's 140-year-old *Idea of a University,* an ideal grounded in "a residential community of students and teachers devoted to the intellect." By definition ideals do not correspond to realities, but do you find the ideal of *alma mater* (Latin, "bountiful mother") appealing? If so, in what ways exactly? Why?
2. Which of the demographic trends delineated in paragraphs 4–6 seem most incompatible with the survival and vitality of the residential college?
3. As the subtitle of the article, "an obituary," would suggest, its view of student culture is gloomy and largely negative: Students are said to be afraid and tired, anxious about money, burdened with personal problems, inclined toward escapism, overly demanding of teachers and college services, socially alienated and fragmented, and so on. Would you say the sketch is accurate? fair? balanced? How much do the attitudes and behaviors described reflect American culture in general rather than student culture in particular? How different are they from the attitudes and behaviors of your parents and their parents?
4. Current college students are routinely described as taking an instrumental view of college, seeing it as only a means to an end, not as an end in itself. That is, "task-oriented students who focus on jobs" *is* the common view "we" take of "you." What intrinsic value might college have? How could it be an end in itself? Have your classes so far helped you to detect and appreciate the intrinsic value of learning and the overall college experience?

For Analysis and Convincing

If we are feeling charitable, we might describe the authors' suggestions at the end of the article as too general and obvious; if we are feeling less charitable, as vague and unhelpful. Can we do better?

Write an essay offering your own portrait of your generation of students or an essay that assesses the image offered here. Your portrait should reflect the demographics and other characteristics of your school. Then, working from the situation as you depict it, offer more concrete and detailed suggestions for coping with student problems and for improving campus life at your school. Address your essay to your school's student governing body.

For Inquiry and Dialogue

If the residential college is dying or dead, as these authors claim and as a good deal of independent evidence supports, what model might replace it? Could we, for example, build a sense of student community and interaction between students and teachers via the electronic media, especially computers, as some have suggested? If student groups are fragmenting into smaller and smaller communities, how can we get these groups back together and engaged in useful dialogue? In short, a key question to think about and discuss is, How can we recapture something of the values represented by the residential college in an environment that does not lend itself to a closely knit community of students and teachers?

LOIS BERNSTEIN

Photograph

When the University of Chicago was founded in the late 19th century, its trustees chose for its original buildings the English Gothic architectural style of Oxford University rather than a more contemporary design. The photograph below accompanied a recent New York Times *article about the University's refusal to soften its rigorous academic standards and requirements in order to attract more applicants. The students are sitting in Hutchinson Commons, the main dining hall, which was constructed in 1901.*

For Discussion

Architecture is a form of visual rhetoric, similar to public sculpture. The style of the buildings at a college or university makes an argument about the education offered there: its purpose, origins, and values. How do you read the argument implied by the interior of this college dining hall? Discuss the architecture of your own school's campus. Is it all in one style? A mix of styles and periods? Do different buildings seem to make different arguments? Consider these arguments in the context of changing ideas about liberal arts education, as discussed in the readings in this chapter.

MARK EDMUNDSON

On the Uses of Liberal Education: As Lite Entertainment for Bored College Students

This essay and the next one, by Earl Shorris, appeared together in the September 1997 issue of Harper's Magazine. *Each can stand alone as an argument about the liberal arts and culture, but they are far more interesting read together as contrasting perspectives. Mark Edmundson is a professor at the prestigious University of Virginia and thus teaches relatively privileged students of traditional college age, while Shorris, a poverty researcher, discusses an experimental liberal arts program he developed for older, disadvantaged students in New York City. As one might expect, the view from "the top" is radically different from the view at "the bottom." Yet, at a deeper level, the essays connect and illuminate each other in provocative ways.*

Edmundson wrote for people of his age, the sixties generation, not for college students. If you wonder about how professors see you, this essay may enlighten and perhaps irritate. Of course, his view does not represent all professors, nor do University of Virginia students typify the current population. But we think most professors and students will see something of themselves and their institutions in what Edmundson has to say. Furthermore, the issues he raises surely relate to higher education generally.

TODAY IS evaluation day in my Freud class, and everything has changed. The class meets twice a week, late in the afternoon, and the clientele, about fifty undergraduates, tends to drag in and slump, looking disconsolate and a little lost, waiting for a jump start. To get the discussion moving, they usually require a joke, an anecdote, an off-the-wall question—When you were a kid, were your Halloween getups ego costumes, id costumes, or superego costumes? That sort of thing. But today, as soon as I flourish the forms, a buzz rises in the room. Today they write their assessments of the course, their assessments of me, and they are without a doubt wide-awake. "What is your evaluation of the instructor?" asks question number eight, entreating them to circle a number between five (excellent) and one (poor, poor). Whatever interpretive subtlety they've acquired during the term is now out the window. Edmundson: one to five, stand and shoot. 1

And they do. As I retreat through the door—I never stay around for this phase of the ritual—I look over my shoulder and see them toiling away like the devil's auditors. They're pitched into high writing gear, even the ones who struggle to squeeze out their journal entries word by word, stoked on a procedure they have by now supremely mastered. They're playing the informed consumer, letting the provider know where he's come through and where he's not quite up to snuff.

But why am I so distressed, bolting like a refugee out of my own classroom, where I usually hold easy sway? Chances are the evaluations will be much like what they've been in the past—they'll be just fine. It's likely that I'll be commended for being "interesting" (and I am commended, many times over), that I'll be cited for my relaxed and tolerant ways (that happens, too), that my sense of humor and capacity to connect the arcana of the subject matter with current culture will come in for some praise (yup). I've been hassled this term, finishing a manuscript, and so haven't given their journals the attention I should have, and for that I'm called—quite civilly, though—to account. Overall, I get off pretty well.

Yet I have to admit that I do not much like the image of myself that emerges from these forms, the image of knowledgeable, humorous detachment and bland tolerance. I do not like the forms themselves, with their number ratings, reminiscent of the sheets circulated after the TV pilot has just played to its sample audience in Burbank. Most of all I dislike the attitude of calm consumer expertise that pervades the responses. I'm disturbed by the serene belief that my function—and, more important, Freud's, or Shakespeare's, or Blake's—is to divert, entertain, and interest. Observes one respondent, not at all unrepresentative: "Edmundson has done a fantastic job of presenting this difficult, important & controversial material in an enjoyable and approachable way."

5 Thanks but no thanks. I don't teach to amuse, to divert, or even, for that matter, to be merely interesting. When someone says she "enjoyed" the course—and that word crops up again and again in my evaluations—somewhere at the edge of my immediate complacency I feel encroaching self-dislike. That is not at all what I had in mind. The off-the-wall questions and the sidebar jokes are meant as lead-ins to stronger stuff—in the case of the Freud course, to a complexly tragic view of life. But the affability and the one-liners often seem to be all that land with the students; their journals and evaluations leave me little doubt.

I want some of them to say that they've been changed by the course. I want them to measure themselves against what they've read. It's said that some time ago a Columbia University instructor used to issue a harsh two-part question. One: What book did you most dislike in the course? Two: What intellectual or characterological flaws in you does that dislike point to? The hand that framed that question was surely heavy. But at least it compels one to see intellectual work as a confrontation between two people, student and author, where the stakes matter. Those Columbia students were being asked to relate the quality of an encounter, not rate the action as though it had unfolded on the big screen.

Why are my students describing the Oedipus complex and the death drive as being interesting and enjoyable to contemplate? And why am I coming across as an urbane, mildly ironic, endlessly affable guide to this intellectual territory, operating without intensity, generous, funny, and loose?

Because that's what works. On evaluation day, I reap the rewards of my partial compliance with the culture of my students and, too, with the culture of the university as it now operates. It's a culture that's gotten little exploration. Current critics tend to think that liberal-arts education is in crisis because universities have been invaded by professors with peculiar ideas: deconstruction, Lacanianism, feminism, queer theory. They believe that genius and tradition are out and that P.C., multiculturalism, and identity politics are in because of an invasion by tribes of tenured radicals, the late millennial equivalents of the Visigoth hordes that cracked Rome's walls.

But mulling over my evaluations and then trying to take a hard, extended look at campus life both here at the University of Virginia and around the country eventually led me to some different conclusions. To me, liberal-arts education is as ineffective as it is now not chiefly because there are a lot of strange theories in the air. (Used well, those theories can be illuminating.) Rather, it's that university culture, like American culture writ large, is, to put it crudely, ever more devoted to consumption and entertainment, to the using and using up of goods and images. For someone growing up in America now, there are few available alternatives to the cool consumer worldview. My students didn't ask for that view, much less create it, but they bring a consumer [worldview] to school, where it exerts a powerful, and largely unacknowledged, influence. If we want to understand current universities, with their multiple woes, we might try leaving the realms of expert debate and fine ideas and turning to the classrooms and campuses, where a new kind of weather is gathering.

10 From time to time I bump into a colleague in the corridor and we have what I've come to think of as a Joon Lee fest. Joon Lee is one of the best students I've taught. He's endlessly curious, has read a small library's worth, seen every movie, and knows all about showbiz and entertainment. For a class of mine he wrote an essay using Nietzsche's Apollo and Dionysus to analyze the pop group The Supremes. A trite, cultural-studies bonbon? Not at all. He said striking things about conceptions of race in America and about how they shape our ideas of beauty. When I talk with one of his other teachers, we run on about the general splendors of his work and presence. But what inevitably follows a JL fest is a mournful reprise about the divide that separates him and a few other remarkable students from their contemporaries. It's not that some aren't nearly as bright—in terms of intellectual ability, my students are all that I could ask for. Instead, it's that Joon Lee has decided to follow his interests and let them make him into a singular and rather eccentric man; in his charming way, he doesn't mind being at odds with most anyone.

It's his capacity for enthusiasm that sets Joon apart from what I've come to think of as the reigning generational style. Whether the students are sorority/fraternity types, grunge aficionados, piercer/tattooers, black or white, rich or middle class (alas, I teach almost no students from truly poor backgrounds), they are, nearly across the board, very, very self-contained. On good days they display a light, appealing glow; on bad days, shuffling disgruntlement. But there's little fire, little passion to be found. . . .

How did my students reach this peculiar state in which all passion seems to be spent? I think that many of them have imbibed their sense of self from consumer culture in general and from the tube in particular. They're the progeny of 100 cable channels and omnipresent Blockbuster outlets. TV, Marshall McLuhan famously said, is a cool medium. Those who play best on it are low-key and nonassertive; they blend in. Enthusiasm, à la Joon Lee, quickly looks absurd. The form of character that's most appealing on TV is calmly self-interested though never greedy, attuned to the conventions, and ironic. Judicious timing is preferred to sudden self-assertion. The TV medium is inhospitable to inspiration, improvisation, failures, slipups. All must run perfectly.

Naturally, a cool youth culture is a marketing bonanza for producers of the right products, who do all they can to enlarge that culture and keep it grinding. The Internet, TV, and magazines now teem with what I call persona ads, ads for Nikes and Reeboks and jeeps and Blazers that don't so much endorse the capacities of the product per se as show you what sort of person you will be once you've acquired it. The jeep ad that features hip, outdoorsy kids whipping a Frisbee from mountaintop to mountaintop isn't so much about what jeeps can do as it is about the kind of people who own them. Buy a Jeep and be one with them. The ad is of little consequence in itself, but expand its message exponentially and you have the central thrust of current consumer culture—buy in order to be.

Most of my students seem desperate to blend in, to look right, not to make a spectacle of themselves. . . . The specter of the uncool creates a subtle tyranny. It's apparently an easy standard to subscribe to, this Letterman-like, Tarantino-like cool, but once committed to it, you discover that matters are rather different. You're inhibited, except on ordained occasions, from showing emotion, stifled from trying to achieve anything original. You're made to feel that even the slightest departure from the reigning code will get you genially ostracized. This is a culture tensely committed to a laid-back norm.

Am I coming off like something of a crank here? Maybe. Oscar Wilde, 15
who is almost never wrong, suggested that it is perilous to promiscuously contradict people who are much younger than yourself. Point taken. But one of the lessons that consumer hype tries to insinuate is that we must never rebel against the new, never even question it. If it's new—a new need, a new product, a new show, a new style, a new generation—it must be good. So maybe, even at the risk of winning the withered, brown laurels of crankdom, it pays to resist newness-worship and cast a colder eye.

Praise for my students? I have some of that too. What my students are, at their best, is decent. They are potent believers in equality. They help out at the soup kitchen and volunteer to tutor poor kids to get a stripe on their resumes, sure. But they also want other people to have a fair shot. And in their commitment to fairness they are discerning; there you see them at their intellectual best. If I were on trial and innocent, I'd want them on the jury.

What they will not generally do, though, is indict the current system. They won't talk about how the exigencies of capitalism lead to a reserve army of the unemployed and nearly inevitable misery. That would be getting too loud, too brash. For the pervading view is the cool consumer perspective, where passion and strong admiration are forbidden. "To stand in awe of nothing, Numicus, is perhaps the one and only thing that can make a man happy and keep him so," says Horace in the Epistles, and I fear that his lines ought to hang as a motto over the university in this era of high consumer capitalism.

It's easy to mount one's high horse and blame the students for this state of affairs. But they didn't create the present culture of consumption. (It was largely my own generation, that of the Sixties, that let the counterculture search for pleasure devolve into a quest for commodities.) And they weren't the ones responsible, when they were six and seven and eight years old, for unplugging the TV set from time to time or for hauling off and kicking a hole through it. It's my generation of parents who sheltered these students, kept them away from the hard knocks of everyday life, making them cautious and overfragile, who demanded that their teachers, from grade school on, flatter them endlessly so that the kids are shocked if their college profs don't reflexively suck up to them.

Of course, the current generational style isn't simply derived from culture and environment. It's also about dollars. Students worry that taking too many chances with their educations will sabotage their future prospects. They're aware of the fact that a drop that looks more and more like one wall of the Grand Canyon separates the top economic tenth from the rest of the population. There's a sentiment currently abroad that if you step aside for a moment, to write, to travel, to fall too hard in love, you might lose position permanently. We may be on a conveyor belt, but it's worse down there on the filth-strewn floor. So don't sound off, don't blow your chance. . . .

From the start, the contemporary university's relationship with students 20
has a solicitous, nearly servile tone. As soon as someone enters his junior year in high school, and especially if he's living in a prosperous zip code, the informational material—the advertising—comes flooding in. Pictures, testimonials, videocassettes, and CD ROMs (some bidden, some not) arrive at the door from colleges across the country, all trying to capture the student and his tuition cash. The freshman-to-be sees photos of well-appointed dorm rooms; of elaborate phys-ed facilities; of fine dining rooms; of expertly kept sports fields; of orchestras and drama troupes; of students working alone (no overbearing grown-ups in range), peering with high seriousness into computers and microscopes; or of students arrayed outdoors in attractive conversational garlands.

Occasionally—but only occasionally, for we usually photograph rather badly; in appearance we tend at best to be styleless—there's a professor teaching a class. (The college catalogues I received, by my request only, in the late Sixties were austere affairs full of professors' credentials and course descriptions; it was clear on whose terms the enterprise was going to unfold.) A college financial officer recently put matters to me in concise, if slightly melodramatic, terms: "Colleges don't have admissions offices anymore, they have marketing departments." Is it surprising that someone who has been approached with photos and tapes, bells and whistles, might come in thinking that the Freud and Shakespeare she had signed up to study were also going to be agreeable treats?

How did we reach this point? In part the answer is a matter of demographics and (surprise) of money. Aided by the G.I. bill, the college-going population in America dramatically increased after the Second World War. Then came the baby boomers, and to accommodate them, schools continued to grow. Universities expand easily enough, but with tenure locking faculty in for lifetime jobs, and with the general reluctance of administrators to eliminate their own slots, it's not easy for a university to contract. So after the baby boomers had passed through—like a fat meal digested by a boa constrictor—the colleges turned to energetic promotional strategies to fill the empty chairs. And suddenly college became a buyer's market. What students and their parents wanted had to be taken more and more into account. That usually meant creating more comfortable, less challenging environments, places where almost no one failed, everything was enjoyable, and everyone was nice.

Just as universities must compete with one another for students, so must the individual departments. At a time of rank economic anxiety, the English and history majors have to contend for students against the more success-insuring branches, such as the sciences and the commerce school. In 1968, more than 21 percent of all the bachelor's degrees conferred in America were in the humanities; by 1993, that number had fallen to about 13 percent. The humanities now must struggle to attract students, many of whose parents devoutly wish they would study something else.

One of the ways we've tried to stay attractive is by loosening up. We grade much more softly than our colleagues in science. In English, we don't give many Ds, or Cs for that matter. (The rigors of Chem 101 create almost as many English majors per year as do the splendors of Shakespeare.) A professor at Stanford recently explained grade inflation in the humanities by observing that the undergraduates were getting smarter every year; the higher grades simply recorded how much better they were than their predecessors. Sure.

25 Along with softening the grades, many humanities departments have relaxed major requirements. There are some good reasons for introducing more choice into curricula and requiring fewer standard courses. But the move, like many others in the university now, jibes with a tendency to serve—and not challenge—the students. Students can also float in and out of classes during the first two weeks of each term without making any commitment. The common name for this time span—shopping period—speaks volumes about the consumer mentality that's now in play. Usually, too, the kids can drop courses up until the last month with only an innocuous "W" on their transcripts. Does a course look too challenging? No problem. Take it pass-fail. A happy consumer is, by definition, one with multiple options, one who can always have what he wants. And since a course is something the students and their parents have bought and paid for, why can't they do with it pretty much as they please?

A sure result of the university's widening elective leeway is to give students more power over their teachers. Those who don't like you can simply avoid you. If the clientele dislikes you en masse, you can be left without students, period. My first term teaching I walked into my introduction to poetry course and found it inhabited by one student, the gloriously named Bambi Lynn Dean. Bambi and I chatted amiably awhile, but for all that she and the pleasure of her name could offer, I was fast on the way to meltdown. It was all a mistake, luckily, a problem with the scheduling book. Everyone was waiting for me next door. But in a dozen years of teaching I haven't forgotten that feeling of being ignominiously marooned. For it happens to others, and not always because of scheduling glitches. I've seen older colleagues go through hot embarrassment at not having enough students sign up for their courses: they graded too hard, demanded too much, had beliefs too far out of keeping with the existing disposition. It takes only a few such instances to draw other members of the professoriat further into line. . . .

How does one prosper with the present clientele? Many of the most successful professors now are the ones who have "decentered" their classrooms. There's a new emphasis on group projects and on computer-generated exchanges among the students. What they seem to want most is to talk to one another. A classroom now is frequently an "environment," a place highly conducive to the exchange of existing ideas, the students' ideas. Listening to one another, students sometimes change their opinions. But what they generally can't do is acquire a new vocabulary, a new perspective, that will cast issues in a fresh light.

The Socratic method—the animated, sometimes impolite give-and-take between student and teacher—seems too jagged for current sensibilities. Students frequently come to my office to tell me how intimidated they feel in class; the thought of being embarrassed in front of the group fills them with dread. I remember a student telling me how humiliating it was to be corrected by the teacher, by me. So I asked the logical question: "Should I let a major factual error go by so as to save discomfort?" The student—a good student, smart and earnest—said that was a tough question. He'd need to think about it.

Disturbing? Sure. But I wonder, are we really getting students ready for Socratic exchange with professors when we push them off into vast lecture rooms, two and three hundred to a class, sometimes face them with only grad students until their third year, and signal in our myriad professorial ways that we often have much better things to do than sit in our offices and talk with them? How bad will the student–faculty ratios have to become, how teeming the lecture courses, before we hear students righteously complaining, as they did thirty years ago, about the impersonality of their schools, about their decline into knowledge factories? "This is a firm," said Mario Savio at Berkeley during the Free Speech protests of the Sixties, "and if the Board of Regents are the board of directors, . . . then . . . the faculty are a bunch of employees and we're the raw material. But we're a bunch of raw material that don't mean . . . to be made into any product."

30 Teachers who really do confront students, who provide significant challenges to what they believe, can be very successful, granted. But sometimes such professors generate more than a little trouble for themselves. A controversial teacher can send students hurrying to the deans and the counselors, claiming to have been offended. ("Offensive" is the preferred term of repugnance today, just as "enjoyable" is the summit of praise.) Colleges have brought in hordes of counselors and deans to make sure that everything is smooth, serene, unflustered, that everyone has a good time. To the counselor, to the dean, and to the university legal squad, that which is normal, healthy, and prudent is best. . . .

Then how do those who at least occasionally promote genius and high literary ideals look to current students? How do we appear, those of us who take teaching to be something of a performance art and who imagine that if you give yourself over completely to your subject you'll be rewarded with insight beyond what you individually command?

I'm reminded of an old piece of newsreel footage I saw once. The speaker (perhaps it was Lenin, maybe Trotsky) was haranguing a large crowd. He was expostulating, arm waving, carrying on. Whether it was flawed technology or the man himself, I'm not sure, but the orator looked like an intricate mechanical device that had sprung into fast-forward. To my students, who mistrust enthusiasm in every form, that's me when I start riffing about Freud or Blake. But more and more, as my evaluations showed, I've been replacing enthusiasm and intellectual animation with stand-up routines, keeping it all at arm's length, praising under the cover of irony.

It's too bad that the idea of genius has been denigrated so far, because it actually offers a live alternative to the demoralizing culture of hip in which most of my students are mired. By embracing the works and lives of extraordinary people, you can adapt new ideals to revise those that came courtesy of your parents, your neighborhood, your clan—or the tube. The aim of a good liberal-arts education was once, to adapt an observation by the scholar Walter Jackson Bate, to see that "we need not be the passive victims of what we deterministically call 'circumstances' (social, cultural, or reductively psychological-personal), but that by linking ourselves through what Keats calls an 'immortal free-masonry' with the great we can become freer—freer to be ourselves, to be what we most want and value."

But genius isn't just a personal standard; genius can also have political effect. To me, one of the best things about democratic thinking is the conviction that genius can spring up anywhere. Walt Whitman is born into the working class and thirty-six years later we have a poetic image of America that gives a passionate dimension to the legalistic brilliance of the Constitution. A democracy needs to constantly develop, and to do so it requires the most powerful visionary minds to interpret the present and to propose possible shapes for the future. By continuing to notice and praise genius, we create a culture in which the kind of poetic gamble that Whitman made—a gamble in which failure would have entailed rank humiliation, depression, maybe suicide—still takes place. By rebelling against established ways of seeing and saying things, genius helps us to apprehend how malleable the present is and how promising and fraught with danger is the future. If we teachers do not endorse genius and self-overcoming, can we be surprised when our students find their ideal images in TV's latest persona ads?

35 A world uninterested in genius is a despondent place, whose sad denizens drift from coffee bar to Prozac dispensary, unfired by ideals, by the glowing image of the self that one might become. As Northrop Frye says in a beautiful and now dramatically unfashionable sentence, "The artist who uses the same energy and genius that Homer and Isaiah had will find that he not only lives in the same palace of art as Homer and Isaiah, but lives in it at the same time." We ought not to deny the existence of such a place simply because we, or those we care for, find the demands it makes intimidating, the rent too high.

What happens if we keep trudging along this bleak course? What happens if our most intelligent students never learn to strive to overcome what they are? What if genius, and the imitation of genius, become silly, outmoded ideas? What you're likely to get are more and more one-dimensional men and women. These will be people who live for easy pleasures, for comfort and prosperity, who think of money first, then second, and third, who hug the status quo; people who believe in God as a sort of insurance policy (cover your bets); people who are never surprised. They will be people so pleased with themselves (when they're not in despair at the general pointlessness of their lives) that they cannot imagine humanity could do better. They'll think it their highest duty to clone themselves as frequently as possible. They'll claim to be happy, and they'll live a long time.

It is probably time now to offer a spate of inspiring solutions. Here ought to come a list of reforms, with due notations about a core curriculum and various requirements. What the traditionalists who offer such solutions miss is that no matter what our current students are given to read, many of them will simply translate it into melodrama, with flat characters and predictable morals. (The unabated capitalist culture that conservative critics so often endorse has put students in a position to do little else.) One can't simply wave a curricular wand and reverse acculturation.

Perhaps it would be a good idea to try firing the counselors and sending half the deans back into their classrooms, dismantling the football team and making the stadium into a playground for local kids, emptying the fraternities, and boarding up the student-activities office. Such measures would convey the message that American colleges are not northern outposts of Club Med. A willingness on the part of the faculty to defy student conviction and affront them occasionally—to be usefully offensive—also might not be a bad thing. We professors talk a lot about subversion, which generally means subverting the views of people who never hear us talk or read our work. But to subvert the views of our students, our customers, that would be something else again.

Ultimately, though, it is up to individuals—and individual students in particular—to make their own way against the current sludgy tide. There's still the library, still the museum, there's still the occasional teacher who lives to find things greater than herself to admire. There are still fellow students who have not been cowed. Universities are inefficient, cluttered, archaic places, with many unguarded corners where one can open a book or gaze out onto the larger world and construe it freely. Those who do as much, trusting themselves against the weight of current opinion, will have contributed something to bringing this sad dispensation to an end. As for myself, I'm canning my low-key one-liners; when the kids' TV-based tastes come to the fore, I'll aim and shoot. And when it's time to praise genius, I'll try to do it in the right style, full-out, with faith that finer artistic spirits (maybe not Homer and Isaiah quite, but close, close), still alive somewhere in the ether, will help me out when my invention flags, the students doze, or the dean mutters into the phone. I'm getting back to a more exuberant style; I'll be expostulating and arm waving straight into the millennium, yes I will.

Questions for Discussion

1. This essay links with the previous one in at least one important way: both see a "consumer mentality" in contemporary students and both are critical of it. But to what extent is it *appropriate* to view colleges and universities as vendors, selling a service in demand, much like any other business? To what extent is this economic understanding limited?
2. The sixties generation is often described as anticommercial and antibusiness, an attitude clearly present in this essay's negative comments on capitalism. To what extent is Edmundson's view a continuation of the rebellions of the sixties or perhaps guilt-ridden compensation for his obviously becoming part of "the system"? If we "read" him this way, must we also dismiss what he has to say? Is his critique any less valid?
3. The more or less conscious cultivation of "cool" or "laid back" extends beyond the sixties to at least "the beats" of the fifties, and arguably further, and thus provides some common ground for half a century or more of young adult experience. Such an attitude has always been vulnerable to Edmundson's charge of lacking "passion and strong admiration." To what extent is "cool" an appropriate and functional way of coping with modern society? Is passion necessary for a meaningful life? If we should have "strong admirations," for what or whom should we have them? Should these commitments be unqualified and uncritical—that is, total?
4. In a part of his essay not printed here, Edmundson contends that "some measure of self-dislike, or self-discontent . . . [is] a prerequisite for getting an education that matters" and that "my students . . . usually lack the confidence to acknowledge . . . their ignorance." What is "an education that matters"? What does self-discontent have to do with it? Is his charge true? Are you and your friends too content with yourselves and too insecure to admit ignorance?

For Analysis and Persuasion

Edmundson claims to want his students to be "changed by [his] course," to "measure themselves against what they've read." As he goes on to explain, "intellectual work [should be] a *confrontation* between two people, student and author, where the stakes matter" (our emphasis).

If he is right, most education is wrong, for very little of it changes us, takes our measure, or confronts us with anything whose stakes are higher than meeting a requirement. But there are exceptions. In an essay describe a course, a work, or a teacher (or all three) that did ignite the fire Edmundson admires, that did change you. Then analyze the experience: What was it, exactly, that made the difference?

In the second part of your essay, which you can think of as an "open letter" to college teachers, advocate whatever it was that made the difference so that professors themselves might be moved to alter their attitudes and approaches. Be tactful—don't make your essay merely an indictment of teachers. And be thoughtful—perhaps what worked for you won't work all the time or in all classes or subjects.

For Inquiry

The unifying theme of Edmundson's essay is power—the power of money and of economic forces generally, the power of the media to shape culture, the power of students over professors, and so on. The last he may exaggerate, because student evaluations alone almost never make or break a professor's career. But in any case professors must be evaluated as teachers somehow, and part of this process nearly everywhere are student evaluations.

Secure a copy of the current instrument or instruments used at your school. Consider it/them carefully. Are they as blunt and unsubtle as Edmundson depicts them? Do they encourage professors to entertain rather than instruct? Based on your analysis, explore ways to improve teacher evaluations. If you know or can find out what committees charged with designing evaluations have considered, ponder their ideas and approaches as well. Then consider how the evaluations are used. Can they be applied more constructively? If so, what are the options? What are the "up" and "down" sides of each?

Design your inquiry as an independent report to whatever committee or committees are charged with creating and assessing student evaluations.

EARL SHORRIS

On the Uses of Liberal Education: As a Weapon in the Hands of the Restless Poor

Earl Shorris was several years into research for a book on poverty and thought he had heard it all—until he met a remarkable young woman, a prison inmate, who gave him the idea for an experimental curriculum in the liberal arts for poor people. The lengthy story of how he developed his idea and found modest financial support for it we have left out, the better to highlight what counts most—attitudes, course content, the students, teaching methods, and results, all of which he reports with disarming honesty, in an account of genuine power.

We agree with Shorris that his course of study cannot reach everyone nor solve by itself the massive and complicated problem of poverty in the United States. But its success is worth pondering, especially when we consider the billions we spend on poverty every year, money that brings relief but no solution. Perhaps the big question implicit in this essay is one we need to address: Do Americans really want to empower *the poor, give them weapons to resist their condition, make them more personally and socially effective? If so, what role can a liberal arts education play?*

NEXT MONTH I will publish a book about poverty in America, 1
but not the book I intended. The world took me by surprise—not once, but again and again. The poor themselves led me in directions I could not have imagined, especially the one that came out of a conversation in a maximum-security prison for women that is set, incongruously, in a lush Westchester suburb fifty miles north of New York City.

I had been working on the book for about three years when I went to the Bedford Hills Correctional Facility for the first time. The staff and inmates had developed a program to deal with family violence, and I wanted to see how their ideas fit with what I had learned about poverty.

Numerous forces—hunger, isolation, illness, landlords, police, abuse, neighbors, drugs, criminals, and racism, among many others—exert themselves on the poor at all times and enclose them, making up a "surround of force" from which, it seems, they cannot escape. I had come to understand that this was what kept the poor from being political and that the absence of politics in their lives was what kept them poor. I don't mean "political" in the sense of voting in an election but in the way Thucydides used the word: to mean activity with other people at every level, from the family to the neighborhood to the broader community to the city-state.

By the time I got to Bedford Hills, I had listened to more than six hundred people, some of them over the course of two or three years. Although my method is that of the bricoleur, the tinkerer who assembles a thesis of the bric-a-brac he finds in the world, I did not think there would be any more surprises. But I had not counted on what Viniece Walker was to say.

. . . Viniece Walker came to Bedford Hills when she was twenty years 5
old, a high school dropout who read at the level of a college sophomore, a graduate of crackhouses, the streets of Harlem, and a long alliance with a brutal man. On the surface Viniece has remained as tough as she was on the street. She speaks bluntly, and even though she is HIV positive and the virus has progressed during her time in prison, she still swaggers as she walks down the long prison corridors. While in prison, Niecie, as she is known to her friends, completed her high school requirements and began to pursue a college degree (psychology is the only major offered at Bedford Hills, but Niecie also took a special interest in philosophy). She became a counselor to women with a history of family violence and a comforter to those with AIDS.

Only the deaths of other women cause her to stumble in the midst of her swaggering step, to spend days alone with the remorse that drives her to seek redemption. She goes through life as if she had been imagined by Dostoevsky, but even more complex than his fictions, alive, a person, a fair-skinned and freckled African-American woman, and in prison. It was she who responded to my sudden question, "Why do you think people are poor?"

We had never met before. The conversation around us focused on the abuse of women. Niecie's eyes were perfectly opaque—hostile, prison eyes. Her mouth was set in the beginning of a sneer.

"You got to begin with the children," she said, speaking rapidly, clipping out the street sounds as they came into her speech.

She paused long enough to let the change of direction take effect, then resumed the rapid, rhythmless speech. "You've got to teach the moral life of downtown to the children. And the way you do that, Earl, is by taking them downtown to plays, museums, concerts, lectures, where they can learn the moral life of downtown."

I smiled at her, misunderstanding, thinking I was indulging her. "And 10
then they won't be poor anymore?"

She read every nuance of my response, and answered angrily, "And they won't be poor no more.

"What you mean is—"

"What I mean is what I said—a moral alternative to the street."

She didn't speak of jobs or money. In that, she was like the others I had listened to. No one had spoken of jobs or money. But how could the "moral life of downtown" lead anyone out from the surround of force? How could a museum push poverty away? Who can dress in statues or eat the past? And what of the political life? Had Niecie skipped a step or failed to take a step? The way out of poverty was politics, not the "moral life of downtown." But to enter the public world, to practice the political life, the poor had first to learn to reflect. That was what Niecie meant by the "moral life of downtown." She did not make the error of divorcing ethics from politics. Niecie had simply said, in a kind of shorthand, that no one could step out of the panicking circumstance of poverty directly into the public world.

Although she did not say so, I was sure that when she spoke of the 15
"moral life of downtown" she meant something that had happened to her. With no job and no money, a prisoner, she had undergone a radical transformation. She had followed the same path that led to the invention of politics in ancient Greece. She had learned to reflect. In further conversation it became clear that when she spoke of "the moral life of downtown" she meant the humanities, the study of human constructs and concerns, which has been the source of reflection for the secular world since the Greeks first stepped back from nature to experience wonder at what they beheld. If the political life was the way out of poverty, the humanities provided an entrance to reflection and the political life. The poor did not need anyone to release them; an escape route existed. But to open this avenue to reflection and politics a major distinction between the preparation for the life of the rich and the life of the poor had to be eliminated.

Once Niecie had challenged me with her theory, the comforts of tinkering came to an end; I could no longer make an homage to the happenstance world and rest. To test Niecie's theory, students, faculty, and facilities were required. Quantitative measures would have to be developed; anecdotal information would also be useful. And the ethics of the experiment had to be considered: I resolved to do no harm. There was no need for the course to have a "sink or swim" character; it could aim to keep as many afloat as possible. . . .

On an early evening that same week, about twenty prospective students were scheduled to meet in a classroom. . . . Most of them came late. Those who arrived first slumped in their chairs, staring at the floor or greeting me with sullen glances. A few ate candy or what appeared to be the remnants of a meal. The students were mostly black and Latino, one was Asian, and five were white; two of the whites were immigrants who had severe problems with English. When I introduced myself, several of the students would not shake my hand, two or three refused even to look at me, one girl giggled, and the last person to volunteer his name, a young man dressed in a Tommy Hilfiger sweatshirt and wearing a cap turned sideways, drawled, "Henry Jones, but they call me Sleepy, because I got these sleepy eyes—"

"In our class, we'll call you Mr. Jones."

He smiled and slid down in his chair so that his back was parallel to the floor.

Before I finished attempting to shake hands with the prospective stu- 20
dents, a waiflike Asian girl with her mouth half-full of cake said, "Can we get on with it? I'm bored."

I liked the group immediately.

. . . "You've been cheated," I said. "Rich people learn the humanities; you didn't. The humanities are a foundation for getting along in the world, for thinking, for learning to reflect on the world instead of just reacting to whatever force is turned against you. I think the humanities are one of the ways to become political, and I don't mean political in the sense of voting in an election but in the broad sense." I told them Thucydides' definition of politics.

"Rich people know politics in that sense. They know how to negotiate instead of using force. They know how to use politics to get along, to get power. It doesn't mean that rich people are good and poor people are bad. It simply means that rich people know a more effective method for living in this society.

"Do all rich people, or people who are in the middle, know the humanities? Not a chance. But some do. And it helps. It helps to live better and enjoy life more. Will the humanities make you rich? Yes. Absolutely. But not in terms of money. In terms of life.

"Rich people learn the humanities in private schools and expensive uni- 25
versities. And that's one of the ways in which they learn the political life. I think that is the real difference between the haves and have-nots in this country. If you want real power, legitimate power, the kind that comes from the people and belongs to the people, you must understand politics. The humanities will help.

"Here's how it works: We'll pay your subway fare; take care of your children, if you have them; give you a snack or a sandwich; provide you with books and any other materials you need. But we'll make you think harder, use your mind more fully, than you ever have before. You'll have to read and think about the same kinds of ideas you would encounter in a first-year course at Harvard or Yale or Oxford.

"You'll have to come to class in the snow and the rain and the cold and the dark. No one will coddle you, no one will slow down for you. There will be tests to take, papers to write. And I can't promise you anything but a certificate of completion at the end of the course. I'll be talking to colleges about giving credit for the course, but I can't promise anything. . . . You must do it because you want to study the humanities, because you want a certain kind of life, a richness of mind and spirit. That's all I offer you: philosophy, poetry, art history, logic, rhetoric, and American history.

"Your teachers will all be people of accomplishment in their fields," I said, and I spoke a little about each teacher. "That's the course. October through May, with a two-week break at Christmas. It is generally accepted in America that the liberal arts and the humanities in particular belong to the elites. I think you're the elites."

The young Asian woman said, "What are you getting out of this?"

"This is a demonstration project. I'm writing a book. This will be proof, 30
I hope, of my idea about the humanities. Whether it succeeds or fails will be up to the teachers and you."

All but one of the prospective students applied for admission to the course. . . .

Of the fifty prospective students who showed up . . . for personal interviews [to gain admission to the course], a few were too rich (a postal supervisor's son, a fellow who claimed his father owned a factory in Nigeria that employed sixty people) and more than a few could not read. Two home-care workers from Local 1199 could not arrange their hours to enable them to take the course. Some of the applicants were too young: a thirteen-year-old and two who had just turned sixteen. . . .

Some of those who came for interviews were too poor. I did not think that was possible when we began, and I would like not to believe it now, but it was true. There is a point at which the level of forces that surround the poor can become insurmountable, when there is no time or energy left to be anything but poor. Most often I could not recruit such people for the course; when I did, they soon dropped out.

Over the days of interviewing, a class slowly assembled. I could not then imagine who would last the year and who would not. One young woman submitted a neatly typed essay that said, "I was homeless once, then I lived for some time in a shelter. Right now, I have got my own space granted by the Partnership for the Homeless. Right now, I am living alone, with very limited means. Financially I am overwhelmed by debts. I cannot afford all the food I need . . ."

35 A brother and sister, refugees from Tashkent, lived with their parents in the farthest reaches of Queens, far beyond the end of the subway line. They had no money, and they had been refused admission by every school to which they had applied. I had not intended to accept immigrants or people who had difficulty with the English language, but I took them into the class.

I also took four who had been in prison, three who were homeless, three who were pregnant, one who lived in a drugged dream-state in which she was abused, and one whom I had known for a long time and who was dying of AIDS. As I listened to them, I wondered how the course would affect them. They had no public life, no place; they lived within the surround of force, moving as fast as they could, driven by necessity, without a moment to reflect. Why should they care about fourteenth-century Italian painting or truth tables or the death of Socrates?

Between the end of recruiting and the orientation session that would open the course, I made a visit to Bedford Hills to talk with Niecie Walker. It was hot, and the drive up from the city had been unpleasant. I didn't yet know Niecie very well. She didn't trust me, and I didn't know what to make of her. While we talked, she held a huge white pill in her hand. "For AIDS," she said.

"Are you sick?"

"My T-cell count is down. But that's neither here nor there. Tell me about the course, Earl. What are you going to teach?"

40 "Moral philosophy."

"And what does that include?"

She had turned the visit into an interrogation. I didn't mind. At the end of the conversation I would be going out into "the free world"; if she wanted our meeting to be an interrogation, I was not about to argue. I said, "We'll begin with Plato: the *Apology,* a little of the *Crito,* a few pages of the *Phaedo* so that they'll know what happened to Socrates. Then we'll read Aristotle's *Nicomachean Ethics.* I also want them to read Thucydides, particularly Pericles' Funeral Oration in order to make the connection between ethics and politics, to lead them in the direction I hope the course will take them. Then we'll end with *Antigone,* but read as moral and political philosophy as well as drama."

"There's something missing," she said, leaning back in her chair, taking on an air of superiority.

The drive had been long, the day was hot, the air in the room was dead and damp. "Oh, yeah," I said, "and what's that?"

"Plato's Allegory of the Cave. How can you teach philosophy to poor 45
people without the Allegory of the Cave? The ghetto is the cave. Education is
the light. Poor people can understand that."

At the beginning of the orientation at the Clemente Center a week later, each teacher spoke for a minute or two. Dr. Inclan and his research assistant, Patricia Vargas, administered the questionnaire he had devised to measure, as best he could, the role of force and the amount of reflection in the lives of the students. I explained that each class was going to be videotaped as another way of documenting the project. Then I gave out the first assignment: "In preparation for our next meeting, I would like you to read a brief selection from Plato's *Republic:* the Allegory of the Cave."

I tried to guess how many students would return for the first class. I hoped for twenty, expected fifteen, and feared ten. [My wife] Sylvia, who had agreed to share the administrative tasks of the course, and I prepared coffee and cookies for twenty-five. We had a plastic container filled with subway tokens. Thanks to Starling Lawrence, we had thirty copies of Bernard Knox's *Norton Book of Classical Literature,* which contained all of the texts for the philosophy section except the *Republic* and the *Nicomachean Ethics.*

At six o'clock there were only ten students seated around the long table, but by six-fifteen the number had doubled, and a few minutes later two more straggled in out of the dusk. I had written a time line on the blackboard, showing them the temporal progress of thinking—from the role of myth in Neolithic societies to The Gilgamesh Epic and forward to the Old Testament, Confucius, the Greeks, the New Testament, the Koran, the Epic of Son-Jara, and ending with Nahuatl and Maya poems, which took us up to the contact between Europe and America, where the history course began. The time line served as context and geography as well as history: no race, no major culture was ignored. "Let's agree," I told them, "that we are all human, whatever our origins. And now let's go into Plato's cave."

I told them that there would be no lectures in the philosophy section of the course; we would use the Socratic method, which is called maieutic dialogue. "'Maieutic' comes from the Greek word for midwifery. I'll take the role of midwife in our dialogue. Now, what do I mean by that? What does a midwife do?"

50 It was the beginning of a love affair, the first moment of their infatuation with Socrates. Later, Abel Lomas would characterize that moment in his no-nonsense fashion, saying that it was the first time anyone had ever paid attention to their opinions.

Grace Glueck began the art history class in a darkened room lit with slides of the Lascaux caves and next turned the students' attention to Egypt, arranging for them to visit the Metropolitan Museum of Art to see the Temple of Dendur and the Egyptian Galleries. They arrived at the museum on a Friday evening. Darlene Codd brought her two-year-old son. Pearl Lau was late, as usual. One of the students, who had told me how much he was looking forward to the museum visit, didn't show up, which surprised me. Later I learned that he had been arrested for jumping a turnstile in a subway station on his way to the museum and was being held in a prison cell under the Brooklyn criminal courthouse. In the Temple of Dendur, Samantha Smoot asked questions of Felicia Blum, a museum lecturer. Samantha was the student who had burst out with the news, in one of the first sessions of the course, that people in her neighborhood believed it "wasn't no use goin' to school because the white man wouldn't let you up no matter what." But in a hall where the statuary was of half-human, half-animal female figures, it was Samantha who asked what the glyphs meant, encouraging Felicia Blum to read them aloud, to translate them into English. Toward the end of the evening, Grace led the students out of the halls of antiquities into the Rockefeller Wing, where she told them of the connections of culture and art in Mali, Benin, and the Pacific Islands. When the students had collected their coats and stood together near the entrance to the museum, preparing to leave, Samantha stood apart, a tall, slim young woman, dressed in a deerstalker cap and a dark blue peacoat. She made an exaggerated farewell wave at us and returned to Egypt—her ancient mirror.

Charles Simmons began the poetry class with poems as puzzles and laughs. His plan was to surprise the class, and he did. At first he read the poems aloud to them, interrupting himself with footnotes to bring them along. He showed them poems of love and of seduction, and satiric commentaries on those poems by later poets. "Let us read," the students demanded, but Charles refused. He tantalized them with the opportunity to read poems aloud. A tug-of-war began between him and the students, and the standoff was ended not by Charles directly but by Hector Anderson. When Charles asked if anyone in the class wrote poetry, Hector raised his hand.

"Can you recite one of your poems for us?" Charles said.

Until that moment, Hector had never volunteered a comment, though he had spoken well and intelligently when asked. He preferred to slouch in his chair, dressed in full camouflage gear, wearing a nylon stocking over his hair and eating slices of fresh cantaloupe or honeydew melon.

55 In response to Charles's question, Hector slid up to a sitting position. "If you turn that camera off," he said. "I don't want anybody using my lyrics." When he was sure the red light of the video camera was off, Hector stood and recited verse after verse of a poem that belonged somewhere in the triangle

formed by Ginsberg's *Howl,* the Book of Lamentations, and hip-hop. When Charles and the students finished applauding, they asked Hector to say the poem again, and he did. Later Charles told me, "That kid is the real thing." Hector's discomfort with Sylvia and me turned to ease. He came to our house for a small Christmas party and at other times. We talked on the telephone about a scholarship program and about what steps he should take next in his education. I came to know his parents. As a student, he began quietly, almost secretly, to surpass many of his classmates.

Timothy Koranda was the most professorial of the professors. He arrived precisely on time, wearing a hat of many styles—part fedora, part Borsalino, part Stetson, and at least one-half World War I campaign hat. He taught logic during class hours, filling the blackboard from floor to ceiling, wall to wall, drawing the intersections of sets here and truth tables there and a great square of oppositions in the middle of it all. After class, he walked with students to the subway, chatting about Zen or logic or Heisenberg.

On one of the coldest nights of the winter, he introduced the students to logic problems stated in ordinary language that they could solve by reducing the phrases to symbols. He passed out copies of a problem, two pages long, then wrote out some of the key phrases on the blackboard. "Take this home with you," he said, "and at our next meeting we shall see who has solved it. I shall also attempt to find the answer."

By the time he finished writing out the key phrases, however, David Iskhakov raised his hand. Although they listened attentively, neither David nor his sister Susana spoke often in class. She was shy, and he was embarrassed at his inability to speak perfect English.

"May I go to blackboard?" David said. "And will see if I have found correct answer to zis problem."

60 Together Tim and David erased the blackboard, then David began covering it with signs and symbols. "If first man is earning this money, and second man is closer to this town . . . ," he said, carefully laying out the conditions. After five minutes or so, he said, "And the answer is: B will get first to Cleveland!"

Samantha Smoot shouted, "That's not the answer. The mistake you made is in the first part there, where it says who earns more money."

Tim folded his arms across his chest, happy. "I shall let you all take the problem home," he said.

When Sylvia and I left the Clemente Center that night, a knot of students was gathered outside, huddled against the wind. Snow had begun to fall, a slippery powder on the gray ice that covered all but a narrow space down the center of the sidewalk. Samantha and David stood in the middle of the group, still arguing over the answer to the problem. I leaned in for a moment to catch the character of the argument. It was even more polite than it had been in the classroom, because now they govern themselves.

One Saturday morning in January, David Howell telephoned me at home. "Mr. Shores," he said, Anglicizing my name, as many of the students did.

65 "Mr. Howell," I responded, recognizing his voice.

"How you doin', Mr. Shores?"

"I'm fine. How are you?"

"I had a little problem at work."

Uh-oh, I thought, bad news was coming. David is a big man, generally good-humored but with a quick temper. According to his mother, he had a history of violent behavior. In the classroom he had been one of the best students, a steady man, twenty-four years old, who always did the reading assignments and who often made interesting connections between the humanities and daily life. "What happened?"

"Mr. Shores, there's a woman at my job, she said some things to me and I said some things to her. And she told my supervisor I had said things to her, and he called me in about it. She's forty years old and she don't have no social life, and I have a good social life, and she's jealous of me."

"And then what happened?" The tone of his voice and the timing of the call did not portend good news.

"Mr. Shores, she made me so mad, I wanted to smack her up against the wall. I tried to talk to some friends to calm myself down a little, but nobody was around."

"And what did you do?" I asked, fearing this was his one telephone call from the city jail.

"Mr. Shores, I asked myself, 'What would Socrates do?'"

David Howell had reasoned that his co-worker's envy was not his problem after all, and he had dropped his rage.

One evening, in the American history section, I was telling the students about Gordon Wood's ideas in *The Radicalism of the American Revolution.* We were talking about the revolt by some intellectuals against classical learning at the turn of the eighteenth century, including Benjamin Franklin's late-life change of heart, when Henry Jones raised his hand.

"If the Founders loved the humanities so much, how come they treated the natives so badly?"

I didn't know how to answer this question. There were confounding explanations to offer about changing attitudes toward Native Americans, vaguely useful references to views of Rousseau and James Fenimore Cooper. For a moment I wondered if I should tell them about Heidegger's Nazi past. Then I saw Abel Lomas's raised hand at the far end of the table. "Mr. Lomas," I said.

Abel said, "That's what Aristotle means by incontinence, when you know what's morally right but you don't do it, because you're overcome by your passions."

The other students nodded. They were all inheritors of wounds caused by the incontinence of educated men; now they had an ally in Aristotle, who had given them a way to analyze the actions of their antagonists.

Those who appreciate ancient history understand the radical character of the humanities. They know that politics did not begin in a perfect world but in a society even more flawed than ours: one that embraced slavery, denied the rights of women, practiced a form of homosexuality that verged on pedophilia, and endured the intrigues and corruption of its leaders. The genius of that society originated in man's re-creation of himself through the recognition of his humanness as expressed in art, literature, rhetoric, philosophy, and the unique notion of freedom. At that moment, the isolation of the private life ended and politics began.

The winners in the game of modern society, and even those whose fortune falls in the middle, have other means to power: they are included at birth. They know this. And they know exactly what to do to protect their place in the economic and social hierarchy. As Allan Bloom, author of the nationally best-selling tract in defense of elitism, *The Closing of the American Mind,* put it, they direct the study of the humanities exclusively at those young people who "have been raised in comfort and with the expectation of ever increasing comfort."

In the last meeting before graduation, the Clemente students answered the same set of questions they'd answered at orientation. Between October and May, students had fallen to AIDS, pregnancy, job opportunities, pernicious anemia, clinical depression, a schizophrenic child, and other forces, but of the thirty students admitted to the course, sixteen had completed it, and fourteen had earned credit from Bard College. Dr. Inclan found that the students' self-esteem and their abilities to divine and solve problems had significantly increased; their use of verbal aggression as a tactic for resolving conflicts had significantly decreased. And they all had notably more appreciation for the concepts of benevolence, spirituality, universalism, and collectivism.

It cost about $2,000 for a student to attend the Clemente Course. Compared with unemployment, welfare, or prison, the humanities are a bargain. But coming into possession of the faculty of reflection and the skills of politics leads to a choice for the poor—and whatever they choose, they will be dangerous: they may use politics to get along in a society based on the game, to escape from the surround of force into a gentler life, to behave as citizens, and nothing more; or they may choose to oppose the game itself. No one can predict the effect of politics, although we all would like to think that wisdom goes our way. That is why the poor are so often mobilized and so rarely politicized. The possibility that they will adopt a moral view other than that of their mentors can never be discounted. And who wants to run that risk? . . .

On May 14, 1997, Viniece Walker came up for parole for the second 85
time. She had served more than ten years of her sentence, and she had been the best of prisoners. In a version of the Clemente Course held at the prison, she had been my teaching assistant. After a brief hearing, her request for parole was denied. She will serve two more years before the parole board will reconsider her case.

A year after graduation, ten of the first sixteen Clemente Course graduates were attending four-year colleges or going to nursing school; four of them had received full scholarships to Bard College. The other graduates were attending community college or working full-time. Except for one: she had been fired from her job in a fast-food restaurant for trying to start a union.

Questions for Discussion

1. This essay requires us to think about familiar terms in unfamiliar ways. What does Shorris mean by "the political"? How does this relate to "the moral life of downtown," also called "the moral alternative to the street"? How do most college students know about the political in Shorris's sense? What prevents most poor people from knowing?
2. "You've been cheated," Shorris tells his prospective students, denied an education in the humanities, and therefore "a foundation . . . for learning to reflect on the world instead of just reacting to whatever force is turned against you." What does "reflect" mean here? What sort of practical consequences can it have? To what extent has your education encouraged reflection?
3. One interesting feature of Shorris's course on moral philosophy is his concentration on classical Greece, on major works by Plato, Aristotle, the historian Thucydides, and the playwright Sophocles. Does this focus surprise you? What might justify it? Should the classics be part of your curriculum?
4. How would you characterize the attitudes, approaches, and methods used by the professors? How important a role did they play in the success of the courses? Compare them to your high school instruction and what you've encountered so far in college. Are they comparable? If so, in what ways? If not, how do you explain the differences?
5. Near the end of the essay, Shorris reports how the class handled a thorny question: "If the Founders [of the United States] loved the humanities so much, how come they treated the natives so badly?" Is Abel's answer adequate? What's the point of Shorris's commentary on the culture in which ancient Greek thought and art arose? How do you respond to what he says?
6. Read carefully the last four paragraphs and note the details about what happened to the students. How successful would you say the curriculum was? What are its limitations? On what does its long-term impact depend? What measures might be taken to improve the odds of more students completing the course?

For Inquiry and Persuasion

It is not hard to imagine what Shorris's critics will say. In teaching his students how to "get along" with European white culture, some will say, he is only encouraging acquiescence to the system, trying to make white people out of people of color, and devaluing by neglect the cultures to which his students belong. Others will say that most poor people do not need a liberal education but rather basic literacy skills, the ability to read and write, coupled with training in some marketable skill, such as data processing.

List on the board these and any other criticisms that occur to you. After extensive class discussion, write an essay either supporting Shorris's program as part of what poor people need for self-improvement or advocating something else. Direct your essay to public school systems whose student populations include people from backgrounds similar to Shorris's group. As preparation for your paper, you may wish to visit such schools and/or talk to members of the faculty.

For Inquiry

As a class select one or two of the works Shorris had his students study in his moral philosophy course. Read them and, paying special attention to their moral and political "lessons," discuss what we can learn from them about how to live better.

Do they have the virtues Shorris believes they have? Understanding them is more difficult than works written closer to our place and time, works that are not necessarily less insightful or profound. Is the struggle with the classics worth it? Did you gain as much from them as some of Shorris's students apparently did? Why or why not?

For Inquiry and Convincing

Anyone who reads Shorris's essay together with the previous one by Edmundson is likely to detect an apparent paradox, which can be expressed in at least two ways. The liberal arts were created by the privileged classes and largely taught to the privileged for the past 2,500 years. So why do they serve now as at best only "lite entertainment" for the very class of student who belongs to the tradition of privilege? Put another way, both Edmundson and Shorris want their courses to change their students, transforming how they understand the world and how they behave in it, but only Shorris believes that change has actually occurred. Edmundson should have the easier time. Why doesn't he?

Write an essay in which you render this paradox less paradoxical. Tie your explanation to your own experiences with the liberal arts, to your background, to the way your classes have been taught. At the end make a case for how the liberal arts might be taught better. Or, if you believe the paradox has little or nothing to do with teaching, make a case for what must change to reenergize the liberal arts.

JOHN TAGG

The Decline of the Knowledge Factory: Why Our Colleges Must Change

In the 1960s "the system" was often a topic of discussion. Many of the conversations were not especially helpful, but implicit in all of them was an insight we must not forget: often what's wrong with society has little to do with particular individuals or the roles they play, with philosophies, or with cultural gaps between generations; rather, the problems may be traced to the way a society is structured in general and to an institution's organization in particular. Individuals may or may not like "the system," but they are caught up in it anyway and realize the powerful forces invested in maintaining the status quo. Understandably, they turn to the practical business of getting the system to pay off for them rather than trying to change it. And so change itself becomes difficult and for many people beyond imagining. It's just "the way things are."

In this article from the journal World and I *(June 1998), John Tagg depicts "the system" at most of our colleges and universities well. We must understand it to grasp why things are as they are and what impedes* all *proposals for change that go beyond mere tinkering. Whether Tagg's own proposals amount to tinkering or represent meaningful change to "the system" is a question we should keep in mind as we read.*

DO COLLEGES WORK?

IN 1991, Ernest Pascarella of the University of Illinois, Chicago, 1
. . . and Patrick Terenzini of the Center for the Study of Higher Education at Pennsylvania State University published a massive volume, *How College Affects Students: Findings and Insights from Twenty Years of Research.* Their assessments are carefully weighted and qualified, and they find, not surprisingly, that college students learn a good deal while in college and change in many ways. College does make a difference. But perhaps their most striking conclusion is that while attending college makes a difference, the particular college one attends makes hardly any predictable difference at all.

One of the foundational assumptions that guides parents, students, alumni, and taxpayers in thinking about colleges is that a greater investment in human and economic resources produces a better product in terms of educational outcome. Conventional thinking holds that those who run these institutions have some coherent conception of quality, and that this conception of quality is embodied in the best colleges, which others seek to emulate. Parents pay the breathtaking tuition charged by Ivy League institutions, and legislators invest public money in enormous state universities, because they believe quality is worth paying for—and because they believe that while they may not be able to define just what that quality consists of, those professionals who govern higher education can define it and, given adequate resources, create it.

> But Pascarella and Terenzini found that there is little consistent evidence to indicate that college selectivity, prestige, or educational resources have any important net impact on students in such areas as learning, cognitive and intellectual development, other psychosocial changes, the development of principled moral reasoning, or shifts in other attitudes and values. Nearly all of the variance in learning and cognitive outcomes is attributable to individual aptitude differences among students attending different colleges. Only a small and perhaps trivial part is uniquely due to the quality of the college attended.

In other words, if colleges know what quality is in undergraduate education, they apparently do not know how to produce it.

In 1993 Alexander Astin, director of the Higher Education Research Institute at UCLA, published a new study: *What Matters in College: Four Critical Years Revisited.* Astin attempted to assess the effects of college using longitudinal studies of students at many varied institutions and finding correlations between the institutions' characteristics and selected student outcomes. His research, like Pascarella and Terenzini's, leaves us with a disappointing picture, a picture of colleges that attend least to what matters most and often act in ways that seem almost designed to assure they fail at their avowed mission.

Astin's research reveals that what colleges actually do bears little resemblance to what we would be likely to extract from college catalogs or commencement speeches. This probably should not surprise us. Harvard organizational theorist Chris Argyris has demonstrated that the way people say they act in business organizations—their "espoused theory," Argyris calls it—has little relationship with their "theory-in-use," which governs how they actually behave. Astin has discovered essentially the same thing in American colleges:

> Institutions espouse high-sounding values, of course, in their mission statements, college catalogues, and public pronouncements by institutional leaders. The problem is that the explicitly stated values—which always include a strong commitment to undergraduate education—are often at variance with the actual values that drive our decisions and policies.

For an outsider—and for not a few insiders—the first barrier to realistically assessing baccalaureate education is simply finding it in the morass of muddled missions that make up the contemporary multiversity. Astin quotes "one of our leading higher education scholars" as dismissing research about undergraduate learning with the remark, "The modern American university is not a residential liberal arts college." Indeed. Astin responds that *5*

> all types of institutions claim to be engaged in the same enterprise: the liberal education of the undergraduate student. While it is true

> that certain kinds of institutions also do other things—research, vocational education, and graduate education, to name just a few—does having multiple functions "give permission" to an institution to offer baccalaureate education programs that are second-rate? Does engaging in research and graduate education justify shortchanging undergraduate education? Does engaging in vocational education justify offering mediocre transfer education?

The answer to that question today is, for all practical purposes, "yes." A multiplicity of functions does justify mediocrity and incoherence in undergraduate education, at least to the not very exacting standards of most of our colleges.

WHAT HAPPENED?

Why are our colleges failing? Because they have substituted standardized processes for educational substance. They have become bureaucratized assembly lines for academic credit and have largely ceased, at the institutional level, to know or care what their students learn.

If we look at higher education as it exists today, what we see is counterintuitive. In a nation with over thirty-five hundred colleges serving more than fourteen million students, we find an amazing homogeneity. Despite the vast number of colleges, they display more sameness than difference. Why?

Today's system of higher education is a product of the postwar world. With the impetus of the GI Bill of Rights, rapid economic growth, and the baby boom, the college population surged after World War II. Between 1950 and 1970 college enrollment more than tripled. The percentage of Americans over twenty-five who completed a bachelor's degree doubled between the end of the war and 1970 and nearly doubled again by 1993. And the most dramatic growth has taken place in public colleges. In 1947 less than half of the nation's college students attended public institutions. By 1993 nearly 80 percent did.

Today's colleges have developed as part of a nationwide system of higher education, and hence they have become nearly interchangeable. In such a system, colleges, especially public colleges, have been able to thrive only by growing. Thus their operations have become standardized and focused on providing more of their product to more students. The mission of colleges in this system is to offer classes. My colleague Robert Barr has labeled the governing set of assumptions, attitudes, and rules that define colleges in this system—the theory-in-use of most colleges—the Instruction Paradigm. In the Instruction Paradigm, the product of colleges is classes; colleges exist for the purpose of offering more instruction to more students in more classes.

10 In this system, the "atom" of the educational universe is the one-hour block of lecture and the "molecule" is the three-unit course. The parts of the educational experience have transferrable value only in the form of completed credit hours. For almost any student at nearly any college today, the essential meaning of "being a student" is accumulating credit hours.

A credit hour is a measurement of time spent in class. I do not mean to suggest that credit is automatic for students who merely show up. They must, of course, pass the course. But the amount of credit, the weight of the course in the transcript, is based on the length of time the student sits in a room. What the student does in the room, what the teacher does in the room, what they think after they leave the room—these things are irrelevant to academic credit. The qualifications and experience and attitudes of the teacher are irrelevant to academic credit—three units from a creative scholar passionately interested in her subject and her students are equal to three units from a bored grad student who finds teaching a largely avoidable irritation. The attitude and involvement of the student are irrelevant to academic credit—three units earned by a committed and involved student who finds a whole new way of thinking and a life-changing body of ideas in a course are equal to three units earned by a student who thinks about the course only long enough to fake temporary knowledge with borrowed notes.

Public funding mechanisms in most states reward colleges for offering courses, credit hours. Not for grades, not for course completion, and certainly not for learning. States pay colleges for students sitting in classrooms. You get what you pay for.

The Knowledge Factory

The Instruction Paradigm college of the postwar period is a knowledge factory: The student passes through an assembly line of courses. As the students pass by, each faculty member affixes a specialized part of knowledge. Then the students move on down the assembly line to the next instructor, who bolts on another fragment of knowledge. The assembly line moves at a steady pace. Each instructor has exactly one semester or quarter to do the same job for every student, who is assumed to be as like every other as the chassis of a given model of car. The workers on this line tend to view their jobs narrowly, as defined by the part of knowledge that it is their business to affix. No one has the job of quality control for the finished product.

In the college as knowledge factory, students learn that the only value recognized by the system, the only fungible good that counts toward success, is the grade on the transcript. It is a fractured system dedicated to the production of parts, of three-unit classes. The reason colleges fail is that the parts don't fit together. They don't add up to a coherent whole. They add up to a transcript but not an education.

Most of the lower division, the first two years of college, is dominated 15
by general education requirements. These requirements at most colleges consist of lists of classes—in a variety of categories such as the humanities, social science, and physical science—from which the student may choose. William Schaefer, emeritus professor of English and former executive vice chancellor at UCLA, describes general education as "a conglomeration of unrelated courses dedicated to the proposition that one's reach should never exceed one's grasp."

The incoherence of the curriculum flows from the internal organizational dynamic of the knowledge factory. Required classes are shaped by the dominant organizational unit of college faculties: academic departments. At nearly all colleges, the fundamental duty and allegiance of the faculty is to their home departments. Most academic departments hire their own faculty. Most faculty members literally owe their jobs not to the college as an institution but to their departments. Most of the crucial decisions about a faculty member's workload and duties are primarily departmental decisions. As Schaefer notes, "Departments have a life of their own—insular, defensive, self-governing, compelled to protect their interests because the faculty positions as well as the courses that justify funding those positions are located therein."

Departments become large by bolting more of their distinctive parts onto more student chassis in the educational assembly line, by offering those bread-and-butter required general education courses that garner large guaranteed enrollments. But these are often just the kinds of innocuous survey courses that faculty prefer not to teach. And the highest rewards in most universities are reserved not for those who teach undergraduates but for those who are recognized for their research contributions to their academic disciplines. Academic departments have achieved the "best" of both worlds by hiring large numbers of graduate students or part-time instructors, at low salaries and often with no benefits, to teach undergraduate courses, while freeing up senior faculty for research activities.

Our great research universities have for many years subsidized their research programs and graduate schools at the expense of undergraduate programs. They have, in effect, pawned their undergraduate colleges to buy faculty the jewel of research time. There is no penalty to pay for this transaction, because undergraduate programs are funded based on seat time; learning doesn't count; the failure of students to learn exacts no cost to the department or the institution.

Academic departments are ostensibly organized in the service of "disciplines"—coherent and discrete bodies of knowledge or methods of study. While many of the academic disciplines that make up the sciences and humanities are of ancient and proud lineage, their configuration in the modern university is largely a product of academic politics. And their trajectory in the development and deployment of general education courses is almost entirely a product of competition between departments for campus resources. On the academic assembly line of the knowledge factory, each part must be different, so the incentive is to emphasize what makes a discipline unlike others and to shape all knowledge into these highly differentiated disciplines.

Even skills of universal relevance to virtually everything we do in life 20
have become the property of one department or another. Thus, writing in the student's native language becomes the concern of the Department of English; speaking the student's native language is relegated to the Department of Communication. Quantitative reasoning belongs to the Department of Mathematics. The atomized curriculum has taken an increasingly conspicuous toll: the inability of students to think globally or to transfer methods of analysis from one subject or problem to another. The evidence mounts that what students

learn in one course they do not retain and transfer to their experience in other courses or to their lives and their work. The fragments never fit together. This has led to a growing demand for the teaching of "critical thinking." But even the subject of thought itself becomes in the knowledge factory an object of competitive bidding among academic departments. Adam Sweeting, director of the Writing Program at the Massachusetts School of Law at Andover, warns that "if we are not careful, the teaching of critical thinking skills will become the responsibility of one university department, a prospect that is at odds with the very idea of a university."

But then much about the modern university is at odds with the very idea of a university. The competition between "academic disciplines" for institutional turf generates a bundle of fragments, a mass of shards, and no coherent whole at all. It lacks precisely that quality of discipline that provided the rationale for the enterprise from the beginning. It creates a metacurriculum in which students learn that college is a sequence of disconnected parts, valuable only as credits earned. And what comes off the assembly line of the knowledge factory in the end is an "education" that might have been designed by Rube Goldberg, with marketing advice from the Edsel team.

The result is an institution that satisfies nobody. College faculties complain bitterly, often about the administration, but most often about the students. History and philosophy professors complain that students can't write. English professors complain that students know little about history and culture. Science professors complain that students have only a rudimentary grasp of mathematics. And everyone complains that students can't think. Yet grades have never been higher. The mean grade point average of all college graduates in 1994 was 3.0 on a scale of 4. It seems unfair to penalize students with poor grades for deficiencies that really fall outside the scope of the course, deficiencies that could not possibly be addressed in a three-unit, one-semester class. So the professors blame the students or the administration and fight pitched battles in the faculty senate. Yet nothing seems to work, because the deficiencies that plague students are almost by definition problems that cannot be addressed in any three-unit class. But three-unit classes are all there are; they are what the college is made of.

Perhaps least satisfied with the knowledge factory are the students. Those students who come to college from high school today come hoping for something better, but with no framework of educational value to bring to the experience themselves. For many of them, the defining experience of college becomes drunkenness. While some colleges have begun belatedly to recognize the costs of the culture of irresponsibility that has grown up on many campuses, it remains the case that substance abuse is one of the few measurable outcomes of a college education. A commission chaired by former Health, Education, and Welfare Secretary Joseph Califano Jr. reported in 1994 that a third of college students are binge drinkers and that the number of college women who reported that they drink in order to get drunk had tripled since 1973, now matching the rate for men.

William Willimon, dean of the chapel at Duke University, and Thomas Naylor, emeritus professor of economics at Duke, have characterized the chaos and aimlessness that college is for many students in their book *The Abandoned Generation: Rethinking Higher Education.* They offer an especially telling statement of the experience of the knowledge factory from a University of Michigan senior:

> So you get here and they start asking you, "What do you think you want to major in?" "Have you thought about what courses you want to take?" And you get the impression that that's what it's all about—courses, majors. So you take the courses. You get your card punched. You try a little this and a little that. Then comes GRADUATION. And you wake up and you look at this bunch of courses and then it hits you: They don't add up to anything. It's just a bunch of courses. It doesn't mean a thing.

Do Colleges Have a Future?

The knowledge factory is breaking down as we approach the twenty- 25
first century. The transformation to the knowledge society means that the demand for higher education will increase both in quantity and quality: More students will require more sophisticated knowledge and skills. But this transformation has also brought into existence something new on the higher education landscape: competition.

Competition has emerged for two reasons. First, private employers who need skilled employees have found that the graduates of conventional colleges are poorly prepared to do the work they need to do. Many corporations have either established their own "universities" or sought the support of outside vendors to provide educational services. The second reason competition has burgeoned is that contemporary information technology has made possible immediate access to educational services from anywhere. Education is no longer bound to the campus. Hence many providers can compete to serve students who were formerly too distant. The competition is real. Stan Davis and Jim Botkin—in *The Monster under the Bed,* their book about the growing imperative for corporate education—offer little hope to the conventional college: "Employee education is not growing 100 percent faster than academe, but 100 times—or 10,000 percent—faster."

In the face of such competition, if conventional colleges hold fast to the Instruction Paradigm and continue to grant degrees on seat time, many of those colleges will wither and die—going down, we can hardly doubt, in a blaze of acrimony as the nation's great minds fulminate in faculty senates across the land. If colleges are to thrive, and in some cases if they are even to survive, they must change.

Colleges need to make a paradigm shift, to set aside a whole body of assumptions and implicit rules and adopt a fundamentally different perspective, a new theory-in-use. They must recognize that the Instruction Paradigm mistakes a means for an end, confuses offering classes with producing learning. To put that end in its proper place would be to embrace what Barr calls "the Learning Paradigm." From the perspective of the Learning Paradigm, the central defining functions of the knowledge factory are trivial. What counts is what students learn. That the mission of colleges is to produce learning should be fairly noncontroversial, since it is consistent with what nearly all college faculty and administrators already say in public.

The problem is that most colleges do not assess in any meaningful way what students have learned. They can tell you what classes their students have taken but not what their graduates know or what they can do. The shift to the Learning Paradigm would require that colleges begin to take learning seriously, to assess and measure it, and to take responsibility for producing it.

A large and growing number of faculty and administrators have seen that *30*
major changes in the way colleges do business are both desirable and inevitable. The prestigious California Higher Education Policy Center, in a 1996 report, urged that "colleges and universities . . . begin a transition toward making student learning, not the time spent on courses taken, the principal basis on which degrees and certificates are rewarded."

Excellent models of such colleges exist. Alverno College in Milwaukee has for decades been developing "assessment-as-learning," an approach that seeks to both monitor and guide students' development toward the mastery of a set of core competencies that define a liberal education. The new Western Governors' University will reward students with credit only when they have established through rigorous assessment that they have mastered the required skills. According to Alan Guskin, chancellor of Antioch University, more than two hundred colleges across the country are seriously discussing major restructuring.

Nonetheless, if we contrast the glacial rate at which colleges and universities seem inclined to change with the lightning speed with which the society they serve is transforming itself, we must be disturbed by the contrast. Many believe that undergraduate colleges cannot meet the challenge of the knowledge society. Davis and Botkin, for example, foresee that "corporations will continue to need traditional universities to carry out basic education and research. Nevertheless they will increasingly take on teaching themselves." Drucker predicts: "Thirty years from now the big university campuses will be relics. Universities won't survive. . . . Such totally uncontrollable expenditures, without any visible improvement in either the content or the quality of education, means that the system is rapidly becoming untenable. Higher education is in deep crisis."

Should we, after all, care? What matter if many of our colleges pass away or diminish into support institutions for market-driven forces that can adapt more flexibly to the needs of a changing world? What would be lost? Perhaps not much. Perhaps a great deal. For colleges hold a place in American society that no other institution is likely to fill. They hold the place of liberal education, of education for liberty, of the kind of experience through which children grow into citizens, through which men and women learn the exercise of the freedom that is tempered by choosing responsibility. I say that colleges "hold the place" of liberal education today because I cannot say that they serve the function. But they remain the institutional focus of the ideal, which survives as an ideal. . . .

Changing the governing paradigm, becoming learning-driven institutions, may seem a daunting task for today's knowledge factories. It seems a little like asking the post office to become a church. Yet the reason that the ideal of liberal education survives in our cultural imagination is that it addresses an ongoing need, the need to nurture in the young the development of both heart and mind, the need to set young people on a course that offers not just facility but maturity, not just cleverness but wisdom. . . .

Questions for Discussion

1. The first article in this chapter strongly supports the remark that Tagg quotes with evident disapproval—that "the modern American university is not a residential liberal arts college." The cold facts—demographic data—back up this contention, so that how we *feel* about the diminishing role of the traditional college is one thing, and well-documented trends another. Read or reread the first article. How does it "speak to" Tagg's argument? What considerations does it raise for his proposals he does not address?
2. Tagg is right, of course, to say that "the 'atom' of the educational universe is the one-hour block of lecture and the 'molecule' is the three-unit course" and that therefore "the essential meaning of 'being a student' is accumulating credit hours." But would his proposed shift from the Instructional Paradigm to the Learning Paradigm necessarily change this? Why or why not?
3. "The evidence mounts," Tagg alleges, "that what students learn in one course they do not retain and transfer to their experience in other courses or to their lives and work." Is this true? Do you see connections among the courses you're taking? Do you see applications to your life and work? Tagg blames this problem on the "atomized curriculum." Do you agree? That is, would a more coherent curriculum *necessarily* result in more connection and application? Is the problem structural, or does it somehow involve more than how "the system" is organized?
4. What is the relation between knowledge and learning? Is knowing a lot about some subject the same thing as understanding it? If not, what's the difference? What sort of educational structure and approach to teaching would best promote both?

For Research, Inquiry, and Convincing

All shrewd people know the difference between an organization's "espoused theory" and its "theory-in-use"—the difference between public relations and reality, between what we say we are doing and what we are actually doing. There's always a gap because we want to present ourselves to the world in the best possible light while also coping with realities within the organization that may be known only to insiders and that may be discomforting or embarrassing.

Problems arise when the gap becomes too great—when the official rhetoric no longer represents merely a favorable spin but rather becomes an outright lie. The result is cynicism and eventual loss of organizational cohesion, pride, and spirit.

Investigate the distinction by examining the official rhetoric of your school. Collect a representative body of it and, as a class, analyze what it says, implies, and promises, paying special attention to the image or character of the school it tries to project. Compare the image with the reality—what you have experienced, what your classmates think is going on—and, if possible, with the impressions of older students, your professors, and the administration.

Then write a paper addressed to your fellow students or prospective students assessing some aspect of the official rhetoric. How honest is it? Is there a tolerably good match between the said and the done? If not, how could it change and still present your school positively?

Additional Suggestions for Writing

1. *Persuasion.* With the exception of Shorris's, all the selections in this chapter have a negative view of present practices in higher education and of current college students. In this sense they tend to be one-sided, mainly "gloom and doom," as we say. But matters are rarely this simple. For example, the decline of the residential college is matched by greater educational opportunity for more students, who can live at home more cheaply and attend school part-time while holding down a job. Loss of coherence in the curriculum has produced fewer required courses and more options to meet requirements—more freedom of choice. Consumerism has forced colleges to listen more to their students and respond to their needs better, including greater regard for how well professors "reach" students. And so on. We do not have to be Pollyannas, "all sunshine and light," to see that what is bad from one perspective can be good, or at least not so bad, from another.

   Write a response to any one of the negative articles or to some significant part of one. Conceive of it in the genre of a letter to the editor of a journal, but direct it to the readership the essay tried to reach. Argue for the "up" side of the negative points the author raised, and try to persuade your readers that things are not as bad as the author contends.
2. *Exploration.* One of the best remedies for confusion is to return again and again to basic questions. So far as higher education and the college experience are concerned, perhaps the basic question is what *you* want from it—not what the college or some "expert" says you should want, or what your parents say they want, or even what you think you should want, but rather what you are actually here for.

Over a period of perhaps a week or two, take time to record in your writer's notebook everything you have done, and ponder it from the standpoint of both apparent motives and deeper or hidden ones. Why are you doing what you're doing? What do your choices say about your real motivations?

Write an essay exploring your genuine motives. Good, bad, or indifferent, what are they exactly? Where do they come from? What motives do you admire that you wish you had? Compare your thoughts with those of your classmates. In class discussion address this question: Will our motives likely change over the next few years? In what specific ways? Why?

CHAPTER SIXTEEN

Race and Class

Prejudice—in its root meaning "prejudge, to evaluate someone or something before knowing the facts, in advance of a particular encounter with the individual thing or person that provokes judgment"—is a more subtle and difficult concept than most people realize. We want to say that prejudice is simply wrong and shameful—for instance, the history of black people in the United States certainly proves that prejudice can be wrong and shameful. We could point also to the treatment of Native Americans, Chinese and Japanese immigrants, Hispanics, and many others whose skin color and cultures marked them as different from the white majority. Hence, we hope to end prejudice and overcome prejudice in ourselves and our institutions. "You're prejudiced" becomes one of the worst of accusations, something that we fear as much as past generations feared steps to undo prejudice, such as integration.

We fear the accusation because most of us know we're guilty. When we encounter anyone for the first time, we don't see that person as an individual. Rather, we see classes of attributes: the person is male or female; is young, middle-aged, or old; dresses this way or that; speaks with a certain accent; and so on, through a host of categories through which we *discriminate*—that is, perceive—*all* people we meet. The problem is that each of the categories carries certain cultural expectations. If the person is female, for example, we expect her to be more or less conventionally feminine, and we are likely to judge her negatively to the degree she doesn't act the part. Of course, not all prejudices result in negative evaluations. When Americans hear a cultivated, upper-class British accent, for example, many will associate the speaker with high intelligence and sophistication, investing that person with all sorts of "positives" he or she may not actually have.

The point is that prejudice and the tendency to discriminate are as inevitable as breathing. We can and should eliminate or reduce some kinds of prejudice, but we can't cease to prejudge things and people and remain human. Simply by living in a society and speaking a language whose words carry positive and negative associations, we will necessarily have prejudices and discriminate. Nor is discrimination always bad. For instance, as a juror in a criminal case, we may be asked to decide whether the accused is legally sane. We can and should make such judgments—indeed, the law says we must.

This chapter is about prejudice in the wrong and shameful sense. What exactly makes some kinds of prejudice wrong and shameful? We would not criticize a home loan company for denying the application of a person whose financial condition should exclude them from moving into an exclusive neighborhood he or she can't afford. But if a person can qualify and is denied simply because he or she is black and the neighborhood is "exclusive" in the sense of all white, that would be not only wrong but also actionable, justification for a lawsuit. The difference is clear: a person's finances are relevant to a loan application; skin color is not. Accordingly, prejudice is justified in the first case, and entirely without justification in the second.

Similarly, colleges discriminate among applicants routinely, and no one blames a school for rejecting a student because grades and test scores don't measure up. But sometimes, of course, students get in because, say, a parent has "pull"—there is money in the family and significant contributions have been made or promised. This is wrong, as is favoring students who come from prosperous neighborhoods, because, just as race should have nothing to do with loan qualifications, so wealth should have no bearing on qualifications for college admission.

The preceding are examples of racism and classism, prejudice based on skin color and socioeconomic background or standing. The articles in this chapter are about both—as well as about how one can merge with or substitute for the other and how both tend to overlap with other kinds of unwarranted bias, such as ethnic or cultural favoritism. Inevitably, the articles emphasize the black-white division, which has plagued us for about 400 years now, since the beginning of the slave trade and long before there was a United States. We cannot forget this dreadful history, but here we focus on what many have called the "new racism," subtler kinds of discrimination and animosity that progress in civil rights and integration have not as yet touched. We also wanted to bring class issues into the picture because Americans generally resist acknowledging the harsh realities of class-based prejudices. We need to recognize, confront, and understand them better.

Among the issues raised by the readings in this chapter are the following: First, what is the future of race and race-oriented prejudice? Are we headed toward a society of "beige and brown," in which skin color differences are less discernible and may well cease to matter? Second, what is "equal opportunity," the core value of most American thinking on issues of social justice and equity? To what extent does equal opportunity exist? Is it an adequate response to the dehumanizing effects of present and past discrimination? Finally, is there a new racism? If so, what forms does it take? How exactly does it differ from older practices? What strategies will reduce prejudice and help victims cope better?

These and other key questions must concern us as we struggle with an old problem that now often takes unfamiliar, confusing, and complicated routes in (and out) of our awareness. One thing we can be sure of as we explore the territory: we have not and will not escape prejudging everything and everybody we encounter. And so we must examine our prejudices carefully and honestly, discarding those that hurt and harm and cultivating those that promote tolerance and understanding.

BRUCE ROBERTS

Photograph

Before the civil rights era of the 1960s, it was common to see blatant discrimination, especially in the South. This photograph of segregated restrooms reveals a great deal about the prejudices of an earlier time. The photograph was taken in South Carolina in 1965.

For Discussion

Rhetorically, the doors are an argument, made by the white majority to members of both white and black races. Discuss the argument in terms of rhetorical context, as described on pages 12–13.

RYSZARD KAPUSCINSKI

Second Thoughts about America's Racial Paradise

The following two-part article appeared in the New Perspectives Quarterly *(1991), published by the Center for the Study of Democratic Institutions. We include the headnote written by the editors of* NPQ, *which explains the unusual circumstances of its composition.*

The article provides a European's perspective on racism in the United States. The author is clearly a prophet of sorts, focusing more on what might be or could be than on what is. And yet if we recognize that his vision is, as even he admits, "perhaps . . . overly naive and idealistic," we must yet grant its appeal—and its challenge. What do we see when we consider race in the United States? What perspective will allow us to understand best what is unfolding before our eyes?

Author most recently of *The Soccer War,* Ryszard Kapuscinski has spent the last several decades reporting on the Third World for the Eastern European press.

In 1988, *NPQ* invited the acclaimed writer to Los Angeles to comment on a city that had become dubbed the "capital of the Third World." We reproduce a portion of his ode to LA's multiculturalism below.

After the beating of Rodney King by white cops, we asked Kapuscinski for his second thoughts, which he sent to us from Warsaw.

How is it, we asked him to ponder, that the same city celebrated for its inter-ethnic peace and remarkable cultural diversity—a city which attracts immigrants of color from all over the world seeking a new chance—was also the setting of the brutal beating of a black man by white police worthy of South Africa?

Is the multicultural paradise beginning to fray as the American economy falters? At the outset of the 1990s, LA's two major economic pillars—real estate and aerospace—have begun to crumble. Is violent inter-ethnic conflict on the horizon without the social glue of economic growth?

In such an eventuality, will Los Angeles remain, as Kapuscinski has postulated, a premonition of the future?

1988—TRADITIONAL history has been a history of nations. But for the first time since the Roman Empire, there is the possibility of creating the history of a civilization. Now is the first chance, on a new basis with new technologies, to create a civilization of unprecedented openness and 1 pluralism. A civilization of the polycentric mind. A civilization that leaves behind forever the ethnocentric, tribal mentality. The mentality of destruction.

Los Angeles is a premonition of this new civilization. Linked more to the Third World and Asia than to the Europe of America's racial and cultural roots, Los Angeles and Southern California will enter the 21st century as a multi-racial and multicultural society. This is absolutely new. There is no previous example of a civilization that is being simultaneously created by so many races, nationalities, and cultures. This new type of cultural pluralism is completely unknown in the history of mankind.

America is becoming more plural every day because of the unbelievable facility of the new Third World immigrants to put a piece of their original culture inside of American culture. The notion of a "dominant" American culture is changing every moment. It is incredible coming to America to find you are somewhere else—in Seoul, in Taipei, in Mexico City. You can travel inside Korean culture right on the streets of Los Angeles. Inhabitants of this vast city are veritable tourists in the place of their own residence.

There are large communities of Laotians, Vietnamese, Cambodians, Mexicans, Salvadorans, Guatemalans, Iranians, Japanese, Koreans, Armenians, Chinese. We find here Little Taipei, Little Saigon, Little Tokyo, Koreatown, Little Central America, the Iranian neighborhood in Westwood, the Armenian community in Glendale or Hollywood, and the vast Mexican-American areas of East Los Angeles. Eighty-one languages, few of them European, are spoken in the elementary school system of the city of Los Angeles.

This transformation of American culture anticipates the general trend in 5
the composition of mankind. Ninety percent of the immigrants to this city are from the Third World. At the beginning of the 21st century, nearly 90 percent of the world's population will be dark-skinned; the white race will be no more than 11 percent of all human beings living on our planet.

Usually, the contact between developed and underdeveloped worlds has the character of exploitation—just taking people's labor and resources and giving them nothing. And the border between races has usually been a border of tension, of crisis.

But this Pacific Rim civilization being created is a new relationship between development and underdevelopment. Here, there is openness. There is hope. And a future. There is a multicultural crowd. But it is not fighting. It is cooperating, peacefully competing, building. For the first time in 400 years of relations between the nonwhite Western world and the white Western world, the general character of the relationship is cooperation and construction, not exploitation or destruction.

Unlike any other place on the planet, Los Angeles shows us the potential of development once the Third World mentality merges with an open sense of possibility, a culture of organization, a Western conception of time.

In 1924, the Mexican philosopher Jose Vasconcellos wrote a book entitled *La Raza Cosmica.* He dreamt of the possibility that, in the future, mankind would create one human race, a mestizo race.[1] All races on the planet would merge into one type of man. *La Raza Cosmica* is being born in Los Angeles, in the cultural sense if not the anthropological sense. A vast mosaic of different races, cultures, religions and moral habits are working toward one common aim. From the perspective of a world submerged in religious, ethnic, and racial conflict, this harmonious cooperation is something unbelievable. It is truly striking.

For the destructive, paralyzed "Third World" where I have spent most 10
of my life, it is important, simply, that such a possibility as Los Angeles exists.

1991—Several thoughts crossed my mind almost simultaneously when I learned that white policemen in Los Angeles had beaten up a black man named Rodney G. King. The first thought—or, rather, feeling—was of surprise. Perhaps I have an overly naive and idealistic view of Los Angeles. My visit there left me with the impression of a city that, despite its indisputable problems with traffic jams, excessive pollution, and drugs, is nevertheless a model of the harmonious coexistence of people of various races, languages, and religions. I have widely voiced this positive assessment. Meantime, in my exemplar of racial harmony, white cops had beaten up a black man!

Because the whole unpleasant incident came to light through the sole fact that someone had recorded it on a videocamera, my second thought was of the revolution brought about in the world (a revolution that continues and develops) by this small, practically pocket-size object. Beware! Your every gesture can from now on be observed and registered without your knowledge or consent!

The vigilant eye of the meddlesome camera watches us from a thousand places—from windows, from balconies, from rooftops, from stationary or moving cars, from behind bushes. We can be filmed by someone who is standing at a bus stop, or sitting at a table in a bar. We can be filmed at all times, almost everywhere, and, potentially, by everyone. This is precisely what happened to the policemen who beat up Rodney King. They fell into the net of that ubiquitous lens, which has itself become a kind of weapon that is virtually universally accessible.

Next, as my attention was drawn to the enormous publicity given the deplorable incident by the American mass media, I thought—fortunate Americans! It is a fortunate country, a fortunate nation, that is able to call forth such a storm of anger and protests because somebody beat up somebody else.

After all, Los Angeles lies on the same planet on which on the very day, 15
at the very instant, that the policemen were beating up Rodney King, there perished in various wars or from hunger thousands upon thousands of people, in Ethiopia, in Mozambique, in Afghanistan, in Iraq; and it didn't occur to anyone to raise a voice of indignation and protest against these massive and

[1]*Mestizo* refers specifically to a person of mixed European and Native American blood; Vasconcellos's *La Raza Cosmica* (*The Cosmic Race*) envisions a world in which all races are blended.

cruel deaths. I thought—although it is an absurd thought—that it is fortunate to be one of the beaten in America, for afterwards one can demand a million dollars for every blow (as Rodney King has cleverly done), while the wretches in Africa and the Middle East, although they are harmed by fate in a truly horrible way, can't even count on a handful of rice and a few drops of water. (At that moment I found myself on slippery ground—for one cannot use a greater wrong to excuse a lesser one.)

Nevertheless, I decided to read once again what the American press had written about the incident. And upon rereading, one thing struck me—that the indignation did not result only from the fact of someone having been so badly beaten, but from the fact that *white* policemen had beaten up a *black* citizen. Whites beat up a black—that was the real cause of the press's anger and disapproval. While at first I was inclined to belittle and make light of the entire Rodney King incident, as I began to appreciate all its racial implications, the outrage of American public opinion started to seem understandable and justified. For today humanity is threatened by three powder kegs, variously dispersed around our planet: One keg is nationalism, the second, racism, and the third, religious fundamentalism.

The point is not to allow one of these kegs to explode in our own house, in our own country; for such an explosion would demolish our present order in its entirety. It would bring about its ruin. And the best way to prevent such an explosion is to snuff out even the smallest incident while it is still but a flicker.

For our increasingly irrational and unpredictable world, even something of seemingly little importance can serve as the catalyst of a larger and devastating conflict. That is why I understand the voice of criticism and censure raised against the Los Angeles policemen: They were playing with dangerous, easily spreading fire.

Questions for Discussion

1. What meanings would you attach to the terms "openness," "pluralism," and "the polycentric mind" (paragraph 1)? Are these "good" terms to you—that is, do they have positive connotations? How do you react to the extreme racial and ethnic diversity of cities like Los Angeles and New York? How do you account for your reaction?
2. Kapuscinski is attracted to Los Angeles because, in his view, it represents "a civilization that leaves behind forever the ethnocentric, tribal mentality. The mentality of destruction" (paragraph 1). How do you understand the notion of ethnocentricity? In your view, is the author justified in condemning the tribal mentality so completely? Is it "the mentality of destruction"?
3. With what is the author comparing the "racial paradise" of the United States? What can we learn from seeing our own racial problems in the

context of, say, conflicts in the Middle East or the former Yugoslavia? How do you react to the label "fortunate Americans" (paragraph 14)?

4. In paragraph 16 Kapuscinski refers to "three powder kegs"—nationalism, racism, and religious fundamentalism. How would you define each of these "isms"? How do they figure in world problems? How do they figure in tensions and conflicts within the United States?

For Inquiry and Convincing

Find out all you can about the Rodney King episode, including the subsequent rioting, the trials of both the police officers involved and rioters arrested in other acts of brutality, and the aftermath for Los Angeles residents generally. Write an essay that agrees or disagrees (or does some of both) with Kapuscinski's evaluation of this event.

MICHAEL LIND

The Beige and the Black

We may hope for mutual understanding among the races and toleration of racial differences, but nothing indicates the actual breakdown of old racial tensions more clearly and profoundly than large numbers of racially mixed couples. Hence, many respond favorably to The Cosmic Race, *Jose Vasconcellos's 1924 book, which predicted the end of race through interracial marriage. In the previous selection Ryszard Kapuscinski refers to this possibility as part of his vision of Los Angeles as a new civilization, free of racial and ethnic hostilities.*

Perhaps the cosmic race will eventually emerge; however, as this article argues, the next fifty years will likely see only part of the vision realized. Americans of European, Hispanic, Asian, and Native American ancestry are intermarrying at significant and increasing rates. African Americans intermarry as well, but at much lower percentages. Thus, even as the old racial divide between white and black weakens, a new line may form separating "the beige"— "a white-Asian-Hispanic . . . majority"—from "the black," especially from impoverished African Americans segregated in our inner cities.

Michael Lind is the Washington editor of Harper's. *This article appeared originally in the* New York Times Magazine *(August 16, 1998).*

JUST WHEN you think you're ready for 21st-century America, it changes on you yet again. A few years ago, predictions that whites would eventually become a minority group in the United States galvanized the multicultural left—and horrified the nativist right. More recently, news of the growing number of mixed-race Americans has inspired the political center with a vision of a true racial melting pot, one in which white and black alike will blend into a universal brown. But a closer look at demographic trends suggests that neither of these futures—a nonwhite majority, a uniformly "beige" society—will very likely come to pass. Instead, shifting patterns of racial intermarriage suggest that the next century may see the replacement of the historic white-black dichotomy in America with a troubling new division, one between beige and black. 1

Racial intermarriage has long been a source of anxiety in America. After World War II, Senator Theodore G. Bilbo of Mississippi defended white supremacy in a book titled *Take Your Choice: Separation or Mongrelization.* Like other racists of his era, Bilbo believed that an inevitable result of dismantling segregation would be the amalgamation of the races through intermarriage. He was right: since the U.S. Supreme Court, in *Loving v. Virginia* (1967), struck down the last antimiscegenation laws of the states, marriage across racial lines has grown at a remarkable rate.

Between 1960 and 1990, interracial marriages in this country skyrocketed by more than 800 percent. Roughly 1 in 25 American married couples today are interracial. In fact, there are at least three million children of mixed-race parentage in the United States—and this figure doesn't even include the millions of Hispanic mestizos and black Americans who have European and Indian ancestors. Perhaps the best-known multiracial American is Tiger Woods, who has described himself as "Cablinasian": a mix of Caucasian, black, Native American and Asian.

Oddly, the U.S. Census Bureau has yet to account properly for the presence of mixed-race Americans. As a result, many of its projections are off target. For example, the bureau has famously predicted that in 2050, whites will make up 52.7 percent of the U.S. population. (In 1990, it was 75.7 percent.) Hispanics will account for 21.1 percent of the population; blacks, 15 percent, and Asians, 10.1 percent. Presumably, 2050 will be white America's last stand. But this projection is dubious, because it assumes that for the next half-century there will be absolutely no intermarriage among the four major conventionally defined racial groups in the United States: whites, blacks, Hispanics and Asians. Each group is supposed to somehow expand—or decline—in hermetic isolation.

But according to an analysis of the 1990 U.S. Census data for persons 5
ages 25–34 by Reynolds Farley, a demographer with the Russell Sage Foundation, 31.6 percent of native-born Hispanic husbands and 31.4 percent of native-born Hispanic wives had white spouses. The figures were even higher for Asians: 36 percent for native-born Asian husbands and 45.2 percent for native-born Asian wives. (In fact, Asian wives were as likely to marry white Americans as they were to marry Asian-Americans.) The highest intermarriage rates are those of American Indians. Majorities of American Indian men (52.9 percent) and American Indian women (53.9 percent) married whites rather than American Indians (40.3 percent and 37.2 percent, respectively). And these figures, which themselves document the creolization of America, undoubtedly understate the extent of racial intermarriage that the 2000 Census will reveal.

Of course intermarriage rates vary by region. White men in California in 1990 were more than six times as likely as Midwestern white men to marry outside their race. Overall, interracial marriages are more than twice as common in California (1 in 10 new couples) as in the rest of the country (1 in 25). According to the magazine *Interrace,* San Jose, San Diego and Oakland are among the Top 10 cities for interracial couples. America's racial complexion, then, will change more quickly on the coasts than in the heartland.

Nevertheless, the overall increase in intermarriage means that both multicultural liberals and nativist conservatives have misunderstood the major demographic trends in this country. There is not going to be a nonwhite majority in the 21st century. Rather, there is going to be a mostly white mixed-race majority. The only way to stop this is to force all Hispanic and Asian-Americans from now on to marry within their officially defined groups. And that is not going to happen.

Thus, the old duality between whites and nonwhites is finally breaking down. But don't cheer just yet. For what seems to be emerging in the United

States is a new dichotomy between blacks and nonblacks. Increasingly, whites, Asians and Hispanics are creating a broad community from which black Americans may be excluded.

Disparities in interracial marriages underline this problem. Black-white marriages have risen from a reported 51,000 in 1960 (when they were still illegal in many states) to 311,000 in 1997. Marriages between white men and black women, though still uncommon, rose from 27,000 in 1980 to 122,000 in 1995. Although black out-marriage rates have risen, they remain much lower than out-marriage rates for Hispanics, Asians and American Indians. For the 25–34 age group, only 8 percent of black men marry outside their race. Less than 4 percent of black women do so.

While many blacks frown upon marriage by blacks to members of other 10
groups—such relationships are viewed by some as disloyal—it seems very unlikely that such conservative attitudes are more pronounced among black Americans than among whites or Hispanic or Asian immigrants. The major cause of low black out-marriage rates may well be antiblack prejudice—the most enduring feature of the eroding American caste system. Furthermore, antiblack prejudice is often picked up by immigrants, when it is not brought with them from their countries of origin.

In the past, the existence of an "untouchable" caste of blacks may have made it easier for Anglo-Americans to fuse with more recent European immigrants in an all-encompassing "white" community. Without blacks as a common "other," the differences between Anglo-Americans, German-Americans, Irish-Americans and Italian-Americans might have seemed much more important. Could this be occurring again? A Knight-Ridder poll taken in May 1997 showed that while respondents were generally comfortable with intermarriage, a full 3 in 10 respondents opposed marriage between blacks and whites.

In the 21st century, then, the U.S. population is not likely to be crisply divided among whites, blacks, Hispanics, Asians and American Indians. Nor is it likely to be split two ways, between whites and nonwhites. Rather, we are most likely to see something more complicated: a white-Asian-Hispanic melting-pot majority—a hard-to-differentiate group of beige Americans—offset by a minority consisting of blacks who have been left out of the melting pot once again.

The political implications of this new racial landscape have not yet been considered. On the positive side, the melting away of racial barriers between Asians, Latinos and whites will prevent a complete Balkanization of American society into tiny ethnic groups. On the negative side, the division between an enormous, mixed-race majority and a black minority might be equally unhealthy. The new mixed-race majority, even if it were predominantly European in ancestry, probably would not be moved by appeals to white guilt. Some of the new multiracial Americans might disingenuously invoke an Asian or Hispanic grandparent to include themselves among the victims rather than the victimizers. Nor would black Americans find many partners for a "rainbow coalition" politics, except perhaps among recent immigrants.

One political response to a beige-and-black America might be a movement to institutionalize binationalism. In Canada, Anglophones and Francophones have been declared the country's two "founding nations." Blacks, as a quasi-permanent minority, might insist upon a status different from that of voluntary immigrants who merge with the majority in a few generations. Such compromises, however, are difficult to maintain. If most immigrants blend into one of the two founding nations—the Anglophone majority in Canada, the mixed-race majority in the U.S.—then working out a stable modus vivendi between the expanding community and the shrinking community becomes almost impossible.

The other possibility is that black Americans will, in time, participate in 15
the melting pot at rates comparable with other groups. Such a result cannot and should not be the aim of public policy—how can you legislate romance?—but it may be an incidental result of greater social mobility and economic equality. The evidence suggests that the association of people as equals erodes even the oldest and deepest prejudice in American life.

According to the 1990 census, white men 25–34 in the U.S. military were 2.3 times as likely to marry nonwhite women as civilians. And white women in the same age group who served in the military in the 1980's were seven times as likely as their civilian counterparts to have black husbands. Indeed, for all groups except for Asian men, military service makes out-marriage much more likely. The reason for this is clear: the U.S. military is the most integrated institution in American society because it is the most egalitarian and meritocratic. It is also—not coincidentally—the least libertarian and least tolerant of subcultural diversity. It may be that in the nation as a whole, as in the military, the integration of individuals can be achieved only at the price of the sacrifice of lesser differences to a powerful common identity.

In the end, racial intermarriage is a result, not a cause, of racial integration. Racial integration, in turn, is a result of social equality. The civil rights revolution abolished racial segregation by law, but not racial segregation by class. Ending racial segregation by class might—just might—bring about an end to race itself in America. It is certainly worth a try.

Questions for Discussion

1. "Intermarriage rates vary by region," Lind notes. There are far more mixed-race couples on both U.S. coasts than in the heartland, the interior regions of the country. Does this matter? If so, in what ways?
2. Intermarriage is also more common in big cities than in small towns or rural communities. Does this matter? If so, in what ways?
3. How do you explain the lower rate of out-marriage for black women as opposed to black men?

4. According to a 1997 Knight-Ridder poll Lind cites, thirty percent of Americans continue to oppose marriage between whites and blacks. How do you account for the opposition?
5. In the next-to-last paragraph Lind discusses the military and intermarriage. How does he interpret the data? What implications do you see for American society in general?

For Inquiry

"Racial intermarriage is a result, not a cause, of racial integration. Racial integration, in turn, is a result of social equality." So Lind claims, and his logic seems compelling.

Investigate his assertions in the context of interracial dating. If you have had experience with it, examine your relationship(s). Talk with classmates and/or with friends who also have had experience with it. If you feel comfortable approaching interracial couples on campus you don't know or don't know well, get their input, too.

How much does integration have to do with interracial dating? Are the people involved always social equals—that is, do they come from the same socioeconomic class and share other similarities in background? Are such factors as important in dating as they are in marriage? Why or why not?

In a short essay discuss the conclusions you've reached, and compare them with those of other class members.

ABIGAIL and STEPHAN THERNSTROM

Black Progress: How Far We've Come—And How Far We Have to Go

A persistent problem in assessing race relations is how to characterize current conditions. In their controversial 1997 book Americans in Black and White: One Nation Indivisible, *Abigail and Stephan Thernstrom argue that blacks have made extraordinary gains over the past half-century and that most of the advance had little to do with government programs. Further progress, they contend, depends on narrowing the "skills gap" between black and white—that is, on effective education—not on affirmative action, which they see as contributing little to the total picture. They urge optimism about the future of race relations.*

Abigail Thernstrom is a senior fellow at the Manhattan Institute in New York; Stephan Thernstrom the Winthrop Professor of History at Harvard. The following article, which appeared in the Brookings Review *(Spring 1998), summarizes their book's argument.*

LET'S START with a few contrasting numbers. Sixty and 2.2. In 1940, 60 percent of employed black women worked as domestic servants; today the number is down to 2.2 percent, while 60 percent hold white-collar jobs. Forty-four and 1. In 1958, 44 percent of whites said they would move if a black family became their next door neighbor; today the figure is 1 percent. Eighteen and 86. In 1964, the year the Great Civil Rights act was passed, only 18 percent of whites claimed to have a friend who was black; today 86 percent say they do, while 87 percent of blacks assert they have white friends. 1

Progress is the largely suppressed story of race and race relations over the past half-century. And thus it's news that more than 40 percent of African Americans now consider themselves members of the middle class. Forty-two percent own their own homes, a figure that rises to 75 percent if we look just at black married couples. Black two-parent families earn only 13 percent less than those who are white. Almost a third of the black population lives in suburbia.

Because these are facts the media seldom report, the black underclass continues to define black America in the view of much of the public. Many assume blacks live in ghettos, often in high-rise public housing projects. Crime and the welfare check are seen as their main source of income. The stereotype crosses racial lines. Blacks are even more prone than whites to exaggerate the extent to which African Americans are trapped in inner-city poverty. In a 1991 Gallup poll, about one-fifth of all whites, but almost half of black respondents, said that at least three out of four African Americans were impoverished urban residents. And yet, in reality, blacks who consider themselves to be middle class outnumber those with incomes below the poverty line by a wide margin.

A Fifty-Year March Out of Poverty

Fifty years ago most blacks were indeed trapped in poverty, although they did not reside in inner cities. When Gunnar Myrdal published *An American Dilemma* in 1944, most blacks lived in the South and on the land as laborers and sharecroppers. (Only one in eight owned the land on which he worked.) A trivial 5 percent of black men nationally were engaged in non-manual, white-collar work of any kind; the vast majority held ill-paid, insecure, manual jobs—jobs that few whites would take. As already noted, six out of ten African-American women were household servants who, driven by economic desperation, often worked 12-hour days for pathetically low wages. Segregation in the South and discrimination in the North did create a sheltered market for some black businesses (funeral homes, beauty parlors, and the like) that served a black community barred from patronizing "white" establishments. But the number was minuscule.

Beginning in the 1940s, however, deep demographic and economic 5
change, accompanied by a marked shift in white racial attitudes, started blacks down the road to much greater equality. New Deal legislation, which set minimum wages and hours and eliminated the incentive of southern employers to hire low-wage black workers, put a damper on further industrial development in the region. In addition, the trend toward mechanized agriculture and a diminished demand for American cotton in the face of international competition combined to displace blacks from the land.

As a consequence, with the shortage of workers in northern manufacturing plants following the outbreak of World War II, southern blacks in search of jobs boarded trains and buses in a Great Migration that lasted through the mid-1960s. They found what they were looking for: wages so strikingly high that in 1953 the average income for a black family in the North was almost twice that of those who remained in the South. And through much of the 1950s wages rose steadily and unemployment was low.

Thus by 1960 only one out of seven black men still labored on the land, and almost a quarter were in white-collar or skilled manual occupations. Another 24 percent had semiskilled factory jobs that meant membership in the stable working class, while the proportion of black women working as servants had been cut in half. Even those who did not move up into higher-ranking jobs were doing much better.

A decade later, the gains were even more striking. From 1940 to 1970, black men cut the income gap by about a third, and by 1970 they were earning (on average) roughly 60 percent of what white men took in. The advancement of black women was even more impressive. Black life expectancy went up dramatically, as did black homeownership rates. Black college enrollment also rose—by 1970 to about 10 percent of the total, three times the prewar figure.

In subsequent years these trends continued, although at a more leisurely pace. For instance, today more than 30 percent of black men and nearly 60 percent of black women hold white-collar jobs. Whereas in 1970 only 2.2

percent of American physicians were black, the figure is now 4.5 percent. But while the fraction of black families with middle-class incomes rose almost 40 percentage points between 1940 and 1970, it has inched up only another 10 points since then.

Affirmative Action Doesn't Work

Rapid change in the status of blacks for several decades followed by a 10
definite slowdown that begins just when affirmative action policies get their start: that story certainly seems to suggest that racial preferences have enjoyed an inflated reputation. "There's one simple reason to support affirmative action," an op-ed writer in the *New York Times* argued in 1995. "It works." That is the voice of conventional wisdom.

In fact, not only did significant advances predate the affirmative action era, but the benefits of race-conscious politics are not clear. Important differences (a slower overall rate of economic growth, most notably) separate the pre-1970 and post-1970 periods, making comparison difficult.

We know only this: some gains are probably attributable to race-conscious educational and employment policies. The number of black college and university professors more than doubled between 1970 and 1990; the number of physicians tripled; the number of engineers almost quadrupled; and the number of attorneys increased more than six-fold. Those numbers undoubtedly do reflect the fact that the nation's professional schools changed their admissions criteria for black applicants, accepting and often providing financial aid to African-American students whose academic records were much weaker than those of many white and Asian-American applicants whom these schools were turning down. Preferences "worked" for these beneficiaries, in that they were given seats in the classroom that they would not have won in the absence of racial double standards.

On the other hand, these professionals make up a small fraction of the total black middle class. And their numbers would have grown without preferences, the historical record strongly suggests. In addition, the greatest economic gains for African Americans since the early 1960s were in the years 1965 to 1975 and occurred mainly in the South, as economists John J. Donahue III and James Heckman have found. In fact, Donahue and Heckman discovered "virtually no improvement" in the wages of black men relative to those of white men outside of the South over the entire period from 1963 to 1987, and southern gains, they concluded, were mainly due to the powerful antidiscrimination provisions in the 1964 Civil Rights Act.

With respect to federal, state, and municipal set-asides, as well, the jury is still out. In 1994 the state of Maryland decided that at least 10 percent of the contracts it awarded would go to minority- and female-owned firms. It more than met its goal. The program therefore "worked" if the goal was merely the narrow one of dispensing cash to a particular, designated group. But how well do these sheltered businesses survive long-term without extraordinary protection from free-market competition? And with almost 30 percent of black families still living in poverty, what is their trickle-down effect? On neither score is the picture reassuring. Programs are often fraudulent, with white contractors offering minority firms 15 percent of the profit with no obligation to do any of the work. Alternatively, set-asides enrich those with the right connections. In Richmond, Virginia, for instance, the main effect of the ordinance was a marriage of political convenience—a working alliance between the economically privileged of both races. The white business elite signed on to a piece-of-the-pie for blacks in order to polish its image as socially conscious and secure support for the downtown revitalization it wanted. Black politicians used the bargain to suggest their own importance to low-income constituents for whom the set-asides actually did little. Neither cared whether the policy in fact provided real economic benefits—which it didn't.

Why Has the Engine of Progress Stalled?

In the decades since affirmative action policies were first instituted, 15
the poverty rate has remained basically unchanged. Despite black gains by numerous other measures, close to 30 percent of black families still live below the poverty line. "There are those who say, my fellow Americans, that even good affirmative action programs are no longer needed," President Clinton said in July 1995. But "let us consider," he went on, that "the unemployment rate for African Americans remains about twice that of whites." Racial preferences are the president's answer to persistent inequality, although a quarter-century of affirmative action has done nothing whatever to close the unemployment gap.

Persistent inequality is obviously serious, and if discrimination were the primary problem, then race-conscious remedies might be appropriate. But while white racism was central to the story in 1964, today the picture is much more complicated. Thus while blacks and whites now graduate at the same rate from high school today and are almost equally likely to attend college, on average they are not equally educated. That is, looking at years of schooling in assessing the racial gap in family income tells us little about the cognitive skills whites and blacks bring to the job market. And cognitive skills obviously affect earnings.

The National Assessment of Educational Progress (NAEP) is the nation's report card on what American students attending elementary and secondary schools know. Those tests show that African-American students, on average, are alarmingly far behind whites in math, science, reading, and writing. For instance, black students at the end of their high school career are almost four years behind white students in reading; the gap is comparable in other subjects. A study of 26- to 33-year-old men who held full-time jobs in 1991 thus found that when education was measured by years of school completed, blacks earned 19 percent less than comparably educated whites. But when word knowledge, paragraph comprehension, arithmetical reasoning, and mathematical knowledge became the yardstick, the results were reversed. Black men earned 9 percent more than white men with the same education—that is, the same performance on basic tests.

Other research suggests much the same point. For instance, the work of economists Richard J. Murnane and Frank Levy has demonstrated the increasing importance of cognitive skills in our changing economy. Employers in firms like Honda now require employees who can read and do math problems at the ninth-grade level at a minimum. And yet the 1992 NAEP math tests, for example, revealed that only 22 percent of African-American high school seniors but 58 percent of their white classmates were numerate enough for such firms to consider hiring them. And in reading, 47 percent of whites in 1992 but just 18 percent of African Americans could handle the printed word well enough to be employable in a modern automobile plant. Murnane and Levy found a clear impact on income. Not years spent in school but strong skills made for high long-term earnings.

The Widening Skills Gap

Why is there such a glaring racial gap in levels of educational attainment? It is not easy to say. The gap, in itself, is very bad news, but even more alarming is the fact that it has been widening in recent years. In 1971, the average African-American 17-year-old could read no better than the typical white child who was six years younger. The racial gap in math in 1973 was 4.3 years; in science it was 4.7 years in 1970. By the late 1980s, however, the picture was notably brighter. Black students in their final year of high school were only 2.5 years behind whites in both reading and math and 2.1 years behind on tests of writing skills.

Had the trends of those years continued, by today black pupils would be 20
performing about as well as their white classmates. Instead, black progress came to a halt, and serious backsliding began. Between 1988 and 1994, the racial gap in reading grew from 2.5 to 3.9 years; between 1990 and 1994, the racial gap in math increased from 2.5 to 3.4 years. In both science and writing, the racial gap has widened by a full year.

There is no obvious explanation for this alarming turnaround. The early gains doubtless had much to do with the growth of the black middle class, but the black middle class did not suddenly begin to shrink in the late 1980s. The poverty rate was not dropping significantly when educational progress was occurring, nor was it on the increase when the racial gap began once again to widen. The huge rise in out-of-wedlock births and the steep and steady decline in the proportion of black children growing up with two parents do not explain the fluctuating educational performance of African-American children. It is well established that children raised in single-parent families do less well in school than others, even when all other variables, including income, are controlled. But the disintegration of the black nuclear family—presciently noted by Daniel Patrick Moynihan as early as 1965—was occurring rapidly in the period in which black scores were rising, so it cannot be invoked as the main explanation as to why scores began to fall many years later.

Some would argue that the initial educational gains were the result of increased racial integration and the growth of such federal compensatory education programs as Head Start. But neither desegregation nor compensatory education seems to have increased the cognitive skills of the black children exposed to them. In any case, the racial mix in the typical school has not changed in recent years, and the number of students in compensatory programs and the dollars spent on them have kept going up.

What about changes in the curriculum and patterns of course selection by students? The educational reform movement that began in the late 1970s did succeed in pushing students into a "New Basics" core curriculum that included more English, science, math, and social studies courses. And there is good reason to believe that taking tougher courses contributed to the temporary rise in black test scores. But this explanation, too, nicely fits the facts for the period before the late 1980s but not the very different picture thereafter. The number of black students going through "New Basics" courses did not decline after 1988, pulling down their NAEP scores.

We are left with three tentative suggestions. First, the increased violence and disorder of innercity lives that came with the introduction of crack cocaine and the drug-related gang wars in the mid-1980s most likely had something to do with the reversal of black educational progress. Chaos in the streets and within schools affects learning inside and outside the classroom.

In addition, an educational culture that has increasingly turned teachers 25
into guides who help children explore whatever interests them may have affected black academic performance as well. As educational critic E. D. Hirsch, Jr., has pointed out, the "deep aversion to and contempt for factual knowledge that pervade the thinking of American educators" means that students fail to build the "intellectual capital" that is the foundation of all further learning. That will be particularly true of those students who come to school most academically disadvantaged—those whose homes are not, in effect, an additional school. The deficiencies of American education hit hardest those most in need of education.

And yet in the name of racial sensitivity, advocates for minority students too often dismiss both common academic standards and standardized tests as culturally biased and judgmental. Such advocates have plenty of company. Christopher Edley, Jr., professor of law at Harvard and President Clinton's point man on affirmative action, for instance, has allied himself with testing critics, labeling preferences the tool colleges are forced to use "to correct the problems we've inflicted on ourselves with our testing standards." Such tests can be abolished—or standards lowered—but once the disparity in cognitive skills becomes less evident, it is harder to correct.

Closing that skills gap is obviously the first task if black advancement is to continue at its once-fast pace. On the map of racial progress, education is the name of almost every road. Raise the level of black educational performance, and the gap in college graduation rates, in attendance at selective professional schools, and in earnings is likely to close as well. Moreover, with educational parity, the whole issue of racial preferences disappears.

The Road to True Equality

Black progress over the past half-century has been impressive, conventional wisdom to the contrary notwithstanding. And yet the nation has many miles to go on the road to true racial equality. "I wish I could say that racism and prejudice were only distant memories, but as I look around I see that even educated whites and African Americans . . . have lost hope in equality," Thurgood Marshall said in 1992. A year earlier *The Economist* magazine had reported the problem of race as one of "shattered dreams." In fact, all hope has not been "lost," and "shattered" was much too strong a word, but certainly in the 1960s the civil rights community failed to anticipate just how tough the voyage would be. (Thurgood Marshall had envisioned an end to all school segregation within five years of the Supreme Court's decision in *Brown v. Board of Education*.) Many blacks, particularly, are now discouraged. A 1997 Gallup poll found a sharp decline in optimism since 1980; only 33 percent of blacks (versus 58 percent of whites) thought both the quality of life for blacks and race relations had gotten better.

Thus, progress—by many measures seemingly so clear—is viewed as an illusion, the sort of fantasy to which intellectuals are particularly prone. But the ahistorical sense of nothing gained is in itself bad news. Pessimism is a self-fulfilling prophecy. If all our efforts as a nation to resolve the "American dilemma" have been in vain—if we've been spinning our wheels in the rut of ubiquitous and permanent racism, as Derrick Bell, Andrew Hacker, and others argue—then racial equality is a hopeless task, an unattainable ideal. If both blacks and whites understand and celebrate the gains of the past, however, we will move forward with the optimism, insight, and energy that further progress surely demands.

Questions for Discussion

1. The Thernstroms contend that "the black underclass continues to define black America in the view of much of the public." Is this true? What do you think of when "black America" is mentioned? How do you explain your image of it?
2. To what forces do the Thernstroms attribute most of the economic and social gains of black Americans since World War II? Do you agree with their analysis? Why or why not?
3. What is your attitude toward the future of race relations? On what do you base your stance? How did you acquire your attitude?

A. RAMEY

Photograph

In 1998, when California's Proposition 209 went into effect, ending affirmative action programs in public employment and at public colleges and universities, students on many California campuses demonstrated against the law and their schools' compliance with it. The intense moment captured in the photograph below shows police barring the doors of a building on UCLA's campus as students attempted to occupy it.

For Discussion

The photograph raises many issues for discussion. Most obviously, the policy of affirmative action is still under debate, as voters in other states have attempted to introduce legislation similar to California's. Look into the effects of Proposition 209 and the Hopwood court decision in Texas. What has been the effect on minority enrollment at schools there? The essays in this chapter by Linda Darling-Hammond and Abigail and Stephan Thernstrom address the question of whether equal education opportunity already exists. Discuss their opposing views on the need for affirmative action.

LINDA DARLING-HAMMOND

Unequal Opportunity: Race and Education

The key principle of social justice in the thinking of most Americans is equal opportunity, as contrasted with equal results. That is, we favor a fair chance for all but believe that outcomes should be different based on individual talent and drive. This article argues that, so far as funding for our school systems is concerned, there is no equity and therefore no genuinely fair chance for all children to get a good education.

Linda Darling-Hammond is an educational researcher at Columbia University Teacher's College and author of The Right to Learn *(1997). This essay appeared in the same issue of the* Brookings Review *as the previous selection.*

W. E. B. Du Bois was right about the problem of the 21st century. 1
The color line divides us still. In recent years, the most visible evidence of this in the public policy arena has been the persistent attack on affirmative action in higher education and employment. From the perspective of many Americans who believe that the vestiges of discrimination have disappeared, affirmative action now provides an unfair advantage to minorities. From the perspective of others who daily experience the consequences of ongoing discrimination, affirmative action is needed to protect opportunities likely to evaporate if an affirmative obligation to act fairly does not exist. And for Americans of all backgrounds, the allocation of opportunity in a society that is becoming ever more dependent on knowledge and education is a source of great anxiety and concern.

At the center of these debates are interpretations of the gaps in educational achievement between white and non-Asian minority students as measured by standardized test scores. The presumption that guides much of the conversation is that equal opportunity now exists; therefore, continued low levels of achievement on the part of minority students must be a function of genes, culture, or a lack of effort and will (see, for example, Richard Herrnstein and Charles Murray's *The Bell Curve* and Stephan and Abigail Thernstrom's *America in Black and White*).

The assumptions that undergird this debate miss an important reality: educational outcomes for minority children are much more a function of their unequal access to key educational resources, including skilled teachers and quality curriculum, than they are a function of race. In fact, the U.S. educational system is one of the most unequal in the industrialized world, and students routinely receive dramatically different learning opportunities based on their social status. In contrast to European and Asian nations that fund schools centrally and equally, the wealthiest 10 percent of U.S. school districts spend nearly 10 times more than the poorest 10 percent, and spending ratios of 3 to 1 are common within states. Despite stark differences in funding, teacher quality, curriculum, and class sizes, the prevailing view is that if students do not achieve, it is their own fault. If we are ever to get beyond the problem of the color line, we must confront and address these inequalities.

The Nature of Educational Inequality

Americans often forget that as late as the 1960s most African-American, Latino, and Native American students were educated in wholly segregated schools funded at rates many times lower than those serving whites and were excluded from many higher education institutions entirely. The end of legal segregation followed by efforts to equalize spending since 1970 has made a substantial difference for student achievement. On every major national test, including the National Assessment of Educational Progress, the gap in minority and white students' test scores narrowed substantially between 1970 and 1990, especially for elementary school students. On the Scholastic Aptitude Test (SAT), the scores of African-American students climbed 54 points between 1976 and 1994, while those of white students remained stable.

Even so, educational experiences for minority students have continued 5
to be substantially separate and unequal. Two-thirds of minority students still attend schools that are predominantly minority, most of them located in central cities and funded well below those in neighboring suburban districts. Recent analyses of data prepared for school finance cases in Alabama, New Jersey, New York, Louisiana, and Texas have found that on every tangible measure—from qualified teachers to curriculum offering—schools serving greater numbers of students of color had significantly fewer resources than schools serving mostly white students. As William L. Taylor and Dianne Piche noted in a 1991 report to Congress:

> Inequitable systems of school finance inflict disproportionate harm on minority and economically disadvantaged students. On an inter-state basis, such students are concentrated in states, primarily in the South, that have the lowest capacities to finance public education. On an intra-state basis, many of the states with the widest disparities in educational expenditures are large industrial states. In these states, many minorities and economically disadvantaged students are located in property-poor urban districts which fare the worst in educational expenditures . . . (or) in rural districts which suffer from fiscal inequity.

Jonathan Kozol's 1991 *Savage Inequalities* described the striking differences between public schools serving students of color in urban settings and their suburban counterparts, which typically spend twice as much per student for populations with many fewer special needs. Contrast MacKenzie High School in Detroit, where word processing courses are taught without word processors because the school cannot afford them, or East St. Louis Senior High School, whose biology lab has no laboratory tables or usable dissecting kits, with nearby suburban schools where children enjoy a computer hookup to Dow Jones to study stock transactions and science laboratories that rival those in some industries. Or contrast Paterson, New Jersey, which could not afford the qualified teachers needed to offer foreign language courses to most high school students, with Princeton, where foreign languages begin in elementary school.

Even within urban school districts, schools with high concentrations of low-income and minority students receive fewer instructional resources than others. And tracking systems exacerbate these inequalities by segregating many low-income and minority students within schools. In combination, these policies leave minority students with fewer and lower-quality books, curriculum materials, laboratories, and computers; significantly larger class sizes; less qualified and experienced teachers; and less access to high-quality curriculum. Many schools serving low-income and minority students do not even offer the math and science courses needed for college, and they provide lower-quality teaching in the classes they do offer. It all adds up.

What Difference Does It Make?

Since the 1966 Coleman report, *Equality of Educational Opportunity,* another debate has raged as to whether money makes a difference to educational outcomes. It is certainly possible to spend money ineffectively; however, studies that have developed more sophisticated measures of schooling show how money, properly spent, makes a difference. Over the past 30 years, a large body of research has shown that four factors consistently influence student achievement: all else equal, students perform better if they are educated in smaller schools where they are well known (300 to 500 students is optimal), have smaller class sizes (especially at the elementary level), receive a challenging curriculum, and have more highly qualified teachers.

Minority students are much less likely than white children to have any of these resources. In predominantly minority schools, which most students of color attend, schools are large (on average, more than twice as large as predominantly white schools and reaching 3,000 students or more in most cities); on average, class sizes are 15 percent larger overall (80 percent larger for non-special education classes); curriculum offerings and materials are lower in quality; and teachers are much less qualified in terms of levels of education, certification, and training in the fields they teach. And in integrated schools, as UCLA professor Jeannie Oakes described in the 1980s and Harvard professor Gary Orfield's research has recently confirmed, most minority students are segregated in lower-track classes with larger class sizes, less qualified teachers, and lower-quality curriculum.

10 Research shows that teachers' preparation makes a tremendous difference to children's learning. In an analysis of 900 Texas school districts, Harvard economist Ronald Ferguson found that teachers' expertise—as measured by scores on a licensing examination, master's degrees, and experience—was the single most important determinant of student achievement, accounting for

roughly 40 percent of the measured variance in students' reading and math achievement gains in grades 1–12. After controlling for socioeconomic status, the large disparities in achievement between black and white students were almost entirely due to differences in the qualifications of their teachers. In combination, differences in teacher expertise and class sizes accounted for as much of the measured variance in achievement as did student and family background.

Ferguson and Duke economist Helen Ladd repeated this analysis in Alabama and again found sizable influences of teacher qualifications and smaller class sizes on achievement gains in math and reading. They found that more of the difference between the high- and low-scoring districts was explained by teacher qualifications and class sizes than by poverty, race, and parent education.

Meanwhile, a Tennessee study found that elementary school students who are assigned to ineffective teachers for three years in a row score nearly 50 percentile points lower on achievement tests than those assigned to highly effective teachers over the same period. Strikingly, minority students are about half as likely to be assigned to the most effective teachers and twice as likely to be assigned to the least effective.

Minority students are put at greatest risk by the American tradition of allowing enormous variation in the qualifications of teachers. The National Commission on Teaching and America's Future found that new teachers hired without meeting certification standards (25 percent of all new teachers) are usually assigned to teach the most disadvantaged students in low-income and high-minority schools, while the most highly educated new teachers are hired largely by wealthier schools. Students in poor or predominantly minority schools are much less likely to have teachers who are fully qualified or hold higher-level degrees. In schools with the highest minority enrollments, for example, students have less than a 50 percent chance of getting a math or science teacher with a license and a degree in the field. In 1994, fully one-third of teachers in high-poverty schools taught without a minor in their main field and nearly 70 percent taught without a minor in their secondary teaching field.

Studies of underprepared teachers consistently find that they are less effective with students and that they have difficulty with curriculum development, classroom management, student motivation, and teaching strategies. With little knowledge about how children grow, learn, and develop, or about what to do to support their learning, these teachers are less likely to understand students' learning styles and differences, to anticipate students' knowledge and potential difficulties, or to plan and redirect instruction to meet students' needs. Nor are they likely to see it as their job to do so, often blaming the students if their teaching is not successful.

15 Teacher expertise and curriculum quality are interrelated, because a challenging curriculum requires an expert teacher. Research has found that both students and teachers are tracked: that is, the most expert teachers teach the

most demanding courses to the most advantaged students, while lower-track students assigned to less able teachers receive lower-quality teaching and less demanding material. Assignment to tracks is also related to race: even when grades and test scores are comparable, black students are more likely to be assigned to lower-track, nonacademic classes.

When Opportunity Is More Equal

What happens when students of color do get access to more equal opportunities? Studies find that curriculum quality and teacher skill make more difference to educational outcomes than the initial test scores or racial backgrounds of students. Analyses of national data from both the High School and Beyond Surveys and the National Educational Longitudinal Surveys have demonstrated that, while there are dramatic differences among students of various racial and ethnic groups in course-taking in such areas as math, science, and foreign language, for students with similar course-taking records, achievement test score differences by race or ethnicity narrow substantially.

Robert Dreeben and colleagues at the University of Chicago conducted a long line of studies documenting both the relationship between educational opportunities and student performance and minority students' access to those opportunities. In a comparative study of 300 Chicago first graders, for example, Dreeben found that African-American and white students who had comparable instruction achieved comparable levels of reading skill. But he also found that the quality of instruction given African-American students was, on average, much lower than that given white students, thus creating a racial gap in aggregate achievement at the end of first grade. In fact, the highest-ability group in Dreeben's sample was in a school in a low-income African-American neighborhood. These children, though, learned less during first grade than their white counterparts because their teacher was unable to provide the challenging instruction they deserved.

When schools have radically different teaching forces, the effects can be profound. For example, when Eleanor Armour-Thomas and colleagues compared a group of exceptionally effective elementary schools with a group of low-achieving schools with similar demographic characteristics in New York City, roughly 90 percent of the variance in student reading and mathematics scores at grades 3, 6, and 8 was a function of differences in teacher qualifications. The schools with highly qualified teachers serving large numbers of minority and low-income students performed as well as much more advantaged schools.

Most studies have estimated effects statistically. However, an experiment that randomly assigned seventh grade "at-risk" students to remedial, average, and honors mathematics classes found that the at-risk students who took the honors class offering a pre-algebra curriculum ultimately outperformed all other students of similar backgrounds. Another study compared African-American high school youth randomly placed in public housing in the

Chicago suburbs with city-placed peers of equivalent income and initial academic attainment and found that the suburban students, who attended largely white and better-funded schools, were substantially more likely to take challenging courses, perform well academically, graduate on time, attend college, and find good jobs.

What Can Be Done?

. . . Last year the National Commission on Teaching and America's Fu- 20
ture issued a blueprint for a comprehensive set of policies to ensure a "caring, competent, and qualified teacher for every child," as well as schools organized to support student success. Twelve states are now working directly with the commission on this agenda, and others are set to join this year. Several pending bills to overhaul the federal Higher Education Act would ensure that highly qualified teachers are recruited and prepared for students in all schools. Federal policymakers can develop incentives, as they have in medicine, to guarantee well-prepared teachers in shortage fields and high-need locations. States can equalize education spending, enforce higher teaching standards, and reduce teacher shortages, as Connecticut, Kentucky, Minnesota, and North Carolina have already done. School districts can reallocate resources from administrative superstructures and special add-on programs to support better-educated teachers who offer a challenging curriculum in smaller schools and classes, as restructured schools as far apart as New York and San Diego have done. These schools, in communities where children are normally written off to lives of poverty, welfare dependency, or incarceration, already produce much higher levels of achievement for students of color, sending more than 90 percent of their students to college. Focusing on what matters most can make a real difference in what children have the opportunity to learn. This, in turn, makes a difference in what communities can accomplish.

An Entitlement to Good Teaching

The common presumption about educational inequality—that it resides primarily in those students who come to school with inadequate capacities to benefit from what the school has to offer—continues to hold wide currency because the extent of inequality in opportunities to learn is largely unknown. We do not currently operate schools on the presumption that students might be entitled to decent teaching and schooling as a matter of course. In fact, some state and local defendants have countered school finance and desegregation cases with assertions that such remedies are not required unless it can be proven that they will produce equal outcomes. Such arguments against equalizing opportunities to learn have made good on Du Bois's prediction that the problem of the 20th century would be the problem of the color line.

But education resources do make a difference, particularly when funds are used to purchase well-qualified teachers and high-quality curriculum and to create personalized learning communities in which children are well known. In all of the current sturm und drang about affirmative action, "special treatment," and the other high-volatility buzzwords for race and class politics in this nation, I would offer a simple starting point for the next century's efforts: no special programs, just equal educational opportunity.

Questions for Discussion

1. Darling-Hammond provides much evidence of funding inequities in our school systems. How does the funding system work? What social and political forces operate to keep it in place?
2. Darling-Hammond mentions that many modern, industrialized nations fund their schools centrally—that is, by the equivalent of our federal government. How do you respond to the idea of Washington handling the funding of our schools? Would such an approach work in the United States?
3. According to Darling-Hammond, what makes the greatest difference in student learning and achievement? How exactly is the level of funding related to this difference?
4. How would you define a "prepared teacher"? Is preparation the same thing as effectiveness?

For Research and Convincing

Investigate school funding in the city and state where your university is located, or in a neighboring city or state. Are there inequities? How great are they? Do the inequities correlate with educational achievement? By what measures?

Write a paper assessing the school system's (or systems') success in providing equal opportunity. If reform is needed, indicate what should be done. Address your essay to an appropriate authority, such as a state legislator or education agency.

For Inquiry

Inquire into the positions of Darling-Hammond and the Thernstroms on the question of the education gap between whites and minorities. How does each define the gap—or example, what do the Thernstroms mean by a "skills gap" and how is that different from an education gap? Does Darling-Hammond recognize a difference between a skills gap and an education gap? How do the two essays differ in their assessment of how the educational system itself fails to correct the gap? What problems does each essay identify? Evaluate the two arguments and do some additional research to determine what you think is the best explanation of the gap.

SHELBY STEELE

The Recoloring of Campus Life

The following personal and reflective essay centers on what the author calls "concentrated microsocieties," our college campuses. In recent years there has been much discussion of a "new racism" on campuses across the country. Shelby Steele, a professor of English at San Jose State University who attended college in the 1960s, argues that today's campus racism is indeed new; he tries to explain why it exists and how it works. His essay appeared originally in 1989 in Harper's, *an eclectic monthly magazine offering essays on various current topics. Much discussed and often reprinted, "The Recoloring of Campus Life" may well be a contemporary classic.*

IN THE past few years, we have witnessed what the National Institute Against Prejudice and Violence calls a "proliferation" of racial incidents on college campuses around the country. Incidents of on-campus "intergroup conflict" have occurred at more than 160 colleges in the last three years, according to the institute. The nature of these incidents has ranged from open racial violence—most notoriously, the October 1986 beating of a black student at the University of Massachusetts at Amherst after an argument about the World Series turned into a racial bashing, with a crowd of up to 3,000 whites chasing twenty blacks—to the harassment of minority students, to acts of racial or ethnic insensitivity, with by far the greatest number falling in the last two categories. At Dartmouth College, three editors of the *Dartmouth Review,* the off-campus right-wing student weekly, were suspended last winter for harassing a black professor in his lecture hall. At Yale University last year a swastika and the words "white power" were painted on the school's Afro-American cultural center. Racist jokes were aired not long ago on a campus radio station at the University of Michigan. And at the University of Wisconsin at Madison, members of the Zeta Beta Tau fraternity held a mock slave auction in which pledges painted their faces black and wore Afro wigs. Two weeks after the president of Stanford University informed the incoming freshman class last fall that "bigotry is out, and I mean it," two freshmen defaced a poster of Beethoven—gave the image thick lips—and hung it on a black student's door. 1

In response, black students around the country have rediscovered the militant protest strategies of the Sixties. At the University of Massachusetts at Amherst, Williams College, Penn State University, UC Berkeley, UCLA, Stanford, and countless other campuses, black students have sat in, marched, and rallied. But much of what they were marching and rallying about seemed less a response to specific racial incidents than a call for broader action on the part of the colleges and universities they were attending. Black students have demanded everything from more black faculty members and new courses on racism to the addition of "ethnic" foods in the cafeteria. There is the sense in these demands that racism runs deep.

Of course, universities are not where racial problems tend to arise. When I went to college in the mid-Sixties, colleges were oases of calm and understanding in a racially tense society; campus life—with its traditions of tolerance and fairness, its very distance from the "real" world—imposed a degree of broad-mindedness on even the most provincial students. If I met whites who were not anxious to be friends with blacks, most were at least vaguely friendly to the cause of our freedom. In any case, there was no guerrilla activity against our presence, no "mine field of racism" (as one black student at Berkeley recently put it) to negotiate. I wouldn't say that the phrase "campus racism" is a contradiction in terms, but until recently it certainly seemed an incongruence.

But a greater incongruence is the generational timing of this new problem on the campuses. Today's undergraduates were born after the passage of the 1964 Civil Rights Act. They grew up in an age when racial equality was for the first time enforceable by law. This too was a time when blacks suddenly appeared on television, as mayors of big cities, as icons of popular culture, as teachers, and in some cases even as neighbors. Today's black and white college students, veterans of *Sesame Street* and often of integrated grammar and high schools, have had more opportunities to know each other—whites and blacks—than any previous generation in American history. Not enough opportunities, perhaps, but enough to make the notion of racial tension on campus something of a mystery, at least to me.

To try to unravel this mystery I left my own campus, where there have 5
been few signs of racial tension, and talked with black and white students at California schools where racial incidents had occurred: Stanford, UCLA, Berkeley. I spoke with black and white students—and not with Asians and Hispanics—because, as always, blacks and whites represent the deepest lines of division, and because I hesitate to wander onto the complex territory of other minority groups. A phrase by William H. Gass—"the hidden internality of things"—describes with maybe a little too much grandeur what I hoped to find. But it *is* what I wanted to find, for this is the kind of problem that makes a black person nervous, which is not to say that it doesn't unnerve whites as well. Once every six months or so someone yells "nigger" at me from a passing car. I don't like to think that these solo artists might soon make up a chorus or, worse, that this chorus might one day soon sing to me from the paths of my own campus.

I have long believed that trouble between the races is seldom what it appears to be. It was not hard to see after my first talks with students that racial tension on campus is a problem that misrepresents itself. It has the same look, the archetypal pattern, of America's timeless racial conflict—white racism and black protest. And I think part of our concern over it comes from the fact that it has the feel of a relapse, illness gone and come again. But if we are seeing the same symptoms, I don't believe we are dealing with the same illness. For one thing, I think racial tension on campus is the result more of racial equality than inequality.

How to live with racial difference has been America's profound social problem. For the first 100 years or so following emancipation it was controlled by a legally sanctioned inequality that acted as a buffer between the races. No longer is this the case. On campuses today, as throughout society, blacks enjoy equality under the law—a profound social advancement. No student may be kept out of a class or a dormitory or an extracurricular activity because of his or her race. But there is a paradox here: On a campus where members of all races are gathered, mixed together in the classroom as well as socially, differences are more exposed than ever. And this is where the trouble starts. For members of each race—young adults coming into their own, often away from home for the first time—bring to this site of freedom, exploration, and now, today, equality very deep fears and anxieties, inchoate feelings of racial shame, anger, and guilt. These feelings could lie dormant in the home, in familiar neighborhoods, in simpler days of childhood. But the college campus, with its structures of interaction and adult-level competition—the big exam, the dorm, the "mixer"—is another matter. I think campus racism is born of the rub between racial difference and a setting, the campus itself, devoted to interaction and equality. On our campuses, such concentrated micro-societies, all that remains unresolved between blacks and whites, all the old wounds and shames that have never been addressed, present themselves for attention—and present our youth with pressures they cannot always handle.

I have mentioned one paradox: racial fears and anxieties among blacks and whites bubbling up in an era of racial equality under the law, in settings that are among the freest and fairest in society. And there is another, related paradox, stemming from the notion of—and practice of—affirmative action. Under the provisions of the Equal Employment Opportunity Act of 1972, all state governments and institutions (including universities) were forced to initiate plans to increase the proportion of minority and women employees—in the case of universities, of students too. Affirmative action plans that establish racial quotas were ruled unconstitutional more than ten years ago in *University of California Regents v. Bakke.*[1] But quotas are only the most controversial aspect of affirmative action; the principle of affirmative action is reflected in various university programs aimed at redressing and overcoming past patterns of discrimination. Of course, to be conscious of patterns of discrimination—the fact, say, that public schools in the black inner cities are more crowded and

[1]Allan Bakke, a white applicant turned down for admission by a California State University medical school, sued the California system, claiming discrimination because the school's policy of maintaining a sixteen percent minority enrollment meant that minority applicants with lower grade point averages were admitted instead of him. The case was settled in 1978, when a divided U.S. Supreme Court ruled that specific quotas such as those in effect in the California system were not permissible; Bakke was subsequently admitted to the program. However, the Court ruling also stated that race could be considered by college administrators in an effort to achieve a diverse student body. The full legal implications of the ruling have thus been ambiguous.

employ fewer top-notch teachers than white suburban public schools, and that this is a factor in student performance—is only reasonable. However, in doing this we also call attention quite obviously to difference: in the case of blacks and whites, racial difference. What has emerged on campus in recent years—as a result of the new equality and affirmative action, in a sense, as a result of progress—is a *politics of difference,* a troubling, volatile politics in which each group justifies itself, its sense of worth and its pursuit of power, through difference alone.

In this context, racial, ethnic, and gender differences become forms of sovereignty, campuses become balkanized, and each group fights with whatever means are available. No doubt there are many factors that have contributed to the rise of racial tension on campus: What has been the role of fraternities, which have returned to campus with their inclusions and exclusions? What role has the heightened notion of college as some first step to personal, financial success played in increasing competition, and thus tension? Mostly what I sense, though, is that in interactive settings, while fighting the fights of "difference," old ghosts are stirred, and haunt again. Black and white Americans simply have the power to make each other feel shame and guilt. In the "real" world, we may be able to deny these feelings, keep them at bay. But these feelings are likely to surface on college campuses, where young people are groping for identity and power, and where difference is made to matter so greatly. In a way, racial tension on campus in the Eighties might have been inevitable.

10 I would like, first, to discuss black students, their anxieties and vulnerabilities. The accusation that black Americans have always lived with is that they are inferior—inferior simply because they are black. And this accusation has been too uniform, too ingrained in cultural imagery, too enforced by law, custom, and every form of power not to have left a mark. Black inferiority was a precept accepted by the founders of this nation; it was a principle of social organization that relegated blacks to the sidelines of American life. So when today's young black students find themselves on white campuses, surrounded by those who historically have claimed superiority, they are also surrounded by the myth of their inferiority.

Of course it is true that many young people come to college with some anxiety about not being good enough. But only blacks come wearing a color that is still, in the minds of some, a sign of inferiority. Poles, Jews, Hispanics, and other groups also endure degrading stereotypes. But two things make the myth of black inferiority a far heavier burden—the broadness of its scope and its incarnation in color. There are not only more stereotypes of blacks than of other groups, but these stereotypes are also more dehumanizing, more focused on the most despised of human traits—stupidity, laziness, sexual immorality, dirtiness, and so on. In America's racial and ethnic hierarchy, blacks have clearly been relegated to the lowest level—have been burdened with an ambiguous, animalistic humanity. Moreover, this is made unavoidable for blacks by the sheer visibility of black skin, a skin that evokes the myth of inferiority on sight. And today this myth is sadly reinforced for many black students by affirmative action programs, under which blacks may often enter college with lower test scores and high-school grade point averages than whites. "They see me as an affirmative action case," one black student told me at UCLA.

So when a black student enters college, the myth of inferiority compounds the normal anxiousness over whether he or she will be good enough. This anxiety is not only personal but also racial. The families of these students will have pounded into them the fact that blacks are not inferior. And probably more than anything, it is this pounding that finally leaves a mark. If I am not inferior, why the need to say so?

This myth of inferiority constitutes a very sharp and ongoing anxiety for young blacks, the nature of which is very precise: It is the terror that somehow, through one's actions or by virtue of some "proof" (a poor grade, a flubbed response in class), one's fear of inferiority—inculcated in ways large and small by society—will be confirmed as real. On a university campus, where intelligence itself is the ultimate measure, this anxiety is bound to be triggered.

A black student I met at UCLA was disturbed a little when I asked him if he ever felt vulnerable—anxious about "black inferiority"—as a black student. But after a long pause, he finally said, "I think I do." The example he gave was of a large lecture class he'd taken with more than 300 students. Fifty or so black students sat in the back of the lecture hall and "acted out every stereotype in the book." They were loud, ate food, came in late—and generally got lower grades than the whites in the class. "I knew I would be seen like them, and I didn't like it. I never sat by them." Seen like what? I asked, though we both knew the answer. "As lazy, ignorant, and stupid," he said sadly.

Had the group at the back been white fraternity brothers, they would 15
not have been seen as dumb *whites,* of course. And a frat brother who worried about his grades would not worry that he would be seen "like them." The terror in this situation for the student I spoke with was that his own deeply buried anxiety would be given credence, that the myth would be verified, and that he would feel shame and humiliation not because of who he was but simply because he was black. In this lecture hall his race, quite apart from his performance, might subject him to four unendurable feelings—diminishment, accountability to the preconceptions of whites, a powerlessness to change those preconceptions, and, finally, shame. These are the feelings that make up his racial anxiety, and that of all blacks on any campus. On a white campus a black is never far from these feelings, and even his unconscious knowledge that he is subject to them can undermine his self-esteem. There are blacks on every campus who are not up to doing good college-level work. Certain black students may not be happy or motivated or in the appropriate field of study—*just like whites.* (Let us not forget that many white students get poor grades, fail, drop out.) Moreover, many more blacks than whites are not quite prepared for college, may have to catch up, owing to factors beyond their control: poor previous schooling, for example. But the white who has to catch up will not

be anxious that his being behind is a matter of his whiteness, of his being *racially* inferior. The black student may well have such a fear.

This, I believe, is one reason why black colleges in America turn out 34 percent of all black college graduates, though they enroll only 17 percent of black college students. Without whites around on campus the myth of inferiority is in abeyance and, along with it, a great reservoir of culturally imposed self-doubt. On black campuses feelings of inferiority are personal; on campuses with a white majority, a black's problems have a way of becoming a "black" problem.

But this feeling of vulnerability a black may feel in itself is not as serious a problem as what he or she does with it. To admit that one is made anxious in integrated situations about the myth of racial inferiority is difficult for young blacks. It seems like admitting that one *is* racially inferior. And so, most often, the student will deny harboring those feelings. This is where some of the pangs of racial tension begin, because denial always involves distortion.

In order to deny a problem we must tell ourselves that the problem is something different than what it really is. A black student at Berkeley told me that he felt defensive every time he walked into a class and saw mostly white faces. When I asked why, he said, "Because I know they're all racists. They think blacks are stupid." Of course it may be true that some whites feel this way, but the singular focus on white racism allows this student to obscure his own underlying racial anxiety. He can now say that his problem—facing a class full of white faces, *fearing* that they think he is dumb—is entirely the result of certifiable white racism and has nothing to do with his own anxieties, or even that this particular academic subject may not be his best. Now all the terror of his anxiety, its powerful energy, is devoted to simply *seeing* racism. Whatever evidence of racism he finds—and looking this hard, he will no doubt find some—can be brought in to buttress his distorted view of the problem, while his actual deep-seated anxiety goes unseen.

Denial, and the distortion that results, places the problem *outside* the self and in the world. It is not that I have any inferiority anxiety because of my race; it is that I am going to school with people who don't like blacks. This is the shift in thinking that allows black students to reenact the protest pattern of the Sixties. Denied racial anxiety-distortion-reenactment is the process by which feelings of inferiority are transformed into an exaggerated white menace—which is then protested against with the techniques of the past. Under the sway of this process, black students believe that history is repeating itself, that it's just like the Sixties, or Fifties. In fact, it is the not yet healed wounds from the past, rather than the inequality that created the wounds, that is the real problem.

This process generates an unconscious need to exaggerate the level of 20
racism on campus—to make it a matter of the system, not just a handful of students. Racism is the avenue away from the true inner anxiety. How many students demonstrating for a black "theme house"—demonstrating in the style of the Sixties, when the battle was to win for blacks a place on campus—

might be better off spending their time reading and studying? Black students have the highest dropout rate and lowest grade point average of any group in American universities. This need not be so. And it is not the result of not having black theme houses.

It was my very good fortune to go to college in 1964, when the question of black "inferiority" was openly talked about among blacks. The summer before I left for college I heard Martin Luther King, Jr., speak in Chicago, and he laid it on the line for black students everywhere. "When you are behind in a footrace, the only way to get ahead is to run faster than the man in front of you. So when your white roommate says he's tired and goes to sleep, you stay up and burn the midnight oil." His statement that we were "behind in a footrace" acknowledged that because of history, of few opportunities, of racism, we were, in a sense, "inferior." But this had to do with what had been done to our parents and their parents, not with inherent inferiority. And because it was acknowledged, it was presented to us as a challenge rather than a mark of shame.

Of the eighteen black students (in a student body of 1,000) who were on campus in my freshman year, all graduated, though a number of us were not from the middle class. At the university where I currently teach, the dropout rate for black students is 72 percent, despite the presence of several academic-support programs; a counseling center with black counselors; an Afro-American studies department; black faculty, administrators, and staff; a general education curriculum that emphasizes "cultural pluralism"; an Educational Opportunities Program; a mentor program; a black faculty and staff association; and an administration and faculty that often announce the need to do more for black students.

It may be unfair to compare my generation with the current one. Parents do this compulsively and to little end but self-congratulation. But I don't congratulate my generation. I think we were advantaged. We came along at a time when racial integration was held in high esteem. And integration was a very challenging social concept for both blacks and whites. We were remaking ourselves—that's what one did at college—and making history. We had something to prove. This was a profound advantage; it gave us clarity and a challenge. Achievement in the American mainstream was the goal of integration, and the best thing about this challenge was its secondary message—that we *could* achieve.

There is much irony in the fact that black power would come along in the late Sixties and change all this. Black power was a movement of uplift and pride, and yet it also delivered the weight of pride—a weight that would burden black students from then on. Black power "nationalized" the black identity, made blackness itself an object of celebration and allegiance. But if it transformed a mark of shame into a mark of pride, it also, in the name of pride, required the denial of racial anxiety. Without a frank account of one's anxieties, there is no clear direction, no concrete challenge. Black students today do not get as clear a message from their racial identity as my generation got. They are not filled with the same urgency to prove themselves, because black pride has said, You're already proven, already equal, as good as anybody.

The "black identity" shaped by black power most powerfully contributes 25
to racial tensions on campuses by basing entitlement more on race than on constitutional rights and standards of merit. With integration, black entitlement was derived from constitutional principles of fairness. Black power changed this by skewing the formula from rights to color—if you were black, you were entitled. Thus, the United Coalition Against Racism (UCAR) at the University of Michigan could "demand" two years ago that all black professors be given immediate tenure, that there be special pay incentives for black professors, and that money be provided for an all-black student union. In this formula, black becomes the very color of entitlement, an extra right in itself, and a very dangerous grandiosity is promoted in which blackness amounts to specialness.

Race is, by any standard, an unprincipled source of power. And on campuses the use of racial power by one group makes racial or ethnic or gender *difference* a currency of power for all groups. When I make my difference into power, other groups must seize upon their difference to contain my power and maintain their position relative to me. Very quickly a kind of politics of difference emerges in which racial, ethnic, and gender groups are forced to assert their entitlement and vie for power based on the single quality that makes them different from one another.

On many campuses today academic departments and programs are established on the basis of difference—black studies, women's studies, Asian studies, and so on—despite the fact that there is nothing in these "difference" departments that cannot be studied within traditional academic disciplines. If their rationale truly is past exclusion from the mainstream curriculum, shouldn't the goal now be complete inclusion rather than separateness? I think this logic is overlooked because these groups are too interested in the power their difference can bring, and they insist on separate departments and programs as a tribute to that power.

This politics of difference makes everyone on campus a member of a minority group. It also makes racial tensions inevitable. To highlight one's difference as a source of advantage is also, indirectly, to inspire the enemies of that difference. When blackness (and femaleness) becomes power, then white maleness is also sanctioned as power. A white male student at Stanford told me, "One of my friends said the other day that we should get together and start up a white student union and come up with a list of demands."

It is certainly true that white maleness has long been an unfair source of power. But the sin of white male power is precisely its use of race and gender as a source of entitlement. When minorities and women use their race, ethnicity, and gender in the same way, they not only commit the same sin but also, indirectly, sanction the very form of power that oppressed them in the first place. The politics of difference is based on a tit-for-tat sort of logic in which every victory only calls one's enemies to arms.

This elevation of difference undermines the communal impulse by making 30
each group foreign and inaccessible to others. When difference is celebrated rather than remarked, people must think in terms of difference, they must find

meaning in difference, and this meaning comes from an endless process of contrasting one's group with other groups. Blacks use whites to define themselves as different, women use men, Hispanics use whites and blacks, and on it goes. And in the process each group mythologizes and mystifies its difference, puts it beyond the full comprehension of outsiders. Difference becomes an inaccessible preciousness toward which outsiders are expected to be simply and uncomprehendingly reverential. But beware: In this world, even the insulated world of the college campus, preciousness is a balloon asking for a needle. At Smith College, graffiti appears: "Niggers, Spics, and Chinks quit complaining or get out."

Most of the white students I talked with spoke as if from under a faint cloud of accusation. There was always a ring of defensiveness in their complaints about blacks. A white student I spoke with at UCLA told me: "Most white students on this campus think the black student leadership here is made up of oversensitive crybabies who spend all their time looking for things to kick up a ruckus about." A white student at Stanford said: "Blacks do nothing but complain and ask for sympathy when everyone really knows they don't do well because they don't try. If they worked harder, they could do as well as everyone else."

That these students felt accused was most obvious in their compulsion to assure me that they were not racists. Oblique versions of some-of-my-best-friends-are stories came ritualistically before or after critiques of black students. Some said flatly, "I am not a racist, but. . . ." Of course, we all deny being racists, but we only do this compulsively, I think, when we are working against an accusation of bias. I think it was the color of my skin, itself, that accused them.

This was the meta-message that surrounded these conversations like an aura, and in it, I believe, is the core of white American racial anxiety. My skin not only accused them, it judged them. And this judgment was a sad gift of history that brought them to account whether they deserved such an accounting or not. It said that wherever and whenever blacks were concerned, they had reason to feel guilt. And whether it was earned or unearned, I think it was guilt that set off the compulsion in these students to disclaim. I believe it is true that in America black people make white people feel guilty.

Guilt is the essence of white anxiety, just as inferiority is the essence of black anxiety. And the terror that it carries for whites is the terror of discovering that one has reason to feel guilt where blacks are concerned—not so much because of what blacks might think but because of what guilt can say about oneself. If the darkest fear of blacks is inferiority, the darkest fear of whites is that their better lot in life is at least partially the result of their capacity for evil—their capacity to dehumanize an entire people for their own benefit, and then to be indifferent to the devastation their dehumanization has wrought on successive generations of their victims. This is the terror that whites are vulnerable to regarding blacks. And the mere fact of being white is sufficient to feel it, since even whites with hearts clean of racism benefit from being white—benefit at the expense of blacks. This is a conditional guilt having nothing to do with individual intentions or actions. And it makes for a very powerful anxiety because it threatens whites with a view of themselves as inhuman, just as inferiority threatens blacks with a similar view of themselves. At the dark core of both anxieties is a suspicion of incomplete humanity.

So the white students I met were not just meeting me; they were also 35
meeting the possibility of their own inhumanity. And this, I think, is what explains how some young white college students in the late Eighties can so frankly take part in racially insensitive and outright racist acts. They were expected to be cleaner of racism than any previous generation—they were born into the Great Society. But this expectation overlooks the fact that, for them, color is still an accusation and judgment. In black faces there is a discomforting reflection of white collective shame. Blacks remind them that their racial innocence is questionable, that they are the beneficiaries of past and present racism, and that the sins of the father may well have been visited on the children.

And yet young whites tell themselves that they had nothing to do with the oppression of black people. They have a stronger belief in their racial innocence than any previous generation of whites, and a natural hostility toward anyone who would challenge that innocence. So (with a great deal of individual variation) they can end up in the paradoxical position of being hostile to blacks as a way of defending their own racial innocence.

I think this is what the young white editors of the *Dartmouth Review* were doing when they shamelessly harassed William Cole, a black music professor. Weren't they saying, in effect, I am so free of racial guilt that I can afford to ruthlessly attack blacks and still be racially innocent? The ruthlessness of that attack was a form of denial, a badge of innocence. The more they were charged with racism, the more ugly and confrontational their harassment became. Racism became a means of rejecting racial guilt, a way of showing that they were not ultimately racists.

The politics of difference sets up a struggle for innocence among all groups. When difference is the currency of power, each group must fight for the innocence that entitles it to power. Blacks sting whites with guilt, remind them of their racist past, accuse them of new and more subtle forms of racism. One way whites retrieve their innocence is to discredit blacks and deny their difficulties, for in this denial is the denial of their own guilt. To blacks this denial looks like racism, a racism that feeds black innocence and encourages them to throw more guilt at whites. And so the cycle continues. The politics of difference leads each group to pick at the sore spots of the other.

Men and women who run universities—whites, mostly—also participate in the politics of difference, although they handle their guilt differently than many of their students. They don't deny it, but still they don't want to *feel* it. And to avoid this *feeling* of guilt they have tended to go along with whatever blacks put on the table rather than work with them to assess their real needs.

University administrators have too often been afraid of their own guilt and have relied on negotiation and capitulation more to appease that guilt than to help blacks and other minorities. Administrators would never give white students a racial theme house where they could be "more comfortable with people of their own kind," yet more and more universities are doing this for black students, thus fostering a kind of voluntary segregation. To avoid the anxieties of integrated situations, blacks ask for theme houses; to avoid guilt, white administrators give them theme houses.

When everyone is on the run from his anxieties about race, race relations 40
on campus can be reduced to the negotiation of avoidances. A pattern of demand and concession develops in which each side uses the other to escape itself. Black studies departments, black deans of student affairs, black counseling programs, Afro houses, black theme houses, black homecoming dances and graduation ceremonies—black students and white administrators have slowly engineered a machinery of separatism that, in the name of sacred difference, redraws the ugly lines of segregation.

Black students have not sufficiently helped themselves, and universities, despite all their concessions, have not really done much for blacks. If both faced their anxieties, I think they would see the same thing: Academic parity with all other groups should be the overriding mission of black students, and it should also be the first goal that universities have for their black students. Blacks can only *know* they are as good as others when they are, in fact, as good—when their grades are higher and their dropout rate lower. Nothing under the sun will substitute for this, and no amount of concessions will bring it about.

Universities and colleges can never be free of guilt until they truly help black students, which means leading and challenging them rather than negotiating and capitulating. It means inspiring them to achieve academic parity, nothing less, and helping them see their own weaknesses as their greatest challenge. It also means dismantling the machinery of separatism, breaking the link between difference and power, and skewing the formula for entitlement away from race and gender and back to constitutional rights.

As for the young white students who have rediscovered swastikas and the word "nigger," I think they suffer from an exaggerated sense of their own innocence, as if they were incapable of evil and beyond the reach of guilt. But it is also true that the politics of difference creates an environment which threatens their innocence and makes them defensive. White students are not invited to the negotiating table from which they see blacks and others walk away with concessions. The presumption is that they do not deserve to be there because they are white. So they can only be defensive, and the less mature among them will be aggressive. Guerrilla activity will ensue. Of course this is wrong, but it is also a reflection of an environment where difference carries power and where whites have the wrong "difference."

I think universities should emphasize commonality as a higher value than "diversity" and "pluralism"—buzzwords for the politics of difference. Difference that does not rest on a clearly delineated foundation of commonality not only is inaccessible to those who are not part of the ethnic or racial group but is antagonistic to them. Difference can enrich only the common ground.

Integration has become an abstract term today, having to do with little 45
more than numbers and racial balances. But it once stood for a high and admirable set of values. It made difference second to commonality, and it asked members of all races to face whatever fears they inspired in each other. I doubt the word will have a new vogue, but the values, under whatever name, are worth working for.

Questions for Discussion

1. Steele claims that "racial tension on campus [now] is the result more of racial equality than inequality" (paragraph 6). How does he support this contention? Do you find it convincing? Why or why not? Test his assertion against what you see around you. Are blacks and other minorities treated equally on your campus?
2. Steele has much to say about what he calls a "politics of difference" (paragraph 8) on college campuses. How exactly does he depict it? In paragraphs 26–30 he presents an argument against it. What reasons make up the case? Judging from what you know of American history, is this politics of difference new? Is it restricted to college campuses?
3. How does Steele view the influence of black power? Do you find it persuasive? Why or why not?
4. How does Steele explain the anxieties of black and white students? Do you agree that "at the dark core of both anxieties is a suspicion of incomplete humanity" (paragraph 34)? How might this diagnosis apply to women on campus? to gay men and lesbians? to minority races other than blacks?

For Research, Discussion, and Convincing

Conduct research as Steele did—by interviewing students. (Chapter 9 provides guidelines for conducting interviews.) Talk to members of all races and significant ethnic groups on your campus. Pose the kind of questions Steele did, along with any questions his conclusions suggest to you. Record or take careful notes about what your interviewees say. Then meet as a class and discuss how to interpret and explain the responses.

Finally, write an essay about some aspect of difference on your campus—it need not be black versus white. Attempt, as Steele does, to get to "the hidden internality of things" (paragraph 5), the deeper sources of tension and anxiety. Propose ways to cope better with the aspect of difference you isolate for analysis.

PATRICIA J. WILLIAMS

The Distribution of Distress

The previous selection explored the "new racism" on campus; this one takes us from the campus to society at large and explores prejudice of several kinds, some of it masked so well that we do not recognize it as prejudice. Chief among these is classism, *prejudice based not on skin color or ethnic origin but on socioeconomic differences. If, as the American social critic H. L. Mencken contended, class is the "dirty little secret" of American life, this author tells it eloquently and memorably.*

Patricia Williams is a law professor, columnist for The Nation, *and author of* Seeing a Color-Blind Future: The Paradox of Race *(1997), from which the following selection comes.*

1 MANY YEARS ago, I was standing in a so-called juice bar in Berkeley, California. A young man came in whom I had often seen begging in the neighborhood. A more bruised-looking human one could not imagine: he was missing several teeth, his clothes were in rags, his blond hair was matted, his eyes red-rimmed, his nails long and black and broken. On this particular morning he came into the juice bar and ordered some sort of protein drink from the well-scrubbed, patchouli-scented young woman behind the counter. It was obvious that his presence disturbed her, and when he took his drink and mumbled, "Thanks, little lady," she exploded.

"Don't you dare call me 'little lady'!" she snarled with a ferocity that turned heads. "I'm a *woman* and you'd better learn the difference!"

"Sorry," he whispered with his head bowed, like a dog that had been kicked, and he quite literally limped out of the store.

"Good riddance," the woman called after him.

5 This took place some fifteen years ago, but I have always remembered the interchange because it taught me a lot about the not so subliminal messages that can be wrapped in the expression of Virtue Aggrieved, in which antibias of one sort is used to further the agenda of bias of another kind.

In an abstract sense, I understood the resentment for girlish diminutives. Too often as a lawyer I have been in courtroom situations where coy terms of endearment were employed in such a way that "the little lady, God-bless-her" became a marginalizing condescension, a precise condensation of "She thinks she's a lawyer, poor thing." Yet in this instance, gender power was clearly not the issue, but rather the emotional venting of a revulsion at this man's dirty and bedraggled presence. It wasn't just that he had called her a little lady; she seemed angry that he had dared address her at all.

If, upon occasion, the ploughshare of feminism can be beaten into a sword of class prejudice, no less can there be other examples of what I call battling biases, in which the impulse to antidiscrimination is defeated by the intrusion or substitution of a different object of enmity. This revolving door of revulsions is one of the trickiest mechanisms contributing to the enduring nature of prejudice; it is at heart, I suppose, a kind of traumatic reiteration of injurious encounters, preserving even as it transforms the overall history of rage.

I was in England several years ago when a young Asian man was severely beaten in East London by a young white man. I was gratified to see the immediate renunciation of racism that ensued in the media. It was a somewhat more sophisticated and heartfelt collective self-examination than sometimes occurs in the United States in the wake of such incidents, where, I fear, we are much more jaded about all forms of violence. Nevertheless, what intrigued me most about the media coverage of this assault was the unfortunate way in which class bias became a tool for the denunciation of racism.

"Racial, Ethnic, or Religious Prejudice Is Repugnant," screamed the headlines.

Hooray, I thought. 10

And then the full text: "It is repugnant, *particularly*"—and I'm embellishing here—"when committed by a miserable low-class cockney whose bestial nature knows no plummeted depth, etc. etc."

Oh dear, I thought.

In other words, the media not only defined anti-Asian and anti-immigrant animus as ignorance, as surely it is, but went on to define that ignorance as the property of a class, of "the" lower classes, implying even that a good Oxbridge education inevitably lifts one above that sort of thing. As surely it does not.

And therein lies a problem, I think. If race or ethnicity is not a synonym for either ignorance or foreignness, then neither should class be an explanatory trashbin for racial prejudice, domestic incivility, and a host of other social ills. If the last fifty years have taught us nothing else, it is that our "isms" are no less insidious when beautifully polished and terribly refined.

None of us is beyond some such pitfalls, and in certain contexts type- 15
casting can even be a necessary and helpful way of explaining the social world. The hard task is to untangle the instances where the categoric helps us predict and prepare for the world from those instances where it verges on scapegoating, projection, and prejudice.

To restate the problem, I think that the persistence of racism, ethnic and religious intolerance, as well as gender and class bias, is dependent upon recirculating images in which the general and the particular duel each other endlessly.

"*En garde,* you heathenish son of an inferior category!"

"Brute!" comes the response. "I am inalienably endowed with the unique luminosity of my rational individualism; it is you who are the guttural eruption of an unspeakable subclassification . . ."

Thrust and parry, on and on, the play of race versus ethnicity versus class versus blood feud. One sword may be sharper or quicker, but neither's wound is ever healed.

Too often these tensions are resolved simply by concluding that stereo- 20
typing is just our lot as humans so let the consequences fall where they may. But stereotyping operates as habit not immutable trait, a fluid project that rather too easily flows across the shifting ecology of human relations. And racism is a very old, very bad habit.

This malleability of prejudice is underscored by a little cultural comparison. If class bias has skewed discussions of racism in the British examples I have just described, it is rather more common in the United States for race to consume discussions of class altogether. While I don't want to overstate the cultural differences between the United States and the United Kingdom—there is enough similarity to conclude that race and class present a generally interlocking set of problems in both nations—the United States does deem itself classless with almost the same degree of self-congratulation that the United Kingdom prides itself on being largely free of a history of racial bias. Certainly these are good impulses and desirable civic sentiments, but I am always one to look closely at what is deemed beyond the pale. *It will never happen here* . . . The noblest denials are at least as interesting study as the highest ideals.

Consider: for a supposedly classless society, the United States nevertheless suffers the greatest gap of any industrialized nation between its richest and poorest citizens. And there can be no more dramatic and ironic class consciousness than the Dickensian characteristics ascribed to those in the so-called underclass, as opposed to the rest—what are we to call them, the *over*class? Those who are deemed to have class versus those who are so far beneath the usual indicia of even lower class that they are deemed to have no class at all.

If this is not viewed by most Americans as a problem of class stasis, it is perhaps because class denominations are so uniformly understood to be stand-ins for race. The very term *underclass* is a *euphemism* for blackness, class operating as euphemism in that we Americans are an upbeat kind of people and class is usually thought to be an easier problem than race.

Middle-classness, on the other hand, is so persistently a euphemism for whiteness, that middle-class black people are sometimes described as "honorary whites" or as those who have been deracinated in some vaguely political sense. More often than I like to remember, I have been told that my opinion about this or that couldn't possibly be relevant to "real," "authentic" black people. Why? Simply because I don't sound like a Hollywood stereotype of the way black people are "supposed" to talk. "Speaking white" or "Talking black." No in-between. Speaking as a black person while sounding like a white person has, I have found, engendered some complicated sense of betrayal. "*You're* not black! You're not *white!*" No one seems particularly interested in the substantive ideas being expressed; but everyone is caught up with the question of whether anyone should have to listen to a white-voiced black person.

It is in this way that we often talk about class and race such that we 25
sometimes end up talking about neither, because we insist on talking about

race as though it were class and class as though it were race, and it's hard to see very clearly when the waters are so muddied with all that simile and metaphor.

By the same token, America is usually deemed a society in which the accent with which one speaks Does Not Matter. That is largely true, but it is not so where black accents are concerned. While there is much made of regional variations—New Yorkers, Minnesotans, and Southerners are the butts of a certain level of cheap satire—an accent deemed "black" is the one with some substantial risk of evoking outright discrimination. In fact, the speech of real black people ranges from true dialects to myriad patois, to regional accents, to specific syntactical twists or usages of vocabulary. Yet language identified as black is habitually flattened into some singularized entity that in turn becomes synonymous with ignorance, slang, big lips and sloppy tongues, incoherent ideas, and very bad—terribly unruly!—linguistic acts. Black speech becomes a cipher for all the other stereotypes associated with racial discrimination; the refusal to understand becomes rationalized by the assumption of incomprehensibility.

My colleague Professor Mari Matsuda has studied cases involving accent discrimination. She writes of lawsuits whose transcripts revealed an interesting paradox. One case featured a speaker whose accent had been declared incomprehensible by his employer. Nevertheless, his recorded testimony, copied down with no difficulty by the court reporter, revealed a parlance more grammatically accurate, substantively coherent, and syntactically graceful than any other speaker in the courtroom, including the judge. This paradox has always been the subject of some interest among linguists and sociolinguists, the degree to which language is understood in a way that is intimately linked to relations among speakers.

"Good day," I say to you. Do you see me as a genial neighbor, as part of your day? If so, you may be generously disposed to return the geniality with a hearty "Hale fellow, well met."

"Good day," I say. Do you see me as an impudent upstart the very sound of whose voice is an unwelcome intrusion upon your good day? If so, the greeting becomes an act of aggression; woe betide the cheerful, innocent upstart.

"Shall we consider race?" I say to you. If you are disposed to like me, 30
you might hear this as an invitation to a kind of conversation we have not shared before, a leap of faith into knowing more about each other.

"Shall we consider race?" I say. *Not* "Shall I batter you with guilt before we riot in the streets?" But only: "Shall we *consider* race?" Yet if I am that same upstart, the blood will have boiled up in your ears by now, and very shortly you will start to have tremors from the unreasonable audacity of my meddlesome presumption. Nothing I actually say will matter, for what matters is that I am out of place . . .

This dynamic, this vital ingredient of the willingness to hear, is apparent in the contradiction of lower-status speech being simultaneously understood yet not understood. Why is the sound of black voices, the shape of black bodies so overwhelmingly agreeable, so colorfully comprehensible in some contexts, particularly in the sports and entertainment industries, yet deemed so utterly incapable of effective communication or acceptable presence when it comes to finding a job as a construction worker?

This is an odd conundrum, to find the sight and the sound of oneself a red flag. And it is a kind of banner, one's face and one's tongue, a banner of family and affiliation—that rhythm and stress, the buoyance of one's mother's tongue; that plane of jaw, that prominence of brow, the property of one's father's face. What to make of those social pressures that would push the region of the body underground in order to allow the purity of one's inner soul to be more fully seen? When Martin Luther King, Jr., urged that we be judged by the content of our character, surely he meant that what we looked like should not matter. Yet just as surely that enterprise did not involve having to deny the entirely complicated symbolic character of one's physical manifestation. This is a hard point, I confess, and one fraught with risk of misunderstanding. The color of one's skin is a part of ourselves. It does not matter. It is precious, and yet it should not matter; it is important and yet it must not matter. It is simultaneously our greatest vanity and anxiety, and I am of the opinion, like Martin Luther King, that none of this should matter.

Yet let me consider the question of self-erasure. I've written elsewhere about my concern that various forms of biotechnological engineering have been turned to such purposes—from skin lighteners to cosmetic surgery to the market for sperm with blond hair and eggs with high IQs. Consider the boy I read about who had started some sort of computer magazine for children. A young man of eleven, celebrated as a computer whiz, whose family had emigrated from Puerto Rico, now living in New York. The article recounted how much he loved computers because, he said, nobody judged him for what he looked like, and he could speak without an accent. What to make of this freedom as disembodiment, this technologically purified mental communion as escape from the society of others, as neutralized social space. What a delicate project, this looking at each other, seeing yet not staring. Would we look so hard, judge so hard, be so hard—what would we look like?—if we existed unself-consciously in our bodies—sagging, grayhaired, young, old, black, white, balding and content?

Let me offer a more layered illustration of the way in which these issues 35
of race and class interact, the markers of class distinction and bias in the United Kingdom emerging also in the United States as overlapping substantially with the category of race. A few years ago, I purchased a house. Because the house was in a different state than where I was located at the time, I obtained my mortgage by telephone. I am a prudent little squirrel when it comes to things financial, always tucking away sufficient stores of nuts for the winter, and so I meet all the criteria of a quite good credit risk. My loan was approved almost immediately.

A short time after, the contract came in the mail. Among the papers the bank forwarded were forms documenting compliance with what is called the Fair Housing Act. It is against the law to discriminate against black people in the housing market, and one of the pieces of legislation to that effect is the Fair Housing Act, a law that monitors lending practices to prevent banks from doing what is called "red-lining." Red-lining is a phenomenon whereby banks circle certain neighborhoods on the map and refuse to lend in those areas for reasons based on race. There are a number of variations on the theme. Black people cannot get loans to purchase homes in white areas; or black people cannot get start-up money for small businesses in black areas. The Fair Housing Act thus tracks the race of all banking customers to prevent such discrimination. Unfortunately, some banks also use the racial information disclosed on the Fair Housing forms to engage in precisely the discrimination the law seeks to prevent.

I should repeat that to this point my entire mortgage transaction had been conducted by telephone. I should also say that I speak what is considered in the States a very Received-Standard-English, regionally northeastern perhaps, but not marked as black. With my credit history, with my job as a law professor, and no doubt with my accent, I am not only middle-class but match the cultural stereotype of a good white person. It is thus perhaps that the loan officer of this bank, whom I had never met in person, had checked off a box on the Fair Housing form indicating that I *was* "white."

Race shouldn't matter, I suppose, but it seemed to in this case, and so I took a deep breath, crossed out "white," checked the box marked "black," and sent the contract back to the bank. That will teach them to presume too much, I thought. A done deal, I assumed.

Suddenly said deal came to a screeching halt. The bank wanted more money as a down payment, they wanted me to pay more points, they wanted to raise the rate of interest. Suddenly I found myself facing great resistance and much more debt.

What was most interesting about all this was that the reason the bank gave for its newfound recalcitrance was not race, heaven forbid—racism doesn't exist anymore, hadn't I heard? No, the reason they gave was that property values in that neighborhood were suddenly falling. They wanted more money to cover the increased risk.

Initially, I was surprised, confused. The house was in a neighborhood that was extremely stable; prices in the area had not gone down since World War II, only slowly, steadily up. I am an extremely careful shopper and I had uncovered absolutely no indication that prices were falling at all.

It took my real estate agent to make me see the light. "Don't you get it," he sighed. "This is what they always do."

And even though I work with this sort of thing all the time, I really hadn't gotten it: for of course, *I* was the reason the prices were in peril.

The bank was proceeding according to demographic data that show any time black people move into a neighborhood in the States, whites are overwhelmingly likely to move out. In droves. In panic. In concert. Pulling every imaginable resource with them, from school funding to garbage collection to social workers who don't want to work in black neighborhoods to police whose too frequent relation to black communities is a corrupted one of containment rather than protection.

It's called a tipping point, this thing that happens when black people 45
move into white neighborhoods. The imagery is awfully catchy you must admit: the neighborhood just tipping right on over like a terrible accident, whoops! Like a pitcher I suppose. All that nice fresh wholesome milk spilling out, running away . . . leaving the dark, echoing, upended urn of the inner city.

This immense fear of "the black" next door is one reason the United States is so densely segregated. Only two percent of white people have a black neighbor, even though black people constitute approximately thirteen percent of the population. White people fear black people in big ways, in small ways, in financial ways, in utterly incomprehensible ways.

As for my mortgage, I threatened to sue and eventually procured the loan on the original terms. But what was fascinating to me about this whole incident was the way in which it so exemplified the new problems of the new rhetoric of racism. For starters, the new rhetoric of racism never mentions race. It wasn't race but risk with which the bank was concerned. Second, since financial risk is all about economics, my exclusion got reclassified as just a consideration of class, and there's no law against class discrimination, after all, for that would present a restraint on one of our most precious liberties, the freedom to contract or not. If public schools, trains, buses, swimming pools, and neighborhoods remain segregated, it's no longer a racial problem if someone who just happens to be white keeps hiking the price for someone who just accidentally and purely by the way happens to be black. White people set higher prices for the "right," the "choice" of self-segregation. If black people don't move in, it's just that they can't *afford* to. Black people pay higher prices for the attempt to integrate, even as the integration of oneself is a threat to one's investment by lowering its value.

By this measure of mortgage worthiness, the ingredient of blackness is cast not just as a social toll but as an actual tax. A fee, an extra contribution at the door, an admission charge for the higher costs of handling my dangerous propensities, my inherently unsavory properties. I was not judged based on my independent attributes or individual financial worth as a client; nor even was I judged by statistical profiles of what my group actually do. (For, in fact, anxiety-stricken, middle-class black people make grovelingly good cake-baking neighbors when not made to feel defensive by the unfortunate, historical welcome strategies of bombs, burnings, or abandon.)

Rather, I was being evaluated based on what an abstraction of White Society writ large thinks we—or I—do, and that imagined "doing" was treated and thus established as a self-fulfilling prophecy.

However rationalized, this form of discrimination is a burden: one's very 50
existence becomes a lonely vacuum when so many in society not only devalue

me, but devalue *themselves* and their homes for having me as part of the landscaped view from the quiet of their breakfast nook.

I know, I know, I exist in the world on my own terms surely. I am an individual and all that. But if I carry the bank's logic out with my individuality rather than my collectively imagined effect on property values as the subject of this type of irrational economic computation, then *I,* the charming and delightful Patricia J. Williams, become a bit like a car wash in your backyard. Only much worse in real price terms. I am more than a mere violation of the nice residential comfort zone in question; my blackness can rezone altogether by the mere fortuity of my relocation.

"Dumping district," cringes the nice, clean actuarial family next door; "there goes the neighborhood . . ." as whole geographic tracts slide into the chasm of impecuniousness and disgust. I am the economic equivalent of a medical waste disposal site, a toxic heap-o'-home.

In my brand-new house, I hover behind my brand-new kitchen curtains, wondering whether the very appearance of my self will endanger my collateral yet further. When Benetton ran an advertisement that darkened Queen Elizabeth II's skin to a nice rich brown, the *Sun* newspaper ran an article observing that this "obviously cheapens the monarchy." Will the presentation of my self so disperse the value of my own, my ownership, my property?

This is madness, I am sure, as I draw the curtain like a veil across my nose. In what order of things is it *rational* to thus hide and skulk?

It is an intolerable logic. An investment in my property compels a selling 55
of myself.

I grew up in a white neighborhood where my mother's family had been the only black people for about fifty years. In the 1960s, Boston began to feel the effects of the great migration of Southern blacks to the north that came about as a result of the Civil Rights Movement. Two more black families moved into the neighborhood. There was a sudden churning, a chemical response, a collective roiling with streams of froth and jets of steam. We children heard all about it on the playground. The neighborhood was under siege. The blacks were coming. My schoolmates' parents were moving out *en masse.*

It was remarkable. The neighborhood was entirely black within about a year.

I am a risk pool. I am a car wash.

I was affected, I suppose, growing up with those children who frightened themselves by imagining what it would be like to touch black bodies, to kiss those wide unkissable lips, to draw the pure breath of life through that crude and forbidden expanse of nose; is it really possible that a gentle God—their God, dear God—would let a *human* heart reside within the wet charred thickness of black skin?

I am, they told me, a jumble of discarded parts: low-browed monkey 60
bones and infected, softly pungent flesh.

In fact, my price on the market is a variable affair. If I were crushed and sorted into common elements, my salt and juice and calcinated bits are worth approximately five English pounds. Fresh from the kill, in contrast, my body parts, my lungs and liver, heart and healthy arteries, would fetch some forty thousand. There is no demand for the fruit of my womb, however; eggs fresh from their warm dark sanctuary are worthless on the open market. "Irish Egg Donor Sought," reads an ad in the little weekly newspaper that serves New York City's parent population. And in the weird economy of bloodlines, and with the insidious variability of prejudice, "Irish eggs" command a price of upwards of five thousand pounds.

This silent market in black worth is pervasive. When a certain brand of hiking boots became popular among young people in Harlem, the manufacturer pulled the product from inner-city stores, fearing that such a trend would "ruin" the image of their boot among the larger market of whites.

It's funny . . . even shoes.

Last year I had a funny experience in a shoe store. The salesman would bring me only one shoe, not two.

"I can't try on a pair?" I asked in disbelief. 65

"When you pay for a pair," he retorted. "What if there were a hundred of you," he continued. "How would we keep track?"

I was the only customer in the store, but there were a hundred of me in his head.

In our Anglo-American jurisprudence there is a general constraint limiting the right to sue to cases and controversies affecting the individual. As an individual, I could go to the great and ridiculous effort of suing for the minuscule amount at stake in waiting for the other shoe to drop from his hand; but as for the real claim, the group claim, the larger defamation to all those other hundreds of me . . . well, that will be a considerably tougher row to hoe.

I am one, I am many.

70 I am amiable, orderly, extremely honest, and a very good neighbor indeed. I am suspect profile, market cluster, actuarial monster, statistical being.

My particulars battle the generals.

"Typecasting!" I protest.

"Predictive indicator," assert the keepers of the gate.

"Prejudice!" I say.

"Precaution," they reply. 75

Hundreds, even thousands, of me hover in the breach.

Questions for Discussion

1. Williams opens her essay with two examples of what she calls "battling biases," one kind of enmity substituting for another. Have you witnessed "this revolving door of revulsions" yourself? When? Under what circumstances? Did you recognize the prejudice of the person resisting prejudice or not?
2. "In certain contexts," Williams says, "typecasting can be a necessary and helpful way of explaining the social world." What contexts? Can you offer

examples of when typecasting was necessary and useful? When does typecasting "verge on scapegoating, projection, and prejudice"?

3. Williams alleges that, in contrast to Britain, a very class-conscious society, in the United States "it is rather more common . . . for race to consume discussions of class altogether." Do you see her point in your own experience? Why might class prejudice mask itself as race prejudice in the United States?
4. Williams says that accent prejudice—judging people based on their speech, which often reveals regional and class origins—is more a problem for blacks than for other races. Can you think of examples of stereotyping based on speech differences involving other races? How did the stereotypes affect your behavior?

For Research and Inquiry

Much has been written in recent years about the problems of the black middle class, the forty percent or so of African Americans whom most would say are relatively well off. Williams gives us some insight into the tensions and conflicts of black middle-class life, but let's find out more by reading some of the literature and discussing these problems openly with students from all racial and social backgrounds.

What does the literature identify as sources of problems? Are the difficulties serious? Are they essentially different from the struggles of the white majority or from other minorities? If so, how exactly? Are the problems temporary, or are they likely to remain problems for many years to come? What strategies do blacks use to cope with their situation? Does the rest of middle-class America need to be aware of the resentments of black members of their class? Would awareness by itself be helpful?

Compare what the literature says with your own experience or the experiences of classmates whose backgrounds might provide special insight into the issue and questions.

After full class discussion, write an essay offering a tentative "reading"—that is, interpretation—of black middle-class consciousness. Consider especially the future: Will race/class problems be different from those faced by your parents?

For Further Research and Discussion

1. For most of U.S. history racial conflict stemmed from the unequal balance of power between white Europeans on the one hand and Native Americans, blacks, and Hispanics on the other. But more recently, racial tensions have been complicated by the influx of many new racial and ethnic minorities. Who are they? What do you know about them?

   Divide the class into groups, and with your group do intensive research on one of the United States' new minorities; summarize the results of your group research to the rest of the class. Then ask, How do the background and conditions of these new minorities resemble those of the older ones? How are they unique?

2. Much has been written about the breakdown of the American family—especially the black family. Find out as much as you can about what is happening to the black family and why. How much of our present racial problems can be traced to the virtual disappearance of the traditional family, especially in urban ghettos?

Additional Suggestions for Writing

1. *Persuading.* Much has been written about so-called voluntary segregation, such as the black theme houses Steele mentions. Write an essay for your school paper or some other suitable publication arguing for or against such theme houses.
2. *Inquiry.* Examine yourself for traces of racism, new or old. In what ways and to what degree are you guilty of race stereotyping, avoiding people of other races, and so forth? Do you sometimes feel the "racial anxiety" that Steele found in both black and white students? Where did you acquire whatever residual racism you have? What can you do to overcome it? What should universities do to help students and professors recognize and cope with latent racism?
3. *Research and Convincing.* The Thernstroms contend that affirmative action is at most responsible for increasing the size of the black professional class, a small percentage of the black middle class. Is this true? Conduct research into affirmative action in an effort to confirm or disconfirm their contention.

   Write a letter to the editor of the *Brookings Review* that takes a definite stance on the Thernstroms's view of the impact of affirmative action. Support your stance with recent and authoritative information on the program.

CHAPTER SEVENTEEN

The Twenty-First Century

There is nothing new about human concern for the future. Ancient kings employed soothsayers to interpret the stars, dreams, and other natural phenomena, believing that, properly interpreted, they revealed events to come. And whether allied with the ruling class or against them, prophets arise in all ages whose visions and warnings influence cultures far beyond their time and place.

However, the quality of our engagement with the future is a relatively new development. For most of human history, change was gradual, hardly perceptible across even several generations. People lived where their kind had always lived and worked the same land as their parents and their parents' parents before them. They knew almost nothing about the world outside their immediate experience, and they seldom traveled. Life was cyclical, organized by the rhythm of the seasons. Now, at least in the prosperous regions of the globe, change is rapid and time-compressed, as our science-driven technologies alter the way we live at a pace unimaginable only a century ago. Separated from nature and concentrated in cities, we may change careers several times, move often, and flit from here to there all over the globe. We seldom do what our parents did and may reside hundreds or thousands of miles away from where we were raised, in communities we know mainly as images seen from our automobiles. On those rare occasions when we have time to reflect, we may wonder where we're going, what our place will be, and how well we will cope. Understandably, then, human concern for the future has become an anxiety-ridden obsession to predict and control nearly everything in a world too complex and too interconnected to grasp fully, much less predict or control.

The approach of a new millennium, of course, only intensified this future obsession and spawned a host of visionaries ranging from the paranoid to the pollyanna. "End-of" prophets abound, with their stories of environmental collapse, social and cultural implosion, political disintegration, and the like, while, in sharp contrast, others imagine a new-age technological paradise in which all human problems have magically been solved, all needs met. In this chapter we have avoided millennialism in all its guises, whether of apocalyptic doom or fantasy fulfillment, opting instead for cooler, more balanced visions of the future well grounded in current knowledge and common sense. Futuristic "sound and fury" is available everywhere in popular novels, books, movies, and television shows; we offer instead something far less common, insights that might actually help us understand and cope with the near future, our world a decade or two hence. Anything more than this is truly idle speculation.

When we think about the future, what should we be thinking about?

First, we should never forget the strangeness of the concept "future" itself. Unlike most concepts that designate "here and now" things, people, and events, the future is never anything more than the "not yet." "It" never arrives except as a projection from the present, and all prophecy, whatever else it may be, arises from a critique of the prophet's time and place. Furthermore, the world we experience is largely the spinning out of past ways and ideas and decisions and actions, none of which can be withdrawn or leaped past into the entirely new. Change is real, and occasionally events transform our world significantly, but still the best guide to the future is an understanding of history.

Second, as we attempt to imagine the future, we need to ask *whose* future we have in mind. People speak carelessly of "our" future when they actually mean some fairly restricted group. Just as the present of the upper ten percent of American society in income differs markedly from everybody else's, and especially from that of the poor, so will their futures. And just as the present of the United States, Canada, Germany, and Japan (among other relatively affluent countries) differs markedly from that of, say, the countries of western Africa or from India and its neighbors, so their futures will hardly be the same. When future talk forgets these and other differences—forgets that "our world" is really many different worlds—it drifts off without any anchor in reality and imagines possibilities that cannot possibly come to pass.

Third, we should ponder the implications of a rift that is as old as the Industrial Revolution but that is growing wider and deeper as technological innovation accelerates. As one of the writers in this chapter points out, computing power doubles on average every eighteen months. But people and cultures evolve much more slowly, and most of our basic needs and desires remain very much what they have always been. We have to eat and sleep, for example, and most of us want the companionship of other human beings—hence the wisdom of the old French proverb "The more things change, the more they remain the same." Such a thought is comforting, until we consider the consequences of rapid technological change in the context of the "same old human being." Once we could only lob rocks at each other, but now it's missiles; once we had to endure natural epidemics, but now germ warfare allows us to create them. And so on—not only does technology enhance the age-old human capacity for killing one another, it also creates new problems for every "solution" it offers. Modern medical knowledge, for instance, has played a major role in extending our lives, but it provides no insight into how to make another decade or two of life fruitful or how to support an aging population of retired people whose medical bills are inevitably much higher than those of the general population. Clearly, somehow, our social and political awareness and our capacity to rethink old, established ways need to catch up with technological change. But how? What can bridge the chasm between human purposes and these ever-changing new instruments we have in our hands?

Finally, contemplating the future raises questions as old as philosophy itself. Is the future largely fated, the result of impersonal forces that carry us in certain directions regardless of our wishes? Or is the future primarily a combination of chance and human choices, not scripted in advance, and thus open to and effected by the human will and imagination? Must things be and become what they are and must be, or might they have been otherwise? If we answer yes to the first, we tend toward passive resignation, stress adjustment to circumstances, and lose much of our anxiety about the future because there is little we can do about it; if we agree to the second, action and resistance become reasonable, but we also increase our anxiety because we are at least partly responsible for what happens. To some extent we can combine these two views into a third possibility, as the great leader of modern India, Mahatma Gandhi, did: Fate, he said, is the cards we are dealt; free will is how we play them.

Regardless of what we decide, thinking about the future involves both exposing our philosophy and confronting its consequences, especially its resources for coping with events. It also exposes and confronts us with our limitations, for everything that exists has some kind of future, and we cannot think about everything. The following articles, then, can help us imagine only *part* of the future and that only from *limited* perspectives. Such is the human condition, which the future, for all of its surprises, will not overcome.

MICHIO KAKU

Choreographers of Matter, Life, and Intelligence

It is only fitting that we should look to science and technology for our first "take" on the future, for these two closely allied forces have called the tune in the developed world since the Industrial Revolution. Michio Kaku, a distinguished professor and theoretical physicist at the City College of New York and a best-selling author of many books about science for the general public, is well placed to speak for science and technology with authority and in language we can understand. We are moving, he contends, from a fundamentally complete understanding of matter, life, and intelligence to what he calls the Age of Mastery, when we can use our knowledge of physics, molecular biology, and computers to manipulate nature almost at will.

The following selection is the first chapter from Kaku's 1997 book Visions: How Science Will Revolutionize the 21st Century.

"There are three great themes in science in the twentieth century—the atom, the computer, and the gene."

—HAROLD VARMUS, *NIH director*

"Prediction is very hard, especially when it's about the future."

—YOGI BERRA

THREE CENTURIES ago, Isaac Newton wrote: ". . . to myself I seem to have been only like a boy playing on a seashore, and diverting myself in now and then finding a smoother pebble or a prettier shell than ordinary, whilst the great ocean of truth lay all undiscovered before me." When Newton surveyed the vast ocean of truth which lay before him, the laws of nature were shrouded in an impenetrable veil of mystery, awe, and superstition. Science as we know it did not exist. 1

Life in Newton's time was short, cruel, and brutish. People were illiterate for the most part, never owned a book or entered a classroom, and rarely ventured beyond several miles of their birthplace. During the day, they toiled at backbreaking work in the fields under a merciless sun. At night, there was usually no entertainment or relief to comfort them except the empty sounds of the night. Most people knew firsthand the gnawing pain of hunger and chronic, debilitating disease. Most people would live not much longer than age thirty, and would see many of their ten or so children die in infancy.

But the few wondrous shells and pebbles picked up by Newton and other scientists on the seashore helped to trigger a marvelous chain of events. A profound transformation occurred in human society. With Newton's mechanics came powerful machines, and eventually the steam engine, the motive force which reshaped the world by overturning agrarian society, spawning factories and stimulating commerce, unleashing the industrial revolution, and opening up entire continents with the railroad.

By the nineteenth century, a period of intense scientific discovery was well underway. Remarkable advances in science and medicine helped to lift people out of wretched poverty and ignorance, enrich their lives, empower them with knowledge, open their eyes to new worlds, and eventually unleash complex forces which would topple the feudal dynasties, fiefdoms, and empires of Europe.

By the end of the twentieth century, science had reached the end of an 5
era, unlocking the secrets of the atom, unraveling the molecule of life, and creating the electronic computer. With these three fundamental discoveries, triggered by the quantum revolution, the DNA revolution, and the computer revolution, the basic laws of matter, life, and computation were, in the main, finally solved.

That epic phase of science is now drawing to a close; one era is ending and another is only beginning. . . .

Clearly, we are on the threshold of yet another revolution. Human knowledge is doubling every ten years. In the past decade, more scientific knowledge has been created than in all of human history. Computer power is doubling every eighteen months. The Internet is doubling every year. The number of DNA sequences we can analyze is doubling every two years. Almost daily, the headlines herald new advances in computers, telecommunications, biotechnology, and space exploration. In the wake of this technological upheaval, entire industries and lifestyles are being overturned, only to give rise to entirely new ones. But these rapid, bewildering changes are not just quantitative. They mark the birth pangs of a new era.

Today, we are again like children walking on the seashore. But the ocean that Newton knew as a boy has largely disappeared. Before us lies a new ocean, the ocean of endless scientific possibilities and applications, giving us the potential for the first time to manipulate and mold these forces of Nature to our wishes.

For most of human history, we could only watch, like bystanders, the beautiful dance of Nature. But today, we are on the cusp of an epoch-making transition, from being *passive observers of Nature to being active choreographers of Nature*. . . . The Age of Discovery in science is coming to a close, opening up an Age of Mastery.

Emerging Consensus among Scientists

What will the future look like? Science fiction writers have sometimes 10
made preposterous predictions about the decades ahead, from vacationing on Mars to banishing all diseases. And even in the popular press, all too often an eccentric social critic's individual prejudices are substituted for the consensus within the scientific community. (In 1996, for example, *The New York Times Magazine* devoted an entire issue to life in the next 100 years. Journalists,

sociologists, writers, fashion designers, artists, and philosophers all submitted their thoughts. Remarkably, *not a single scientist* was consulted.)

The point here is that predictions about the future made by professional scientists tend to be based much more substantially on the realities of scientific knowledge than those made by social critics, or even those by scientists of the past whose predictions were made before the fundamental scientific laws were completely known. . . .

As a research physicist, I believe that physicists have been particularly successful at predicting the broad outlines of the future. Professionally, I work in one of the most fundamental areas of physics, the quest to complete Einstein's dream of a "theory of everything." As a result, I am constantly reminded of the ways in which quantum physics touches many of the key discoveries that shaped the twentieth century.

In the past, the track record of physicists has been formidable: we have been intimately involved with introducing a host of pivotal inventions (TV, radio, radar, X-rays, the transistor, the computer, the laser, the atomic bomb), decoding the DNA molecule, opening new dimensions in probing the body with PET, MRI, and CAT scans, and even designing the Internet and the World Wide Web. Physicists are by no means seers who can foretell the future (and we certainly haven't been spared our share of silly predictions!). Nonetheless, it is true that some of the shrewd observations and penetrating insights of leading physicists in the history of science have opened up entirely new fields.

There undoubtedly will be some astonishing surprises, twists of fate, and embarrassing gaps in this vision of the future: I will almost inevitably overlook some important inventions and discoveries of the twenty-first century. But by focusing on the interrelations between the three great scientific revolutions, and by consulting with the scientists who are actively bringing about this revolution and examining their discoveries, it is my hope that we can see the direction of science in the future with considerable insight and accuracy.

Over the past ten years, while working on this book, I have had the rare 15
privilege of interviewing over 150 scientists, including a good many Nobel Laureates, in part during the course of preparing a weekly national science radio program and producing science commentaries.

These are the scientists who are tirelessly working in the trenches, who are laying the foundations of the twenty-first century, many of whom are opening up new avenues and vistas for scientific discovery. In these interviews, as well as through my own work and research, I was able to go back over the vast panorama of science laid out before me and draw from a wide variety of expertise and knowledge. These scientists have graciously opened their offices and their laboratories and shared their most intimate scientific ideas with me. I've tried to return the favor by capturing the raw excitement and vitality of their scientific discoveries, for it is essential to instill the romance and excitement of science in the general public, especially the young, if democracy is to remain a vibrant and resonating force in an increasingly technological and bewildering world.

The fact is that there *is* a rough consensus emerging among those engaged in research about how the future will evolve. Because the laws behind the quantum theory, computers, and molecular biology are now well established, it is possible for scientists to generally predict the paths of scientific progress in the future. *This is the central reason why the predictions made here, I feel, are more accurate than those of the past.*

What is emerging is the following. . . .

The Quantum Revolution

Since time immemorial, people have speculated what the world was made of. The Greeks thought that the universe was made of four elements: water, air, earth, and fire. The philosopher Democritus believed that even these could be broken down into smaller units, which he called "atoms." But attempts to explain how atoms could create the vast, wondrous diversity of matter we see in Nature always faltered. Even Newton, who discovered the cosmic laws which guided the motion of planets and moons, was at a loss to explain the bewildering nature of matter.

All this changed in 1925 with the birth of the quantum theory, which 20
has unleashed a thundering tidal wave of scientific discovery that continues to surge unabated to this day. The quantum revolution has now given us an almost complete description of matter, allowing us to describe the seemingly infinite multiplicity of matter we see arrayed around us in terms of a handful of particles, in the same way that a richly decorated tapestry is woven from a few colored strands.

The quantum theory, created by Erwin Schrödinger, Werner Heisenberg, and many others, reduced the mystery of matter to a few postulates. First, that energy is not continuous, as the ancients thought, but occurs in discrete bundles, called "quanta." (The photon, for example, is a quantum or packet of light.) Second, that subatomic particles have both particle and wavelike qualities, obeying a well-defined equation, the celebrated Schrödinger wave equation, which determines the probability that certain events occur. With this equation, we can mathematically predict the properties of a wide variety of substances before creating them in the laboratory. The culmination of the quantum theory is the Standard Model, which can predict the properties of everything from tiny subatomic quarks to giant supernovas in outer space.

In the twentieth century, the quantum theory has given us the ability to understand the matter we see around us. In the next century, the quantum revolution may open the door to the next step: the ability to manipulate and choreograph new forms of matter, almost at will.

The Computer Revolution

In the past, computers were mathematical curiosities; they were supremely clumsy, messy contraptions, consisting of a complex mass of gears, levers, and cogs. During World War II, mechanical computers were replaced by vacuum tubes, but they were also monstrous in size, filling up entire rooms with racks of thousands of vacuum tubes.

The turning point came in 1948, when scientists at Bell Laboratories discovered the transistor, which made possible the modern computer. A decade after that, the laser was discovered, which is essential to the Internet and the information highway. Both are quantum mechanical devices. . . .

Today, tens of millions of transistors can be crammed into an area the 25
size of a fingernail. In the future, our lifestyles will be irrevocably changed when microchips become so plentiful that intelligent systems are dispersed by the millions into all parts of our environment.

In the past, we could only marvel at the precious phenomenon called intelligence; in the future, we will be able to manipulate it according to our wishes.

The Biomolecular Revolution

Historically, many biologists were influenced by the theory of "vitalism"—i.e., that a mysterious "life force" or substance animated living things. This view was challenged when Schrödinger, in his 1944 book *What Is Life?,* dared to claim that life could be explained by a "genetic code" written on the molecules within a cell. It was a bold idea: that the secret of life could be explained by using the quantum theory.

James Watson and Francis Crick, inspired by Schrödinger's book, eventually proved his conjecture by using X-ray crystallography. By analyzing the pattern of X-rays scattered off a DNA molecule, they were able to reconstruct the detailed atomic structure of DNA and identify its double-helical nature. Since the quantum theory also gives us the precise bonding angles and bonding strength between atoms, it enables us to determine the position of practically all the individual molecules in the genetic code of a complex virus like HIV.

The techniques of molecular biology will allow us to read the genetic code of life as we would read a book. Already, the complete DNA code of several living organisms, like viruses, single-cell bacteria, and yeast, have been completely decoded, molecule for molecule.

The complete human genome will be decoded by the year 2005, giving 30
us an "owner's manual" for a human being. This will set the stage for twenty-first century science and medicine. Instead of watching the dance of life, the biomolecular revolution will ultimately give us the nearly godlike ability to manipulate life almost at will.

From Passive Bystanders to Active Choreographers of Nature

Some commentators, witnessing these historic advances in science over the past century, have claimed that we are seeing the demise of the scientific enterprise. John Horgan, in his book *The End of Science,* writes: "If one believes in science, one must accept the possibility—even the probability—that the great era of scientific discovery is over. . . . Further research may yield no more great revelations or revolutions, but only incremental, diminishing returns."

In one limited sense, Horgan is right. Modern science has no doubt uncovered the fundamental laws underlying most of the disciplines of science: the quantum theory of matter, Einstein's theory of space-time, the Big Bang theory of cosmology, the Darwinian theory of evolution, and the molecular basis of DNA and life. Despite some notable exceptions (e.g., determining the nature of consciousness and proving that superstring theory, my particular field of specialization, is the fabled unified field theory), the "great ideas" of science, for the most part, have probably been found.

Likewise, the era of reductionism—i.e., reducing everything to its smallest components—is coming to a close. Reductionism has been spectacularly successful in the twentieth century, unlocking the secrets of the atom, the DNA molecule, and the logic circuits of the computer. But reductionism has probably, in the main, run its course.

However, this is just the beginning of the romance of science. These scientific milestones certainly mark a significant break with the ancient past, when Nature was interpreted through the prism of animism, mysticism, and spiritualism. But they only open the door to an entirely new era of science.

The next century will witness an even more far-reaching scientific revolution, as we make the transition from unraveling the secrets of Nature to becoming masters of Nature.

Sheldon Glashow, a Nobel Laureate in physics, describes this difference metaphorically when he tells the story of a visitor named Arthur from another planet meeting earthlings for the first time:

"Arthur [is] an intelligent alien from a distant planet who arrives at Washington Square [in New York City] and observes two old codgers playing chess. Curious, Arthur gives himself two tasks: to learn the rules of the game, and to become a grand master." By carefully watching the moves, Arthur is gradually able to reconstruct the rules of the game: how pawns advance, how queens capture knights, and how vulnerable kings are. However, just knowing the rules does not mean that Arthur has become a grand master! As Glashow adds: "Both kinds of endeavors are important—one more 'relevant,' the other more 'fundamental.' Both represent immense challenges to the human intellect."

In some sense, science has finally decoded many of the fundamental "rules of Nature," but this does not mean that we have become grand masters. Likewise, the dance of elementary particles deep inside stars and the rhythms of DNA molecules coiling and uncoiling within our bodies have been largely deciphered, but this does not mean that we have become master choreographers of life.

In fact, the end of the twentieth century, which ended the first great phase in the history of science, has only opened the door to the exciting developments of the next. We are now making the transition from amateur chess players to grand masters, from observers to choreographers of Nature.

From Reductionism to Synergy

Similarly, this is creating a new approach in the way in which scientists 40
view their own discipline. In the past, the reductionist approach has paid off handsomely, eventually establishing the foundation for modern physics, chemistry, and biology.

At the heart of this success was the discovery of the quantum theory, which helped to spark the other two revolutions.

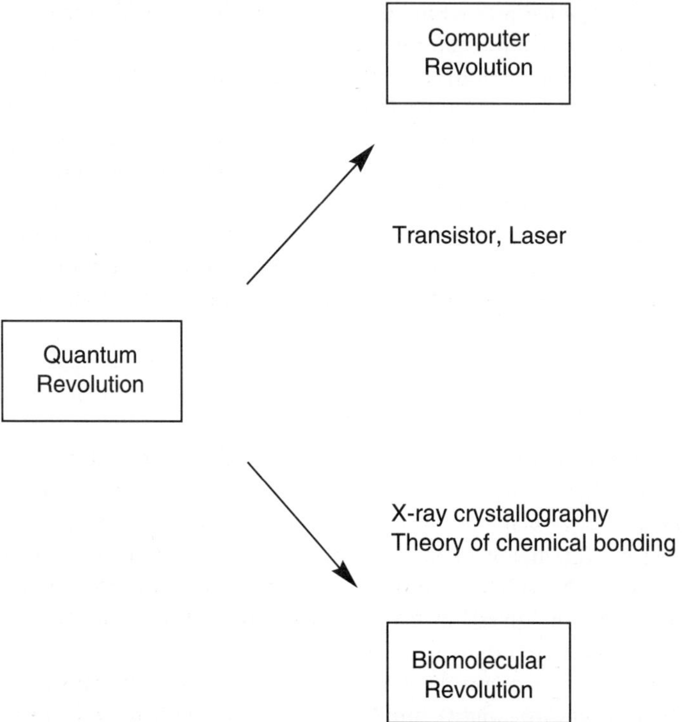

The quantum revolution gave birth to the computer and biomolecular revolutions via the transistor, laser, X-ray crystallography, and the theory of molecular bonds.

But since the quantum theory helped to initiate these other revolutions in the 1950s, they have since matured and grown on their own, largely independent of physics and of each other. The watchword was specialization, as scientists probed deeper and deeper into their subdisciplines, smugly ignoring the developments in other fields. But now the heyday of reductionism has probably passed. Seemingly impenetrable obstacles have been encountered which cannot be solved by the simple reductionist approach. This is heralding a new era, one of *synergy* between the three fundamental revolutions.

The twenty-first century, unlike the previous ones, will be typified by synergy, the cross-fertilization between all three fields, which will mark a sharp turning point in the development of science. The cross-pollination between these three revolutions will be vastly accelerated and will enrich the development of science, giving us unprecedented power to manipulate matter, life, and intelligence. . . .

The new relationship between the three revolutions is an intensely dynamic one. Often, when an impasse is reached in one area, usually a totally unexpected development in another field is found to contain the solution. For example, biologists once despaired of ever deciphering the millions of genes which contain the blueprint for life. But the recent torrent of genes being discovered in our laboratories is being driven largely by a development in another field: the exponential increase in computer power, which is mechanizing and automating the gene-sequencing process. Similarly, silicon computer chips will eventually hit a roadblock as they become too clumsy for the computer of the next century. But new advances in DNA research are making possible a new type of computer architecture which actually computes on organic molecules. Thus, discoveries in one field nourish and fertilize discoveries in totally unrelated fields. The whole is more than the sum of its parts.

45 One of the consequences of this intense synergy between these revolutions is that the steady pace of scientific discovery is accelerating at an ever-increasing rate.

The Wealth of Nations

This acceleration of science and technology into the next century will necessarily have vast repercussions on the wealth of nations and our standard of living. For the past three centuries, wealth was usually accumulated by those nations which were endowed with rich natural resources or which amassed large amounts of capital. The rise of the Great Powers of Europe in the nineteenth century and the United States in the twentieth century follows this classic textbook principle.

However, as Lester C. Thurow, former dean of MIT's Sloan School of Management, has stressed, in the coming century, there will be a historic movement in wealth away from nations with natural resources and capital. In the same way that shifts in the earth's tectonic plates can generate powerful earthquakes, this seismic shift in wealth will reshape the distribution of power on the planet. Thurow writes: "In the twenty-first century, brainpower and imagination, invention, and the organization of new technologies are the key strategic ingredients." In fact, many nations which are richly endowed with abundant natural resources will find their wealth vastly reduced because, in the marketplace of the future, commodities will be cheap, trade will be global, and markets will be linked electronically. Already, the commodity prices of many natural resources plummeted some 60 percent from the 1970s to the 1990s, and, in Thurow's estimation, will plummet another 60 percent by 2020.

Even capital itself will be reduced to a commodity, racing around the globe electronically. Many nations which are barren of natural resources will flourish in the next century because they placed a premium on those technologies which can give them a competitive edge in the global marketplace. "Today, knowledge and skills now stand alone as the only source of comparative advantage," Thurow asserts.

As a consequence, some nations have drawn up lists of the key technologies which will serve as the engines of wealth and prosperity into the next century. A typical list was compiled in 1990 by Japan's Ministry of International Trade and Industry. That list included:

- microelectronics
- biotechnology
- the new material science industries
- telecommunications
- civilian aircraft manufacturing
- machine tools and robots
- computers (hardware and software)

Without exception, every one of the technologies singled out to lead 50
the twenty-first century are deeply rooted in the quantum, computer, and DNA revolutions.

The point is that these three scientific revolutions are not only the key to scientific breakthroughs in the next century; they are also the dynamic engines of wealth and prosperity. *Nations may rise and fall on their ability to master these three revolutions.* In any activity, there are winners and losers. The winners will likely be those nations which fully grasp the vital importance of these three scientific revolutions. Those who would scoff at the power of these revolutions may find themselves marginalized in the global marketplace of the twenty-first century.

Time Frames for the Future

In making predictions about the future, it is crucial to understand the time frame being discussed, for, obviously, different technologies will mature at different times. The time frames of the predictions made [here] fall into three categories: those breakthroughs and technologies that will evolve between now and the year 2020, those that will evolve from 2020 to 2050, and those that will emerge from 2050 to the end of the twenty-first century. (These are not absolute time frames; they represent only the general period in which certain technologies and sciences will reach fruition.)

To the Year 2020

From now to the year 2020, scientists foresee an explosion in scientific activity such as the world has never seen before. In two key technologies, computer power and DNA sequencing, we will see entire industries rise and fall on the basis of breathtaking scientific advances. Since the 1950s, the power of our computers has advanced by a factor of roughly *ten billion.* In fact, because both computer power and DNA sequencing double roughly every two years, one can compute the rough time frame over which many scientific breakthroughs will take place. This means that predictions about the future of computers and biotechnology can be quantified with reasonable statistical accuracy through the year 2020.

For computers, this staggering growth rate is quantified by Moore's law, which states that computer power doubles roughly every eighteen months. (This was first stated in 1965 by Gordon Moore, co-founder of the Intel Corp. It is not a scientific law, in the sense of Newton's laws, but a rule-of-thumb which has uncannily predicted the evolution of computer power for several decades.) Moore's law, in turn, determines the fate of multibillion-dollar computer corporations, which base their future projections and product lines on the expectation of continued growth. By 2020, microprocessors will likely be as cheap and plentiful as scrap paper, scattered by the millions into the environment, allowing us to place intelligent systems everywhere. This will change everything around us, including the nature of commerce, the wealth of nations, and the way we communicate, work, play, and live. This will give us smart homes, cars, TVs, clothes, jewelry, and money. We will speak to our appliances, and they will speak back. Scientists also expect the Internet will wire up the entire planet and evolve into a membrane consisting of millions of computer networks, creating an "intelligent planet." The Internet will eventually become a "Magic Mirror" that appears in fairy tales, able to speak with the wisdom of the human race.

Because of revolutionary advances in our ability to etch ever-smaller 55
transistors onto silicon wafers, scientists expect this relentless drive to continue to generate newer and more powerful computers up to 2020, when the iron laws of quantum physics eventually take over once again. By then, the size of microchip components will be so small—roughly on the scale of molecules—that quantum effects will necessarily dominate and the fabled Age of Silicon will end.

The growth curve for biotechnology will be equally spectacular in this period. In biomolecular research, what is driving the remarkable ability to decode the secret of life is the introduction of computers and robots to automate the process of DNA sequencing. This process will continue unabated until roughly 2020, until literally thousands of organisms will have their complete DNA code unraveled. By then, it may be possible for anyone on earth to have their personal DNA code stored on a CD. We will then have the Encyclopedia of Life.

This will have profound implications for biology and medicine. Many genetic diseases will be eliminated by injecting people's cells with the correct gene. Because cancer is now being revealed to be a series of genetic mutations, large classes of cancers may be curable at last, without invasive surgery or chemotherapy. Similarly, many of the microorganisms involved in infectious diseases will be conquered in virtual reality by locating the molecular weak spots in their armor and creating agents to attack those weak spots. Our molecular knowledge of cell development will be so advanced that we will be able to grow entire organs in the laboratory, including livers and kidneys.

From 2020 to 2050

The prediction of explosive growth of computer power and DNA sequencing from now through 2020 is somewhat deceptive, in that both are driven by known technologies. Computer power is driven by packing more and more transistors onto microprocessors, while DNA sequencing is driven by computerization. Obviously, these technologies cannot indefinitely continue to grow exponentially. Sooner or later, a bottleneck will be hit.

By around 2020, both will encounter large obstacles. Because of the limits of silicon chip technology, eventually we will be forced to invent new technologies whose potentials are largely unexplored and untested, from optical computers, molecular computers, and DNA computers to quantum computers. Radically new designs must be developed, based on the quantum theory, which will likely disrupt progress in computer science. Eventually, the reign of the microprocessor will end, and new types of quantum devices will take over.

If these difficulties in computer technology can be overcome, then the 60
period 2020 to 2050 may mark the entrance into the marketplace of an entirely new kind of technology: true robot automatons that have common sense, can understand human language, can recognize and manipulate objects in their environment, and can learn from their mistakes. It is a development that will likely alter our relationship with machines forever.

Similarly, biotechnology will face a new set of problems by 2020. The field will be flooded with millions upon millions of genes whose basic functions are largely unknown. Even before 2020, the focus will shift away from DNA sequencing to understanding the basic functions of these genes, a process which cannot be computerized, and to understand polygenic diseases and traits—i.e., those involving the complex interaction of multiple genes. The shift to polygenic diseases may prove to be the key to solving some of the most pressing chronic diseases facing humanity, including heart disease, arthritis, autoimmune diseases, schizophrenia, and the like. It may also lead to cloning humans and to isolating the fabled "age genes" which control our aging process, allowing us to extend the human life span.

Beyond 2020, we also expect some amazing new technologies germinating in physics laboratories to come to fruition, from new generations of lasers and holographic three-dimensional TV to nuclear fusion. Room-temperature superconductors may find commercial applications and generate a "second industrial revolution." The quantum theory will give us the ability to manufacture machines the size of molecules, thereby opening up an entirely new class of machines with unheard-of properties called nanotechnology. Eventually, we may be able to build ionic rocket engines that may ultimately make interplanetary travel commonplace.

From 2050 to 2100 and Beyond

. . . Although any predictions this far into the future are necessarily vague, it is a period that will likely be dominated by several new developments. Robots may gradually attain a degree of "self-awareness" and consciousness of their own. This could greatly increase their utility in society, as they are able to make independent decisions and act as secretaries, butlers, assistants, and aides. Similarly, the DNA revolution will have advanced to the point where biogeneticists are able to create new types of organisms involving the transfer of not just a few but even hundreds of genes, allowing us to increase our food supply and improve our medicines and our health. It may also give us the ability to design new life forms and to orchestrate the physical and perhaps even the mental makeup of our children, which raises a host of ethical questions.

The quantum theory, too, will exert a powerful influence in the next century, especially in the area of energy production. We may also see the beginnings of rockets that can reach the nearby stars and plans to form the first colonies in space.

Beyond 2100, some scientists see a further convergence of all three revo- 65
lutions, as the quantum theory gives us transistor circuits and entire machines the size of molecules, allowing us to duplicate the neural patterns of the brain on a computer. In this era, some scientists have given serious thought to extending life by growing new organs and bodies, by manipulating our genetic makeup, or even by ultimately merging with our computerized creations.

Toward a Planetary Civilization

When confronted with dizzying scientific and technological upheaval on this scale, there are some voices that say we are going too far, too fast, that unforeseen social consequences will be unleashed by these scientific revolutions. . . .

. . . [T]o where are we rushing? If one era of science is ending and another is just beginning, then where is this all leading to?

This is exactly the question asked by astrophysicists who scan the heavens searching for signs of extraterrestrial civilizations which may be far more advanced than ours. There are about 200 billion stars in our galaxy, and trillions of galaxies in outer space. Instead of wasting millions of dollars randomly searching all the stars in the heavens for signs of extraterrestrial life, astrophysicists engaged in this search have tried to focus their efforts by theorizing about the energy characteristics and signatures of civilizations several centuries to millennia more advanced than ours.

Applying the laws of thermodynamics and energy, astrophysicists who scan the heavens have been able to classify hypothetical extraterrestrial civilizations into three types, based on the ways they utilize energy. Russian astronomer Nikolai Kardashev and Princeton physicist Freeman Dyson label them Type I, II, and III civilizations.

Assuming a modest yearly increase in energy consumption, one can extrapolate centuries into the future when certain energy supplies will be exhausted, forcing society to advance to the next level. 70

A Type I civilization is one that has mastered all forms of terrestrial energy. Such a civilization can modify the weather, mine the oceans, or extract energy from the center of their planet. Their energy needs are so large that they must harness the potential resources of the entire planet. Harnessing and managing resources on this gigantic scale requires a sophisticated degree of cooperation among their individuals with elaborate planetary communication. This necessarily means that they have attained a truly planetary civilization, one that has put to rest most of the factional, religious, sectarian, and nationalistic struggles that typify their origin.

Type II civilizations have mastered stellar energy. Their energy needs are so great that they have exhausted planetary sources and must use their sun itself to drive their machines. Dyson has speculated that, by building a giant sphere around their sun, such a civilization might be able to harness their sun's total energy output. They have also begun the exploration and possible colonization of nearby star systems.

Type III civilizations have exhausted the energy output of a single star. They must reach out to neighboring star systems and clusters, and eventually evolve into a galactic civilization. They obtain their energy by harnessing collections of star systems throughout the galaxy.

(To give a sense of scale, the United Federation of Planets described in *Star Trek* probably qualifies for an emerging Type II status, as they have just attained the ability to ignite stars and have colonized a few nearby star systems.)

This system of classifying civilizations is a reasonable one because it relies 75
on the available supply of energy. Any advanced civilization in space will eventually find three sources of energy at their disposal: their planet, their star, and their galaxy. There is no other choice.

With a modest growth rate of 3 percent per year—the growth rate typically found on earth—one can calculate when our planet might make the transition to a higher status in the galaxy. For example, astrophysicists estimate that, based on energy considerations, a factor of ten billion may separate the energy demands between the various types of civilizations. Although this staggering number at first seems like an insurmountable obstacle, a steady 3 percent growth rate can overcome even this factor. In fact, we can expect to reach Type I status within a century or two. To reach Type II status may require no more than about 800 years. But attaining Type III status may take on the order of 10,000 years or more (depending on the physics of interstellar travel). But even this is nothing but the twinkling of an eye from the perspective of the universe.

Where are we now? you might ask. At present, we are a Type 0 civilization. Essentially, we use dead plants (coal and oil) to energize our machines. On this planetary scale, we are like children, taking our first hesitant and clumsy steps into space. But by the close of the twenty-first century, the sheer power of the three scientific revolutions will force the nations of the earth to cooperate on a scale never seen before in history. By the twenty-second century, we will have laid the groundwork of a Type I civilization, and humanity will have taken the first step toward the stars.

Already the information revolution is creating global links on a scale unparalleled in human history, tearing down petty, parochial interests while creating a global culture. Just as the Gutenberg printing press made people aware of worlds beyond their village or hamlet, the information revolution is building and forging a common planetary culture out of thousands of smaller ones.

What this means is that our headlong journey into science and technology will one day lead us to evolve into a true Type I civilization—a planetary civilization which harnesses truly planetary forces. The march to a planetary civilization will be slow, accomplished in fits and starts, undoubtedly full of unexpected twists and setbacks. In the background always lurks the possibility of a nuclear war, the outbreak of a deadly pandemic, or a collapse of the environment. Barring such a collapse, however, I think it is safe to say that the progress of science has the potential to create forces which will bind the human race into a Type I civilization.

Far from witnessing the end of science, we see that the three scientific 80
revolutions are unleashing powerful forces which may eventually elevate our civilization to Type I status. So when Newton first gazed alone at the vast, uncharted ocean of knowledge, he probably never realized that the chain reaction of events that he and others initiated would one day affect all of modern society, eventually forging a planetary civilization and propelling it on its way to the stars.

Questions for Discussion

1. Kaku claims special authority for his projections of the future. How does he attempt to secure his claim? Are you persuaded that his vision is more trustworthy than most? Why or why not?
2. Explain in your own words what Kaku means by the key concept of *synergy*. Why does he think it is so important to the development of science in the twenty-first century?
3. Summarize the developments Kaku thinks will unfold for each time period—that is, from now until 2020, from 2020 to 2050, and from 2050 to 2100. Try to imagine how routine, daily life might be effected by these changes: How will our lives be different from what they are now?
4. Kaku's vision is hopeful, optimistic. He thinks, for example, that our energy needs will force us to develop what he calls a "planetary civilization," in which "factional, religious, . . . and nationalistic struggles" have been largely overcome. How do you respond to the idea of a planetary civilization? Do you think that energy needs alone can motivate us to overcome divisiveness and strife?

For Research and Convincing

Let's put one of Kaku's contentions to the test—namely, whether he articulates an emerging consensus among scientists about the future. Locate other statements in print about the future from reputable scientists in a number of fields. Ask scientists at your school to read "Choreographers of Matter, Life, and Intelligence," and then talk to them about their reactions—or even, if your instructor likes the idea, invite them to class to discuss it.

Write an essay addressed to other students in your class evaluating Kaku's claim that his views represent an emerging consensus. In what ways do other scientists agree with him? In what ways do they differ? How important are the differences? Remembering that "consensus" doesn't mean total agreement in every detail, would you say Kaku's claim is justified?

For Persuasion

In many ways Kaku represents the classic Enlightenment mind—a strong faith in scientific reason and endless progress, all based on the promise of human *mastery* of nature. We cannot deny the appeal of this attitude, nor can we casually dismiss its successes and benefits, from the invention of electric lighting to gene therapy for preventing or treating disease. But it is also precisely this outlook in general and the goal of mastery in particular that has drawn heavy fire from many critics both within and outside of science. Should we strive to master nature? Or should we rather learn how to live in harmony with it?

Write a brief, two- to three-page essay stating your view. In class discussion present your opinions to the class and listen carefully to what your classmates say. Then form groups based on similarities in opinion and write a longer, better developed essay together representing your group's point of view.

Photograph

This photograph of a display at the World's Fair in 1940 is amusing, with its now crude-seeming robot Electro and his faithful mechanical dog Sparko. Our future as many envisioned it sixty years ago included robot servants in every American home—just as, a few decades before 1940, the promise was a car in every garage. We have the cars but not the robots, which should remind us how difficult it is to project exactly when a technology will mature.

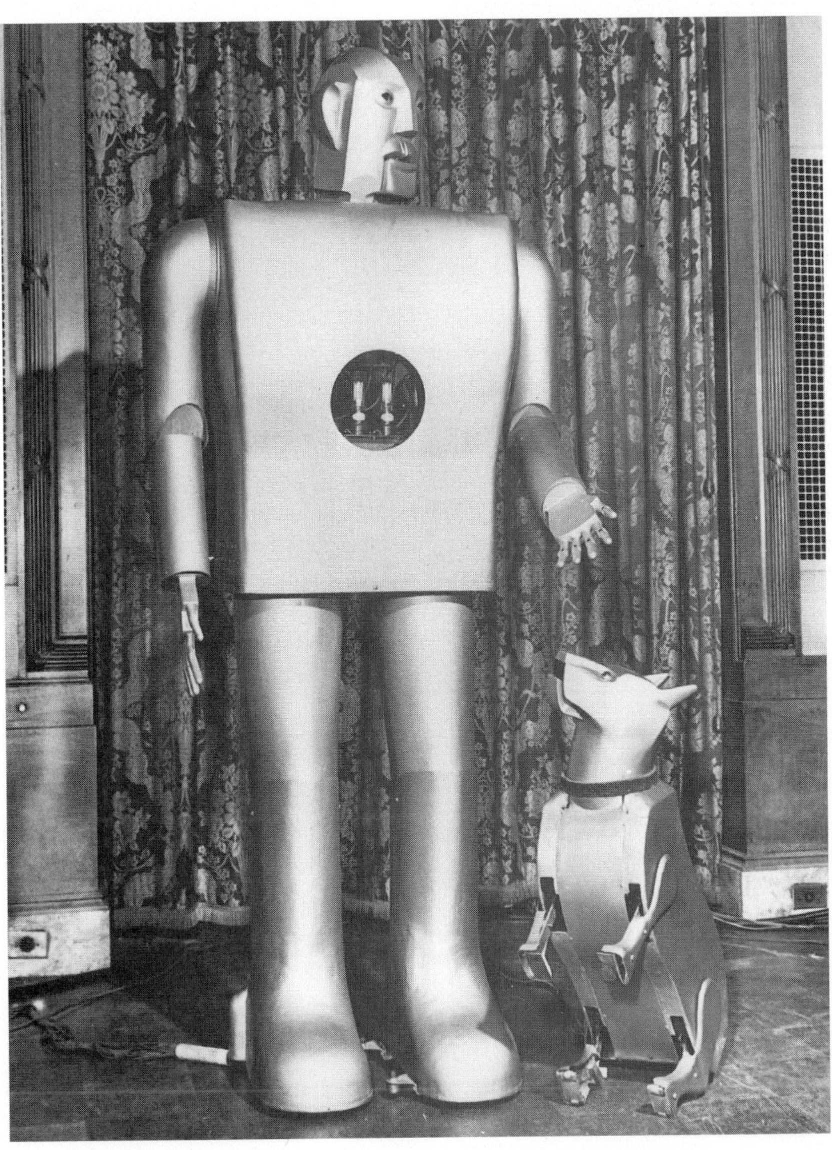

For Discussion

Collect and examine some contemporary images of the future, especially those featuring high-tech devices or environments. Which of them seem likely "prophecies" of technologies we will actually use?

LARRY KING

Future Talk

Larry King is the host of a well-known talk show on Cable News Network. The following four brief selections are excerpts from interviews transcribed for his 1998 book Future Talk. *They all deal with the present and future of what might be called the human condition, as contrasted with the previous selection's focus on advanced science and high technology, which largely ignore people and their endless, intractable problems—all that "messy stuff" so-called hard science cannot reduce to orderly laws nor solve by elegant technological manipulation. Clearly, before we get too carried away by what science and technology can do, we must ponder the human condition, only part of which can be touched or improved by technology alone.*

MARIAN WRIGHT EDELMAN

Marian Wright Edelman is the founder and president of the Children's Defense Fund. Because the future is always the future of children and young people, we begin with her observations.

LK: We're coming to the end of the twentieth century. Both parents 1
work. The traditional family structure seems pulled and stressed. Where do you think we're going?

Edelman: A nation that doesn't stand up for its children is a nation that is falling. I think we're going to hell because a child drops out of school every nine seconds, a child is arrested every fourteen seconds, every twenty-five seconds a child is born to an unmarried mother, and in the richest nation on earth the economy is booming and we let a child be born into poverty every thirty-two seconds. And the worst thing of all is, we have become numb.

LK: Is there a country now that does a good job?

Edelman: There are many countries doing far, far better. Japan, England, Canada, and the Scandinavian countries are just a few. In many countries health coverage for children is a given. The United States is eighteenth in the gap between rich and poor children but we're also the country leading the world in the number of millionaires and billionaires. That says something.

LK: What legislation would you like to see in place in the next cen- 5
tury to make this country better for children?

Edelman: First priority is health coverage for 10 million uninsured children, nine out of ten of whom live with parents who work every day. . . . I want to see a high-quality comprehensive child care system in place which includes parental support from business, such as policies on parental leave. I want to see parent support groups which allow children the opportunity to go to after-school and weekend summer programs so they don't come home to an empty house. Congregations are going to have to get involved in mentoring and tutoring and homework centers and, in general, show that adults can be there. We have wonderful models working right now but we lack the resources to bring them to scale and quality.

LK: What do you say to those in the next century who want to bring children into the world? What questions should they be asking themselves?

Edelman: Everybody needs to ask, "Am I prepared to put this child first in my life for the rest of my lifetime?" Parenting, in many ways, never ends. Another question would be, "Do we recognize this is the most important decision that we're going to make?" I would urge them to ask, "Are we ready and able to provide this child with a stable life, and are we prepared to be good role models?" Each person thinking about children should say, "What kind of values am I trying to transmit to these children and to their children and to the future?" And then parents should ask, "If I want this child to grow up and not be a racist, or intolerant of people who are different, or violent, or a drug user, am I going to be able to reflect that value in my household?" Our children do what we do. If we don't vote, they won't. It's the most important role in a society. . . .

LK: What will new parents face in the next century?

Edelman: We need to redefine success. We need to teach our children 10
that it is not about things. We need to focus on heroes rather than celebrities. We need to focus on spiritual values rather than material values. Parents are going to need to think anew and decide what it is they want this country to stand for. I think we have lost our way.

LK: Will business become more family-friendly?

Edelman: It will happen, but it depends on a critical mass of citizens demanding it. Business will look at its bottom line. The demand will come for the public sector to do it, and once that happens the private sector will do it. They have been slow in my view, and it's going to require a different atmosphere before it happens.

LK: Will parental leave policies be in place in the next century?

Edelman: It would be desirable but business in large part opposes parental leave. I'd hope business will become a leader rather than an opposer. It will happen. . . .

LK: You've talked about the role of the religious community through- 15
out this interview. Is it going to become more visible and active?

Edelman: Absolutely. The religious community needs to be the moral locomotive rather than the moral caboose. It's beginning. And we should all know they can't do it alone.

LK: We hear of the pendulum swinging one way and then another. Do you see it swinging toward a parent staying home with children again in the next century?

Edelman: There is deep concern in America about what has happened to the family. Keep in mind, taking care of children at home is a lot cheaper than putting children in day care. I hope parents will have a choice. Let's not call it welfare. Let's call it parental support until those children go to school. Other industrialized countries do it. We'll save an awful lot in future prison costs because we either invest in children right now or we invest in them later in far more negative ways.

LK: What scares you about the next century?

Edelman: We have lost our sense of what is important as a nation. We are a nation that says all men, and I include women in that, are created equal, and yet we are so far away from that in the practices we see. There is racial division. We don't need to go back and refight the Civil War, and we don't need another postwar Reconstruction era. But we can see the division between the haves and have-nots grow. In the past twenty-five years we have seen children killed by guns and drugs and a breakdown in parental and community responsibility. I worry we will value things and not people. If we can't give this value to our children we can't give it to the rest of the world, which is so desperately in need of a leader. . . .

MARJORIE MARGOLIES-MEZVINSKY

Formerly a member of the U.S. House of Representatives, Marjorie Margolies-Mezvinsky is now president of the Women's Campaign Fund. Her comments remind us that our future will be shaped significantly by politics and that the future of women in politics may shape policy more than we might imagine.

LK: Let's say it's the year 2010. What will have changed in the way issues are handled in Congress?

Mezvinsky: We have raised the American public, whoever "we" are, to pay attention only to what it wants to hear rather than what it needs to hear. Somehow that's going to have to change. This means talking responsibly about entitlements. I think in the year 2010 we will be looking right down the barrel of a real crisis with regard to Social Security, Medicare, and any other entitlement. So I'm hoping there will be responsible people who are directing legislation that say, "This may cost me big but we have to talk very seriously about making sacrifices." We've got to talk in the future about coming together and figuring out how the next generation is going to be in the loop. I can tell you, as somebody who tried to talk about it, it's like painting a target on your chest.

LK: So the problem is, obviously, the system, which could use a little work, but the American people need a little work too.

Mezvinsky: You turn on your television around election time and everyone is "dissing" on one another and the American public says, "I knew you were a sleazebag because all politicians are sleazebags, so the real issue is who is the least sleazy?" What has settled in is an unwillingness to really listen to what we need to listen to.

LK: How will this "unwillingness" change into a willingness? A strong leader? Use of the media? A president?

Mezvinsky: A combination of them all . . .

LK: Isn't there an irony in that we have all these media available to us but we can't understand, or don't want to understand, the issues that are important?

Mezvinsky: Maybe the real irony is that the people who joke about our Founding Fathers not wanting government to work except in times of crisis are right. . . . I think the Founding Fathers wanted change to be slow and deliberate.

LK: What are some of the important changes that have occurred in Congress that the public might have missed or not paid attention to?

Mezvinsky: The 103rd Congress voted on the Family Medical Leave Act. It took seven years to get that through, and had the women not been there, it wouldn't have happened. I think we saw a chipping away at the misguided notion the Second Amendment is absolute and everyone has the right to bear any kind of arms. . . . I don't think we would have had the automatic weapons ban had women not been in Congress.

LK: How come people missed it?

Mezvinsky: People are human. . . . [W]e're all trying to put together our days, pick up the kids, make dinner, make sure our parents are okay. Sure there's lack of interest, and sure there's frustration involved, and sure the tax articles are just so darn complicated and dry. It's b-o-r-i-n-g. And I'm not sure of the answer. . . .

LK: What scares you about this coming century?

Mezvinsky: Our inability to face facts. Our willingness to seek easy answers. You talk to somebody about Social Security and they say it's a contract the government made with the people. What good is the contract if the government can't keep its part of the deal? People are living longer and requiring more support than people ever dreamed when Social Security was created. So today we hear, "The government is breaking its contract with the people," when what we really need to be saying is "Let's sit down and take a long hard look at this contract and figure out how to make it work even when the times change." I'll say it again: People need to listen to what they need to hear, not just what they want to hear.

LK: Do you see this willingness occurring?

Mezvinsky: No I don't. People say government shouldn't come into their lives. Well, dissect your day and you will realize it does come into your life. By the time you get into your car in the morning you have had . . . government interference. It's important people understand that and I think they fundamentally don't because it's not easy to look at. I got a call when I was in office from a woman who wanted to know, "When will government stay out of my Medicare?" And the answer is "When you no longer have Medicare."

MAYA ANGELOU

A celebrated poet and author of I Know Why the Caged Bird Sings, *Maya Angelou teaches in the English department at Wake Forest University. Her concerns are mainly artistic and spiritual—that is, with matters, like child-rearing and politics, that may evolve with the times but change little compared to the breakneck speed of technological innovation.*

LK: What changes will we face in the next century? 1

Angelou: I would imagine the center of the human will not change. . . . We've been saying, "Don't kill each other" and "Don't be cruel" for centuries. I don't think it's going to change. . . .

LK: Who are we right now?

Angelou: We are fearful children right now standing around a . . . fire. We like the fire and we like each other but we're afraid of each other. Because we don't trust ourselves we find it impossible to trust each other. So what we use more often than not is might to protect our fear. We use our power. We are duped sometimes because we live such short lives and it's over so soon. We can't see much positive change for our positive acts, and as a result, we become disheartened and cynical.

LK: We don't have hope? 5

Angelou: Oh, we have hope, but if it remains targeted to things, then we are lost. If we can aim it at sensitivity and humanitarianism, then we're going to be fine. I know this sounds awfully soft but that's what we've got to do.

LK: So how are you going to do that?

Angelou: It's a combination of church and state and academia and personal. It's unique and it's general and it's complex and it's simple. I don't think any portion of society can be less a participant than another. I would like very much to have every politician and lobbyist reread the Preamble to the Constitution and hear the dream of those men two hundred years ago.

LK: Are you optimistic that in another one hundred years when somebody is writing a book about the twenty-second century, they will look back at the twenty-first and say, "They did okay"?

Angelou: Yes. But I have to realize two hundred years ago, the people 10
who wrote "We the people" had the incredible gall to own other individuals. Look at how we have changed! Even the idea is unacceptable and incomprehensible. At the same time they wanted to "ensure domestic tranquillity" and

they wanted to "provide for the common good." So I can look back two hundred years and admire those men. . . . [I]n the twenty-first century, I hope people will look back at us and say, "Gee, they rioted in the streets and there was vulgarity in the neighborhoods and communication and they abused children and they were cruel to women and had restrictions against people of different color, and yet they actually tried to stop war. One country which had absolutely nothing to do with another country tried to stop the killing." That is optimistic. . . .

LK: What scares you about the next century?

Angelou: Isolation. . . . [W]e are weakened when we are separated. . . . [A]ll together is when we are at our best and our strongest, and you can see that when we have a crisis. Something pushes us to each other when there's a hurricane or a fire. I hate the crisis but I love to turn on the television and hear that firefighters have gone from Nebraska to California to help.

LK: What would you say to high school students in the year 2009 who, this evening, have been assigned to read a poem but are leaning toward turning on the television or hanging out with friends someplace?

Angelou: My first encouragement is to read it aloud. And read it to someone else. There's nothing so wonderful as having help in a required endeavor. We run together. We jog together. We walk together. High school students will be amazed to hear their voices read those words written by someone else, maybe two years or two hundred years earlier. When you read to someone else you are doing the reading but you are also doing the listening.

LK: And the English teacher should also read aloud to the class?

Angelou: Yes, it's the same thing. I read to my students and I can see them physically begin to relax. Teachers have become, I'm sorry to say [so], superficially sophisticated, that we don't read to students.

LK: Is the role of the artist going to change in the next century?

Angelou: I think the poet and the painter and the choreographer are all reaching for the same thing they've always reached for.

LK: Do they ever grab hold of it?

Angelou: On occasion. Michelangelo got it when he did the *Pieta.*

LK: Did you ever get it?

Angelou: Only in a line or two.

LK: So the role remains the same?

Angelou: I think so. The artist is always trying to show the truth of our experience, not necessarily the facts. Sometimes the facts obscure the truth because there are so many facts. But if you hit the truth you know it whether it's Confucius or Martin Luther King. You know the truth whether it is spoken to you or you hear it in a piece of music. Haydn got it and so did Ray Charles. . . .

LK: If someone on a school board in the next century is reading these words right now, and he faces cutting arts out of the school budget, what do you say to that person?

Angelou: It should be the last thing to cut back. We are forever talking about protecting the life of the environment but we never talk about protecting the life of the soul. . . .

ELAINE PAGELS

A distinguished scholar of religion at Princeton, Elaine Pagels speculates on the future of our notion of the divine and what may shape religious organizations and practices. Whether we are believers or not, we must reckon with religion in forming any adequate view of the future. Its political impact alone makes it impossible to ignore.

LK: We seem to be traveling faster, we are learning so much, every- 1
one says there's going to be change-change-change, and I'm wondering what this is going to do to God.

Pagels: You're talking about quantitative changes: changes in speed, medical advances, travel, communications, and the like. They've changed our lives. But they have also pressed with urgency the kinds of questions religion involves: What does it mean, and what do we think about living and dying, and what is it for? I work on a bioethics committee at a hospital where medical technology raises the questions about values of life in a very radical and practical way. These questions are becoming all the more acute. . . .

LK: So advances in science are forcing answers?

Pagels: No, they are forcing questions that may be becoming more urgent than before. These are questions about what we ultimately value and what we find worthwhile about human beings.

LK: Are we starting on a road of having a different perception of a 5
divine presence? . . .

Pagels: People used to locate God in the corners of their ignorance, you know, "This is what we don't know so that belongs to God." That is, I hope, no longer going to be the case. Certainly our perceptions are changing. The enormous awareness from communications and cultural transformations is making people aware of other cultures. Buddhists don't talk about God in the way Westerners do and yet they engage in issues involving the spiritual dimension of life, and that is going to come to the fore. The question of how one perceives a spiritual life is as powerful as ever. . . .

LK: Okay, if our idea of a God is changing, one can presume our idea of Satan is changing also.

Pagels: Well, the people who have taken Satan seriously have tried to account for certain things that have happened, certain atrocities of human violence . . . such as the Holocaust. . . . I think fewer people today think they have to invoke a supernatural presence to account for this. Instead, many people are suggesting that human nature and human culture has enough depth, weirdness, and mystery in it to account for these things. . . .

LK: Death. How is our perception changing, and where do you see it moving?

Pagels: I think of Walt Whitman's comment that death is different than 10
what we supposed and luckier. People are now looking at the possibility that near-death experiences, be they actual or simply a chemical change in the brain, are a window to visions of angels. I thought we would have more confidence in the possibility of other realities and more awareness of the limits of our rational moments, and that, while it doesn't tell us everything, does tell us a great deal. Now people are aware that scientific answers have limits and that we are not going to learn everything from them. . . .

LK: Will there be more religions?

Pagels: I would guess the answer is yes, but what they will look like, I don't know. Certainly the groups that exist are often breaking into different variations, and there may be others that join as a result. But I do think there will be new religions and quite new perceptions. . . .

LK: . . . Will religions become more tolerant of each other?

Pagels: The only religions I know of that are genuinely intolerant are the three Western religions: Judaism, Christianity, and Islam. But we are going to see a borrowing from one for another, a mingling, and as a result, we will not see these as much as separate paths as we have seen in the past. Now, some people will say this waters one of them or all of them down. Some would even call it a betrayal. But I think people are going to move the boundaries in an attempt to become more open, and that will set in motion others who get nervous and, therefore, more and more rigid. The answer, then, is we'll probably see both. There is going to be a lot of discussion in the next century about this because people are becoming aware these traditions aren't just made in heaven, that they have their own depth, history, culture, and limits. . . .

LK: Eastern spirituality has attracted those in the West. That going to 15
continue?

Pagels: Absolutely. Westerners are going toward it not only to seek God but to help transform internal states; dealing with anger, loneliness, distress, and isolation. In this technological age people can be very lonely and very isolated and unhappy.

In meditation, solitude is seen as an illusion; we are, in fact, part of a living network of beings that extends throughout this universe. It's a sense of community and a sense of self in the universe. Look at the best-seller list: books about near-death experiences, angels, and so on. This shows that many people are becoming aware of levels of human experience that aren't explicable in scientific terms or psychological terms or reducible to those. I think many people are coming to the sense that there may be more. . . .

LK: Let's talk about the mix of religion and politics. We have the Christian Coalition and the Pat Robertsons and so on. Is this something new?

Pagels: This is probably as ancient as religion itself. . . . [I]f people have religious convictions then those convictions have practical implications that have to do with whether or not you can kill or commit suicide or perform an abortion. The interaction of religion and politics will increase in intensity in the next thirty or forty years.

LK: Is this clash of religion and politics driven by technology? 20

Pagels: I don't think so. It's always been intensely engaged. New technology, instead of making religion irrelevant (which is what some people assumed before) in fact is raising the issues acutely. For example, now we can keep people alive who, five years ago, would have died. So the questions about termination of life are becoming increasingly acute because they seem to be much more in our hands. For instance, it is now legal in some cases to terminate pregnancy at a stage in which the fetus can be kept alive outside of the womb. So what do you do about it? Technologically you can support babies born very premature. Can you legally kill or abort them? These are fundamental questions about our values.

LK: We then are going to hear more from religious action groups like the Christian Coalition?

Pagels: Absolutely. There are many people who see, first of all, how the world is changing and how technology is giving us so many more options, for example, to have a baby when you otherwise wouldn't have had a baby, or to prolong life in a very radical way. Those ethical questions are frightening and complex to many people who say, "Let's go back to the old answers because if it's good enough for Moses, it's good enough for me." But of course Moses, or Jesus or Paul or any of those traditional figures, did not face the world we live in. I'm not saying one can't look at Jewish or Christian tradition and deal with those questions, but we have to explore those issues in other ways as well. . . .

Questions for Discussion

1. As noted, these selections share a focus on the human condition. What else pulls them together?
2. "I think we have lost our way," Edelman says. "We" who? What does she seem to have in mind by "our way"? Would any of the other three interviewees agree with her? Do you? Why or why not?
3. Compare what Edelman has to say about the role of the religious community in social and political reform with Pagel's views on similar themes. Do they reinforce each other or not?
4. Margolies-Mezvinsky worries about "our inability to face facts," pointing especially to entitlement programs like Social Security. As she sees it, what exactly is the nature of the problem? Can you think of other pressing issues we cannot seem to grapple with realistically and honestly? Are the barriers the same in all cases?

5. Angelou is apologetic about her concerns "sound[ing] awfully soft." What does she mean? "Soft" as compared to what? Is it fair or useful to characterize her concerns or those of the other interviewees as soft?
6. "We never talk about protecting the life of the soul," Angelou complains. What is this life? What nurtures it? What undermines it or causes it to get little attention?
7. Pagels seems to think that our idea of God is changing. From what? To what? Suppose she is right. What difference might it make in how people behave?

For Inquiry

Just how different men and women are and why is a subject of intense scientific and humanistic study, as well as a common topic of popular debate. Remembering that prophecy tells us at least as much about the prophet as it does the future, we can study the question of gender difference by comparing the "future talk" of men and women. As a class project collect a significant sample of speculations about the future from both men and women. Try to make your sample diverse by including people of different backgrounds and occupations. King's book and the other selections in this chapter are a good place to begin. Divide what you find into equitable parts, and assign each part to a class group for assessment.

After extensive discussion write individual or group papers exploring the implications of the research. Is there a "feminine" brand of prophecy that differs from its "masculine" counterpart? If so, in what ways? Try to account for the differences in some reasonable and consistent way.

MAX DUBLIN

The Power of Prophecy

No inquiry into the future can afford to ignore the genre of prophecy itself, especially how it persuades and what effect it has on our thought and actions. The following trenchant critique of recent prophets and trend-chasers indicts them for being not merely often mistaken about the future but morally vacuous and irresponsible in their attitudes and approach.

Max Dublin is a published poet and Research Fellow at the University of Toronto, who did his college work at the University of Chicago and Harvard. We offer here an excerpt from the Prologue to his 1991 book Futurehype: The Tyranny of Prophecy.

. . . the Erewhonians are a meek people, easily led by the nose, and quick to offer up common sense at the shrine of logic.

—SAMUEL BUTLER

• • •

PREDICTING THE future has become so integral to the fabric of modern consciousness that few people feel compelled to question it, and fewer still feel the need to defend it. And yet, in surveying the landscape of modern prophecy, it was shocking to discover how much of what even our most respectable prophets have to say about the future is blatantly false, that is, either deeply flawed intellectually, or morally questionable, or both. It is true that their predictions and visions are logical, up to a point, but when you look at them closely, many of even the most respectable prophecies today still fly in the face of common sense and/or common decency. And there seem to be no real people in these visions of the future, no real life in the rich and sometimes puzzling way in which we experience it—only banal abstractions of life and neat little caricatures of people. 1

Since it is obvious that our prophets and our prophetic leaders in government, in the media and in industry have a powerful impact on our lives, and since so much of what they say turns out to be false, in the end I found myself thinking more and more not so much about *what* they have to say, but *how* they say it. I became concerned about the nature of their appeal, the techniques and rhetoric that make our prophets credible and persuasive, and also about how prophecy shapes our world and how we think about the future. The more I learned about modern prophecy, and the more I thought about the role our prophets have come to play in the development of our world, the more contradictions I discovered, and the more striking—and troubling—did these contradictions appear.

The first of these contradictions to strike me, and perhaps the one that really got me going . . . , goes something like this: on the one hand, a great many present-day prophets . . . have proclaimed that present trends allow for almost endless possibilities for developing the world of the future; on the other hand, however, many of the same futurologists . . . also take great pains to explain to their followers that the world of the future will only be *thus and so.* And sometimes they even go on to warn that those who are not willing to prepare for this specific future, or for a short list of possible futures, will run into any number of difficulties and dangers, and perhaps be hopelessly left behind . . .

Endless possibilities, but very few real choices—unless, of course, you are willing to run the risks and pay the costs of "bucking trends."

Not everyone has such a respectful, if not worshipful, view of trends. 5
George Orwell, who many people have mistakenly considered to be a prophet, was actually, in his time, a severe detractor of modern prophets, and especially of trend-chasers. . . . In a long essay about James Burnham, a prominent American futurologist and trend-follower of his time, Orwell cast a very different light on trend-chasing when he made the following criticism of Burnham's political predictions: "The prediction that Russia would gang up with Japan against the U.S.A. was written early in 1944, soon after the conclusion of a new Russo-Japanese treaty. The prophecy of Russian world conquest was written in the winter of 1944, when the Russians were advancing rapidly in eastern Europe while the Western Allies were still held up in Italy and northern France. It will be seen that at each point Burnham is predicting *a continuation of the thing that is happening*" (emphasis in original).[1]

However, Orwell's critique went much further than merely pointing out the intellectual fallacy of "predicting a continuation of the thing that is happening." Orwell argued that this way of thinking was the consequence of a moral failing. He wrote: "The tendency to do this is not simply a bad habit, like inaccuracy or exaggeration, which one can correct by taking thought. It is a major mental disease, and its roots lie partly in cowardice and partly in the worship of power, which is not fully separable from cowardice."[2] Later in this critique Orwell went on to elaborate how our experience teaches us that such predictions are false and to describe how the worship of power works in political prophecies, but his observations are generally applicable to all sorts of prophecies, not only the political ones. He wrote:

> Power worship blurs political judgement because it leads, almost unavoidably, to the belief that present trends will continue. Whoever is winning at the moment will always seem to be invincible. . . . This habit of mind leads also to the belief that things will happen more quickly, completely, and catastrophically than they ever do in practice. The rise and fall of empires, the disappearance of cultures and religions, are expected to happen with earthquake suddenness, and processes which have barely started are talked about as though they were already at an end. . . . The slowness of historical change, the fact that any epoch always contains a great deal of the last epoch, is never

> sufficiently allowed for. Such manner of thinking is bound to lead to mistaken prophecies, because, even when it gauges the direction of events rightly, it will miscalculate their tempo. Within the space of five years Burnham foretold the domination of Russia by Germany and of Germany by Russia. In each case he was obeying the same instinct: the instinct to bow down before the conqueror of the moment, to accept the existing trend as irreversible.[3]

It might be nice to think that the differences between how Orwell and [contemporary futurologists] think about trends are merely intellectual, a gentleman's disagreement to be sorted out over drinks at the club. . . . But the reason that this and the other contradictions of modern prophecy . . . are *not* merely intellectual is that predictions are not merely exercises of the mind. Predictions have power: there is no rhetorical or propaganda device more powerful than prophecy. Predictions do not simply describe the world—they *act* on it. How do they do this? For one thing, predictions are seldom neutral, seldom merely descriptive. Usually predictions—even weather forecasts—are also prescriptive; they contain a strong element of advice and warning. . . .

But even when predictions have no advice or warning built into them, they still act powerfully on their audiences because they naturally function in the same way that promises do in the sense that they create expectations, and there is no question but that people will act on the basis of these kinds of expectations. But false predictions—and, as I will show in this book, most predictions, except for the most obvious and short-range ones do, in fact, turn out to be false—are like false promises, that is to say, they act like lies. And false predictions are destructive in the same way that lies are because, when uttered with conviction, they disarm and inspire us and put us into false positions. Furthermore, these false positions, like all false positions, encourage us to act in ways we never would if we really understood where we stood and what we were doing, in ways that are typically self-defeating. . . .

Because it is capable of influencing us this way, modern prophecy, in all of its different manifestations, should be considered a force in its own right—a force which, like all sources of power, is liable to be abused. It does not merely monitor the development of our civilization, as futurologists . . . like to claim it does, but actually shapes it, often in decidedly harmful ways. By saying this, however, I have a great deal more in mind than the now commonplace observation that polling often affects the outcome of elections. . . . The effect of prophecy on a society is much more powerful than this. Because of its power, there is, and always has been, a great deal of manipulative, exploitative and destabilizing potential in prophecy—and often this is precisely what false prophecy is all about. . . .

It is characteristic of science, in its quest for objectivity, to exclude and avoid ethical considerations. Therefore it is natural for modern prophecy, which has scientific pretensions, to do the same thing. But a prophecy with scientific pretenses, and especially one which on this basis often manages to avoid or mask ideological and ethical issues rather than facing them head-on, is a disturbing development in the history of the world. There have always been false prophets, but before scientism began to obscure ethical questions by claiming to transcend them, all forms of prophecy were deeply and explicitly grounded in ethical thinking, for the simple reason that they were a part of religious practice. Prophets were spiritual leaders and foretelling the future was only one part of the extremely complex roles they played in their nations and societies. One only has to recall the prophets of ancient Greece and Israel during what may be regarded as the golden age of prophecy to realize how integral this grounding used to be.

Consider, for example, the role that prophecy played in the life and times of King Oedipus of Thebes. We are all familiar with the bare bones of this story. A young man kills a stranger, who turns out to be his father, and through a series of quirks becomes king and marries another stranger, who turns out to be his mother. For committing these crimes he dooms himself to a miserable destiny of blindness and exile. What is interesting, however, is how all of this is revealed, for the most important work of revelation is left to a prophet by the name of Tiresias. Tiresias, the famous blind prophet of Oedipus's kingdom of Thebes, far from thrusting himself into the political fray, as our modern prophets like to do, was actually at the outset a very reluctant oracle. In fact, when first questioned by Oedipus, Tiresias was adamantly unwilling to talk. He knew the truth would eventually come out, that it would bring doom to his king and shame to the city, and so the prophet preferred not to be the one to break this terrible news. Describing his predicament, Tiresias himself says in Sophocles's version of this story, "Alas, how terrible is wisdom when/It brings no profit to the man that's wise!"[4]

But Oedipus, true to character, immediately became incensed with Tiresias for this reluctance. It was only at this point, when Oedipus had once again displayed his famous temper, that Tiresias hinted at all of the crimes that would eventually be revealed. Ultimately it was Oedipus's temper, now brandished at Tiresias himself, that reminded the prophet of the original source of this tragedy, the earlier occasion when Oedipus had lost his temper and killed another old man during an altercation on the road, a stranger who turned out to be his father. "You blame my temper," the prophet reproached King Oedipus, "but do not see/your own that lives within you."[5]

In the end, when Tiresias was forced to reveal the source of present misery and to foretell the coming doom of King Oedipus, he did so by way of a moral chastisement. Tiresias did not merely glibly predict the future for Oedipus, he did it in the context of raising explicit moral issues. He not only predicted that horrible things were in store for Oedipus but he also explained that it was the King's own reprehensible behavior that had doomed him. Tiresias indicted Oedipus in the harshest way possible by maintaining that it was nothing less fundamental than Oedipus's own character, his unruly temper, that had shaped his destiny. Character is destiny said Tiresias to King Oedipus;

I predict that all of these horrible things will happen to you and they will happen as a consequence of the way you have lived your life.

Like Tiresias, most of the Old Testament prophets also chastised the Children of Israel, reminding them of their moral shortcomings. In the case of the Hebrew prophets, however, the prophecy-cum-chastisement took a somewhat different form: the call of the prophet was often an exhortation to the Israelites to better themselves so that they would be worthy of the great destiny that had been prepared for them, so that it would not be delayed by their undesirable behavior. Moses, the first and greatest of these prophets, forced them to wander through the desert for forty years to expiate their sin and prepare themselves for their destiny. Elijah, in his turn, called upon them to live a more spiritual life, and Isaiah censured them for materialism and land-grabbing. Isaiah said, "Woe to those who add house to house/and join field to field/until everywhere belongs to them/and they are the sole inhabitants of the land" (Isaiah, 5:8).

In a sense the *foresight* which these ancient prophets possessed was fundamentally part of their more general and profound *insight* into human nature. It was a vehicle for making an honest and open moral argument about the future. There have always been charlatans in the prophecy business, but moral intelligence based on a profound understanding of the complexity of human nature has always been an integral part of true prophecy. In modern prophecy, however, this is hardly the case. Trendiness and the managerial/technological juggernaut that drives most modern forecasting generally have little if anything to do with ethics. Elijah predicted of the Children of Israel, "You will be a light unto the nations." Today our prophets are just as likely to predict, "You will sell computer chips, or armaments or banking services to the nations."

Typically, the only thing that is left of a moral argument in the prophecy 15
of our times is lip service to progress and a great deal of the power of prediction to make us act is based on the rhetoric of progress. However, contrary to popular conceptions—conceptions which are often promoted by futurologists themselves for obvious self-serving reasons—prediction has very little, if anything, to do with progress. In fact, in our time prediction has often acted as a hindrance to real progress. This is true because, first of all, governments often use rosy predictions as a mechanism for avoiding coming to grips with the intractable problems of the present. A great deal of time, energy and money is spent making and fostering these kinds of predictions—and the often foolish interventions that are based on them—instead of taking responsibility for the present situation and tackling the problems at hand. Second, and perhaps more important, predictions often retard progress: when one speaks of progress it is important to be specific because we do not all agree on what it is, and because progress in one area often means regress in another. For example, although the arms race is now presumably over, its progress was characteristically based on predictions of future military superiority or a future state of "parity." Since the

end of World War II this kind of futuristic propaganda served as an excuse for constantly postponing the talks and negotiations that were necessary to create progress in peace.*

Divorced from the progressivism of earlier periods, prophecy has also largely lost what was left, as recently as the turn of this century, of the moral and ethical basis for gazing forward. Because of this rupture we have developed an ethic about forecasting that is often self-serving but ethically indifferent. Fitting ourselves into a vulgar Darwinian definition of our humanity, in following our false prophets we are always "adaptive" and "exploitative" creatures rather than morally purposive ones. Therefore we are not so much concerned about what the future will be because, on the basis of our values, we want it to be a certain way; rather we want to know what the future will be because we think this is the only way we can protect ourselves and perhaps take advantage of it. Worse than this, many people have come to think that the future must be good merely because it is the next step, because it is there, because the next step is said to be inevitable. In our time false prophecy consistently substitutes the ethic of inevitability for the ethic of responsibility. What this amounts to—instead of futuregazing tied to truly progressive thinking—is a bland, pervasive, sterile and rather mechanical *futurity.* The future is the place to go to and we should want to go there simply because it is the next place to go. . . .

Since what is always at stake in our relationship with our prophets is nothing less than what we want to become, and since the very act of prediction has the power to influence what we will become, the questions we must pose for ourselves in this relationship are these: Will we make our own choices, or will we accept the ready-made ones with which they present us, and based on which, if they are leaders in positions of power, they often act in our behalf? Will we buy into their dreams, or will we assert the right that is the precursor to real growth, the right to dream our own dreams?

Dreaming our own dreams, that is, pursuing a diverse and rich economic and cultural development, may appear to be a luxury in our time when we are possessed by the need to predict the future in order to be purposive in conquering it. In fact it is not a luxury but one of the most compelling of necessities. It is necessary because of the diversity it promotes. It is one of the few things that can keep our civilization diverse enough so that, as time unfolds, we retain choices through the skills and knowledge that we have preserved and developed by continual cultivation. . . .

*In spite of the fact that the cold war has largely died down, the end of the arms race is greatly exaggerated: in spite of the disarmament treaties of the last few years new weapons systems are still scheduled to come on board until the end of the century. A conference of NATO defense ministers in April 1990 issued a communique that the Alliance will continue to adhere to its first strike policy because they are unwilling to relinquish a policy that has supposedly served them so well in the past. This is a typical incidence in which "clinging to the past" is called "looking to the future."

NOTES

1. George Orwell, "James Burnham and the Managerial Revolution," in *Collected Essays, Journalism and Letters,* vol. 4 (New York: Harcourt, 1968) 172–73.
2. Orwell 173.
3. Orwell 174.
4. Sophocles, *Oedipus the King,* in *Greek Tragedies,* vol. 1, trans. David Grene (Chicago: U of Chicago P, 1973) 123.
5. Sophocles 124.

Questions for Discussion

1. Dublin claims that much contemporary prophecy is "either deeply flawed intellectually, or morally questionable, or both." What does he mean by "deeply flawed intellectually"? Whom or what does he blame for the lack of moral engagement with the future?
2. Dublin cites George Orwell, author of *1984* and *Animal Farm.* Summarize Orwell's critique of futurism. Which of his points seem strongest to you? Why?
3. "Predictions do not simply describe the world," Dublin contends, "they *act* on it" (his emphasis). What does he mean? Can you cite examples of decisions you've made or the decisions of others you know that were based on knowledge about trends?
4. What's the point (or points) of Dublin's discussion of ancient Greek and Hebrew prophecy? How, according to Dublin, can we tell false prophets from true ones?

For Analysis and Convincing

Choose any other selection in this chapter or your own example of contemporary prophecy for analysis according to Dublin's views and categories. Who is your author's audience? How does he or she attempt to persuade? (See Chapter 6 on arguing to persuade for additional guidance.) Are the prophecies offered consistent and reasonable? Does the author see us as having choices about the future? Does he or she engage the future with some awareness that our choices have ethical dimensions and consequences?

Write a paper explaining and justifying your evaluation. In other words, make a case for your assessment, and back it up by referring to and citing from the text you are analyzing.

ROBERT D. KAPLAN

The Coming Anarchy

Any effort to imagine the future of our entire globe must take into account the so-called developing world. But it's very difficult to grasp. First, it is many worlds, not one; poverty and slums in West Africa, for example, as Robert Kaplan points out, is not the same thing as poverty and slums in Turkey. Second, the cultures of the developing world are so different from ours as to seem remote and alienating. Third, the sheer complexity of these countries and regions scattered all over the globe daunts us; can we really begin to understand what is going on? Finally, although we may feel pity for the suffering masses in Africa, or India, or South America, still their problems are not our problems, and the problems they have seem so overwhelming, so beyond solution, that we understandably turn our attention elsewhere.

Despite the difficulties, however, we must think seriously about the developing world, and this article offers a good beginning. And despite the author's doubts about the validity of maps, read it with globe or atlas in hand, following him as he describes what he saw in his extensive travels. We need not agree with his conclusions to learn much from his experience and knowledge.

Robert Kaplan is a distinguished journalist whose work frequently appears in the Atlantic Monthly. *The following excerpt is from an article published in the February 1994 issue of that journal.*

THE MINISTER'S eyes were like egg yolks, an aftereffect of some of the many illnesses, malaria especially, endemic in his country. There was also an irrefutable sadness in his eyes. He spoke in a slow and creaking voice, the voice of hope about to expire. Flame trees, coconut palms, and a ballpoint-blue Atlantic composed the background. None of it seemed beautiful, though. "In forty-five years I have never seen things so bad. We did not manage ourselves well after the British departed. But what we have now is something worse—the revenge of the poor, of the social failures, of the people least able to bring up children in a modern society." Then he referred to the recent coup in the West African country Sierra Leone. "The boys who took power in Sierra Leone come from houses like this." The Minister jabbed his finger at a corrugated metal shack teeming with children. "In three months these boys confiscated all the official Mercedes, Volvos, and BMWs and willfully wrecked them on the road." The Minister mentioned one of the coup's leaders, Solomon Anthony Joseph Musa, who shot the people who had paid for his schooling, "in order to erase the humiliation and mitigate the power his middle-class sponsors held over him." 1

Tyranny is nothing new in Sierra Leone or in the rest of West Africa. But it is now part and parcel of an increasing lawlessness that is far more significant than any coup, rebel incursion, or episodic experiment in democracy. Crime was what my friend—a top-ranking African official whose life would be threatened were I to identify him more precisely—really wanted to talk about. Crime is what makes West Africa a natural point of departure for my report on what the political character of our planet is likely to be in the twenty-first century.

The cities of West Africa at night are some of the unsafest places in the world. Streets are unlit; the police often lack gasoline for their vehicles; armed burglars, carjackers, and muggers proliferate. "The government in Sierra Leone has no writ after dark," says a foreign resident, shrugging. . . . In Abidjan, effectively the capital of the Cote d'Ivoire, or Ivory Coast, restaurants have stick- and gun-wielding guards who walk you the fifteen feet or so between your car and the entrance, giving you an eerie taste of what American cities might be like in the future. An Italian ambassador was killed by gunfire when robbers invaded an Abidjan restaurant. The family of the Nigerian ambassador was tied up and robbed at gunpoint in the ambassador's residence. After university students in the Ivory Coast caught bandits who had been plaguing their dorms, they executed them by hanging tires around their necks and setting the tires on fire. In one instance Ivorian policemen stood by and watched the "necklacings," afraid to intervene. Each time I went to the Abidjan bus terminal, groups of young men with restless, scanning eyes surrounded my taxi, putting their hands all over the windows, demanding "tips" for carrying my luggage even though I had only a rucksack. In cities in six West African countries I saw similar young men everywhere—hordes of them. They were like loose molecules in a very unstable social fluid, a fluid that was clearly on the verge of igniting.

"You see," my friend the Minister told me, "in the villages of Africa it is perfectly natural to feed at any table and lodge in any hut. But in the cities this communal existence no longer holds. You must pay for lodging and be invited for food. When young men find out that their relations cannot put them up, they become lost. They join other migrants and slip gradually into the criminal process." . . .

A Premonition of the Future

West Africa is becoming the symbol of worldwide demographic, envi- 5
ronmental, and societal stress, in which criminal anarchy emerges as the real "strategic" danger. Disease, overpopulation, unprovoked crime, scarcity of resources, refugee migrations, the increasing erosion of nation-states and international borders, and the empowerment of private armies, security firms, and international drug cartels are now most tellingly demonstrated through a West African prism. West Africa provides an appropriate introduction to the issues, often extremely unpleasant to discuss, that will soon confront our civilization. To remap the political earth the way it will be a few decades hence—as I intend to do in this article—I find I must begin with West Africa. . . .

In Sierra Leone, as in Guinea, as in the Ivory Coast, as in Ghana, most of the primary rain forest and the secondary bush is being destroyed at an alarming rate. I saw convoys of trucks bearing majestic hardwood trunks to coastal ports. When Sierra Leone achieved its independence, in 1961, as much as 60 percent of the country was primary rain forest. Now six percent is. In the Ivory Coast the proportion has fallen from 38 percent to eight percent. The deforestation has led to soil erosion, which has led to more flooding and more mosquitoes. Virtually everyone in the West African interior has some form of malaria.

Sierra Leone is a microcosm of what is occurring, albeit in a more tempered and gradual manner, throughout West Africa and much of the underdeveloped world: the withering away of central governments, the rise of tribal and regional domains, the unchecked spread of disease, and the growing pervasiveness of war. West Africa is reverting to the Africa of the Victorian atlas. It consists now of a series of coastal trading posts, such as Freetown and Conakry, and an interior that, owing to violence, volatility, and disease, is again becoming, as [the novelist] Graham Greene once observed, "blank" and "unexplored." . . .

. . . I got a general sense of the future while driving from the airport to downtown Conakry, the capital of Guinea. The forty-five-minute journey in heavy traffic was through one never-ending shantytown: a nightmarish Dickensian spectacle to which Dickens himself would never have given credence. The corrugated metal shacks and scabrous walls were coated with black slime. Stores were built out of rusted shipping containers, junked cars, and jumbles of wire mesh. The streets were one long puddle of floating garbage. Mosquitoes and flies were everywhere. Children, many of whom had protruding bellies, seemed as numerous as ants. When the tide went out, dead rats and the skeletons of cars were exposed on the mucky beach. In twenty-eight years Guinea's population will double if growth goes on at current rates. Hardwood logging continues at a madcap speed, and people flee the Guinean countryside for Conakry. It seemed to me that here, as elsewhere in Africa and the Third World, man is challenging nature far beyond its limits, and nature is now beginning to take its revenge.

Africa may be as relevant to the future character of world politics as the Balkans were a hundred years ago, prior to the two Balkan wars and the First World War. Then the threat was the collapse of empires and the birth of nations based solely on tribe. Now the threat is more elemental: nature unchecked. Africa's immediate future could be very bad. The coming upheaval, in which foreign embassies are shut down, states collapse, and contact with the outside world takes place through dangerous, disease-ridden coastal trading posts, will loom large in the century we are entering. (Nine of twenty-one U.S. foreign-aid missions to be closed over the next three years are in Africa—a prologue to a consolidation of U.S. embassies themselves.) Precisely because much of Africa is set to go over the edge at a time when the Cold War has ended, when environmental and demographic stress in other parts of the globe is becoming critical, and when the post–First World War system of nation-states—not just in the Balkans but perhaps also in the Middle East—is about to be toppled, Africa suggests what war, borders, and ethnic politics will be like a few decades hence.

To understand the events of the next fifty years, then, one must under- 10
stand environmental scarcity, cultural and racial clash, geographic destiny, and the transformation of war. The order in which I have named these is not accidental. Each concept except the first relies partly on the one or ones before it, meaning that the last two—new approaches to mapmaking and to warfare—are the most important. They are also the least understood. I will now look at each idea, drawing upon the work of specialists and also my own travel experiences in various parts of the globe besides Africa, in order to fill in the blanks of a new political atlas.

The Environment as a Hostile Power

• • •

It is time to understand "the environment" for what it is: the national-security issue of the early twenty-first century. The political and strategic impact of surging populations, spreading disease, deforestation and soil erosion, water depletion, air pollution, and, possibly, rising sea levels in critical, overcrowded regions like the Nile Delta and Bangladesh—developments that will prompt mass migrations and, in turn, incite group conflicts—will be the core foreign-policy challenge from which most others will ultimately emanate, arousing the public and uniting assorted interests left over from the Cold War. In the twenty-first century water will be in dangerously short supply in such diverse locales as Saudi Arabia, Central Asia, and the southwestern United States. A war could erupt between Egypt and Ethiopia over Nile River water. Even in Europe tensions have arisen between Hungary and Slovakia over the damming of the Danube, a classic case of how environmental disputes fuse with ethnic and historical ones. The political scientist and erstwhile Clinton adviser Michael Mandelbaum has said, "We have a foreign policy today in the shape of a doughnut—lots of peripheral interests but nothing at the center." The environment, I will argue, is part of a terrifying array of problems that will define a new threat to our security, filling the hole in Mandelbaum's doughnut and allowing a post–Cold War foreign policy to emerge inexorably by need rather than by design.

Our Cold War foreign policy truly began with George F. Kennan's famous article, signed "X," published in *Foreign Affairs* in July of 1947, in which Kennan argued for a "firm and vigilant containment" of a Soviet Union that was imperially, rather than ideologically, motivated. It may be that our post–Cold War foreign policy will one day be seen to have had its beginnings in an even bolder and more detailed piece of written analysis: one that appeared in the journal *International Security*. The article, published in the fall of 1991 by Thomas Fraser Homer-Dixon, who is the head of the Peace and Conflict Studies Program at the University of Toronto, was titled "On the Threshold:

Environmental Changes as Causes of Acute Conflict." Homer-Dixon has, more successfully than other analysts, integrated two hitherto separate fields—military-conflict studies and the study of the physical environment.

In Homer-Dixon's view, future wars and civil violence will often arise from scarcities of resources such as water, cropland, forests, and fish. Just as there will be environmentally driven wars and refugee flows, there will be environmentally induced . . . "hard regimes." Countries with the highest probability of acquiring hard regimes, according to Homer-Dixon, are those that are threatened by a declining resource base yet also have "a history of state [read 'military'] strength." Candidates include Indonesia, Brazil, and, of course, Nigeria. Though each of these nations has exhibited democratizing tendencies of late, Homer-Dixon argues that such tendencies are likely to be superficial "epiphenomena" having nothing to do with long-term processes that include soaring populations and shrinking raw materials. Democracy is problematic; scarcity is more certain.

Indeed, the Saddam Husseins of the future will have more, not fewer, opportunities. In addition to engendering tribal strife, scarcer resources will place a great strain on many peoples who never had much of a democratic or institutional tradition to begin with. Over the next fifty years the earth's population will soar from 5.5 billion to more than nine billion. Though optimists have hopes for new resource technologies and free-market development in the global village, they fail to note that, as the National Academy of Sciences has pointed out, 95 percent of the population increase will be in the poorest regions of the world, where governments now—just look at Africa—show little ability to function, let alone to implement even marginal improvements. . . .

While a minority of the human population will be, as Francis Fukuyama 15
would put it, sufficiently sheltered so as to enter a "post-historical" realm, living in cities and suburbs in which the environment has been mastered and ethnic animosities have been quelled by bourgeois prosperity, an increasingly large number of people will be stuck in history, living in shantytowns where attempts to rise above poverty, cultural dysfunction, and ethnic strife will be doomed by a lack of water to drink, soil to till, and space to survive in. In the developing world environmental stress will present people with a choice that is increasingly among totalitarianism (as in Iraq), fascist-tending mini-states (as in Serb-held Bosnia), and road-warrior cultures (as in Somalia). Homer-Dixon concludes that "as environmental degradation proceeds, the size of the potential social disruption will increase." . . .

"Think of a stretch limo in the potholed streets of New York City, where homeless beggars live. Inside the limo are the air-conditioned post-industrial regions of North America, Europe, the emerging Pacific Rim, and a few other isolated places, with their trade summitry and computer-information highways. Outside is the rest of mankind, going in a completely different direction."

We are entering a bifurcated world. Part of the globe is inhabited by Hegel's and Fukuyama's Last Man, healthy, well fed, and pampered by technology. The other, larger, part is inhabited by Hobbes's First Man, condemned to a life that is "poor, nasty, brutish, and short." Although both parts will be threatened by environmental stress, the Last Man will be able to master it; the First Man will not. . . .

Environmental scarcity will inflame existing hatreds and affect power relationships, at which we now look.

Skinhead Cossacks, Juju Warriors

In the summer, 1993, issue of *Foreign Affairs,* Samuel P. Huntington, of Harvard's Olin Institute for Strategic Studies, published a thought-provoking article called "The Clash of Civilizations?" The world, he argues, has been moving during the course of this century from nation-state conflict to ideological conflict to, finally, cultural conflict. I would add that as refugee flows increase and as peasants continue migrating to cities around the world—turning them into sprawling villages—national borders will mean less, even as more power will fall into the hands of less educated, less sophisticated groups. In the eyes of these uneducated but newly empowered millions, the real borders are the most tangible and intractable ones: those of culture and tribe. Huntington writes, "First, differences among civilizations are not only real; they are basic," involving, among other things, history, language, and religion. "Second . . . interactions between peoples of different civilizations are increasing; these increasing interactions intensify civilization consciousness." Economic modernization is not necessarily a panacea, since it fuels individual and group ambitions while weakening traditional loyalties to the state. It is worth noting, for example, that it is precisely the wealthiest and fastest-developing city in India, Bombay, that has seen the worst intercommunal violence between Hindus and Muslims. Consider that Indian cities, like African and Chinese ones, are ecological time bombs—Delhi and Calcutta, and also Beijing, suffer the worst air quality of any cities in the world—and it is apparent how surging populations, environmental degradation, and ethnic conflict are deeply related. . . .

Most people believe that the political earth since 1989 has undergone 20
immense change. But it is minor compared with what is yet to come. The breaking apart and remaking of the atlas is only now beginning. The crack-up of the Soviet empire and the coming end of Arab-Israeli military confrontation are merely prologues to the really big changes that lie ahead. Michael Vlahos, a long-range thinker for the U.S. Navy, warns, "We are not in charge of the environment and the world is not following us. It is going in many directions. Do not assume that democratic capitalism is the last word in human social evolution."

Before addressing the questions of maps and of warfare, I want to take a closer look at the interaction of religion, culture, demographic shifts, and the distribution of natural resources in a specific area of the world: the Middle East.

The Past Is Dead

. . .

Slum quarters in Abidjan terrify and repel the outsider. In Turkey it is the opposite. The closer I got to Golden Mountain the better it looked, and the safer I felt. I had $1,500 worth of Turkish lira in one pocket and $1,000 in traveler's checks in the other, yet I felt no fear. Golden Mountain was a real neighborhood. The inside of one house told the story: The architectural bedlam of cinder block and sheet metal and cardboard walls was deceiving. Inside was a home—order, that is, bespeaking dignity. I saw a working refrigerator, a television, a wall cabinet with a few books and lots of family pictures, a few plants by a window, and a stove. Though the streets become rivers of mud when it rains, the floors inside this house were spotless.

Other houses were like this too. Schoolchildren ran along with briefcases strapped to their backs, trucks delivered cooking gas, a few men sat inside a cafe sipping tea. One man sipped beer. Alcohol is easy to obtain in Turkey, a secular state where 99 percent of the population is Muslim. Yet there is little problem of alcoholism. Crime against persons is infinitesimal. Poverty and illiteracy are watered-down versions of what obtains in Algeria and Egypt (to say nothing of West Africa), making it that much harder for religious extremists to gain a foothold.

My point in bringing up a rather wholesome, crime-free slum is this: its existence demonstrates how formidable is the fabric of which Turkish Muslim culture is made. A culture this strong has the potential to dominate the Middle East once again. Slums are litmus tests for innate cultural strengths and weaknesses. Those peoples whose cultures can harbor extensive slum life without decomposing will be, relatively speaking, the future's winners. Those whose cultures cannot will be the future's victims. Slums—in the sociological sense—do not exist in Turkish cities. The mortar between people and family groups is stronger here than in Africa. Resurgent Islam and Turkic cultural identity have produced a civilization with natural muscle tone. Turks, history's perennial nomads, take disruption in stride. . . .

In Turkey several things are happening at once. In 1980, 44 percent of 25
Turks lived in cities; in 1990 it was 61 percent. By the year 2000 the figure is expected to be 67 percent. Villages are emptying out as . . . developments grow around Turkish cities. This is the real political and demographic revolution in Turkey and elsewhere, and foreign correspondents usually don't write about it.

Whereas rural poverty is age-old and almost a "normal" part of the social fabric, urban poverty is socially destabilizing. As Iran has shown, Islamic extremism is the psychological defense mechanism of many urbanized peasants threatened with the loss of traditions in pseudo-modern cities where their values are under attack, where basic services like water and electricity are unavailable, and where they are assaulted by a physically unhealthy environment. The American ethnologist and orientalist Carleton Stevens Coon wrote in 1951 that Islam "has made possible the optimum survival and happiness of millions of human beings in an increasingly impoverished environment over a fourteen-hundred-year period." Beyond its stark, clearly articulated message, Islam's very militancy makes it attractive to the downtrodden. It is the one religion that is prepared to fight. A political era driven by environmental stress, increased cultural sensitivity, unregulated urbanization, and refugee migrations is an era divinely created for the spread and intensification of Islam, already the world's fastest-growing religion. . . .

In Turkey . . . Islam is painfully and awkwardly forging a consensus with modernization, a trend that is less apparent in the Arab and Persian worlds (and virtually invisible in Africa). In Iran the oil boom—because it put development and urbanization on a fast track, making the culture shock more intense—fueled the 1978 Islamic Revolution. But Turkey, unlike Iran and the Arab world, has little oil. Therefore its development and urbanization have been more gradual. Islamists have been integrated into the parliamentary system for decades. The tensions I noticed in Golden Mountain are natural, creative ones: the kind immigrants face the world over. While the world has focused on religious perversity in Algeria, a nation rich in natural gas, and in Egypt, parts of whose capital city, Cairo, evince worse crowding than I have seen even in Calcutta, Turkey has been living through the Muslim equivalent of the Protestant Reformation.

Resource distribution is strengthening Turks in another way vis-à-vis Arabs and Persians. Turks may have little oil, but their Anatolian heartland has lots of water—the most important fluid of the twenty-first century. Turkey's Southeast Anatolia Project, involving twenty-two major dams and irrigation systems, is impounding the waters of the Tigris and Euphrates rivers. Much of the water that Arabs and perhaps Israelis will need to drink in the future is controlled by Turks. The project's centerpiece is the mile-wide, sixteen-story Ataturk Dam, upon which are emblazoned the words of modern Turkey's founder: "Ne Mutlu Turkum Diyene" ("Lucky is the one who is a Turk"). . . .

Erduhan Bayindir, the site manager at the dam, told me that "while oil can be shipped abroad to enrich only elites, water has to be spread more evenly within the society. . . . It is true, we can stop the flow of water into Syria and Iraq for up to eight months without the same water overflowing our dams, in order to regulate their political behavior." . . .

The Lies of Mapmakers

. . .

Consider the map of the world, with its 190 or so countries, each sig- 30
nified by a bold and uniform color: this map, with which all of us have grown up, is generally an invention of modernism, specifically of European colonialism. Modernism, in the sense of which I speak, began with the rise of nation-states in Europe and was confirmed by the death of feudalism at the end of the Thirty Years' War—an event that was interposed between the Renaissance

and the Enlightenment, which together gave birth to modern science. People were suddenly flush with an enthusiasm to categorize, to define. The map, based on scientific techniques of measurement, offered a way to classify new national organisms, making a jigsaw puzzle of neat pieces without transition zones between them. "Frontier" is itself a modern concept that didn't exist in the feudal mind. And as European nations carved out far-flung domains at the same time that print technology was making the reproduction of maps cheaper, cartography came into its own as a way of creating facts by ordering the way we look at the world.

In his book *Imagined Communities: Reflections on the Origin and Spread of Nationalism,* Benedict Anderson, of Cornell University, demonstrates that the map enabled colonialists to think about their holdings in terms of a "totalizing classificatory grid. . . . It was bounded, determinate, and therefore—in principle—countable." To the colonialist, country maps were the equivalent of an accountant's ledger books. Maps, Anderson explains, "shaped the grammar" that would make possible such questionable concepts as Iraq, Indonesia, Sierra Leone, and Nigeria. The state, recall, is a purely Western notion, one that until the twentieth century applied to countries covering only three percent of the earth's land area. Nor is the evidence compelling that the state, as a governing ideal, can be successfully transported to areas outside the industrialized world. Even the United States of America, in the words of one of our best living poets, Gary Snyder, consists of "arbitrary and inaccurate impositions on what is really here."

Yet this inflexible, artificial reality staggers on, not only in the United Nations but in various geographic and travel publications (themselves by-products of an age of elite touring which colonialism made possible) that still report on and photograph the world according to "country." . . .

According to the map, the great hydropower complex emblemized by the Ataturk Dam is situated in Turkey. Forget the map. This southeastern region of Turkey is populated almost completely by Kurds. About half of the world's 20 million Kurds live in "Turkey." The Kurds are predominant in an ellipse of territory that overlaps not only with Turkey but also with Iraq, Iran, Syria, and the former Soviet Union. The Western-enforced Kurdish enclave in northern Iraq, a consequence of the 1991 Gulf War, has already exposed the fictitious nature of that supposed nation-state.

On a recent visit to the Turkish-Iranian border, it occurred to me what a risky idea the nation-state is. Here I was on the legal fault line between two clashing civilizations, Turkic and Iranian. Yet the reality was more subtle: as in West Africa, the border was porous and smuggling abounded, but here the people doing the smuggling, on both sides of the border, were Kurds. In such a moonscape, over which peoples have migrated and settled in patterns that obliterate borders, the end of the Cold War will bring on a cruel process of natural selection among existing states. No longer will these states be so firmly propped up by the West or the Soviet Union. Because the Kurds overlap with nearly everybody in the Middle East, on account of their being cheated out of a state in the post–First World War peace treaties, they are emerging, in effect, as the natural selector—the ultimate reality check. They have destabilized Iraq and may continue to disrupt states that do not offer them adequate breathing space, while strengthening states that do.

Because the Turks, owing to their water resources, their growing econ- 35
omy, and the social cohesion evinced by the most crime-free slums I have encountered, are on the verge of big-power status, and because the 10 million Kurds within Turkey threaten that status, the outcome of the Turkish-Kurdish dispute will be more critical to the future of the Middle East than the eventual outcome of the recent Israeli-Palestinian agreement.

America's fascination with the Israeli-Palestinian issue, coupled with its lack of interest in the Turkish-Kurdish one, is a function of its own domestic and ethnic obsessions, not of the cartographic reality that is about to transform the Middle East. The diplomatic process involving Israelis and Palestinians will, I believe, have little effect on the early- and mid-twenty-first-century map of the region. Israel, with a 6.6 percent economic growth rate based increasingly on high-tech exports, is about to enter Homer-Dixon's stretch limo, fortified by a well-defined political community that is an organic outgrowth of history and ethnicity. Like prosperous and peaceful Japan on the one hand, and war-torn and poverty-wracked Armenia on the other, Israel is a classic national-ethnic organism. Much of the Arab world, however, will undergo alteration, as Islam spreads across artificial frontiers, fueled by mass migrations into the cities and a soaring birth rate of more than 3.2 percent. Seventy percent of the Arab population has been born since 1970—youths with little historical memory of anticolonial independence struggles, postcolonial attempts at nation-building, or any of the Arab-Israeli wars. . . .

Like the borders of West Africa, the colonial borders of Syria, Iraq, Jordan, Algeria, and other Arab states are often contrary to cultural and political reality. As state control mechanisms wither in the face of environmental and demographic stress, "hard" Islamic city-states or shantytown-states are likely to emerge. . . . Whatever the outcome of the peace process, Israel is destined to be a Jewish ethnic fortress amid a vast and volatile realm of Islam. In that realm, the violent youth culture of the Gaza shantytowns may be indicative of the coming era. . . .

A New Kind of War

To appreciate fully the political and cartographic implications of postmodernism—an epoch of themeless juxtapositions, in which the classificatory grid of nation-states is going to be replaced by a jagged-glass pattern of city-states, shanty-states, nebulous and anarchic regionalisms—it is necessary to consider, finally, the whole question of war.

"Oh, what a relief to fight, to fight enemies who defend themselves, enemies who are awake!" Andre Malraux wrote in *Man's Fate.* I cannot think of a more suitable battle cry for many combatants in the early decades of the twenty-first century. The intense savagery of the fighting in such diverse cultural settings as Liberia, Bosnia, the Caucasus, and Sri Lanka—to say nothing of what obtains in American inner cities—indicates something very troubling that those of us inside the stretch limo, concerned with issues like middle-class entitlements and the future of interactive cable television, lack the stomach to contemplate. It is this: a large number of people on this planet, to whom the comfort and stability of a middle-class life is utterly unknown, find war and a barracks existence a step up rather than a step down.

40 "Just as it makes no sense to ask 'why people eat' or 'what they sleep for,'" writes Martin Van Creveld, a military historian at the Hebrew University in Jerusalem, in *The Transformation of War,* "so fighting in many ways is not a means but an end. Throughout history, for every person who has expressed his horror of war there is another who found in it the most marvelous of all the experiences that are vouchsafed to man, even to the point that he later spent a lifetime boring his descendants by recounting his exploits." When I asked Pentagon officials about the nature of war in the twenty-first century, the answer I frequently got was "Read Van Creveld." The top brass are enamored of this historian not because his writings justify their existence but, rather, the opposite: Van Creveld warns them that huge state military machines like the Pentagon's are dinosaurs about to go extinct, and that something far more terrible awaits us.

The degree to which Van Creveld's *Transformation of War* complements Homer-Dixon's work on the environment, Huntington's thoughts on cultural clash, my own realizations in traveling by foot, bus, and bush taxi in more than sixty countries, and America's sobering comeuppances in intractable-culture zones like Haiti and Somalia is startling. The book begins by demolishing the notion that men don't like to fight. "By compelling the senses to focus themselves on the here and now," Van Creveld writes, war "can cause a man to take his leave of them." As anybody who has had experience with Chetniks in Serbia, "technicals" in Somalia, Tontons Macoutes in Haiti, or soldiers in Sierra Leone can tell you, in places where the Western Enlightenment has not penetrated and where there has always been mass poverty, people find liberation in violence. In Afghanistan and elsewhere, I vicariously experienced this phenomenon: worrying about mines and ambushes frees you from worrying about mundane details of daily existence. If my own experience is too subjective, there is a wealth of data showing the sheer frequency of war, especially in the developing world since the Second World War. Physical aggression is a part of being human. Only when people attain a certain economic, educational, and cultural standard is this trait tranquilized. In light of the fact that 95 percent of the earth's population growth will be in the poorest areas of the globe, the question is not whether there will be war (there will be a lot of it) but what kind of war. And who will fight whom? . . .

Because, as Van Creveld notes, the radius of trust within tribal societies is narrowed to one's immediate family and guerrilla comrades, truces arranged with one Bosnian commander, say, may be broken immediately by another Bosnian commander. The plethora of short-lived ceasefires in the Balkans and the Caucasus constitute proof that we are no longer in a world where the old rules of state warfare apply. . . .

Also, war-making entities will no longer be restricted to a specific territory. Loose and shadowy organisms such as Islamic terrorist organizations suggest why borders will mean increasingly little and sedimentary layers of tribalistic identity and control will mean more. "From the vantage point of the present, there appears every prospect that religious . . . fanaticisms will play a larger role in the motivation of armed conflict" in the West than at any time "for the last 300 years," Van Creveld writes. This is why analysts like Michael Vlahos are closely monitoring religious cults. Vlahos says, "An ideology that challenges us may not take familiar form, like the old Nazis or Commies. It may not even engage us initially in ways that fit old threat markings." Van Creveld concludes, "Armed conflict will be waged by men on earth, not robots in space. It will have more in common with the struggles of primitive tribes than with large-scale conventional war." While another military historian, John Keegan, in his new book *A History of Warfare,* draws a more benign portrait of primitive man, it is important to point out that what Van Creveld really means is re-primitivized man: warrior societies operating at a time of unprecedented resource scarcity and planetary overcrowding. . . .

Future wars will be those of communal survival, aggravated or, in many cases, caused by environmental scarcity. These wars will be subnational, meaning that it will be hard for states and local governments to protect their own citizens physically. This is how many states will ultimately die. As state power fades—and with it the state's ability to help weaker groups within society, not to mention other states—peoples and cultures around the world will be thrown back upon their own strengths and weaknesses, with fewer equalizing mechanisms to protect them. Whereas the distant future will probably see the emergence of a racially hybrid, globalized man, the coming decades will see us more aware of our differences than of our similarities. . . .

The Last Map

. . . Imagine cartography in three dimensions, as if in a hologram. In this 45
hologram would be the overlapping sediments of group and other identities atop the merely two-dimensional color markings of city-states and the remaining nations, themselves confused in places by shadowy tentacles, hovering overhead, indicating the power of drug cartels, mafias, and private security agencies. Instead of borders, there would be moving "centers" of power, as in the Middle Ages. Many of these layers would be in motion. Replacing fixed and abrupt lines on a flat space would be a shifting pattern of buffer entities, like . . . the Latino buffer entity replacing a precise U.S.-Mexican border. To this protean cartographic hologram one must add other factors, such as

migrations of populations, explosions of birth rates, vectors of disease. Henceforward the map of the world will never be static. This future map—in a sense, the "Last Map"—will be an ever-mutating representation of chaos. . . .

None of this even takes into account climatic change, which, if it occurs in the next century, will further erode the capacity of existing states to cope. India, for instance, receives 70 percent of its precipitation from the monsoon cycle, which planetary warming could disrupt.

Not only will the three-dimensional aspects of the Last Map be in constant motion, but its two-dimensional base may change too. The National Academy of Sciences reports that "as many as one billion people, or 20 per cent of the world's population, live on lands likely to be inundated or dramatically changed by rising waters. . . . Low-lying countries in the developing world such as Egypt and Bangladesh, where rivers are large and the deltas extensive and densely populated, will be hardest hit. . . . Where the rivers are dammed, as in the case of the Nile, the effects . . . will be especially severe."

Egypt could be where climatic upheaval—to say nothing of the more immediate threat of increasing population—will incite religious upheaval in truly biblical fashion. Natural catastrophes, such as the October, 1992, Cairo earthquake, in which the government failed to deliver relief aid and slum residents were in many instances helped by their local mosques, can only strengthen the position of Islamic factions. In a statement about greenhouse warming which could refer to any of a variety of natural catastrophes, the environmental expert Jessica Tuchman Matthews warns that many of us underestimate the extent to which political systems, in affluent societies as well as in places like Egypt, "depend on the underpinning of natural systems." She adds, "The fact that one can move with ease from Vermont to Miami has nothing to say about the consequences of Vermont acquiring Miami's climate."

Indeed, it is not clear that the United States will survive the next century in exactly its present form. Because America is a multi-ethnic society, the nation-state has always been more fragile here than it is in more homogeneous societies like Germany and Japan. James Kurth, in an article published in *The National Interest* in 1992, explains that whereas nation-state societies tend to be built around a mass-conscription army and a standardized public school system, "multicultural regimes" feature a high-tech, all-volunteer army . . . operating in a culture in which the international media and entertainment industry has more influence than the "national political class." In other words, a nation-state is a place where everyone has been educated along similar lines, where people take their cue from national leaders, and where everyone (every male, at least) has gone through the crucible of military service, making patriotism a simpler issue. Writing about his immigrant family in turn-of-the-century Chicago, Saul Bellow states, "The country took us over. It was a country then, not a collection of 'cultures.'"

During the Second World War and the decade following it, the United 50
States reached its apogee as a classic nation-state. During the 1960s, as is now clear, America began a slow but unmistakable process of transformation. The signs hardly need belaboring: racial polarity, educational dysfunction, social fragmentation of many and various kinds. . . .

Issues like West Africa could yet emerge as a new kind of foreign-policy issue, further eroding America's domestic peace. The spectacle of several West African nations collapsing at once could reinforce the worst racial stereotypes here at home. That is another reason why Africa matters. We must not kid ourselves: the sensitivity factor is higher than ever. The Washington, D.C., public school system is already experimenting with an Afrocentric curriculum. Summits between African leaders and prominent African-Americans are becoming frequent, as are Pollyanna-ish prognostications about multiparty elections in Africa that do not factor in crime, surging birth rates, and resource depletion. The Congressional Black Caucus was among those urging U.S. involvement in Somalia and in Haiti. At the *Los Angeles Times* minority staffers have protested against, among other things, what they allege to be the racist tone of the newspaper's Africa coverage, allegations that the editor of the "World Report" section, Dan Fisher, denies, saying essentially that Africa should be viewed through the same rigorous analytical lens as other parts of the world.

Africa may be marginal in terms of conventional late-twentieth-century conceptions of strategy, but in an age of cultural and racial clash, when national defense is increasingly local, Africa's distress will exert a destabilizing influence on the United States.

This and many other factors will make the United States less of a nation than it is today, even as it gains territory following the peaceful dissolution of Canada. Quebec, based on the bedrock of Roman Catholicism and Francophone ethnicity, could yet turn out to be North America's most cohesive and crime-free nation-state. . . . "Patriotism" will become increasingly regional as people in Alberta and Montana discover that they have far more in common with each other than they do with Ottawa or Washington, and Spanish-speakers in the Southwest discover a greater commonality with Mexico City. . . . As Washington's influence wanes, and with it the traditional symbols of American patriotism, North Americans will take psychological refuge in their insulated communities and cultures. . . .

. . . When the Berlin Wall was falling, in November of 1989, I happened to be in Kosovo, covering a riot between Serbs and Albanians. The future was in Kosovo, I told myself that night, not in Berlin. The same day that Yitzhak Rabin and Yasser Arafat clasped hands on the White House lawn, my Air Afrique plane was approaching Bamako, Mali, revealing corrugated-zinc shacks at the edge of an expanding desert. The real news wasn't at the White House, I realized. It was right below.

Questions for Discussion

1. Judging from the article, what does Kaplan mean by "anarchy"? With what concept of social order is anarchy contrasted? Some parts of the developing world—Turkey, for example—seem better equipped to cope than others. To what does Kaplan attribute such relative stability?
2. Kaplan quotes Michael Vlahos, "a long-range thinker for the U.S. Navy," who warns us "not [to] assume that democratic capitalism is the last word in human social evolution." That is, the developed world, especially the United States, should not attempt to encourage the spread of its system throughout the world. Why not? What in Kaplan's article supports Vlahos's contention that democratic capitalism won't work everywhere?
3. According to Kaplan, what is "wrong"—reality-distorting—with our maps of the world? Even the United States, he says, is falsely conceived in that we accept conventional boundaries between countries too uncritically. How must we think to overcome this neat-and-definite-boundaries notion of the world?
4. "To understand the events of the next fifty years," Kaplan claims, "one must understand environmental scarcity, cultural and racial clash, geographical destiny, and the transformation of war." In three or four sentences summarize what he has to say about each factor. How might they interact? Which of these seem most important in the long run?
5. In many ways Kaplan challenges us to think "outside the box," in ways different from how we are accustomed to thinking about international politics. Which of his views surprised you the most? Did they change or modify your understanding in some way? How exactly?

For Research and Mediation

If nothing else, Kaplan's article should make us aware of our ignorance about the developing world and thereby encourage us to "dig in," find out more about it. Select a region of the developing world the class finds especially interesting, and as a class research project, read extensively about it and share all information. Look especially for interpretations of the future that differ from Kaplan's. Attempt to specify why they differ. If your school has an expert or experts on the region, consult with them to determine how their interpretations relate to Kaplan's and the other sources you've read.

Then select a single source whose views differ sharply from Kaplan's. In groups or individually write an essay attempting to combine the best of both into a coherent view of what's likely to happen over, say, the next ten years. Use your research to explain and support your case.

For Inquiry

Kaplan refers to three sources who influenced his views strongly: Thomas Fraser Homer-Dixon, Samuel P. Huntington, and Martin Van Creveld. Choose one and read the source work Kaplan cites. Study it carefully, comparing what it says to how Kaplan understood and used it. Then draft questions you would ask Kaplan, the source you've selected, or both if you could engage them in dialogue.

Form class groups based on the source selected, and compare questions. Draft a master list of the questions that seem most useful. Working separately, write out answers to several of the questions as you think Kaplan or your source or both would respond, and then meet as a group to compare them. To conclude this inquiry into sources, in a brief, two- to three-page essay discuss the questions and answers that stimulated your thinking the most.

ADRIAN BERRY

Have We Got Company?

Futurists speculate endlessly about "wild cards," more or less improbable events that nevertheless could happen and that would alter human life drastically. Among these the most intriguing is contact with extraterrestrial intelligence. Adrian Berry, a renowned British journalist who specializes in topics of scientific interest, explores this possibility in our final selection, a chapter from his book The Next 500 Years: Life in the Coming Millennium *(1996).*

Far and few, far and few,
Are the lands where the Jumblies live;
Their heads are green, and their hands are blue;
And they went to sea in a sieve.

—EDWARD LEAR, "The Jumblies"

So deep is the conviction that there must be life out there beyond the dark, one thinks that if they are more advanced than ourselves they may come across space at any moment, perhaps in our generation. Later, contemplating the infinity of time, one wonders if perchance their messages came long ago, hurtling into the swamp muck of the steaming coal forests, the bright projectile clambered over by hissing reptiles, and the delicate instruments running mindlessly down with no report.

—LOREN EISELEY, *The Immense Journey*

WITHIN 500 years, and probably in much less time, we shall know for certain whether ours is the only advanced technological society in our Milky Way galaxy. 1

It is probably also safe to assert that the discovery of an alien civilisation will have a more profound impact on the way we think and behave than any other possible single scientific discovery.

The reason for this is plain. It is not merely a matter of the effects it would have on our religions, or on our self-esteem—and these would be considerable—it is political, military and commercial.[1] It is a question of "spheres of interest." A rival civilisation would look upon the galaxy or on parts of it, in exactly the same way as our descendants will, property to be seized and then held by right of conquest. Throughout our history, this has been the ultimate way to establish claims of property over virgin or disputed lands. Force is the final arbiter.

Unfortunately, if another civilisation is discovered, the chances are overwhelming that its technology will be superior to ours. If they were inferior to us in power, we would have no way of detecting their presence since they would not yet have invented radio. And as for their being our approximate equals, the probability of that is infinitesimally low. In the ten billion years since the galaxy was formed, it seems almost inconceivable that two civilisations could arise with histories exactly parallel in time, with both discovering radio, electronics and rocketry in the same century. That only leaves the possibility that they will be thousands, or even millions, of years in advance of us.

What would they be like? They could not be human—that is far too improbable—but would they be human-*like?* Would their bodies be based, like ours, on oxygen and carbon, or on some totally unknown arrangement of elements? Having multi-fingered hands, two eyes, two ears, a mouth and a nose seems to us very efficient, but can better organs be adapted, and in better ways? We have no means of knowing the answers to these questions; we can only guess at them and that very unproductively. We are still as ignorant as the Dutch astronomer Christian Huygens who wrote in the seventeenth century:

> Were we to meet with a Creature of a much different shape from Man, with Reason and Speech, we should be much surprised and shocked at the Sight. For if we try to imagine or paint a Creature like a Man in every Thing else, but that has a Neck four times as long, and great round Eyes five or six times as big, we cannot look upon't without the utmost Aversion, altho' at the same time we can give no account of our Dislike. For 'tis a very ridiculous Opinion, that the common People have got, that 'tis impossible a rational Soul should dwell in another Shape than ours. This can proceed from nothing but the Weakness, Ignorance, and Prejudice of Men.[2]

Whatever they looked like, because of their technical superiority we would be as helpless in the face of their machinations as people of the Stone Age would be in the face of ours. In the words of Arthur C. Clarke's Third Law: "A sufficiently advanced technology is indistinguishable from magic." And despite this superiority, there is no guarantee whatsoever that they would be benevolent. As H. G. Wells once remarked, if they proclaim that their sole wish is to "serve" mankind, we should ask ourselves most seriously whether that means that they wish to serve us fried or baked.

So what are the chances that we are alone in the galaxy, or that we "have company"? One of the famous rhetorical questions in science is that asked by the Italian physicist Enrico Fermi in 1943: "Where are they?" There is still no answer to this so-called Fermi Paradox. Yet this is a galaxy of some 250 *billion* suns. It occupies a region of space so vast that a beam of light travelling a billion kilometres every hour will take 100,000 years to traverse it. Why, therefore, in all this immensity, do we observe no intelligent radio signals, no artificial rearranging of stars, that would indicate advanced life or super-advanced technology?

Let us consider the matter statistically, and as conservatively as possible. Of those 250,000 million stars, suppose that 50 billion are sufficiently like the Sun in stability and age to have Earth-sized, habitable worlds. Imagine that one billion actually *have* such planets. Suppose that 500 million of these possess life in the form of primitive plants and animals. On a minority of these, say 100 million, imagine that animals have evolved to the extent of being able to manipulate tools. Is it not a reasonable supposition that on a hundredth of these, the worlds of a million suns, there have evolved advanced civilisations capable of radio communication and space travel?[3] In some quarters, this is a widely held opinion. It was even more so in the nineteenth century when, with the encouragement of scientists, every educated person assumed that the universe (separate and widely dispersed galaxies were not yet known) teemed with advanced life.* Religion also influenced the argument. If there were so many millions of stars that *didn't* harbour life, then why would God have troubled to create them? As one historian reports:

> Remarkable above all is the extent to which this idea was discussed. From Capetown to Copenhagen, from Dorpat to Dundee, from Saint Petersburg to Salt Lake City, terrestrials talked of extraterrestrials. Their conclusions appeared in books and pamphlets, in penny newspapers and ponderous journals, in sermons and scriptural commentaries, in poems and plays, and even in a hymn and on a tombstone. Oxford dons and observatory directors, sea captains and heads of state, radical reformers and ultra-montane conservatives, the orthodox as well as the heterodox—all had their say.[4]

But the people of the nineteenth century had not invented radio, and their beliefs could be no more than speculations. Today, having developed the appropriate technology, we have begun the search for these alleged beings in earnest. In 1993, NASA began its $10-million-a-year project SETI ("The Search for Extraterrestrial Intelligence"), in which radio telescopes focused on nearby stars and examined millions of frequencies. As a publicly funded project, it lasted only a year. It could not survive politics and ignorance. Members of Congress could not understand the project. One of them, according to its chief supporter, the astronomer Professor Frank Drake, declared:

> Of course there are flying saucers and advanced civilisations in outer space. But we don't need to spend millions to find these rascally creatures. We need only 75 cents to buy a tabloid at the local supermarket. Conclusive evidence of these crafty critters can be found at checkout counters from coast to coast.[5]

As I have related elsewhere, the project was privatised, and is now called Project Phoenix, with radio searches continuing in both hemispheres, north and south, in California and Australia, so that the entire sky can be surveyed.

*In 1835, the American journalist Richard Adams Locke increased the circulation of the *New York Sun* by more than 30,000 copies with his fictitious claim that a civilisation of winged beings had been found on the Moon. He supported this hoax by "quoting" the astronomer Sir John Herschel who was at the time working in South Africa and whom sceptics could not easily contact. A more recent example of the widespread popular belief in alien life was the panic reaction to Orson Welles's 1938 radio broadcast of H. G. Wells's *The War of the Worlds*. Thousands of Americans fled their homes, imagining the events Welles was recounting to be real.

No early success is expected, and proponents hope that the project can be continued for at least a century, moving—as suggested earlier—to the far side of the Moon when that becomes feasible.

So what is the answer to Fermi's Paradox? What are the prospects that Project Phoenix or its successors will find one or more alien civilisations? This is not only a question of profound importance for our descendants in the next five centuries; it is also perhaps the single most interesting question in astronomy. Surprisingly, astronomers are diametrically divided about the answer to it. One side in this dispute has been best represented by Carl Sagan and Iosif Shklovskii who, in their *Intelligent Life in the Universe,* argue from the statistics quoted above that the minimum number of civilisations, in this galaxy alone, must lie between 50,000 and a million.[6] At the other extreme are Michael Hart, Frank Tipler and others, who maintain that this number is zero, and that it is a waste of time and money even to look for these "little green men." If these aliens existed, says this school of thought, they should long ago have arrived on Earth. And if they had come, and departed, they would surely have left unmistakable signs of their presence. But they plainly have not been here. Hart, in a paper entitled "An Explanation for the Absence of Extraterrestrials on Earth," declares that the reason that they have not come is that they do not exist.[7]

The idea of them "coming here" might seem strange in view of . . . the technical difficulties of star travel. . . . [A] ship that managed to travel to the nearest star—just over four light years away—in a voyage time (as experienced by the astronauts) of two years would be doing very well. But the diameter of the galaxy is 100,000 light years, not two. Would it not take billions of years for an alien civilisation to explore the entire galaxy?

The answer to this question is no, for their ships would be able to 10
reproduce themselves. A single ship could be replaced by millions of identical ones which would set out to explore in different directions, enabling a huge area to be colonised in a comparatively short time.

This has happened at least once in the history of the Earth. The vast expanses of the Pacific and Indian Oceans contain tens of thousands of habitable islands. They fill an area, stretching from east to west from Africa to South America, and from north to south from Hawaii to New Zealand, of some 170 million square kilometres, one third of the surface of the globe. Yet primitive peoples using only catamaran canoes managed to settle this entire area within a mere 2,500 years.[8] These boats, able to do twelve knots in a favourable wind, and carrying up to fifty passengers and domestic animals, would settle a single island. Then, using local materials, the mariners would build new boats and on each of them set out for many more islands. On arrival at each of these new islands, fresh boats would eventually set out, and so forth, until every available niche in the two vast oceans had been settled by humanity.

Aliens—or ourselves—would be able to reproduce their craft in exactly the same way. We have known since 1948 of the possibility of building "von Neumann machines," computers that could (although this has not yet been done) produce identical copies of themselves. The computer pioneer John von Neumann wrote in that year his paper "The General and Logical Theory of Automata," which showed how such machines could be constructed.[9] This work was considered at the time to be little more than an academic curiosity, but the great surprise came in 1953 when Francis Crick and James D. Watson cracked the genetic code and discovered the secret of organic reproduction. It turned out to be essentially the same as the sequence for *machine* reproduction as proposed five years earlier by von Neumann![10] If terrestrials can discover a science, so can any other intelligence. If aliens wish to occupy every habitable planet in the galaxy, they can easily do so if they allow themselves a million years or so in which to do it.

But there are no signs of aliens *anywhere,* let alone on Earth. Hart's conclusion accords with what we observe. Everywhere we look, even in those regions where the stars appear to be so crowded as to form a milk-like mass, whatever spectrum we use, whether radio, optical, infrared, ultraviolet or gamma ray, we find nothing but natural "noise," the everlasting and meaningless chaos emitted by ordinary astrophysical events. Even in the "globular clusters" surrounding our galaxy that contain some stars sixteen billion years old, 60 per cent older than the oldest galactic stars, there is not even a rumour of life. The Sun is only five billion years old. If suns three times as old cannot produce advanced civilisation, is there a chance of finding it anywhere? Moreover, we have not even found so much as a single alien bacterium. Neither the *Viking* spacecraft that landed on Mars in 1976 with instruments specifically designed to find life, nor studies of meteorites, have found even the lowliest alien life forms. In short, although all statistical probability seems to point in the opposite direction, there is as yet no evidence whatever—apart from the microbes that man and his instruments take with them when they explore other planets—*of life, in any form, existing beyond the Earth.*

And of advanced creatures? There is of course the possibility that they do not visit us because they do not choose to. This is known as the "Contemplation Hypothesis," namely that most advanced civilisations have no interest in space exploration and are primarily concerned with spiritual contemplation. Hart has this to say of it:

> It might be a perfectly adequate explanation of why, in the year 600,000 BC, the inhabitants of Vega III chose not to visit the Earth. However, as we know, civilisations and cultures change. The Vegans of 599,000 BC could well be less interested in spiritual matters and more interested in space travel. A similar possibility could exist in 598,000 BC, and so forth.
>
> Even if we assume that the Vegans' social and political structure is so rigid that no changes even occur over hundreds of thousands of years, or that their basic psychological makeup is such that they always remain uninterested in space travel, there is still a problem. The Contemplation Hypothesis might explain why the *Vegans* have never vis-

> ited the Earth, but it still would not explain why the civilisations which developed on Procyon VI, Sirius II, and Altair IV have also failed to come here. The Hypothesis is not sufficient to explain the absence of extraterrestrials on Earth unless we assume that it will hold for *every* such race—regardless of its biological, psychological, social or political structure—and at *every* stage in their history after they achieve the ability to engage in space travel. That assumption is not plausible, and so the Hypothesis must be rejected.[11]

With the same logic, we can also refute the "Self-Destruction Hypothesis," that alien civilisations no longer exist because they have blown themselves up in nuclear wars, been destroyed by epidemics of plague or suffered extinction through catastrophic climate changes on their home planets. Some of them may indeed have suffered such fates. But of the tens of thousands, or hundreds of thousands, of civilisations postulated by Sagan and Shklovskii, is it likely that they have *all* done so? After all, the only civilisation that is known to exist—ours—has most emphatically not done so; nor does it seem likely that any of these fates await us.

A scientific theory, if it is to win respect, must be based on evidence. *15*
And that means evidence of what *has* happened rather than what might. Speculation has no more validity in science than it does in a criminal court. The only evidence we have of the behaviour of technological races is from our own. While a large number of people on Earth are no doubt devoted to spiritual and other kinds of contemplation, a sufficiently large minority is interested in exploration. We have explored every part of the globe and every part of the universe that it has so far been possible to explore. From the tourists who visit the Antarctic to the astronomers who peer at the remotest galaxies, we exhibit evidence of being passionately fond of investigating unknown places, visiting them personally whenever we get the chance. It is reasonable to predict that a large number of extraterrestrial civilisations—if they existed—would show the same traits. As Michael Hart points out, this fact is *not* proof that they must *all* behave as we do. But it *does* caution us against giving credence to any prediction that most extraterrestrials will behave in the *reverse* way.[12] It is inconceivable that any such obvious abode of possible life as the Sun could have been accidentally overlooked by roving aliens or their robots. The conclusion therefore seems irrefutable that there are no such rovers.

Are or *were?* It is just possible that the searchers for alien intelligence are looking in the wrong dimension. They ought ideally—although they cannot—to be exploring time instead of space. As Arthur C. Clarke and Gentry Lee suggest in their 1993 novel *Rama Revealed,* there may have been hundreds of millions of alien civilisations in the remote past, and there will be many more in the distant future. But we find no traces of them today because none last more than a few million years. After that, for some reason or another, they become extinct. Loren Eiseley suggested the same in the quotation I gave at the beginning of this chapter.

Superficially, the idea seems attractive. The galaxy has been a stable aggregation of stars for about ten billion years. If an advanced star-faring civilisation lasts, say, for two million years, that is a mere 0.02 percent of the galaxy's history, a flash in the immensities of time that vanishes and leaves no trace.

But this notion accords too much with the Self-Destruction Hypothesis to be plausible. They could not *all* become extinct within a few million years. Some, perhaps the majority, would have survived. And yet we see no sign of them. The Hypothesis defies the probabilities of time as well as space. No advanced alien races in this galaxy survived any threats of extinction for the simple reason that none of them existed in the first place.*

For when a planet has life upon it, how likely is intelligence to evolve from it? Biologists think the probabilities are vanishingly small. They point to the extraordinarily long time it took to appear on Earth, and the unlikely accidents that made it happen.[13] After the planet was formed 4.6 billion years ago, no life appeared on it for nearly a billion years. And when it did, it was single-celled life, like amoebas and algae. Nothing interesting happened for *another three billion years.* Then came the great Cambrian "explosion" of 500 million years ago, when sophisticated animals bred everywhere. Within a few hundred million years the oceans were full of fish and the land of giant reptiles. This situation might have continued indefinitely had not a giant comet or asteroid struck the planet 65 million years ago, killing most of the dinosaurs. If that had not happened, there would have been no apes and no people. (There seems to have been no chance that the dinosaurs themselves would have developed intelligence or civilisation. Throughout the 150 million years of their dominance they showed no signs of doing so—despite the cunning showed by the velociraptors in *Jurassic Park.*) And so, according to the viewpoint of the biologists, the coming of intelligence on Earth may be a unique event, unlikely to be repeated elsewhere in the universe, let alone the galaxy.

Perhaps this argument is too extreme. It may be that in the vast profusion 20
of stars that exists anything that can happen will happen. Round and round the argument goes. The truth—whatever it turns out to be—will affect our future profoundly; but frustratingly, we do not yet know what that truth is.

There is one final possibility that there exists one or more alien civilisation . . . that has learned to exploit a significant amount of the resources of its parent galaxy. If it had done so, the signs might even be visible. These beings, deploying unimaginable technological resources, might have even rearranged the positions of some of the stars to suit their purposes. Are there, perhaps, suspicious arrangements of stars? Clusters that appear to form equal-sided triangles, perfect squares or long straight lines? One can easily find such geometric shapes by poring over charts of the night sky. Perhaps they should be investigated.

*Moreover, one can see no reason why they *should* become extinct. Once a civilisation has spread itself among the planets of many suns, it would surely be indestructible. No *local* disaster, like a nuclear war or asteroid impact, could ever threaten the entirety of it. One day on Earth, this will be seen as a powerful argument for building starships.

But cold water was poured on this idea in one of the most elegant and cheapest experiments ever conducted, by a British Astronomer Royal, Professor Sir Martin Rees. I suggested the theory to him at lunch one day, and he responded by taking the salt cellar and scattering a few hundred grains over the table where we were sitting. "Notice that I dropped the salt at random," he said. "Look at the shapes some of them have formed." And there indeed among the salt grains were many unusual shapes, all the triangles, squares and lines one could want. In short, the components of a galaxy of 250 billion suns will assume many a bizarre outline, a phenomenon to which, without other evidence, no significance should be attached at all.

These conclusions could of course be wrong. Perhaps a few weeks after this book has gone to press, the managers of Project Phoenix will announce that they have found unmistakable artificial signals coming from a planet circling Proxima Centauri, the closest star to the Sun and the first southern star which, in early 1995, the Project decided to investigate. If such signals were confirmed, the sensational news would surely drive out the rubbish of day-to-day politics and cover the front pages of every newspaper in the world.

I have taken bets that this will not happen, despite being offered very poor odds. We don't have company. There will be no opposition when we occupy the worlds of neighbouring suns. Every planet that we find will remain ours by right of conquest.

NOTES

1. For a fascinating account of the effect that the discovery of an alien civilisation would have on our religious beliefs, see Davies, *Are We Alone? Implications of the Discovery of Extraterrestrial Life* (London: Penguin, 1994).
2. Christian Huygens, *New Conjectures Concerning the Planetary Worlds, Their Inhabitants and Productions,* published about 1670. Quoted by Carl Sagan and Iosif Shklovskii, *Intelligent Life in the Universe* (San Francisco: Holden-Day, 1966), 448.
3. This is my own simplified popularisation of the famous Drake equation, first presented by the astronomer Frank Drake at a conference on hypothetical alien civilisations in 1961. It ran: $N = R_* f_p n_e f_l f_i f_c L$. In this equation, N is the number of civilisations that now exist. R_* is the rate at which stars were being formed in the galaxy when our own solar system was being formed. f_p is the fraction of stars that have planets. n_e is the number of planets in each solar system with an environment suitable for life. f_l is the fraction of suitable planets on which life appears. f_i is the fraction of planets on which intelligence emerges. f_c is the fraction of intelligent societies that develop the desire and the ability to communicate with other worlds. And L is the amount of time that each such society lasts in its communicative state. (For a full discussion, see Sullivan, *We Are Not Alone* ch. 17).

   It will be seen at once that information revealed by this equation is extremely tenuous. For if *any* of the factors has a value of zero, then the number of civilisations is zero! But rather than being intended as a practical guide to finding alien civilisations, Drake meant the equation as a mathematical essay to show how little we know.

4. Michael Crowe, *The Extraterrestrial Life Debate, 1750–1900* (Cambridge: Cambridge UP, 1986). Quoted by Davies 6
5. I have been unable to identify this Congressman, but the speech appears typical of the mental attitude that brought about the cancellation of Government-funded SETI in 1993 as well as that of the Texas super-colliding atom-smashing machine in the same year. Both were major blows to science. Drake tells the story of the former in his *Is Anyone Out There?*
6. Sagan and Shklovskii ch. 29.
7. Michael H. Hart, "An Explanation for the Absence of Extraterrestrials on Earth," *Quarterly Journal of the Royal Astronomical Society* 16: 128–35. See also, in the same vein, Frank J. Tipler, "Extraterrestrial Intelligent Beings Do Not Exist," *Quarterly Journal of the Royal Astronomical Society* 21: 267–81.
8. See, for example, P. S. Bellwood, "The Peopling of the Pacific," *Scientific American,* Nov. 1980; William Howells, *The Pacific Islanders* (London: Weidenfeld, 1973); R. H. MacArthur and E. O. Wilson, *The Theory of Island Biogeography* (Princeton: Princeton UP, 1967). See also Chapters 13 and 14 of my 1983 book *The Super-Intelligent Machine.*
9. This work is reproduced in von Neumann, *Collected Works* (Oxford: Pergammon, 1963). 288–328.
10. This point was vividly made in Freeman J. Dyson's Vanuxem lecture delivered at Princeton University on 26 Feb. 1970.
11. Hart.
12. Hart.
13. Davies, ch. 4.

Questions for Discussion

1. Berry claims that within the next 500 years "we shall know for certain whether ours is the only advanced technological society in our Milky Way." Given other things he says about the size of the galaxy and the number of stars in it, is this a plausible claim?
2. According to Berry, why is it likely than any extraterrestrial civilization will be more advanced than ours? Do you find his reasoning compelling? Why or why not?
3. What is paradoxical about Fermi's Paradox? Do you consider Fermi's skepticism warranted? Why or why not?
4. How does Berry say that we, or any advanced technological society, will colonize other star systems? Does his analogy seem convincing? Is there any other way to explore space?
5. Berry discounts the possibility that advanced societies may have evolved elsewhere and ceased to exist before we had the technology to locate them.

What is his reasoning? If you had to counter this thesis, what would you say?

For Inquiry and Convincing

In a footnote omitted from our selection, Berry contends that we should "reject, in its entirety, the UFO 'industry.'" He claims it is "kept going by cranks." Is this evaluation justified, or can we view at least some of the UFO reports as worthy of analysis and thought and some of the reporters as credible?

Write an essay addressed to skeptics like Berry that makes the best case you can for not discounting the possibility of UFOs.

For Persuasion

Berry claims confidently that any civilization will view other worlds as "property to be seized and then held by right of conquest." Yet we see this motive in decline in our own civilization since World War II, and so far our visits to the moon have not resulted in "claiming" it as the European explorers claimed territory in the New World. Write an essay arguing against the universality and permanence of the colonial motives, including the use of force to arbitrate claims.

Additional Suggestions for Writing

1. *Persuasion.* Is futurism, prophecy, and trend projection worth the time and effort? Write an essay attacking or defending this obsession in our society. Address it to your college-educated peers, who will be about forty years old in 2020.
2. *Convincing.* As we said in the introduction to this chapter, everything that currently exists has some kind of future. Choose any topic, activity, or event that interests you and that you know at least partly through experience. Make a case for the future you think it will have over the next twenty years. Address it to a readership that has some stake in its future and concrete, personal experience with it.

APPENDIX A

Editing and Proofreading

Editing and proofreading are the final steps in creating a finished piece of writing. Too often, however, these steps are rushed, as writers race to meet a deadline. Ideally, you should distinguish between the acts of revising, editing, and proofreading. Because each step requires that you pay attention to something different, you cannot reasonably expect to do them well if you try to do them all at once.

Our suggestions for revising appear in each of Chapters 4–7 on the aims of argument. Revising means shaping and developing the whole argument, with an eye to audience and purpose; when you revise, you are ensuring that you have accomplished your aim. Editing, on the other hand, means making smaller changes within paragraphs and sentences. When you edit, you are thinking about whether your prose will be a pleasure to read. Editing improves the sound and rhythm of your voice. It makes complicated ideas more accessible to readers and usually makes your writing more concise. Finally, proofreading means eliminating errors. When you proofread, you correct everything you find that will annoy readers, such as misspellings, punctuation mistakes, and faulty grammar.

In this appendix we offer some basic advice on what to look for when editing and proofreading. For more detailed help consult a handbook on grammar and punctuation and a good book on style, such as Joseph Williams's *Ten Lessons in Clarity and Grace* or Richard Lanham's *Revising Prose.* Both of these texts guided our thinking in the advice that follows.

EDITING

Most ideas can be phrased in a number of ways, each of which gives the idea a slightly distinctive twist. Consider the following examples:

In New York City about 74,000 people die each year.

In New York City death comes to one in a hundred people each year.

Death comes to one in a hundred New Yorkers each year.

To begin an article on what becomes of the unknown and unclaimed dead in New York, Edward Conlon wrote the final of these three sentences. We can only speculate about the possible variations he considered, but because openings are so crucial, he almost certainly cast these words quite deliberately.

For most writers such deliberation over matters of style occurs during editing. In this late stage of the writing process, writers examine choices made earlier, perhaps unconsciously, while drafting and revising. They listen to how sentences sound, to patterns of rhythm both within and among sentences. Editing is like an art or craft; it can provide you the satisfaction of knowing you've said something gracefully and effectively. To focus on language this closely, you will need to set aside enough time following the revision step.

In this section we discuss some things to look for when editing your own writing. Don't forget, though, that editing does not always mean looking for weaknesses. You should also recognize passages that work well just as you wrote them, that you can leave alone or play up more by editing passages that surround them.

Editing for Clarity and Conciseness

Even drafts revised several times may have wordy and awkward passages; these are often places where a writer struggled with uncertainty or felt less than confident about the point being made. Introductions often contain such passages. In editing you have the opportunity to take one more stab at clarifying and sharpening your ideas.

Express Main Ideas Forcefully

Emphasize the main idea of a sentence by stating it as directly as possible, using the two key sentence parts (*subject* and *verb*) to convey the two key parts of the idea (*agent* and *act*).

As you edit, first look for sentences that state ideas indirectly rather than directly; such sentences may include (1) overuse of the verb *to be* in its various forms (*is, was, will have been,* and so forth), (2) the opening words "There is . . ." or "It is . . . ," (3) strings of prepositional phrases, or (4) many vague nouns. Then ask, "What is my true subject here, and what is that subject's action?" Here is an example of a weak, indirect sentence:

> It is a fact that the effects of pollution are more evident in lower-class neighborhoods than in middle-class ones.

The writer's subject is pollution. What is the pollution's action? Limply, the sentence tells us its "effects" are "evident." The following edited version makes pollution the agent that performs the action of a livelier verb, "fouls." The edited sentence is more specific—without being longer.

> *Pollution* more frequently *fouls* the air, soil, and water of lower-class neighborhoods than of middle-class ones.

Editing Practice

The following passage, about a plan for creating low-income housing, contains two weak sentences. In this case the weakness results from wordiness. (Note the overuse of vague nouns and prepositional phrases.) Decide for each sentence what the true subject is, and make that word the subject of the verb. Your edited version should be much shorter.

> As in every program, there will be the presence of a few who abuse the system. However, as in other social programs, the numbers would not be sufficient to justify the rejection of the program on the basis that one person in a thousand will try to cheat.

Choose Carefully between Active and Passive Voice

Active voice and passive voice indicate different relationships between subjects and verbs. As we have noted, ideas are usually clearest when the writer's true subject is also the subject of the verb in the sentence—that is, when it is the agent of the action. In the passive voice, however, the agent of the action appears in the predicate or not at all. Rather than acting as agent, the subject of the sentence *receives* the action of the verb.

The following sentence is in the passive voice:

> The air of poor neighborhoods is often fouled by pollution.

There is nothing incorrect about the use of the passive voice in this sentence, and in the context of a whole paragraph, passive voice can be the most emphatic way to make a point. (Here, for example, it allows the word "pollution" to fall at the end of the sentence, a strong position.) But, often, use of the passive voice is not a deliberate choice at all but rather a vague and unspecific way of stating a point.

Consider the following sentences, in which the main verbs have no agents:

> It *is believed* that dumping garbage at sea is not as harmful to the environment as *was* once *thought.*
>
> Ronald Reagan *was considered* the "Great Communicator."

Who thinks such dumping is not so harmful? environmental scientists? industrial producers? Who considered Reagan a great communicator? speech professors? news commentators? Such sentences are clearer when they are written in the active voice:

> Some environmentalists believe that dumping garbage at sea is not as harmful to the environment as they used to think.
>
> Media commentators considered Ronald Reagan the "Great Communicator."

In editing for the passive voice, look over your verbs. Passive voice is easily recognized because it always contains (1) some form of *to be* as a helping verb and (2) the main verb in its past participle form (which ends in *-ed, -d, -t, -en,* or *-n,* or may in some cases be irregular: *drunk, sung, lain,* and so on).

When you find a sentence phrased in the passive voice, decide who or what is performing the action; the agent may appear after the verb, or not at all. Then decide if changing the sentence to the active voice will improve the sentence as well as the surrounding passage.

Editing Practice

1. The following paragraph from a student's argument needs editing for emphasis. It is choking with excess nouns and forms of the verb *to be,* some as part of passive constructions. You need not eliminate all passive voice, but do look for wording that is vague and ineffective. Your edited version should be not only stronger but shorter.

   > Although emergency shelters are needed in some cases (for example, a mother fleeing domestic violence), they are an inefficient means of dealing with the massive numbers of people they are bombarded with each day. The members of a homeless family are in need of a home, not a temporary shelter into which they and others like them are herded, only to be shuffled out when their thirty-day stay is over to make room for the next incoming herd. Emergency shelters would be sufficient if we did not have a low-income housing shortage, but what is needed most at present is an increase in availability of affordable housing for the poor.

2. Select a paragraph of your own writing to edit; focus on using strong verbs and subjects to carry the main idea of your sentences.

Editing for Emphasis

When you edit for emphasis, you make sure that your main ideas stand out so that your reader will take notice. Following are some suggestions to help.

Emphasize Main Ideas by Subordinating Less Important Ones

Subordination refers to distinctions in rank or order of importance. Think of the chain of command at an office: the boss is at the top of the ladder, the middle management is on a lower (subordinate) rung, the support staff is at an even lower rung, and so on.

In writing, subordination means placing less important ideas in less important positions in sentences in order to emphasize the main ideas that should stand out. Writing that lacks subordination treats all ideas equally; each idea may consist of a sentence of its own or be joined to another idea by a coordinator (*and, but,* and *or*). Such a passage follows, with its sentences numbered for reference purposes.

> (1) It has been over a century since slavery was abolished, and a few decades since lawful, systematic segregation came to an unwilling halt. (2) Truly, blacks have come a long way from the darker days that lasted for more than three centuries. (3) Many blacks have entered the mainstream, and there is a proportionately large contingent of middle-class blacks. (4) Yet an even greater percentage of blacks are immersed in truly pathetic conditions. (5) The inner-city black poor are enmeshed in devastating socioeconomic problems. (6) Unemployment among inner-city black youths has become much worse than it was even five years ago.

Three main ideas are important here—that blacks have been free for some time, that some have made economic progress, and that others are trapped in poverty—and of these three, the last is probably intended to be the most important. Yet, as we read the passage, these key ideas do not stand out. In fact, each point receives equal emphasis and sounds about the same, with the repeated subject-verb-object syntax. The result seems monotonous, even apathetic, though the writer is probably truly disturbed about the subject. The following edited version that subordinates some of the points is more emphatic. We have italicized the main points.

> *Blacks have come a long way* in the century since slavery was abolished and in the decades since lawful, systematic segregation came to an unwilling halt. Yet, while many blacks have entered the mainstream and the middle class, *an even greater percentage are immersed in truly pathetic conditions.* To give just one example of these devastating socioeconomic problems, *unemployment among inner-city black youths is much worse now than it was even five years ago.*

While different editing choices are possible, this version plays down sentences 1, 3, and 5 in the original, so that sentences 2, 4, and 6 stand out.

As you edit, look for passages that sound wordy and flat because all the ideas are expressed with equal weight in the same subject-verb-object pattern. Then single out your most important points, and try out some options for subordinating the less important ones. The key is to put main ideas in main clauses, and modifying ideas in modifying clauses or phrases.

Modifying Clauses Like simple sentences, modifying clauses contain a subject and verb. They are formed in two ways: (1) with relative pronouns and (2) with subordinating conjunctions.

Relative pronouns introduce clauses that modify nouns, with the relative pronoun relating the clause to the noun it modifies. There are five relative pronouns: *that, which, who, whose,* and *whom.* The following sentence contains a relative clause:

> Alcohol advertisers are trying to sell a product *that is by its very nature harmful to users.*
>
> —JASON RATH (student)

Relative pronouns may also be implied:

> I have returned the library book [that] *you loaned me.*

Relative pronouns may also be preceded by prepositions, such as *on, in, to,* or *during:*

> Drug hysteria has created an atmosphere *in which civil rights are disregarded.*

Subordinating conjunctions show relationships among ideas. It is impossible to provide a complete list of subordinating conjunctions in this short space, but here are the most common and the kinds of modifying roles they perform:

> To show time: *after, as, before, since, until, when, while*
> To show place: *where, wherever*
> To show contrast: *although, though, whereas, while*
> To show cause and effect: *because, since, so that*
> To show condition: *if, unless, whether, provided that*
> To show manner: *how, as though*

By introducing it with a subordinating conjunction, you can convert one sentence into a dependent clause that can modify another sentence. Consider the following two versions of the same idea:

> Pain is a state of consciousness, a "mental event." It can never be directly observed.
>
> *Since pain is a state of consciousness, a "mental event,"* it can never be directly observed.
>
> —PETER SINGER, "Animal Liberation"

Modifying Phrases Unlike clauses, phrases do not have a subject and a verb. Prepositional phrases and infinitive phrases are most likely already in your repertoire of modifiers. (Consult a handbook if you need to review these.) Here, we remind you of two other useful types of phrases: (1) participial phrases and (2) appositives.

Participial phrases modify nouns. Participles are created from verbs, so it is not surprising that the two varieties represent two verb tenses. The first is present participles ending in *-ing:*

> *Hoping to eliminate harassment on campus,* many universities have tried to institute codes for speech and behavior.
>
> The desperate Haitians fled here in boats, *risking all.*
>
> —CARMEN HAZAN-COHEN (student)

The second is past participles ending in *-ed, -en, -d, -t,* or *-n:*

> Women themselves became a resource, *acquired by men much as the land was acquired by men.*
>
> —GERDA LERNER

> *Linked more to the Third World and Asia than to the Europe of America's racial and cultural roots,* Los Angeles and Southern California will enter the 21st century as a multi-racial and multicultural society.
>
> —RYSZARD KAPUSCINSKI

Notice that modifying phrases should immediately precede the nouns they modify.

An *appositive* is a noun or noun phrase that restates another noun, usually in a more specific way. Appositives can be highly emphatic, but more often they are tucked into the middle of a sentence or added to the end, allowing a subordinate idea to be slipped in. When used like this, appositives are usually set off with commas:

> Rick Halperin, *a professor at Southern Methodist University,* noted that Ted Bundy's execution cost Florida taxpayers over six million dollars.
>
> —DIANE MILLER (student)

Editing Practice

1. Edit the following passage as needed for emphasis, clarity, and conciseness, using subordinate clauses, relative clauses, participial phrases, appositives, and any other options that occur to you. If some parts are effective as they are, leave them alone.

> The monetary implications of drug legalization are not the only reason it is worth consideration. There is reason to believe that the United States would be a safer place to live if drugs were legalized. A large amount of what the media has named "drug-related" violence is really prohibition-related violence. Included in this are random shootings and murders associated with black-market transactions. Estimates indicate that at least 40 percent of all property crime in the United States is committed by drug users so they can maintain their habits. That amounts to a total of 4 million crimes per year and $7.5 billion in stolen property. Legalizing drugs would be a step toward reducing this wave of crime.

2. Edit a paragraph of your own writing with an eye to subordinating less important ideas through the use of modifying phrases and clauses.

Vary Sentence Length and Pattern

Even when read silently, your writing has a sound. If your sentences are all about the same length (typically fifteen to twenty words) and all structured according to a subject-verb-object pattern, they will roll along with the monotonic rhythm of an assembly line. Obviously, one solution to this problem is to open some of your sentences with modifying phrases and clauses, as we discussed in the previous section. Here, we offer some other strategies, all of which add emphasis by introducing something unexpected.

1. Use a short sentence after several long ones.

> [A] population's general mortality is affected by a great many factors over which doctors and hospitals have little influence. For those diseases and injuries for which modern medicine can affect the outcome, however, which country the patient lives in really matters. Life expectancy is not the same among developed countries for premature babies, for children born with spina bifida, or for people who have cancer, a brain tumor, heart disease, or chronic renal failure. *Their chances of survival are best in the United States.*
>
> —JOHN GOODMAN

2. Interrupt a sentence.

> The position of women in that hippie counterculture was, *as a young black male leader preached succinctly,* "prone."
>
> —BETTY FRIEDAN

> Symbols and myths—*when emerging uncorrupted from human experience*—are precious. Then it is the poetic voice and vision that informs and infuses—*the poet-warrior's, the prophet-seer's, the dreamer's*—reassuring us that truth is as real as falsehood. And ultimately stronger.
>
> —OSSIE DAVIS

3. Use an intentional sentence fragment. The concluding fragment in the previous passage by Ossie Davis is a good example.
4. Invert the order of subject-verb-object.

> Further complicating negotiations is the difficulty of obtaining relevant financial statements.
>
> —REGINA HERZLINGER

> This creature, with scarcely two thirds of man's cranial capacity, was a fire user. Of what it meant to him beyond warmth and shelter, we know nothing; with what rites, ghastly or benighted, it was struck or maintained, no word remains.
>
> —LOREN EISELY

Use Special Effects for Emphasis

Especially in persuasive argumentation, you will want to make some of your points in deliberately dramatic ways. Remember that just as the crescendos stand out in music because the surrounding passages are less intense, so the special effects work best in rhetoric when you use them sparingly.

Repetition Deliberately repeating words, phrases, or sentence patterns has the effect of building up to a climactic point. In Chapter 6 we noted how Martin Luther King, Jr., in the emotional high point of his "Letter from Birmingham Jail," used repeated subordinate clauses beginning with the phrase "when you" to build up to his main point: ". . . then you will understand why we find it difficult to wait" (paragraph 14, page 116). Here is another example, from the conclusion of an argument linking women's rights with environmental reforms:

> Environmental justice goes much further than environmental protection, a passive and paternalistic phrase. *Justice requires that* industrial nations pay back the environmental debt incurred in building their wealth by using less of nature's resources. *Justice prescribes that* governments stop siting hazardous waste facilities in cash-poor rural and urban neighborhoods and now in the developing world. *Justice insists that* the subordination of women and nature by men is not only a hazard; it is a crime. *Justice reminds us that* the Earth does not belong to us; even when we "own" a piece of it, we belong to the Earth.
>
> —H. PATRICIA HYNES

Paired Coordinators Coordinators are conjunctions that pair words, word groups, and sentences in a way that gives them equal emphasis and that also shows a relationship between them, such as contrast, consequence, or addition. In grade school you may have learned the coordinators through the mnemonic *FANBOYS,* standing for *for, and, nor, but, or, yet, so.*

Paired coordinators emphasize the relationship between coordinated elements; the first coordinator signals that a corresponding coordinator will follow. Some paired coordinators are:

both ______________ and ______________
not ______________ but ______________
not only ______________ but also ______________
either ______________ or ______________
neither ______________ nor ______________

The key to effective paired coordination is to keep the words that follow the marker words as grammatically similar as possible. Pair nouns with nouns, verbs with verbs, prepositional phrases with prepositional phrases, and whole sentences with whole sentences. (Think of paired coordination as a variation on repetition.) Here are some examples:

> Feminist anger, or any form of social outrage, is dismissed breezily—*not* because it lacks substance *but* because it lacks "style."
>
> —SUSAN FALUDI

> Alcohol ads that emphasize "success" in the business and social worlds are useful examples *not only* of how advertisers appeal to people's envy *but also* of how ads perpetuate gender stereotypes.
>
> —JASON RATH (student)

Emphatic Appositives While an appositive (a noun or noun phrase that restates another noun) can subordinate an idea, it can also emphasize an idea if it is placed at the beginning or the end of a sentence, where it will command attention. Here are some examples:

> *The poorest nation in the Western hemisphere,* Haiti is populated by six million people, many of whom cannot obtain adequate food, water, or shelter.
>
> —SNEED B. COLLARD III

> [Feminists] made a simple, though serious, ideological error when they applied the same political rhetoric to their own situation as women versus men: *too literal an analogy with class warfare, racial oppression.*
>
> —BETTY FRIEDAN

Note that at the end of a sentence, an appositive may be set off with a colon or a dash.

Emphatic Word Order The opening and closing positions of a sentence are high-profile spots, not to be wasted on weak words. The following sentence, for example, begins weakly with the filler phrase "there are":

> *There are* several distinctions, all of them false, that are commonly made between rape and date rape.

A better version would read:

> My opponents make several distinctions between rape and date rape; all of these are false.

Even more important are the final words of every paragraph and the opening and closing of the entire argument.

Editing Practice

1. Select one or two paragraphs from a piece of published writing you have recently read and admired. Be ready to share it with the class, explaining how the writer has crafted the passage to make it work.
2. Take a paragraph or two from one of your previous essays, perhaps even an essay from another course, and edit it to improve clarity, conciseness, and emphasis.

Editing for Coherence

Coherence refers to what some people call the "flow" of writing; writing flows when the ideas connect smoothly, one to the next. In contrast, when writing is incoherent, the reader must work to see how ideas connect and infer points that the writer, for whatever reason, has left unstated.

Incoherence is a particular problem with writing that contains an abundance of direct or indirect quotations. In using sources, be careful always to lead into the quotation with some words of your own, showing clearly how this new idea connects with what has come before.

Because finding incoherent passages in your own writing can be difficult, ask a friend to read your draft to look for gaps in the presentation of ideas. Here are some additional suggestions for improving coherence.

Move from Old Information to New Information

Coherent writing is easy to follow because the connections between old information and new information are clear. Sentences refer back to previously introduced information and set up reader expectations for new information to come. Notice how every sentence fulfills your expectations in the following excerpts from an argument on animal rights by Steven Zak.

> The credibility of the animal-rights viewpoint . . . need not stand or fall with the "marginal human beings" argument.

Next, you would expect to hear why animals do not have to be classed as "marginal human beings"—and you do:

> Lives don't have to be qualitatively the same to be worthy of equal respect.

At this point you might ask upon what else we should base our respect. Zak answers this question in the next sentence:

> One's perception that another life has value comes as much from an appreciation of its uniqueness as from the recognition that it has characteristics that are shared by one's own life.

Not only do these sentences fulfill reader expectations, but each also makes a clear connection by referring specifically to the key idea in the sentence before it, forming an unbroken chain of thought. We have italicized the words that accomplish this linkage and connected them with arrows.

> The credibility of the animal rights viewpoint . . . need not stand or fall with the "*marginal human beings*" argument.
>
> Lives don't have to be *qualitatively the same* to be worthy of *equal respect.*
>
> One's perception that *another life has value* comes as much from an *appreciation of its uniqueness* as from the recognition that it has characteristics that are shared by one's own life.
>
> One can imagine that the lives of various kinds of animals *differ radically. . . .*

In the following paragraph, reader expectations are not so well fulfilled:

> We are presently witness to the greatest number of homeless families since the Great Depression of the 1930s. The cause of this phenomenon is a shortage of low-income housing. Mothers with children as young as two weeks are forced to live on the street because there is no room for them in homeless shelters.

While these sentences are all on the subject of homelessness, the second leads us to expect that the third will take up the topic of shortages of low-income housing. Instead, it takes us back to the subject of the first sentence and offers a different cause—no room in the shelters.

Looking for ways to link old information with new information will help you find problems of coherence in your own writing.

Editing Practice

1. In the following paragraph underline the words or phrases that make the connections back to the previous sentence and forward to the next, as we did earlier with the passage from Zak.

> The affluent, educated, liberated women of the First World, who can enjoy freedoms unavailable to any women ever before, do not feel as free as they want to. And they can no longer restrict to the subconscious their sense that this lack of freedom has something to do with—with apparently frivolous issues, things that really should not matter. Many are ashamed to admit that such trivial concerns—to do with physical appearance, bodies, faces, hair, clothes—matter so much. But in spite of shame, guilt, and denial, more and more women are wondering if it isn't that they are entirely neurotic alone but rather that something important is indeed at stake that has to do with the relationship between female liberation and female beauty.
>
> —NAOMI WOLF

2. The following student paragraph lacks coherence. Read through it, and put a slash (/) between sentences expressing unconnected ideas. You may try to rewrite the paragraph, rearranging sentences and adding ideas to make the connections tighter.

> Students may know what AIDS is and how it is transmitted, but most are not concerned about AIDS and do not perceive themselves to be at risk. But college-age heterosexuals are the number-one high-risk group for this disease (Gray and Sacarino 258). "Students already know about AIDS. Condom distribution, public or not, is not going to help. It just butts into my personal life," said one student surveyed. College is a time for exploration and that includes the discovery of sexual freedom. Students, away from home and free

to make their own decisions for maybe the first time in their lives, have a "bigger than life" attitude. The thought of dying is the farthest from their minds. Yet at this point in their lives, they are most in need of this information.

Use Transitions to Show Relationships between Ideas

Coherence has to be built into a piece of writing; as we discussed earlier, the ideas between sentences must first cohere. However, sometimes readers need help in making the transition from one idea to the next, so you must provide signposts to help them see the connections more readily. For example, a transitional word like *however* can prepare readers for an idea in contrast to the one before it, as in the second sentence in this paragraph. Transitional words can also highlight the structure of an argument ("These data will show three things: first . . . , second . . . , and third . . ."), almost forming a verbal path for the reader to follow. Following are examples of transitional words and phrases and their purposes:

To show order: *first, second, next, then, last, finally*
To show contrast: *however, yet, but, nevertheless*
To show cause and effect: *therefore, consequently, as a result, then*
To show importance: *moreover, significantly*
To show an added point: *as well, also, too*
To show an example: *for example, for instance*
To show concession: *admittedly*
To show conclusion: *in sum, in conclusion*

The key to using transitional words is similar to the key to using special effects for emphasis: Don't overdo it. To avoid choking your writing with these words, anticipate where your reader will genuinely need them, and limit their use to these instances.

Editing Practice

Underline the transitional words and phrases in the following passage of published writing:

> When people believe that their problems can be solved, they tend to get busy solving them.
>
> On the other hand, when people believe that their problems are beyond solution, they tend to position themselves so as to avoid blame. Take the woeful inadequacy of education in the predominantly black central cities. Does the black leadership see the ascendancy of black teachers, school administrators, and politicians as an asset to be

used in improving those dreadful schools? Rarely. You are more likely to hear charges of white abandonment, white resistance to integration, conspiracies to isolate black children, even when the schools are officially desegregated. In short, white people are accused of being responsible for the problem. But if the youngsters manage to survive those awful school systems and achieve success, leaders want to claim credit. They don't hesitate to attribute that success to the glorious Civil Rights movement.

—WILLIAM RASPBERRY

PROOFREADING

Proofreading is truly the final step in writing a paper. After proofreading you ought to be able to print your paper out one more time; but if you do not have time, most instructors will be perfectly happy to see the necessary corrections done neatly in ink on the final draft.

Following are some suggestions for proofreading.

Spelling Errors

If you have used a word processor, you may have a program that will check your spelling. If not, you will have to check your spelling by reading through again carefully, with a dictionary at hand. Consult the dictionary whenever you feel uncertain. You might consider devoting a special part of your writer's notebook to your habitual spelling errors: some students always misspell *athlete,* for example, while others leave the second *n* out of *environment.*

Omissions and Jumbled Passages

Read your paper out loud. Physically shaping your lips around the words can help locate missing words, typos (*saw* instead of *was*), or the remnants of some earlier version of a sentence that did not get fully deleted. Place a caret (∧) in the sentence, and write the correction or addition above the line, or draw a line through unnecessary text.

Punctuation Problems

Apostrophes and commas give writers the most trouble. If you have habitual problems with these, you should record your errors in your writer's notebook.

Apostrophes

Apostrophe problems usually occur in forming possessives, not contractions, so here we discuss only the former. If you have problems with possessives, you may also want to consult a good handbook or seek a private tutorial with your instructor or your school's writing center.

Here are the basic principles to remember.

1. Possessive pronouns—*his, hers, yours, theirs, its*—never take an apostrophe.
2. Singular nouns become possessive by adding *-'s.*

   A single parent's life is hard.

   A society's values change.

   Do you like Mr. Voss's new car?

3. Plural nouns ending in *-s* become possessive by simply adding an apostrophe.

   Her parents' marriage is faltering.

   Many cities' air is badly polluted.

   The Joneses' house is up for sale.

4. Plural nouns that do not end in *-s* become possessive by adding *-'s.*

   Show me the women's (men's) room.

   The people's voice was heard.

If you err by using apostrophes where they don't belong in nonpossessive words ending in *-s,* remember that a possessive will always have a noun after it, not some other part of speech such as a verb or a preposition. You may even need to read each line of print with a ruler under it to help you focus more intently on each word.

Commas

Because commas indicate a pause, reading your paper aloud is a good way to decide where to add or delete them. A good handbook will elaborate on the following basic principles. The example sentences have been adapted from an argument by Mary Meehan, who opposes abortion.

1. Use a comma when you join two or more main clauses with a coordinating conjunction.

   Main clause, conjunction (and, but, or, nor, so, yet) *main clause.*

   Feminists want to have men participate more in the care of children, but abortion allows a man to shift total responsibility to the woman.

2. Use a comma after an introductory phrase or dependent clause.

   Introductory phrase or clause, main clause.

   To save the smallest children, the Left should speak out against abortion.

3. Use commas around modifiers such as relative clauses and appositives, unless they are essential to the noun's meaning. Be sure to put the comma at both ends of the modifier.

   __________, *appositive,* __________

__________, *relative clause,* __________

One member of the 1972 Presidential commission on population growth was Graciela Olivarez, a Chicana who was active in civil rights and anti-poverty work. Olivarez, who later was named to head the Federal Government's Community Services Administration, had known poverty in her youth in the Southwest.

4. Use commas with a series.

__x__, __y__, and __z__

The traditional mark of the Left has been its protection of the underdog, the weak, and the poor.

Semicolons

Think of a semicolon as a strong comma. It has two main uses.

1. Use a semicolon to join two main clauses when you choose not to use a conjunction. This works well when the two main clauses are closely related or parallel in structure.

   Main clause; main clause.

   Pro-life activists did not want abortion to be a class issue; they wanted to end abortion everywhere, for all classes.

   As a variation, you may wish to add a transitional adverb to the second main clause. The adverb indicates the relationship between the main clauses, but it is not a conjunction, so a comma preceding it would not be correct.

   Main clause; transitional adverb (however, therefore, thus, moreover, consequently), *main clause.*

   When speaking with counselors at the abortion clinic, many women change their minds and decide against abortion; however, a woman who is accompanied by a husband or boyfriend often does not feel free to talk with the counselor.

2. Use semicolons between items in a series if any of the items themselves contain commas.

   ___,___; ___,___; ___,___

   A few liberals who have spoken out against abortion are Jesse Jackson, a Civil Rights leader; Richard Neuhaus, a theologian; the comedian Dick Gregory; and politicians Mark Hatfield and Mary Rose Oakar.

Colons

The colon has two common uses.

1. Use a colon to introduce a quotation when both your own lead-in and the words quoted are complete sentences that can stand alone. (See the section

in Chapter 9 entitled "Incorporating and Documenting Source Material in the Text of Your Argument" for more on introducing quotations.)

Main clause in your words: "Quoted sentence(s)."

Mary Meehan criticizes liberals who have been silent on abortion: "If much of the leadership of the pro-life movement is right-wing, that is due largely to the default of the Left."

2. Use a colon before an appositive that comes dramatically at the end of a sentence, especially if the appositive contains more than one item.

Main clause: appositive, appositive, and appositive.

Meehan argues that many pro-choice advocates see abortion as a way to hold down the population of certain minorities: blacks, Puerto Ricans, and other Latins.

Grammatical Errors

Grammatical mistakes can be hard to find, but once again we suggest reading aloud as one method of proofing for them; grammatical errors tend not to "sound right" even if they look like good prose. Another suggestion is to recognize your habitual errors and then look for particular grammatical structures that lead you into error.

Introductory Participial Phrases

Constructions such as these often lead writers to create dangling modifiers. To avoid this pitfall, see the discussion of participial phrases earlier in this appendix. Remember that an introductory phrase dangles if it is not immediately followed by the noun it modifies.

Incorrect: Using her conscience as a guide, our society has granted each woman the right to decide if a fetus is truly a "person" with rights equal to her own.

(Notice that the implied subject of the participial phrase is "each woman," when in fact the subject of the main clause is "our society"; thus, the participial phrase does not modify the subject.)

Corrected: Using her conscience as a guide, each woman in our society has the right to decide if a fetus is truly a "person" with rights equal to her own.

Paired Coordinators

If the words that follow each of the coordinators are not of the same grammatical structure, then an error known as nonparallelism occurs. To correct this error, line up the paired items one over the other. You will see that the correction often involves simply adding a word or two to, or deleting some words from, one side of the paired coordinators.

> not only __________ but also __________
>
> *Incorrect:* Legal abortion not only protects women's lives, but also their health.
>
> *Corrected:* Legal abortion protects not only women's lives but also their health.

Split Subjects and Verbs

If the subject of a sentence contains long modifying phrases or clauses, by the time you get to the verb you may make an error in agreement (using a plural verb, for example, when the subject is singular) or even in logic (for example, having a subject that is not capable of being the agent that performs the action of the verb). Following are some typical errors:

> The *goal* of the courses grouped under the rubric of "Encountering Non-Western Cultures" *are* . . .

Here, the writer forgot that *goal,* the subject, is singular.

> During 1992 *the Refugee Act of 1980,* with the help of President Bush and Congress, *accepted* 114,000 immigrants into our nation.

The writer here should have realized that the agent doing the accepting would have to be the Bush administration, not the Refugee Act. A better version would read:

> During 1992 the Bush administration accepted 114,000 immigrants into our nation under the terms of the Refugee Act of 1980.

Proofreading Practice

Proofread the following passage for errors of grammar and punctuation.

> The citizens of Zurich, Switzerland tired of problems associated with drug abuse, experimented with legalization. The plan was to open a central park, Platzspitz, where drugs and drug use would be permitted. Many European experts felt, that it was the illegal drug business rather than the actual use of drugs that had caused many of the cities problems. While the citizens had hoped to isolate the drug problem, foster rehabilitation, and curb the AIDS epidemic, the actual outcome of the Platzspitz experiment did not create the desired results. Instead, violence increased. Drug-related deaths doubled. And drug users were drawn from not only all over Switzerland, but from all over Europe as well. With thousands of discarded syringe packets lying around, one can only speculate as to whether the spread of AIDS was curbed.

The park itself was ruined and finally on February 10, 1992, it was barred up and closed. After studying the Swiss peoples' experience with Platzspitz, it is hard to believe that some advocates of drug legalization in the United States are urging us to participate in the same kind of experiment.

APPENDIX B

Keeping a Writer's Notebook

In the past you may have kept a journal, diary, lab notebook, or some other written record with daily or weekly entries. A writer's notebook resembles these in that it records experiences and activities; it differs from them, however, in that it primarily records preparations for writing something else, such as a major essay or a term paper for one of your courses. You may have turned in a lab notebook for a grade, for example, but a writer's notebook has no other function than to help you sort out what you learn, accomplish, and think as you go through the stages of creating a finished piece of writing. A writer's notebook contains the writing you do before you write; it is a place to sketch out ideas, assess research, order what you have to say, and determine strategies and goals for writing.

WHY KEEP A NOTEBOOK?

Short, simple, and routine kinds of writing—personal letters, notes to friends, memos, and the like—require little preparation. We simply sit down and write them. But much writing in college and in professional setings, demands weeks, months, or—in the case of a book—even years of work. Some projects require extensive research and consultation, which involve compiling and assessing large amounts of data and working one's way through complex chains of reasoning. Under such conditions even the best memory must fail without the aid of a notebook. Given life's distractions, we often forget too much and recall imprecisely what we do manage to remember. With a writer's notebook we can preserve the idea that came to us as we were walking across campus or staring into space over our morning coffee. Throughout this book we encourage you to use a writer's notebook extensively as you criticize and create arguments.

WAYS OF USING A NOTEBOOK

What sort of notebook entries might be appropriate? The simple answer is anything that helps, whatever you want to write down for future reference. Following are some more specific possibilities for using a writer's notebook.

To Explore Issues You Encounter in and out of Class

Your notebook is a place for freewriting—that is, private exploration for your eyes only. Such writing should not be judged as good or bad. Don't worry about organization, spelling, grammar, or any of the things that might concern you if someone else were to read your entries.

If you have been assigned a topic, write down your first impressions and opinions about it. If you will be choosing some of your own topics in a course, use the notebook to respond to controversial issues in the news or on campus. Your notebook can then become a source of ideas for your essays. Bring it with you to each class session so you can record ideas that come up during class discussions. In fact, a notebook can make you a better contributor to class discussion because it's easier to share your ideas publicly if you have roughed them out in writing first; use your notebook to respond to ideas presented in class and in every reading assignment.

To Copy Down and Analyze Assignments

If your instructor gives you a handout explaining an assignment, staple it to a page in the notebook. If not, write down the assignment word for word from the board or as it is dictated to you. In addition, take notes as your instructor explains the assignment. After class take time to look over the assignment more carefully. What are the key words? Circle them and make sure you know exactly what they mean. Underline due dates and such information as paper length and format. Record any questions you have about the assignment, and ask your instructor for clarification at the first appropriate opportunity; you may also want to jot down your instructor's answers.

To Work Out a Timetable for Completing an Assignment

One way to avoid procrastination is to divide the time you have for completing an assignment into blocks: preparation, writing and rewriting, editing, making a final copy, and proofreading. Work out in your notebook how many days you can devote to preparation and research, how many to writing a first draft, how many to revising, how many to editing, and how many to the final typing and proofreading. Draft a tentative schedule for yourself. Your schedule will probably change as you complete the assignment, but mapping one out and attempting to stick to it should help you make steady progress and avoid scrambling at the last moment to get your paper in on time.

To Make Notes as You Research

No matter the type of research, you should have a place to record ideas, questions, and preliminary conclusions that occur to you as you read and to discuss your ideas with others, conduct experiments, compile surveys and questionnaires, consult with experts, and pursue other types of information about your topic. Keep your notebook handy at all times, and write down as soon as possible whatever comes to mind, no matter how promising or unpromising it may initially seem. You can assess the value of your notes later when you have completed your research, but there will be nothing to assess if you do not keep a written record of your thoughts during the process.

To Respond to Arguments You Hear or Read

Your most immediate written responses to what you read are likely to be brief comments in a book's margins. Marginal annotation is a good habit to develop, but an equally good habit is to follow up your reading by jotting down more extended responses in your notebook. You might evaluate a text's strengths and weaknesses, compare the argument with other arguments you have read on the same topic, and make notes about how you might use material in the text to build your own argument (noting down page numbers at this point will make it easier to use such information in your paper later).

To Write a Rhetorical Prospectus

A *prospectus* details a plan for a proposed work. A rhetorical prospectus gets you thinking not just about *what* you want to say but about the rhetorical context in which you will say it: *to whom, how,* and—most importantly—*why* you are writing. In real-life arguments these elements are simply a given, but to write a successful argument for a class assignment, you usually have to create a rhetorical situation for yourself. In your notebook, explore the following:

Your *thesis:* What are you claiming?
Your *aim:* What do you want to accomplish?
Your *audience:* Who should read this? Why? What are these people like?
Your *persona:* What is your relationship to the audience? How do you want them to perceive you?
Your *subject matter:* What does your thesis obligate you to discuss? What do you need to learn more about? How do you plan to get the information?
Your *organizational plan:* What should you talk about first? Where might that lead? What might you end with? (This need not be a complete outline; an overview will suffice.)

If you have trouble with the prospectus, discuss it with your instructor at a conference or with a tutor at the writing center, if your school has one.

To Record Useful Feedback

A student writer has at least two sources of feedback on ideas and drafts—other students and the instructor. Many writing classes are now designed to encourage such interaction. Throughout this book we suggested points in the writing process when seeking feedback may be a good idea. Examples of such times include the following:

When your *initial ideas* have taken shape. Seeking feedback now helps you discover how well you can explain your ideas to others and how they respond.

After you and other students have *completed research* on common or similar topics. Feedback at this point allows you to share information and to compare evaluations of the sources.

At the completion of a *first draft.* At this point feedback uncovers what you need to do in a second draft in order to accommodate readers' needs, objections, and questions.

At the end of the *revising process.* This sort of feedback helps eliminate surface problems, such as awkward sentences, usage errors, misspellings, and typos.

You will benefit most from feedback opportunities if you prepare yourself with specific questions to ask your instructor or classmates. What concerns *you* about how the project is going? Use your notebook to jot down such questions, and leave room to sum up the comments you receive. The suggestion that seems too good to forget during a conference may elude your recall a day or two later at your word processor.

To Assess a Graded Paper

We seldom learn all we can from the comments of instructors. If the comments are positive, we tend to bask in the warmth of praise; if not, we tend to be embarrassed, frustrated, even angry. Neither response is likely to make us better writers.

The best approach is to let the feelings play themselves out: bask when you can, and feel discouraged when you have to. Then resolve to sit down and look over the comments carefully, writing down in your notebook what you find useful for future reference. On the positive side, what did you do well? What did you learn that might carry over to the next assignment? On the not-so-positive side, can you detect any pattern in the shortcomings and errors your instructor has pointed out? If so, list the types of problems you discover, and refer to them at an appropriate time when revising or editing or when composing your next essay. If, for example, you did not develop and support your points well, revise with this in mind or devote special attention to this issue as you plan and draft in the future. If you have a tendency to misplace the apostrophe in plural possessives, check all plural possessive apostrophes in subsequent final drafts.

It is natural to want to be done with a paper once you have turned it in, to get a grade and forget about it. Resist this desire long enough to record anything you can learn from your instructor's comments. The self-assessment preserved in your notebook will help you apply what you have learned to future assignments in future semesters.

Following Through

What issues do you currently have strong opinions about? Although you can look to today's newspaper or the evening news for inspiration, think as well about events you've noticed on campus, at your job, or around your town—a change in course requirements for your planned major, a conflict over some aspect of your work environment, or a proposed land development near your house. Write a notebook entry in which you list several possible topics for written arguments. Then pick one or two, and create the briefest of arguments—a statement of your position followed by a statement of your best reason for holding that position. Think about who the audience for such an argument could be. Think also about your aim: Would you be arguing to inquire, convince, persuade, or negotiate?

CREDITS

Text Credits

JONATHAN ALTER, "Degrees of Discomfort" from *Newsweek,* March 12, 1990. Copyright © 1990 Newsweek, Inc. All rights reserved. Reprinted by permission.

RUSSELL A. BARKLEY, "Attention-Deficit Hyperactivity Disorder" from *Scientific American,* September 1998. Reprinted with permission. Copyright © 1998 by Scientific American, Inc. All rights reserved.

W. LANCE BENNETT, "Escaping the News Prison" from *News: The Politics of Illusion, Third Edition.* Copyright © 1996, 1988, 1983 by Longman Publishers USA. Reprinted by permission of Addison-Wesley Educational Publishers Inc.

ADRIAN BERRY, *The Next 500 Years: Life in the Coming Millennium.* Copyright © 1996 by Adrian Berry. Used with permission of W. H. Freeman and Company.

PETER BRIMELOW, "Time to Rethink Immigration." Copyright © 1992 by Peter Brimelow. Reprinted by permission of The Wylie Agency, Inc.

LINDA CHAVEZ, "What to Do About Immigration." Reprinted from *Commentary,* March, 1995 by permission. All rights reserved.

MATTHEW CONOLLY, "Euthanasia Is Not the Answer" from a speech delivered at the Hemlock Society's Second National Voluntary Euthanasia Conference, February 9, 1985. Reprinted with permission of the author.

STEPHANIE COONTZ, *The Way We Really Are.* Copyright © 1997 by Basic Books, a division of HarperCollins Publishers, Inc. Reprinted by permission of Basic Books, a member of Perseus Books, L.L.C.

LINDA DARLING-HAMMOND, "Unequal Opportunity: Race and Education" from *Brookings Review,* Spring 1998, pp. 28–33. Reprinted by permission of Brookings Institution Press.

MIDGE DECTER, "The Madness of the American Family" from *Policy Review,* September/October 1998. Reprinted with permission of Policy Review, a publication of The Heritage Foundation.

MAX DUBLIN, "The Power of Prophecy," from *Futurehype: The Tyranny of Prophecy.* Copyright © 1989, 1991 by Max Dublin. Used by permission of Dutton, a division of Penguin Putnam Inc.

MARK EDMUNDSON, "On the Uses of Liberal Education: As Lite Entertainment for Bored College Students." Copyright © 1997 by Harper's Magazine. All rights reserved. Reproduced from the September issue of *Harper's Magazine* by special permission.

JAMES FALLOWS, "Public Journalism: An Attempt to Connect the Media with the Public" from *Breaking the News.* Copyright © 1996 by James Fallows. Reprinted by permission of Pantheon Books, a division of Random House, Inc.

SUSAN FALUDI, "The Backlash Against Feminism" from *Backlash.* Copyright © 1991 by Susan Faludi. Reprinted by permission of Crown Publishers, Inc.

JACK FULLER, "What Is News?" from *News Values: Ideas for an Information Age,* pp. 4–37. Copyright © 1996. Reprinted by permission of The University of Chicago Press and the author.

PETER J. GOMES, "Homophobic? Reread Your Bible" from *The New York Times,* August 17, 1992. Copyright © 1992 by The New York Times Co. Reprinted by permission.

ANGELA J. GRELLHESL, "Mediating the Speech Code Controversy." Reprinted by permission of the author.

PETER HAMILL, "Confessions of a Heterosexual" as appeared in *Esquire,* August 1990. Reprinted by permission of International Creative Management, Inc.

BETTY HOLCOMB, Reprinted with the permission of Scribner, a Division of Simon & Schuster from *Not Guilty* by Betty Holcomb. Copyright © 1998 by Betty Holcomb.

SIDNEY HOOK, "In Defense of Voluntary Euthanasia" from *The New York Times,* March 1, 1987. Copyright © 1987 by The New York Times Co. Reprinted by permission.

MICHIO KAKU, From *Visions: How Science Will Revolutionize the 21st Century.* Copyright © 1997 by Michio Kaku. Used by permission of Doubleday, a division of Random House, Inc.

ROBERT D. KAPLAN, "The Coming Anarchy." Originally published in *The Atlantic Monthly,* February 1994. All Rights Reserved. Copyright © 1994 by Robert D. Kaplan. Reprinted by permission of Brandt & Brandt Literary Agents, Inc.

RYSZARD KAPUSCINSKI, "Second Thoughts About America's Racial Paradise," *New Perspectives Quarterly,* Summer 1991. Reprinted by permission of the publisher.

DAVID KENNEDY, "Can We Still Afford to Be a Nation of Immigrants?" *The Atlantic Monthly,* November 1996. Copyright © 1996 David M. Kennedy, as first published in The Atlantic Monthly. With permission from the publisher.

LARRY KING, From *Future Talk.* Copyright © 1998 by Larry King. Reprinted by permission of HarperCollins Publishers, Inc.

MARTIN LUTHER KING, JR., "Letter from a Birmingham Jail." Copyright © 1968 by Martin Luther King, Jr., copyright renewed 1996 by The Estate of Martin Luther King, Jr. Reprinted by arrangement with The Heirs to the Estate of Martin Luther King, Jr., c/o Writers House, Inc. as agent for the proprietor.

CASSANDRA LANGER, *A Feminist Critique.* Copyright © 1996 by Westview Press. Reprinted by permission of Westview Press, a member of Perseus Books, L.L.C.

MICHAEL LEVIN, "The Case for Torture," *Newsweek,* June 7, 1982. Reprinted with permission of the author.

ARTHUR LEVINE AND JEANETTE S. CURETON, "College Life: An Obituary" from *Change* 30, May/June 1998, pp. 12–19. Copyright © 1998 Heldref Publications. Reprinted with permission of the Helen Dwight Reid Educational Foundation. Published by Heldref Publications, 1319 Eighteenth St., NW, Washington, DC 20036-1802.

MICHAEL LIND, "The Beige and the Black" from *The New York Times,* August 16, 1998. Reprinted by permission of International Creative Management, Inc. Copyright © 1998 by Michael Lind.

WILLIAM F. MAY, "Rising to the Occasion of our Death." Copyright © 1993 Christian Century Foundation. Reprinted by permission from the 7/11/93 issue of *The Christian Century.*

MARGARET LIU McCONNELL, "Living with Roe v. Wade," *Commentary,* November 1990. Reprinted with permission of the author.

TONI A. H. McNARON, Excerpted and reprinted from "In or Out in the Classroom" as included in Poison Ivy by Tonia McNaron by permission of Temple University Press. Copyright © 1997 by Temple University. All rights reserved.

NICOLAUS MILLS, "Lifeboat Ethics and Immigration Fears." This article first appeared in *Dissent,* Winter 1996 and is reprinted with permission.

ELIZABETH MITCHELL, "An Odd Break with the Human Heart." Reprinted by permission of the author.

WILLIAM MURCHISON, "Should Dallas Drop Ban: City Shouldn't Ignore Morality," from *The Dallas Morning News' Viewpoint,* January 17, 1992. Reprinted with permission of The Dallas Morning News.

JEFFREY NICKEL, "Everybody's Threatened by Homophobia." Reprinted from *Christopher Street,* Issue 185, August 17, 1992, with permission.

ANNE MARIE O'KEEFE, "The Case Against Drug Testing" from *Psychology Today* magazine, June 1987. Copyright © 1987 Sussex Publishers, Inc. Reprinted with permission from Psychology Today magazine.

DAVID POPENOE, "A World Without Fathers" from *Life Without Father: Compelling New Evidence That Fatherhood and Marriage Is Indispensable for the Good of Children and Society,* New York: The Free Press, 1996 (paperback edition Cambridge, MA: Harvard Univ. Press, 1999). Reprinted by permission of David Popenoe, Professor of Sociology and Co-Director, National Marriage Project, Rutgers University, New Brunswick, NJ.

PATRICK PUGH, "Legalization of Euthanasia: A Means to a More Comfortable Dying Process." Reprinted by permission of the author.

ANNA QUINDLEN, "Public and Private: Making the Mosaic" from *The New York Times,* May 20, 1991. Copyright © 1991 by The New York Times Company. Reprinted by permission.

JAMES RACHELS, *The End of Life: Euthanasia and Morality.* Copyright © 1986 James Rachels. Reprinted by permission of Oxford University Press.

JONATHAN RAUCH, "Beyond Oppression," *The New Republic,* May 10, 1993. Copyright © 1993 The New Republic, Inc. Reprinted by permission of The New Republic.

DEBORAH RHODE, Reprinted by permission of the publisher from *Speaking of Sex,* Cambridge, Mass.: Harvard University Press, Copyright © 1997 by the President and Fellows of Harvard College.

KATIE ROIPHE, "The Independent Woman (and Other Lies)" from *Esquire Magazine,* February 1997. Copyright © 1997 by Katie Roiphe. Reprinted by permission of International Creative Management, Inc.

ROGER ROSENBLATT, "How to End the Abortion War" from *The New York Times,* January 19, 1992. Copyright © 1992 by The New York Times Company. Reprinted by permission.

MICHAEL SCHUDSON, "In All Fairness" from *Media Studies Journal,* "What's Fair?", Vol. 12, No. 2 (Spring/Summer 1998), pp. 34–41. Reprinted by permission.

JOEY SHANKS, "An Uncomfortable Position." Reprinted by permission of the author.

EARL SHORRIS, "On the Uses of Liberal Education: As a Weapon in the Hands of the Restless Poor." Copyright © 1997 by Harper's Magazine. All rights reserved. Reproduced from the September issue of *Harper's Magazine* by special permission.

LESLIE MARMON SILKO, "The Border State Patrol" reprinted with the permission of Simon & Schuster, Inc. from *Yellow Woman and a Beauty of the Spirit* by Leslie Marmon Silko. Copyright © 1996 by Leslie Marmon Silko.

ARLENE SKOLNICK, "The Paradox of Perfection" from the *Wilson Quarterly,* Summer 1980. Copyright © 1980 by The Woodrow Wilson International Center for Scholars. Reprinted by permission.

CHRISTINA HOFF SOMMERS, reprinted with the permission of Simon & Schuster, Inc., from *Who Stole Feminism?* Copyright © 1994 by Christina Hoff Sommers.

JUSTIN SPIDEL, "Who Should Have the Right to Marry?" Reprinted with permission from the author.

JIM SQUIRES, "The Impossibility of Fairness" from *Media Studies Journal,* "What's Fair?", Vol. 12, No. 2 (Spring/Summer 1998), pp. 66–71. Reprinted by permission.

SHELBY STEELE, "The Recoloring of Campus Life." Copyright © 1989 by Harper's Magazine. All rights reserved. Reproduced from the February issue of *Harper's Magazine* by special permission.

JOHN TAGG, "The Decline of the Knowledge Factory: Why Our Colleges Must Change" from the *The World and I,* Vol. 13, June 1998, pp. 292–304. Reprinted by permission.

CINDY TARVER, "An Appeal to Prejudice." Reprinted by permission of the author.

ABIGAIL AND STEPHAN THERNSTROM, "Black Progress: How Far We've Come—And How Far We Have to Go" from *Brookings Review,* Spring 1998, pp. 12–17. Reprinted by permission of Brookings Institution Press.

BARBARA DAFOE WHITEHEAD, *The Divorce Culture.* Copyright © 1997 by Barbara Dafoe Whitehead. Reprinted by permission of Alfred A. Knopf, Inc.

KELLY WILLIAMS, "Ad Analysis." Reprinted by permission of the author.

PATRICIA WILLIAMS, "The Distribution of Distress" from *Seeing a Color-Blind Future: The Paradox of Race.* Copyright © 1997 by Patricia Williams. Reprinted by permission of Farrar, Straus & Giroux, Inc.

ELLEN WILLIS, "Abortion: Whose Right to Life Is It Anyway?" Copyright © 1985 by Ellen Willis. Reprinted by permission of the Charlotte Sheedy Literary Agency.

NAOMI WOLF, "The Beauty Myth" from *The Beauty Myth.* Copyright © 1991 by Naomi Wolf. By permission of William Morrow and Company, Inc.

AMBER YOUNG, "Capital Punishment: Society's Self-Defense." Reprinted with permission of the author.

Photo Credits

Page 199 Mike Keefe, dePIXion studios, inc. **Page 200** *Top:* By permission of Jim McCloskey; *Bottom:* By permission of Mike Luckovich and Creators Syndicate. **Page 201** By permission of Gary Varvel. **Page 202** Courtesy of Department of Defense. **Page 203** *Top:* © Barbara Alper/Stock, Boston Inc.; *Bottom:* © Richard Pasley/Stock, Boston Inc. **Page 204** © Bruce Young/Corbis-Bettmann. **Page 209** By permission of Yan Nascimbene. **Page 212** © 1998 Terese Winslow. **Page 217** © Stephen Rose/Liason Agency. **Page 330** © David Maung/Impact Visuals. **Page 390** Kirk Anderson, Ladysmith, WI. **Page 427** Lawman Jeans ad by permission of Lawman Sportswear Inc. **Page 483** The New Yorker Collection 1997 Tom Cheny from cartoonbank.com. All rights reserved. **Page 515** Doonesbury © 1993 G. B. Trudeau. Reprinted with permission of Universal Press Syndicate. All rights reserved. **Page 567** © The New Yorker Collection 1998 Mike Twohy from cartoonbank.com. All rights reserved. **Page 598** © Lois Bernstein. **Page 636** © Bruce Roberts/Photo Researchers, Inc. **Page 654** © A. Ramey/PhotoEdit. **Page 703** © Corbis Images.

INDEX

Boldfaced numbers indicate page on which term is defined.